百年律师看天津

ONE HUNDRED YEARS OF LAWYERS
ACCUMULATED HISTORY FOCUSED ON TIANJIN

上册

天津市律师协会　编著

丁立莹　编译

图书在版编目（CIP）数据

百年律师看天津/天津市律师协会编著. -- 天津：天津古籍出版社, 2021.6
ISBN 978-7-5528-1091-2

Ⅰ.①百… Ⅱ.①天… Ⅲ.①律师业务 - 概况 - 天津 Ⅳ.①D926.5

中国版本图书馆CIP数据核字(2021)第076754号

百年律师看天津
BAINIAN LÜSHI KAN TIANJIN

编　　著：	天津市律师协会
编　　译：	丁立莹
出 版 人：	张　玮
出版发行：	天津古籍出版社
	天津市西康路35号　邮政编码：300051
策　　划：	唐　舰
责任编辑：	郑　伟
责任校对：	王羽茜
装帧设计：	雅迪云印（天津）科技有限公司
印　　制：	雅迪云印（天津）科技有限公司
经　　销：	全国新华书店发行
版　　次：	2021年6月第1版　2021年6月第1次印刷
开　　本：	889mm×1194mm　1/16
印　　张：	36
字　　数：	700千字
定　　价：	580.00元（上、下册）

编委会

编委会主任
刘基智

编委会副主任
柴续泰　才　华

编委会委员
冯志东　牛同栩　丁立莹　李　雯　马　军

序

王红卫

光影交错，回眸百年。天津是中国近代律师业发源地之一，是现代律师成长的摇篮，也是新时代律师发展的沃土。在举国上下欢庆建党百年之际，《百年律师看天津》正式出版问世了。这是天津律师行业发展的一项重大成果，是广大天津律师的一笔宝贵财富。此书全面回顾了天津律师行业跌宕起伏的不凡历程，为社会各界提供了深刻感受律师在法治建设和社会发展中发挥重要作用的宣传窗口。

从中国最早开展法学高等教育的北洋学堂，到严复远赴伦敦代理开平矿务局诉讼，开创中国参与国际诉讼的先河，再到为天津被捕的新民主主义革命人士挺身辩护，天津律师在纷繁乱世中为社会正义奔走疾呼、为国家命运殚精竭虑，彰显了追求公正、不畏强权的风骨气节，高扬了崇尚法治、保障人权的价值追求，成为中国近现代发展史难以忘却的记忆。

伴随着中华民族开天辟地、改天换地、翻天覆地的历史巨变，天津律师行业茁壮成长，日渐成熟。1979年12月，司法部下发《关于律师工作的通知》，中国大陆律师制度正式宣告重启。我国律师从"国家法律工作者"，到"为社会提供法律服务的执业人员"，到"维护当事人的合法权益、维护法律的正确实施、维护社会公平和正义的执业人员"，再到"依法治国队伍的一支重要力量"，天津律师队伍也由28人发展到8807人，实现了从小到大、从弱到强的历史性跨越，不断焕发着百舸争流、千帆竞发的生机活力。广大律师认真履行辩护代理职责，发挥专业优势参政议政，热心参与公益法律服务，成为贯穿立法、执法、司法、守法各环节的重要力量，获得了人民群众的高度信赖和社会各界的一致认可。

1934	1935	1936	1937	1938	1939	1940	1941	1942	1943	1944	1945	1946
1960	1961	1962	1963	1964	1965	1966	1967	1968	1969	1970	1971	1972
1986	1987	1988	1989	1990	1991	1992	1993	1994	1995	1996	1997	1998
2012	2013	2014	2015	2016	2017	2018	2019	2020	2021	……		

　　当前，世界正经历百年未有之大变局，我国正处于实现中华民族伟大复兴的关键时期。天津市委、市政府确定了到2035年基本建成社会主义现代化大都市的远景目标。天津律师业正面临着难得的历史机遇，使命更加光荣、责任更加重大、挑战更加艰巨。广大律师要充分发扬前辈们爬坡过坎、勇立潮头的优良传统，继续担起维护社会公平正义、推进全面依法治市、服务高质量发展的重任，坚持以习近平新时代中国特色社会主义思想为指导，深入践行习近平法治思想，坚定拥护党的领导，拥护社会主义法治，坚定不移走中国特色社会主义法治道路，坚持以人民为中心，在构建新发展格局中找准定位，全面把握新时代法律服务新需求，依法依规诚信执业、积极履行社会责任，彰显律师使命担当、树立行业新风正气，共同推动律师行业规模化专业化规范化国际化发展，在天津律师发展史上留下浓墨重彩的崭新一笔。

　　征途漫漫，惟有奋斗。站在"两个一百年"的历史交汇点上，希望广大天津律师永葆"闯"的精神、"创"的劲头、"干"的作风，不断谱写天津律师行业发展新的辉煌篇章，为全面建设社会主义现代化大都市贡献更大力量！

目 录
CONTENTS

百年律师看天津
ONE HUNDRED YEARS OF LAWYERS ACCUMULATED HISTORY FOCUSED ON TIANJIN

上 册
Volume 1

001 绪 论
INTRODUCTION

020 传统讼师与近代律师的萌芽
THE ORIGIN OF
TRADITIONAL SHYSTER AND MODERN LAWYER

044 清末律师制度的确立与天津的司法尝试
ESTABLISHMENT OF LAWYER SYSTEM IN
THE LATE QING DYNASTY AND
TIANJIN'S JUDICIAL ATTEMPT

078 民国初期至20世纪30年代的天津律师
TIANJIN LAWYERS FROM THE EARLY
REPUBLIC OF CHINA TO THE 1930S

222 七七事变至新中国成立前的天津律师
TIANJIN LAWYERS IN THE PERIOD FROM
THE JULY 7 INCIDENT OF 1937 TO THE FOUNDING
OF THE PEOPLE'S REPUBLIC OF CHINA

1934	1935	1936	1937	1938	1939	1940	1941	1942	1943	1944	1945	1946
1960	1961	1962	1963	1964	1965	1966	1967	1968	1969	1970	1971	1972
1986	1987	1988	1989	1990	1991	1992	1993	1994	1995	1996	1997	1998
2012	2013	2014	2015	2016	2017	2018	2019	2020	2021	……		

绪 论
INTRODUCTION

中国近代史学界公认的法典意义上律师制度的建立，是北洋政府于1912年9月16日颁布的《律师暂行章程》。这是中国历史上第一部律师法典。

The establishment of the lawyer system in the sense of a code recognized by the modern history of China was the *Provisional Regulation of Lawyers* promulgated by the Beiyang Government on September 16, 1912. This is the first lawyer's law in Chinese history.

文化或制度的建立，并不是一蹴而就的，尤其是在新旧杂陈、动荡变迁的清末民初。受农耕社会沿袭千年亲亲尊尊的宗法准则的影响，旧思想、旧势力对代表民主与法治的新职业群体的禁止、限制和戒备，使得律师这个群体在完成于禁锢中生存、在发展中模仿、在壮大中规范的历史进程中付出了极大的艰辛，而这段"萌芽于讼师，催化于西律，产生于清末，施行于北洋"的律师文化的起源更经历了一个自外而内、上下齐动，并且抗争与融合对立统一的过程。民间讼师这个独特社会群体的存在，在几千年的传统社会中实实在在地扮演了与近代律师极为相似的角色。同时，在外国传教士、洋律师享受的治外法权所体现的司法结构中，在清政府意欲变法图强的格局下，一个可完成自我规制的新兴法律职业阶层——律师，终于在民国元年横空出世了。

The establishment of culture or system did not happen overnight, especially in the late Qing Dynasty and the beginning of the Republic of China when the old and the new were mixed and turbulent. Affected by the patriarchal norms that the

1921	1922	1923	1924	1925	1926	1927	1928	1929	1930	1931	1932	1933
1947	1948	1949	1950	1951	1952	1953	1954	1955	1956	1957	1958	1959
1973	1974	1975	1976	1977	1978	1979	1980	1981	1982	1983	1984	1985
1999	2000	2001	2002	2003	2004	2005	2006	2007	2008	2009	2010	2011

farming society has inherited for thousands of years, the old ideas and forces have played a role in representing democracy and the rule of law. The prohibition, restriction and guard against the new professional group of the lawyers have made the lawyers this group have completed the historical process of survival in imprisonment, imitating in development, and standardizing in growth. The origin of the lawyer culture, which was catalyzed by western Law, was born in the late Qing Dynasty, and was implemented in Beiyang, has experienced a process of struggle and integration of opposites and unity from the outside to the inside. The existence of the unique social group of civil litigators has played a role very similar to modern lawyers in traditional society for thousands of years. At the same time, in the judicial structure embodied by the extraterritorial rights enjoyed by foreign missionaries and foreign lawyers, and under the pattern of the Qing government's desire to reform the law, a new class of legal professions that can complete self-regulation——lawyers, finally born in the first year of the Republic of China.

在催生律师职业复杂而渐进的过程中，有诸多翔实的史料从不同角度指向天津，研究近代百年中国律师制度的起步和发展，在源头上，无论如何是绕不开天津的。

In the complex and gradual process of giving birth to the lawyer profession, there are many informative historical materials pointing to Tianjin from different angles. To study the start and development of the Chinese lawyer system in the modern century, Tianjin cannot be avoided at the source.

一

乾隆五十八年（1793），中西方文明一次巨大的碰撞发生在天津。无论是清政府欲借助西方文明来拯救传统文明，还是东西方文明的必然碰撞，都使天津走向世界并成为了面向西方文明的"桥头堡"。

1934	1935	1936	1937	1938	1939	1940	1941	1942	1943	1944	1945	1946
1960	1961	1962	1963	1964	1965	1966	1967	1968	1969	1970	1971	1972
1986	1987	1988	1989	1990	1991	1992	1993	1994	1995	1996	1997	1998
2012	2013	2014	2015	2016	2017	2018	2019	2020	2021	……		

1793年8月11日，英国马戛尔尼使团抵达天津时绘制的天津图景

A picture of Tianjin drawn by the British Macartney Mission when they arrived in Tianjin on August 11, 1793

In 1793, the great collision between Chinese and Western civilizations occurred in Tianjin. Whether it is the Qing government's desire to use Western civilization to save traditional civilization, or the inevitable collision of Eastern and Western civilization, Tianjin has become the world's "bridgehead" facing Western civilization.

天津市和平区的安徽路与青岛道，在英租界时期被称为马开内道。这是为了纪念1793年8月11日马戛尔尼勋爵受英王乔治三世委派，到清王朝为乾隆皇帝祝贺83岁寿辰而在天津大沽口登陆的一段历史，此后便以"马戛尔尼"（时译马开内）命名英租界中的一条道路。

1921	1922	1923	1924	1925	1926	1927	1928	1929	1930	1931	1932	1933
1947	1948	1949	1950	1951	1952	1953	1954	1955	1956	1957	1958	1959
1973	1974	1975	1976	1977	1978	1979	1980	1981	1982	1983	1984	1985
1999	2000	2001	2002	2003	2004	2005	2006	2007	2008	2009	2010	2011

Anhui Road and Qingdao Road in Heping District of Tianjin City were called Macartney Road during the British concession period. This is to commemorate a period of history when Lord Macartney was appointed by King George III of England on August 11, 1793 to congratulate Emperor Qianlong on his 83rd birthday and landed in Dagu Port, Tianjin. "Macartney" was named a road in the British concession.

马戛尔尼使团访华是中英两国间的第一次对话。天津，又是英国使团到达中国后，清政府正式接待的第一站。尽管清王朝对使团所赠礼物，诸如天体运行仪、油画、钟表以及英人的装束、礼节、典籍等都有焕然一新的感觉，但是天朝上国的夜郎自大还是将其视为"域外岛夷"的"藩属小部"。面对西方文明的第一次"貌似拜谒，实为挑战"的出使，清王朝不但闭目塞听，而且还因马戛尔尼拒绝向皇帝行跪拜礼而下令"减其供给，减其礼待"。47年后，鸦片战争在南方诸省展开，清政府最后妥协开放五口通商。不过，"占领天津，控制北京"才是侵略者的目标。随着侵略程度的加深和列强利益需求的扩大，西方文明试图在司法领域改变中国"就地正法""先斩后奏"的传统制度。"政审合一""诸法合体"的弊端也让中华民族的有识之士上下求索，并尝试建立新秩序。两者相伴而生，渐至发达。革新思想家严复早在19世纪末就已指出："夫泰西之所以能无刑讯而情得者，非徒司法折狱之有术，而无情者不得尽其辞也，有辩护之律师，有公听之助理，抵瑕蹈隙，曲证旁搜，盖数听之余……吾国治狱，无此具也。"律师一词，可见已深入人心。在立法还没有出现律师这一概念时，晚清民间已经把精于词讼的状士称呼为律师了。

The Macartney delegation's visit to China is the first dialogue between China and Britain. Tianjin was also the first stop officially received by the Qing government after the British delegation arrived in China. Although the Qing Dynasty gave gifts to the delegation, such as celestial movement instruments, oil paintings, clocks, and British costumes, etiquette, and classics, all had a new feel, but the arrogant Yelang of the heavenly kingdom still regarded them as the "small part of the vassal" of the "outside the island barbarian". Facing Western civilization's first mission of "looks like a visit, but actually a challenge", the Qing Dynasty not only closed its eyes and listened to it, but also ordered "reduction of its supply and reduction of its supply" because of Macartney's refusal to bow down to the emperor. 47 years later, the Opium War started in the southern provinces, and the Qing government finally compromised and opened up five ports to trade. However, "occupy Tianjin and control Beijing" is the target of the aggressors. With the deepening of the degree of aggression and the expansion of the interests of the powers, Western civilization tried to change China's traditional system of "justifying the law on the spot" and "being cut before playing" in the judicial field. The shortcomings of the "integration of politics and trial" and the "combination of all laws" have also made the Chinese people of insight search up and down and try to establish a new order. The two came together and gradually developed. Innovative thinker Yan Fu pointed out as early as the end of the 19th century: "The reason why western countries cannot extort confessions by torture is not only because of the judicial and prison system, but also because the accused cannot fully defend themselves. I have heard of many cases. However, in China's criminal system, there is no defense link, and the examination is not clear." The word lawyer is deeply rooted in the hearts of the people. Before the concept of a lawyer appeared in the legislation, the folks in the late Qing Dynasty had already called lawyers who were good at litigation as lawyers.

二

同治九年（1870）的天津教案让直隶总督第一次直面洋律师出庭代理案件的新情况。

The Tianjin Religious Case in 1870 allowed Zhili Governor to face the new situation of foreign lawyers appearing in court for the first time.

西方律师辩护思想的输入天津是与划定租界后的领事裁判权紧密联系在一起的。天津最早的会审公堂在紫竹林租界一带，而怡和洋行的洋律师也随着咸丰十年（1860）的天津开埠而活跃起来。同治九年爆发了震惊中外的天

1921	1922	1923	1924	1925	1926	1927	1928	1929	1930	1931	1932	1933
1947	1948	1949	1950	1951	1952	1953	1954	1955	1956	1957	1958	1959
1973	1974	1975	1976	1977	1978	1979	1980	1981	1982	1983	1984	1985
1999	2000	2001	2002	2003	2004	2005	2006	2007	2008	2009	2010	2011

清朝官员审案场景
Qing Dynasty officials trial scene

津教案，民众杀死法国领事丰大业、火烧望海楼教堂，险些引发战争。在侵略军大兵压境的情况下，曾国藩选择了委曲求全，他用死刑犯调包教案中的犯人，凑够人数在西大道公开问斩。西方列强的洋律师团首次进入天津的法庭参加诉讼，这个案件也对清政府产生了深远的影响。按照清廷的行事风格，领事、神父、洋商等多人被杀的惊天大案，肇事者早就应该"斩立决"了，可洋人偏要"遵循程序"，派出了律师公堂诉讼、质问对诘。这不得不令有识之士深思，也最终令清政府在世纪之交开启了改良司法、建立律师制度的革新之路。

The introduction of western lawyers' defense ideas in Tianjin is closely related to the consular jurisdiction after the delimitation of the concession. The earliest adjudicative office in Tianjin was in the Zizhulin concession area, and the foreign

1934	1935	1936	1937	1938	1939	1940	1941	1942	1943	1944	1945	1946
1960	1961	1962	1963	1964	1965	1966	1967	1968	1969	1970	1971	1972
1986	1987	1988	1989	1990	1991	1992	1993	1994	1995	1996	1997	1998
2012	2013	2014	2015	2016	2017	2018	2019	2020	2021	……		

lawyer of Jardine Matheson also became active with the opening of Tianjin in 1860. In 1870, the Tianjin Religious Case that shocked both China and foreign countries broke out. The people killed the French consul Fontanier and burned the Church of Our Lady of Victory, almost triggering a war. When the invading army was under pressure, Zeng Guofan replaced the prisoners in the Religious Case with the death row prisoners, and made up enough people and kill on West Avenue. For the first time, a group of foreign lawyers from western powers entered a court in Tianjin to participate in litigation. This case also had a profound impact on the Qing government. According to the Qing court's style of acting, the consuls, priests, foreign merchants and other people were killed in a shocking case. The perpetrators should have "executed the decision" long ago, but the foreigners had to "follow the procedure" and sent a lawyer to litigate and question in court. This had to make people of insight think deeply, and finally led the Qing government to open the road of reforms such as improving the judiciary and establishing a lawyer system at the turn of the century.

三

光绪三十一年（1905）中国人首次越洋诉讼——严复参与了开平矿务局在英国伦敦高等法院的国际股权诉讼纠纷案。

In 1905, the Chinese people's first overseas litigation——Yan Fu participated in the international stockrights litigation dispute of Kaiping Mining Bureau in London's High Court, England.

翻检《朱批奏折》《录副奏折》《刑案汇览》等档案文献，我们不难发现，在传统社会的话语体系中，统治者总是将包揽词讼的"讼棍""哗徒"描述为"架词唆讼"者，充满了根深蒂固的负面情感。比如乾隆二十九年（1764）制定的《积惯讼棍例》中规定："若系积惯讼棍，串

1921	1922	1923	1924	1925	1926	1927	1928	1929	1930	1931	1932	1933
1947	1948	1949	1950	1951	1952	1953	1954	1955	1956	1957	1958	1959
1973	1974	1975	1976	1977	1978	1979	1980	1981	1982	1983	1984	1985
1999	2000	2001	2002	2003	2004	2005	2006	2007	2008	2009	2010	2011

通胥吏，播弄乡愚，恐吓诈财，一经审实，即依棍徒生事扰害例，发云贵、两广极边烟瘴充军。"不过，广大民众与之相反，他们将讼师刻画成利用文刀剑笔"劫富济贫""才智出众"的豪侠形象。更重要的是，尽管存在截然对立的官民认知，但由于诉讼当事人对法律服务的客观需求以及愚昧官员不断制造冤假错案，因此"笔砚贩子"始终能够经久不衰地存在着。

If we look through the archives and documents such as *Zhu Pi Zou Zhe*, *Lu Fu Zou Zhe*, and *Criminal Case Summary*, we can easily find that in the discourse system of traditional society, the governor always describ the agent ad litem as shyster and the troubler. Those who are described as "arguing and instigating" are full of deep-rooted negative emotions. For example, the *Accumulation of Lawsuits Law* enacted in 1764 stipulates: "If the lawsuits are used to accumulate lawsuits, collude with subordinate staff, play tricks on the country, intimidate and swindle money, once the case is verified, you will be prosecuted by sticks. Cases of harassment are sent to the borders of Yunnan, Guizhou, Guangdong and Guangxi." On the contrary, the majority of the people portray the litigants as heroes who use their swords and pens to "rob the rich and help the poor" and "excellent intellect". More importantly,

开平矿务有限公司发行的股票

Kaiping Mining Co.,Ltd. issued stocks

光绪二十八年（1902）开平矿务有限公司发行的金融券

Financial bonds issued by Kaiping Mining Co., Ltd. in 1902

despite the existence of diametrically opposed cognitions between officials and the people, due to the objective needs of litigants for legal services and the constant unjust, false and wrong cases created by ignorant officials, the "shyster" has always been in resquest for a long time.

光绪二十七年（1901），思想家严复在天津就任开平矿务有限公司华部总办。四年后，他作为诉讼代理人，代理张翼（醇亲王奕谭侍从、工部侍郎）和开平矿务局在英国伦敦高等法院起诉德璀琳、开平矿务有限公司的股权诉讼。严复此次在英国参与诉讼的经历，开启了中国人越洋诉讼的先河。

In 1901, the thinker Yan Fu served as the Chinese General Office of Kaiping Mining Bureau in Tianjin. Four years later, he represented Zhang Yi (the attendant of the Chun Prince Yixuan, the attendant of the Gong Ministry) and the Kaiping Mining Bureau in London's High Court to sued Gustav von Detring and Kaiping Mining Co., Ltd. in equity litigation. Yan Fu's experience of participating in litigation in the UK opened the first Chinese litigation overseas.

严复这段鲜为人知的伦敦法院诉讼经历无疑说明了清廷在与洋人利用诉讼规则的对抗中，不得不选用具有法律技巧的专业人士来提供帮助。清政府对律师既排斥又依赖的矛盾心理，逐渐摧毁了民族记忆里讼师咆哮公堂的负面形象，取而代之的是对律师欲言还羞的实际需求。

This little-known London's High Court litigation experience by Yan Fu undoubtedly shows that the Qing goverment had to choose professionals with legal skills to help in the confrontation with foreigners using the rules of litigation. The ambivalence of the Qing government's rejection and reliance on lawyers gradually destroyed the negative image of lawyers roaring in court in national memory, and replaced it with the actual need for lawyers to speak and be ashamed.

丁立莹律师采访严复侄曾孙严孝潜老师
Lawyer Ding Liying interviewed Yan Fu's great-grandson of nephew teacher Yan Xiaoqian

四

北洋大学法科——中国最早的法学教育机构，孕育近代法学家和近代律师的摇篮。光绪二十五年（1899），第一批中国未来的法学家和律师毕业。

Law Department of Beiyang University——the earliest legal education institution in China, gave birth to modern jurists and modern lawyers. In 1899, the first batch of Chinese future jurists and lawyers graduated.

1934	1935	1936	1937	1938	1939	1940	1941	1942	1943	1944	1945	1946
1960	1961	1962	1963	1964	1965	1966	1967	1968	1969	1970	1971	1972
1986	1987	1988	1989	1990	1991	1992	1993	1994	1995	1996	1997	1998
2012	2013	2014	2015	2016	2017	2018	2019	2020	2021	……		

鸦片战争以后，国门洞开，中国被迫纳入资本主义世界体系。伴随着康有为、梁启超的变法维新，盛宣怀于光绪二十一年八月（1895年10月）创办了天津北洋西学学堂（即著名的北洋大学，今天津大学前身），并开设了法科，招收与西方接触较早的天津及东南沿海等地的学生，同时聘任洋教习，如讲授法律的美籍学者林文德（天津注册的职业律师）、讲授世界史的任纳福等。全英文的授课以及丰富且处于学术前沿的律法总论、罗马律例、万国公法、商务律例、格致学、身理学、国策学等课程，为法科学生从事政治或法律工作作好了充分的准备。一代代的法科毕业生也为日后的汇通中西、法制变革、开启民智、民族抗争作出了巨大的贡献。

After the Opium War, the gate of the country was opened and China was forced to join the world system. Following the reforms of Kang Youwei and Liang Qichao, Sheng Xuanhuai opened the Tianjin Western Studies School (renamed Beiyang University, the predecessor of Tianjin University today) and recruited students from Tianjin and the southeast coast that had earlier contacts with the West. At the same time, foreign teachers were hired, such as American scholar Edgar Pierce Allen (registered professional lawyer of Tianjin) who teaches law, Renocg who teaches world history, etc. The English-language teaching and the rich and academic frontier law, Roman law, universal law, business law, Gezhi, Shenli, national policy and other courses, provided a sufficient basis for law students to engage in politics or law. Generations of law graduates have also made great contributions to the future integration of China and the West, the reform of the legal system, the opening of the people's wisdom, and the national struggle.

光绪二十五年（1899），天津北洋大学堂颁发了第一届毕业证书。诞生在天津的中国第一张大学文凭——"钦字第壹号"文凭授予了王宠惠，他后来也成为了民国第一法学家。优秀的毕业生还有日后成为北洋大学校长的赵天麟、革命先驱张太雷、联合国国际法院大法官徐谟、著名法学家吴经熊等。另外，1912年毕业的法科学生很多都成为了天津著名的执业律师，其中包括钱俊（曾为周恩来领导学生运动被捕审判案辩护）、张务滋（著名华洋商务律师）、贾文范（中国第一个翻译、研究《罗马法》并出版译著的律师）、吴大业、苏企田等。民国初年的北洋大学法科毕业生引领并开拓了中国司法界和律师业的实务，为中国律师的发展写下了浓墨重彩的一笔。

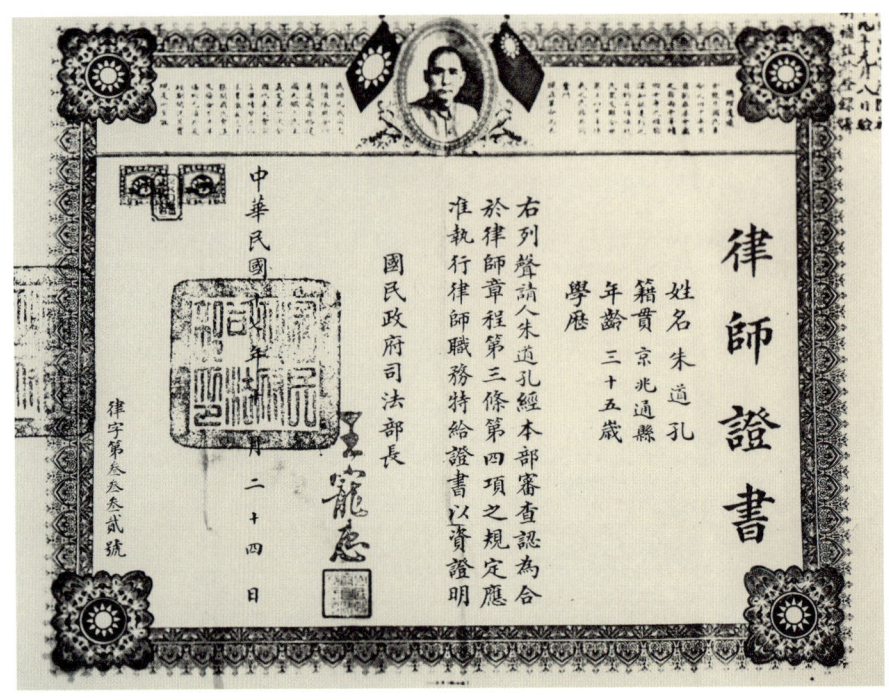

王宠惠为天津律师朱道孔签发的律师证
Lawyer certificate issued by Wang Chonghui to Tianjin lawyer Zhu Daokong

In 1899, Tianjin Beiyang University issued the first graduation certificate. The first university diploma in China, the "Qinzi No.1", born in Tianjin, was awarded to Wang Chonghui, who later became the number one jurist in the Republic of China. Outstanding graduates include Zhao Tianlin, who will become president of Beiyang University, revolutionary pioneer Zhang Tailei, Justice Xu Mo of United Nations International Court of Justice, and famous jurist Wu Jingxiong. In addition, many law students who graduated in 1912 became well-known practicing lawyers in Tianjin, including Qian Jun (who used to defend Zhou Enlai's arrest and trial for leading the student movement), Zhang Wuzi (famous Chinese and foreign business lawyer), and Jia Wenfan (Chinese first lawyer who translated, studied and published the translation of *Roman Law*), Wu Daye, Su Qitian, etc. The Beiyang University law graduates in the early years of the Republic of China led and pioneered the practice of China's judicial circle and the lawyer industry, and wrote a strong mark in the history of the development of Chinese lawyers.

1934	1935	1936	1937	1938	1939	1940	1941	1942	1943	1944	1945	1946
1960	1961	1962	1963	1964	1965	1966	1967	1968	1969	1970	1971	1972
1986	1987	1988	1989	1990	1991	1992	1993	1994	1995	1996	1997	1998
2012	2013	2014	2015	2016	2017	2018	2019	2020	2021	……		

五

中国律师最早的执业舞台——光绪三十二年（1906）天津在全国率先试办审判厅。

The earliest practice stage for Chinese lawyers——Tianjin took the lead in setting up adjudicative office in the country in 1906.

早在光绪二十八年二月初二（1902年3月11日），清政府便下诏："慎选熟悉中西律例者，保送来京，听候简派，开馆编纂。"随后，沈家本、伍廷芳开始"参酌各国法律，悉心考订"，并在给光绪皇帝的奏折中阐述了设立律师的必要性："夫以华人讼案，借外人辩护，已觉扞格不通……且领事治外之权，因之更形滋蔓，后患何堪设想！"光绪三十二年（1906），沈家本、伍廷芳主持完成了《大清刑事民事诉讼法草案》，直接引进了西方诉讼制度和律师制度。这是中国第一部诉讼法规草案，也是中国第一部明确规定律师辩护制度的法律草案，不过终因各地督抚以"招致祸患"为由，百般阻挠而胎死腹中。在清政府着手进行司法改革的背景下，直

天津地方法院
Tianjin District Court

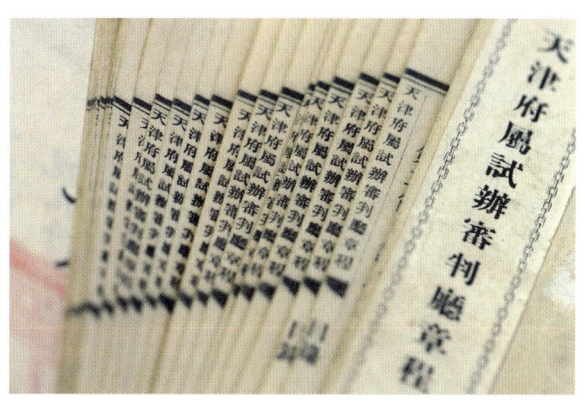

天津府属试办审判厅章程
Regulation on Tianjin Pilot Adjudicative Office

1921	1922	1923	1924	1925	1926	1927	1928	1929	1930	1931	1932	1933
1947	1948	1949	1950	1951	1952	1953	1954	1955	1956	1957	1958	1959
1973	1974	1975	1976	1977	1978	1979	1980	1981	1982	1983	1984	1985
1999	2000	2001	2002	2003	2004	2005	2006	2007	2008	2009	2010	2011

20 世纪前期的天津地方法院
Tianjin District Court in the early 20th century

隶总督兼北洋大臣袁世凯于光绪三十二年决定在天津试办审判厅，并令天津知府凌福彭拟定章程、筹建审判厅。光绪三十三年二月十日（1907年3月23日），天津高等审判分厅正式对外办公，全国最早的地方审判机构、检察机构在天津成立。

As early as March 11, 1902, the Qing government issued an order: "Carefully select those who are familiar with Chinese and Western laws, and recommend them to Beijing, waiting for the briefing, and opening the library for compilation." After that, Shen Jiaben and Wu Tingfang began to "consider the Western laws and carefully study the rules". In the memorial to Emperor Guangxu, they explained the necessity of setting up a lawyer: "Using a Chinese case and borrowing a foreigner to defend his case, we has found it to be unreasonable. Moreover, the consul's power of extraterritoriality has become more tainted. How can the future troubles be imagined?" In 1906, Shen Jiaben and Wu Tingfang presided over the completion of *The Draft Criminal and Civil Procedure Law of Qing Dynasty* and directly introduced the Western litigation system and lawyer system. This is the first draft of China's litigation regulations, and it is also China's first draft law that clearly stipulates the lawyer's defense system. However, it was still aborted due to various interruptions by local governors on the grounds of "causing disaster". Under the background of the Qing government embarking on judicial reform, Yuan Shikai, the Governor of Zhili and the Minister of Beiyang, decided in 1906 to set up a adjudicative office in Tianjin and ordered the Magistrate of Tianjin, Ling Fupeng, to draw up a charter and prepare for the establishment of a adjudicative office. On March 23, 1907, the Tianjin High Adjudicative Branch officially opened its doors to the outside world, and the country's earliest local judicial and procuratorial institutions were established in Tianjin.

天津高等审判分厅与此前在天津设立的全国最早的警察机构和最早的近代监狱（习艺所）共同形成了近代天津完备的司法体系。宣统元年（1909）和宣统二年（1910），清政府先后颁布了《各级审判厅试办章程》和《法院编制法》，以法律的形式明确了律师存在的合法性，比如"充京师及各省法政学堂，律师历三年以上者；候补推事，候补检察官，充任京、省法政学堂教习五年以上者"等等。作为律师执业的重要舞台，审判厅成立以后，民间讼师也再度活跃起来。通过对欧美的司法制度的考察，清政府深刻地认识到："各国审判制度虽略有不同，但律师之保障权利，征东西之各国，殆无不一致。我国省城及商埠审判厅业于年前次第成立，自应及时筹设律师。"民间的诉求和司法机器的运转，使得法律职业共同体的形成完全不能脱离律师制度，清政府的各级审判厅对于及时引进律师的尝试，始终在曲折中前行。

The Tianjin High Adjudicative Branch and the country's earliest police agency and the earliest modern prison (workshop) previously established in Tianjin have formed a complete judicial system in modern Tianjin. In 1909 and 1910, the Qing government successively promulgated the *Trial Regulations for Adjudicative Offices at All Levels* and the *Court Preparation Law*, clarified the legality of the existence of lawyers in the form of law. For example, those who once held positions in the capital and the law and politics schools of various provinces, have a lawyer with more than three years of experience, alternate judge, alternate prosecutor, those who have served as a teacher in the Beijing or Provincial School of Law and Political Science for more than five years, etc. As an important stage for lawyers to practice, after the adjudicative office was established, civil shysters are also active again. Through the inspection of the European and American judicial systems, the Qing government deeply realized: "Although the trial systems of different countries are slightly different, the protection of the rights of lawyers is the same in all countries in the East and the West. Adjudicative offices in our country's provincial cities and commercial ports have been established years ago, so it is natural that lawyers should be established in time." The demands of the common people and the operation of the judicial apparatus make the formation of a legal professional community completely inseparable from the lawyer system. The adjudicative offices at all levels of the Qing government always tried to bring in lawyers in a timely manner.

六

天津律师运用自身法律技能，在全国最早参与民族救亡运动，为周恩来等新民主主义革命志士"被捕""审判"进行辩护。

Tianjin lawyers used their own legal skills to participate in the national salvation movement for the first time in the country, defending the "arrest" and "trial" of Zhou Enlai and others, patriots of the new democratic revolution.

在五四运动爆发的同年，周恩来在天津成立了最著名的学生革命团体——觉悟社。1919年12月，周恩来、马千里、于方舟等人创设天津学生联合会，以鲜明的斗争姿态，组织各界联合会、国民大会，进行抵制日货、反对当局暴政的斗争，成为天津反帝反封建斗争的一面旗帜。1920年1月29日，周恩来等人向当局请愿，要求释放被逮捕的爱国志士，却被以"骚扰罪""妨害安全罪"而"逮捕",后由检察官起诉到天津地方审判厅"审判"。这件事引起了关心国家命运的天津律师梁锡纶、钱俊、兰兴周和北京律师刘崇佑等人的愤慨,他们纷纷站出来为周恩来等爱国志士奔走、辩护。钱俊律师在法庭上慷慨陈词:"国势危亡,岂忍束手待毙?国民分子,天良而发,奋力呼号,热诚所激,不应受刑。"兰兴周律师辩护称:"检察官起诉之各项,殊与事实不符,委未允当。"经过多名律师的不懈努力,北洋政府不得不提前释放了爱国志士。

In the same year that the May Fourth Movement broke out, Zhou Enlai established the most famous student revolutionary group——Juewushe in Tianjin. In December 1919, Zhou Enlai, Ma Qianli, Yu Fangzhou, etc. founded the Tianjin Student Union. They organized various federations and the National Assembly with a clear fighting posture. They carried out an unrelenting struggle to boycott Japanese goods and oppose the tyranny of the authorities, and became a banner of anti-imperialist and anti-feudal struggle in Tianjin. On January 29, 1920, Zhou Enlai and others petitioned the authorities for the release of the arrested patriots, but were "arrested" for "harassment" and "security obstruction", and then prosecuted by the prosecutor to Tianjin Local Adjudicative Office. This incident aroused the indignation of Tianjin lawyers Liang Xilun, Qian Jun, Lan Xingzhou, and Beijing lawyer Liu Chongyou who were concerned about the country's destiny. They all stood up and defended Zhou Enlai and other patriots. Lawyer Qian Jun gave a generous statement in the court: "The country is in danger, how can you bear to die? The nationals, for the sake of nature, screaming hard, and enthusiasm, should not be punished." Lawyer Lan Xingzhou defended: "Every prosecutor prosecuted each other. This item is inconsistent with the facts, and the commission has not been approved." After the unremitting efforts of many lawyers, the Beiyang Government had to release the patriots early.

七

洋务运动和清末新政在天津创造了中国企业的诸多第一,也为律师提供了广阔的执业舞台。

1921	1922	1923	1924	1925	1926	1927	1928	1929	1930	1931	1932	1933
1947	1948	1949	1950	1951	1952	1953	1954	1955	1956	1957	1958	1959
1973	1974	1975	1976	1977	1978	1979	1980	1981	1982	1983	1984	1985
1999	2000	2001	2002	2003	2004	2005	2006	2007	2008	2009	2010	2011

The Westernization Movement and the New Deal in the late Qing Dynasty created many firsts in Chinese enterprises in Tianjin, and also provided a broad practice stage for lawyers.

在清末民国变革的宏大背景下，天津因为特殊的地理位置和开放、包容的文化底蕴，出现了一大批"中国之最"。这里有世界上规模最大的火药厂——天津机器局，有最早的邮政、电报通讯系统，最早的军事学院、高等院校，最早的运营铁路和股份制农场，最早的警察和监狱……这一时期，华洋纠纷不断发生，天津律师就成为了沟通中西方法制的纽带，如张务滋律师曾代理高介臣控诉美商兴泰洋行的买卖合同欠款案件，钱俊律师代理李雅泉控告英商仁记洋行票据拨款纠纷案件以及比商电车公司控告孙恩元损害涉外赔偿案件等等。20世纪上半叶，前清的遗老遗少、下野政客、失势军阀云集津城，寓居租界，购地买楼，成为了近代中国绝无仅有的风景，而曾在政府或大理院任职的曹汝霖、董康、章士钊、林行规、江庸、林棨等知名人士都在天津成为了执业律师。

In the context of the changes in the late Qing Dynasty and the Republic of China, Tianjin, because of its special geographical location and open and inclusive cultural heritage, appeared with a large number of "China's best". Here is the world's largest gunpowder factory——Tianjin Machinery Bureau, the earliest postal and telegraph communication systems, the earliest military academies, colleges and universities, the earliest railway operations and joint-stock farms, the earliest police and prison... During this period, disputes between China and foreign countries continued to occur, and Tianjin lawyers became the link between Chinese and Western legal systems. For example, lawyer Zhang Wuzi represented Gao Jiechen in suing Young & Tyle for arrears in the sales contract, Qian Jun represented Li Yaquan suing Fobes & Co., William for bill appropriation disputes, and Tianjin Tramways & Lighting Co., Ltd. sued Sun Enyuan for damages in foreign-related compensation cases, and so on. In the first half of the 20th century, survivals of the former Qing Dynasty, politicians, and defeated warlords gathered in Tianjin to live in concessions and purchase land and buildings, which became the unique scenery in modern China. Cao Rulin, Dong Kang, Zhang Shizhao, Lin Xinggui, Jiang Yong, Lin Qi and other celebrities who served in the government and the Daliyuan have become practicing lawyers in Tianjin.

1934	1935	1936	1937	1938	1939	1940	1941	1942	1943	1944	1945	1946
1960	1961	1962	1963	1964	1965	1966	1967	1968	1969	1970	1971	1972
1986	1987	1988	1989	1990	1991	1992	1993	1994	1995	1996	1997	1998
2012	2013	2014	2015	2016	2017	2018	2019	2020	2021	……		

天津自设立之日起就发挥着"九河要津,天子经由"的桥头堡作用。九国租界,不仅书写了一段民族屈辱与抗争的历史,而且为天津的变革与发展带来了契机。西方文明以天津为跳板进入中国,天津也自然而然地成为了清政府应对华洋共处纷杂局面并推行各种革新举措的中心。从利顺德到劝业场,从大公报馆到饮冰室,百年间风云际会,天津涌现出了一大批博古通今、学贯中西的律师。当代律师自应追寻、挖掘先辈的优良传统,推陈出新,继往开来,为民族的伟大复兴贡献自己的力量。

Since the establishment of Tianjin, Tianjin has always played the role of a bridgehead of "the important fund of the Nine Rivers through which the emperor passes". The nine-nation concession not only wrote a history of national humiliation and resistance, but also brought opportunities for Tianjin's reform and development. Western civilization entered China using Tianjin as a springboard, and Tianjin naturally became the center of the Qing government's response to the chaotic situation of Chinese and foreign coexistence and various innovative measures. From the Astor Hotel to Quanye Bazaar, from *Ta-Kung-Pao* Office to Yinbing Chamber, a hundred years of turmoil have emerged in Tianjin, with a large number of lawyers who have learned Chinese and Western skills. Contemporary lawyers should pursue and excavate the fine traditions of their ancestors, bring forth the new, carry forward the past, and contribute to the great revival of the nation.

传统讼师与近代律师的萌芽

THE ORIGIN OF TRADITIONAL SHYSTER AND MODERN LAWYER

律师溯源：传统社会的讼师 /022
THE ORIGIN OF LAWYERS: SHYSTER IN TRADITIONAL SOCIETY

清季司法主权的丧失 /027
THE LOSS OF JUDICIAL SOVEREIGNTY IN THE LATE QING DYNASTY

一、领事裁判权和会审公廨制度 /027
1. Consular Jurisdiction and Joint Trial System

二、天津教案的影响 /031
2. The Influence of Tianjin Religious Case

北洋大学法科：中国最早的法学教育机构 /036
LAW DEPARTMENT OF BEIYANG UNIVERSITY: THE EARLIEST LEGAL EDUCATION INSTITUTION IN CHINA

律师溯源：
传统社会的讼师

THE ORIGIN OF LAWYERS: SHYSTER IN TRADITIONAL SOCIETY

律师制度起源于西方，古希腊、古罗马时期的诉讼代理人、辩护人堪称西方律师的雏形。英国是近代律师制度的发源地。最初，英国律师分为出庭律师和诉状律师。到了13世纪后半期爱德华一世在位时，随着巡回审判、陪审制度、令状制度的推行，出庭律师和诉状律师逐渐结合，构成了英国职业律师群体，为西方近代律师制度的形成奠定了基础。

The lawyer system originated in the west, and the lawsuit agents and defenders in ancient Greece and Roma could be regarded as the rudiment of western lawyers. Britain was the birthplace of modern lawyer system. At first, British lawyers included barrister and solicitor. When Edward I was in power in the second half of the 13th century, with the implementation of the circuit trial, jury system and writ system, the barrister and the solicitor gradually combined to form a group of professional lawyers in Britain, which laid the foundation for the modern western lawyer system.

讼师是古代中国专门替人写诉状、咨询、打官司的人。作为这一群体最普遍的称呼，讼师一词最早出现在南宋，此前称作"教令人者""为人作词牒者"或"诈伪之民"；南宋以后，讼师还有"讼师官鬼""把持人""假儒衣冠""无赖宗室""茶食人""哗鬼讼师""刀笔先生""讼棍""法家"的叫法，不一而足。

In ancient China, shysters were the person who wrote complaint, consultation,

1934	1935	1936	1937	1938	1939	1940	1941	1942	1943	1944	1945	1946
1960	1961	1962	1963	1964	1965	1966	1967	1968	1969	1970	1971	1972
1986	1987	1988	1989	1990	1991	1992	1993	1994	1995	1996	1997	1998
2012	2013	2014	2015	2016	2017	2018	2019	2020	2021	……		

and lawsuit for the people. As the most common name for this group, the appellation of shyster first appeared in the Southern Song Dynasty. Previously, it was called "a person who teaches others" "a person who writes a word for others" or "a deceitful people". After the Southern Song Dynasty, shysters were also known as "officials act as shysters" "controllers" "fake Confucian clothes" "rogue clansmen" "tea eaters" "evildoers act as shysters" "Mr. Knife Pen" "shyster" and "legalists".

中国很早就出现了诉讼代理人，西周晚期的𤷍匜便有目前最早的记录。𤷍匜1975年3月出土于陕西省岐山县董家村窖藏，铭文铸于器盖和腹底内壁，内容连属，共154字（有合文三）。铭文记载了一起民告官的案件，除法官、原告、被告外，参加庭审的还有四人，分别是诉讼代理人、证人和两名书记员；诉讼代理人还向法庭提供了讼词和辩护词。

𤷍匜铭文

Inscription of Ying Yi bronze ware

In ancient China, there were lawsuit agents for a long time, and it was first recorded in Ying Yi bronze ware in the late Western Zhou Dynasty. Ying Yi was unearthed in the cellar of Dongjia village, Qishan County, Shanxi Province in March 1975, and 154 character inscriptions were found on the lid and inside of the vessel. The inscription recorded a case which the people sued the officials. The case included a judge, a plaintiff, a defendant, a lawsuit agent, a witness, and two clerks. Moreover, the lawsuit agent also provided the court with the statement of suit and defense.

春秋时期郑国的邓析是后人普遍认可的最早的职业讼师，他将刑法写在竹简上，称作《竹刑》。邓析广收门徒，讲授法律，向他学讼的人不在少数。邓析帮人打官司，以擅长辩论著称，"以非为是，以是为非，是非无度"，荀子称其"持之有效，言之有理"。不过，邓析与官方的争辩和他私著《竹刑》的行为令统治者感到不满。于是，邓析被以"小人乱郑"之名处死，而他本人也成了讼师的鼻祖。

In the Spring and Autumn Period, Deng Xi of the state of Zheng was the earliest

旧式审判
Traditional trial

litegator generally recognized by later generations. He wrote the criminal law on bamboo slips, which was called *Bamboo Punishment*. Deng Xi recruited disciples and taught them law during that time. Deng Xi was known for being good at debating, and would take wrong as right, right as wrong, right and wrong without limit. Xunzi appraised Deng Xi who was effective and reasonable. However, Deng's argument with the government and his behavior in writing *Bamboo Punishment* made the rulers feel dissatisfied, so he was executed by the ruler and he was regarded as the originator of shyster.

秦朝秉承法家传统,以吏为师。两汉则以《春秋》等儒家经典为审案的重要依据。两宋是讼师发展的重要阶段。宋仁宗时,民间健讼之风初露端倪,"兴讼""健讼""嚣讼"之词屡见不鲜。宋都南迁之后,长江流域的经济得到了进一步发展,民间田地、房屋、财产流转交易增多,商业贸易行为繁盛,争利好讼之风渐盛,且成为全国普遍现象。讼师也在宋代成为了一种社会职业。明清两代,民间的诉讼观念已相当普遍,讼师参与的助讼活动不仅涉及田产、钱债、继承、婚姻等民事领域,而且在刑事诉讼中也发挥着重要的作用。

The Qin Dynasty inherited the legalist tradition of taking officials as judges. In the Han Dynasty, the judge takes *The Spring and Autumn Annals* and other Confucian classics as the important basis for the trial. Song Dynasty was an important stage of the development of shysters. During the reign of Emperor Renzong of the Song Dynasty, the ethos of civil litigation was beginning to appear, the words of "raising litigation", "being good at litigation" and "clamour litigation" became popular. After the capital of Song Dynasty moved to the south, the economy of the Changjiang River Basin got further development, the transaction of land, houses and property increased, the commercial trade activities flourished, and the trend of dispute for profits and lawsuits gradually flourished, which became a common phenomenon in the whole country. Shyster also became a social profession in Song Dynasty. In the Ming and Qing Dynasties, the concept of civil litigation had been quite common. The litigation activities participated by the shysters not only involved in the fields of property, money, debt, inheritance, marriage and other civil fields, but also played an important role in criminal proceedings.

1921	1922	1923	1924	1925	1926	1927	1928	1929	1930	1931	1932	1933
1947	1948	1949	1950	1951	1952	1953	1954	1955	1956	1957	1958	1959
1973	1974	1975	1976	1977	1978	1979	1980	1981	1982	1983	1984	1985
1999	2000	2001	2002	2003	2004	2005	2006	2007	2008	2009	2010	2011

由此可见，中国古代的讼师发挥着近代律师的功能，而最早将"律师"用于提供法律服务人群的做法可追溯到同治十年（1871）。当时天津教案刚刚结束，清政府派崇厚出使法国道歉。陪同出访的翻译之一、京师同文馆培养的高才生张德彝创造性地使用了"律师"这个词。他在《随使法国记》中三次提到欧洲人向他介绍律师的活动，因为他们不是通常意义上的律师，而是担任政府法律顾问的高级专家，所以张德彝没有选择在中国社会地位不高的"讼师"进行对译，而是以"律师"相称。此后，律师一词逐渐流行开来。民元初创之时，《时报》刊登了一篇题为《新陈代谢》的文章，提到了一系列新旧更替的事物，其中就有"律师兴，讼师灭"，反映了时人对新生事物——律师的接受。

It could be seen that the ancient Chinese shysters played the function of modern lawyers, and the first time to use the word "lawyer" in providing legal services could be traced back to 1871. At that time, the Tianjin Religious Case had just ended, and the Qing government sent Chonghou to France to apologize. Zhang Deyi, one of the translators accompanying him and a talented student trained by Beijing Tongwen library, creatively used the word "lawyer". In the *French Envoy*, he mentioned three times that Europeans introduced lawyers to him, because the lawyers were not ordinary lawyers, but senior experts who served as legal advisers to the government. Therefore, Zhang Deyi did not choose "shysters" with low social status in China to translate, but used "lawyers" instead. Since then, the word of lawyer had gradually became popular. At the beginning of the Republic of China, the *Times* published an article entitled *Metabolism*, which mentioned a series of new and old things. Among them, the phrase "lawyers prosper, shysters perish" reflected people's acceptance of lawyers.

清季司法主权的丧失

THE LOSS OF JUDICIAL SOVEREIGNTY IN THE LATE QING DYNASTY

一、领事裁判权和会审公廨制度

1. Consular Jurisdiction and Joint Trial System

鸦片战争结束后,中英《南京条约》规定:"凡系大英国人,无论本国、属国军民等,今在中国所管辖各地方被禁者,大清大皇帝准即释放。""凡系中国人,前在英人所据之邑居住者,或与英人有来往者,或有跟随及伺候英国官人者,均由大皇帝俯降御旨,誊录天下,恩准全然免罪;且凡系中国人,为英国事被拿监禁受难者,亦加恩释放。"《南京条约》中这些条款的签订标志着中国开始丧失司法主权。第二年,中英双方再次签订《五口通商章程》,其中"英人华民交涉词讼一款"规定:"倘遇有交涉词讼,管事官(即领事)不能劝息,又不能将就,即移请华官公同查明其事,既得实情,即为秉公定断,免滋讼端。其英人如何科罪,由英国议定章程、法律,发给管事官(即领事)照办。华人如何科罪,应治以中国之法。"这无疑是领事裁判权制度在中国的开端。此后,凡在中国享有领事裁判权的国家,其侨民可不受中国法律的管辖,无论发生怎样违反中国法律的行为,或者成为民事、刑事诉讼当事人,中国的司法机关都无权裁判,只能由该国领事或该国设在中国的司法机构依据其本国法律进行裁判。咸丰八年(1858)《(中英)天津条约》第十五款"英国属民相涉案件,不论人、产,皆归英官查办"和第十六款"英国民人有犯事者,皆由英国惩办"的签订则使列强巩固并扩大了已攫取的领事裁判权。

After the Opium War, the *Treaty of Nanjing* stipulated that "the Great Emperor of the Qing Dynasty will release all the British who are forbidden in China, regardless of their own country, military and civil affairs". "All those who are Chinese, who lived in the cities where the British lived, who have contacts with

1921	1922	1923	1924	1925	1926	1927	1928	1929	1930	1931	1932	1933
1947	1948	1949	1950	1951	1952	1953	1954	1955	1956	1957	1958	1959
1973	1974	1975	1976	1977	1978	1979	1980	1981	1982	1983	1984	1985
1999	2000	2001	2002	2003	2004	2005	2006	2007	2008	2009	2010	2011

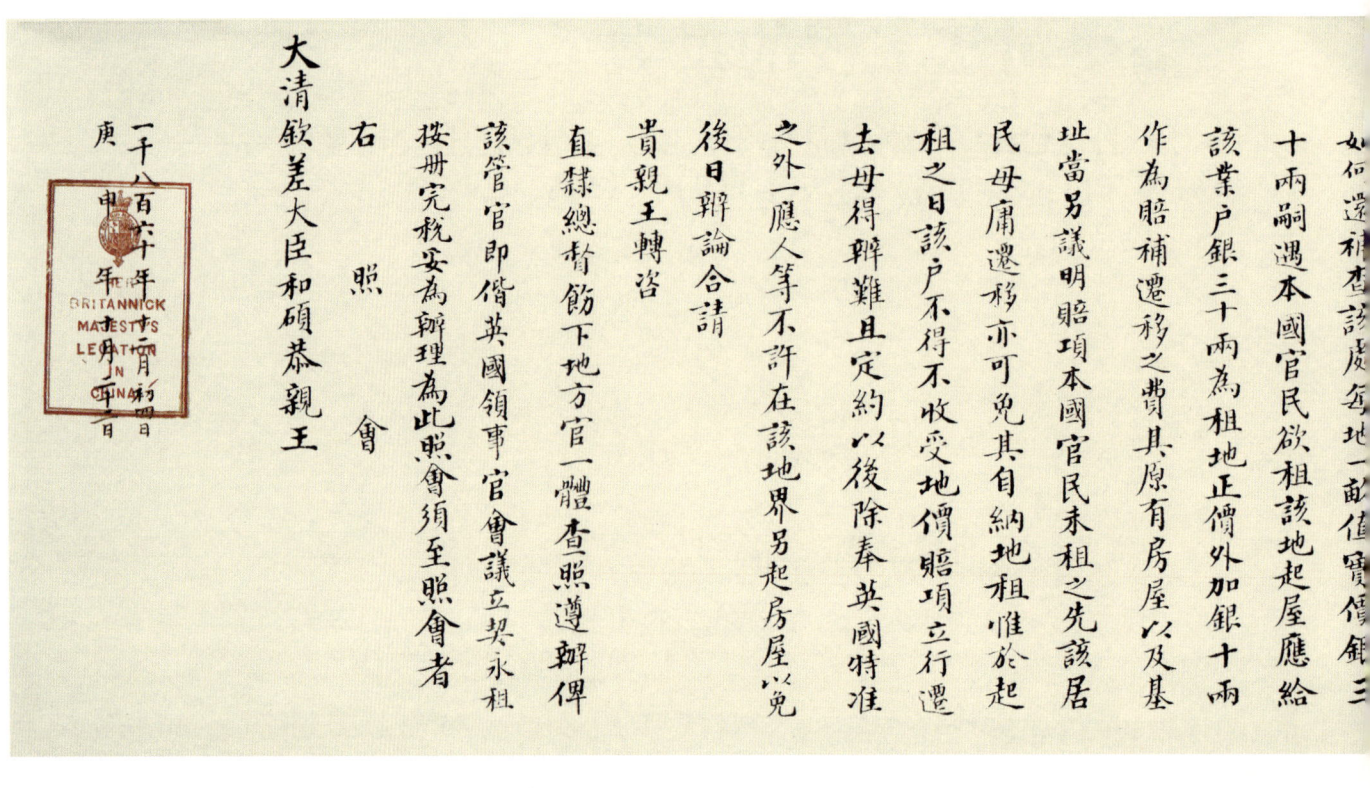

咸丰十年十月（1860年12月）英国驻华公使普鲁斯照会清政府要求在天津设立租界

In December 1860, British Minister Proust sent a note to the Qing government demanding the establishment of a concession in Tianjin

the British, or who follow and wait for the British officials, will be given the imperial edict by the Great Emperor, transcribed from the world, and will be free from all guilt. Moreover, all those who are Chinese and imprisoned for British affairs will be released with grace." The signing of these clauses in the *Treaty of Nanjing* marked the beginning of China's loss of judicial sovereignty. In the following year, China and Britain signed the *Five Ports Trade Constitution* again, in which "the English and Chinese people's litigations" stipulates: "If there is a litigation, the steward (i.e. the consul) cannot persuade or make do with it. He will ask the Chinese officials and the public to find out the matter. When the truth is obtained, he will make a fair decision and avoid litigation. The British were punished in accordance with the articles of association and laws agreed upon by the United Kingdom, and sent them to the bailiff (i.e. the consul). Chinese people should be punished according to Chinese law. " This was undoubtedly the beginning of consular jurisdiction system in China. Since then, any country with consular jurisdiction in China might not be subject to the jurisdiction of Chinese law. No matter how it violated Chinese law or became a party to civil or criminal proceedings, the Chinese judicial organ had no right to make a judgment. It could only make a judgment by the consul of that country or the judicial organ of that country in China in accordance with its domestic law. In 1858, the *Treaty of Tianjin* between China and Britain was signed. The signing of the article 15 "Cases involving the British people, regardless of person or property, shall be investigated and dealt with by the British officials" and the article 16 "If the British people have offenders, they shall be punished by the British" consolidated and expanded the jurisdiction seized by the powers.

与领事裁判权相关，中国的司法主权受到列强侵犯的另一个重要表现就是会审公廨制度的建立。同治三年（1864），清政府采纳英国驻沪领事巴夏礼的建议，在上海英租界设立理事衙门（又称"洋泾浜北首理事衙门"），由中外官员共同审理华洋之间的案件。会审公廨制度严重破坏了中国的司法主权，它令外国领事、陪审官可以根据利益的需要直接干预审判；而纯粹华人之间的案子，外国陪审官也会以各种各样的理由介入，清政府的司法主权遭到了进一步的侵犯。

Related to consular jurisdiction, another important manifestation of the infringement of China's judicial sovereignty by foreign powers was the establishment of the joint trial system. In 1864, the Qing government adopted the proposal of British Consul Harry Parkes in Shanghai and set up a council yamen (also known as "the northern head Council yamen of the Pidgin Creek") in the British concession of Shanghai, where Chinese and foreign officials jointly tried the cases between China and foreign countries. The joint trial system had seriously damaged China's judicial sovereignty, which enabled foreign consuls and jurors to directly intervene in judicial activities according to their own interests. In the case of only Chinese litigants existed, foreign jurors would intervene in the trial for various reasons, which further infringed the judicial sovereignty of the Qing government.

领事裁判权使洋人获得了保障利益的治外法权，会审公廨制度又成了列强干预司法、干预审判的工具，不仅严重侵蚀了中国的司法主权，而且大大超出了保护外国侨民不受中国法律制裁的本意，成了在华洋人攫取各种利益的保护伞。至19世纪末，清政府逐渐认识到丧失司法主权对国家政权造成的危害，并开始有意识地作出反应，而清末司法改革也呼之欲出。

Consular jurisdiction gave foreigners extraterritoriality to protect their interests, and the system of joint trial had become a tool for foreign powers to intervene in justice and trial, which not only seriously eroded China's judicial sovereignty, but also went far beyond the original intention of protecting foreign nationals from Chinese legal sanctions and became a protective umbrella for foreigners in China to seize various interests. By the end of the 19th century, the Qing government gradually realized the harm of the loss of judicial sovereignty to the state power, and began to respond consciously, and the judicial reform in the late Qing Dynasty was about to come out.

二、天津教案的影响
2. The Influence of Tianjin Religious Case

咸丰十年（1860）第二次鸦片战争结束以后，天津被迫开为通商口岸，英、美、法三国率先胁迫清政府将海河西岸的紫竹林一带划为租界，从此拉开了天津近代历史的序幕。随着领事裁判权的确立，天津的司法主权也开始受到挑战。如果说会审公廨制度是洋人平缓攫取上海司法主权工具的话，那么天津教案就是有关洋人观审、会审的一次激烈的碰撞与爆发。

After the end of the Second Opium War in 1860, Tianjin was forced to open as a trading port. Britain, the United States, and France took the lead in coercing the Qing government to delimit the Zizhulin area on the west bank of the Haihe River as a concession, which opened the prelude of Tianjin's modern history. With the establishment of consular jurisdiction, Tianjin's judicial sovereignty began to be challenged. If the joint trial system was a tool for foreigners to seize the judicial sovereignty of Shanghai, then the Tianjin Religious Case was a fierce collision and outbreak of the joint trial of foreigners.

咸丰十一年（1861）年末，法国天主教遣使会神父和仁爱会的修女购买了天津三岔河口北岸望海楼旧址及其西侧崇禧观的一公顷土地。同治八年（1869），法国神父谢福音拆除崇禧观和附近民房以建造望海楼教堂，引起了当地百姓极大的愤慨。第二年夏，天津爆发瘟疫，法国人开办的育婴堂中30余名儿童死亡，关于天主教神父和修女派人用药迷拐孩子并挖眼剖心制药的谣言随即流传开来。

At the end of 1861, the French Catholic missionary priest and the nuns of Daughters of Charity purchased one hectare of the former site of Wanghai building on the north bank of sanchahekou in Tianjin and Chongxi Temple on the west side. In 1869, the French priest Chevrier demolished Chongxi Temple and nearby houses to

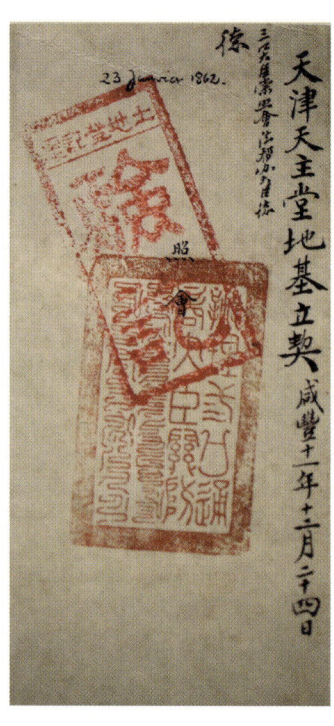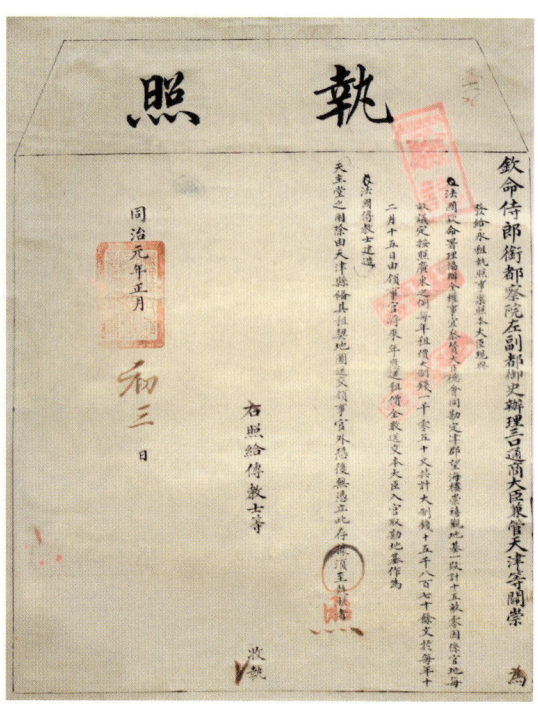

咸丰十一年（1861）年末天津天主堂地基立契（左）
In early 1862, the foundation contract of Tianjin Catholic Church (left)

同治元年（1862）望海楼教堂的永租执照（右）
The permanent license of the Church of Our Lady of Victory in 1862 (right)

build the Church of Our Lady of Victory, which aroused great indignation of the local people. In the summer of the next year, a plague broke out in Tianjin, and more than 30 children died in the French nursery. Rumors spreaded that Catholic priests and nuns sent people to abduct children with drugs and made drugs by digging their eyes and dissecting their hearts.

民间组织水火会开始主动组织捉拿人贩子，不久即捕获一名叫武兰珍的迷拐犯。武兰珍供称其作案所用迷药是法国天主教仁慈堂所提供。未经核实的消息不胫而走，聚集在教堂外的愤怒市民与教堂人员发生口角，抛砖互殴。

The non-governmental organization Shuihuohui began to take the initiative to arrest the traffickers, and soon captured a abductor named Wu Lanzhen. Wu Lanzhen confessed that the drug used in her crime was provided by the French Catholic Mercy Church. The unverified news spreaded like wildfire, and angry citizens gathered outside the church quarreled with church staff, and fought each other with brick.

1934	1935	1936	1937	1938	1939	1940	1941	1942	1943	1944	1945	1946
1960	1961	1962	1963	1964	1965	1966	1967	1968	1969	1970	1971	1972
1986	1987	1988	1989	1990	1991	1992	1993	1994	1995	1996	1997	1998
2012	2013	2014	2015	2016	2017	2018	2019	2020	2021	……		

仁慈堂修女本拟请民众派代表入内调查真相，不过被法国领事丰大业阻止。他带人闯入三口通商大臣驻地和天津府衙，要求崇厚、张光藻派兵镇压，却没得到满意的结果。丰大业后于狮子林浮桥上遇到静海知县刘杰，辩论中，丰大业向刘杰开枪，射到挡在前面的刘杰家人刘七。围观百姓被丰大业的开枪行为激怒，打死了丰大业、领事馆秘书西蒙、领事馆翻译夫妇、神父谢福音以及多名法国、俄国商人，望海楼教堂、育婴堂以及教堂旁的法国领事馆均遭到焚毁，酿成了震惊中外的天津教案。

The nun of Mercy Church originally asked the people to send representatives to investigate the truth, but she was blocked by the French consul Fontanier. He led people to break into the residence of Three-port Commerce Minister and Tianjin government, and demanded Chonghou and Zhang Guangzao to send troops to suppress them, but he didn't get satisfactory results. Fontanier met Liu Jie later, the county magistrate of Jinghai, on the Shizilin bridge. During the debate, Fontanier shot Liu Qi, a family member who was standing in front of Liu Jie. Enraged by Fontanier's shooting, the onlookers killed Fontanier, the consulate secretary Simon, the consulate interpreter and his wife, priest Chevrier, and a number of French and Russian businessmen. The Church of Our Lady of Victory, the French nursery and the French Consulate beside the church were all burned, resulting in a shocking Tianjin Religious Case.

天津教案爆发后，涉案国法、俄、西、美、普、比、英纷纷出面干涉，威胁清政府要公平妥善的处理。最终，清政府在法国的要求下，判决处死变乱中为首的16人，4人缓刑，充军流放25人，并将天津知府张光藻、静海知县刘杰革职，充军发配到黑龙江，赔偿法国损失46万两白银，赔偿俄、英、美各两万两白银，并派崇厚出使法国道歉。

After the outbreak of the Tianjin Religious Case, France, Russia, Spain, the United States, Prussia, Belgium and Britain intervened one after another, and they threated the Qing government to deal with it fairly and properly. Finally, at the request of France, the Qing government sentenced 16 people to death, 4 to probation, 25 to exile, and sent Zhang Guangzao, the magistrate of Tianjin, and Liu Jie, the magistrate of Jinghai, to Heilongjiang Province. Moreover the Qing government

焚毁后的仁慈堂
Mercy Church after burning

compensated France for the loss of 460000 taels of silver, Russia, Britain, and the United States for 20000 taels of silver, and sent Chonghou to France to apologize.

天津教案不仅在当时引起了巨大的轰动，而且影响深远。清政府的立法权、司法权都受到了极大的干涉和削弱。曾国藩和清政府本不想处罚地方官员，但迫于各国公使、领事的压力，最终不得不将府县官员撤职。同时，拥有观审权、会审权的外国代表在审案时，往往对中国法官施加压力，要求清政府满足自己的要求。于是，地方官权量利弊，大多采取隐瞒案件真相的手段，牺牲一些普通民众来了结案件，从而严重破坏了司法的公正。

Tianjin Religious Case not only caused a huge sensation at that time, but also had a far-reaching impact. The legislative and judicial powers of the Qing government were greatly interfered and weakened. Zeng Guofan and the Qing government did not want to punish local officials, but under the pressure of ministers and

1934	1935	1936	1937	1938	1939	1940	1941	1942	1943	1944	1945	1946
1960	1961	1962	1963	1964	1965	1966	1967	1968	1969	1970	1971	1972
1986	1987	1988	1989	1990	1991	1992	1993	1994	1995	1996	1997	1998
2012	2013	2014	2015	2016	2017	2018	2019	2020	2021	……		

consuls of various countries, they had to remove the officials from their posts. At the same time, the foreign representatives who had the power of observation and joint trial often exerted pressure on the Chinese judges to meet their own requirements. As a result, local officials closed the case by sacrificing ordinary people and concealing the facts of the case, thus it seriously undermined the judicial justice.

总之，天津教案的处理充分暴露了清政府司法主权的丧失，不过也为督促清季司法改革，甚至废除领事裁判权，增添了一枚重重的砝码。

In a word, the handling of Tianjin Religious Case fully exposed the loss of judicial sovereignty of the Qing government, but also added a heavy weight to urge the judicial reform in the Qing Dynasty and even abolished the consular jurisdiction.

第一代仁慈堂
The first Mercy Church

1921	1922	1923	1924	1925	1926	1927	1928	1929	1930	1931	1932	1933
1947	1948	1949	1950	1951	1952	1953	1954	1955	1956	1957	1958	1959
1973	1974	1975	1976	1977	1978	1979	1980	1981	1982	1983	1984	1985
1999	2000	2001	2002	2003	2004	2005	2006	2007	2008	2009	2010	2011

北洋大学法科：
中国最早的法学教育机构

LAW DEPARTMENT OF BEIYANG UNIVERSITY: THE EARLIEST LEGAL EDUCATION INSTITUTION IN CHINA

光绪二十一年（1895），直隶津海关道兼直隶津海关监督、"中国实业之父"盛宣怀通过直隶总督兼北洋大臣王文韶禀奏德宗皇帝设立新式学堂。同年八月十八日（10月2日），德宗皇帝御笔钦准，成立天津北洋西学学堂（1896年更名为天津北洋大学堂，1903年改称北洋大学堂，民国成立后改称北洋大学及国立北洋大学，今天津大学的前身）。这是中国近代历史上第一所官办大学，10月2日也成为了中国第一所大学的建校纪念日。

In 1895, Sheng Xuanhuai, the "Master of Chinese industry" and the supervisor of Zhili Tianjin Customs Dao, sent a letter to Emperor Dezong to set up the new school through Wang Wenshao, the Governor of Zhili and Minister of Beiyang. On October 2 of the same year, Emperor Dezong established Tianjin Western Studies School (renamed Tianjin Beiyang University in 1896, renamed Beiyang University in 1903, renamed Beiyang University and National Beiyang University after the founding of the Republic of China, the predecessor of Tianjin University today). This was the first official university in modern Chinese history, and October 2 had become the anniversary of the founding of the first university in China.

针对清王朝在处理内政外交事务上急需法律人才以及开发矿产资源、发展机械加工工业的实际，北洋西学学堂开设了律例学、工程学、矿务学、电学等学科，并随着社会的变化，及时添设新的专业。

1934	1935	1936	1937	1938	1939	1940	1941	1942	1943	1944	1945	1946
1960	1961	1962	1963	1964	1965	1966	1967	1968	1969	1970	1971	1972
1986	1987	1988	1989	1990	1991	1992	1993	1994	1995	1996	1997	1998
2012	2013	2014	2015	2016	2017	2018	2019	2020	2021	……		

In view of the fact that the Qing Dynasty was in urgent need of legal talents in dealing with domestic and foreign affairs, as well as the development of mining resources and mechanical processing industry, Tianjin Western Studies School opened disciplines such as law, engineering, mining, electricity, etc., and added new specialties in time with the change of society.

律例学即为法科，由美籍学者林文德等人讲授，包括大清律例、各国通商条约、万国公法等课程。近代著名法学家、政治家、外交家王宠惠便是北洋西学学堂头等学堂第一班25人中的一员，也是北洋大学法科的首批毕业生之一。王宠惠（1881—1958），字亮畴，广东东莞人。光绪二十一年，刚刚成立的北洋西学学堂在全国招考学员，王宠惠在香港报名参加考试，并以优异的成绩进入北洋西学学堂头等学堂攻读法律。光绪二十五年（1899），王宠惠以最优成绩毕业，并获得了第一张中国大学毕业文凭，又称"钦字第壹号"文凭。

Legal science was the law department, taught by American scholar Edgar Pierce Allen and others, including the laws of the Qing Dynasty, international trade treaties, universal public law and other courses. Wang Chonghui, a famous jurist, politician and diplomat in modern times, was one of the 25 students in the first class of Tianjin Western Studies School, and also one of the first batch of graduates of law department in Beiyang University. Wang Chonghui (1881-1958), born in Dongguan, Guangdong Province. In 1895, the newly established Tianjin Western Studies School recruited students from all over the country. Wang Chonghui signed up for the examination in Hong Kong and entered the first-class school of Tianjin Western Studies School to study law with excellent results. In 1899, Wang Chonghui graduated with the best results and obtained the first Chinese university diploma, also known as "Qinzi No.1" diploma.

此后不久，天津大学堂因义和团运动和八国联军侵华而陷于停顿。光绪二十八年（1902），直隶总督兼北洋大臣袁世凯将其恢复，并于第二年更名为北洋大学堂。重建后的北洋大学法科开设了国文、国史、英文（兼习法文或德文）、西史、生理、天文、大清律例要义、宪法史、宪法、法律总义、法律学原理、罗马法律史、合同律例、刑法、交涉法、罗马法、商法、损伤赔偿法、田产学、成案比较、船法、诉讼法则、约章、理财学、兵学等多门课程。

盛宣怀、丁家立与北洋大学堂师生合影
A group photo of Sheng Xuanhuai, Tenney Charles Daniel and teachers and students of Beiyang University

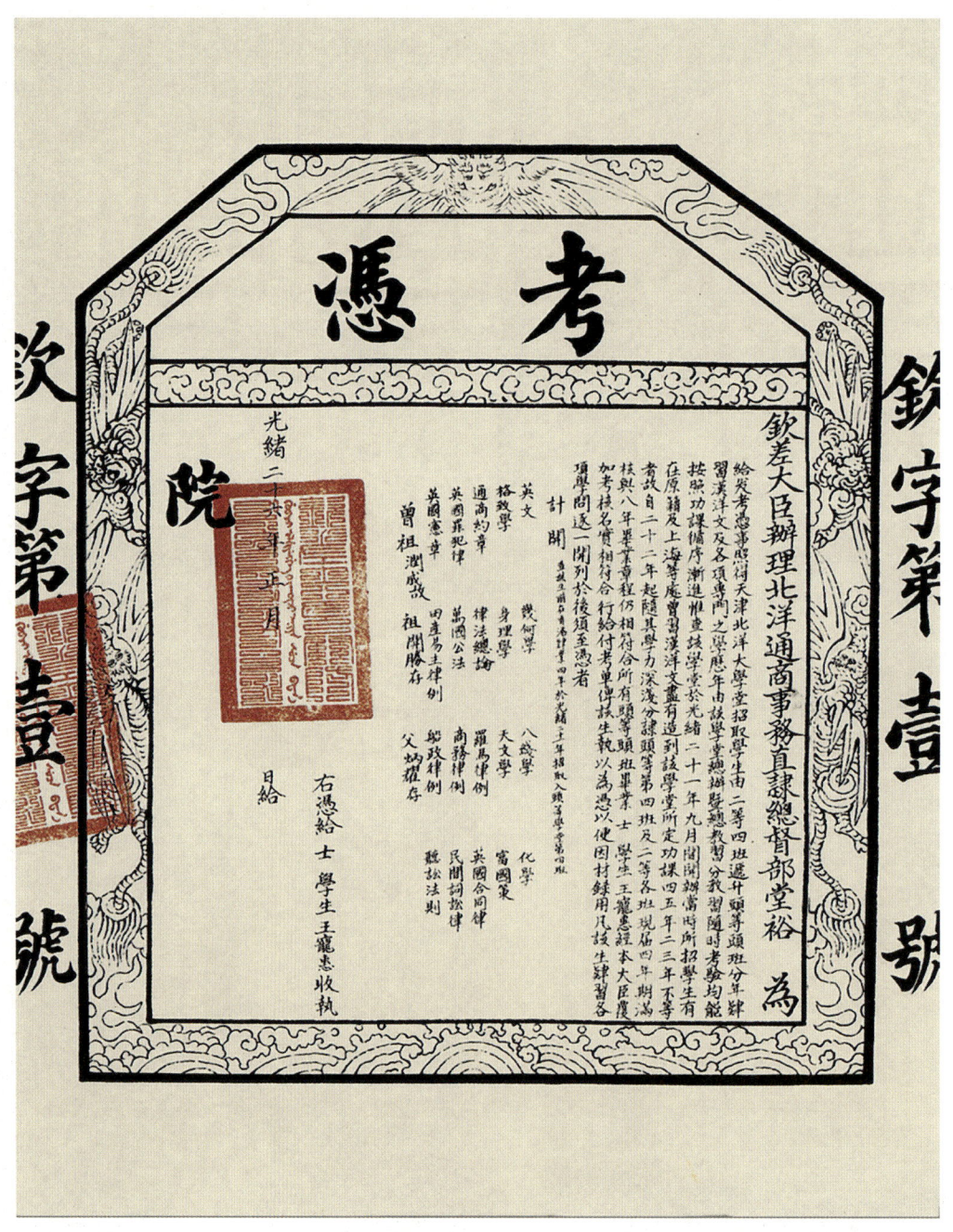

王宠惠"钦字第壹号"文凭
Wang Chonghui's "Qinzi No.1" diploma

Shortly after that, Tianjin University came to a standstill because of the Yihetuan Movement and the invasion of China by the Eight-Power Allied Forces. In 1902, Yuan Shikai, Governor of Zhili and Minister of Beiyang, restored and renamed it Beiyang University in the following year. After reconstruction, the courses of law department were Chinese, Chinese history, English (learning French or German), western history, physiology, astronomy, laws and regulations of Qing Dynasty, history of constitution, constitution, general meaning of law, principles of law, history of Roman law, contract law, criminal law, negotiation law, Roman law, commercial law, damage compensation law, field science, case comparison, shipping law, procedural law, charter, financial management, military science, etc.

1913年,北洋大学根据北洋政府新颁布的《大学规程》对法科课程进行了调整和充实,新开设必修课宪法、行政法、刑法、民法、商法、破产法、刑事诉讼法、民事诉讼法、国际公法、国际私法、罗马法、法制法、法理法、经济法,选修课比较法制史、财政学,并任选英吉利法、德意志法或法兰西法一种。1917年2月,北洋政府教育部发布训令,要求北洋大学所有法律正科班(即本科班)办至毕业为止。1920年6月,北洋大学法科乙班为该校最后一届法律专业毕业班。此后,北洋大学法科停办,并于1924年并入北京大学。

In 1913, Beiyang University adjusted and enriched the law courses according to the new *University Regulations* issued by the Beiyang Government. It opened new compulsory courses such as constitution, administrative law, criminal law, civil law, commercial law, bankruptcy law, criminal procedure law, civil procedure law, international public law, international private law, Roman law, legal law, legal theory law, economic law, and elective courses such as comparative legal history, finance, and choose English law, German law or French law. In February 1917, the Ministry of Education of the Beiyang Government issued an instruction, requiring all the law major classes (undergraduate classes) of Beiyang University to be run until graduation. In June 1920, class B of law department in Beiyang University was the last graduating class of law major. After that, the law department of Beiyang University was closed down and merged into Peking University in 1924.

1913年北洋大学法科乙班师生合影

A group photo of teachers and students in class B of the law department of Beiyang University in 1913

民国时期的北洋大学法科共培养了88名法律专业毕业生，人数虽然不多，但由于北洋大学在课程设置、教学安排、教科书选择等方面一直处于先进水平，并始终保持严谨治学、严格要求、艰苦朴素的校风，因而形成了北洋大学独特的学术传统和校园风貌，培养出了一批法学名家和知名律师，赵天麟、冯熙远、张太雷、吴经熊、贾文范、钱俊、张务滋、吴大业以及清朝末年的王宠惠都先后毕业于北洋大学法科，为20世纪上半叶的中国司法作出了卓越的贡献。

During the period of the Republic of China, a total of 88 law graduates were trained in the law department of Beiyang University. Although the number was small, because Beiyang University had always been at an advanced level in curriculum, teaching arrangement, textbook selection, etc., and had always maintained the school spirit of rigorous scholarship, strict requirements, hardship and simplicity, it had

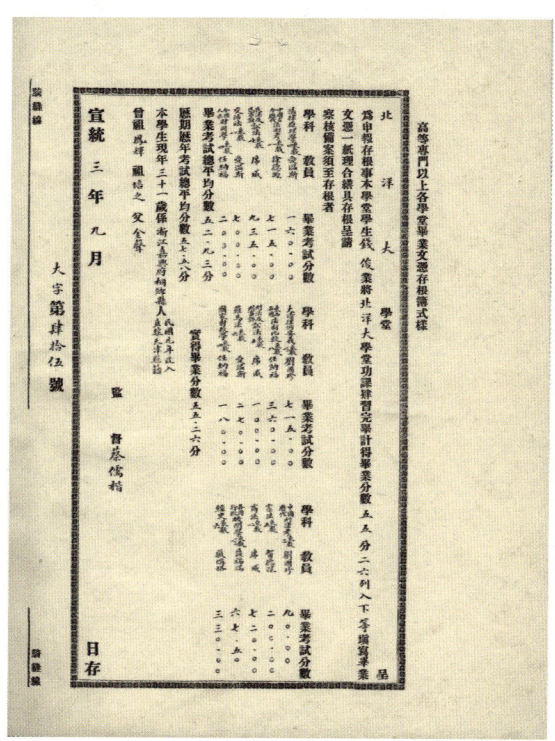

钱俊律师宣统三年（1911）北洋大学堂毕业文凭存根
Lawyer Qian Jun's diploma stub of Beiyang University in 1911

formed its unique academic tradition and campus style. Zhao Tianlin, Feng Xiyuan, Zhang Tailei, Wu Jingxiong, Jia Wenfan, Qian Jun, Zhang Wuzi, Wu Daye and Wang Chonghui, who graduated from the law department of Beiyang University, had made outstanding contributions to Chinese justice in the first half of the 20th century.

清末律师制度的确立与天津的司法尝试

ESTABLISHMENT OF LAWYER SYSTEM IN
THE LATE QING DYNASTY AND
TIANJIN'S JUDICIAL ATTEMPT

严复与开平矿权纠纷 / 046
YAN FU AND KAIPING'S DISPUTE OVER MINERAL RIGHTS

清末司法改革与律师制度的确立 / 053
THE JUDICIAL REFORM AND THE ESTABLISHMENT OF LAWYER SYSTEM IN THE LATE QING DYNASTY

一、司法改革 / 054
1. Judicial Reform

二、律师制度的确立 / 057
2. The Establishment of Lawyer System

北洋法政专门学堂的设立 / 062
ESTABLISHMENT OF BEIYANG SPECIAL SCHOOL OF LAW AND POLITICS

天津审判厅的尝试 / 068
ATTEMPT OF TIANJIN ADJUDICATIVE OFFICE

严复与开平矿权纠纷
YAN FU AND KAIPING'S DISPUTE OVER MINERAL RIGHTS

清末思想家严复（1854—1921）在天津生活了20余年，曾利用其掌握的法律知识，陪同开平矿务局督办张翼到伦敦高等法院起诉英国开平矿务公司。这是中国人第一次到国外参与中国公司的诉讼维权活动。

Yan Fu (1854-1921), a thinker in the late Qing Dynasty, lived in Tianjin for more than 20 years. He used his legal knowledge to accompany Zhang Yi, the supervisor of Kaiping Mining Bureau, to sue British Kaiping Mining Company in London's High Court. This is the first time that Chinese people have gone abroad to participate in litigation rights protection activities of Chinese companies.

严复字几道，初名传初，福建侯官（今闽侯县）人。光绪三年（1877）赴英国抱士穆德大学学习，后入格林尼次海军大学学习。其间，严复广泛接触英国社会，遂成为一个具有西方民主思想、向西方寻找真理的先进的中国人。光绪六年（1880），北洋大臣李鸿章在天津创办北洋水师学堂，调严复任总教习，光绪十六年（1890）任总办。七年后，严复与夏曾佑、王修植在天津创办《国闻报》，成为维新派在北方重要的宣传阵地。这一时期，严复还集中精力介译西方学术名著，如《天演论》《原富》《法意》《名学》《群己权界论》《名学浅说》《群学肄言》《社会通诠》等。光绪二十六年（1900）义和团运动发生后，严复离开天津，迁居上海，从此脱离水师学堂。此后，严复曾协助马相伯创办复旦公学（复旦大学的前身），担任袁世凯总统府外交法律顾问、约法会议议员等职。

Yan Fu was named Jidao, original name of Chuanchu, born in Houguan(now Minhou

County), Fujian Province. In 1877, he went to the University of Portsmouth in England to study, and then went to the Greenwich Naval College. In the meantime, Yan Fu made extensive contact with British society, and became an advanced Chinese with western democratic thoughts and seeking truth from the west. In 1880, Li Hongzhang, Minister of Beiyang, founded Beiyang Marine College in Tianjin, and transferred Yan Fu as the general teacher. In 1890, he served as the director. Seven years later, Yan Fu, Xia Zengyou and Wang Xiuzhi founded *Guowen Newspaper* in Tianjin, which became an important propaganda position of reformists in the north. During this period, Yan Fu also concentrated on introducing and translating western academic classics, such as *Evolution of Heaven*, *The Wealth of Nations*, *Spirit of Law*, *Ming Xue*, *On the Group's Right Boundary*, *On Ming Xue*, *The Study of Sociology*, *General Interpretation of Society* and so on. In 1900, after the Yihetuan Movement, Yan Fu left Tianjin and moved to Shanghai, and then left the Naval Academy. After that, Yan Fu helped Ma Xiangbo to establish Fu Dan College (the predecessor of Fu Dan University), and served as diplomatic legal adviser to Yuan Shikai's presidential palace, and a member of the conference on treaty making.

光绪二十六年五月（1900年6月），开平煤矿被八国联军霸占。开平矿务局督办张翼以保护开平矿务局产业之名，授权德璀琳全权处理，并委托德璀琳吸收洋股投资，将开平矿务局变为中外合办的公司。德璀琳以开平矿务局代理总办的身份，与墨林公司的代理人胡佛签订了卖约，把开平的股权卖到了胡佛名下，后在伦敦依据英国法律注册成立了新公司——开平矿务有限公司。光绪二十六年十二月（1901年2月），张翼又签订了移交约和副约，将原开平矿务局的产业移交给开平矿务有限公司。虽然副约中有"督办、中国股东享有的权利"及"设立中国董事会"等条款，但这些规定并没有得到认可和执行。

In June 1900, Kaiping Coal Mine was occupied by the Eight-Power Allied Forces. In the name of protecting Kaiping Mining Bureau's industry, the official of Kaiping Mining Bureau Zhang Yi, authorized Gustav von Detring to handle the industry with full authority, and entrusted Gustav von Detring to absorb foreign investment, turning Kaiping Mining Bureau into a Sino-foreign joint venture company. As acting general manager of Kaiping Mining Bureau, Gustav von Detring signed the Sale

1921	1922	1923	1924	1925	1926	1927	1928	1929	1930	1931	1932	1933
1947	1948	1949	1950	1951	1952	1953	1954	1955	1956	1957	1958	1959
1973	1974	1975	1976	1977	1978	1979	1980	1981	1982	1983	1984	1985
1999	2000	2001	2002	2003	2004	2005	2006	2007	2008	2009	2010	2011

开平矿务局办公楼
Kaiping Mining Bureau Office Building

Contract with Hoover, the agent of Morlin Company, and sold the equity of Kaiping to Hoover, and then registered and established a new company Kaiping Mining Co., Ltd. in London according to English law. In February 1901, Zhang Yi signed the Transfer Contract and the Sub-Contract, transferring the former Kaiping Mining Bureau industry to Kaiping Mining Co., Ltd. Although there are clauses such as "supervision, rights enjoyed by Chinese shareholders" and "establishment of Chinese board of directors" in the Sub-Contract, these provisions have not been recognized and implemented.

光绪二十七年正月（1901年3月），严复应张翼之邀，从上海回到天津就职开平矿务有限公司华部总办。不久，严复参与制定了《开平矿务有限公司试办章程》，并公告老股东更换新公司股票。不过，由于英方的私下操纵，开平矿务局实际上已被外国资本控制。此后，由于英方不允许在唐山的厂矿悬挂龙旗，因此袁世凯十分愤怒，上书《请饬外务部声明产地权利折》，弹劾张翼。于是德宗皇帝责成张翼赶紧设法收回。

In March 1901, at the invitation of Zhang Yi, Yan Fu returned to Tianjin to work for the General Office of China Department of Kaiping Mining Company. Soon, Yan Fu participated in the formulation of *Kaiping Mining Company's Trial Articles of Association*, and then announced that the old shareholders would replace the shares of the new company. Due to the private manipulation of the British side, Kaiping Mining Bureau has actually been controlled by foreign capital. Subsequently, the British side did not allow the dragon flag to be hoisted in Tangshan factories and mines. Yuan Shikai was very angry. He submitted to the Foreign Affairs Department a memorial named *Petition to Foreign Affairs Department to Declare Ownership of Real Estate* to declare the right of origin and to impeach Zhang Yi. Emperor Guangxu instructed Zhang Yi to try to recover it quickly.

张翼让严复代拟《遵旨回奏开平矿务情形折》，不过收回开平矿务的事毫无进展。光绪二十九年十一月（1903年12月）和转年二月（1904年4月），袁世凯又两次参劾张翼，张翼只能被迫选择法律途径解决问题。光绪三十年（1904）年末，在张翼的再三邀请和委托下，严复同其一起赴英国伦敦高等法院进行诉讼。

Zhang Yi asked Yan Fu to draft a memorial named *Response on the Situation of Kaiping Mining*, but there was no progress in recovering Kaiping. In December 1903 and April 1904, Yuan Shikai participated in impeaching Zhang Yi twice, Zhang Yi was forced to choose legal means to solve the problem. At the end of 1904, under the repeated invitation and entrustment of Zhang Yi, Yan Fu went to London's High Court in England with him for litigation.

1905年1月，伦敦高等法院正式开庭，张翼在英国委托的代理律师列举了大量原始资料，控诉墨林公司和开平矿务有限公司的欺诈行为。诉讼要求主要有两点：一、判令副约有效，并要求被告履行副约条款；如认为副约无效，则应宣告移交约是由欺诈手段获得的，应予撤销，被告无权取得移交约中的权益。二、向英方索赔经济损失。同年3月，伦敦高等法院作出判决：一、副约与移交约合法有效，二者视为一份文件，副约应当遵守执行。被告如不遵守副约，就不得享受移交约所载产业及其利益，法院将尽力把矿产及产业收回，交还原告。二、不支持索赔要求。判决后，被告提出上诉。1906年1月，法庭经过审理后判决：墨林公司及开平矿务公司应遵守副约的约定；按照副约的条款，张翼取得不超过该公司章程给予董事兼总经理的权利，副约中没有给予张翼督办的权利，张翼不得行使；驳回张翼其他主张赔偿的要求。张翼和开平矿务局一无所获。

In January 1905, London's High Court officially opened its session. Zhang Yi's attorney in England cited a large number of original materials and accused Morlin and Kaiping Company of fraud. Litigation requirements: first, order the Sub-Contract to be valid and require the defendant to perform the terms of the Sub-Contract. If the Sub-Contract is considered invalid, it should be declared that the Transfer Contract was obtained by fraudulent means and should be revoked; the defendant has no right to acquire the rights and interests in the Transfer Contract. Second, claim for economic losses from the British side. In March of the same year, London's High Court made a judgment: first, the Sub-Contract and the Transfer Contract are legal and valid, and they are regarded as one document. The Sub-Contract shall be observed and implemented. If the defendant fails to comply with the Sub-Contract, he will not enjoy the property and its benefits as stated in the Transfer Contract, and the court will try its best to recover the minerals and property and return them to the plaintiff. Second, do not support the claim. After the verdict, the defendant appealed. In January 1906, after trial by the court, it was decided that Morlin Company and Kaiping Company should abide by the agreement of the Sub-Contract. According to the terms of the Sub-Contract, Zhang Yi obtained no more than the rights granted to the director and general manager by the company's articles of association. The Sub-Contract did not give Zhang Yi the right to supervise, and Zhang Yi could not exercise it; reject Zhang Yi's other claims for compensation. Zhang Yi and Kaiping Mining Bureau achieved nothing.

在庭审期间，被告的举证内容暴露了张翼中饱私囊的问题。严复识破张翼的嘴脸后，加上张翼始终不兑现答应给严复的法律服务"代理费"，严复就终止了对张翼的法律服务和翻译帮助，并离开了伦敦。几年之后，严复撰写了《关于开平矿案的说帖》，分析了案件，指出："今有限公司系英国法人，既非条约，又未经特别允许，并未向中国农工商部正式挂号，其在开平执管地产，开采矿苗，实属违背中国法律。"纵然如此，在当时的政治环境下，以严复微不足道的一己之力也是无法为开平矿务局争取利益的。

During the trial, the content of the defendant's evidence exposed the problem of Zhang Yi's self-enrichment. After Yan Fu saw through Zhang Yi's face, and Zhang Yi never fulfilled the promise of "agency fee" for Yan Fu's legal services, Yan Fu terminated his legal services and translation assistance to Zhang Yi and left London. A few years later, Yan Fu wrote *Notes on Kaiping Mining Case*, analyzed the case, and pointed out that: "Today Limited Company is a British legal person, neither a treaty nor a special permission, and has not been officially registered in the Ministry of Agriculture, Industry and Commerce of China. It is against Chinese law to manage real estate and develop mining seedlings in Kaiping." However, in the political environment at that time, it was impossible to win benefits for Kaiping Mining Bureau with Yan Fu's insignificant efforts.

光绪二十六年（1900）以后，严复开始翻译法国启蒙思想家孟德斯鸠的名著《法意》（通译为《论法的精神》），至宣统元年（1909）脱稿。原书31卷，严复据英译本译出29卷。《法意》是探讨法律的性质、研究国家政治制度的法学和政治学理论专著。就律师制度而言，严复

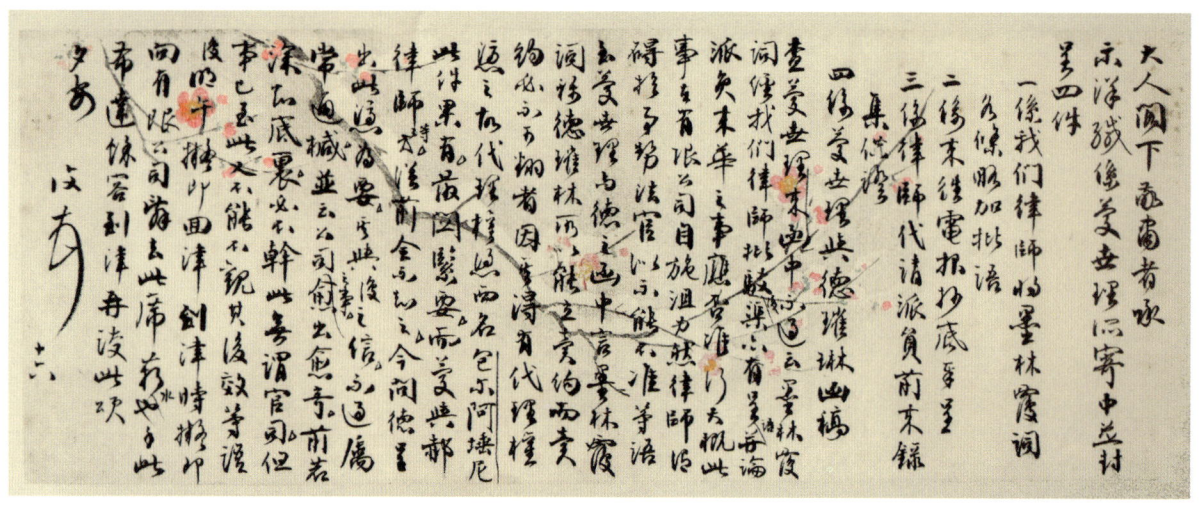

严复与林文德律师的通信
Correspondence between Yan Fu and lawyer Edgar Pierce Allen

在《法意》所撰按语中说:"夫泰西之所以能无刑讯而情得者,非徒司法折狱之有术,而无情者不得尽其辞也,有辩护之律师,有公听之助理,抵瑕蹈隙,曲证旁搜,盖数听之余,其狱之情,靡不得者。而吾国治狱,无此具也,又况诪张之民,誓言无用,鹘突之宰,惟勘不明,则舍刑讯,几无术矣。"严复明确指出了律师在取证、诉讼中的重要作用。

After 1900, Yan Fu began to translate French Enlightenment thinker Montesquieu's famous book *Fa Yi* (now translated as *The Spirit of Law*), and the manuscript was released in 1909. The original book consists of 31 volumes, and Yan Fu translated 29 volumes according to the English version. *Fa Yi* is a monograph on the theory of law and politics, which explores the nature of law and studies the national political system. As far as the lawyer system was concerned, Yan Fu pointed out the important role of lawyers in obtaining evidence and litigation in the preface of *Fa Yi*. He said, "The reason why western countries cannot extort confessions by torture is not only because of the judicial and prison system, but also because the accused cannot fully defend themselves. I have heard of many cases. However, in China's criminal system, there is no defense link, and the examination is not clear. Therefore, we should establish a defense system by lawyers."

清末司法改革与律师制度的确立

THE JUDICIAL REFORM AND THE ESTABLISHMENT OF LAWYER SYSTEM IN THE LATE QING DYNASTY

如果说严复作为代理人远赴英国参与诉讼只是精英人物个案的话,那么晚清十年间的变法修律则为中国律师制度的确立打下了坚实的基础。

If Yan Fu, as an agent, went to England to participate in litigation only as a case of elite figures, then the reform and revision of law in the late Qing Dynasty laid a solid foundation for the establishment of China's lawyer system.

光绪二十七年(1901),清政府被迫与十一国签订了《辛丑各国和约》(即《辛丑条约》),中国完全沦为半殖民半封建社会。民族危机空前加剧,清政府的统治已到了岌岌可危的地步。面对内忧外患,清政府不得不认真考虑变法图强。恰逢光绪二十八年(1902)中英双方签订《续议通商行船条约》,其中第十二款规定:"中国深欲整顿律例,以期与各西国律例改同一律,英国允愿尽力协助,以成此举,一俟查悉中国律例情形及其审断办法及一切相关事宜,皆臻妥善,英国即允弃其治外法权。"英国的"允诺"坚定了清政府改变现行司法体制、废除治外法权的信心,变法修律的大幕也由此拉开。

In 1901, the Qing government was forced to sign the *Final Protocol for the Settlement of the Disturbances of 1900*, which completely reduced China to a semi-colonial and semi-feudal society. The national crisis intensified unprecedentedly, and the Qing government's rule was in jeopardy. Facing internal and external troubles, the Qing government had to seriously consider reforming the political system. In 1902, China and Britain signed the *Treaty of Renewing Trade and Shipping*, which stipulated in the 12th paragraph: "China is eager to rectify its laws with a view to bringing them into conformity with those of western countries, and Britain is willing to do its best to assist in order to achieve this. Once China's laws and regulations, their adjudication methods and all related matters have been properly investigated, Britain will give up its extraterritorial jurisdiction." Britain's "promise" strengthened the Qing government's confidence in changing the current judicial system and abolishing extraterritorial jurisdiction, and the curtain of legal reform was opened.

一、司法改革
1. Judicial Reform

为进行变法修律，清政府根据张之洞等人的保荐，于光绪二十八年四月初六日（1902年5月13日）着派沈家本、伍廷芳为修订法律大臣，"将一切现行律例，按照交涉情形，参酌各国法律，悉心考订，妥为拟议。务期中外通行，有裨治理"。

According to the sponsorship of Zhang Zhidong and others, the Qing government appointed Shen Jiaben and Wu Tingfang as the Minister of Law Revision on May 13, 1902, "All the existing laws and regulations should be carefully examined and properly proposed according to the negotiation situation, taking into account the laws of various countries. In order to make it applicable both at home and abroad, which would benefit the governance".

沈家本（1840—1913），字子惇，浙江归安（今湖州市）人。光绪九年（1883）进士，十九年（1893）任天津知府，后任通永道、山西按察使、刑部侍郎、修订法律大臣等职。平生专心法律之学，著有《历代刑法考》《刑案汇览》《汉律摭遗》《明律目笺》等。

Shen Jiaben (1840-1913), named Zidun, a native of Gui'an(now Huzhou City), Zhejiang Province. In 1883, he was listed Jinshi of the Qing Dynasty. In 1893, he was appointed as the Magistrate of Tianjin and later served as Tongyong Dao, Shanxi Provincial Magistrate, Assistant Minister of Punishments, and Minister of Law Revision. He has devoted himself to the study of law in his life and has written *The Examination of Criminal Law in Past Dynasties*, *A Survey of Criminal Cases*, *Han Law's Legacy*, *Ming Law's Notes* and so on.

伍廷芳（1842—1922），字文爵，号秩庸，广东新会人。同治十三年（1874）自费赴英国伦敦林肯法律学院学习，三年后考取大律师资格，被香港聘为法官兼立法局议员。光绪八年（1882）起协助李鸿章办理洋务十余年，后任清政府驻美国、西班牙及秘鲁公使。回国后，先后任商约大臣、修订法律大臣、会办商务大臣、外交部右侍郎、刑部右侍郎等职。辛亥革命后，曾作为南方民军全权代表与袁世凯派出的唐绍仪在上海举行南北议和谈判。袁世凯死后，曾任黎元洪政府代总理，孙中山护法军政府外交总长、财长。陈炯明叛变中，登上永丰舰与孙中山会晤。后因英美等国协助陈炯明夺取广州，气愤之下，病发而逝世。

Wu Tingfang (1842-1922), born in Xinhui, Guangdong Province, was named Wenjue and Zhiyong. In 1874, he studied at Lincoln Law School in London, England at his own expense. Three years later, he was admitted as a barrister and was hired as a judge and Legislative Council member by Hong Kong. In 1882, he assisted Li Hongzhang in handling foreign affairs for more than ten years, and later served as the Minister of the Qing government in the United States, Spain and Peru. After returning to China, he served as Minister of Commerce and Contract, Minister of Law Revision, Minister of Commerce, Assistant Minister of Foreign Affairs, Assistant Minister of Criminal Department, etc. After the Revolution of 1911, as the plenipotentiary of the Southern People's Army, Wu Tingfang and Tang Shaoyi sent by Yuan Shikai held the North-South peace talks in Shanghai. After Yuan Shikai's death, he served as Acting Prime Minister of Li Yuanhong government, Foreign Minister and Finance Minister of Sun Yat-sen's government. During Chen Jiongming's mutiny, he boarded the Yongfeng ship to meet Sun Yat-sen. Later, as Britain, America and other countries helped Chen Jiongming seize Guangzhou, he died of illness in anger.

废除治外法权是清政府司法改革的原初动力之一。而借鉴列强的既有法律，又是清末司

1921	1922	1923	1924	1925	1926	1927	1928	1929	1930	1931	1932	1933
1947	1948	1949	1950	1951	1952	1953	1954	1955	1956	1957	1958	1959
1973	1974	1975	1976	1977	1978	1979	1980	1981	1982	1983	1984	1985
1999	2000	2001	2002	2003	2004	2005	2006	2007	2008	2009	2010	2011

法改革的重要方式。修律期间，清政府聘请各国法律专家担任顾问，积极组织力量翻译各国法典、法规，为修订新律提供蓝本。

Abolishing extraterritorial jurisdiction is one of the original motive forces of judicial reform of the Qing government. Drawing lessons from the existing laws of the great powers is also an important way of judicial reform in the late Qing Dynasty. During the revision of the law, the Qing government hired legal experts from various countries as consultants, and actively organized efforts to translate the codes and regulations of various countries, which provided a blueprint for revising the new law.

在翻译外国法律的基础上，清廷又设立了修订法律馆、宪政编查馆，为全面修订以《大清律》为主体的固有法律制度、法律体系作好了准备。从光绪三十年（1904）颁布的《钦定大清商律》开始，清政府先后起草、颁布了一系列新法典或单行法规，其中包括《钦定宪法大纲》《大清新刑律草案》《大清民律草案》《大清现行刑律》《国际条例》《违警律草案》《商律》《大清民商事诉讼草案》《大清刑事民事诉讼法草案》《法院编制法》等。

On the basis of translating foreign laws, the Qing court set up Law Revision Library and a Constitutional Compilation Library, which prepared for the comprehensive revision of the inherent legal system with the *Qing Law* as the main body. Since the *Imperial Qing Commercial Law* promulgated in 1904, the Qing government has drafted and promulgated a series of new codes or separate regulations, *Imperial Constitution Outline*, *Qing Criminal Law Draft*, *Qing Civil Law Draft*, *Qing Current Criminal Law*, *International Regulations*, *The Draft Police Law*, *The Commercial Law*, *The Draft Civil and Commercial Litigation of Qing Dynasty*, *The Draft Criminal and Civil Procedure Law of Qing Dynasty*, and the *Court Preparation Law*.

清末司法改革从形式上结束了行政与司法合一、皇帝总揽司法大权的传统，初步确立了司法与行政分立的原则，标志着司法与行政分离的开始，并直接关系到民国时期的司法制度建设，对中国社会的发展产生了深远的影响。

The judicial reform in the late Qing Dynasty formally ended the tradition of the unity of administration and justice, and the emperor took over the judicial power. It initially established the principle of separation between justice and administration, marked the beginning of separation between justice and administration, and directly related to the construction of judicial system in the Republic of China, which had a far-reaching impact on the development of Chinese society.

程序法与实体法的分离则突出表现在《大清刑事民事诉讼法草案》的提出上，而这部草案，又为律师制度的确立，奠定了坚实的基础。

The separation between procedural law and substantive law is highlighted in the proposal of *The Draft of Criminal and Civil Procedure Law of Qing Dynasty*, which laid a solid foundation for the establishment of lawyer system.

二、律师制度的确立
2. The Establishment of Lawyer System

在清末变法修律的过程中，律师制度在中国得以初步确立。光绪三十二年四月初三日（1906年4月25日），伍廷芳和沈家本在《修律大臣伍廷芳等奏呈刑事民事诉讼法折》中首次正式对律师的概念和基本作用作出了解释，文中说："按律师一名代言人，日本谓之辩护士。盖人因讼对簿公庭，惶悚之下，言语每多失措，故用律师代理一切质问、对诘、覆问各事宜。"此外，该折还就律师的来源、外籍律师干涉华人诉讼以及因外籍律师而加重治外法权危害的问题进行了阐述。

In the process of reforming the law in the late Qing Dynasty, the lawyer system was initially established in China. On April 25th, 1906, Wu Tingfang and Shen Jiaben officially explained the concept and basic role of lawyers for the first time in the *Paper of Criminal and Civil Procedure Law Presented by Wu Tingfang, Minister of Law Revision*, which said: "Assign a lawyer as a spokesperson, Japan is called a defender. The people went to court because of the lawsuit, and when they were embarrassed, they lost their heads every time they spoke. Therefore, they used lawyers to represent all questions, cross-examine and answer questions." In addition, this paper also expounds the source of lawyers, the interference of foreign lawyers in Chinese litigation and the aggravation of extraterritorial harm caused by foreign lawyers.

在《修律大臣伍廷芳等奏呈刑事民事诉讼法折》撰成前一个月，伍廷芳、沈家本即奉旨修订完成了《大清刑事民事诉讼法草案》，并于光绪三十二年四月初二日（1906年4月24日）奉旨公布。《草案》包括总则、刑事规则、民事规则、刑事民事通用规则、中外交涉案五章二百六十条及颁行例三条。其中第四章"刑事民事通用规则"第一节即为"律师"，共九条内容，就律师资格的获得、注册、责任、处分方式和外国律师问题作出了规定。此外，《草案》中还有多处提及律师，占《草案》总条款数的12%。《草案》仿效英美司法理念和制度，第一次将实体法和程序法区分开来，并尝试引入西方的律师制度和陪审制度，初步建构起了中国的律师制度。

One month before the publication of the *Paper of Criminal and Civil Procedure Law Presented by Wu Tingfang, Minister of Law Revision*, Wu Tingfang and Shen Jiaben completed the revision of *The Draft of Criminal and Civil Procedure Law of Qing Dynasty*, which was published on April 24, 1906. The *Draft* includes general rules, criminal rules, civil rules, general rules of criminal and civil affairs, 260 articles in five chapters concerning China-foreign affairs and three promulgations. Among them, the first section of Chapter IV "General Rules of Criminal Civil Affairs" is "Lawyer", which consists of nine articles, and provides rules for the qualification of lawyers, registration, responsibilities, punishment methods and foreign lawyers. In addition, there are many references to lawyers in the *Draft*, accounting for 12% of the total articles in the *Draft*. The *Draft* imitates the judicial ideas and systems of Britain and America, distinguishes the substantive law from the procedural law for the first time, and tries to introduce the western lawyer system and jury system, thus initially constructing the lawyer system of China.

《大清刑事民事诉讼法草案》完成后，由朝廷转发各省督抚、都统体察情形，悉心研究。地方督抚纷纷提出质疑，认为《草案》与传统诉讼体制区别太大，难以为社会所接受。其中，张之洞的反对意见最为激烈,他在《遵旨核议新编刑事民事诉讼法折》中说:"若果不察情势,贸然举行,而自承审官、陪审员以至律师、证人等无专门学问、无公共道德,骤欲行此规模外人貌合神离之法,势必良懦冤抑,强暴纵恣,盗已起而莫惩,案久悬而不结,此臣所谓难挽法权而转滋狱讼者也。"并在"条单"中明确表达了对施行律师制度的担忧。

After the completion of *The Draft of Criminal and Civil Procedure Law of Qing Dynasty*, it was forwarded by the court to the governors of all provinces, and the commanders observed the situation and studied it carefully. Local governors have raised questions. All thought that the *Draft* is too different from the traditional litigation system to be accepted by the society. Among them, Zhang Zhidong's objection is the most fierce. He said in the *Review of the New Criminal and Civil Procedure Law in Accordance with the Purposes*: "If you don't observe the situation and rush to hold it, and the self-supporting judges, jurors and even lawyers and witnesses have no specialized knowledge and public morality, then the rape will be rampant, and the theft has started without punishment. The case would be pending unresolved for a long time." In the "Bill", the author clearly expressed his concern about the implementation of the lawyer system.

尽管伍廷芳、沈家本两人多次向朝廷阐述律师制度和陪审制度的好处,指出它们可以促进公正裁判、防止包庇贿赂,但由于两人提出的《草案》过于超前,加之强调礼教的张之洞一派的强烈反对,因此律师制度只能停留在纸面上,清政府并未实施这部法律。

Although Wu Tingfang and Shen Jiaben have repeatedly explained to the court the advantages of lawyer system and jury system, pointing out that they can promote fair judgment and prevent harboring bribery, because the *Draft* put forward by them is too advanced, and the strong opposition of Zhang Zhidong, which emphasizes ethics, the lawyer system can only stay on paper, and the Qing government has not implemented this law.

原计划与《大清刑事民事诉讼法草案》配套实施的《各级审判厅试办章程》于光绪三十三年十月二十九日(1907年12月4日)颁行,虽然其中没有出现"律师"二字,但它对代理人、代诉人的规定，可以视为律师制度的延续。

The *Trial Regulations for Adjudicative Offices at All Levels*, which was originally planned to be implemented in conjunction with *The Draft of Criminal and Civil Procedure Law of Qing Dynasty*, was promulgated on December 4th, 1907. Although the word "lawyer" did not appear in it, its provisions on agents and litigants can be regarded as the continuation of the lawyer system.

《章程》第三章"诉讼"第一节"起诉"中第四十八条规定"凡民事案件，非本人或其代理人不得诉讼"，确立了代理人参与诉讼的合法性；第五十二条规定"职官、妇女、老幼、废疾为原告时，得委任他人代诉"，延续了传统司法中官吏不躬坐狱讼、老幼废疾可委托代理的原则。不仅如此，《章程》还对代诉人的身份进行了规范，并提出了登记的要求。它规定妇女、未成丁者、有心疾及疯癫者和积惯讼棍"不得充当代诉人"；第五十六条则明确规定"委任状应填写左列各项"："一、委任人及代诉人之姓名、籍贯、年龄、住所、职业；二、代诉人与委任人之关系；三、委任之原因；四、委任之权限；五、代诉之年月日。"总的来说，《各级审判厅试办章程》基本保持了传统司法审判的面貌，因此没有遭到更多的非议，不过它对代理人、代诉人的规定比较完善，为律师制度的确立铺平了道路。

Article 48 in Section 1 "Prosecution" of Chapter 3 "Litigation" of the *Articles of Association* stipulates that "in civil cases, no lawsuit shall be filed unless he or his agent", which establishes the legality of the agent's participation in litigation; Article 52 stipulates that "when officials, women, old and junior, and invalid are plaintiffs, they should appoint others to represent them", which continues the principle that officials in traditional justice do not appear in person in litigation, and old, junior and invalid can entrust agents. Not only that, the *Articles of Association* also regulates the identity of the representative and puts forward the requirement of registration. It stipulates that women, immature people, people with heart diseases and madness, and habitual litigants "shall not act as litigants"; Article 56 clearly stipulates that "the following items should be filled in the letter of appointment": "1. The name, place of origin, age, residence and occupation of the appointor and the agent; 2. The relationship between the agent and the appointer; 3. Reasons for appointment; 4. The authority of appointment; 5. Date, month and day of the lawsuit. " Generally speaking, the *Trial Regulations for Adjudicative Offices at All Levels* basically keeps the appearance of traditional judicial trials, so it has not been criticized more, but its regulations on agents and attorneys are relatively perfect, paving the way for the establishment of the lawyer system.

宣统二年（1910），清政府颁行了《法院编制法》，在第七章"法庭之开闭及秩序"中重申了伍廷芳、沈家本在《大清刑事民事诉讼法草案》中对律师制度的阐释，进一步明确了关于律师代理和律师辩护的相关规定，标志着近代律师制度的初步确立。

In 1910, the Qing government enacted the *Court Preparation Law*. In the seventh chapter, "Opening and Closing of Courts and Order", Wu Tingfang and Shen Jiaben reiterated the interpretation of the lawyer system in *The Draft of Criminal and Civil Procedure Law of Qing Dynasty*, and further clarified the relevant provisions on lawyer representation and lawyer defense, marking the initial establishment of the modern lawyer system.

事实上，《大清刑事民事诉讼法草案》遭到否决后，清政府曾要求沈家本等修律大臣吸收反对意见，对《草案》进行修订。宣统二年年末，沈家本完成了《大清刑事诉讼法草案》和《大清民事诉讼法草案》，并送交宪政编查馆核议。然而，随着辛亥革命的爆发，两部《草案》同样未能颁布、实施。不过，它们中的许多内容最终为民国初年的北洋政府所采纳并实施。

In fact, after *The Draft of Criminal and Civil Procedure Law of Qing Dynasty* was rejected, the Qing government asked Shen Jiaben and other Ministers of Law Revision to absorb the objections and revise the *Draft*. At the end of 1910, Shen Jiaben completed the *Draft of Criminal Procedure Law of Qing Dynasty* and the *Draft of Civil Procedure Law of Qing Dynasty*, and sent them to the Constitutional Compilation and Research Ministry for review. However, with the outbreak of the Revolution of 1911, the two *Drafts* also failed to be promulgated and implemented. However, many of them were finally adopted and implemented by the Beiyang Government in the early years of the Republic of China.

北洋法政专门学堂的设立
ESTABLISHMENT OF BEIYANG SPECIAL SCHOOL OF LAW AND POLITICS

清末司法的近代化，首先是法律人才的近代化，而其关键就在于全新的法律教育模式。于是，在变法修律之初，清政府就着手改革教育，创办新式学堂，培养新式人才。

The modernization of judicature in the late Qing Dynasty, first of all, is the modernization of legal talents, and the key lies in the brand-new legal education mode. Therefore, at the beginning of the law reform, the Qing government began to reform education, set up new schools and train new talents.

光绪二十八年（1902），清廷颁布《钦定学堂章程》，直到光绪三十一年（1905）宣布："自丙午科为始，所有乡会试一律停止。各省岁科考试，亦停止。"正式终结了中国持续1300年的科举考试制度。

In 1902, the Qing court promulgated *The School Rules Made by Imperial Order*, until 1905, it is declared: "All township examinations will be stopped from the beginning of Bingwu. The annual examinations in various provinces have also stopped." It officially ended the imperial examination system which lasted for 1300 years in China.

早在甲午战争结束后，北洋大学、京师大学堂、南洋公学、震旦学堂等新式学堂就先后设立了法律或政治学科。《钦定学堂章程》中大学专门学科分为政治、格致、文学、商务、农业、医术、工艺七科，其中政治分为政治学和法律学二目。而光绪三十年（1904）颁布的《奏定学堂章

1934	1935	1936	1937	1938	1939	1940	1941	1942	1943	1944	1945	1946
1960	1961	1962	1963	1964	1965	1966	1967	1968	1969	1970	1971	1972
1986	1987	1988	1989	1990	1991	1992	1993	1994	1995	1996	1997	1998
2012	2013	2014	2015	2016	2017	2018	2019	2020	2021	……		

程》更加明确地将政法科分为法律门和政治门，奠定了具有近代意义的法政教育基础。

As early as after the Sino-Japanese War of 1894-1895, Beiyang University, Jingshi University, Nanyang Public College, Zhendan School and other new schools have successively set up legal or political subjects. In *The School Rules Made by Imperial Order*, the specialized disciplines of universities are divided into seven subjects: politics, ethics, literature, commerce, agriculture, medical skills and crafts, among which politics is divided into two subjects: political science and law. However, in 1904, *The Rules of Zouding School* more clearly divided politics and law into law and politics, which laid the foundation of modern legal education.

1906年日俄战争中日本的胜利也激发了国人立宪的热情，全国掀起了法政学习之风，各地的法律学堂、法政学堂如雨后春笋般纷纷建立。其中最著名，影响力也最大的就是天津的北洋法政专门学堂。

Japan's victory in the Russo-Japanese War in 1906 also stimulated the enthusiasm of Chinese people for constitutionalism. The whole country set off a wind of studying law and politics, and law schools and law and politics schools all over the country mushroomed. Among them, the most famous and influential one is Tianjin Beiyang Special School of Law and Politics.

光绪三十二年（1906），袁世凯听取赴日考察的阎凤阁等人的建议，决定仿照日本法政学堂的模式，以"改良直隶全省吏治，培养佐理新政人才"为宗旨，创办一所北洋法政专门学堂。同年六月，袁世凯委任日本东京中央大学法学学士黎渊为监督（校长），筹建学堂。光绪三十三年（1907），北洋法政学堂校舍在新开河河坝下（今志成道33号）建成，蔚为壮观。

In 1906, Yuan Shikai listened to the suggestions of Yan Fengge and others who visited Japan, and decided to set up a Beiyang Special School of Law and Politics, following the model of Japanese law and politics school, with the aim of "improving the official management of Zhili province and cultivating talents who assisted in the New Deal". In June of the same year, Yuan Shikai appointed Li Yuan, who

位于天津老三岔河口北岸的直隶总督衙门辕门
The Yuanmen of Zhili Governor's Yamen located on the north bank of the old Sancha River Estuary in Tianjin

graduated from Tokyo Central University in Japan with a bachelor's degree in law, as the supervisor (principal) to build the school. In 1907, the school building of Beiyang Law and Politics School was built under Xinkaihe River Dam (now No. 33 Zhicheng Road), which was spectacular.

学堂分设本科、简易科两类，亦称专门类、速成类。本科六年，其中预科、正科各三年。正科又分设政治、法律两科。政治科为政治、经济专业，法律科为本国法和国际法专业。正科毕业后授予证书并给予安置。正科三年的必修课程包括大清律例、大清会典、宪法、刑法、国际公法、国际私法、银行法、货币法、商法、西方政治学、财政学、经济学、应用经济学、地方自治、社会学、政治哲学、政治史、外交史、通商史等。此外，还有两门外语，第一外语是日语，第二外语可任选英、德、法语之一。

直隶总督衙门
Zhili Governor's Yamen

    Schools are divided into two categories: undergraduate and simple, also known as specialized and accelerated. Undergraduate course is six years. Among them, the preparatory course and the regular course each have three years. The formal course is divided into politics and law. Politics is a major in politics and economics, while law is a major in national law and international law. After graduating from formal course, student will be awarded a certificate and placed. The three-year compulsory courses of formal course include laws and regulations of the Qing Dynasty, conventions of the Qing Dynasty, constitution, criminal law, public international law, private international law, banking law, monetary law, commercial law, western political science, finance, economics, applied economics, local autonomy, sociology, political philosophy, political history, diplomatic history, trade history, etc. In addition, there are two foreign languages, the first foreign language is Japanese, and the second foreign language can choose one of English, German and French.

简易科分绅班和职班两种，学制一年半。绅班为行政科，招收直隶地方府县保送生，不过也要参加入学考试；职班为司法科，专收外地在职人员，主要培养法律人才。

There are two kinds of simple subjects: gentry class and vocational class, with a school system of one and a half years. The gentry class is an administrative subject, recruiting students from local prefectures and counties in Zhili, but also taking the entrance examination. The vocational class is the Judicial Department, which specializes in recruiting foreign in-service personnel, mainly training legal talents.

辛亥革命后，北洋法政专门学堂更名为北洋法政专门学校。1914年，保定法政专门学校、天津高等商业专门学校并入该校，改称直隶省公立法政专门学校，设法律、政治、商业三科。1928年，改称河北省立法政专门学校，1929年更名为河北省立法商学院，设法律、政治、经济、商业四科，学制四年，另附高中班和高、初两级商科职业班，并开始招收女生。1937年天津沦陷后学校被日军封闭。1947年复校，新中国成立后并入北京政法学院和南开大学。

After the Revolution of 1911, Beiyang Special School of Law and Politics was renamed Beiyang Law School. In 1914, Baoding Legal and Political College and Tianjin Higher Commercial College were merged into the school, and renamed Zhili Provincial Public Legal and Political College, with three subjects: law, politics and business. In 1928, it was renamed Hebei Legislative and Political College, and in 1929, it was renamed Hebei Legislative Business School. It has four subjects: law, politics, economy and business, with a four-year academic system, plus high school classes and high and junior business vocational classes and began to recruit female students. After the fall of Tianjin in 1937, the school was closed by the Japanese army. It was reopened in 1947 and merged into Beijing Institute of Political Science and Law and Nankai University after the founding of the People's Republic of China.

北洋法政专门学堂先后培养出夏勤、潘云超、童冠贤、杨亦周、崔敬伯、朱道孔等一大批法律、政治、经济、商务方面的人才。更重要的是，北洋法政专门学堂还具有光荣的革命传统，中国共产党主要创始人之一李大钊即为该校专门科第一期学生，攻读六年，成绩优异。在校期间，曾参加天津第四次国会请愿活动，并于1912年加入中国社会党。毕业后，李大钊曾多次回到母校。1923年12月30日，李大钊参加母校18周年校庆，并发表演讲《十八年来的回顾》，对母校的革命传统给予了高度评价，他说："那时中国北方政治运动首推天津，天津以北洋法政为中心，所以我校在政治运动史上是很重要的。"除李大钊外，辛亥革命烈士、同盟会会员白雅雨曾在学堂任史地教员，传播反清思想，进行革命活动，后参加滦州起义，失败被捕后，坚贞不屈，英勇就义。抗日名将张自忠、佟麟阁青年时代也曾在北洋法政专门学堂读书。

Beiyang Special School of Law and Politics has trained a large number of talents in law, politics, economy and commerce, such as Xia Qin, Pan Yunchao, Tong Guanxian, Yang Yizhou, Cui Jingbo and Zhu Daokong. More importantly, Beiyang Special School of Law and Politics also has a glorious revolutionary tradition. Li Dazhao, one of the main founders of the Communist Party of China, the student of the first period in specialized section of this school, studied for six years and achieved outstanding results. In school, he participated in the fourth congressional petition in Tianjin and joined the Chinese Socialist Party in 1912. After graduation, Li Dazhao returned to his alma mater many times. On December 30, 1923, Li Dazhao attended the 18th anniversary celebration of his alma mater and delivered a speech *Review in the Past Eighteen Years*, which spoke highly of the revolutionary tradition of his alma mater, and he said: "At that time, Tianjin was the first to push the political movement in northern China, and Tianjin was centered on Beiyang law and politics, so our school is very important in the history of political movement." In addition to Li Dazhao, Bai Yayu, a martyr of the Revolution of 1911 and a member of the League, once worked as a teacher of history and geography in the school, spreading anti-Qing thoughts, carrying out revolutionary activities, and then taking part in Luanzhou Uprising. After failing and being arrested, he was unyielding and died bravely. Zhang Zizhong and Tong Linge, famous anti-Japanese generals, also studied in Beiyang Special School of Law and Politics in their youth.

天津审判厅的尝试

ATTEMPT OF TIANJIN ADJUDICATIVE OFFICE

  天津是中国最早设立地方审判、检察机构,警察和监狱的城市,是20世纪初清政府司法改革的先行试点。

Tianjin was the first city in China to set up local judicial and procuratorial organs, police and prisons, and it was the first pilot of judicial reform of the Qing government in the early 20th century.

  光绪三十二年九月二十日(1906年11月6日),清政府仿行宪政,宣布参照日本的司法制度,将刑部改为法部,专掌司法;将大理寺改为大理院,为全国最高审判机关;同时附设总检察厅,为全国最高检察机关,原都察院撤销。同时,各省要分期筹设各级审判厅。不过,这将面临人才、经费、经验等诸多方面的问题,于是袁世凯建议:"惟有逐渐分析,择一二处先行试办,视情形实无窒碍,然后以次推行。"由此,清政府决定先选择一地作为试点,总结经验教训后,再向全国推广,而直隶总督所在地天津便成了不二之选。

On November 6, 1906, the Qing government imitated constitutionalism and announced that it would change the criminal department into the legal department with reference to the Japanese judicial system, specializing in justice; Dalisi was changed into Daliyuan, which was the highest judicial organ in China, and the General Prosecutor's Office was attached as the highest procuratorial organ in China. The former Duchayuan was abolished. At the same time, the provinces should set up adjudicative offices at all levels by stages. However, this will face many problems such as talents, funds, experience, etc., so Yuan Shikai suggested: "Only by gradual analysis, choose one or two places to try it out first, depending on the situation, and then implement it." Therefore, the Qing government decided to choose one place as a pilot, sum up the experience and lessons, and then spread it to the whole country, and Tianjin, where the governor of Zhili is located, became the best choice.

早在光绪二十九年（1903），直隶总督兼北洋大臣袁世凯为试行审判改革，在天津设立发审公所（后更名谳法研究所、审判研究所），由凌福彭主持，培养审判改革人才。第二年，天津又在全国率先创立罪犯习艺所。这些都为天津作为清政府司法改革的试点奠定了基础。

As early as 1903, Yuan Shikai, Governor of Zhili and Minister of Beiyang, set up a adjudicative office in Tianjin (later renamed as Law Research Institute and Judicial Research Institute), which was presided over by Ling Fupeng to train

袁世凯在天津设立的警察局
Police station founded by Yuan Shikai in Tianjin

judicial reform talents. In the following year, Tianjin took the lead in setting up a criminal art institute in China. All these laid the foundation for Tianjin as a pilot of judicial reform of Qing government.

光绪三十二年（1906）秋，袁世凯为试办审判厅，令天津知府凌福彭拟定章程并筹办。十月，《天津府属试办审判厅章程》拟成，成为全国第一个地方性试办审判厅的法规。根据《章程》，府一级设高等审判分厅，县一级设地方审判厅，县以下按巡警所定区域设乡谳局（后根据《法院编制法》改称初级审判厅）。

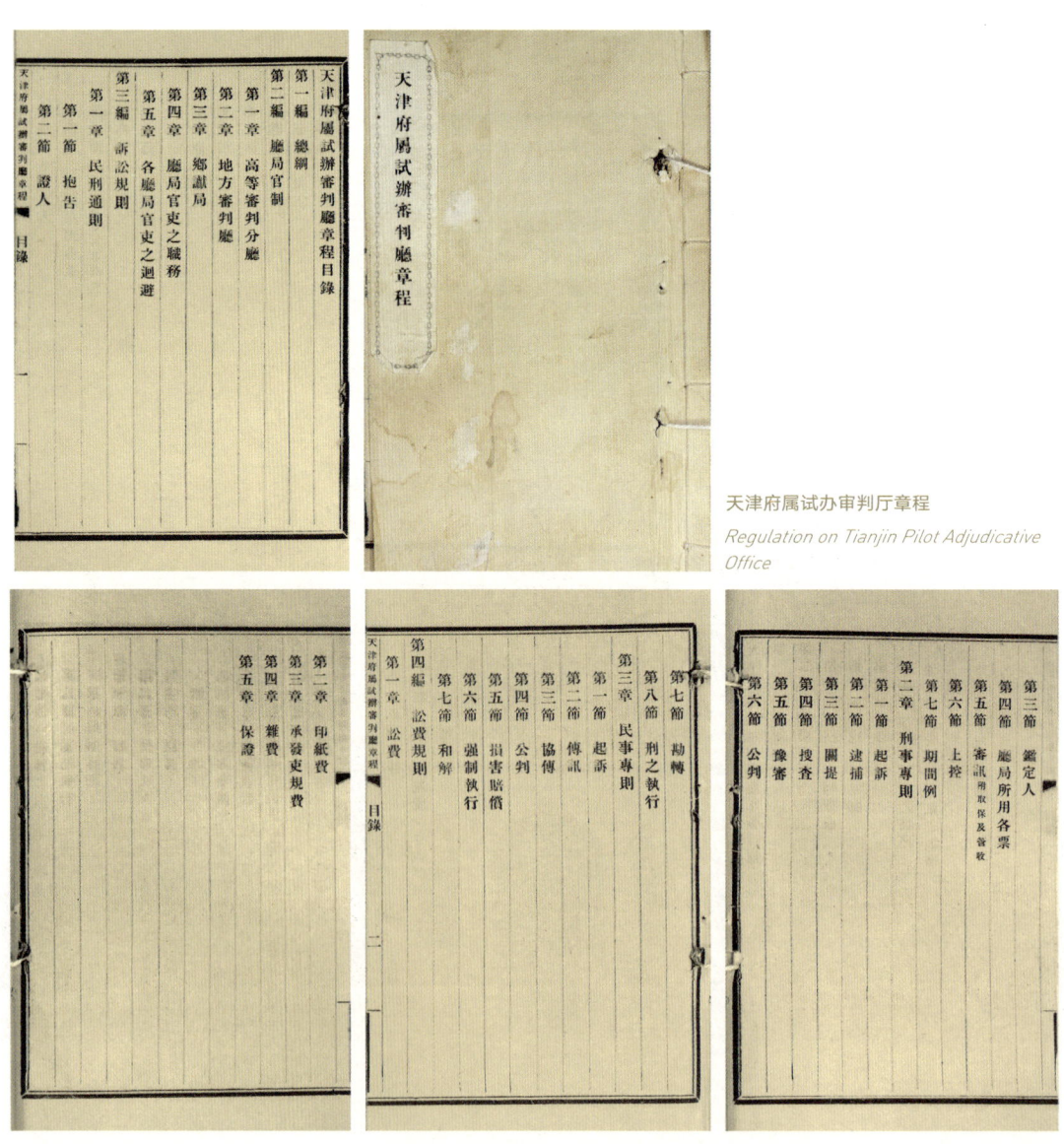

天津府属试办审判厅章程
Regulation on Tianjin Pilot Adjudicative Office

In the autumn of 1906, Yuan Shikai set up a adjudicative office, and ordered Ling Fupeng, the Magistrate of Tianjin, to draw up the articles of association and organize the adjudicative office. In October, the *Regulation on Tianjin Pilot Adjudicative Office* was drafted, which became the first local adjudicative office law in China. According to the *Regulation*, there is a high adjudicative office at the government level, a local adjudicative office at the county level, and a township bureau at the level below county according to the area determined by the patrolman (later renamed the primary adjudicative office according to the *Court Preparation Law*).

天津府高等审判分厅称为直隶高等审判分厅，厅长由天津知府兼任，内设民事审判厅和刑事审判厅各一，审判为合议制，审理不服地方审判厅判决的民事、刑事案件。由初级审判厅起诉者，以此厅为终审。天津县地方审判厅称为天津地方审判厅，厅长由天津知县兼任。高等审判分厅和天津地方审判厅均于光绪三十三年二月十日（1907年3月23日）举行开厅典礼，正式对外办公，厅址都设在天津县衙所在地，并于同年十一月二十日（1907年12月24日）共同迁至河北李公祠东侧新址办公。

The High Adjudicative Branch of Tianjin Government is called Zhili High Adjudicative Branch, and its director is concurrently appointed by Tianjin Magistrate. There are one civil adjudicative division and one criminal adjudicative

直隶高等检察厅官印
The official seal of the High Procuratorial Office of Zhili

直隶高等审判厅官印
The official seal of the High Adjudicative Office of Zhili

天津审判厅所在的天津县衙
Tianjin County Government where
Tianjin Adjudicative Office is located

division, and the trial is collegiate, which tries civil and criminal cases that refuse to accept the judgment of the local adjudicative office. If the prosecution is conducted by the primary adjudicative office, this office shall be the final judgment. Tianjin County Local Adjudicative Office is called Tianjin Local Adjudicative Office, and its director is concurrently appointed by Tianjin Magistrate. On March 23, 1907, the opening ceremony was held for the High Adjudicative Branch and the Tianjin Local Adjudicative Office, which were both located in the seat of Tianjin County Government. On December 24, 1907, they moved to the new office on the east side of Li Hongzhang Temple in Hebei.

此外，直隶高等审判分厅内还设有检事长（兼地方审判厅检事官），配备有书记官和司法巡警。宣统元年（1909）年末，天津高等检察分厅正式成立。地方审判厅内设有检事官，配备有书记官和司法巡警。后成立检察局，并于光绪三十三年六月十二日（1907年7月21日）改称检察厅，与同级审判厅并立。

In addition, there is also a prosecutor (who is also the prosecutor of the local adjudicative office) in the High Adjudicative Branch of Zhili, equipped with clerks and judicial patrol officers. At the end of 1909, Tianjin High Procuratorate Branch was formally established. There are prosecutors, clerks and judicial patrol

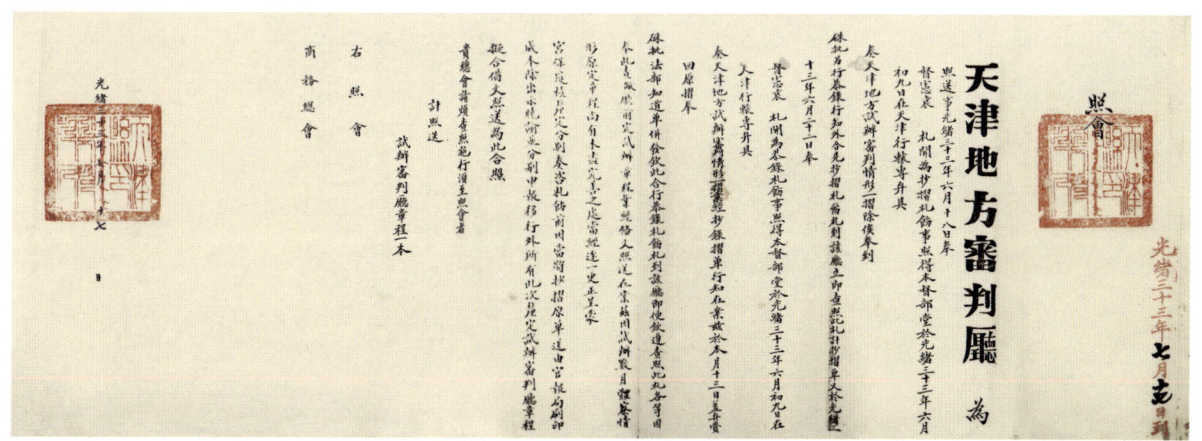

光绪三十三年（1907）照会试办天津地方审判厅章程
Articles of Association of Tianjin Local Adjudicative Office by Note in 1907

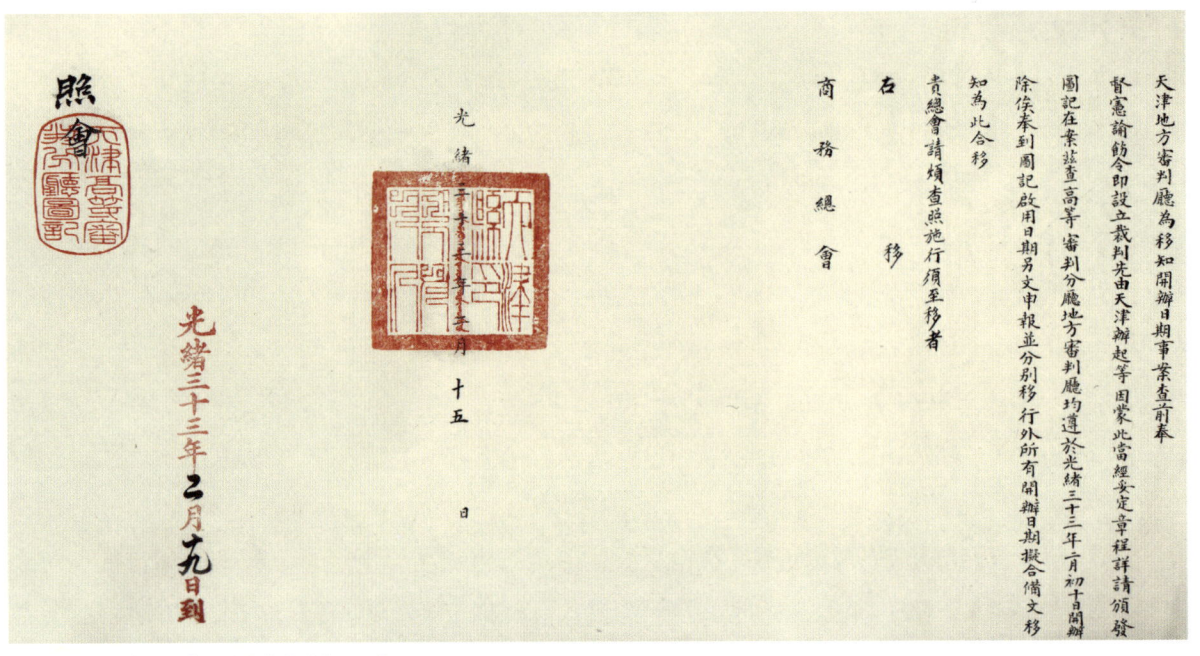

光绪三十三年（1907）天津高等审判分厅照会
Note of Tianjin High Adjudicative Branch in 1907

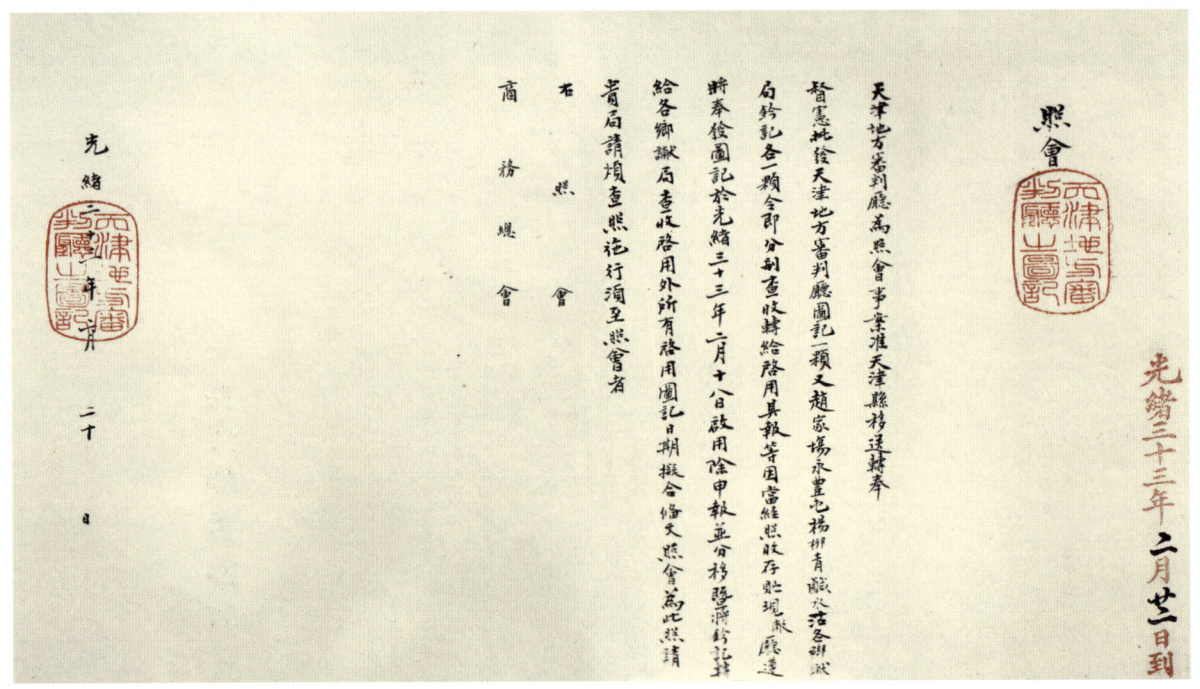

光绪三十三年（1907）天津地方审判厅照会批乡谳局
Tianjin Local Adjudicative Office approved the Township Bureau by note in 1907

officers in the local adjudicative office. After that, the procuratorial bureau was established, and it was renamed as the procuratorial office on July 21, 1907, and it stood side by side with the adjudicative office at the same level.

审判厅创办初期，天津设有永丰屯（后为第一初级审判厅）、赵家场（后为第二初级审判厅）、咸水沽（后为第三初级审判厅）和杨柳青（后为第四初级审判厅）四个乡谳局。四局均于光绪三十三年三月初一日（1907年4月13日）开局，三月初六日（4月18日）开始放告。每座乡谳局设承审官、检事官、书记官各一名。审判为独任制，分刑事与民事。当时的承审官一般都由候补知州、知县，候补通判充任。宣统元年（1909）年末，天津县第一初级检察厅、第二初级检察厅、第三初级检察厅、第四初级检察厅相继成立，均设有检事官、典簿、录事等职。宣统三年三月（1911年4月），天津第一、第二初级审判厅合二为一，厅址位于南马路天津县衙内，位于咸水沽和杨柳青的初级审判厅未作变更。

At the beginning of the establishment of the adjudicative office, Tianjin had four township bureaus: Yongfengtun (later the first junior adjudicative office), Zhaojiachang (later the second junior adjudicative office), Xianshuigu (later the third junior adjudicative office) and Yangliuqing (later the fourth junior adjudicative office). The four bureaus started on April 13, 1907 and began to be announced on April 18. Each township bureau shall have an examining officer, a prosecutor and a clerk. The trial is independent, divided into criminal and civil. At that time, the assessors were generally appointed by alternate magistrate, magistrate and alternate judge. At the end of 1909, the first, second, third and fourth primary procuratorates in Tianjin County were established one after another, all of which were equipped with prosecutors, bookkeepers and record clerks. In April 1911, the first and second primary adjudicative offices in Tianjin were merged into one, and the address of the courtrooms was located at Tianjin County Government, South Road, while the primary adjudicative offices in Xianshuigu and Yangliuqing were unchanged.

《天津府属试办审判厅章程》共四编一百四十六条（后改为一百四十五条），按照司法行政区划，承认裁判权的相对独立，并实行审、检分立制度；在审判组织原则方面，废除了独裁

1921	1922	1923	1924	1925	1926	1927	1928	1929	1930	1931	1932	193
1947	1948	1949	1950	1951	1952	1953	1954	1955	1956	1957	1958	195
1973	1974	1975	1976	1977	1978	1979	1980	1981	1982	1983	1984	198
1999	2000	2001	2002	2003	2004	2005	2006	2007	2008	2009	2010	201

制，采取合议制，同时实行回避制度。又设立了承发吏、检验吏和司法警察，改变了民事、刑事不分的旧制度。不仅为我国实行地方司法自治提供了一个新样本，而且还促进了全国审判新体系的建设。

There are 146 articles (later changed to 145 articles) in the *Regulation on Tianjin Pilot Adjudicative Office*, according to the judicial administrative divisions, the *Regulation* recognized the relative independence of jurisdiction and

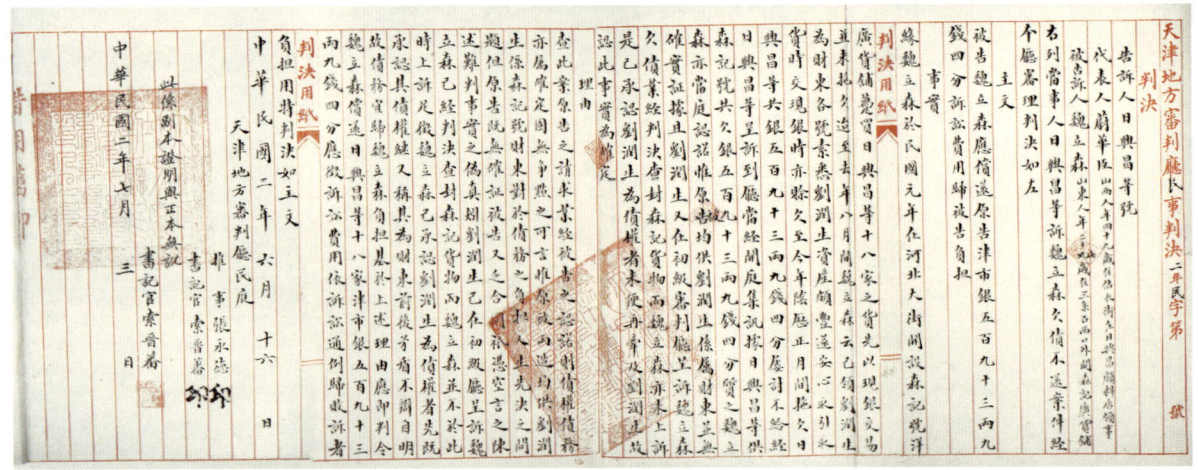

1913年天津地方审判厅民事判决书
Civil judgment of Tianjin Local Adjudicative Office in 1913

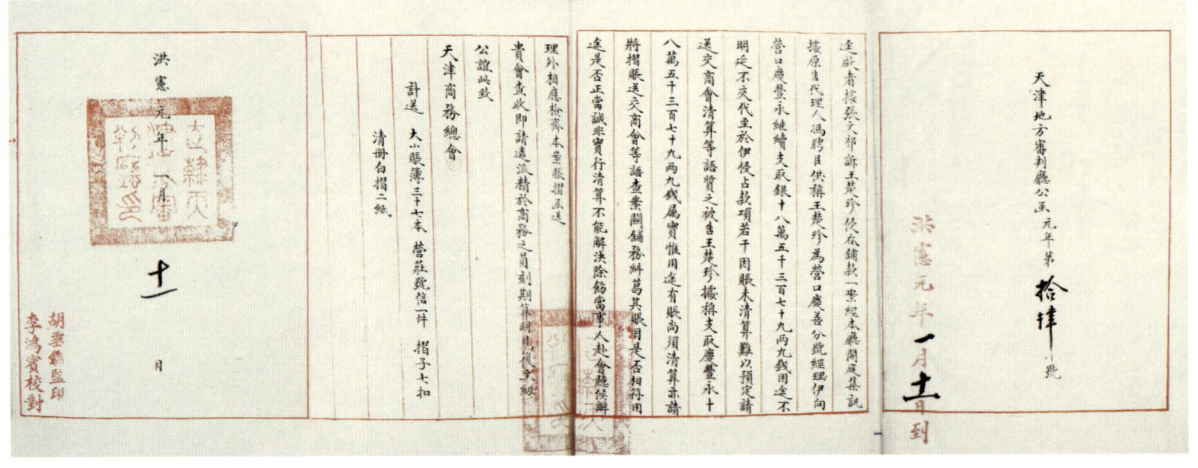

1916年天津地方审判厅致天津商务总会公函
Official letter from Tianjin Local Adjudicative Office to Tianjin Chamber of Commerce in 1916

implemented the system of separation of trial and prosecution; in the principle of trial organization, dictatorship was abolished, collegial system was adopted, and avoidance system was implemented at the same time. It also set up the officials of inheritance and inspection, set up the judicial police, and changed the old system of civil and criminal separation. It not only provided a new sample for the implementation of local judicial autonomy in China, but also promoted the construction of a new national trial system.

设立天津各级审判厅的尝试取得了极好的效果，被清廷法部确认为"前事之师"并向全国各省推广。截至宣统三年六月（1911年7月），清政府共设立高等审判分厅23所、地方审判厅62所、初级审判厅88所。各级审判厅的设立是清末司法改革的重要一环，标志着中国法院近代化的开端。

The attempt to set up adjudicative offices at all levels in Tianjin has achieved excellent results, which was recognized as a "teacher of ahead" by the Ministry of Justice of the Qing Dynasty and popularized in all provinces of China. By July 1911, the Qing government had set up 23 high adjudicative branches, 62 local adjudicative offices and 88 junior adjudicative offices. The establishment of adjudicative offices at all levels is an important part of judicial reform in the late Qing Dynasty, which marks the beginning of the modernization of Chinese courts.

民国初期至20世纪30年代的天津律师

TIANJIN LAWYERS FROM THE EARLY REPUBLIC OF CHINA TO THE 1930S

《律师暂行章程》《律师章程》与民国律师制度的确立 / 080
PROVISIONAL REGULATION OF LAWYERS, REGULATION OF LAWYERS AND THE ESTABLISHMENT OF LAWYER SYSTEM IN THE REPUBLIC OF CHINA

一、南京临时政府积极促成民国律师制度的确立 / 080
1. Nanjing Provisional Government Actively Promoted the Establishment of Lawyer System in the Republic of China

二、《律师暂行章程》的出台及其特征 / 085
2. The Promulgation and Characteristics of the *Provisional Regulation of Lawyers*

三、《律师暂行章程》的修订与律师法律体系的初步建立 / 089
3. Revision of the *Provisional Regulation of Lawyers* and Preliminary Establishment of Lawyer's Legal System

四、《律师章程》与律师法律体系的完善 / 090
4. *Regulation of Lawyers* and Perfection of Lawyer's Legal System

律师公会制度及天津律师公会 / 094
BAR ASSOCIATION SYSTEM AND TIANJIN BAR ASSOCIATION

一、律师公会的基本特征 / 094
1. Basic Characteristics of the Bar Association

二、律师公会的组织机构 / 096
2. Organization of the Bar Association

三、律师公会的自治权 / 101
3. Autonomy of the Bar Association

四、律师公会的职能与社会价值 / 115
4. Function and Social Value of the Bar Association

律师诉讼书状 / 128
LAWYERS' LITIGATION PLEADINGS

民国初创二十年的天津律师业 / 135
TIANJIN LAWYERS IN THE FIRST TWENTY YEARS OF THE REPUBLIC OF CHINA

一、天津律师数量的变化 / 137
1. Changes in the Number of Lawyers in Tianjin

二、天津律师的年龄、籍贯及学历特点 / 139
2. Tianjin Lawyers' Age, Native Place and Educational Background Characteristics

三、天津律师的类型 / 141
3. Types of Tianjin Lawyers

四、与天津相关的知名律师 / 144
4. Well-known Lawyers Related to Tianjin

五、在天津执业的女律师 / 172
5. Female Lawyers Practicing in Tianjin

民国大案中的天津律师 / 184
TIANJIN LAWYERS IN THE CASE OF THE REPUBLIC OF CHINA

一、周恩来等各界代表案 / 184
1. The Case of Zhou Enlai and Other Representatives from All Walks of Life

二、溥仪状告天津兴业银行案 / 197
2. The Case of Puyi Sued Tianjin Xingye Bank

三、文绣、溥仪离婚案 / 206
3. Divorce Case of Wenxiu and Puyi

四、施剑翘案 / 217
4. The Case of Shi Jianqiao

《律师暂行章程》《律师章程》与民国律师制度的确立

PROVISIONAL REGULATION OF LAWYERS, REGULATION OF LAWYERS AND THE ESTABLISHMENT OF LAWYER SYSTEM IN THE REPUBLIC OF CHINA

一、南京临时政府积极促成民国律师制度的确立

1. Nanjing Provisional Government Actively Promoted the Establishment of Lawyer System in the Republic of China

1911年10月10日武昌起义爆发，由此拉开了辛亥革命的序幕，清末预备立宪及蕴含其中的司法改革也随之中断。1912年1月1日，中华民国南京临时政府成立。以孙中山为代表的资产阶级革命派在废除封建专制制度、打破旧的国家机器的基础上，仿效西方资本主义国家，建立了现代意义上的共和国。同时，临时政府还仿照西方国家的法治原则，确定了全面建设新型法律制度的蓝图，其中就涉及司法审判体制改革，并且特别重视律师辩护制度的建立。

On October 10, 1911, Wuchang Uprising broke out, which opened the prelude of the Revolution of 1911, and the preparatory constitutionalism and judicial reform in the late Qing Dynasty were also interrupted. On January 1, 1912, Nanjing Provisional Government of the Republic of China was established. The bourgeois revolutionaries represented by Sun Yat-sen, on the basis of abolishing the feudal autocratic system and breaking the old state machine, imitated the western capitalist countries and established the republic in the modern sense. At the same time, the Provisional Government modeled on the rule of law principle in western countries, and determined the blueprint for building a new legal system in an all-round way, which involved the reform of the judicial trial system, and paid special attention to the establishment of the lawyer defense system.

在民国律师制度的确立过程中，前清修律大臣、南京临时政府司法总长伍廷芳发挥了重要的作用。他不仅积极主张效仿西方，建立新的法律体系，而且利用司法总长的身份，在审理素有"民国第一案"之称的姚荣泽案中率先实行了律师辩护制度。

Wu Tingfang, former Minister of Law Revision and Minister of Justice of Nanjing Provisional Government, played an important role in the establishment of lawyer system in the Republic of China. He not only actively advocated following the example of the West and establishing a new legal system, but also using the identity of the director of justice, in the trial known as the "first case of the Republic of China", said Yao Rongze case took the lead in the implementation of the lawyer defense system.

姚荣泽本为前清江苏省山阳县（今属淮安市）知县，辛亥革命后任该县司法长。在地方势力的支持下，他杀害了回乡发动独立起义的周实丹和阮式，之后逃匿于南通。在沪军都督陈其美的要求下，临时大总统孙中山电令江苏都督庄蕴宽和南通民军总司令张謇将姚荣泽解送到沪军都督府，并令陈其美"秉公讯办"。

Yao Rongze was originally the Magistrate of Shanyang County (now Huai'an) in Jiangsu Province in the former Qing Dynasty, and served as the magistrate of the county after the Revolution of 1911. With the support of local forces, he killed Zhou Shidan and Ruan Shi, who returned home to launch an independent uprising, and then fled to Nantong. At the request of Chen Qimei, the Shanghai Military Governor, Sun Yat-sen, the interim president, sent a telegram to Zhuang Yunkuan, the Jiangsu Governor, and Zhang Jian, the commander-in-chief of Nantong Civil Army, to deliver Yao Rongze to the Shanghai Military Governor's Office, and ordered Chen Qimei to "do justice".

伍廷芳得知此事，于1912年2月18日致电孙中山，称："廷以为民国方新，对于一切诉讼应

1921	1922	1923	1924	1925	1926	1927	1928	1929	1930	1931	1932	1933
1947	1948	1949	1950	1951	1952	1953	1954	1955	1956	1957	1958	1959
1973	1974	1975	1976	1977	1978	1979	1980	1981	1982	1983	1984	1985
1999	2000	2001	2002	2003	2004	2005	2006	2007	2008	2009	2010	2011

伍廷芳
Wu Tingfang

采文明办法，况此案情节重大，尤须审慎周详，以示尊重法律之意。拟由廷特派精通中外法律之员承审，另选通达事理、公正和平、名望素著者三人为陪审员，并准两造聘请辩护士到堂辩护，审讯时任人旁听。如此，则大公无私，庶无失出失入之弊。"3月2日，伍廷芳又致信陈其美，称："先由辩护士将全案理由提起，再由裁判官动问原告及各人证，两造辩护士盘诘。俟原告及人证既终，再审被告，其审问之法与原告同。然后由两造辩护士各将案由复述结束。"3月19日，伍廷芳在第四次致陈其美的信中强调说："法庭之上，断案之权在陪审员；依据法律为适法之裁判，在裁判官；盘诘驳难之权，在律师。"在姚荣泽案中，伍廷芳司法独立、陪审制、律师到庭辩护以及无罪推定的思想与实践为民国司法的变革树立了良好的开端。最终，在多数陪审员和承审官的认可下，姚荣泽案报请临时大总统减刑，并由袁世凯下令特赦，改判死刑为监禁十年，附加罚金一万元而结案。

When Wu Tingfang learned about this, he sent a telegram to Sun Yat-sen on February 18, 1912, saying: "Ting thought that the Republic of China was new, and civilized methods should be adopted for all lawsuits. However, the circumstances of this case are serious, and it is especially necessary to be careful and thorough to show respect for the law. It is proposed that the court should appoint a person who is proficient in Chinese and foreign laws to take the trial, and choose three people who are sensible, fair, peaceful and famous as jurors, and allow the two companies to hire defenders to defend in court, who will attend the trial. In this way, it is selfless, and there is no malfeasance." On March 2, Wu Tingfang sent a letter to Chen Qimei, saying: "First, the defender raised the reasons of the whole case, then the magistrate questioned the plaintiff and the witnesses, and the two defenders cross-examined. When the plaintiff and the witness are finished, the defendant will be interrogated in the same way as the plaintiff. Then two lawyers will make a final statement. " On March 19, Wu Tingfang emphasized in his fourth letter to Chen Qimei: "Above the court, jurors are responsible for clarifying the facts of the case; judges are responsible for making judgments according to law; lawyers are responsible for defense." In Yao Rongze's case, Wu Tingfang's thought and practice of judicial independence, jury system, lawyer's defense in court and presumption of innocence set a good beginning for the judicial reform of the Republic of China. Finally, with the approval of most jurors and judges, Yao Rongze's case was submitted to the interim president for commutation of sentence, and Yuan Shikai ordered an amnesty, which was commuted to ten years' imprisonment with a fine of 10,000 yuan.

在姚荣泽案实践中，孙中山也十分支持律师辩护制度。他不仅迅速回复伍廷芳的来电，称"所陈姚荣泽案审讯方法极善，即照来电办理可也"，同意伍廷芳的建议，而且明确批复内务部警务司司长孙润宇所拟定的《律师法草案》，称"查律师制度与司法独立相辅相成，夙为文明各国所通行。现各处既纷纷设立律师公会，尤应亟定法律，俾资依据，合将原呈及《草案》发交该局，仰即审核呈复，以便咨送参议院议决。切切！此令"，积极促成《律师法》的制定，以确立民国的律师制度。此外，南京临时政府的各个部门也纷纷行动，从官制、立法、舆论等角度为律师制度的确立创造条件。《司法部官职令（草案）》第二条即拟订了"关于律师之身份事项"的规定。

In Yao Rongze's case, Sun Yat-sen also supported the lawyer defense system. He not only responded to Wu Tingfang's telegram quickly, saying that "he said that the method of judging Yao Rongze's case is very good, and the trial can be conducted according to the telegram", agreeing with Wu Tingfang's suggestion, but also explicitly replyed to the *Lawyers Law Draft* drafted by Sun Runyu, Director of Police Department of the Ministry of Internal Affairs, saying that "the lawyer system and the judicial independence complement each other, which are very popular in many civilized countries. Now bar associations are being set up everywhere, and relevant laws and basis should be formulated. So I handed them the submitted official letter and the *Draft*, and they should review the reply immediately, so that they can submit the submitted official letter and the *Draft* to the Senate for resolution ", actively promoted the formulation of *Lawyers Law*, in order to establish the lawyer system of the Republic of China. In addition, various departments of Nanjing Provisional Government had also taken actions to create conditions for the establishment of lawyer system from the angles of official system, legislation and public opinion. Article 2 of the *Official Order of the Ministry of Justice (Draft)* drew up the provisions on "matters concerning the status of lawyers".

伍廷芳
Wu Tingfang

二、《律师暂行章程》的出台及其特征

2. The Promulgation and Characteristics of the *Provisional Regulation of Lawyers*

1912年3月,袁世凯就任中华民国临时大总统,民国历史从此进入北洋时期。这一时期虽然政局不稳,但在司法领域基本保留了清末司法改革的诸多重要成果,也沿袭了许多南京临时政府的相关政策,为民国律师制度的确立打下了一个良好的基础。1912年6月17日,参议院审议通过了《司法部官制》。这项制度虽然对原南京临时政府拟订的《司法部官职令(草案)》有所修改,但仍然保留了管理律师业务的内容。

In March 1912, Yuan Shikai became the interim president of the Republic of China, and the history of the Republic of China entered the Beiyang Period. Although the political situation was unstable during this period, many important achievements of judicial reform in the late Qing Dynasty were basically retained in the judicial field, and many relevant policies of Nanjing Provisional Government were also followed, which laid a good foundation for the establishment of lawyer system in the Republic of China. On June 17, 1912, the Senate deliberated and adopted the *Official System of the Ministry of Justice*. Although this system has modified the *Official Order of the Ministry of Justice (Draft)* drawn up by the former Nanjing Provisional Government, it still retains the contents of managing lawyers' business.

1912年9月16日,北洋政府司法部以行政命令的形式颁布了《律师暂行章程》,并在第三十七条中规定:"本《章程》于《律师法》及其施行法颁布后即行废止。"这部《暂行章程》是中国历史上第一部通行全国的律师法规,虽然在民国成立九个月后即告完成,但由于它仿照《日本辩护士法》修订而成,因此并不显得粗糙。《律师暂行章程》的出台标志着民国律师制度的确立。

On September 16, 1912, the Ministry of Justice of Beiyang Government promulgated the *Provisional Regulation of Lawyers* in the form of administrative orders, and stipulated in Article 37: "This *Regulation* shall be abolished upon the promulgation of the *Lawyers Law* and its implementation law." This *Provisional Regulation* is the first law for lawyers in China's history. Although it was completed nine months after the founding of the Republic of China, it is not rough because it was revised in imitation of the *Japanese Defender Law*. The promulgation of the *Provisional Regulation of Lawyers* marks the establishment of lawyer system in the Republic of China.

（一）律师自由职业者身份的确立

(a) The Establishment of the Status of Lawyers as Freelancers

律师自由职业者身份的确立是《律师暂行章程》的重要内容之一。该《章程》第十四条规定："律师受当事人之委托或审判衙门之命令，在审判衙门执行法定职务，并得依特别法之规定，在特别审判衙门行其职务。"这里提到了律师履行职务的两种情况。第一种，律师以个人身份独立接受当事人委托，在法庭诉讼或非讼业务中，基于其自身对受委托事件具体情节的了解以及对相关法律条款的理解，提出对委托人有利的法律要求。第二种则是对于因贫穷而无力聘请律师，法庭又认为有必要让律师参与诉讼的当事人，法庭将指派律师为其提供法律服务。虽然律师在这里必须服从法庭指派，承担辩护任务，但在诉讼过程中，律师行为的依据依然是法律本身，依然是独立行使法定职务。因此，无论是以上哪种情况，律师的身份都是自由职业者。

The establishment of the status of lawyers as freelancers is one of the important contents of the *Provisional Regulation of Lawyers*. Article 14 of the *Regulation* stipulates: "Lawyers are entrusted by the parties or ordered by the adjudicative office to perform their statutory duties in the adjudicative office, and may perform their duties in the special adjudicative office according to the provisions of the special law." Two situations in which lawyers perform their duties are mentioned here. First, lawyers independently accept clients' entrustment in their personal capacity, and in court litigation or non-litigation business, based on their own understanding of the specific circumstances of entrusted events and relevant legal provisions, they put forward legal requirements beneficial to clients. The second is that the court will appoint lawyers to provide legal services for those who are unable to hire lawyers because of poverty and think it necessary for lawyers to participate in litigation. Although lawyers here must obey the court's assignment and undertake the defense task, in the process of litigation, lawyers' behavior is still based on the law itself, and they still exercise their statutory duties independently. Therefore, no matter which of the above situations, lawyers are freelancers.

（二）司法机关与律师公会的双重监管体制

(b) The Dual Supervision System of the Judiciary and the Bar Association

作为自由职业者，律师既没有主管机关的直接监管，也没有推选机关的民意监督，因此《律师暂行章程》设立了以登录和惩戒为主要形式的司法机关与行业团体的双重管理监督体制。律师获得资格后，若要正式执业，首先要到省级高等审判（检察）厅进行登录，以确定其资格的真伪。登录过程分两步：第一，向司法总长领取律师证书，而司法总长在发放律师证书时，也将该律师列入总名簿；第二，已领取证书的律师到准备执业区域内的高等审判（检察）厅登录律师名簿。律师开展业务的区域一般以省为单位，登录后，该省高等审判（检察）厅会通知辖区内的各级审判（检察）机构准予该律师执行职务，同时开始对该律师的监督和管理。

As a freelancer, lawyers have neither the direct supervision of the competent authorities nor the supervision of the public opinion of the elected organs. Therefore, the *Provisional Regulation of Lawyers* has established a dual management and supervision system of judicial organs and industry groups with registration and punishment as the main forms. After a lawyer has obtained the lawyer qualification, if he wants to practice formally, he must first register with the provincial high adjudicative (procuratorial) office to determine the authenticity of his qualification. The registration process is divided into two steps: first, get the lawyer certificate from the Minister of Justice, and when the Minister of Justice issues the lawyer certificate, he also lists the lawyer in the general directory; second, lawyers who have received certificates should register the directory of lawyer in the high adjudicative (procuratorial) office in the area where they are going to practice. The area where lawyers conduct business is generally in the province. After registration, the provincial high adjudicative (procuratorial) office will notify the judicial (procuratorial) institutions at all levels within

民国国庆纪念日里的北京中央司法部
Beijing Central Ministry of Justice on the National Day of the Republic of China

its jurisdiction to grant the lawyers permission to perform their duties, and at the same time begin to supervise and manage the lawyers.

登录审核之外，司法机关对于律师最重的处罚就是实施律师惩戒。依据《律师暂行章程》，对于律师的惩戒，必须依法提起诉讼。地方检察长对于执业律师，如认为其行为有违反法律规定、应予惩戒者，即可依其职权，呈请高等检察长，提起对该律师的惩戒诉讼；律师公会对于律师惩戒的声请，也必须经由地方检察长呈请，不得径自呈请。

Apart from registration and auditing, the heaviest punishment for lawyers by judicial organs is to punish lawyers. According to the *Provisional Regulation of Lawyers*, the punishment of lawyers must be brought according to law. If the local procurator-general thinks that lawyer's behavior violates the law and should be punished, he can petition the high procurator-general according to his authority and file a disciplinary lawsuit against the lawyer. The bar association's request for disciplinary action by lawyers must also be petitioned by the local procurator-general, and it is not allowed to petition all the time.

三、《律师暂行章程》的修订与律师法律体系的初步建立
3. Revision of the *Provisional Regulation of Lawyers* and Preliminary Establishment of Lawyer's Legal System

北洋军阀统治时期，内阁频繁更迭，时局动荡，战争不断，不过民国大势已定，制定各类新式法律制度的势头有增无减，律师制度建设也从未停止过。以《律师暂行章程》为例，其实施不到一年时间，就进行了两次修订。此后，北洋政府又对《律师暂行章程》进行了多次修订，并相继颁布了一系列法令法规，其中包括《律师应守义务》《律师登录暂行章程》《律师考试规则》《律师惩戒会暂行规则》《复审查律师惩戒会审查细则》《无领事裁判权国律师出庭暂行章程》《律师甄别章程》等法律及修订案，初步确立了包括资格、条件、考试、职责、义务、惩戒等多方面内容的律师法律体系。

During the reign of the Northern Warlords, the cabinet changed frequently, the current situation was turbulent, and wars continued. However, the general trend of the Republic of China was set, and the momentum of formulating various new legal systems continued unabated, and the construction of lawyer system never stopped. Take the *Provisional Regulation of Lawyers* as an example, it has been revised twice in less than one year. Since then, the Beiyang Government has revised the *Provisional Regulation of Lawyers* for many times, and successively promulgated a series of laws and regulations. These include *Lawyers' Obligations*, *Lawyers' Registration Provisional Regulations*, *Lawyers' Examination Rules*, *Lawyers' Disciplinary Committee Provisional Rules*, *Re-examination Lawyers' Disciplinary Committee Review Rules*, *Provisional Regulation of Lawyers in Countries without Consular Jurisdiction*, *Lawyers' Screening Regulations* and other laws and amendments, which have initially established the lawyer's legal system including qualifications, obligations, examinations, duties, obligations, punishments etc.

1915年7月,司法部又专门制定并颁布了《律师应守义务》五条,并于1916年10月加以修订。《律师应守义务》主要从三个方面限制律师的职业行为:一是律师与当事人的利益关系;二是律师的疏忽责任;三是诚实、信用原则。《律师应守义务》的制定,重在加强对律师执行职务的管理,强化律师执行职务过程中应承担的义务,对于初建时期律师队伍的净化以及律师良好社会形象的树立,起到了积极的作用。

In July 1915, the Ministry of Justice specially formulated and promulgated five articles of *Lawyers' Obligations*, which were revised in October 1916. *Lawyers' Obligations* mainly restricts lawyers' professional behavior from three aspects: first, the interest relationship between lawyers and parties; second, the negligence responsibility of lawyers; third, the principle of honesty and credit. The formulation of *Lawyers' Obligations* focuses on strengthening the management of lawyers in performing their duties, and strengthening the obligations that lawyers should bear in the process of performing their duties, which has played a positive role in the purification of lawyers and the establishment of a good social image of lawyers in the initial construction period.

四、《律师章程》与律师法律体系的完善
4. *Regulation of Lawyers* and Perfection of Lawyer's Legal System

南京国民政府成立以后,北洋时期的律师制度被继续援用,同时综合当时社会的需要,提出了众多修改意见,颁布了新的法律法规。

After the establishment of Nanjing National Government, the lawyer system in Beiyang Period was continuously used. At the same time, considering the needs of the society at that time, many amendments were put forward and new laws and regulations were promulgated.

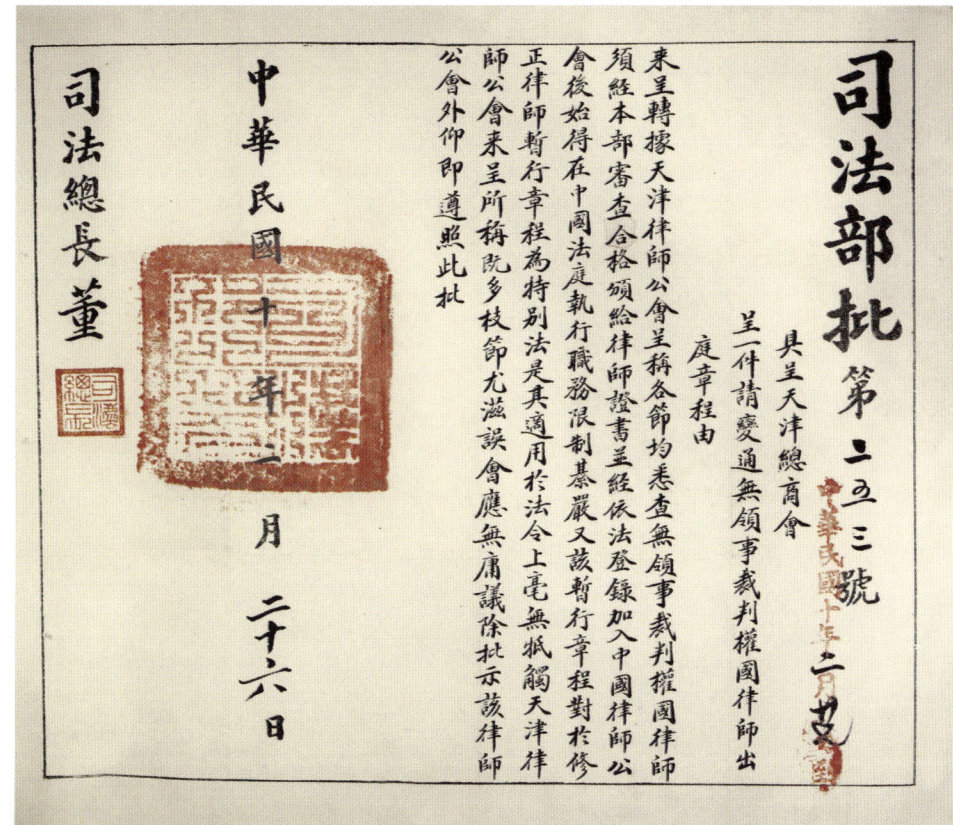

1921年北洋政府司法部关于请变通《无领事裁判权国律师出庭暂行章程》的批复

Reply of the Ministry of Justice of Beiyang Government in 1921 on the modification of the *Provisional Regulation of Lawyers in Countries without Consular Jurisdiction*

1927年7月23日，南京国民政府司法部公布并施行了《律师章程》，也就取代了北洋政府时期的《律师暂行章程》，随后又相继颁布了《甄别律师委员会章程》《高等考试司法官律师考试条例》《律师惩戒委员会规则》《律师公会标准会则》等法律法规。

On July 23, 1927, the Ministry of Justice of Nanjing National Government promulgated and implemented the *Regulation of Lawyers*, which replaced the *Provisional Regulation of Lawyers* during the Beiyang Government. Later, it successively promulgated laws and regulations, such as the *Statutes of the Screening Lawyers Committee*, the *Examination Regulations of Higher Examination for Magistrates and Lawyers*, the *Rules of the Lawyers Disciplinary Committee*, and the *Standards Rules of the Bar Association*.

南京国民政府公布并施行的相关法律，大体以1926年北洋政府修订的《律师暂行章程》为基础，同时添加了许多新的内容。《律师章程》不仅延续了律师的自由职业者身份，而且进行了一系列调整，包括增加律师消极资格的条款；具体规定了律师的检核制度，律师登录限定于两个地方法院和高等法院；增加了新的律师惩戒特别程序，增设了惩戒复审委员会；增加了关于外国律师执行职务的相关规定。

The relevant laws promulgated and implemented by Nanjing National Government were generally based on the *Provisional Regulation of Lawyers* revised by Beiyang Government in 1926. At the same time, many new contents were added. The *Regulation of Lawyers* continued the status of lawyers as freelancers. In addition, a series of adjustments had been made in the *Regulation of Lawyers*, including the provision of increasing the negative qualifications of lawyers; the lawyer's verification system was specified, and the lawyer's login was limited to two district courts and the high court; a new special disciplinary procedure for lawyers had been added, and a disciplinary review committee had been added; the relevant provisions on the

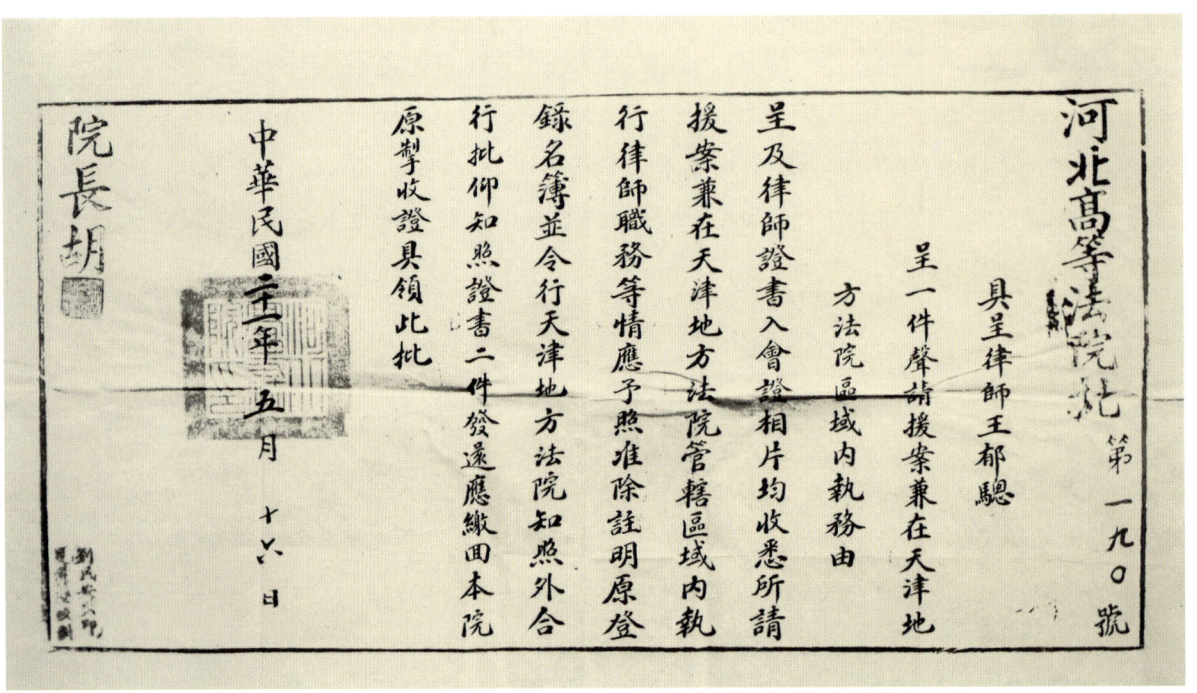

1932年河北高等法院的批复

Reply of Hebei High Court in 1932

performance of duties by foreign lawyers had been added.

相较于《律师暂定章程》，律师资格的变化是《律师章程》的一个显著特色。《律师章程》将律师应具备的资格修改为"中华民国人民满二十一岁以上者"，从而放开了女性从事律师职业的限制，具有相当大的进步意义。

Compared with the *Provisional Regulation of Lawyers*, the change of lawyer qualification was a prominent feature of the *Regulation of Lawyers*. The *Regulation of Lawyers* changed the qualifications that lawyers should have to be "people of the Republic of China who are over 21 years old", thus liberalizing the restrictions on women's engagement as lawyers, which was of great progressive significance.

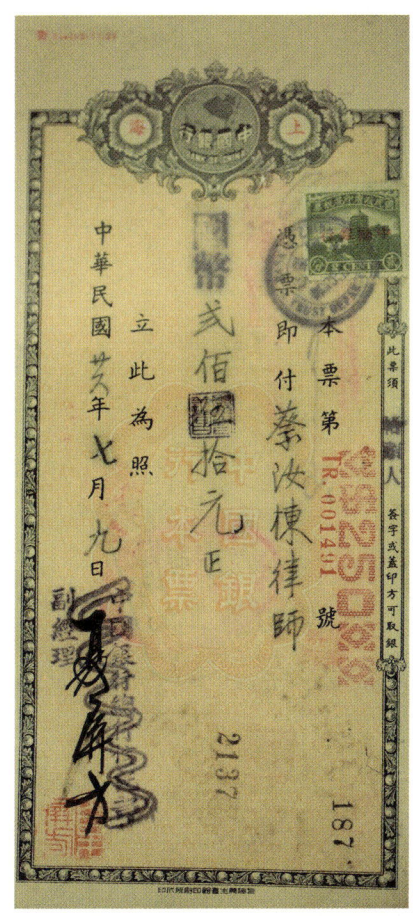

1937年7月上海中国银行付蔡汝栋律师费凭证

Voucher of lawyer fee paid by Bank of China in Shanghai to Cai Rudong in July 1937

《律师章程》及相关法律法规的颁布标志着南京国民政府律师法律体系整体架构的完成，也意味着民国律师制度的完全确立以及逐步完善，并由此促进了民国律师业的发展。

The promulgation of the *Regulation of Lawyers* and related laws and regulations marked the completion of the overall framework of the lawyer legal system of Nanjing National Government, and also means the complete establishment and gradual improvement of the lawyer system in the Republic of China, thus promoting the development of the lawyer industry in the Republic of China.

律师公会制度及天津律师公会
BAR ASSOCIATION SYSTEM AND TIANJIN BAR ASSOCIATION

如果说法官、检察官、律师是民国司法体系中的三大职务的话，那么法院、检察院、律师公会就是司法组织体系中三个互相制衡又共同发挥作用的机构。律师公会的重要性可见一斑。

If judges, prosecutors and lawyers are the three major positions in the judicial system of the Republic of China, then the courts, procuratorates and bar associations are the three institutions in the judicial organization system that balance each other and play a common role. The importance of the bar association can be seen.

一、律师公会的基本特征
1. Basic Characteristics of the Bar Association

北洋政府《律师暂行章程》第二十二条规定："律师非加入律师公会，不得执行职务。"这表明1912年9月16日《律师暂行章程》的公布实施，不仅标志着民国律师制度的确立，而且也意味着律师公会制度的正式建立。

Article 22 of the *Provisional Regulation of Lawyers* of Beiyang Government stipulates, "Lawyers shall not perform their duties unless they join the bar association." This shows that the promulgation and implementation of the *Provisional Regulation of Lawyers* on September 16, 1912 not only marks the establishment of the

1934	1935	1936	1937	1938	1939	1940	1941	1942	1943	1944	1945	1946
1960	1961	1962	1963	1964	1965	1966	1967	1968	1969	1970	1971	1972
1986	1987	1988	1989	1990	1991	1992	1993	1994	1995	1996	1997	1998
2012	2013	2014	2015	2016	2017	2018	2019	2020	2021	……		

1918年天津律师公会会员徽章
Member badge of Tianjin Bar Association in 1918

天津律师公会会员徽章
Member badge of Tianjin Bar Association

lawyer system of the Republic of China, but also means the formal establishment of the bar association system.

天津律师公会经天津市社会团体登记局批准，成立于1913年3月，最初的会址位于河北新区黄纬路诚安里27号。1934年3月10日，天津律师公会会刊《天津律师公会旬刊》第一卷第一号正式出版发行，江庸律师亲笔题写了封面。次年1月，《天津律师公会旬刊》更名为《法令旬刊》，曾为天津著名饭店登瀛楼题写牌匾的北洋寓公张志潭亲笔题签。《法令旬刊》期刊社社长李洪岳，副社长老遇春，副社长兼总编辑朱道孔，编辑有于振宗、尹凤藻、王劲闻、包振等43人。

Tianjin Bar Association was established in March 1913 with the approval of Tianjin Social Organization Registration Bureau. It was originally located at No. 27 Cheng'an Lane, Huangwei Road, Hebei New District. On March 10, 1934, the first volume of *Tianjin Bar Association Quarterly*, the journal of Tianjin Bar Association, was officially published, and Jiang Yong wrote the cover with his own handwriting. In January of the following year, *Tianjin Bar Association Quarterly* was renamed as *Law Quarterly*, and Zhang Zhitan, a resident of Beiyang who once wrote a plaque for Dengyinglou of Tianjin famous restaurant, personally signed it. Li Hongyue, president of *Law Quarterly*, Lao Yuchun, vice president, Zhu Daokong, vice president

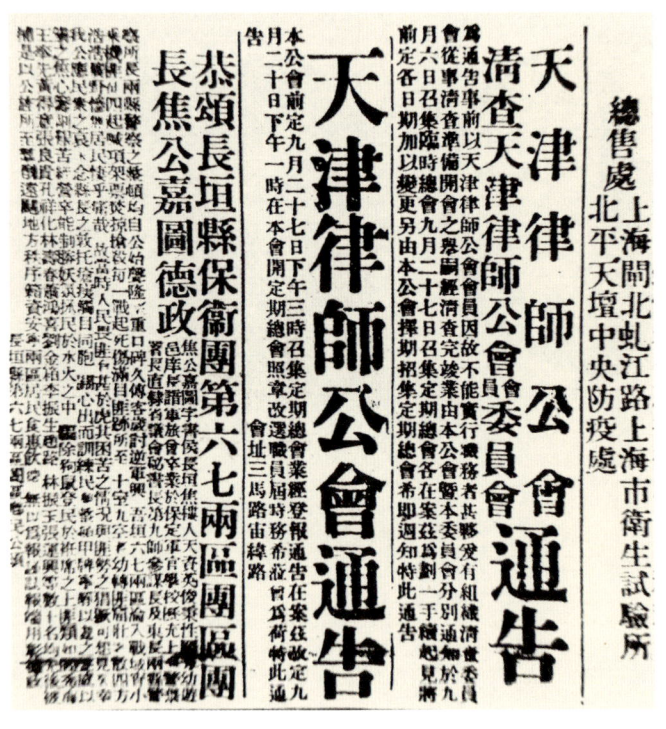

天津律师公会通告
Notice of Tianjin Bar Association

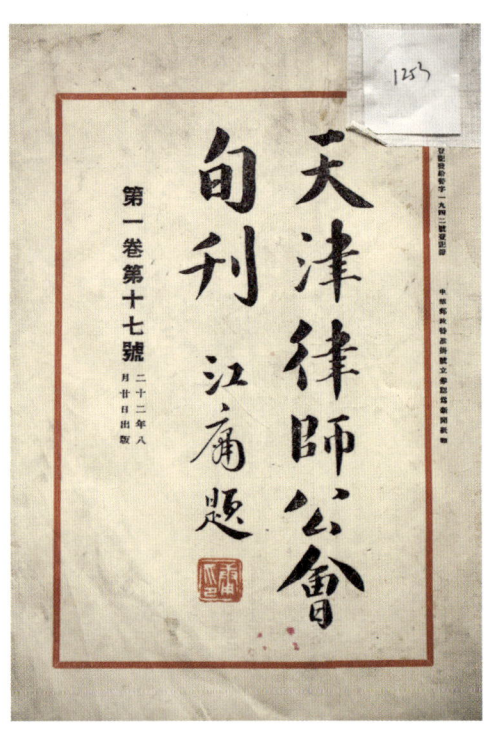

江庸题签的《天津律师公会旬刊》
Tianjin Bar Association Quarterly signed by Jiang Yong

and editor-in-chief, and 43 editors, including Yu Zhenzong, Yin Fengzao, Wang Jinwen and Bao Zhen, etc.

二、律师公会的组织机构
2. Organization of the Bar Association

依据《律师暂行章程》和《律师章程》的规定，律师公会实行会长制度，而在1941年《律师法》颁布后，则实行理事会制度。不过，无论是会长制度还是理事会制度，其组织机构的功能并没有什么不同。律师公会采取代议民主制，无论日常工作还是重大决策都通过召开会议集体讨论决定；如果来不及召开会议，就先由领导层作出决定，然后在下次会议时追认。

According to the *Provisional Regulation of Lawyers* and the *Regulation of*

Lawyers, the bar association implemented the system of president, and after the promulgation of the *Lawyers Law* in 1941, it implemented the system of council. However, whether it is the president system or the council system, its organizational functions are not different. The bar association adopted a representative democracy system, and both daily work and major decisions were decided through collective discussion at meetings. If it is too late to hold a meeting, the leadership will make a decision first, and then make ratification at the next meeting.

律师公会的组织机构包括公会会员大会、常任评议员会和干事会，领导成员则由会长、副会长、评议员、干事组成。其中会长一人，主持一切会务，副会长一人或两人，辅佐会长办理会务。会长因故不能到公会时，由副会长代行其职。常任评议员人数不等，如天津律师公会为九人，上海律师公会为八人，北平律师公会为十二人，集体开会议决公会中一切进行的事务。干事四至八人，执行议决事件并随时处理会务。律师公会一般还设有候补评议员和干事，遇到缺额时递补。

The organization of the bar association includes the Member's General Assembly of the association, the permanent council and the officers council, and the leading members are composed of the president, vice president, councillors and officers. Among them, one president presides over all business meetings, and one or two vice presidents assist the president in handling business meetings. If the president is unable to attend the guild for some reason, the vice president shall take his place. The number of permanent councillors varies. For example, Tianjin Bar Association had 9 members, Shanghai Bar Association had 8 members and Beiping Bar Association had 12 members. Collective meetings are held to decide all the business of the bar association. There are 4-8 officers, who are responsible for deciding events and handling meetings at any time. Generally, the bar association also has alternate councillors and officers, who will be replaced when they encounter vacancies.

从1913年到1949年，天津律师公会共有九人担任过会长，包括梁锡纶、兰兴周、许云舫、许肇铭、李洪岳、张绍曾、刘蓬瀛和朱德武（后两位为理事会制度时期的会长）。此外，据我国《罗马法》研究的先驱贾文范身后的《德教碑》记载，贾文范也曾担任早期天津律师公会会长，不过具体时间并未注明。

From 1913 to 1949, there were nine presidents of Tianjin Bar Association, including Liang Xilun, Lan Xingzhou, Xu Yunfang, Xu Zhaoming, Li Hongyue, Zhang Shaozeng, Liu Pengying and Zhu Dewu (the latter two were presidents of the council system). In addition, according to the *Morality Monument* erected after Jia Wenfan's death, the pioneer of the study of *Roman Law* in China, Jia Wenfan also served as the chairman of the early Tianjin Bar Association, but the specific time was not specified.

公会会员大会是律师公会最高权力机关，有权处理会中一切事务，包括选举等事宜。会员大会分定期总会与临时总会，每年3月和9月，或春季和秋季各举行一次。1920年5月3日的《益世报》曾刊登新闻《律师公会开春季例会》，文中提到："梁锡纶报告了自民国八年（1919）十月至现在之出入款项事宜，复报告此次由本会发出公函共二百五十二封，实得会员复函一百五十五封，今日到会者一百五十四人，除委任代理函件外，实到人数五十三人，与法定人数相合，即可从事投票改选会长。报告毕，由该会职员李思逊并有地方检察官王果苉场监视。

1919 年天津律师公会票选职员通告
Notice of voting staff of Tianjin Bar Association in 1919

1925 年 7 月许云舫任会长期间的改选报道
Report on the re-election of Xu Yunfang as chairman of Tianjin Bar Association in July 1925

惟时至六钟余,选举尚无结果,全场秩序甚形紊乱,会员中有因时间过晚,自由退席者,诚可谓放弃选举大权云。"记录了早期天津律师公会召开春季大会时的情景。公会会长为议长(天津律师公会称主席),负责召集、主持会议;会议表决时,会长与其他评议员权力相同,只有在票数相等的情况下,会长才有最后的决定权。会员大会的召开日期和地点由常任评议员决定,并在开会前两周分函通知各会员,同时登报通告。

The Member's General Assembly of the association is the highest authority of the bar association, and has the right to handle all affairs in the association, including elections, etc. The Member's General Assembly are divided into regular Member's General Assembly and temporary Member's General Assembly, which are held once a year in March and September, or in spring and autumn. On May 3, 1920, *Yishi Daily* published a news report *The Spring Regular Meeting of the Bar Association*, which mentioned, "Liang Xilun reported the payment and withdrawal from October, 1919 to the present, and re-reported that this time, a total of 252 official letters were sent by this council, and 155 replies were received from members. Today, 154 people attended the meeting. In addition to the letter of appointment, the actual number was 53. Meet the quorum, it can vote to re-elect the president. After the

梁锡纶会长
Chairman Liang Xilun

张绍曾会长
Chairman Zhang Shaozeng

刘蓬瀛会长
Chairman Liu Pengying

report was finished, Li Sixun, a staff member of the association, and Wang Guo, a local prosecutor, came to the scene for surveillance. However, until six o'clock, there was no result in the election, and the order of the whole audience was very disordered. Among the members, there were people who quit freely because of the late time, which can be said to give up the right to vote. " It recorded the scene when the Tianjin Bar Association held its spring meeting in the early days. The president of the association is the speaker (called the chairman of Tianjin Bar Association), who is responsible for convening and presiding over the meeting. When voting at a meeting, the president has the same power as other councillors, and only when the votes are equal can the president have the final decision. The date and place of the Member's General Assembly shall be decided by the permanent councillors, and the members shall be notified by letter two weeks before the meeting, and the notice shall be published in the newspaper at the same time.

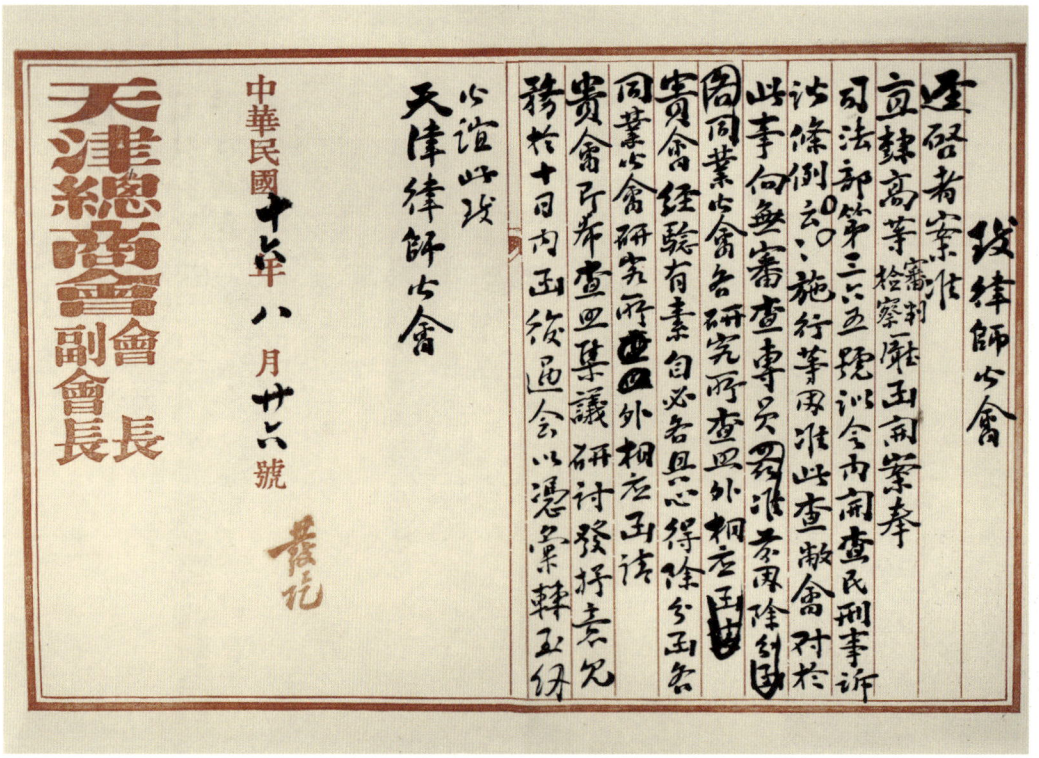

1927年天津总商会致天津律师公会函
Letter from Tianjin General Chamber of Commerce to Tianjin Bar Association in 1927

会员大会需要与会者超过会员总数的一半（如天津律师公会、上海律师公会）或三分之一（如北平律师公会）才能开会。临时总会的召开则需要20名以上会员的提议或常任评议员过半数的决议，并能以专函形式通知到与会者。

The Member's General Assembly requires more than half (such as Tianjin Bar Association and Shanghai Bar Association) or one third (such as Beiping Bar Association) of the total number of members to hold a meeting. The convening of the temporary Member's General Assembly requires the proposal of more than 20 members or the resolution of more than half of the permanent councillors, and can be notified to the participants in the form of a special letter.

常任评议员会由全体常任评议员组成；按照《天津律师公会会则》的规定，常任评议员会每月至少举行一次。干事会是律师公会的执行机构，负责执行会员大会及常任评议员会的议决事项，并处理律师公会的日常事务。

The permanent council consists of all the permanent councillors. According to the *Rules of Tianjin Bar Association*, the permanent council will be held at least once a month. The officers council is the executive body of the bar association, which is responsible for implementing the resolutions of the Member's General Assembly and the permanent council, and handling the daily affairs of the bar association.

三、律师公会的自治权

3. Autonomy of the Bar Association

国家通过《律师暂行章程》《律师章程》赋予律师公会相当程度的自治权，从而使其成为监督、管理律师的重要一环。律师公会的权力主要体现在以下五个方面：

The state has granted a considerable degree of autonomy to the bar association through the *Provisional Regulation of Lawyers* and the *Regulation of Lawyers*, thus making it an important part of supervising and managing lawyers. The power of the bar association is mainly reflected in the following five aspects:

(一)制定律师公会会则的权力

(a) The Power to Formulate the Rules of the Bar Association

《律师暂行章程》规定律师公会有权制定公会会则,《律师章程》第二十九条规定:"律师公会应议定会则,由地方法院院长经高等法院院长呈请司法部长核准。"由此,《律师暂行章程》或《律师章程》成为了制定律师公会会则的法律依据。两部章程对制定公会会则的要求基本一致,包括:一、会长、副会长、常任评议员之选举方法及其职务;二、常任评议员之会议规则;三、维持律师德义方法;四、公费及谢金之最高额;五、其他处理会务之必要方法。可见,法律上对制定律师公会会则的要求并不多,律师公会有较大的自主权。直到1936年2月南京国民政府司法行政部颁布的《律师公会标准会则》,才以训令的形式对律师公会会则的言辞与格式作出了规定。

The *Provisional Regulation of Lawyers* stipulates that the bar association has the Rules to formulate the rules of the association, and Article 29 of the *Regulation of Lawyers* stipulates, "The bar association shall agree on the rules, and the district court president shall apply to the Minister of Justice for approval by the high court president." Therefore, the *Provisional Regulation of Lawyers* or *Regulation of Lawyers* has become the legal basis for formulating the rules of the bar association. The requirements of the two regulations for formulating the rules of the guild are basically the same, including: 1. The election methods and duties of the president, vice president and permanent councillors. 2. Meeting rules of permanent assessors of the Member's General Assembly. 3. Methods of maintaining lawyers' morality and justice. 4. The maximum amount of public expense and gratuity. 5. Other necessary methods for handling business affairs. It can be seen that there are not many legal requirements for formulating the rules of the bar association, and the bar association has greater autonomy. It was not until February 1936, when the Ministry of Justice and Administration of Nanjing National Government promulgated the *Standard Rules of the Bar Association* that the words and format of the rules of the bar association were stipulated in the form of instructions.

（二）入会退会与审查会员资格的权力

(b) The Power to Join, Withdraw and Review the Membership

几乎所有的律师公会会则都规定，只要具备《律师章程》第二条或第三条所规定的律师资格，领有律师证书，并在相关法院进行了登录，律师就具有了公会会员的资格。同时，《律师暂定章程》和《律师章程》也都规定"律师非加入公会不得执行职务"。于是，律师天然就被授予了律师公会会员的身份，而公会似乎没有拒绝的权力，但实际上律师公会不仅有批准律师入会退会的权力，而且拥有律师资格的审定权。

Almost all bar associations stipulate that as long as they have the lawyer qualification stipulated in Article 2 or Article 3 of the *Regulation of Lawyers*, have a lawyer certificate and have registered in the relevant courts, lawyers will have the qualification of members of the association. At the same time, *Provisional Regulation of Lawyers* and *Regulation of Lawyers* also stipulate that "lawyers shall not perform their duties unless they join the guild". Therefore, lawyers are naturally granted the status of members of the bar association, and the association does not seem to have the power to refuse. However, in fact, the bar association not only has the power to approve lawyers' membership and withdrawal, but also has the right to examine and approve lawyers' qualifications.

以《天津律师公会会则》为例，律师公会首先规定会员要缴纳入会费40元和每月经常费一元，如果三个月以上不缴纳经常费，就视为退会。其次，公会列出了六类勒令退会的情况："一、任有俸给之公职者。二、因惩戒受停职或除名之处分者。三、自愿撤销律师登录者。四、法律上规定不许当律师者。五、有精神丧失之常况，由本会常任评议员会决议提交该管法院首席检察官经鉴定属实者。六、有妨害律师风纪之行为而受本条第二款之处分者。"上海律师公会在会员入会时还要求交验律师证书、学校毕业文凭或其他有充当律师资格之证明文件；确定是否登录；填写入会自愿申请书等。

Take the *Rules of Tianjin Bar Association* as an example. First, the bar association stipulates that members should pay an entrance fee of 40 yuan and a monthly recurrent fee of one yuan. If they do not pay the recurrent fee for more than three months, they will be regarded as retiring. Secondly, the guild listed six kinds of cases of being ordered to withdraw from the guild: "1. Those who hold public office with salary. 2. Those who have been suspended or removed from the list due to disciplinary actions. 3. Voluntarily revoking the lawyer's registration. 4. The law is not allowed to be a lawyer. 5. If there is a normal condition of mental loss, it shall be submitted to the chief prosecutor of the competent court by the resolution of the permanent council of this council and verified by authentication. 6. Those who are subject to the second paragraph of this article because of the behavior that impairs the discipline of lawyers. " When members joined the Shanghai Bar Association, they were required to submit a lawyer certificate, school diploma or other certification documents that were qualified to act as lawyers; determine whether to log in; fill in voluntary application for membership, etc.

这些条款充分说明了律师公会在会员入会退会问题上的自主性，而更重要的是，公会实际上还具有严格审查律师资格的权力。按照《律师暂定章程》等法律法规的要求，律师资格的授予应该以考试为主，而整个民国时期都没有进行一场像样的律师资格考试，因此律师资格的取得主要通过法律规定的免试来实现。不过，国家机关往往无法分辨免试条件的真伪，特别是国外文凭的鱼龙混杂，很容易出现骗取律师资格的现象。于是，律师公会利用其专业素养对律师资格进行严格审查，比如天津律师公会的律师登记名簿就比法院多出了"学历及履历""加入律师公会年月日""其他法院之登录号数"三项内容。如此便能将一些假冒者挡在律师公会大门外，以至于一些被律师公会拒绝入会者惊呼"律师公会权力凌驾于国家权力之上"。此外，律师公会也会审查已入会律师的资格，如果发现问题，同样令其退会。

These clauses fully illustrate the autonomy of the bar association in the issue of membership and withdrawal, and more importantly, the association actually has the power to strictly examine the qualifications of lawyers. According to the requirements of the *Provisional Regulation of Lawyers* and other laws and regulations, the granting of lawyer's qualification should be based on examination, but there was no decent lawyer's qualification examination in the whole period of the Republic of China. Therefore, the lawyer's qualification was mainly achieved through the exemption from examination prescribed by law. However, state organs were often unable to distinguish the authenticity of the exemption conditions, especially because foreign diplomas were mixed, and it was easy to cheat lawyers. Therefore, the bar association made use of its professional quality to strictly examine lawyers' qualifications. For example, the directory of lawyers in Tianjin Bar Association had more contents than the courts, such as "educational background and resume", "date of joining the bar association" and "login number of other courts". In this way, some counterfeiters were blocked out of the bar association, so that some people who were rejected by the bar association exclaim that "the power of the bar association is above the state power". In addition, the bar association will also examine the qualifications of lawyers who have joined the club, and if problems are found, they will also be withdrawn.

（三）制定律师收费上限的权力

(c) The Power to Set the Upper Limit of Lawyers' Fees

律师的费用时称"公费"，天津律师公会会长梁锡纶曾于1920年的公会年度报告中指出："旧管共计大洋一千四百四十一元有余，新收共计大洋二百九十余元，开除共计大洋五百一十七元，实在共存大洋一千二百一十四元有余。"足见律师公会的财力之盛。事实上，合理的公费标准是保障律师制度正常运行、维护律师社会形象的重要一环。《律师暂行章程》规定，律师公会对于执业律师在收费方面实行监督，其具体方法是制定律师收费的最高标准，并监督收费的实际情况。

The lawyers' fee was called "public expense". Liang Xilun, chairman of Tianjin Bar Association, pointed out in the annual report of the guild in 1920: "A total of more than 1,441 yuan, with a new revenue of more than 290 yuan, excluding a total of 517 yuan, there is more than 1,214 yuan coexisting." It showed that the bar association had a strong financial capacity. In fact, the reasonable standard of public expense was an important link to ensure the normal operation of the lawyer system and maintain the social image of lawyers. According to the *Provisional*

第九條　職員除書記應由本會僱備外均由本會員選出

第十條　職員之選舉用投票方法以票數多者為當選票數同者以籤法定之

第十一條　職員除書記應務外任期均以一年為限但得被選連任

第十二條　本會分定期總會及常任評議會臨時總會凡開會時均以會長為主席

第五章　集會

第十三條　定期總會於每年三月九月各舉行一次由本會於開會時期兩星期前分函通知各會員並登報通告

第十四條　於必要時經會員二十人以上提議或常任評議員過半數之決議得以專函通知召集臨時總會

第十五條　常任評議員會每月至少舉行一次

第十六條　無論定期總會或臨時總會有會員二分之一到會即可開會

第十七條　凡本會議決事件以多數取決之可否同數取決於主席

第十八條　本會職員如有違反本會則者經臨時會之議決得停止或免除其職務

第十九條　本會開總會時須先期報請所在地地方法院首席檢察官親自或派員屆時蒞會

第六章　職務

第二十條　本會律師職務如左

一　為當事人撰具詞狀及搜集證據提呈法院

二　為當事人依法到庭為言詞辯論及其他訴訟行為

三　依法向兩造當事人及證人發問或提出事實請審判長代為發問

第二十一條　本會律師行為

一　代理法律行為

二　證明契約及其他法律文件

三　代訂契約及其他法律文件

四　辦理仲裁及和解事件

第七章　權利義務

第二十二條　本會律師在各級法院得請求抄閱關於承辦案件一切文卷但以經法院許可者為限

第二十三條　本會律師得通知監獄或看守所接見時間內接見並詢問承辦案內之囚人或被羈押人

第二十四條　本會律師有收受公費之權

第二十五條　本會律師除遵守本會律師章程第十三條至第二十三條之規定外宜遵守本會會則

第二十六條　本會律師受委託其書狀或言詞辯論理由書除留稿存查外須備同式繕本兩份以一份送致法院以一份送致當事人

第二十七條　為各種契約之證明或代訂時須備具同樣之書式三份送致雙方之當事人並存一份備查

第二十八條　前二條之書件須鈐律師本人印章並於騎縫上鈐章為註塗

訴訟物價額在五萬元以上者得以訴訟物價額每審不得超過百分之一

二辦理刑事案件第一審公費總額每審至多不得逾六百元第二審第三審收取公費總額至多不得逾三百元但案情重大或因委任人有特別身分地位者其公費得增加之惟每審公費總額仍以不超過一千元為限

第二辦理民刑訴訟外一切法律行為及行政訴訟其公費得比照乙種一款辦理

第九章　風紀

第三十五條　律師辦理案件須聽當事人自由委任不得唆訟攙越或有阻止當事人和息情事

第三十六條　律師辦理各級法院指定辯護之案件得不收公費

第三十七條　律師不得指示原被告捏造或湮沒證據

第三十八條　無論原被告之律師既受一方委任即不得再受他方之囑託致有不實不盡之情弊

第三十九條　收受公費照本會會則不得濫行收納

第四十條　出庭辯論不得稍存偏頗或涉及無關本案別情

第四十一條　律師並其延聘人和書記均不得沾染嗜好

第四十二條　律師到庭恭將事不得輕慢誚謔

第四十三條　律師辯論時須起立陳述

第四十四條　律師出庭辯論如相對人對於律師有侮辱及不正當之行為得即時聲請庭長依照法院編制法第六十一條辦理

第十章　懲戒

第四十五條　凡本會會員有違反律師章程及本會會則之行為者遵照律師章程第三十五條辦理

第十一章　報告

第四十六條　本會選舉職員之詳情及開會時期處所並議決事項遵照律師章程第三十一條辦理

第十二章　附則

第四十七條　本會則自呈奉　司法行政部核准之日實行

第四十八條　本會則如有未盡事宜得於開總會時修改之仍遵照律師章程第二十九條辦理

天津律师公会会则

Rules of Tianjin Bar Association

天津律師公會會則

第一章 總綱

第一條　本會遵照律師章程組成之定名曰天津律師公會

第二條　本會會員依律師章程第一條第一項及第九條至第十一條之規定得在各級法院及特別審判機關執行職務

第三條　本會會址設在天津河北

第二章 資格

第四條　凡具有律師章程第二條或第三條資格領有律師證書並經呈准登錄者均得爲本會會員

第三章 入會及退會

第五條　凡入會會員須納入會費四十元每月納經常費一元其不納經常費三月以上者視爲退會受前項退會處置後更行入會者祇須補足前欠母庸再納入會費

第六條　凡入會會員由本會發給入會証書登記於會員名簿並呈報各級法院

第七條　有左列行爲之一者經本會總會或常任評議員會之議決令其退會

一　任有俸給之公職者
二　因懲戒受停職或除名之處分者
三　自願撤銷律師登錄者
四　法律上規定不許爲律師者
五　有精神喪失之常況由本會常任評議員會決議提交該管法院首席檢察官經鑑定屬實者
六　有妨害律師風紀之行爲而受本條第二欵之處分者

本會會員退會須呈報各級法院備案並公告之

第四章 職員

第八條　本會職員如左

一　會長一人總理會中一切事務
二　副會長二人佐理會中一切事務
三　常任評議員九人議決會中一切進行事務
四　幹事四人執行議決事件⋯⋯

第二十九條　無論何種事件受託後遇有應守秘密者須嚴守之

第三十條　本會律師受當事人委託後對於該案件所有事實上資料應先詳細詢問並應切實研究案件所適用之法律

第三十一條　本會得請求法院指定律師但非有正當事由不得聲請變更

第三十二條　本會得請求法院指定律師休息至並爲必要之設備

第三十三條　本會事宜會員均有維持之責

第八章 公費

第三十四條　律師受當事人之委託辦理訴訟事件或非訟事件其收取公費法如左

甲　分訟公費辦法

第一　訴訟事件分左列二種辦法由當事人自擇以契約定之

一　討論案情每小時至多不得逾五元
二　閱卷或接見在留人每次至多不得逾十元
三　簡錄文箱或造具清冊每百字至多不得逾一角
四　撰兩造件每件至多不得逾十元
五　撰聲請書每件至多不得逾五元
六　撰和解狀每件至多不得逾二十元
七　民事出庭費每次至多不得逾八十元
八　刑事出庭費每次至多不得逾四十元
九　出具專供委任人參考之意見書及其他文件每件至多不得逾四十元

十　撰民事訴狀第二審上訴狀抗告狀辯訴反訴狀每件至多不得逾六十元

十一　撰刑事訴狀第二審上訴狀抗告狀辯訴狀每件至多不得逾四十元

十二　撰民事訴狀第三審上訴狀辯訴狀每件至多不得逾一百元

十三　撰刑事訴狀第三審上訴狀辯訴狀每件至多不得逾六十元

十四　撰第一審或第二審民事案件追加理由書每件至多不得逾六十元

十五　撰第一審或第二審刑事案件辯護意旨書每件至多不得逾四十元

十六　撰第三審民事案件追加理由書每件至多不得逾一百元

十七　撰第三審刑事案件辯護意旨書每件至多不得逾六十元

十八　辦理民事執行案件或處理和息事項每件至多不得逾三百元

十九　在津埠境內履勘調查公費每日至多不得逾六十元

二十　赴津埠境外辦理一二七八十九各欵事項者除依各該欵收取公費外每日所收日費至多不得逾五十元

Regulation of Lawyers, the bar association shall supervise the fees paid by practicing lawyers. The specific method is to set the highest standards for lawyers' fees and supervise the actual situation of fees.

《天津律师公会会则》就对收取公费的上限作了详细的规定。首先将公费分为分收和总收两种形式，然后罗列出具体要求。比如"讨论案情，每小时至多不得逾五元""阅卷或接见在留人，每次至多不得逾十元""撰函件，每件至多不得逾十元""撰声请书，每件至多不得逾五元""撰和解状，每件至多不得逾二十元""民事出庭费，每次至多不得逾八十元""刑事出庭费，每次至多不得逾四十元"，是为分收。总收则如"办理民事案件，第一、第二两审收取公费总额，每审至多不得逾一千元，第三审收取公费总额，至多不得逾六百元，但诉讼物价额在五万元以上者，得以诉讼物价额为准。其每审公费总额，第一、第二两审均不得超过诉讼物价额百分之二，第三审不得超过百分之一"。

The *Rules of Tianjin Bar Association* provides detailed regulations on the upper limit of collecting public expense. Firstly, the public expense is divided into two forms: divided income and total income, and then the specific requirements are listed. For example, "To discuss the case, it should not exceed five yuan per hour." "Reading or interviewing people should not exceed ten yuan at a time." "Writing letters should not exceed ten yuan at most." "Writing a petition, each piece should not exceed five yuan at most." "Writing a reconciliation, each piece should not exceed twenty yuan at most." "Civil court fees should not exceed eighty yuan at most." "Criminal court fees should not exceed forty yuan at most." The above are the restrictions on single charges, and the restrictions on overall charges are as follows, "In handling civil cases, the first and second trials charge a total of public expense, which shall not exceed 1,000 yuan per trial, and the third trial charge a total of public expense, which shall not exceed 600 yuan at most. However, if the litigation price is more than 50,000 yuan, the litigation price shall prevail. The total amount of public expense per trial shall not exceed 2% of the litigation price in the first and second trials, and shall not exceed 1% in the third trial."

1934	1935	1936	1937	1938	1939	1940	1941	1942	1943	1944	1945	1946
1960	1961	1962	1963	1964	1965	1966	1967	1968	1969	1970	1971	1972
1986	1987	1988	1989	1990	1991	1992	1993	1994	1995	1996	1997	1998
2012	2013	2014	2015	2016	2017	2018	2019	2020	2021	……		

律师公费的标准因不同地区的经济状况和消费水平而有所区别，不过所有的公费都被严格限定在一个区域之内，律师公会反对超出所定标准的私自馈赠，违者将会遭到处罚。如果要改变律师收费标准，就必须由律师公会呈请当地法院转呈中央司法部门批准。

The standard of lawyers' public expense varied with the economic situation and consumption level in different regions, but all public expense were strictly limited in one region. The bar association opposed giving gifts without permission beyond the set standard, and offenders would be punished. If you want to change the lawyers' fees standard, you must apply to the local court by the bar association and submit it to the central judicial department for approval.

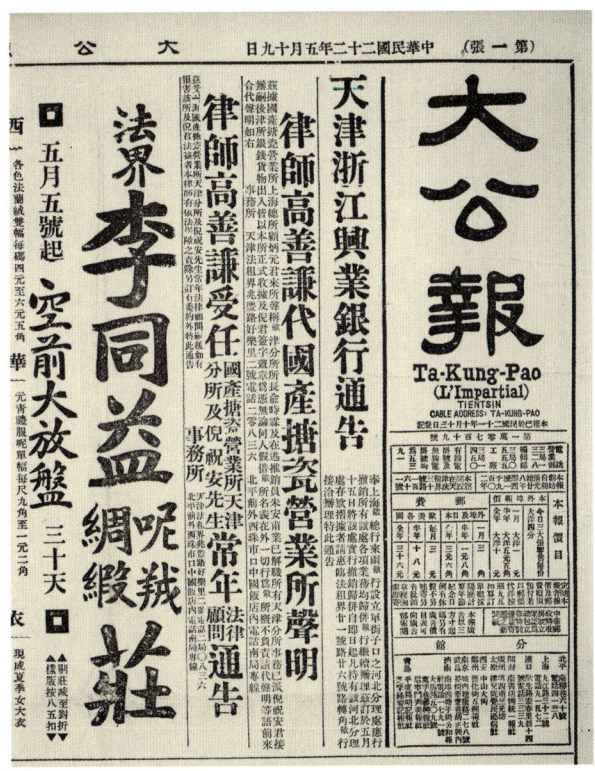

《大公报》刊登高善谦律师担任企业法律顾问的通告
Ta-Kung-Pao published a notice on lawyer Gao Shanqian serving as corporate legal counsel

（四）监管律师从业品德的权力
(d) The Power to Supervise the Professional Ethics of Lawyers

《律师暂行章程》第二十八条规定，律师公会应制定会则，以"维持律师德义"。所谓"律师德义"，就是律师的从业品德。在诉讼活动中，律师的行为不仅对当事人的利益得失发挥着举足轻重的作用，而且会从整体上影响司法体制的运行，影响民众对法律体系的评价，因此仅用是否违法来评价律师是远远不够的，还需要鼓舞律师在一定程度上承担起维护正义、保护民众合法权益的责任，也就是要求律师在执业过程中保持较高的道德水准和职业操守。正是出于这样的考虑，《律师暂行章程》等法律法规赋予了律师公会加强监管律师从业品德的权力。

Article 28 of the *Provisional Regulation of Lawyers* stipulates that the bar association shall formulate rules to "maintain the morality of lawyers". The so-called "lawyer's morality and justice" is the lawyer's professional morality. In litigation activities, lawyers' behavior not only plays a decisive role in the interests of the parties, but also affects the operation of the judicial system as a whole and people's evaluation of the legal system. Therefore, it is far from enough to judge lawyers only by whether they are illegal or not. It is also necessary to encourage lawyers to assume the responsibility of safeguarding justice and protecting the legitimate rights and interests of the people to a certain extent, that is, lawyers are required to maintain high moral standards and professional ethics in the process of practicing. It is out of this consideration that the bar association has been given the power to strengthen the supervision of lawyers' professional ethics by the *Provisional Regulation of Lawyers* and other laws and regulations.

（五）提请惩戒的权力
(e) The Power to Apply for Disciplinary Action

律师的风纪是律师公会非常重视的一项内容，它代表着律师职业道德与执业纪律最基本的要求。《天津律师公会会则》中专设"风纪"一章，规定："第三十六条，律师办理案件须听

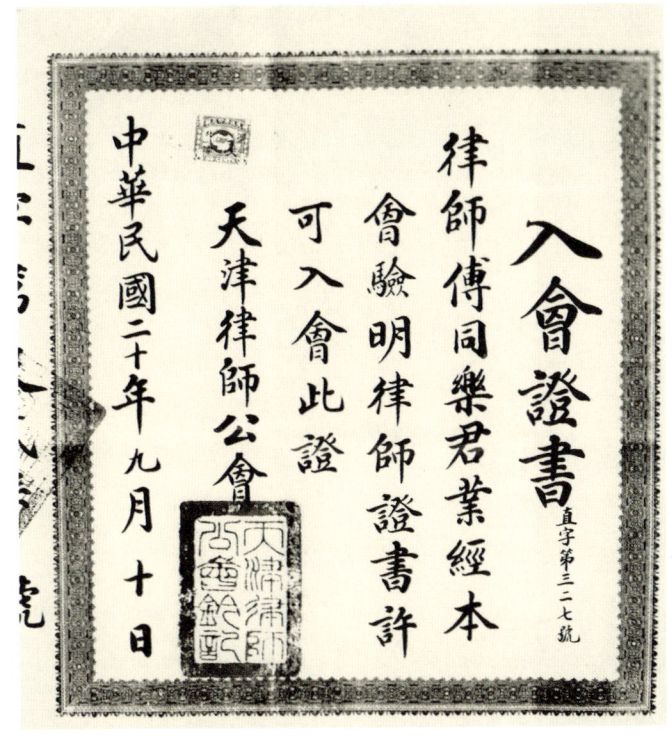

傅同乐律师天津律师公会入会证书
Membership certificate of lawyer Fu Tongle Tianjin Bar Association

天津律师公会钤记
Seal of Tianjin Bar Association

当事人自由委任，不得唆讼挽越或有阻止当事人和息情事。第三十七条，律师不得指示原被告捏造或湮没证据。第三十八条，无论原被告之律师，既受一方委任，即不得再受他方之嘱托，致有不实不尽之情弊。第三十九条，收受公费，须照本会会则，不得滥行收纳。第四十条，出庭辩论，不得稍存偏颇，或涉及无关本案别情。第四十一条，律师并其延聘人及书记均不得沾染嗜好。第四十二条，律师到庭，恪恭将事，不得轻慢诙谐。第四十三条，律师辩论时须起立陈述。第四十四条，律师出庭辩论，如相对人对于律师有侮辱及不正当之行为，得即时声请庭长依照《法院编制法》第六十一条办理。"

Lawyers' discipline is a content that the bar association attached great importance to, and it represented the most basic requirements of lawyers' professional ethics and practice discipline. There was a special chapter on "discipline" in the *Rules of Tianjin Bar Association*, which stipulated, "Article 36, when handling cases, lawyers must listen to the free appointment of the parties, and may not interfere with litigation or prevent the parties from paying interest. Article 37, a lawyer shall not instruct the original defendant to fabricate or annihilate evidence. Article 38, no matter whether the lawyer of the original defendant is appointed by one party, he shall not be entrusted by the other party, which will lead to endless disadvantages. Article 39, to receive public expense, we must follow the rules of this association, and we must not accept them indiscriminately. Article 40, a debate in court shall not be slightly biased or involve other circumstances irrelevant to the case. Article 41, lawyers, their appointees and secretaries shall not be contaminated with bad habits. Article 42, when a lawyer appears in court, he shall be modest and polite, and shall not be rude. Article 43, a lawyer must stand up and make a statement when debating. Article 44, if a lawyer appears in court to debate, if the opposite party insults or misbehaves against the lawyer, he may immediately request the president to handle the matter in accordance with Article 61 of the *Court Preparation Law.* "

对于严重有违风纪，特别是违反《律师暂定章程》《律师章程》以及各公会会则的律师，律师公会有权提请惩戒。1913年12月19日，为了依法实行对律师的惩戒，北洋政府制定了《律师惩戒会暂行规则》，并于1916年10月27日作了修订，随后便成立了律师惩戒会组织，制定了惩戒办法和程序。律师惩戒会由高等审判厅厅长（担任会长）和三名推事组成；另有复审查律师惩戒会，由大理院院长及四名推事组成。

The bar association has the right to apply for disciplinary action against lawyers who seriously violate discipline, especially the *Provisional Regulation of Lawyers*, the *Regulation of Lawyers* and the rules of the associations. On December 19, 1913, in order to punish lawyers according to law, Beiyang Government formulated the *Lawyers' Disciplinary Committee Provisional Rules*, which was revised on October 27, 1916, and then established the organization of lawyers' disciplinary committee, and formulated disciplinary measures and procedures. The lawyers' disciplinary committee is composed of the director of the high adjudicative office (as the president) and three judges; there is also a disciplinary committee for reexamination lawyers, which is composed of the president of Daliyuan and four judges.

遇有违反相关法律法规的律师，律师公会会长可依常任评议员会或会员大会的决议向地方检察长申请惩戒。该地方检察长依职权呈请高等检察长，再由高等检察长向高等审判厅（后为高等法院）提请惩戒，随后由高等审判厅厅长（后为高等法院院长）等人组成的律师惩戒会依法定程序给予相关律师惩戒。如果对惩戒不服，可在20日内向司法总长声明；有理由者，由司法总长交给复审查律师惩戒会复审，复审结果报告司法总长确定，惩戒结果由政府公报公布。

In case of a lawyer who violates relevant laws and regulations, the president of the bar association may apply to the local Minister of Justice for disciplinary action according to the resolution of the permanent council or the Member's General Assembly. The local procurator-general petitioned the high procurator-general ex officio, and then the high procurator-general submitted to the high adjudicative office (later the high court) for disciplinary action. Then the lawyers' disciplinary committee composed of the director of the high adjudicative office (later the president of the high court) gave disciplinary action to the relevant lawyers according to the prescribed procedures. If you are dissatisfied with the punishment, you can declare it to the Minister of Justice within 20 days; if there is any reason, it shall be submitted by the Minister of Justice to the re-examination lawyers' disciplinary committee for review, and the review results shall be reported to the Minister of Justice for confirmation, and the disciplinary results shall be published in the official gazette.

如果司法机关发现律师违法，可直接向律师惩戒机关提请惩戒，不过这往往属于受刑事处罚的律师，更多的违反律师公会会则的惩戒则是由律师公会提请的。律师公会对律师的监管主要体现在律师是否违背了律师公会会则，特别是在德义与风纪两方面。对于严重违背律师风纪的情况，律师公会可以根据公会会则对该律师作出退会处分。20世纪30年代天津律师公会李景光退会案便是非常著名的例证。当时天津律师公会新一届领导机构积极整顿会务、整肃风纪，从中发现会员李景光存在登报招揽，发行彩票，承诺低价、包赢官司等严重违反律师广告规定的行为，于是勒令其退会。后经长达五年的纷争，也包括李景光起诉律师公会，到1938年4月4日，天津律师公会会长李洪岳以天津律师公会公文形式呈报伪天津地方法院检察处，称："本会于民国二十年（1931）十月依据当时有效会则议决，令其退会，呈报钧处之后，以其行为涉及刑事，交付侦查。"李景光退会案也成了民国时期查处时间最长、惩戒最为严厉的案例。

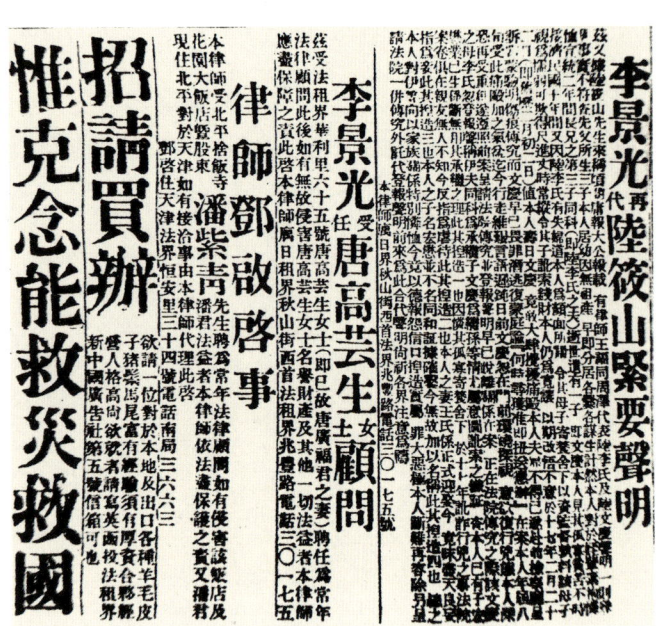

李景光、邓启律师的登报声明与启事
Newspaper statements and announcements made by lawyers Li Jingguang and Deng Qi

李景光律师
Lawyer Li Jingguang

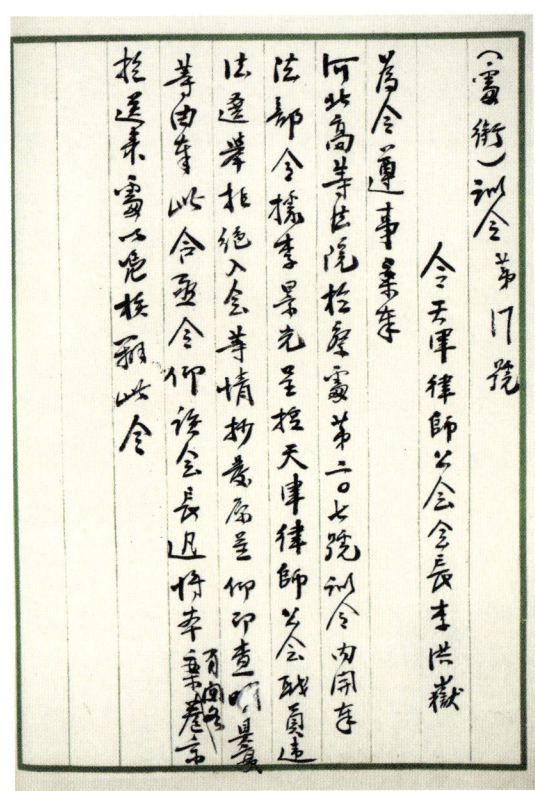

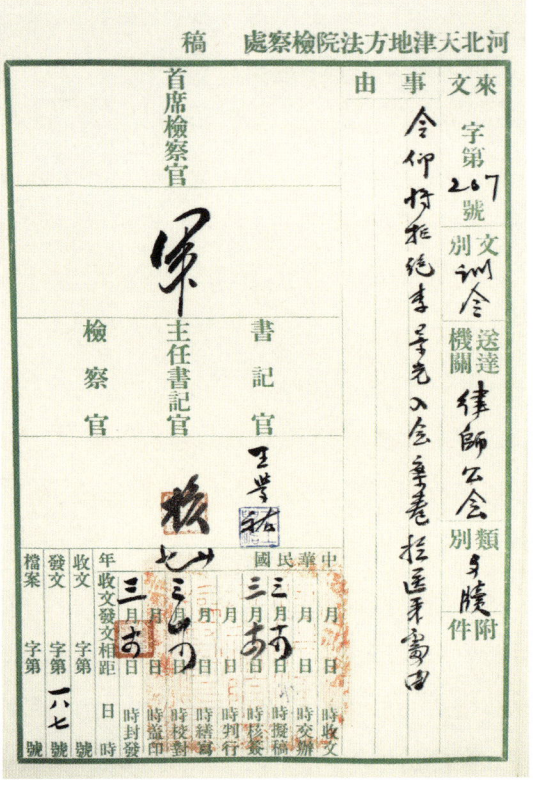

李景光退会案训令
Instructions on Li Jingguang's withdrawal case

If the judiciary finds that a lawyer violates the law, it can directly apply to the lawyer disciplinary authority for disciplinary action, but this is often a lawyer who is subject to criminal punishment, and more disciplinary actions that violate the rules of the bar association are submitted by the bar association. The supervision of lawyers by the bar association is mainly reflected in whether lawyers violate the rules of the bar association, especially in the aspects of morality and discipline. In case of serious violation of lawyers' discipline, the bar association may, according to the rules of the bar association, take disciplinary action against the lawyers. The case of Li Jingguang's withdrawal from Tianjin Bar Association in 1930s is a famous example. At that time, the new leading organization of Tianjin Bar Association actively rectified the conference and discipline, and found that Li Jingguang, a member of Tianjin Bar Association, had serious violations of lawyers' advertising regulations, such as soliciting newspapers, issuing lottery tickets, promising low prices and winning lawsuits, so he was ordered to withdraw from the conference. After five years of disputes, including Li Jingguang suing the Bar Association, on April 4, 1938, Li Hongyue, president of the Tianjin Bar Association, reported to the procuratorate of the puppet Tianjin District Court in the form of the official document of the Tianjin Bar Association, saying, "It was decided in October 1931 according to the then effective meeting, and he was ordered to withdraw from the meeting. After reporting to the office, he involved criminal acts and sent him to the investigation." The case of Li Jingguang's withdrawal from the Tianjin Bar Association also became the case with the longest investigation and the most severe punishment in the Republic of China.

四、律师公会的职能与社会价值
4. Function and Social Value of the Bar Association

对律师的监督、管理是律师公会最基本的职能。除此以外，律师公会还在加强与司法机关沟通、维护律师权益等法制建设以及保障广大贫苦民众的合法权益、国家赔偿制度的建立、收回法权等与国家、社会紧密相关的法律问题上发挥着积极的作用和应有的价值。

The supervision and management of lawyers is the most basic function of the bar association. In addition, the bar association also plays an active role and due value in strengthening communication with judicial organs, safeguarding lawyers' rights and interests and other legal issues closely related to the state and society, such as safeguarding the legitimate rights and interests of the poor people, establishing the state compensation system, and recovering legal rights.

（一）与司法机关沟通，保障律师进行法律服务的权利

(a) To Communicate with the Judicial Organs to Protect the Right of Lawyers to Provide Legal Services

进行法律服务是律师的基本特征之一，而这一过程必然会与司法机关产生联系，因此律师能否与司法机关进行有效沟通，就成了律师工作成败的重要一环，而律师公会为保障律师的基本权利，发挥着重要的作用。一方面，国家通过立法确保律师公会与司法机关沟通的顺畅。《律师暂行章程》第三十条规定，律师公会可就司法总长或审判衙门所咨询之事项作出决议，也可就与律师公会利害相关的问题，向司法总长或审判衙门提出建议。另一方面，律师公会会则保障了律师在司法机关办案的相关权利。如《天津律师公会会则》中规定："第二十二条，本会律师在各级法院得请求抄阅关于承办案件一切文卷，但以经法院许可者为限。第二十三条，本会律师得通知监狱或看守所于接见时间内接见并询问承办案内之囚人或被羁押人。第三十二条，本会得请求法院指定律师休息室并为必要之设备。"

Providing legal services is one of the basic characteristics of lawyers, and this process is bound to have contact with judicial organs. Therefore, whether lawyers can communicate effectively with judicial organs becomes an important part of the success or failure of lawyers' work, and the bar association plays an important role in safeguarding lawyers' basic rights. On the one hand, the state has ensured the smooth communication between the bar association and the judiciary through legislation. Article 30 of the *Provisional Regulation of Lawyers* stipulates that the bar association may make resolutions on matters consulted by the Minister of Justice or the adjudicative office, and may also make suggestions to the Minister of Justice or the adjudicative office on issues related to judicial affairs and the interests of the bar association. On the other hand, the rules of the bar association guarantees lawyers' right to handle cases in judicial organs. For example, the *Rules of Tianjin Bar Association* stipulates, "Article 22, lawyers of this association may request to copy and read all documents about undertaking cases in courts at all levels, but only those permitted by the courts. Article 23, lawyers of the association may notify prisons or detention centers to meet and inquire prisoners or detainees in charge of the case during the interview time. Article 32, the association may request the court to designate a lawyer's lounge and provide it with necessary equipment. "

（二）扶弱济贫及冤狱赔偿运动

(b) Helping the Weak and Helping the Poor and Compensation for Unjust Cases Movement

对于没有聘请律师的刑事案件被告，法院应为其指定义务的辩护律师，同时被指定律师不得拒绝。然而，由于这是无偿的法律辩护，因此有些律师会以种种借口不到庭，或者到庭也不尽力。针对这种情形，律师公会会采取一定的措施，如1928年2月28日，上海律师公会第十八次改组委员会讨论临时法院来函告知指定义务律师往往不到庭，致使重要案件审理颇感困难，拟请由上海律师公会派员轮值，并由法院酌给津贴的问题。

For a defendant in a criminal case who has not hired a lawyer, the court shall appoint an obligatory defense lawyer, and the appointed lawyer shall not refuse. However, because this is a free legal defense, some lawyers will not appear in court under various excuses, or they will not try their best to appear in court. In view of this situation, the bar association will take certain measures. For example, on February 28, 1928, the 18th Reorganization Committee of Shanghai Bar Association discussed the problem that the appointed volunteer lawyers were often absent from the court in a letter from the Provisional Court, which made it difficult to hear important cases. It is proposed that the Shanghai Bar Association should send its staff to rotate on duty and the court should give allowances.

相比于刑事辩护，非刑事案件中更没有保障措施来解决因为贫穷而请不起律师的问题，大多数贫民往往因此而败诉，其合法权益得不到保护，律师保障人权的使命也成了一句空话。有鉴于此，天津律师公会于1935年3月31日正式成立了贫民法律扶助会，"对贫苦民众无偿予以法律上之援助，对于慈善事业，亦屡屡捐助"，帮助处于弱势地位的民众，积极从事社会慈善救助，以实现司法正义的追求。与此同时，全国各地律师公会也相继成立了平民法律扶助会，以改变律师为有钱人服务的形象。

Compared with criminal defense, in non-criminal cases, there are no safeguards to solve the problem that lawyers cannot be hired because of poverty. Most poor people often lose the case, and their legitimate rights and interests are not protected. The mission of lawyers to protect human rights has become empty talk. In view of this, the Tianjin Bar Association formally established the Legal Aid Society for the Poor on March 31, 1935, "providing free legal assistance to the poor people and making repeated donations to charitable causes", helping the people in a weak position and actively engaging in social charity assistance in order to realize the pursuit of judicial justice. At the same time, bar associations all over the country had successively set up civilian legal aid associations to change the image of lawyers serving the rich.

扶弱济贫是律师公会深得人心的重要法律实践，而在民国时期，最具代表性的律师保障人权的案例，便是由各地律师公会共同推动的冤狱赔偿运动。所谓"冤狱赔偿"，是指人民在遭受国家司法机关违法判决、误判或无辜羁押后，除该司法机关应受法律制裁外，国家也应对遭受冤狱的人民进行赔偿的行为。冤狱赔偿运动是20世纪30年代中国律师界同仁为推动国家立法机关制定冤狱赔偿法、实行冤狱赔偿制度而发动法律界及各机关团体向政府请愿的全国性群众运动。此次运动由中华民国律师协会倡导，各地律师公会具体执行，并最终迫使南京国民政府开始了实行国家赔偿制度的准备，只因1937年7月日本全面侵华战争的爆发而终止。

Helping the weak and helping the poor is an important legal practice won by bar associations. In the Republic of China, the most representative case of lawyers' protection of human rights was the Compensation for Unjust Cases Movement jointly promoted by lawyers' associations from all over the world. The so-called "Compensation

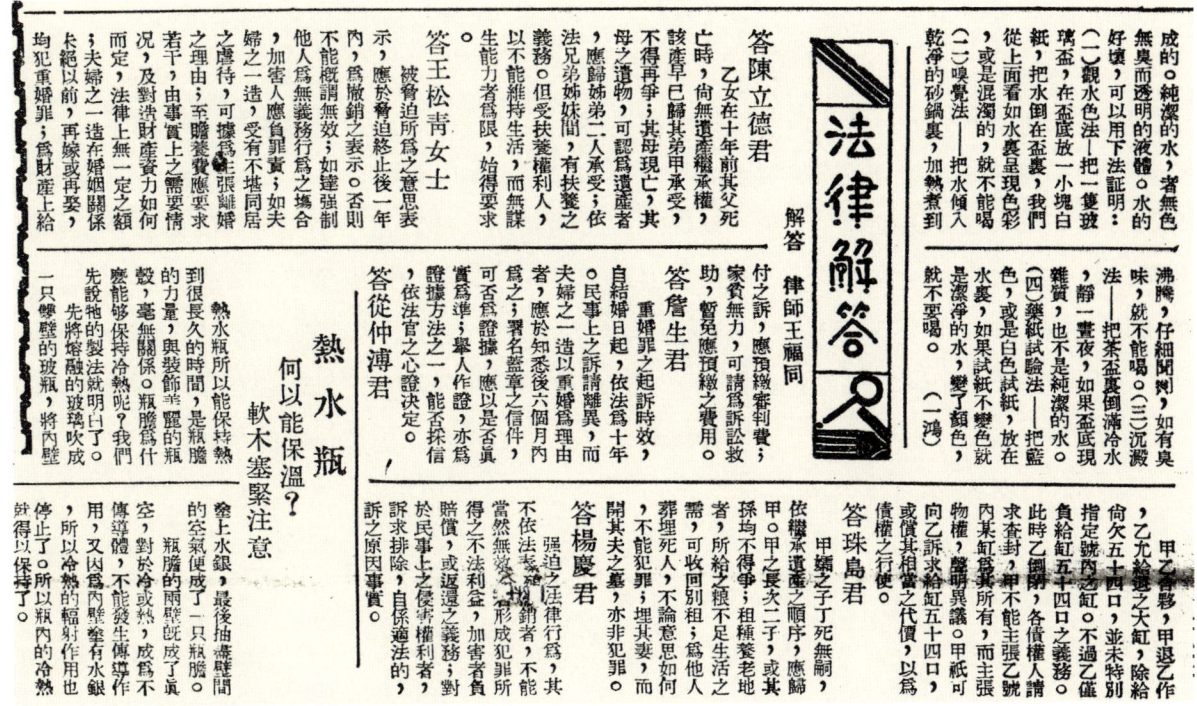

"Legal Answers" column opened by lawyer Wang Futong

for Unjust Cases" refers to the behavior that the state should compensate the people who suffered unjust imprisonment after the people suffered illegal judgment, misjudgment or innocent detention by the state judicial organ, except that the judicial organ should be subject to legal sanctions. The Compensation for Unjust Cases Movement was a national mass movement launched by the legal profession and government organizations to petition the government in order to promote the national legislature to formulate the Compensation for Unjust Cases law and implement the Compensation for Unjust Cases system in 1930s. The movement was initiated by the Lawyers Association of the Republic of China and implemented by local bar associations, which finally forced Nanjing National Government to start the preparation for the implementation of the state compensation system, but ended only with the outbreak of

1921	1922	1923	1924	1925	1926	1927	1928	1929	1930	1931	1932	193
1947	1948	1949	1950	1951	1952	1953	1954	1955	1956	1957	1958	195
1973	1974	1975	1976	1977	1978	1979	1980	1981	1982	1983	1984	198
1999	2000	2001	2002	2003	2004	2005	2006	2007	2008	2009	2010	201

Japan's full-scale war of aggression against China in July 1937.

由于没有国家赔偿制度，因此民国的司法部门或"操行不检，嗜货渎职"，或"学识浅陋，轻率定谳"，或"无辜蒙罪，号泣周闻"，致使冤狱累累。"堂上一笔朱，阶下千滴血"的现实令人民的生命财产安全毫无保障。正因如此，1931年中华民国律师协会在杭州召开第三届代表大会，一致通过了《建议政府对于过误裁判实行国家负赔偿责任之制度案》，可惜未被政府采纳。1933年6月中华民国律师协会第五次代表大会在青岛召开，上海、杭州、苏州的律师公会联署向大会提交了《本会应建议立法院制订冤狱赔偿法案》，依然难逃被政府搁置的命运。不过，这也促使各律师公会下决心发动全国性民间社会运动，以推动政府实施冤狱赔偿制度。

Because there was no state compensation system, the judicial departments of the Republic of China were either "misbehaving, addicted to goods and dereliction of duty", "ignorant, rashly offering", or "innocent people were convicted, and the masses couldn't help crying when they heard it", resulting in numerous unjust sentences. The reality of "a hasty judgment caused a serious cost to people's lives" endangers the safety of people's lives and property. For this reason, the Third Congress of the Lawyers Association of the Republic of China was held in Hangzhou in 1931, and unanimously passed the *Proposal for the Government to Implement the System of State Responsibility for Compensation for Unjust Cases*, but unfortunately it was not adopted by the Government. In June 1933, the Fifth Congress of the Lawyers Association of the Republic of China was held in Qingdao, and the bar associations of Shanghai, Hangzhou and Suzhou jointly submitted to the congress *This Council should Recommend the Legislature to Formulate a Bill on Compensation for Unjust Cases*, which was still doomed to be shelved by the government. However, this also prompted the bar associations to make up their minds to launch a nationwide civil society movement to promote the government to implement the Compensation for Unjust Cases system.

在1934年9月召开的律师协会第六届代表大会上，上海、天津、汉口、九江、广州的律师公会代表组成了冤狱赔偿运动委员会，开始领导全国的冤狱赔偿运动。同年11月12日，律师协会六届一次执行委员会会议推举江庸、李洪岳、沈钧儒、李时蕊等41人为委员会委员,负责推进冤狱赔偿运动。1935年5月5日,冤狱赔偿运动委员会在苏州召开全体会议,通过了《冤狱赔偿运动宣言》和《冤狱赔偿运动工作纲要》。此后,律师协会还制定了《律师公会冤狱赔偿运动工作大纲》,详细规划了冤狱赔偿运动的内容。

At the Sixth Congress of the Lawyers Association held in September 1934, representatives of the bar associations in Shanghai, Tianjin, Hankou, Jiujiang and Guangzhou formed the Committee for Compensation for Unjust Cases Movement, and began to lead the nationwide Compensation for Unjust Cases Movement. On November 12, the same year, the first session of the Sixth Executive Committee of the Lawyers Association elected 41 members, including Jiang Yong, Li Hongyue, Shen Junru and Li Shirui, to be responsible for promoting the Compensation for Unjust Cases Movement. On May 5, 1935, the Committee for Compensation for Unjust Cases Movement held a plenary meeting in Suzhou, and adopted the *Declaration of Compensation for Unjust Cases Movement* and the *Work Outline of Compensation for Unjust Cases Movement*. Since then, the Lawyers Association has also formulated the *Work Outline of the Bar*

李洪岳继任天津律师公会会长的报道

Report on Li Hongyue's succession as chairman of Tianjin Bar Association

Association's Compensation for Unjust Cases Movement, and has planned the contents of the Compensation for Unjust Cases Movement in detail.

1935年6月5日，中华民国律师协会经过长期充分的准备，终于迎来了第一个冤狱赔偿运动宣传周。这一天，全国各地律师公会依照律师协会的决议与安排，在各地发起了冤狱赔偿运动。该运动得到了各地报纸、广播电台的配合与支持，获得了社会舆论的同情，一时间成为举国关注的事件，实现了运动引起政府注意的预期。

On June 5, 1935, the Lawyers Association of the Republic of China finally ushered in the first publicity week of the Compensation for Unjust Cases Movement. On this day, according to the resolution and arrangement of the bar association, the bar associations all over the country launched the Compensation for Unjust Cases Movement. The Movement received the cooperation and support of local newspapers and radio stations, and won the sympathy of public opinion. It became an event of national concern for a time and realized the expectation that the Movement would attract the attention of the government.

到1936年6月，冤狱赔偿运动得到了全国各界的同情与认可，南京国民政府也不得不认真对待举国沸腾的热情。1937年年初，国民政府立法院指派刑法委员会的赵琛、林彬、罗鼎起草冤狱赔偿法。6月2日，刑法委员会开会审查，将草案定名为《无罪被押受刑补偿法》，开启了民国时期国家赔偿制度建设的序幕。不过，随着七七事变的爆发，全面抗战开始，冤狱赔偿法不得不束之高阁，冤狱赔偿运动也就此中断。

By June 1936, the Compensation for Unjust Cases Movement had won sympathy and recognition from all walks of life across the country, and Nanjing National Government had to take seriously the enthusiasm of the whole country. At the beginning of 1937, the Legislature of the National Government appointed Zhao Chen, Lin Bin and Luo Ding of the Criminal Law Committee to draft a law on Compensation for Unjust Cases. On June 2, the Criminal Law Committee held a meeting to review and named the draft *Law on Compensation for Imprisonment and Punishment*, which opened the prelude to the construction of the state compensation system in the

Republic of China. However, with the outbreak of the July 7 Incident of 1937 and the beginning of the All-out Anti-Japanese War of resistance, the Compensation for Unjust Cases law had to be shelved and the Compensation for Unjust Cases Movement was interrupted.

（三）收回法权宣传运动
(c) The Publicity Campaign to Recover Legal Rights

随着民国初年律师制度的确立与发展，到1919年年初巴黎和会召开时，律师及律师公会已能深刻影响民众的热情，中国人民强烈呼吁废除包含领事裁判权在内的众多不平等条约。1920年11月6日，北洋政府公布了《法权讨论委员会条例》，为收回包括领事裁判权在内的法权作好了准备。

With the establishment and development of the lawyer system in the early years of the Republic of China, by the time of the Paris Peace Conference in early 1919, lawyers and bar associations had been able to profoundly influence the enthusiasm of the people, and the Chinese people strongly called for the abolition of many unequal treaties including consular jurisdiction. On November 6, 1920, the Beiyang Government promulgated the *Regulations of the Legal Rights Discussion Committee*, which made preparations for the recovery of legal rights including consular jurisdiction.

1928年年底，南京国民政府完成了与列强的关税自主谈判，基本上实现了关税自主。第二年4月27日，南京国民政府外交部照会英、美、法、荷等国家，提出交涉法权，不过列强以种种借口不愿立即放弃领事裁判权。为配合外交部，司法院于1929年9月17日成立了由20人组成的法权筹备委员会，国民党中央执行委员会宣传部还编印了《撤废领事裁判权运动》一书，对国民进行宣传，推动收回法权的进程。

At the end of 1928, Nanjing National Government completed the tariff autonomy negotiations with the big powers, and basically realized the tariff autonomy. On April 27, the following year, the Ministry of Foreign Affairs of Nanjing National

天津律师公会关于《无领事裁判权国律师出庭暂行章程》的快邮代电
Tianjin Bar Association's *Provisional Regulation of Lawyers in Countries without Consular Jurisdiction* by express mail

快郵代電

各省督軍省長省議會商會教育會報館律師公會公鑒民國九年十二月二十八日政府公報載司法部第一一八六號部令公布無領事裁判權國律師出庭暫行章程在案竊查此項章程於國民公權及我國國情並法律咸有妨害用敢瀝陳利害關係懇請一致力爭以保人民公權而重法律事第一查律師之資格原爲本國人民公權之一種故多數國之立法例皆以本國人民爲限外國人民不得享有此種特權蓋以律師之職務係依訴訟當事人之委託或法院之命令在法院執行法定職務是公法上之職務則充當律師之權當然爲司法機關之輔助機關律師之職務既爲公法上之職務則充當律師之權當然爲司法機關之權利自不待言故此種權利外國人民不得享有是又一般之通例我國律師暫行章程第二條第一欵之規定律師資格爲中華民國人民年滿二十歲以上之男子依此規定是律師之資格惟限於中華民國人民外國人絕對不能承認者也現在文明諸國關於國人民之私權雖取內外人平等主義然查多數國之立法例仍言明除依法令有特別規定外外國人民得與內國人民享有同一之私權云云故普通之職業若即襲失菲中國人不能享有之權利於此更可證明中國人依法令享有之特權交易所之股員或點長等職業多不具特別法令之規定即不許外國人享有是上之公權又爲能無端犧牲中國人民之特殊之權利此非惟與現行法令顯相違背而無端犧牲中國人民之特殊之權利此非惟與現行法令顯相違背而裁判權原爲先進國與外國人民也故此項部令當然不能施行第二查領事裁判權原爲先進國與法制不完備之國家間所締結之一種特別條約以整頓我國自主獨立之法權惟擬提議於國際聯盟同各國要求撤廢領事裁判條約而已故自歐戰告終後全國人民皆提議即行撤廢我國與東西各國所締結之領事裁判條約大半附有界各國有此種條約著除半開化之土耳其外我中華一國而已故自歐戰告終不可故此項令凡爲中華民國人民絕對不能承認者也現在文明諸國關於人民之私權雖取內外人平等主義然查多數國之立法例仍言明除依法令有日今若對於無領事裁判權國之人民付與以司法上特別之權利則有領事裁侯中國法制完備即行撤廢之即爲對於有領事裁判權國之權利更無允許撤廢之日矣若對於無領事裁判權國付與以特殊之權利則必以權利與特殊之判權國之國家則必以權利與特殊之權利爲口實對於領事裁判權國更無允許撤廢權劃絞可領事裁判權之手段欲使有領事裁判權國有鑒於此易爲放棄其領

Government took note of Britain, America, France, Holland and other countries etc., and put forward the right to negotiate, but the powers refused to give up consular jurisdiction immediately under various excuses. In order to cooperate with the Ministry of Foreign Affairs, the judicial court set up a preparatory committee for legal rights consisting of 20 people on September 17, 1929. The Propaganda Department of the Central Executive Committee of the Kuomintang also published the book *Movement for Abolition of Consular Jurisdiction* to publicize the people and promote the process of recovering legal rights.

与此同时，各地律师公会也在全国律师协会的领导下，发起了全国性的收回法权宣传运动。1929年11月7日，上海律师公会代表、法权运动宣传部主任吴迈与宣传部秘书李逢初从上海出发，赶赴南昌、九江、安庆、芜湖、南京、镇江、扬州、杭州、宁波、青岛、大连、沈阳、天津、北平、武汉、长沙等城市，开展撤废领事裁判权、废除一切不平等条约的收回法权宣传运动。宣传团所到之处，民众热烈响应，誓作政府后盾，支持废除领事裁判权。

At the same time, under the leadership of the National Lawyers Association, local bar associations also launched a nationwide publicity campaign to recover legal rights. On November 7, 1929, Wu Mai, a representative of Shanghai Bar Association and director of the Propaganda Department of the Legal Rights Movement, and Li Fengchu, secretary of the Propaganda Department, set off from Shanghai and rushed to Nanchang, Jiujiang, Anqing, Wuhu, Nanjing, Zhenjiang, Yangzhou, Hangzhou, Ningbo, Qingdao, Dalian, Shenyang, Tianjin, Beiping, Wuhan, Changsha and other cities to carry out a publicity campaign to revoke consular jurisdiction and abolish all unequal treaties. Wherever the propaganda group went, the people responded enthusiastically and vowed to be the backing of the government to support the abolition of consular jurisdiction.

其间，吴迈、李逢初等人于1930年4月20日抵达天津。天津律师公会会长许肇铭前来迎接，并提出天津市民对于撤废领事裁判权之事颇感兴趣。第二天，在教育局局长的陪同下，宣传团赴南开大学演讲。南开学子深受鼓舞，拟组织撤废领事裁判权宣传委员会，利用课余时间，向群众进行宣传。事实上，天津律师公会历来就具有抵制法权沦丧的鲜明态度。早在1921年2月26

日司法总长董康批转天津总商会的训令中就有这样的记载："转据天津律师公会呈各节均悉查无领事裁判权国律师须经本部审查合格颁给律师证书。"这里充分展示了天津律师公会在收回法权运动中的努力。

Meanwhile, Wu Mai, Li Fengchu and others arrived in Tianjin on April 20, 1930. Xu Zhaoming, chairman of Tianjin Bar Association, greeted them and pointed out that Tianjin citizens were interested in abolishing consular jurisdiction. The next day, accompanied by the Director of Education Bureau, the propaganda group went to Nankai University to give a speech. Encouraged by this, Nankai students planed to organize a publicity committee to abolish consular jurisdiction and publicized it to the masses in their spare time. In fact, Tianjin Bar Association had always maintained a clear attitude of resisting the loss of legal rights. As early as February 26, 1921, there was such a record in the instructions of the Minister of Justice Dong Kang who approved the Tianjin General Chamber of Commerce, "According to the Tianjin Bar Association, it was found that lawyers in countries without consular jurisdiction must pass the examination of the Ministry and be awarded a lawyer certificate." This fully demonstrated the efforts of Tianjin Bar Association in the movement of recovering legal rights.

律师诉讼书状

LAWYERS' LITIGATION PLEADINGS

律师接受当事人委任,代理诉讼,会涉及一系列的诉讼书状,首当其冲的便是委任状。所谓委任状,是指民事诉讼中的当事人与受委任律师,刑事自诉案件中的自诉人与委任代理人,刑事公诉案件中的被告与委任辩护人,就诉讼代理而签署的授权书状。

When a lawyer accepts the appointment of a client to act as an agent, it will involve a series of pleadings, the first of which is the power of attorney. The so-called power of attorney refers to the power of attorney signed by the parties and appointed lawyers in civil litigation, private prosecutors and appointed agents in criminal private prosecution cases, defendants and appointed defenders in criminal public prosecution cases.

关于委任状,在民事案件中,委任人(即当事人)应将委任契约关于代理权限的委任状副本提交管辖法院,以表明身份并明确权限。在诉讼过程中,如果委任人要解除委任契约,除了必须通知受委任人(即律师)以外,还必须向管辖法院提出书面的解除委任状,并由法院通知对方当事人,否则解除行为不发生效力。如果是受委任人提出解除委任契约,那么在正式通知解除委任契约起五日内,仍应为保护作为委任人的当事人利益从事诉讼上的必要行为。在刑事诉讼中,无论是自诉案件中的诉讼代理人,还是公诉案件中的选任辩护人,都必须向管辖法院提交委任人与受委任人签署的委任状。

With regard to the power of attorney, in civil cases, the appointor (i.e. the party) should submit a copy of the power of attorney in the contract of attorney to the competent court to show his identity and clarify his power. In the process

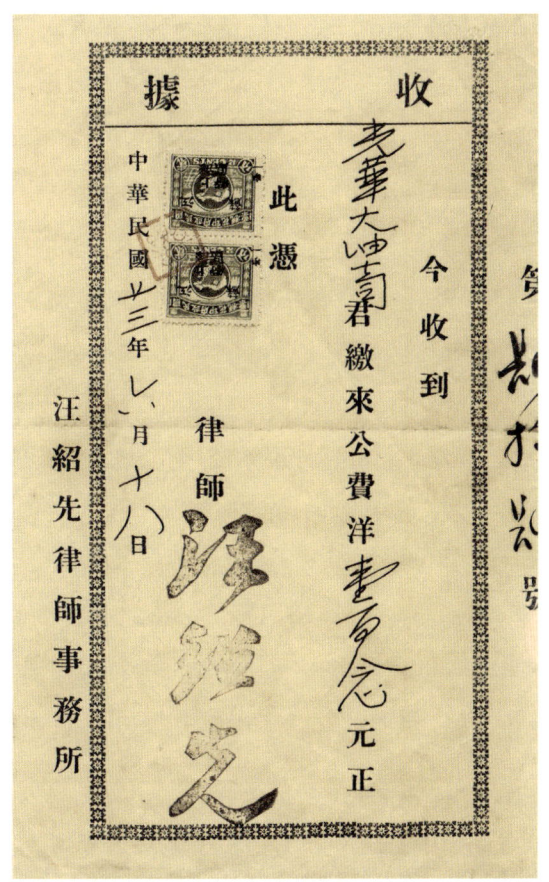

1934年6月汪绍先律师事务所收据
Receipt of Wang Shaoxian Law Firm in June 1934

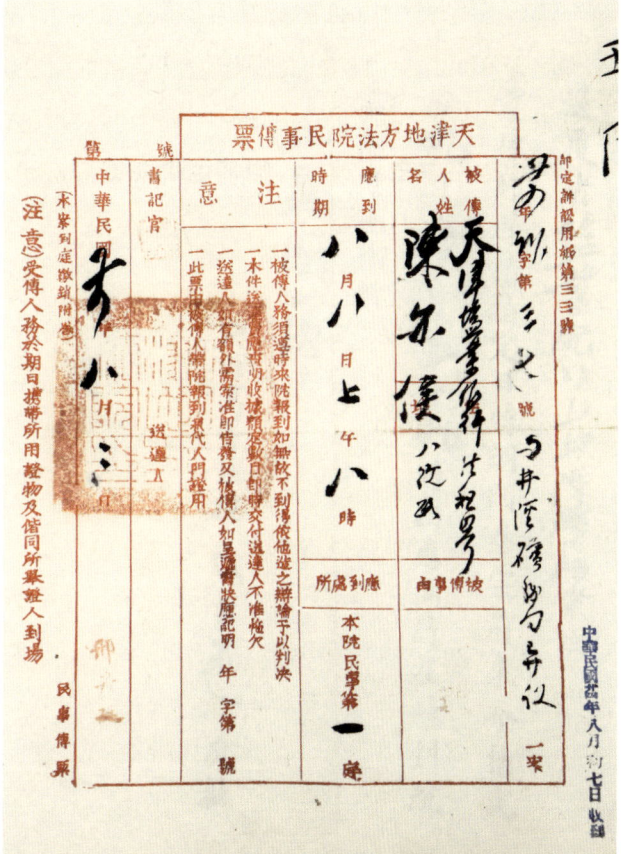

1935年8月天津地方法院民事传票
Civil summons of Tianjin District Court in August 1935

of litigation, if the appointor wants to cancel the appointment contract, he must not only notify the appointee (i.e. lawyer), but also submit a written cancellation letter to the competent court, and the court will notify the other party, otherwise the cancellation will not be effective. If the appointee proposes to terminate the appointment contract, he should still take necessary actions in litigation to protect the interests of the parties who are appointees within five days from the formal notice of termination of the appointment contract. In criminal proceedings, both the agent ad litem in a private prosecution case and the elected defender in a public prosecution case must submit a letter of appointment signed by the appointor and the appointed person to the competent court.

律师在经过书面通知对方当事人，仍不能以调解方式解决时，受委任律师将具体进入诉讼程序。在诉讼活动中，律师作为当事人的受委任人，代理当事人从事一切诉讼活动。无论是在民事诉讼还是刑事诉讼中，律师关于诉讼行为的声明或陈述，除了依法以言辞方式进行外，其他一律以书状形式进行。律师也将根据诉讼活动的不同阶段或不同要求，作出各种不同的书状，主要包括以下14种：

If the lawyer fails to solve the problem through mediation after notifying the other party in writing, the appointed lawyer will enter the litigation procedure concretely. In litigation activities, lawyers, as the appointees of the parties, engage in all litigation activities on behalf of the parties. Whether in civil litigation or criminal litigation, lawyers' statements or statements about litigation behavior are all made in the form of written pleadings, except in the form of words according to law. Lawyers will also make various pleadings according to different stages or requirements of litigation activities, mainly including the following 14 kinds:

诉状，指向法院陈述事件及诉讼要求的书状。刑事告诉人应将刑事诉状提交到检察处，刑事自诉人则应将刑事诉状提交到管辖法院。刑事诉状应包括被告人的姓名、年龄、籍贯、职业、住址，若有可能，还应说明被告的体貌特征、告诉或自诉的事实和理由、案件的证人和证物等。

A petition is an instrument that points to the court to state events and claims. The criminal informant should submit the criminal complaint to the prosecution office, while the criminal private prosecutor should submit the criminal complaint to the competent court. The criminal complaint should include the defendant's name, age, native place, occupation and address. If possible, it should also explain the defendant's physical characteristics, facts and reasons for telling or private prosecution, witnesses and exhibits of the case, etc.

答辩状和辩诉状，在民事诉讼中称"答辩状"，是就对方当事人陈述及要求进行答辩的书状。答辩状应包括答辩的事实、理由以及对于原告请求的全部或部分予以承认或否认。在刑事

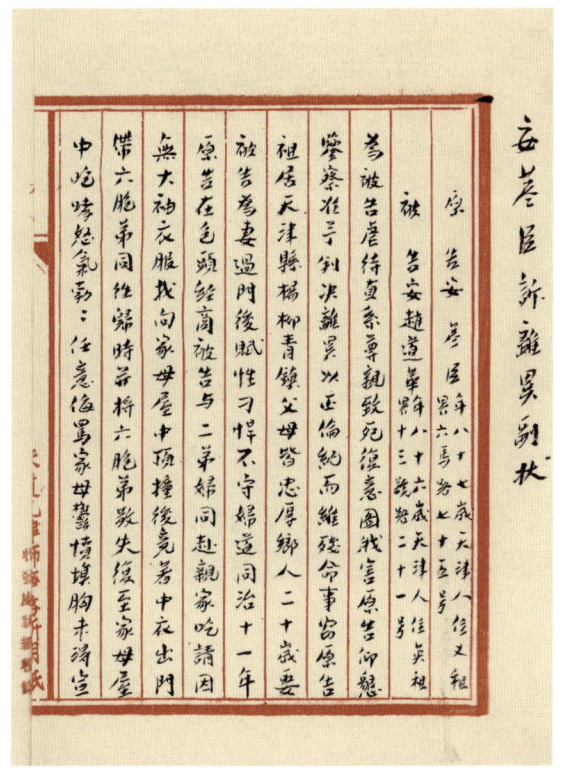 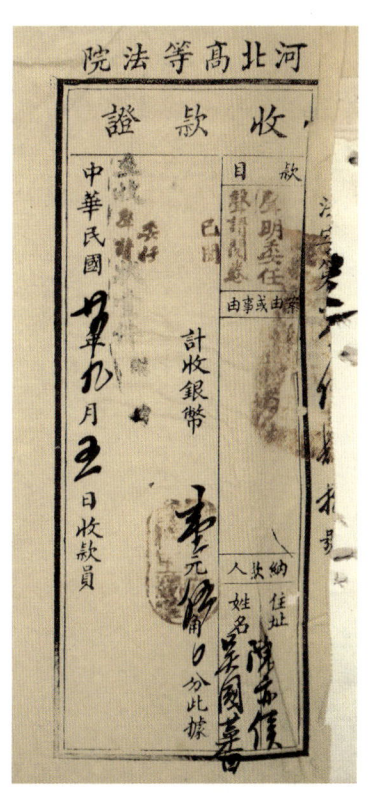

安蓉臣诉离异副状
A copy complaint of An Rongchen's divorce petition

1935年9月河北高等法院收款证
Collection certificate of Hebei High Court in September 1935

诉讼中称"辩诉状",是被告就刑事诉状的指控作出的答辩书状。辩诉状应包括案件事实、辩诉理由以及作为反证的证人和证物等。

The pleadings and counter-pleadings, called "pleadings" in civil litigation, are pleadings to answer the statements and demands of the other party. The pleadings shall include the facts and reasons of the pleadings, and admit or deny all or part of the plaintiff's request. In criminal proceedings, it is called "counter-pleadings", which is the pleadings made by the defendants on the charges of criminal pleadings. The pleadings should include the facts of the case, the reasons for the pleadings, and the witnesses and exhibits as counter-evidence.

抗告状,指在抗告诉讼中向原审法院或抗告审法院陈述事件及要求的书状。民事抗告状应包括对原审判决不服的陈述、不服的程度、要求如何废弃或变更原审判决的声明、抗告的理由

1921	1922	1923	1924	1925	1926	1927	1928	1929	1930	1931	1932	193
1947	1948	1949	1950	1951	1952	1953	1954	1955	1956	1957	1958	195
1973	1974	1975	1976	1977	1978	1979	1980	1981	1982	1983	1984	198
1999	2000	2001	2002	2003	2004	2005	2006	2007	2008	2009	2010	201

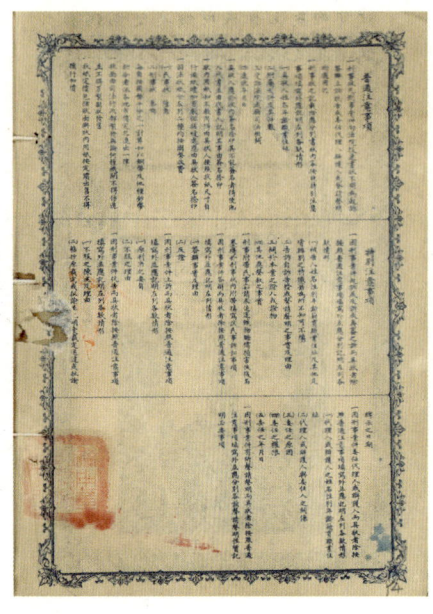 

刑事诉讼中的司法状纸
Judicial paper in criminal proceedings

以及新事实和证据方法。刑事抗告状应包括原裁判的内容和对于原裁判不服的陈述及理由。

Anti-complaint refers to the pleadings that state events and demands to the court of first instance or the court of anti-complaint. Civil complaint should include the statement of dissatisfaction with the judgment of the original trial, the degree of dissatisfaction, the statement of how to abandon or change the judgment of the original trial, the reasons for protest and the new facts and evidence methods. The criminal complaint should include the content of the original referee and the statement and reasons for dissatisfaction with the original referee.

上诉状，指对于原审裁判不服而向上一级法院提起上诉时，用以提出上诉要求的书状。民事上诉状应包括诉讼标的和原因、原审判决的内容、对于原审判决不服的程度、要求废弃或变更原判决的声明、上诉理由、关于上诉理由的证据方法。如果是因为对第一审判决不服而提起上诉，则还应记明新的事实和证据方法。刑事上诉状应记述原判决的要旨以及对原判决不服的理由。

The appeal pleadings refer to the written pleadings used to put forward appeal requirements when appealing to a higher court against the judgment of the original trial. The civil appeal should include the object and reason of the lawsuit, the content of the original judgment, the degree of dissatisfaction with the original judgment, the statement for abandoning or changing the original judgment, the reasons for appeal, and the evidential methods for the reasons for appeal. If you appeal because you are not satisfied with the judgment of the first instance, you should also remember new facts and evidence methods. The criminal appeal shall record the gist of the original judgment and the reasons for dissatisfaction with the original judgment.

声请状，指在民事诉讼中，当事人一方就实体或程序等方面有所请求时所使用的书状。在刑事诉讼中，指有所请求时向法院提交的书状。

Petition refers to the written pleadings used when one of the parties makes a request in terms of entity or procedure in civil litigation. In criminal proceedings, it refers to the written pleadings submitted to the court upon request.

交状，指在民事诉讼中，当事人一方向管辖法院提交与诉讼相关的证物、财产时使用的书状。在刑事诉讼中，指根据法院决定而将案内相关财产、物品交纳法院时使用的书状。

The submitting pleadings refer to pleadings used when one party submits evidence and property related to litigation to the competent court in civil litigation. In criminal proceedings, it refers to the pleadings used when handing over the related property and articles in the case to the court according to the court's decision.

领状，指在民事诉讼中，当事人一方自管辖法院领取与诉讼相关的证物、财产时所使用的书状。在刑事诉讼中，根据法院决定而将案内相关财产、物品领回时使用的书状。

Solicitation refers to the written pleadings used by one of the parties to obtain evidence and property related to litigation from the court of jurisdiction in civil litigation. In criminal proceedings, the pleadings used when taking back the related property and articles in the case according to the court's decision.

限状，指就期限问题向管辖法院提出的请求书状。

The written pleadings refer to the written pleadings submitted to the competent court on the time limit.

保状，指向管辖法院具保时缔结的书状。

The preserving pleadings refer to the written pleadings concluded when the competent court guarantees.

结状，指向管辖法院具结时缔结的书状。

The closing pleadings refer to the pleadings concluded when the competent court makes a statement.

撤回状，指在民事诉讼中，原告在法院作出确定判决前撤回诉讼请求时使用的书状。在刑事自诉案件中，指自诉人在第一审辩论终结前撤回诉讼时使用的书状。

The withdrawal pleadings refer to pleadings used by the plaintiff to withdraw his claim before the court makes a definite judgment in civil litigation. In criminal private prosecution cases, it refers to the pleadings used by the private prosecutor when withdrawing the lawsuit before the end of the first-instance debate.

还有两种民事诉讼中的书状，一是调解状，是指当事人一方提出的请求调解的书状。另一种是和解状，是指双方当事人达成和解时缔结的书状。

There are two kinds of pleadings in civil litigation, one is mediation pleadings, which refer to pleadings submitted by one of the parties requesting mediation. The other is reconciliation pleadings, which refer to the pleadings concluded when both parties reach a settlement.

民国初创二十年的天津律师业

TIANJIN LAWYERS IN THE FIRST TWENTY YEARS OF THE REPUBLIC OF CHINA

咸丰十年（1860）天津开埠，在与西方政治、经济、文化的碰撞与融合中，天津开启了城市近代化的历程。清末民初，天津已发展成为中国北方首屈一指的工商业大都会，城市地位仅次于上海，对于中国政治的走向和经济的发展发挥着举足轻重的作用。与此同时，动荡的局势、复杂的社会状况、交相作用的社会力量也使天津充满了各式各样的矛盾。为解决这些矛盾、缓和社会压力，律师群体逐渐在天津兴盛起来，并不断发展壮大。因此可以说，律师的兴盛是与复杂的社会形态密不可分的。

Tianjin opened its port in 1860. In the collision and integration with western politics, economy and culture, Tianjin started the process of urban modernization. In the late Qing Dynasty and the early Republic of China, Tianjin had developed into the leading industrial and commercial metropolis in northern China, which was second only to Shanghai and played an important role in China's political trend and economic development. At the same time, the turbulent situation, complex social conditions and interactive social forces also filled Tianjin with various contradictions. In order to solve these contradictions and ease the social pressure, the lawyers group gradually flourished in Tianjin and continued to grow and develop. Therefore, it can be said that the prosperity of lawyers is inseparable from complex social forms.

此外，天津律师的崛起也离不开华洋诉讼、涉外案件的客观要求。由于在津执业的外国律师不熟悉中国的法律和程序，特别是随着领事裁判权的弱化，不论是中外纠纷还是洋行间的讼争，外国律师都要到中国法庭代理诉讼，因此他们不得不求助于中国律师，这就为中国律师的发展提供了客观条件。在天津执业的唐宝锷、侯文彪、许日升、王庭兰等人都是通晓西律及外语的律师，他们经常与外国律师合作办案，有效地促进了天津律师的成长。

In addition, the rise of Tianjin lawyers can not be separated from the objective requirements of foreign lawsuits and foreign-related cases. Because foreign lawyers practicing in Tianjin were not familiar with Chinese laws and procedures, especially with the weakening of consular jurisdiction, foreign lawyers had to act in Chinese courts, whether it was disputes between China and foreign countries or disputes between foreign firms, so they had to resort to Chinese lawyers, which provided objective conditions for the development of Chinese lawyers. Tang Baoe, Hou Wenbiao, Xu Risheng and Wang Tinglan, who practiced in Tianjin, were lawyers who were familiar with western law and foreign languages. They often cooperated with foreign lawyers in handling cases, which effectively promoted the growth of Tianjin lawyers.

虽然清末司法改革因清王朝的覆灭而终止，但其种种措施与思想理念已对中国社会产生了深刻的影响。于是，伴随着北洋政府《律师暂行章程》的出台，越来越多的国人，特别是像天津这样高度近代化的大都市的市民，逐渐开始接受律师和律师制度，越来越多有海外留学背景的高官政要、法学名家也纷纷投身律师业，为天津乃至全国律师业的发展打下了良好的基础。

Although the judicial reform in the late Qing Dynasty ended with the fall of the Qing Dynasty, its various measures and ideas had had a profound impact on Chinese society. Therefore, with the promulgation of the *Provisional Regulation of Lawyers* by Beiyang Government, more and more Chinese people, especially the citizens of a highly modernized metropolis like Tianjin, gradually began to accept the lawyer and lawyer system, and more and more high-ranking officials, dignitaries and famous jurists with overseas study backgrounds also joined the lawyer industry, laying a good foundation for the development of lawyer industry in Tianjin and even the whole country.

一、天津律师数量的变化

1. Changes in the Number of Lawyers in Tianjin

民国时期律师制度的演变和律师业的发展始终与社会经济的发展状况紧密相连。总体来看,律师从业者的数量呈上升趋势,而不同地域的基数又有明显差异。沿海、沿江经济较发达的大中城市始终是律师业最发达的地区,其中上海、天津、北京的发展最令人瞩目。

During the Republic of China, the evolution of lawyer system and the development of lawyer industry were always closely related to the economic development of society. On the whole, the number of lawyers was on the rise, and the bases of different regions were obviously different. Large and medium-sized cities with relatively developed economy along the coast and Changjiang River had always been the most developed areas for lawyers, among which Shanghai, Tianjin and Beijing had attracted the most attention.

民国元年的律师极少,仅为17人,第二年增加到47人,到1923年,人数才刚刚破百,达到133人。此后,律师人数增加明显,而这与国内法科院校大量法律人才的培养密不可分。

In the first year of the Republic of China, there were very few lawyers, only 17 people, but only increased to 47 in the second year, and then in 1923, the number just exceeded 100, reaching 133. Since then, the number of lawyers had increased significantly, which was inseparable from the cultivation of a large number of legal talents in domestic law colleges.

到20世纪30年代,在沿海、沿江经济较发达的大中城市,律师的数量有显著的增加。如1931年,执业律师登录在册、满100人的城市包括上海828人,天津760人,北平760人,武汉459人,苏州329人,杭州304人,广州252人,济南234人,保定214人,鄞县176人,南昌144人,镇江144人,怀宁124人,金华112人,开封109人,福州104人。反观同时期的内地城市,即使是一些大城市,其律师的数量也明显偏少,如长沙98人,重庆89人,成都79人,太原38人,西安11人,承德5人,而南宁与桂林直到1934年才分别有16人和29人。

By 1930s, the number of lawyers had increased significantly in large and medium-sized cities with relatively developed economy along the coast and river. For example, in 1931, practicing lawyers were registered, and cities with over 100 people included 828 in Shanghai, 760 in Tianjin, 760 in Beiping, 459 in Wuhan, 329 in Suzhou, 304 in Hangzhou, 252 in Guangzhou, 234 in Jinan, 214 in Baoding, 176 in Yinxian, 144 in Nanchang, 144 in Zhenjiang, 124 in Huaining, 112 in Jinhua, 109 in Kaifeng and 104 in Fuzhou. On the other hand, the number of lawyers in mainland cities in the same period, even some big cities, was obviously less, such as Changsha 98 people, Chongqing 89 people, Chengdu 79 people, Taiyuan 38 people, Xi'an 11 people, Chengde 5 people, while Nanning and Guilin had 16 people and 29 people respectively until 1934.

就天津而言，1921—1937年，随着民法、刑法、商法及各类单行法规的编纂、修订，律师的从业人数激增，天津律师业的发展也进入了民国的鼎盛时期。1928年前后，天津律师进入繁荣期，当年共有律师575人，同时也设立了575处律师事务所，其中多数位于今河北区一带；1929年612人，1930年708人，1931年760人，1932年814人，1933年达到了860人，是天津在民国时期律师人数最多的一年，而此时全国共有律师7651名。尽管1934年降至518人，1935年回到609人，1936年又为537人，但仍比同时期北平律师公会的448人占有很大的优势。

As far as Tianjin was concerned, from 1921 to 1937, with the compilation and revision of civil law, criminal law, commercial law and various special laws and regulations, the number of lawyers increased sharply, and the development of Tianjin lawyers also entered the heyday of the Republic of China. Around 1928, Tianjin lawyers entered a prosperous period. In that year, there were 575 lawyers and 575 law firms were also set up, most of which were located in Hebei District today. There were 612 lawyers in 1929, 708 in 1930, 760 in 1931, 814 in 1932 and 860 in 1933, which was the year with the largest number of lawyers in Tianjin during the Republic of China. At that time, there were 7651 lawyers in China. Although it dropped to 518 in 1934, returned to 609 in 1935 and 537 in 1936, it still had a great advantage over the 448 people in Beiping Bar Association in the same period.

二、天津律师的年龄、籍贯及学历特点
2. Tianjin Lawyers' Age, Native Place and Educational Background Characteristics

民国时期,天津的律师主要以30—49岁的中青年律师为主。在1920年以前,该年龄段的人数占比为50%,此后不断上升,到1946年达到了最高的57%。不过,就该年龄段而言,40—49岁的人数比例要远远高于30—39岁,在1945年,两者甚至相差34个百分点。此外,50—59岁的律师占比基本保持在30%左右,而60岁以上的比例,最高时可达到1945年的19%,最低则仅为1935年的0.3%。总体来看,天津律师年龄最小者35岁,最大者67岁。

During the Republic of China, lawyers in Tianjin were mainly young and middle-aged lawyers aged 30-49. Before 1920, the proportion of people in this age group was 50%, and then it kept rising, reaching the highest 57% in 1946. However, in this age group, the proportion of people aged 40-49 was much higher than that of people aged 30-39. In 1945, the difference between them was even 34 percentage points. In addition, the proportion of lawyers aged 50-59 remained at about 30%, while the highest proportion of lawyers aged over 60 reached 19% in 1945 and the lowest was only 0.3% in 1935. Generally speaking, the youngest lawyer in Tianjin was 35 years old and the oldest was 67 years old.

天津执业律师大部分来自今天津、北京、河北,占比高达67%,其中天津籍占三地总和的12%。京津冀以外的区域主要涉及江苏、安徽、浙江和山东等地,最远者可达福建、广东。另有德籍律师1人、俄籍6人。

Most of the practicing lawyers in Tianjin came from Tianjin, Beijing and Hebei, accounting for 67%, of which Tianjin nationality accounted for 12% of the total of the three places. The area outside the Beijing-Tianjin-Hebei region mainly covers Jiangsu, Anhui, Zhejiang and Shandong provinces, with the farthest reaches reaching Fujian and Guangdong. There are also 1 German lawyer and 6 Russian lawyers.

天津律师有近10%有海外留学经历,其中留日学生约占60%,留学法国、德国、瑞士、苏联和美国的约占40%,而活跃在天津的90%的律师都毕业于国内法政专门学校或各类大学。值得注

意的是，天津律师资格的取得不仅看重学历，而且看重任职经历。以朱道孔事务所为例，在47名律师中，有29名律师在执业前担任过教授、检察官、推事、司法官或政府官员。学历和任职经历并重的选拔方式，使从业者不仅有良好的专业教育背景，而且还有相当丰富的社会经验和对司法诉讼程序的体验，有助于律师工作的开展。

Nearly 10% of lawyers in Tianjin had overseas study experience, of which about 60% were students studying in Japan, and about 40% were studying in France, Germany, Switzerland, the Soviet Union and the United States, while 90% of lawyers active in Tianjin had graduated from domestic specialized schools of law and politics or various universities. It was worth noting that the qualification of Tianjin lawyers not only attached importance to academic qualifications, but also attached importance to working experience. Take Zhu Daokong Law Firm as an example, among 47 lawyers, 29 lawyers had served as professors, prosecutors, judges, or government officials before practicing. The selection method, which paid equal attention to educational background and job experience, made practitioners not only had a good professional education background, but also had rich social experience and experience in judicial proceedings, which was helpful to the development of lawyers' work.

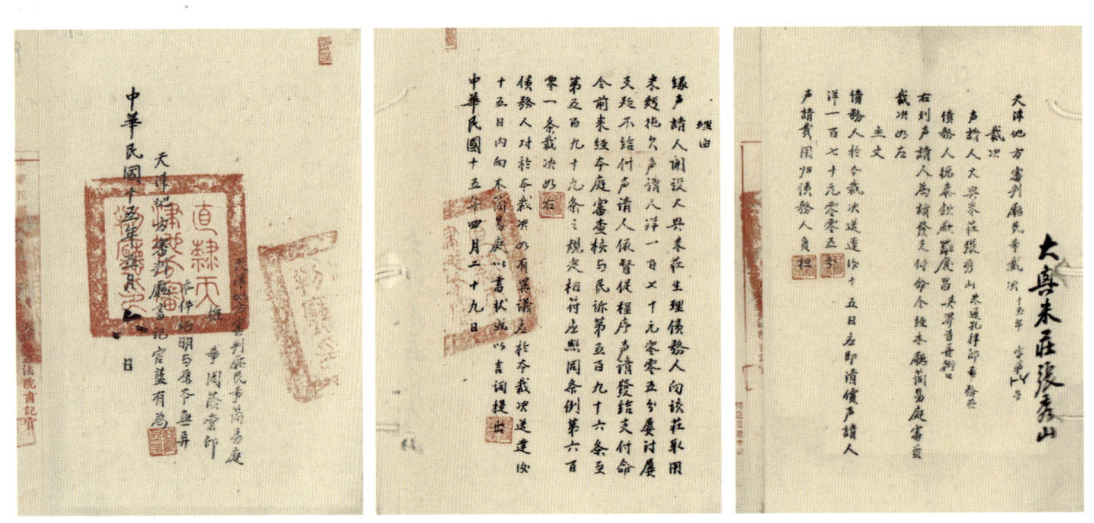

1926年朱道孔律师事务所代理张秀山案天津地方审判厅民事裁决书

The civil award of the Tianjin Local Adjudicative Office of Justice in the case of Zhang Xiushan represented by Zhu Daokong Law Firm in 1926

三、天津律师的类型

3. Types of Tianjin Lawyers

作为民国律师业最发达的城市之一,各类法律从业者云集天津,这里既有唐宝锷、朱道孔一类的知名大律师,也有许多为生计奔波的普通律师,展现了一幅生动的民国律师众生相。大致来说,民国时期的天津律师可以分为以下四种:

As one of the most developed cities in the Republic of China, all kinds of legal practitioners gathered in Tianjin, where there were well-known barristers such as Tang Baoe and Zhu Daokong, as well as many ordinary lawyers running for their livelihood, showing a vivid picture of lawyers in the Republic of China. Generally speaking, Tianjin lawyers in the Republic of China can be divided into the following four types:

第一种是来自政府,特别是司法界的高层,后因各种原因离职而转做律师者。其中在京津两地从事过律师职业的,包括曾任北洋政府司法总长的章士钊、董康、朱深,曾任大理院院长的余棨昌、石志泉、李怀亮,曾任外交总长的罗文干,曾任北京朝阳大学校长的江庸。他们被称作"名律师",专办大案、要案,名望高,收费高,属于社会上流人物,在律师业中凤毛麟角。就天津而言,许多下野的军阀、政客常常聘请这类律师作私人顾问,处理内外事务。天津著名律师李洪岳、朱道孔、张士俊、张绍曾等都曾担任重要人物的法律顾问。

The first kind was from the government, especially from the top of the judiciary, who left for various reasons and turned to be a lawyer. Among them, those who had worked as lawyers in Beijing and Tianjin included Zhang Shizhao, Dong Kang and Zhu Shen, who served as the judicial chief of Beiyang Government; Yu Qichang, Shi Zhiquan and Li Huailiang, who served as the president of Daliyuan; Luo Wengan, who served as the foreign chief; and Jiang Yong, who served as the president of Beijing Chaoyang University. They were called "famous lawyers", specializing in major cases and important cases, with high fame and high fees, belonging to the upper class of society and being rare in the lawyer industry. As far as Tianjin was concerned, many warlords and politicians who were out of office often employed such lawyers as private consultants to handle internal and external affairs. Tianjin famous lawyers Li Hongyue, Zhu Daokong, Zhang Shijun, Zhang Shaozeng, etc. all served as legal advisers to important people.

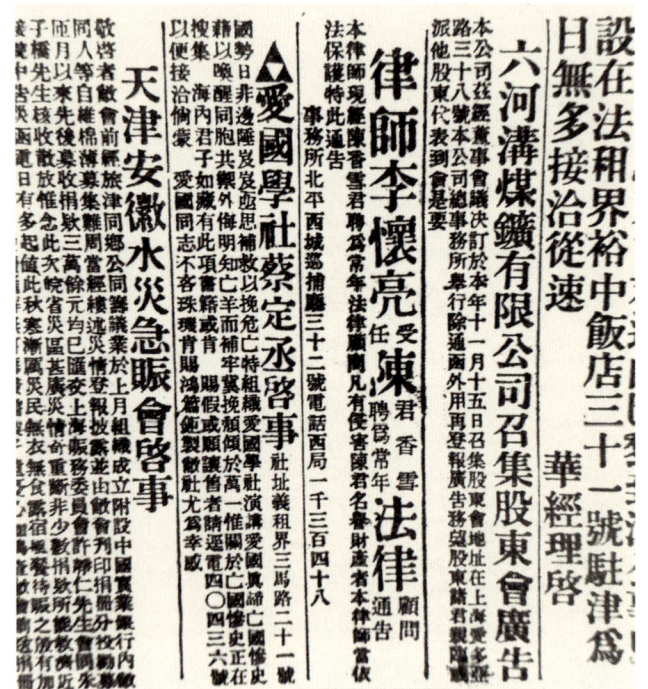

李怀亮律师受聘法律顾问的通告
Notice of lawyer Li Huailiang's appointment of legal counsel

　　第二种是各大学法科及法律专门学校的教师，或者在司法部门有过院长、庭长任职经历的人。他们法学知识渊博，法律功底深厚，又有丰富的司法经验和一定的社会关系与声望，方便从事律师职业。在京津地区较为著名者包括孙观圻、刘盦诒、阮性言，他们都曾在高等审判机关供职；方震甲、老遇春等人则在法科院校讲学多年，律师业务都比较活跃。

　　The second type was the teachers of law departments and specialized law schools in universities, or those who had worked as presidents and presidents in judicial departments. They had profound legal knowledge, profound legal foundation, rich judicial experience, certain social relations and prestige, and were convenient for lawyers. The famous people in Beijing and Tianjin included Sun Guanche, Liu Anyi and Ruan Xingyan, all of whom had served in higher judicial organs. Fang Zhenjia, Lao

Yuchun and others had lectured in law colleges for many years, and their lawyers were active.

第三种是国内法科或专门学校的毕业生以及海外留学生回国后直接进入律师行业，或从其他行业普通职位转入者。这类律师的名望、交游和社会地位都无法与前两种相比，不过他们普遍具有良好的专业背景和业务能力，具备一定的社会关系，执业收入足够维持体面的生活，也构成了民国律师业的主体。

The third type was graduates from domestic law schools or specialized schools and overseas students who directly entered the lawyer industry after returning home, or transfered from ordinary positions in other industries. The reputation, friends and social status of these lawyers could not be compared with the former two, but they generally had good professional background and professional ability, had certain social relations, earned enough to maintain a decent life, and also constituted the main body of the lawyer industry in the Republic of China.

第四种是民国律师业的底层。他们常年围着法院转，不过很少出庭代理诉讼，只在法院门前租一间斗室，或在附近旅馆包个单间，门口挂上某某大律师事务所的牌子。这类律师往往被称为"三不律师"，即文理不通、口才不行、交游不广，他们实际上兼书记和勤杂于一身，终日奔忙，收入无多。同时，他们还要警惕当事人因对诉讼结果不满而对他们的人身伤害。不过，这类律师的人数并不多。

The fourth was the bottom of the lawyer industry in the Republic of China. They went around the court all the year round, but they rarely appeared in court to represent the lawsuit. They only rented a cubicle in front of the court, or packed a single room in a nearby hotel, and hung the sign of so-and-so big law firm at the door. These lawyers were often referred to as "three no lawyers", that was, they had poor liberal arts, poor eloquence and poor friends. In fact, they were both secretaries and handymen, and they were busy all day long with little income. At the same time, they should also be alert to the personal injury caused by dissatisfaction with the outcome of litigation. However, the number of such lawyers was not large.

四、与天津相关的知名律师
4. Well-known Lawyers Related to Tianjin

曹汝霖（1877—1966），字润田，上海人。幼年入私塾，光绪二十六年（1900）赴日本留学，先后就读于早稻田专门学校和东京法学院。光绪三十一年（1905）回国，任商务司行走、商律馆编纂等职，并通过了留学生特科考试。

Cao Rulin (1877-1966), born in Shanghai. He entered private school at an early age and went to Japan to study in 1900. He studied at Waseda Special School and Tokyo Law School successively. In 1905, he returned to China, took the posts of walking in the Department of Commerce and compiling the Commercial Law Museum, and passed the special examination for foreign students.

1912年9月16日，北洋政府司法部颁布了《律师暂行章程》；9月19日，曹汝霖便请领了司法部颁发的律师证书，在家中设事务所，在北京及周边地区执业律师，并在天津日租界宫岛街（今鞍山道）置地购房。由于其证书编号为"一"，遂被称为"民国第一号律师"。

On September 16, 1912, the Ministry of Justice of Beiyang Government promulgated the *Provisional Regulation of Lawyers*. On September 19th, Cao Rulin received the lawyer certificate issued by the Ministry of Justice, set up an office at home, practiced as a lawyer in Beijing and its surrounding areas, and bought a house on land in Miyajima Street (now Anshan Road) of Tianjin Japanese Concession. Because its certificate number was "One", it was called "No.1 Lawyer of the Republic of China".

1919年年初，列强在巴黎和会上将德国在山东的权益转让给日本的消息激起了全国人民的一致反对。曹汝霖却向大总统徐世昌进言"决不可失日本之欢心，必须顺从其意"，同时公开为日本侵占青岛辩护。同年5月4日下午，北京三千余名学生在天安门前集会，高呼"外争主权，内惩国贼""拒绝和约签字"的口号，同时要求惩办卖国贼曹汝霖、陆宗舆、章宗祥。游行学生包围并冲入了曹汝霖的住宅赵家楼，没抓到曹汝霖，而将章宗祥痛打一顿，并且放火烧了赵家楼。在广大工人、学生的爱国斗争下，北洋政府不得不于6月10日罢免了曹、陆、章三

曹汝霖（右二）
Cao Rulin (second from right)

人，并拒绝在《凡尔赛和约》上签字。

At the beginning of 1919, the news that the great powers transferred Germany's rights and interests in Shandong to Japan at the Paris Peace Conference aroused the unanimous opposition of the whole nation. However, Cao Rulin still advised President Xu Shichang that "Japan must never be lost, and must obey its wishes", and at the same time publicly defended Japan's occupation of Qingdao. On the afternoon of May 4, the same year, more than 3,000 students gathered in front of Tian'anmen Square, shouting the slogan of "fighting for sovereignty outside, punishing the country thieves inside" and "refusing to sign the peace treaty", and demanding that the traitors Cao Rulin, Lu Zongyu and Zhang Zongxiang be punished. The marching students surrounded and rushed into Cao Rulin's residence, Zhaojialou. Instead of catching

Cao Rulin, they beat Zhang Zongxiang up and set fire to Zhaojialou. Under the patriotic struggle of workers and students, the Beiyang Government had to recall Cao, Lu and Zhang on June 10 and refused to sign the *Versailles Peace Treaty*.

全面抗战爆发后，曹汝霖公开表示"要以晚节挽回前誉之失"，发誓不在日伪政权任职。虽被日本侵略者视为华北伪政权总理大臣的不二人选，但曹汝霖始终不为所动，仅有一个伪华北政务委员会咨询委员的空衔。解放战争时期，曹汝霖从北平迁居上海，新中国成立前夕又转往台北。后经香港赴日本，受到日本首相吉田茂的庇护。1957年，曹汝霖迁居美国，并于1966年8月4日客死于底特律。

After the outbreak of the All-out Anti-Japanese War, Cao Rulin publicly stated that he would "save the loss of his former reputation with the late festival" and vowed not to serve in the Japanese puppet regime. Although regarded by the Japanese invaders as the best candidate for the Prime Minister of the puppet regime in North China, Cao Rulin remained unmoved, with only one vacant title as an Advisory Member of the puppet North China Administrative Committee. During the War of Liberation, Cao Rulin moved from Beiping to Shanghai, and then moved to Taipei on the eve of the founding of the People's Republic of China. After going to Japan from Hong Kong, he was sheltered by Japanese Prime Minister Shigeru Yoshida. In 1957, Cao Rulin moved to the United States and died in Detroit on August 4, 1966.

在1912年9至12月间，曹汝霖在大理院代理的诉讼案件多达28件，而在大理院当时受理的37件刑事上诉案中，有19件以曹汝霖为被告辩护人，占了总数的一半，彰显了其在民国初年律师界的重要地位。在与袁世凯的谈话中，曹汝霖也曾透露自己律师业务的月收入可达2000大洋，远高于其外交次长的官俸。

From September to December, 1912, Cao Rulin represented as many as 28 lawsuits in Daliyuan. Among the 37 criminal appeals accepted by Daliyuan at that time, Cao Rulin was the defendant's defender in 19 cases, accounting for half of the total, which showed his important position in the lawyers in the early years of the Republic of China. In the conversation with Yuan Shikai, Cao Rulin also revealed

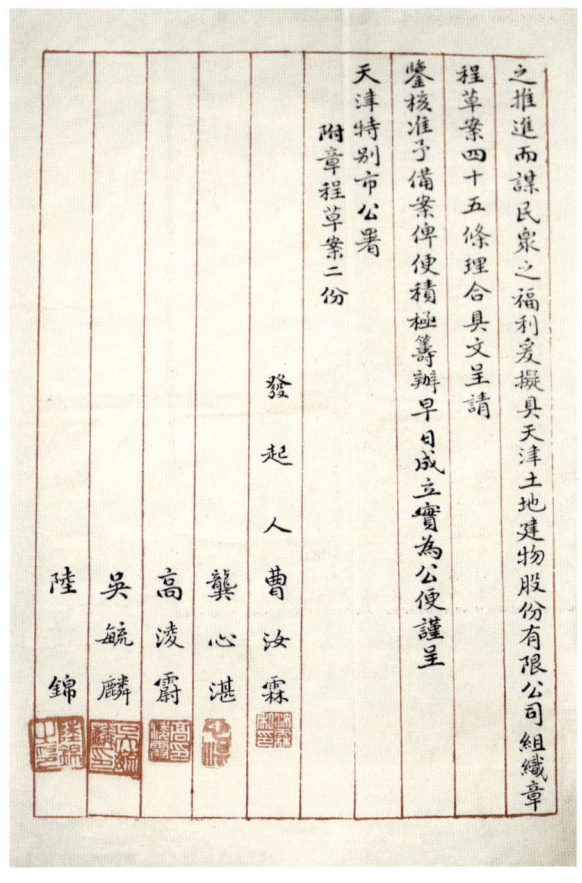

作为章程发起人之首的曹汝霖
Cao Rulin, the first initiator of the articles of association

1946年天津市财政局关于曹汝霖一处房产的投税声请书
1946 Tianjin Finance Bureau's petition for tax on a real estate in Cao Rulin

that the monthly income of his lawyer business can reach 2000 yuan, far higher than the official salary of his Foreign Minister.

唐宝锷（1878—1953）是名震天津的大律师，族名宗鎏，字秀锋、秀丰，生于上海，祖籍广东香山县上恭都唐家村（今珠海市香洲区唐家镇），是唐绍仪的侄辈。其父唐昭航为上海唐族"买办世家""茶叶世家"成员之一，与近代著名企业家、同乡唐廷枢在上海从事多种经营。光绪二十二年（1896），唐宝锷考取首批官派赴日留学生。光绪二十五年（1899）毕业后，任清廷驻日本长崎领事馆代理副领事，两年后调任东京公使馆馆员。因其日语十分流利，所以每逢清廷官员访日，都由唐宝锷担任翻译。与此同时，唐宝锷还在东京早稻田专门学校邦交行政科学习国际法。光绪二十九年（1903）唐宝锷进入早稻田大学政治经济部学习，两年后

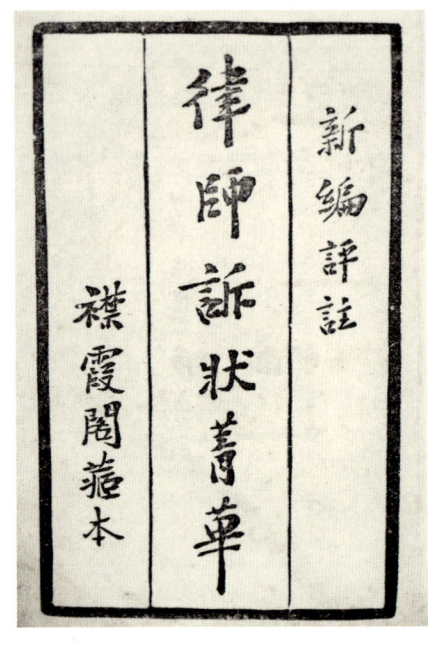

《律师诉状菁华》封面
Cover of *The Lawyer's Complaint Elite*

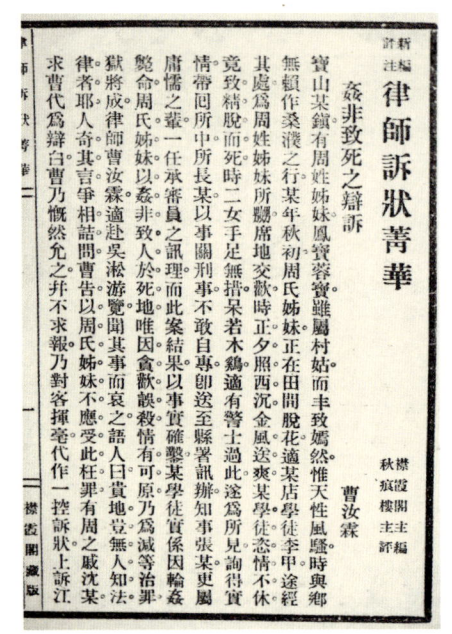

《律师诉状菁华》中收录的曹汝霖的文章
Cao Rulin's articles included in *The Lawyer's Complaint Elite*

获学士学位，成为最早一批正式获得日本高等学校学位的中国留学生中的一员。同年回国后，唐宝锷通过了清廷留学生归国考试，赐进士出身，授翰林院检讨。此后历任北洋司法官养成学校监督（校长）、洋务局会办、陆军部一等首席参事官、川粤铁路督办等职。

Tang Baoe (1878-1953) was a barrister who was famous in Tianjin. He was born in Shanghai with the family name of Zongliu, Xiufeng and Xiufeng. His ancestral home was Tangjia Village, Shanggongdu, Xiangshan County, Guangdong Province (now Tangjia Town, Xiangzhou District, Zhuhai City), and he was Tang Shaoyi's nephew. His father, Tang Zhaohang, was one of the members of the "comprador family" and "tea family" of the Tang family in Shanghai, and engaged in various businesses in Shanghai with Tang Tingshu, a famous modern entrepreneur and fellow countryman. In 1896, Tang Baoe was admitted to the first batch of official students studying in Japan. After graduating in 1899, he served as acting vice consul of the Qing Consulate in Nagasaki, Japan, and was transferred as a librarian of Tokyo Legation two years later. Because of his fluency in Japanese, Tang Baoe acted as an interpreter whenever Qing court officials visited Japan. At the same time, Tang Baoe also studied international law in the Department of Diplomatic Relations Administration of Waseda Special School in Tokyo. In 1903, Tang Baoe entered the Department of Political Science and Economics of Waseda University, and obtained a bachelor's degree two years later, becoming one of the first batch of Chinese students who officially obtained a degree from a Japanese university. After returning to China in the same year, Tang Baoe passed the exam of returning students from the Qing court, and was given a Jinshi background and a review by the Hanlin Academy. Since then, he has served as the supervisor (principal) of Beiyang Judicial Officer Training School, the Office of Foreign Affairs Bureau, the First-class Chief Counselor of the War Department, and the Supervisor of Sichuan-Guangdong Railway.

在南北议和谈判中，唐宝锷出任北方代表唐绍仪的参赞。曹汝霖在1912年9月19日请领了民国第一号律师证书之后，唐宝锷于次日获得了第三号律师证书。此后历任国会众议员、大总统顾问、直隶都督府顾问、绥远将军署高等顾问、荣旗垦务督办署秘书长、归绥警务处处长等职。1921年，唐宝锷定居天津，住在河北造币厂一带。1924年年末退出政界后，开办事务所，专门从事律师职业。

In the North-South negotiation, Tang Baoe became the counsellor of Tang Shaoyi, the representative of the North. After Cao Rulin received the No.1 Lawyer Certificate of the Republic of China on September 19, 1912, Tang Baoe received the No.3 Lawyer Certificate the next day. Since then, he had served as a Member of the House of Representatives, an Adviser to the President, an Adviser to Zhili Governor's Office, a Senior Adviser to Suiyuan General Office, the Secretary General of Rongqi Reclamation Supervision Office, and the Commissioner of Guisui Police. In 1921, Tang Baoe settled in Tianjin and lived in Hebei Mint. After retiring from politics at the end of 1924, he opened a firm and specialized in lawyers.

天津河北四经路（今四马路）事务所是唐宝锷律师生涯中存在时间最长的事务所。1939年7月，这里被日寇强占，改建为昭南橡胶工厂，抗战胜利后成为南洋橡胶厂，即后来的橡胶制品四厂、今巷肆创意产业园的所在地。此外，在天津英租界三德里、法租界葛公使路（今滨江道东段）平和里、日租界旭街19号（今百货大楼对面）、特一区（前德租界）福州路以及林森路

（今新华路南段）均设有唐宝锷律师的办事处或事务所。日本著名律师大木干一既是其数十年的故交，也是他旭街事务所的主要合作者。

Tianjin and Hebei Sijing Road (now Si Road) was the longest-standing firm in Tang Baoe's lawyer career. In July, 1939, it was occupied by the Japanese aggressors and rebuilt into Zhaonan Rubber Factory. After the victory of Anti-Japanese War, it became Nanyang Rubber Factory, which was the location of the fourth rubber products factory and now Xiangsi Creative Industry Park. In addition, lawyers' offices or offices of Tang Baoe have been set up in Sande Lane, the British Concession in Tianjin, Pinghe Lane, Baron Gros Road (now the eastern section of Binjiang Road) in French Concession, No.19 Asahi Street, the Japanese Concession (now opposite to the Department Store), Fuzhou Road and Linsen Road (now the southern section of Xinhua Road) in Special Zone 1. A famous Japanese lawyer, Mikio Oki, was not only an old friend for decades, but also a major partner of his Asahi Street Office.

唐宝锷还被聘为北宁铁路局法律顾问，并作为京津律师代表，多次出席全国律师协会代表大会，担任大会执行委员、会长等职。1948年，唐宝锷停止律师业务，并于1953年在天津病逝。一生翻译《东语正规》《日本明治维新概要》《日本警察法令提要》等20余部著作。

Tang Baoe was also hired as the legal adviser of Beining Railway Bureau, and as a lawyer representative of Beijing and Tianjin, he attended the National Lawyers Association Congress for many times and served as executive member and president of the Congress. Tang Baoe stopped practicing as a lawyer in 1948 and died in Tianjin in 1953. He had translated more than 20 books such as *Formal East Language*, *Summary of Meiji Restoration in Japan* and *Summary of Japanese Police Law* all his life.

江庸（1878—1960），字翊云，号澹翁，福建长汀人，生于四川璧山县（今重庆市璧山区）。乃父江瀚，曾任京师大学堂总教习、文科学长、学部参事、北京大学教授、山西大学教授等职。光绪二十七年（1901），江庸官费赴日留学，初入成城学校普通科，两年后毕业，入早稻田大学师范部法制经济科学习。留学期间，结识了秋瑾、蔡锷、梁启超、蒋方震等人。光绪三十二年（1906）获法学士学位回国，历任京师法政学堂总教习、修订法律馆专任纂修、法律学堂教习、大理院详谳处推事等职。宣统元年（1909）参加归国留学生考试，以一等第四名授大理院正六品推事，兼任京师法律学堂监督。

Jiang Yong (1878-1960), named Yiyun, was also known as Danweng, Fujian Changting, born in Bishan County, Sichuan Province (now Bishan District, Chongqing). Jiang Han, his father, used to be the head teacher, senior of liberal arts, counselor of department of Jingshi University, professor of Peking University and Shanxi University. In 1901, Jiang Yong went to Japan to study abroad at an official fee. He first entered the general course of Chengcheng School. After two years, he graduated and entered the Legal Economics Department of the Normal Department of Waseda University. During his study abroad, he met Qiu Jin, Cai E, Liang Qichao, Jiang Fangzhen and others. In 1906, he returned to China with a bachelor's degree in law. He has served as the Chief Teacher of the Law and Politics School of Jingshi,

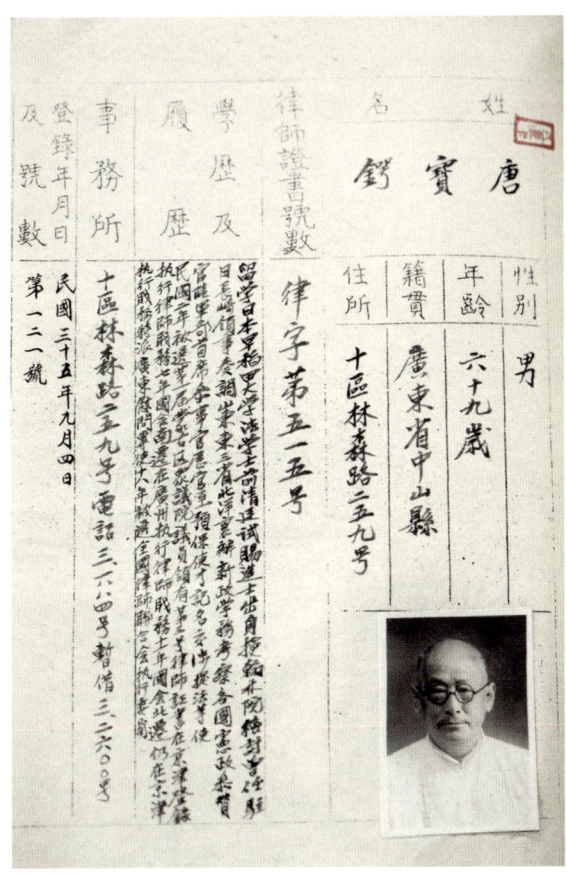

1946 年唐宝锷律师的登记信息

Registration information of lawyer Tang Baoe in 1946

the Full-time Editor of the Revised Law Museum, the Teacher of the Law School, and the Judge of the Department of Xiangyan of the Daliyuan. In 1909, he took the exam for returned students, and won the first-class fourth place to be awarded the sixth level Judge of Daliyuan, and concurrently served as the Supervisor of the Law School of Jingshi.

民国成立后，江庸留任大理院推事，当年9月，兼任高等审判厅厅长。次年，熊希龄组阁，江庸任司法部次长，梁启超任总长。针对袁世凯称帝的图谋，江庸多有评议，并于1915年冬坚辞而去。直到1917年王士珍组阁，江庸才再度出山，任司法部总长。不久，江庸又因拒绝在赦免复辟要犯张镇芳的文件上副署而愤然辞职，得到了舆论的褒扬。此后，江庸又充任日本留学生总监督、法律编查馆总裁兼故宫博物院古物馆馆长以及东方文化事业总委员会委员等职。

After the founding of the Republic of China, Jiang Yong remained as the Judge of Daliyuan, and in September of that year, Jane became the Director of the High Adjudicative Office. The following year, Xiong Xiling formed a Cabinet, Jiang Yong served as Under-Secretary of Justice and Liang Qichao served as Chief. In view of Yuan Shikai's attempt to claim the title of emperor, Jiang Yong had many comments and resigned in the winter of 1915. Until 1917, when Wang Shizhen formed a cabinet, Jiang Yongcai regained his position as the Head of the Ministry of Justice. Soon, Jiang Yong refused to endorse the document on pardoning Zhang Zhenfang, who was a important offender in the restoration, and he resigned angrily. He was praised by public opinion. Since then, Jiang Yong has served as the General Supervisor of Japanese students, the President of the Law Compilation Museum, the Curator of the Antiquities Museum of the Palace Museum, and a Member of the General Committee of Oriental Culture.

1923年10月贿选总统曹锟上台后，江庸辞去所任职务，在京津两地设立律师事务所，开展律师业务。他在天津的律师事务所位于英租界敦桥道（今西安道）福顺里10号。此外，江庸还创办了周刊《法律评论》，自任社长及尚志学会会长。《法律评论》以司法改良为主要议题，同时也涉及律师问题，曾刊登司法部关于律师的各项法令及相关解释，并在"法界消息"栏目中，集中介绍各地律师公会的近期活动。从1927年10月9日第223期开始，《法律评论》增设了

"律师界消息"一栏，专门报道律师新闻，从而正式将律师作为一个群体介绍给公众，意义十分重大。

After Cao Kun took office in October 1923, Jiang Yong resigned and set up law firms in Beijing and Tianjin to carry out lawyer business. His law firm in Tianjin was located at No.10 Fushun Lane, Tunbridge Road (now Xi'an Road), British Concession. In addition, Jiang Yong founded *Law Review*, a weekly magazine, and became the president of Shangzhi Society. The *Law Review* focused on judicial improvement, and also involved lawyers. It had published various decrees and related explanations of lawyers of the Ministry of Justice, and concentrated on the recent activities of local bar associations in the column of "Legal News". Starting from the 223rd issue on October 9, 1927, the *Law Review* added a column of "News of Lawyers" to report the news of lawyers, thus formally introducing lawyers as a group to the public, which is of great significance.

1924年，江庸到广州士敏土厂晋谒孙中山，北返后任国立法政大学校长，三年后出任朝阳大学校长。私立朝阳大学始建于1912年，由江庸与汪有龄、黄群、蹇念益等人凭借"为天地立心，为生民立命"的情怀，集资创办而成。经过多年的努力，最终形成了"北朝阳，南东吴""无朝（阳）不成（法）院，无朝不开庭"的格局。江庸为中国司法人才的培养作出了巨大的贡献。

In 1924, Jiang Yong went to Guangzhou Shimin Soil Factory to visit Sun Yat-sen. After returning to the north, he became the president of National University of Law and Politics, and three years later he became the president of Chaoyang University. Private Chaoyang University, founded in 1912, was founded by raising funds by Jiang Yong, Wang Youling, Huang Qun, Jian Nianyi and others with the feelings of "building a heart for the world and living for the people". After years of hard work, the pattern of "North Chaoyang, South Dongwu", "No court can not be established without Chaoyang, and no court session can be held without Chaoyang" had finally formed. Jiang Yong had made great contributions to the cultivation of judicial talents in China.

"七君子"和他们的辩护律师,前排居中者为江庸
"Seven Gentlemen" and their defense lawyers, front row center for Jiang Yong

九一八事变以后，江庸撰文谴责日本的侵略行径，并指名斥责其学生赵欣伯出任伪职，投敌卖国，同时声明脱离师生关系。1932年，北平大学教授侯外庐因在课堂上宣传与三民主义不相容之主义（即马克思主义），而与许德珩、马哲民等人以"危害民国"罪被捕，时称"许侯马事件"。江庸受聘出任辩护律师，帮助侯外庐等人于第二年获假释出狱。1936年，江庸出任南京国民政府法制委员会委员，并代表中国律师协会出席在奥地利维也纳召开的国际律师协会世界会议。回国后，举家迁往上海。

After the September 18th Incident, Jiang Yong wrote an article condemning Japan's aggression, and reprimand Zhao Xinbo, his student, as a false post, for taking refuge in the enemy and betraying the country, and declared his separation from the teacher-student relationship. In 1932, Hou Wailu, a professor of Beiping University, was arrested with Xu Deheng, Ma Zhemin and others for "endangering the Republic of China" because he publicized the doctrine(Marxism) incompatible

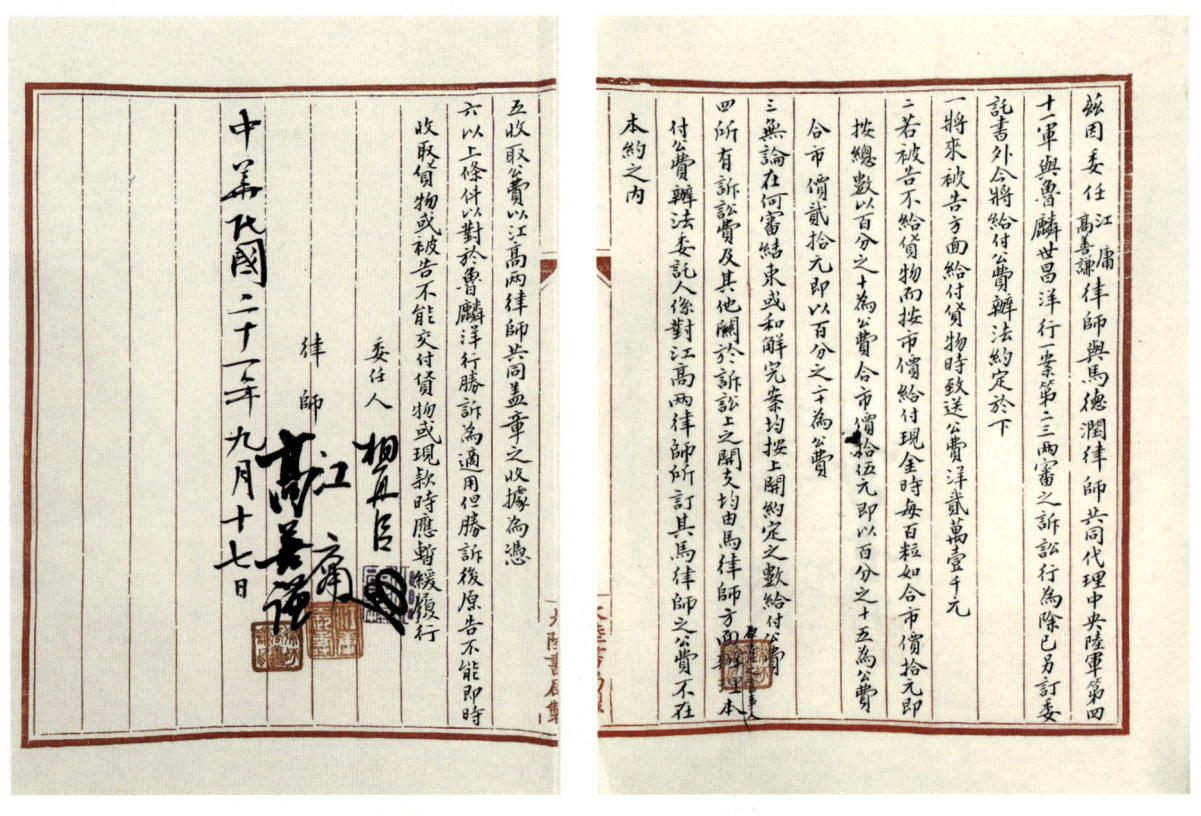

江庸律师受委任事

Appointment of lawyer Jiang Yong

with the Three People's Principles in class, which was called "Xuhouma Incident". Jiang Yong was employed as the defense lawyer, helping Hou Wailu and others to be released on parole in the following year. In 1936, Jiang Yong became a member of the Legal Committee of Nanjing National Povernment, and represented the Chinese Lawyers Association at the International Lawyers Association World Conference held in Vienna, Austria. After returning home, his family moved to Shanghai.

上海沦陷后，江庸拒绝了汉奸温宗尧及日寇畑俊六等人的诱降，并赴重庆从事律师业务。抗战胜利后，江庸回到上海，此后多次拒绝出任国民政府的各类职务。1949年1月，应代总统李宗仁之邀，江庸与颜惠庆、章士钊、邵力子赴北平试探求和，在河北省得到了毛泽东主席的接见。同年秋，毛主席亲笔致函江庸，邀他来北平参加中国人民政治协商会议第一届全体会议。江庸作为特邀代表，被选为全国委员。

After the fall of Shanghai, Jiang Yong refused the lure of Wen Zongyao, the traitor, and Shunroku Hata, the Japanese aggressors, and went to Chongqing to engage in lawyer business. After the victory of Anti-Japanese War, Jiang Yong returned to Shanghai, and then refused to take up various positions in the National Government many times. In January 1949, at the invitation of Acting President Li Zongren, Jiang Yong, Yan Huiqing, Zhang Shizhao and Shao Lizi went to Beiping to try to make peace, and were received by Chairman Mao Zedong in Hebei Province. In the autumn of the same year, Chairman Mao personally sent a letter to Jiang Yong inviting him to Beiping to attend the first plenary session of the Chinese People's Political Consultative Conference. Jiang Yong, as a special representative, was elected as a National Committee Member.

新中国成立后，江庸出任政务院政治法律委员会委员，上海文史馆副馆长、馆长，先后当选第一、第二届全国人民代表大会代表，政协第二届全国委员，上海市各界人民代表会议代表、市政协委员，华东军政委员会人民监察委员会委员。1960年2月9日，因病在上海去世。

After the founding of the People's Republic of China, Jiang Yong became a member of the Political and Legal Committee of the State Council, deputy director and curator of the Shanghai Museum of Literature and History, and was successively elected as a representative of the first and second National People's Congress, the member of second National Committee of the CPPCC, the representative of the Shanghai People's Congress, a member of the Shanghai Political Consultative Conference, and a member of the People's Supervision Committee of the East China Military and Political Commission. On February 9, 1960, he died of illness in Shanghai.

贾文范（1880—1924），字子式，直隶南乐县近德固村（今属河南省濮阳市）人，早年毕业于直隶高等学堂。宣统元年（1909）四月，奉上谕奖给文科举人并补任中书科中书。宣统三年（1911），内阁裁撤，改任农工商部七品京官，八月升任五品主事。民国元年，政府各部改组，贾文范进入国立北洋大学学习，后于1913年12月从北洋大学法科法律学门乙班毕业，被授予法学士学位。1914年11月，任直隶法政专门学校教务主任兼教员，曾编纂《行政法》《法院编制法》等课程讲义。后出于保障人权、巩固法治的目的，贾文范开始执行律师职务，并任天津律师公会会长、直隶省议会议员兼省长公署咨议、直隶省教育会会长等职，多有建树。贾文范治家勤俭，教子有方。长子士钊毕业于法政专门学校，后任陕西警务处视察员、南乐县议会议员；次子士谔毕业于国立北洋大学，候补县长；长女幼英毕业于女子师范大学；次女幼华肄业于河北女子师范学院。

Jia Wenfan (1880—1924),named Zishi, born in Jindegu Village, Nanle County, Zhili Province (now Puyang City, Henan Province), graduated from Zhili Higher School in his early years. In April 1909, he was awarded to the liberal arts Juren by the Imperial edict and supplemented the Zhongshu of Zhongshu Department. In 1911, the cabinet was abolished, and he was appointed as the official of Qipin in the Ministry of Agriculture, Industry and Commerce, and was promoted to master of Wupin in August. In the first year of the Republic of China, various government departments were reorganized, and Jia Wenfan entered the National Beiyang University to study. In December 1913, he graduated from Class B of the Law department of Beiyang University and was awarded a bachelor of law degree. In November, 1914, he served as the academic director and teacher of Zhili Law and Politics College, and compiled the lecture notes of *Administrative Law*, *Court Preparation Law* and other courses. After that, for the purpose of protecting human rights and consolidating the rule of law, Jia Wenfan began to perform his duties as a lawyer, and served as the chairman of Tianjin Bar Association, a member of Zhili Provincial Council and Consultation of the Provincial Governor's Office, the president of Zhili Provincial Education Association. Jia Wenfan was diligent in managing his family and he taught his children well. The eldest son, Shizhao, graduated from the School of Law and Politics, and later served as an inspector of Shanxi Police Force and a member of Nanle County Council; Shie, the second son graduated from the National Beiyang University and was an alternate county magistrate; Youying, the eldest daughter, graduated from Women's Normal University. The second daughter Youhua studied in Hebei Women's Teachers College.

贾文范是中国最早翻译并研究罗马法的学者。罗马法是人类法治史上的丰碑，许多法律制度、原则和精神都源自罗马法；它对包括中国在内的所有国家都产生了深远的影响。提起中国最初的罗马法研究，人们首先想到的是周枏和陈朝璧，前者被誉为"罗马法的活字典"，晚年著成《罗马法原论》，后者于1937年出版《罗马法原理》，是中国罗马法研究的不朽之作。不过，早在1913年，贾文范就翻译并研究了罗马法，成为中国罗马法研究的鼻祖。

Jia Wenfan is the earliest scholar who translated and studied Roman law in China. Roman law is a monument in the history of human rule of law, and many legal systems, principles and spirits are derived from Roman law. It has had a profound impact on all countries including China. When people mention the initial study of Roman law in China, they first think of Zhou Nan and Chen Chaobi. The former is known as the "living dictionary of Roman law", and in his later years he wrote *The Original Theory of Roman Law*, while the latter published *Principles of Roman Law* in 1937, which is an immortal work of Chinese Roman law research. However, as early as 1913, Jia Wenfan translated and studied Roman law, and was the originator of Chinese Roman law research.

贾文范的《罗马法》不仅是一部翻译著作，而且有许多创见。它首先明确了罗马法兼具私法与公法的双重属性，其次将遗产信托理解为信托，指出了罗马法对信托制度的贡献，最后将作为主体资格的人格与作为具体权利的人格权区分开来，高度关注人格权制度的研究，而这些

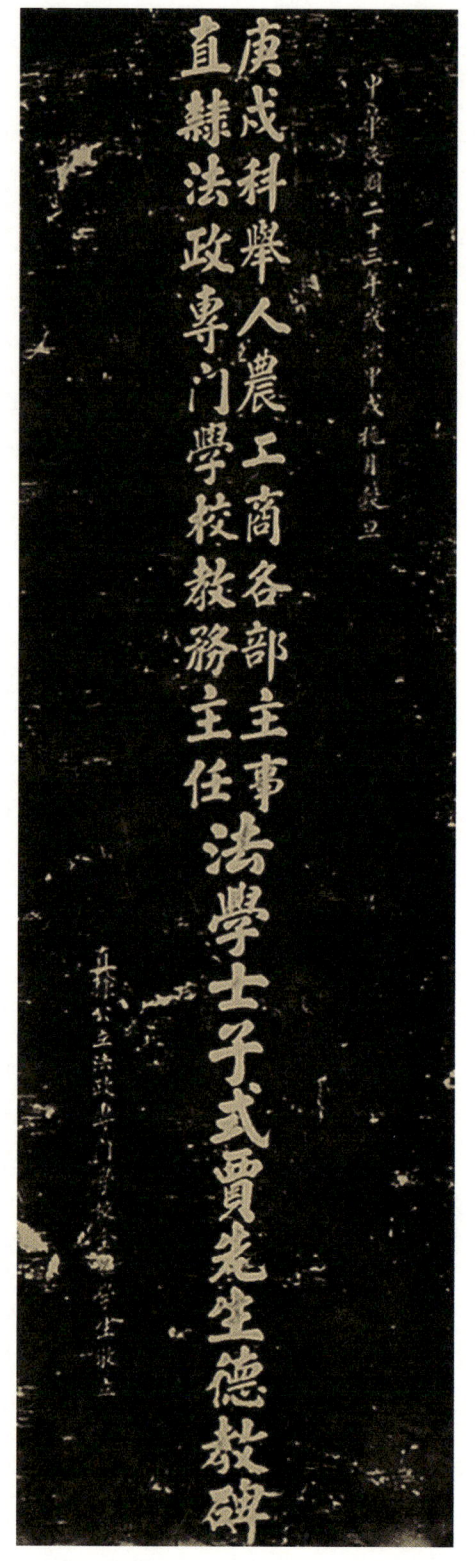

贾文范德教碑

Morality Monument of Jia Wenfan

成果对于当代学界仍具有重要的意义。贾文范的《罗马法》问世之后引起了众多学者的关注，黄右昌1915年出版的《罗马法与现代》以及1931年陈允、应时所著的《罗马法》都在很大程度上参考了贾文范的译著。

Roman Law by Jia Wenfan is not only a translated work, but also has many original ideas. It first clarifies that Roman law has dual attributes of private law and public law, then understands heritage trust as trust, and points out the contribution of Roman law to trust system. Finally, it distinguishes personality as subject qualification from personality right as specific right, and pays great attention to the research of personality right system, which is still of great significance to contemporary academic circles. After Jia Wenfan's *Roman Law* came out, it attracted the attention of many scholars. The *Roman Law and Modernity* published by Huang Youchang in 1915 and the *Roman Law* written by Chen Yun and Ying Shi in 1931 referred to Jia Wenfan's translation to a great extent.

2012年，贾文范的后人在天津大学发起设立了贾文范法学教育公益基金，旨在资助天津大学在法学研究方面有成果的师生。

In 2012, Jia Wenfan's descendants initiated the establishment of Jia Wenfan's Legal Education Public Welfare Fund in Tianjin University, aiming to support the teachers and students who have made research achievements in law in Tianjin University.

林行规（1882—1944），字斐成，浙江鄞县（今属宁波市鄞州区）人。自幼聪颖好学，光绪二十二年（1896）就读于上海南洋公学（今上海交通大学的前身），毕业后入京师译学馆（隶属于北京大学的前身京师大学堂）学习。光绪三十年（1904）公费赴伦敦大学政治经济学院学习，后获博士学位及英国大律师执照，服务于林肯思皇家律师所。

Lin Xinggui (1882-1944), named Feicheng, born in Yinxian County, Zhejiang Province (now Yinzhou District, Ningbo City). Since childhood, he was intelligent and studious. In 1896, he studied at Nanyang Public College in Shanghai (the predecessor of Shanghai Jiao Tong University), and after graduation, he studied at the Translation Institute of Jingshi University (the predecessor of Peking University). In 1904, he went to the academy of political and economy of London University to study at public expense, and later obtained his doctorate and English barrister's license, and served in Lincolns Royal Law Firm.

1912年回国后，林行规担任南京临时政府总统府法律顾问，在"民国第一案"姚荣泽案中任原告律师。北洋政府时期，先后任大理院推事、司法部民事司司长、法院编查会编查员、司法部部长、调查治外法权委员会专门委员等职务。1914年1月至1916年2月，担任北京大学法科学长。

After returning to China in 1912, Lin Xinggui served as legal adviser to the

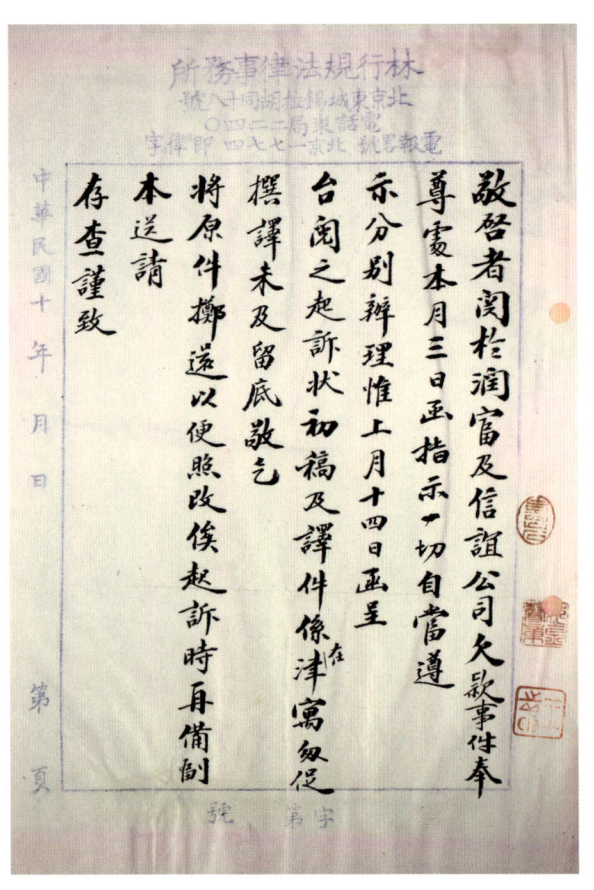 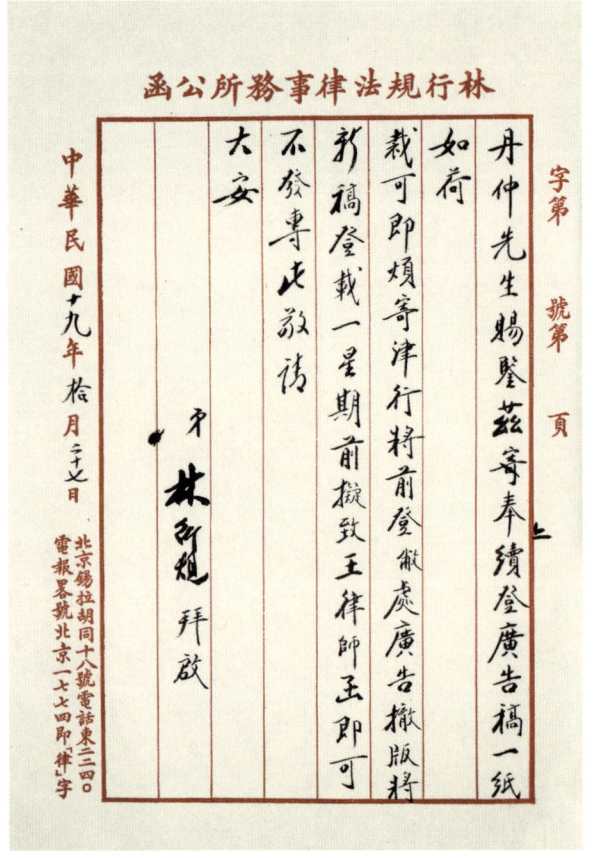

林行规律师函
Lawyer's letter of Lin Xinggui

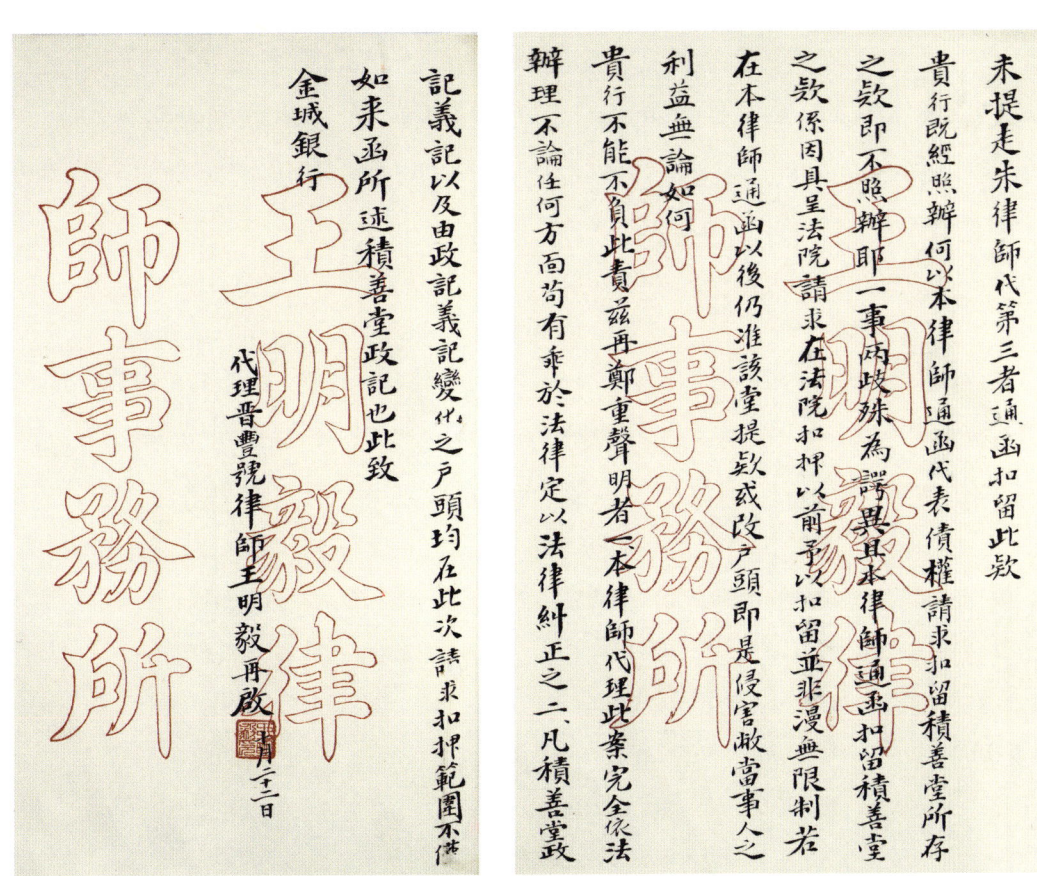

王明毅律师函

Lawyer's letter of Wang Mingyi

Presidential Palace of Nanjing Provisional Government, and served as plaintiff's lawyer in Yao Rongze case, "the first case of the Republic of China". During the period of Beiyang Government, he successively served as the Judge of Daliyuan, the Director of Civil Affairs Department of the Ministry of Justice, the Editor of the Court Compilation Committee, the Minister of Justice, and the special member of the Committee for Investigating Extraterritorial Jurisdiction. From January, 1914 to February, 1916, he served as a senior in the law department of Peking University.

此后，林行规因不满当政者以权凌法而愤然辞职，在天津律师公会登录，于京津间以律师为业，事务所设在天津法租界大法国路新华大楼（今解放北路与滨江道交会处西侧）305和306室，后来成为全国著名的商务涉外律师，并担任北平律师公会会长。20世纪30年代，曾在好友胡适的邀约下，作为何瑞琼女士的律师代理其与北京大学教授梁宗岱的离婚案。林行规以保障民权为己任，常常为穷苦人无偿提供法律援助，深受民众的好评与尊重。应社会各界的邀请，林行规曾出任铁路局、开滦矿务局及多家银行、公司的法律顾问。七七事变后，林行规闭门谢客。1944年6月，因病在北平逝世。

After that, Lin Xinggui resigned angrily because he was dissatisfied with the ruling authority overpowering the law. He registered in Tianjin Bar Association and worked as a lawyer between Beijing and Tianjin. His firm was located in Room 305 and Room 306 of Xinhua Building, France Road, Tianjin French Concession (now on the west side of the intersection of Jiefang North Road and Binjiang Road). Later, he became a famous foreign-related lawyer in China and served as the president of Beiping Bar Association. In 1930s, with the invitation of his friend Hu Shi, he acted as the attorney of Ms. He Ruiqiong in Ms. He Ruiqiong's divorce case with Peking University professor Liang Zongdai. Lin Xinggui took the protection of civil rights as his duty, and often provided free legal aid to the poor, which was highly praised and respected by the people. At the invitation of different sectors of society, Lin Xinggui had served as legal adviser to the Railway Bureau, Kailuan Mining Bureau and many banks and companies. After the July 7 Incident of 1937, Lin Xinggui stopped receiving guests. In June 1944, he died of illness in Beiping.

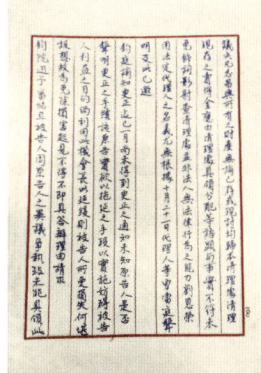
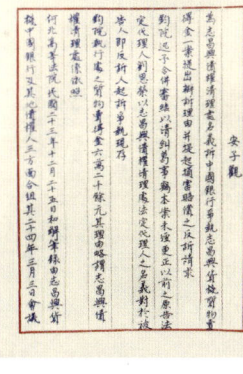
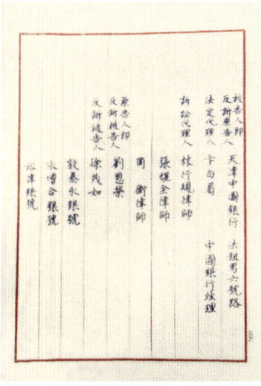

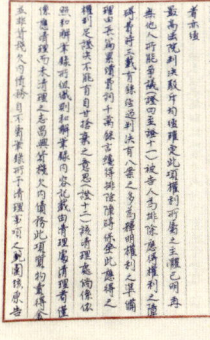
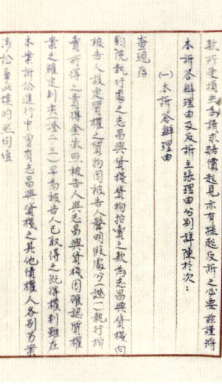
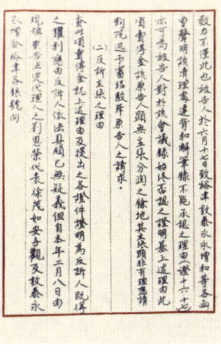

1935年林行规、张煜全、周衡律师书写的诉状

Complaint written by lawyers Lin Xinggui, Zhang Yuquan and Zhou Heng in 1935

孙启濂（1890—1967），字吉臣，湖北汉阳（今属武汉市）人，武昌文华大学肄业，上海圣约翰大学毕业。光绪三十三年（1907）赴美国拉克斯大学留学，毕业后获法学硕士学位。1913年回国后，在北京《东方汉英报》任采访兼校对。1916年任北京《极东新闻》主笔。一年后，受黎元洪约请，任总统府翻译、英文秘书。黎元洪下台后，孙启濂与其同往天津，任其私人秘书兼法律顾问前后十余年，同时兼任南开大学国际法教授。孙启濂在天津长期执业律师，事务所位于其英租界围墙道（今南京路）的住宅中，并与美国律师福克斯在基泰大楼里合办华洋事务所，承办中外诉讼案件。孙启濂曾担任英租界工部局、汇丰银行、太古洋行、花旗银行、天津银钱业商业公会的法律顾问。1929年，孙启濂主动代理天津东郊万辛庄农民控诉德士古石油公司强占耕地一案，并最终胜诉，受到民众的好评。

Sun Qilian (1890-1967), named Jichen, born in Hanyang(now Wuhan), Hubei Province, studied in Wenhua University in Wuchang and graduated from St. John's University in Shanghai. In 1907, he went to Lux University to study abroad, and obtained a master's degree in law after graduation. After returning to China in 1913, he worked as an interview and proofreader for *Oriental Chinese-English*

孙启濂律师
Lawyer Sun Qilian

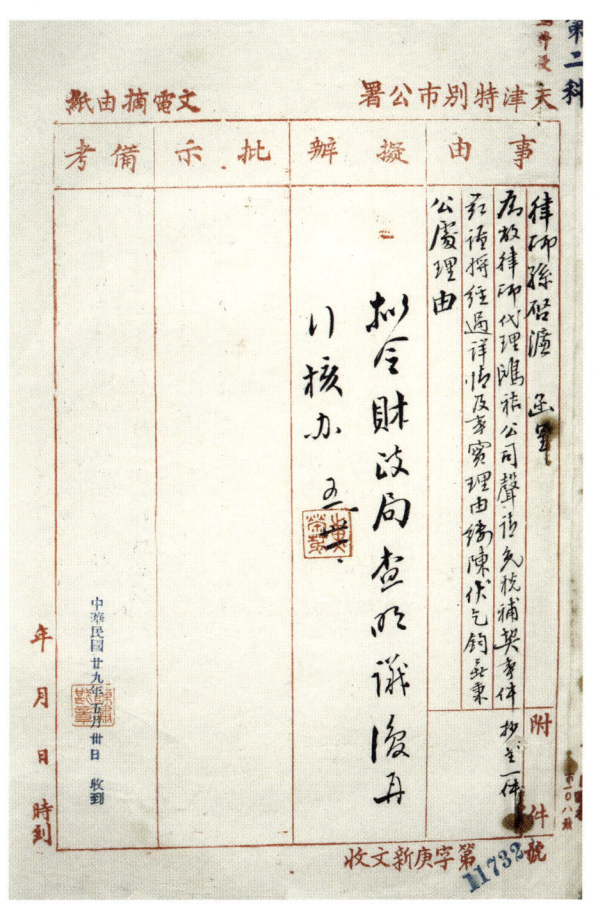 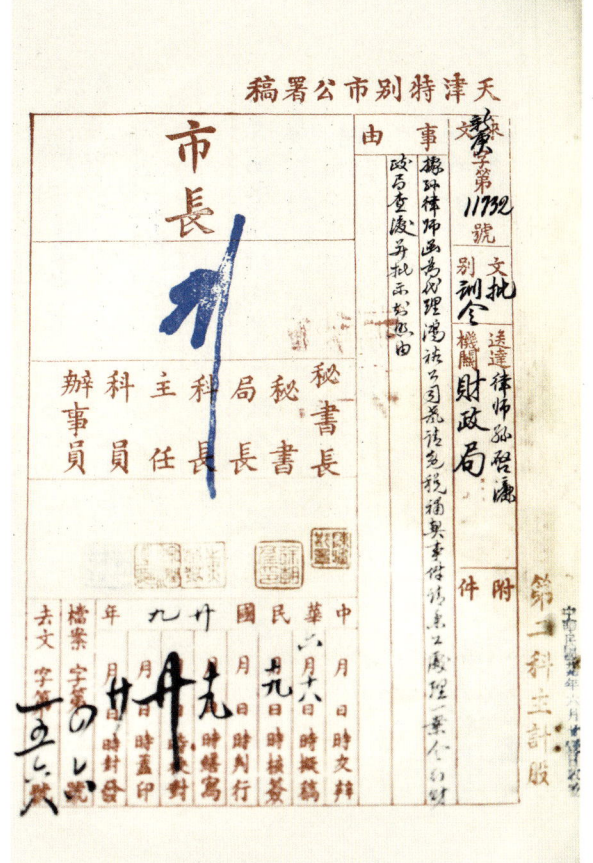

孙启濂律师代理鸿裕公司免税补契事电文
Text of lawyer Sun Qilian for representing Hongyu Company's tax-free supplementary contract

Newspaper in Beijing. In 1916, he was the chief editor of *Jidong News* in Beijing. A year later, at the invitation of Li Yuanhong, he served as translator and English secretary of the presidential palace. After Li Yuanhong stepped down, Sun Qilian went to Tianjin with him and served as his private secretary and legal adviser for more than ten years. He also served as a professor of international law at Nankai University. Sun Qilian had been a lawyer for a long time in Tianjin. His office was located in his residence in the Elgin Avenue of the British Concession (now Nanjing Road). He co-organized Huayang Office with Fox, an American lawyer, in the Jitai Building to undertake Chinese and foreign litigation cases. Sun Qilian once served as legal adviser to the British Concession Bureau, HSBC, Swire International,

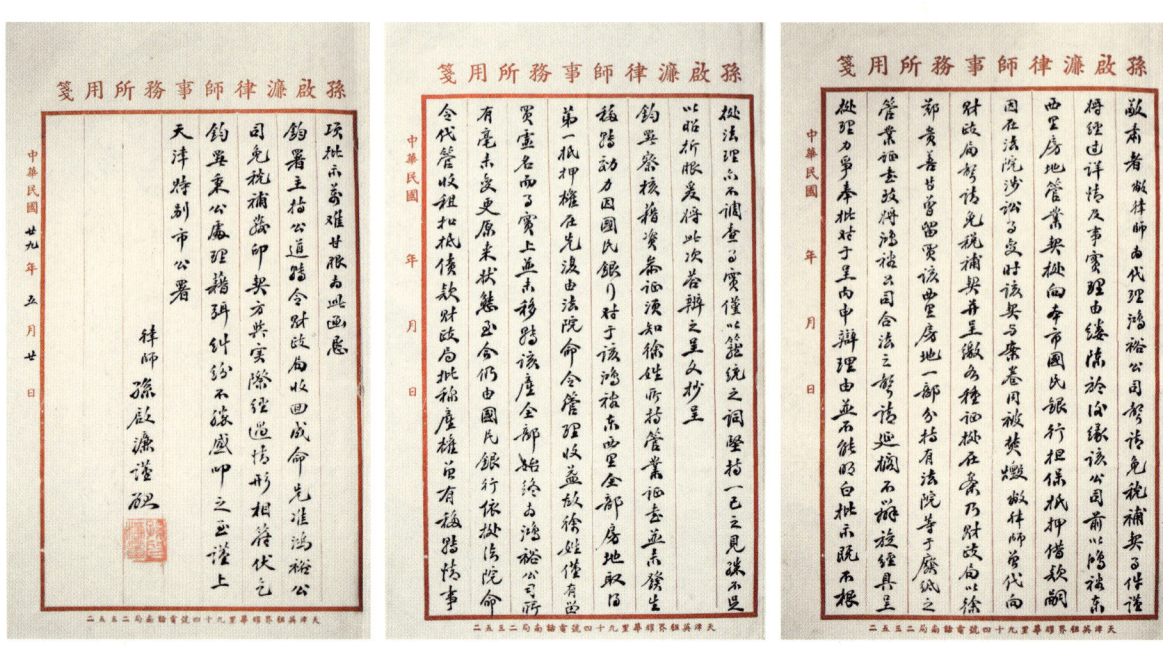

孙启濂律师代理鸿裕公司免税补契事律师函
Lawyer's letter of lawyer Sun Qilian for representing Hongyu Company's tax-free supplementary contract

Citibank, and Tianjin Banking and Money Business Association. In 1929, Sun Qilian took the initiative to represent farmers in Wanxinzhuang, the eastern suburb of Tianjin, to sue Texaco Oil Company for seizing cultivated land, and finally won the case, which was well received by the people.

朱道孔（1892—1969），名锡纯，号仰素，以字行，直隶大兴（今北京大兴区）人。后随父赴津开办工厂，因工厂难以为继，故考学而成为律师。朱道孔法律事务所于1914年2月在天津地方审判厅登记注册，主要承接民事、刑事诉讼案件，办公地点位于河北宙纬路27号。朱道孔曾担任天津律师公会副会长，并兼任曹锟宠姜陈寒蕊的法律顾问。1931年，罗隆基到天津《益世报》作主笔，朱道孔受邀为《益世报》副刊撰稿，并作为"法律问答组"成员为社会提供咨询服务。罗隆基很欣赏朱道孔的才干，两人交往甚密。

Zhu Daokong (1892-1969),named Xichun, was also known as Yangsu, yizixing, born in Daxing, Zhili (now Daxing District, Beijing). After that, he went to Tianjin to set up a factory with his father, and because the factory was unsustainable, he took an examination and became a lawyer. Zhu Daokong Law Firm was registered in Tianjin Local Adjudicative Office in February 1914, mainly undertook civil and criminal litigation cases, and its office is located at No.27 Zhouwei Road, Hebei. Zhu Daokong once served as the vice chairman of Tianjin Bar Association, and also served as the legal adviser of Chen Hanrui, Cao Kun's favorite concubine. In 1931, Luo Longji went to Tianjin *Yishi Daily* as the main writer, and Zhu Daokong was invited to write for the supplement of *Yishi Daily*, and as a member of the "Legal Question and Answer Group", he provided consulting services for the society. Luo Longji appreciates Zhu Daokong's talents, and they have close contacts.

1937年7月天津沦陷后,《益世报》停刊，朱道孔也停止了律师事务，转而在天津律师公会内部组织"黑律师调查组"，揭露黑律师的行径，并于1964年撰成《解放前黑律师的形形色色》一文。抗战胜利后，朱道孔恢复了律师事务所的业务，并继续在复刊的《益世报》做法律顾问。1947年3月，朱道孔还在北平地方法院重新进行了登记注册。

朱道孔律师

Lawyer Zhu Daokong

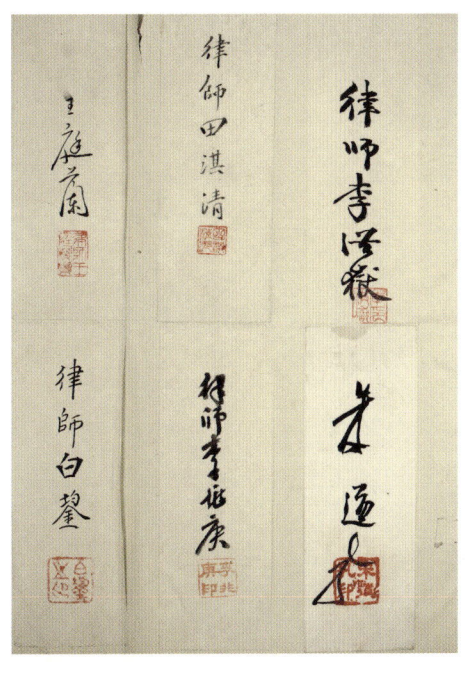

朱道孔律师的签名及印章

Signature and seal of lawyer Zhu Daokong

After the fall of Tianjin in July 1937, *Yishi Daily* was discontinued, and Zhu Daokong also stopped his lawyer affairs. Instead, he organized a "black lawyer investigation team" within Tianjin Bar Association to expose the behavior of black lawyers, and in 1964 he wrote the article *All Kinds of Black Lawyers before Liberation*. After the victory of Anti-Japanese War, Zhu Daokong resumed his business as a law firm and continued to work as a legal consultant in the reissue of *Yishi Daily*. In March 1947, Zhu Daokong re-registered in Beiping District Court.

1949年3月《益世报》停办，朱道孔也终止了律师业务。后经人民政府介绍，到河北省立宁河中学（今天津市宁河区芦台一中）任教，并于1957年4月当选宁河县第一届政协副主席。1958年春，朱道孔因曾应邀赴京与罗隆基叙旧而被错划为右派，"文革"时受到冲击，于1969年不幸去世。1979年被彻底平反。

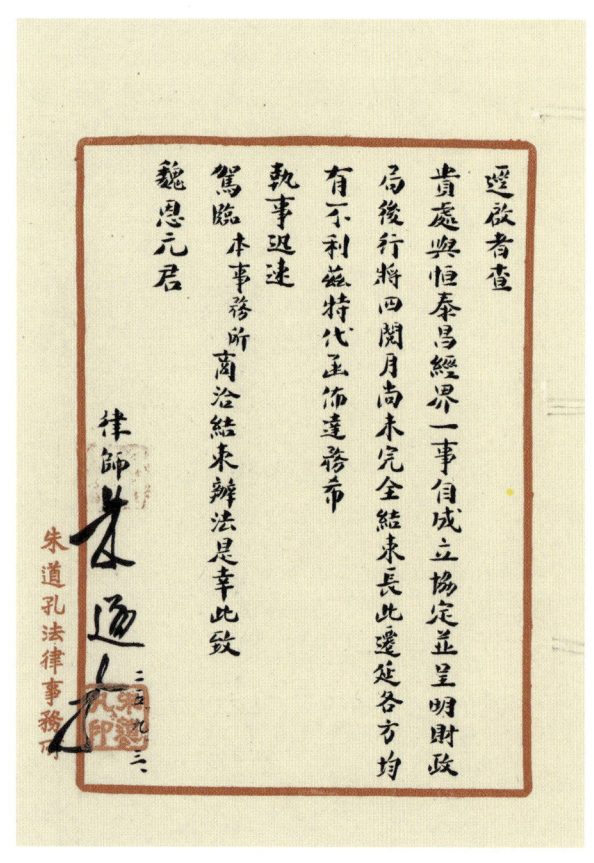

朱道孔律师函
Lawyer's letter of Zhu Daokong

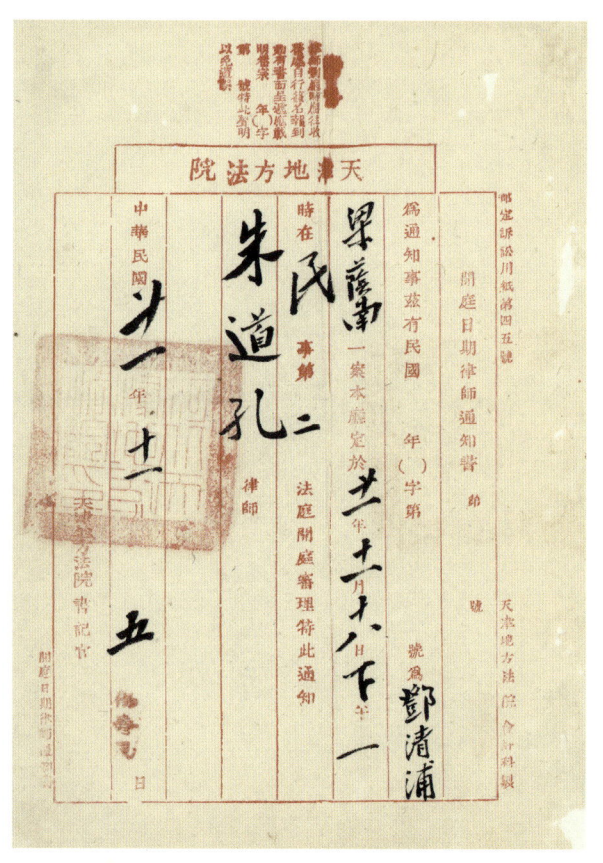

天津地方法院致朱道孔律师开庭通知
Notice of Tianjin District Court to lawyer Zhu Daokong

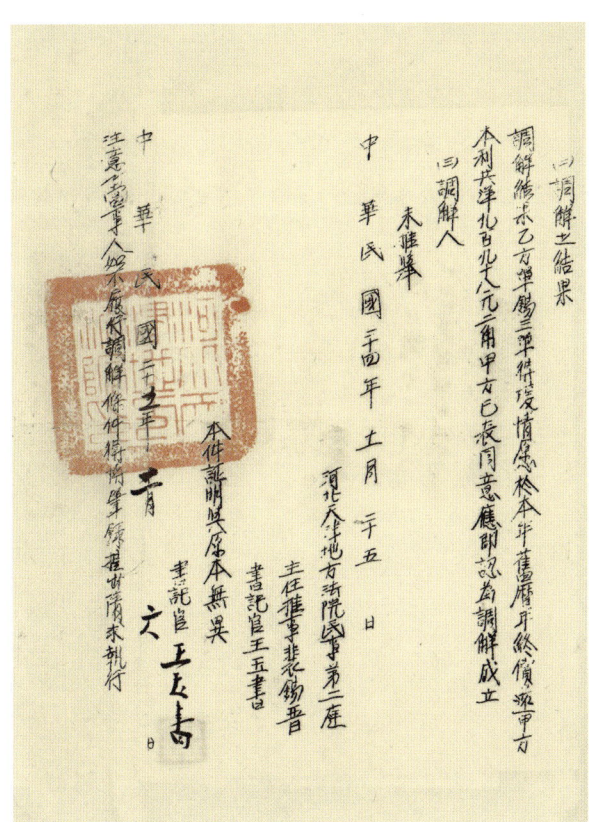
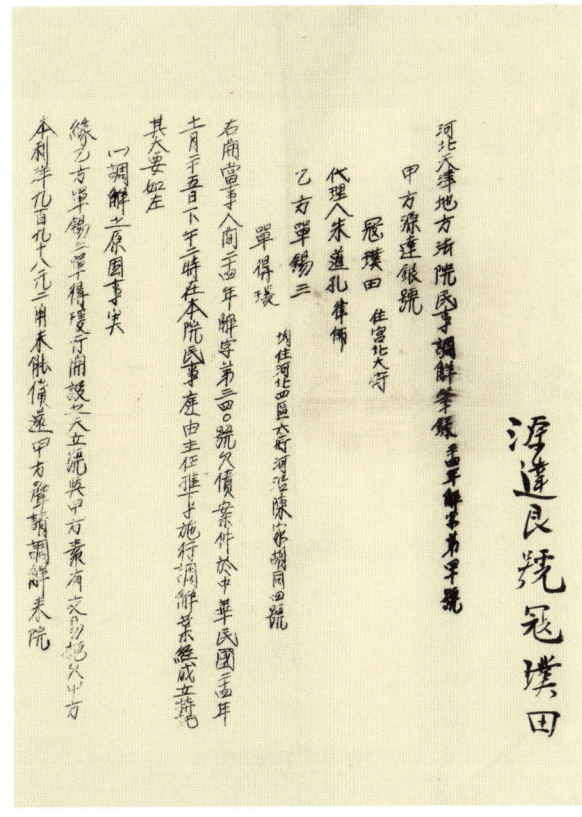

河北天津地方法院民事调解笔录
Record of civil mediation in Tianjin District Court, Hebei Province

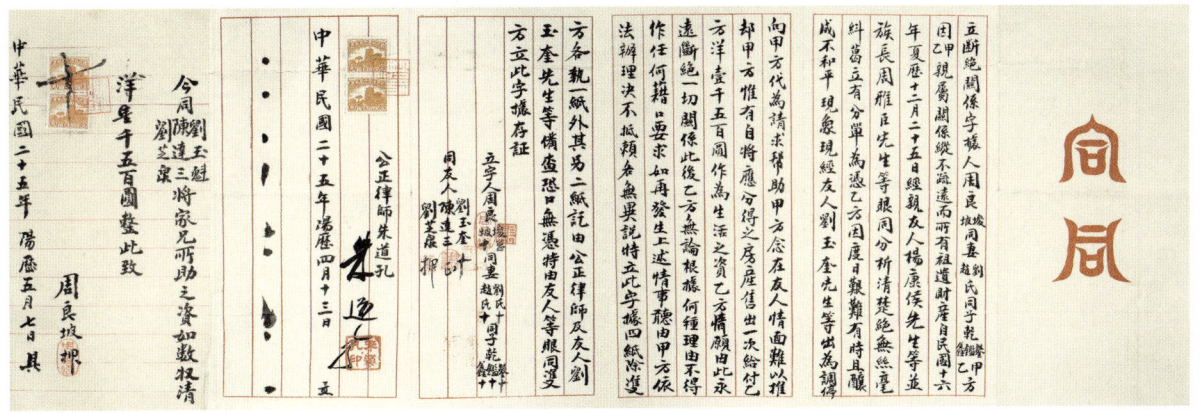

朱道孔律师主持断绝关系字据公证
Lawyer Zhu Daokong presided over the notarization of severance documents

In March 1949, *Yishi Daily* was closed, and Zhu Daokong also terminated his lawyer business. After being introduced by the People Government, he taught at Ninghe Middle School in Hebei Province (now Lutai No.1 Middle School in Ninghe District, Tianjin) and was elected as the vice chairman of the First CPPCC in Ninghe County in April 1957. In the spring of 1958, Zhu Daokong was wrongly classified as a rightist because he was invited to Beijing to catch up with Luo Longji. He was hit by the "Cultural Revolution" and died in 1969. He was completely rehabilitated in 1979.

五、在天津执业的女律师
5. Female Lawyers Practicing in Tianjin

1912年9月16日颁布的《律师暂行章程》第二条规定："充律师者……中华民国人民满二十岁以上之男子。"这就意味着立法所确认的律师从业身份仅仅是赋予男性的权利，女性则被排除在律师这一新兴法律服务行业之外。

Article 2 of the *Provisional Regulation of Lawyers* promulgated on September 16, 1912 stipulates, "A lawyer...a man of the Republic of China who has reached the age of 20." This means that the lawyer's professional status confirmed by the legislation was only conferred for the rights of men, women were excluded from the emerging legal service industry of lawyers.

1926年，第一位华人女律师在上海执业，她便是民国传奇女子郑毓秀。这一年，获得法国巴黎大学博士学位的郑毓秀回到祖国，并在上海法租界开办了魏郑联合律师事务所，以规避女性不能在中国法庭担任律师的规定。一年间，她曾在北伐军逼近上海时，将20多名被捕的国民党人引渡到法租界，也曾担任民主人士杨杏佛的辩护律师，令其成功脱险，又曾作为孟小冬的代理人，助其打赢了与梅兰芳的离婚案。郑毓秀和她的魏郑联合律师事务所由此声名大振。

In 1926, the first Chinese female lawyer to practice in Shanghai was the legendary woman Zheng Yuxiu of the Republic of China. This year, Zheng Yuxiu, who received a doctorate from the University of Paris in France, returned to her motherland and opened the Weizheng United Law Firm in the French Concession of Shanghai to circumvent the rule that women cannot be lawyers in Chinese courts. In one year, as the Northern Expedition Army approached Shanghai, she extradited more than 20 arrested Kuomintang members to the French Concession. She also served as a defense lawyer for the democrat Yang Xingfo, helped her escape danger successfully. She also served as Meng Xiaodong's agent, helped her win the divorce case with Mei Lanfang. Zheng Yuxiu and her Weizheng United Law Firm became famous.

郑毓秀于1927年出任上海审判厅厅长，从此离开律师行业。令人欣慰的是，就在这一年的7月，南京国民政府颁布了《律师章程》，规定"中华民国人民满二十一岁以上者"均可充任律师，从此废除了女性从事律师职业的限制，女律师正式登上了历史舞台。不过，就整个民国时期而言，郑毓秀这样的情况还是比较特殊的，虽然学习法律的女性不在少数，但女律师真可谓凤毛麟角。

Zheng Yuxiu became Director of the Shanghai Adjudicative Office in 1927 and left the lawyer profession. What was gratifying is that in July of this year, Nanjing National Government promulgated the *Regulation of Lawyers*, stipulating that "people of the Republic of China who are over 21 years old" can serve as lawyers, and since then abolished the restrictions on women's practice as lawyers, female lawyers officially stepped onto the stage of history. However, as far as the Republic of China was concerned, Zheng Yuxiu's situation was quite special. Although there were not a few women studying law, female lawyerswere really rare.

天津的律师群体同样以男性为主，直到20世纪三四十年代，才个别出现了活跃在天津律师界的女律师，其中比较著名的有吴缣、马荃、纪清漪、王秀洁、陈以庄和董端懿六人。

Tianjin's lawyers were also dominated by men. It was not until the 1930s and 1940s that there were individual female lawyers active in the Tianjin lawyers' circle. The more famous ones were Wu Jian, Ma Quan, Ji Qingyi, Wang Xiujie, Chen Yizhuang, and Dong Duanyi.

吴缣毕业于北平私立朝阳学院法科法律系，1937年7月3日加入天津律师公会，是较早在天津执业的女律师，事务所位于意租界西马路（今民族路）3号。吴缣生于1911年，祖籍江苏吴县（今苏州市），乃父吴鹏毕业于京师大学堂土木工学门，曾任国民政府铁道部技正（总工程师）。吴缣读中学时，曾任北平第一女子中学学生自治会主席。20世纪40年代初离开天津，赶赴革命圣地延安，并于1941年在陕甘宁边区政府秘书处工作。其妹吴绮曾参加抗日战争、解放战争，新中国成立后担任《中国妇女》杂志社社长、联合国妇女地位委员会第一任中国代表等职。

Wu Jian graduated from the Faculty of Law of Beiping Private Chaoyang College. She joined the Tianjin Bar Association on July 3, 1937. She was an earlier female lawyer practicing in Tianjin. The firm was located at No. 3, West Road (now Minzu Road) in the Italian Concession. Wu Jian was born in 1911, and her ancestral home is Wu County(now Suzhou City), Jiangsu. His father Wu Peng graduated from the Civil Engineering Department of Jingshi University. He was a technician (chief engineer) of the Ministry of Railways of the National Government. When Wu Jian was in middle school, she was the chairman of the Student Self-Government Association of Beiping No.1 Girls' Middle School. In the early 1940s, she left Tianjin and rushed to Yan'an, the sacred place of revolution. In 1941, she worked in the Secretariat of the Shanxi-Gansu-Ningxia Border Region Government. Her sister Wu Qian participated in Anti-Japanese War and the War of Liberation. After the founding of the People's Republic of China, she served as the president of the *Chinese Women* magazine and the first Chinese representative of the UN Commission on the Status of Women.

马荃，直隶河间（今河北省河间市）人，1933年毕业于北平私立朝阳学院法科法律系，次年加入北平律师公会，并与同为朝阳学院毕业的女律师丁聪、李德义合伙开办联合律师事务所，为女同胞伸冤辩护。1936年南京国民政府选举国民大会代表期间，马荃以北平市妇女会会长的身份主持全国妇女国民大会代表竞选委员会北平市分会的工作，呼吁女律师作为身兼职业团体与妇女团体的一分子，应积极参加竞选。1937年，马荃当选北平律师公会评议员。1946年，北平律师公会改组，在重新登录的252名会员中，马荃不仅是唯一的女性，而且当选了公会监事。同年9月21日，马荃来到天津执业，并加入了天津律师公会，其事务所位于第十区营口道四宜里18号。同时，马荃还担任了天津《妇女之友》杂志的法律顾问和南开大学女生训导员。

Ma Quan, born in Hejian, Zhili (now Hejian City, Hebei Province), graduated from the Faculty of Law of Beiping Private Chaoyang College in 1933. She joined the Beiping Bar Association the following year and worked with female lawyers Ding Cong, Li Deyi who graduated from Chaoyang College opened a joint law firm in partnership to defend female compatriots. During the election of representatives to the National Assembly by the Nanjing National Government in 1936, Ma Quan presided over the work of the Beiping Branch of the National Women's National Assembly Representative Election Committee as the president of the Beiping Women's Association. She called on female lawyers should actively participate in the electionto as the part of both professional and women's groups. In 1937, Ma Quan was elected as a member of the Beiping Bar Association. In 1946, the Beiping Bar Association was reorganized. Among the 252 members who re-registered, Ma Quan was not only the only woman, but was also elected as a supervisor of the Association. On September 21 of the same

吴缣天津律师公会会员证书
Tianjin Bar Association membership certificate of Wu Jian

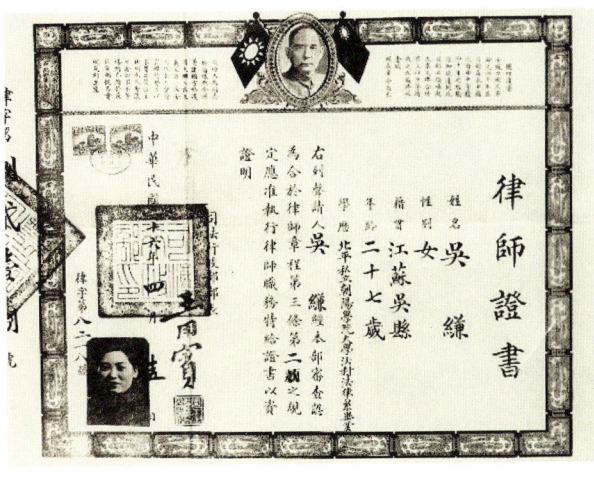

吴缣律师证书
Lawyer certificate of Wu Jian

year, Ma Quan came to Tianjin to practice and joined the Tianjin Bar Association. Her office was located at No.18 Siyi Lane, Yingkou Road, Tenth District. At the same time, Ma Quan also served as the legal counsel of Tianjin *Friends of Women* magazine and the female trainer of Nankai University.

1921	1922	1923	1924	1925	1926	1927	1928	1929	1930	1931	1932	1933
1947	1948	1949	1950	1951	1952	1953	1954	1955	1956	1957	1958	1959
1973	1974	1975	1976	1977	1978	1979	1980	1981	1982	1983	1984	1985
1999	2000	2001	2002	2003	2004	2005	2006	2007	2008	2009	2010	2011

活跃于20世纪三四十年代平津地区的纪清漪是一位爱国、勇敢、充满传奇色彩的女律师。纪清漪是清代著名学者纪昀的嫡系六世孙,出生于直隶献县(今河北省献县),在黑龙江绥化长大。她从小就耳闻目睹了日俄帝国主义对中国东北的侵略,并在心灵深处形成了强烈的爱国主义思想。

Ji Qingyi, who was active in the Pingjin area in the 1930s and 1940s, was a patriotic, brave and legendary female lawyer. Ji Qingyi was the sixth-generation grandson of Ji Yun, a famous scholar in the Qing Dynasty. She was born in Xian County, Zhili Province (now Xian County, Hebei Province), and grew up in Suihua, Heilongjiang. She had heard and witnessed the Japanese-Russian imperialist invasion of Northeast China since she was a child, and formed a strong patriotism in her heart.

1925年,纪清漪考入北京大学政治系,接触到很多进步老师与同学,同时她还参加了东北学生在齐齐哈尔组织的新东北学会。1928年暑假,纪清漪回到齐齐哈尔,参加了新东北学会发起的呼吁东北和平易帜的运动。

In 1925, Ji Qingyi was admitted to the Politics Department of Peking University and met many progressive teachers and classmates. At the same time, she also participated in the New Northeast Society organized by Northeast students in Qiqihar. In the summer of 1928, Ji Qingyi returned to Qiqihar to participate in a campaign initiated by the New Northeast Society to call for peace in the Northeast.

在校期间,纪清漪还负责新东北学会主办的《东北半月刊》的编辑工作。这本刊物是北平《华北日报》的副刊,旨在揭露日本帝国主义侵略东北的阴谋,同时抨击南京国民政府对日妥协的外交政策。1929年,在一个偶然的机会,纪清漪从总编安怀音处得到了臭名昭著的"田中奏章",随后果断地连夜抄写多份,并在和平门里新华印刷厂印了5000份,寄给全国各机关、团体、图书馆、学校,甚至大商店。同时,纪清漪还在扉页上写了这样几句话:"读者啊,如果你的心还在跳,如果你的血还在流,你就应该把这个小册子一字一句的读完。你就应该想一想:你作为一个中国人,你有什么责任!你应该做些什么事情!"纪清漪的行动使更多中国人认清了日本帝国主义的狼子野心。

While in school, Ji Qingyi was also responsible for the editing of the *Northeast Semi-Monthly* sponsored by the New Northeast Society. The publication was a supplement to the *North China Daily* in Beiping. It aimed to reveal the conspiracy of Japanese imperialists to invade the Northeast, and at the same time criticize the Nanjing National Government's compromised foreign policy towards Japan. In 1929, by chance, Ji Qingyi received the infamous "Tanaka Memorial" from the editor-in-chief An Huaiyin, and then decisively copied several copies overnight, and printed 5,000 copies at the Xinhua Printing Factory in Hepingmen and sent them to various institutions, organizations, libraries, schools, and even large stores across the country. At the same time, Ji Qingyi also wrote a few words on the title page, "Reader, if your heart is still beating, if your blood is still flowing, you should read this booklet word by word. You should think about it: as a Chinese, what are your responsibilities! What should you do!" Ji Qingyi's actions have made more Chinese people recognize the wolf ambition of Japanese imperialism.

1931年，纪清漪从北京大学毕业，第二年领取律师证，1933年加入北平律师公会，成为北平首位执业女律师。除在北平挂牌外，纪清漪还在天津兼任律师，同时担任北平市女二中训育主任，并创办了新声女子职业传习所，为女性谋求经济独立而奔走呼号。对于女同胞普遍关心的与财产继承、夫妻财产制度、婚姻、妨害风化以及妨害他人家庭等问题有关的法令、法理，纪清漪特别留心钻研，不仅撰成了《释女子继承权》《青年妇女问题与社会制度》等法理文章，而且还通过北平女青年会及各类学校组织演讲，主动传播、推广相关法律知识。当时的《世界日报》评价纪清漪"有异常魅力""有人类最勇敢的性情，能代表无能力的妇女来打抱不平"。

In 1931, Ji Qingyi graduated from Peking University and received a lawyer's certificate the following year. In 1933, she joined the Beiping Bar Association and became the first practicing female lawyer in Beiping. In addition to listing in Beiping, Ji Qingyi also served as a lawyer in Tianjin, and at the same time as the director of training in Beiping Women's Second Middle School, and founded the

Xinsheng Women's Vocational Training Institute, calling for women to seek economic independence. Ji Qingyi paid special attention to the laws and legal principles related to the issues of property inheritance, husband and wife property system, marriage, obstruction of morals, and obstruction of other people's families that are generally of concern to female compatriots. Not only has she written legal articles such as *Interpretation of Women's Inheritance Rights*, *Young Women's Issues and Social System*, but also organized speeches through the Beiping Young Women's Association and various schools to actively disseminate and promote relevant legal knowledge. At that time, the *World Journal* commented that Ji Qingyi was "unusually attractive" and "has the bravest human temperament, able to represent incompetent women to fight injustices".

七七事变以后，纪清漪远赴西安开展律师业务，并担任山西大同银行法律顾问。抗战胜利后，纪清漪回到天津执业，其事务所先位于第十区常德道57号，后迁至第一区嫩江路122号。

After the July 7 Incident of 1937, Ji Qingyi went to Xi'an to start lawyer business and served as the legal counsel of Shanxi Datong Bank. After the victory of Anti-Japanese War, Ji Qingyi returned to Tianjin to practice. Her office was first located at No. 57 Changde Road, District 10, and then moved to No. 122, Nenjiang Road, District 1.

新中国成立后，纪清漪积极参加社会主义建设事业，在政务院政法委员会参与司法改革，并参加了清理法院积案的工作。"文革"结束后，她当选为第一届中国法学会理事，协助张友渔编纂了《法学词典》，参与撰写了《中国大百科全书·法学卷》，发表了《中国古代法医学初探》等文章。曾任北京市西城区第五、第六届政协委员，北京市文史研究馆馆员等职。1998年1月11日，在北京逝世，享年94岁。

After the founding of the People's Republic of China, Ji Qingyi actively participated in the cause of socialist construction, participated in judicial reform in the Political and Legal Committee of the State Council, and participated in the work of clearing up court cases. After the "Cultural Revolution", she was elected as the first council member of the Chinese Law Society, assisted Zhang Youyu in compiling the *Law Dictionary*, participated in the writing of the *Law Volume of Encyclopedia of China*, and published articles such as *A Preliminary Study of Forensic Medicine in Ancient China*. Served as a member of the Fifth and Sixth CPPCC in Xicheng District, Beijing, and a librarian of the Beijing Municipal Museum of Literature and History. She passed away in Beijing on January 11, 1998 at the age of 94.

凭借着才华与正义，纪清漪接办了许多大案、难案，其中最著名的就是1936年5月为马占山将军代理的"马荣认子案"。

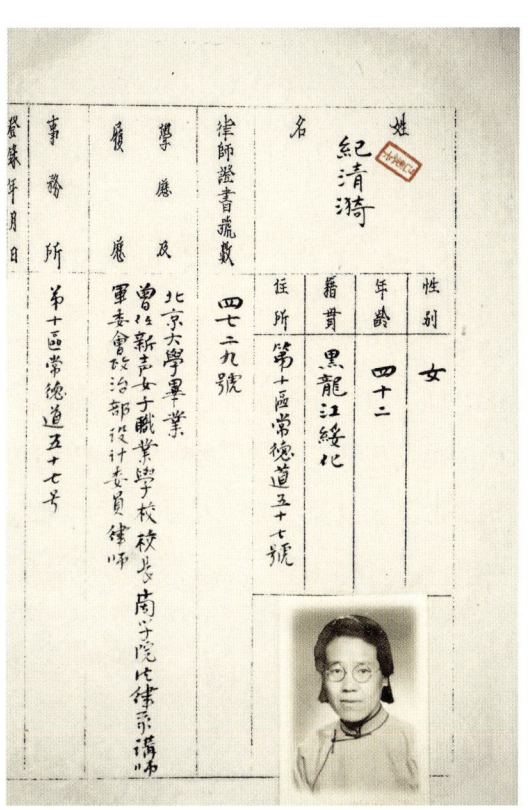

纪清漪律师登记表

Registration form of lawyer Ji Qingyi

Since then, relying on her talent and justice, Ji Qingyi took over many major and difficult cases, the most famous of which was the "Ma Rong's Recognition Case" acted for General Ma Zhanshan in May 1936.

1936年5月，抗日名将马占山自东北归来后寓居在天津英租界。此后，河北丰润县（今丰润区）一个名叫马荣的人多次到马占山的住处吵闹，称马占山是他多年失散的儿子，并认定马占山耳际有"拴马桩"。于是，马占山委托纪清漪律师在天津地方法院刑庭控告马荣妨害名誉，同时在民庭起诉确认与马荣无父子关系。

In May 1936, Ma Zhanshan, a famous anti-Japanese general, lived in Tianjin British Concession after returning from the northeast. Since then, a man named Ma Rong in Fengrun County, Hebei Province, repeatedly went to Ma Zhanshan's residence and claimed that Ma Zhanshan was his long-lost son, and believed that Ma Zhanshan had "malformed ear" in his ears. Therefore, Ma Zhanshan entrusted lawyer Ji Qingyi to accuse Ma Rong of damaging his reputation in the Criminal Court of Tianjin District Court. At the same time, he filed a lawsuit in the civil court to confirm that he has no father-son relationship with Ma Rong.

这起案件实际是由企图栽赃陷害甚至要刺杀马占山的日本侵略者导演的闹剧。它实际经历了三个司法程序，第一起案件是马荣在天津地方检察处控告马占山遗父不养罪，因无证据支持，被不起诉；第二起案件是马荣见控告无果，遂在天津地方法院民庭起诉马占山确认父子关系案；第三起案件是马占山作为原告提起的刑事诉讼，控告马荣妨害名誉。纪清漪是在马占山接到第二起民事案件的传票后接受委托的。在接受委托并听取案情后，纪清漪确定了如下代理思路：一、民事"认子案"积极应诉，且启动检验程序；二、应主动提起刑事诉讼，控告马荣妨害名誉，这样才能有效遏制马荣的险恶用心。代理思路得到马占山的认可后，纪清漪前往天津地方法院报到。

This case was actually a farce directed by a Japanese aggressor who tried to frame up and even assassinate Ma Zhanshan. There were actually three judicial procedures. The first case was that Ma Rong sued Ma Zhanshan's for refusing to support his father in the Tianjin District Procuratorate. He was not prosecuted because he had no evidence to support him; The second case was that Ma Rong found that the accusation failed, so he sued Ma Zhanshan in the Civil Court of Tianjin District Court to confirm the father-son relationship; the third case was a criminal lawsuit filed by Ma Zhanshan as the plaintiff, accusing Ma Rong of the crime of obstructing his reputation. Ji Qingyi accepted the commission after Ma Zhanshan received the subpoena for the second civil case. After accepting the entrustment and hearing the case, Ji Qingyi determined the following agency ideas: 1. Actively respond to the civil "recognition case" and initiate inspection procedures; 2. Proactively initiate criminal proceedings to accuse Ma Rong of damaging his reputation, so as to effectively deter Ma Rong's sinister intentions. After the agency idea was approved by Ma Zhanshan, Ji Qingyi went to Tianjin District Court to report.

马荣在民庭抗告称，马家祖居河北丰润县，光绪十年（1884）腊月初八得子马占山，因家境窘迫，过继姨妈后被其贩卖致下落不明。经马荣多年辗转于平津、东北寻找，最终得知马占山于天津的寓所，几次上门认子，均被马占山拒之门外。痛心疾首之余，对其不念养恩、不尽孝道之举忍无可忍，于是呈状于天津地方法院，要求马占山认父且履行赡养义务。纪清漪代理马占山拟写的刑事抗告状称：

Ma Rong protested in the civil court, claiming that the Ma family lived in Fengrun County, Hebei. His son Ma Zhanshan was born in the eighth day of the twelfth lunar month 1884. Because his family was poor, his son was adopted by aunt and then be sold .After Ma Rong spent many years in searching in Pingjin and Northeast China, he finally learned of Ma Zhanshan's apartment in Tianjin. He came to admit his son several times, but was rejected by Ma Zhanshan. Distressed, he couldn't bear his lack of nourishment and filial piety, so he filed a petition in the Tianjin District Court, requesting Ma Zhanshan to recognize his father and fulfill his maintenance obligations. The criminal anti-complaint written by Ji Qingyi on behalf of Ma Zhanshan stated:

因丰润马荣迭次到宅吵闹，欲强认为其失子。我自东北归来后，即寓居英租界，息影林泉，不问世事。我自十二岁时丧母，仅我兄妹二人随侍老父，始终未离一步。先父在民国六年（1917）九月二十六日故于吉林省怀德县炭窑村。证人张殿元亲自参加葬礼，且远近亲友无人不知，现在津地人证很多，全可出庭作证，倘我有父不认，不说自身良心难逃，亲友亦不相容。在民庭请求确认与马荣无父子关系的同时，我的精神名誉均受打击。对于平日所有往来之本族，向不拒绝接见，力所能及更无不援助。惟该马荣与我毫无关系，连来多次，经我再三解释不听，存心捣乱，迹近诈财，实属无可理喻。马荣多日数次来门任意谩骂，并称因寻子花费千元，居心不良，我名誉精神具受损失。我虽非书香门第，但也守法知理。按照常情而论，若父子失别多年，有机会相见，只有抱头痛哭，哪有咬牙不认之理？我家教严肃且军人出身，并请早日判决，使社会人士明了真相，以正国人听闻。

Because Ma Rong of Fengrun County visited his residence many times to make noise, he wanted to force him to claim his lost son. After I returned from the Northeast, I lived in the British concession and did not care about world affairs. Since I lost my mother when I was twelve years old, I and my sister were the only ones who served my father. My father died in Tanyao Village, Huaide County, Jilin Province on September 26th in 1917. Witness Zhang Dianyuan attended the funeral in person, and everyone knew about it. Now there are many people in Tianjin who can testify in court. If I denied my father, against my conscience, my relatives and friends are incompatible. While the civil court asked to confirm that I had no father-son relationship with Ma Rong, my spiritual reputation was both hit. For all the people who communicate with each other on weekdays, I never refuse to meet, and will help them as much as I can. But Ma Rong has nothing to do with me. He has come here many times. After I have repeatedly explained and refused to listen, it is unreasonable to deliberately make troubles and swindle money. Ma Rong came to the door several times a few days to swear arbitrarily, and said that because he spent thousands of yuan to find a child, he had bad intentions. My reputation and spirit have suffered. Although I am not a scholar, I also abide by the law. Normally, if a father and son have been separated for many years and have a chance to meet each other, they can only cry with each other. How can there be no reason to refuse to recognize each other? My family tutor is serious and has a military background. Please make an early judgment so that people in the community can understand the truth and listen to it as the people of the country.

刑庭胡国桢推事认为，刑案诬告是否成立，有俟于民案是否能认定父子关系，遂裁定先民后刑。在民事审理过程中，马荣坚称马占山为其失子的证据是指称马占山左耳际有"拴马桩",并期以此为证,要求传马占山亲自到庭。纪清漪律师称,马占山乃抗日英雄,如今政坛军界失意,且有日本特务行刺暗杀,原告公开露面于都市,恐有不便。请求法庭考虑原告安全,不宜在法庭公开检验。民事审判长裴锡晋也认为有讯问原告之必要,遂决定偕书记官王玉书、法医士李新民及纪清漪律师共同前往英租界马宅就讯。1936年5月22日,天津地方法院刑庭胡国桢推事判决马荣犯侮辱罪和毁人名誉罪,处有期徒刑六个月。

The judge of the Criminal Court Hu Guozhen believed that whether the false accusation in the criminal case was established depends on whether the relationship between father and son can be determined in the civil case, and he ruled that the civil case should be sentenced firstly. During the civil trial, Ma Rong insisted that the evidence that Ma Zhanshan was his lost son was that Ma Zhanshan had a "malformed ear" in his left ear, and expected to use this as evidence, demanding that Ma Zhanshan appear in court in person. Lawyer Ji Qingyi said that Ma Zhanshan was a hero of Anti-Japanese War. Now the political and military circles were frustrated, and Japanese secret agents were conducting assassinations and assassinations. The plaintiff's public appearance may be inconvenient. Asked the court to consider the safety of the plaintiff, and it was not appropriate to conduct a public examination in court. Civil presiding judge Pei Xijin also believed that it was necessary to interrogate the plaintiff, so he decided to join the clerk Wang Yushu, the forensic doctor Li Xinmin, and the lawyer Ji Qingyi to go to the house in the British Concession for the interrogation. On May 22, 1936, judge Hu Guozhen, the Criminal Division of Tianjin District Court, sentenced Ma Rong to crimes of insult and honour, and sentenced him to six months in prison.

民国大案中的天津律师

TIANJIN LAWYERS IN THE CASE OF THE REPUBLIC OF CHINA

天津律师公会各类档案记录了旧天津外强侵略、内乱不断的社会状况，也呈现了多起在全国产生重大影响的大案要案。那个动荡的年代，与达官贵人、军阀政客关联的案件也折射出了旧社会的专横、贪婪、投机和荒淫无度。这些案件都有律师的辩护和代理，当然，律师也只能在法律框架内为委托人寻求无罪、轻罪或其他的法律帮助。

In many files of Tianjin Bar Association, the social status quo of foreign aggression and constant civil strife in old Tianjin has been recorded, and there have also been many major cases that have a great impact on the whole country. In that turbulent era, the cases related to dignitaries and warlords and politicians also reflected the tyranny, greed, speculation and dissolute of the old society. In these cases, lawyers also participate in defense and representation. Of course, the professional requirements of pattern lawyers were only seeking innocent, misdemeanor or other legal help for clients within the framework of law.

一、周恩来等各界代表案

1. The Case of Zhou Enlai and Other Representatives from All Walks of Life

1919年五四运动爆发，因地处京畿，所以天津各大、中学校师生和爱国青年积极响应，组织学生联合会、女界爱国同志会、各界联合会和国民大会等一系列爱国团体，举行了声势浩大的示威游行和抵制日货运动。

In 1919, the May 4th Movement broke out. Because of its location in Gyeonggi, Tianjin's teachers and students from universities and middle schools and patriotic youth responded actively and organized a series of patriotic groups such as the Student Union, the Women's Patriotic Association, the Federation of all walks of life and the National Convention. There was a massive demonstration and a boycott of Japanese goods.

1920年1月23日，学生联合会调查委员会成员段鸿荫发现东门里魁发成料器庄私藏日货不报，遂组织国民大会成员前往调查。其间与奸商和日本浪人发生冲突，后将魁发成伙计裴唐仙、张云翰带走，监禁起来，次日游街示众。于是，天津警察厅派出军警进行镇压，逮捕了南开学校庶务主任马千里、南开学校学生马骏等20余人，并查封了天津各界联合会和天津学生联合会。

On January 23, 1920, Duan Hongyin, a member of the Investigative Committee of the Student Union, discovered that Japanese goods had not been reported in the Dongmenli Kuifacheng and organized members of the National Assembly to investigate. In the meantime, they clashed with profiteers and Japanese ronin, and later took away Kui Fa's associates Pei Tangxian and Zhang Yunhan, imprisoned them, and paraded the streets the next day. As a result, the Tianjin Police Department sent military police to suppress it, arrested more than 20 people including Ma Qianli, general affairs director of Nankai School, and Ma Jun, a student of Nankai School, and seized the Tianjin Federation of All walks of life and the Tianjin Student Federation.

1月29日，正在南开学校读书、时任天津学生联合会执行科长的周恩来领导天津20多所学校的1000余名学生到直隶公署门前进行大规模的请愿活动，要求驳回日本通牒；拒绝山东问题直接交涉，催办福州惨案的交涉，取消中日军事协约；恢复天津学联原状；释放被拘代表，不干涉人民集会、结社、出版自由。请愿学生随即遭到军警镇压，重伤50余人，周恩来、于方舟、张砚庄、郭隆真四名学生代表被捕，开始羁押在天津警察厅，后转移到天津地方检察厅看守所，由检察官起诉到天津地方审判厅进行"审判"。

On January 29, Zhou Enlai, who was studying in Nankai School and was the executive section chief of the Tianjin Student Federation at the time, led more than 1,000 students from more than 20 schools in Tianjin to conduct a large-scale petition in front of the Zhili Office, demanding the rejection of the Japanese notice; rejecting direct negotiations on the Shandong issue, urging negotiations on the Fuzhou tragedy, canceling the Sino-Japanese military agreement; restoring the Tianjin Student Federation to its original status; releasing detained representatives, and not interfering with the freedom of people's assembly, association, and press. The petition students were immediately suppressed by the military and police, and more than 50 people were seriously injured. Four student representatives, Zhou Enlai, Yu Fangzhou, Zhang Yanzhuang, and Guo Longzhen, were arrested and detained at the Tianjin Police Department. They were later transferred to the Tianjin Local Procuratorate Detention Center, where they were prosecuted by the prosecutor. Finally, the Tianjin Local Adjudicative Office would conduct a "trial."

为营救被捕代表，邓颖超等人积极奔走，不仅聘请了天津律师公会会长梁锡纶、副会长兰兴周和资深律师钱俊，而且从北京请来了著名的刘崇佑律师共同代理诉讼。周恩来等革命志士在给刘崇佑的通信中写道："崇佑先生，省署请愿一案，检厅起诉案由，系注意在强暴胁迫、不服解散，从此点上，我们愿意与先生声明者数事。"

In order to rescue the arrested representatives, Deng Yingchao and others rushed actively, not only hired Tianjin Bar Association chairman Liang Xilun, vice chairman Lan Xingzhou and senior lawyer Qian Jun, but also invited the famous lawyer Liu Chongyou from Beijing to represent the litigation. Zhou Enlai and other revolutionary veterans wrote in their correspondence to Liu Chongyou, "Mr. Chongyou, in the petition case of the Provincial Department, the prosecutors' prosecution is to pay attention to rape, coercion, disobedience, and dissolution. From this point, we are willing to discuss matters with teacher."

1920年6月5日，周恩来在狱中编写完成了《警厅拘留记》，详细记述了从天津抵制日货，商学两届于南开操场集会，引起"魁发成勾引日人殴击学生"，演变成省公署前的流血惨剧，

1934	1935	1936	1937	1938	1939	1940	1941	1942	1943	1944	1945	1946
1960	1961	1962	1963	1964	1965	1966	1967	1968	1969	1970	1971	1972
1986	1987	1988	1989	1990	1991	1992	1993	1994	1995	1996	1997	1998
2012	2013	2014	2015	2016	2017	2018	2019	2020	2021	……		

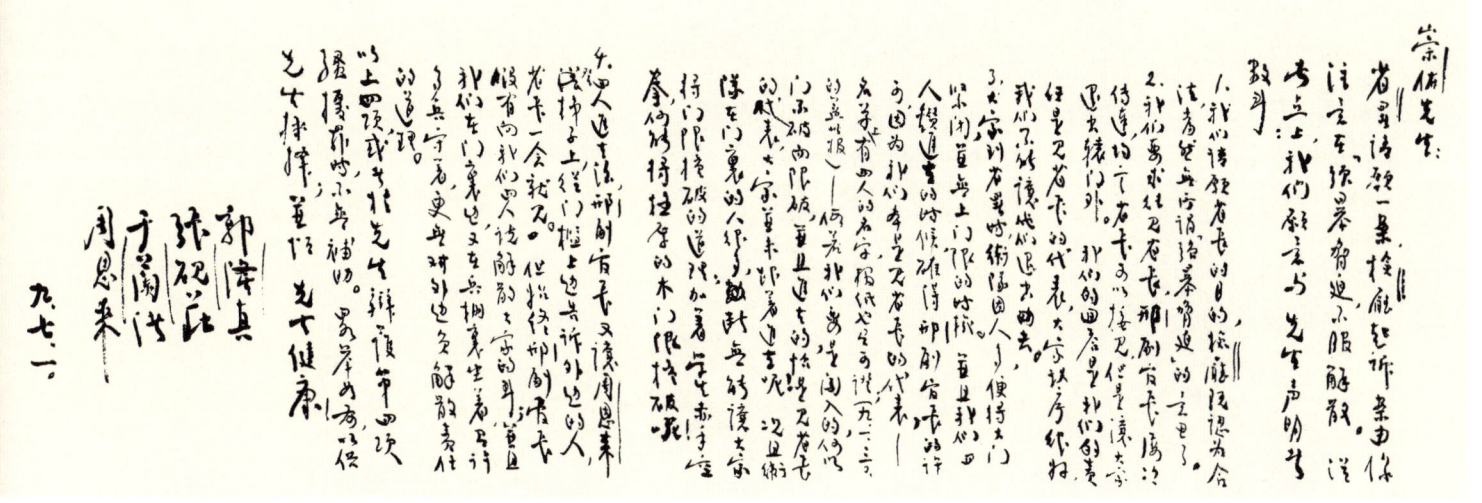

1920年7月1日周恩来等革命志士致刘崇佑律师的信

Letter from Zhou Enlai and other revolutionary veterans to lawyer Liu Chongyou on July 1, 1920

直到共同前往直隶省公署请愿的详细过程。当年11月交给马千里，并在其创办的《新民意报》上刊发。

On June 5, 1920, Zhou Enlai wrote and completed *The Detention Records of the Police Hall* in prison, which described in detail the boycott of Japanese goods from Tianjin. The business and school held two rallies on the Nankai playground, causing "Kui Facheng to seduce the Japanese to assault the students." It turned into a bloodshed before the provincial government office, until the detailed process of petitioning together to the Zhili provincial government office. In November of that year, it was handed over to Ma Qianli and published in the *New Public Opinion* founded by him.

1920年6月26日，被捕代表接到通知，当局已经准许律师阅卷，并将于7月6日开庭。1920年6月30日，刘崇佑律师来到看守所，接见了被捕代表，并告知检察厅移文，被定罪案如下：马千里、夏琴西等十人犯妨害公安罪和私擅监禁罪，李燕豪、郭绪荣等八人犯妨害公务罪，周恩来、于方舟等四人犯骚扰罪。7月6日至8日，经地方检察厅检察官杨占鳌、徐家驹提起公诉，天津地方审判厅开庭审理，审判长俞钟，推事谢越石、丁海瀛，书记官姚赓寿。杨占鳌起立发言："本案发生原因，系因青岛问题，外交失败，激发热诚，而有抵制日货之倡议。此为道德良心，本无违反，仅可与报纸上鼓吹演讲，以资激劝，万不可检察搜索、焚毁日货，虽系激于热诚，而实越法律范围，侵犯营业自由。故依据刑律第三百五十八条之规定，构成妨害安全。"刘崇佑律师答辩道："查国民力争外交，是人民应有心理，应有责任，亦系民主国自卫天职。御外辱、避危险，乃人民应作之事。当局不但不加保护，反来摧残蹂躏，未免贻笑日人。"

On June 26, 1920, the arrested representatives were notified that the authorities had allowed the lawyers to read the files, and the court was scheduled to start on July 6. On June 30, 1920, Lawyer Liu Chongyou came to the detention center, met with the arrested representative, and informed the procuratorate to

周恩来的《警厅拘留记》
The Detention Records of the Police Hall by Zhou Enlai

1934	1935	1936	1937	1938	1939	1940	1941	1942	1943	1944	1945	1946
1960	1961	1962	1963	1964	1965	1966	1967	1968	1969	1970	1971	1972
1986	1987	1988	1989	1990	1991	1992	1993	1994	1995	1996	1997	1998
2012	2013	2014	2015	2016	2017	2018	2019	2020	2021	......		

transfer the text. The convictions were as follows: Ma Qianli, Xia Qinxi and other ten persons committed crimes of obstructing public security and imprisonment without authorization, Eight people including Li Yanhao, Guo Xurong committed the crime of obstructing official duties, and four people including Zhou Enlai and Yu Fangzhou committed the crime of harassment. On July 6-8, prosecutors Yang Zhan'ao and Xu Jiaju of the Local Procuratorate filed public prosecutions, and the Tianjin Local Adjudicative Office opened a trial. The presiding judge Yu Zhong, the judges Xie Yueshi and Ding Haiying, and the clerks Yao Gengshou. Yang Zhan'ao stood up and spoke, "The reason for this case is the Qingdao issue, diplomatic failure, enthusiasm, and an initiative to address Japanese goods. This is not a violation of moral conscience. You can only promote speeches in newspapers to encourage you. Prosecutors are not allowed to search and burn Japanese goods. Although they are driven by enthusiasm, they violate the scope of the law and violate the freedom of business. Therefore, in accordance with Article 358 of the Criminal Law, it constitutes a safety hazard." Lawyer Liu Chongyou replied, "It is not only the people's psychology and responsibility but also the bounden duty of a democratic country to strive for diplomacy. It is the people's duty to resist foreign humiliation and avoid danger. Instead of giving protection, the authorities have destroyed and ravaged them, which makes Japanese people laugh at them."

法庭上，钱俊律师慷慨陈词地说："国势危亡，岂忍束手待毙？国民分子，天良而发，奋力呼号，热诚所激，不应受刑。"兰兴周律师辩护称："检察官起诉之各项，殊与事实不符，委未允当。""马千里等有无强暴胁迫，为本案构成之要件，马千里等虽系国民大会会员，究系与各同业公会共同之核议，自决抵制日货，对于一切行为，纯出自愿，焉得有强暴胁迫？"

In the court, Lawyer Qian Jun generously stated, "The country is in danger and can't bear to die. The nationals, for the sake of nature, work hard to shout, and are motivated by enthusiasm, and should not be sentenced." Lawyer Lan Xingzhou defended, "The prosecutor prosecuted it. All items are inconsistent with the facts, and the commission has not been approved." "Whether Ma Qianli and others have violent coercion is an essential element of this case. Although Ma Qianli and

190

1934	1935	1936	1937	1938	1939	1940	1941	1942	1943	1944	1945	1946
1960	1961	1962	1963	1964	1965	1966	1967	1968	1969	1970	1971	1972
1986	1987	1988	1989	1990	1991	1992	1993	1994	1995	1996	1997	1998
2012	2013	2014	2015	2016	2017	2018	2019	2020	2021	……		

刘崇佑律师撰写的辩护书

Defense note written by lawyer Liu Chongyou

others are members of the National Assembly, they have been jointly approved by various trade associations and self-determined to boycott Japanese goods. For all behaviors, it is purely voluntary, how can there be rape and coercion?"

经过多名律师的不懈努力,北洋政府在判决了各代表有期徒刑两个月后,不得不释放了广大爱国人士。出狱后,各界代表继续传播马克思主义、抵制日货,而周恩来也踏上了革命家的道路。

After the unremitting efforts of many lawyers, the Beiyang Government had to release the patriots after sentenced the representatives to two months' imprisonment. After being released from prison, representatives of all walks of life continued to spread Marxism and boycott Japanese goods, and Zhou Enlai also set foot on the road of revolution.

刘崇佑(1877—1941),字厚诚,号松生,福建侯官(今闽侯县)人,清末民初立宪派活动家、著名进步律师。光绪二十年(1894)乡试中举,会试不第后赴日留学,入早稻田大学攻读法律。光绪三十四年(1908)毕业回国,次年10月,就任新成立的福建省咨议局副议长。宣统三年(1911),与林长民创办了私立福建法政学堂(今福建师范大学的前身之一)。

Liu Chongyou (1877-1941), named HouCheng, was also known as Songsheng, born in Houguan(now Minhou County), Fujian, a constitutionalist activist and a well-known progressive lawyer in the late Qing Dynasty and the early Republic of China. In 1894, he went to Japan to study in Japan after failing the examination, and went to Waseda University to study law. In 1908, he graduated and returned to China. In October of the following year, he became the deputy chairman of the newly established Fujian Provincial Advisory Bureau. In 1911, he and Lin Changmin founded the private Fujian School of Law and Politics (one of the predecessors of Fujian Normal University).

1913年4月8日,中华民国第一届国会在北京召开,汤化龙当选众议院议长,刘崇佑为众议院议员。5月末,进步党成立,梁启超、汤化龙、刘崇佑为党内骨干。7月,刘崇佑参与制

1934	1935	1936	1937	1938	1939	1940	1941	1942	1943	1944	1945	1946
1960	1961	1962	1963	1964	1965	1966	1967	1968	1969	1970	1971	1972
1986	1987	1988	1989	1990	1991	1992	1993	1994	1995	1996	1997	1998
2012	2013	2014	2015	2016	2017	2018	2019	2020	2021	……		

刘崇佑律师
Lawyer Liu Chongyou

定了中华民国宪法（即《天坛宪法草案》）。护国运动后，原进步党人转变为研究系，受到段祺瑞的重用。不过，随着安福系的崛起，研究系走向没落。1918年9月，汤化龙被国民党人暗杀，因刘崇佑与汤化龙私交甚厚，遂对政治心灰意冷，逐渐退出政界，转而在北京丞相胡同开设事务所，专以律师为业，曾任北京《晨报》和中国银行总行的法律顾问，主张"律师应仗人间义"。

On April 8, 1913, the first Congress of the Republic of China was held in Beijing. Tang Hualong was elected Speaker of the House of Representatives and Liu Chongyou was a member of the House of Representatives. At the end of May, the Progressive Party was established, with Liang Qichao, Tang Hualong, and Liu Chongyou as the backbone of the party. In July, Liu Chongyou participated in the formulation of the Constitution of the Republic of China (the *Draft Constitution of the Temple of Heaven*). After the National Defence Movement, the former Progressive Party members were transformed into a research department, which was reused by Duan Qirui. However, with the rise of the Anfu department, the research department declined. In September 1918, Tang Hualong was assassinated by the Kuomintang. Because Liu

Chongyou had a personal relationship with Tang Hualong, he became frustrated with politics and gradually withdrew from the political circle. Instead, he opened an office in Beijing Chengxiang Hutong and worked as a lawyer. He used to work in Beijing. The legal advisers of the *Morning Post* and the Bank of China's head office advocated that "lawyers should act on human justice".

1919年五四运动爆发后，5至8月间相继发生了"北京《益世报》查封案"和"北大学生案"。刘崇佑不畏强权，挺身为报馆和学生的正义之举义务辩护，加之其精于法理、技巧出色，故而在律师界声名大振。

After the May 4th Movement broke out in 1919, the "Beijing *Yishi Daily* seizure case" and the "Peking University student case" occurred successively from May to August. Liu Chongyou was not afraid of power, and stood up to defend the press and students' obligations of justice. In addition, he was proficient in legal principles and excellent in skills, so he became famous in the lawyers circle.

周恩来出狱后，刘崇佑与天津名士严修共同出资500元，帮助周恩来赴法国留学。此后的两年间，刘崇佑每月都会给周恩来汇去20余块银元作生活费，直至周恩来获得奖学金。1941年9月，刘崇佑在上海病逝，身处重庆的周恩来得知后，非常惋惜并赞扬地说："刘崇佑先生是中国一位有正义感的大律师。"新中国成立初期，周恩来专门委托上海市市长陈毅关照刘崇佑的家人，并于1957年11月24日亲自看望刘崇佑的夫人，并指定专人为她解决生活困难。

After Zhou Enlai was released from prison, Liu Chongyou and Tianjin celebrity Yan Xiu jointly contributed 500 yuan to help Zhou Enlai study in France. For the next two years, Liu Chongyou would remit more than 20 silver dollars to Zhou Enlai every month for living expenses until Zhou Enlai received a scholarship. In September 1941, Liu Chongyou died of illness in Shanghai. Zhou Enlai, who was in Chongqing, regretted and said in praise, "Mr. Liu Chongyou is a barrister with a sense of justice in China." In the early days of the founding of the People's Republic of China, Zhou Enlai commissioned Shanghai. Mayor Chen Yi took care of Liu Chongyou's family and personally visited Liu Chongyou's wife on November 24, 1957, and appointed someone to solve her difficulties in life.

钱俊，光绪七年（1881）生于浙江嘉兴桐乡，宣统三年（1911）九月毕业于北洋大学堂。民国元年，改入天津县籍，当年11月5日被司法部授予律师证书，编号84，在司法部直隶律师登录附表中排列14号。钱俊曾代理李雅泉控告英商仁记洋行票据拨款纠纷案。

Qian Jun was born in Tongxiang, Jiaxing, Zhejiang in 1881, and graduated from Beiyang University in September in 1911. In the first year of the Republic of China, he changed to Tianjin County and was awarded a lawyer certificate by the Ministry of Justice on November 5 of that year, No.84, ranked No.14 in the attached table of the Ministry of Justice Zhili Lawyer Registration. Qian Jun once represented Li Yaquan in suing Yingshang Renji Foreign Bank in the dispute over the appropriation of bills.

兰兴周，字绍文，直隶沧县（今属河北省沧州市）人，光绪三十年（1904）赴日留学。先入宏文学院，四年后进入早稻田大学政治经济科学习，宣统二年（1910）改入法政大学法律科，次年学成归国。应北洋法政专门学校之邀，任国际法、诉讼法讲习，同时兼任律师，曾接替梁锡纶担任天津律师公会会长，并于1921年当选第三届顺直省议会议员。1924年3月11日病逝。

Lan Xingzhou, named Shaowen, born in Cang County, Zhili Province(now Cang County, Hebei Province). He went to Japan to study in 1904. He first entered Hongwen College, and four years later, he entered the political and economics department of Waseda University. In 1910, he was changed to the law department of Hosei University. At the invitation of Beiyang College of Law and Politics, he served as a lecturer in international law and procedural law, and also served as a lawyer. He replaced Liang Xilun as the chairman of the Tianjin Bar Association and was elected as a member of the third Shunzhi Provincial Assembly in 1921. He died on March 11, 1924.

梁锡纶（1879—1954），字佩恩，直隶河间（今河北省河间市）人，毕业于直隶法律学堂，1912年11月16日被司法部授予律师证书，编号138，在司法部直隶律师登录附表中排列34号。梁锡纶于1913—1921年担任天津律师公会会长，并于1920年10月4日主持召开了全国律师

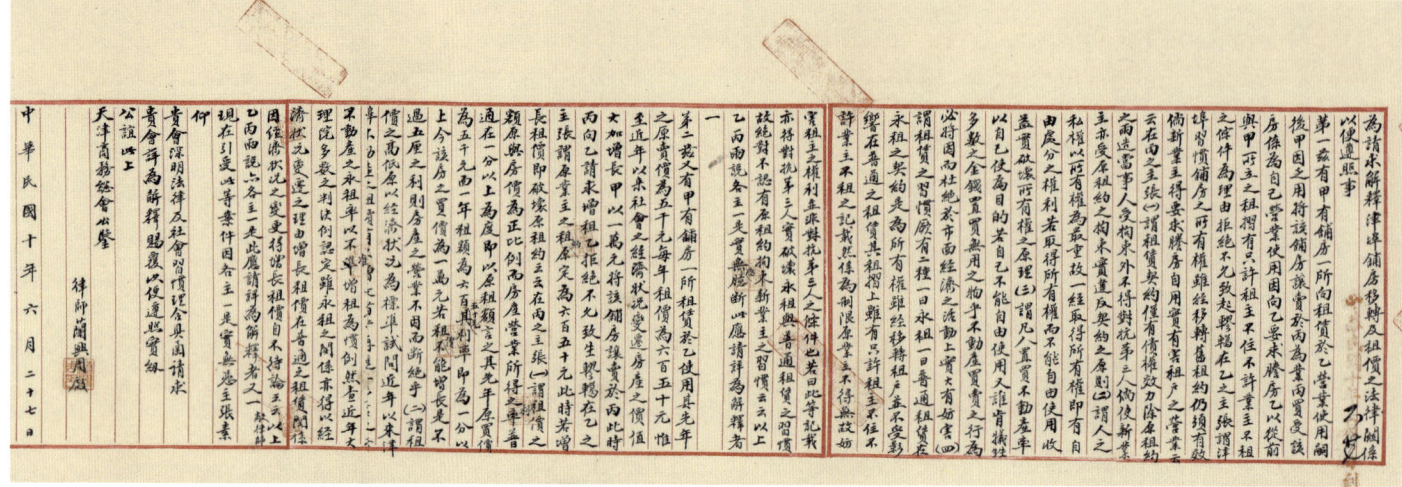

兰兴周律师致函天津商务总会寻求关于津埠
铺房移转及租价之法律关系的解释

Lawyer Lan Xingzhou sent a letter to the Tianjin
General Chamber of Commerce to seek an
explanation on the legal relationship between the
transfer and rental price of Tianjin shops

公会联合会会员大会。1934年,梁锡纶从天津回到原籍,组织成立了河间县律师公会并担任会长。抗战期间,梁锡纶积极拥护中国共产党的抗日政策,主动为八路军组织捐钱捐物,被誉为地方开明士绅。

Liang Xilun (1879-1954), named Peien, born in Hejian, Zhili Province (now Hejian City, Hebei Province). He graduated from Zhili Law School. On November 16, 1912, he was awarded a lawyer certificate by the Ministry of Justice, No.138, the number in the attached table of the Ministry of Zhili lawyer registration was 34. Liang Xilun served as the chairman of Tianjin Bar Association from 1913 to 1921, and presided over the Member's General Assembly of the National Federation of Bar Association on October 4, 1920. In 1934, Liang Xilun returned to his place of origin from Tianjin and organized and established the Hejian County Bar Association and served as its chairman. During Anti-Japanese War, Liang Xilun actively supported the Chinese Communist Party's anti-Japanese policy, actively donating money and materials to the Eighth Route Army organization, and was hailed as a local enlightened gentry.

二、溥仪状告天津兴业银行案

2. The Case of Puyi Sued Tianjin Xingye Bank

1927年11月18日，溥仪将本洋8万元存入陈光远、阮忠极、李荣贵等13人合办的天津兴业银行。次年1月19日又存入本洋1万元，共计9万元，均按每月八厘五毫行息，一年为期。然而到期后，溥仪没能收回本洋，而且1928年10月之后的利息也没能给付。后经多次催讨，毫无效果，于是溥仪将天津兴业银行及其股东李荣贵、陈光远、王廷桢、龚心湛、倪道杰、阮忠极等人告上法庭，要求偿还原告本洋9万元及利息。

On November 18, 1927, Puyi deposited 80,000 yuan of this foreign currency into the Tianjin Xingye Bank cofounded by 13 people including Chen Guangyuan, Ruan Zhongji, and Li Ronggui. On January 19 of the following year, another 10,000 yuan was deposited for the local and foreign countries, a total of 90,000 yuan, all at a monthly interest rate of 8.5 cents for a period of one year. However, after the expiration, Puyi failed to reclaim the foreign capital, and the interest after October 1928 was not paid. After repeated urges to no avail, Puyi sued Tianjin Xingye Bank and its shareholders Li Ronggui, Chen Guangyuan, Wang Tingzhen, Gong Xinzhan, Ni Daojie, Ruan Zhongji and others to court, demanding the repayment of the plaintiff's 90,000 yuan and interest.

此后，法庭多次举行公开审理，不过始终没能达成和解。1929年10月14日，天津地方法院民一庭组织了原被告最后一次辩论。原告溥仪请来林荣、林廷琛、谢道仁三位代理律师，诸被告也延聘了天津有名的大律师，如李荣贵的代理人王明毅，陈光远的代理人李怀亮，王廷桢的代理人张恩寿，龚心湛的代理人孙观圻，倪道杰的代理人金殿选，阮忠极和谢廷绥的代理人朱鸿儒等，律师阵容十分强大。

Since then, the court has held many public hearings, but no settlement has been reached. On October 14, 1929, the First Civil Court of Tianjin District Court organized the last debate of the original defendant. Puyi, the plaintiff, invited Lin Qi, Lin Tingchen and Xie Daoren as attorneys, and the defendants also hired famous barristers in Tianjin, such as Li Ronggui's agent Wang Mingyi, Chen

Guangyuan's agent Li Huailiang, Wang Tingzhen's agent Zhang Enshou, Gong Xinzhan's agent Sun Guanche, Ni Daojie's agent Jin Dianxuan, Ruan Zhongji and Xie Tingyi's agent Zhu Hongru.

1929年10月19日，天津地方法院作出判决，被告天津兴业银行应偿还原告溥仪银洋9万元，其中8万元应自1928年10月18日起，1万元应自同月19日起，均至执行终日止，按月息八厘五毫给付利息。

On October 19, 1929, the Tianjin District Court made a judgment that the defendant Tianjin Xingye Bank should repay the plaintiff Puyi 90,000 yuan, of which 80,000 yuan should be from October 18, 1928, and 10,000 yuan should be from the 19th of the same month. Until the end of execution, interest will be paid at a monthly interest rate of 8.5 cents.

林棨，字肖旭，一字少旭，光绪七年（1881）生，福建侯官（今闽侯县）人。初就读于福州东文学堂，光绪二十五年（1899）冬由该学堂出资赴日留学，先后就读于东京同文书院、早稻田大学邦语政治科，光绪三十年（1904）夏获优等文凭。同年冬回国，在京师大学堂进士馆教授国际法。宣统元年（1909），任京师大学堂法政科监督，是北京大学法学教育的缔造者之一。民国成立后，林棨先后任教育部专门教育司司长，大理院推事，北京、江苏及湖北等地高等审判厅厅长等职。伪满洲国成立后，林棨充任伪执政府秘书处秘书官、伪最高法院院长，直至1939年12月。

Lin Qi, named Xiaoxu, was also known as Shaoxu, was born in 1881, and was born in Houguan(now Minhou County), Fujian. He first studied at Fuzhou Dongwentang. In the winter of 1899, he was funded by the school to study in Japan. he studied at the Tokyo Tongshuyuan and Waseda University's Politics Department. In 1904, he received a diploma in summer. In the winter of the same year, he returned to China and taught international law at the Jinshi Hall of Jingshi University. In 1909, he served as the supervisor of the Department of Law and Politics of Jingshi University. He was one of the founders of Peking University's legal education. After the founding of the Republic of China, Lin Qi successively served as the Director of the Special Education Department of the Ministry of Education, the Judge of the Daliyuan, and the director of the High Adjudicative Office in Beijing, Jiangsu and Hubei. After the establishment of the puppet Manchukuo, Lin Qi served as secretary of the secretariat of the ruling government and president of the supreme court until December 1939.

林棨、林廷琛、谢道仁同为福建人，曾长期为溥仪及小德张提供法律服务，素有"宫廷律师"之称。林棨、林廷琛还因代理文绣、溥仪离婚案及章遏云、倪道杰离婚案而名噪一时。溥仪赴东北后，谢道仁仍在天津执业律师，20世纪30年代曾作为原江西督军陈光远的辩护律师代理其家产争执案，颇负盛名。

Lin Qi, Lin Tingchen, and Xie Daoren are all Fujianese. They have provided legal services for Puyi and Xiao Dezhang for a long time, and were known as "court lawyers". Lin Qi and Lin Tingchen also became famous for representing Wenxiu and Puyi in divorce case and Zhang Eyun and Ni Daojie's divorce case. After Puyi went to the Northeast, Xie Daoren was still practicing as a lawyer in Tianjin. In the

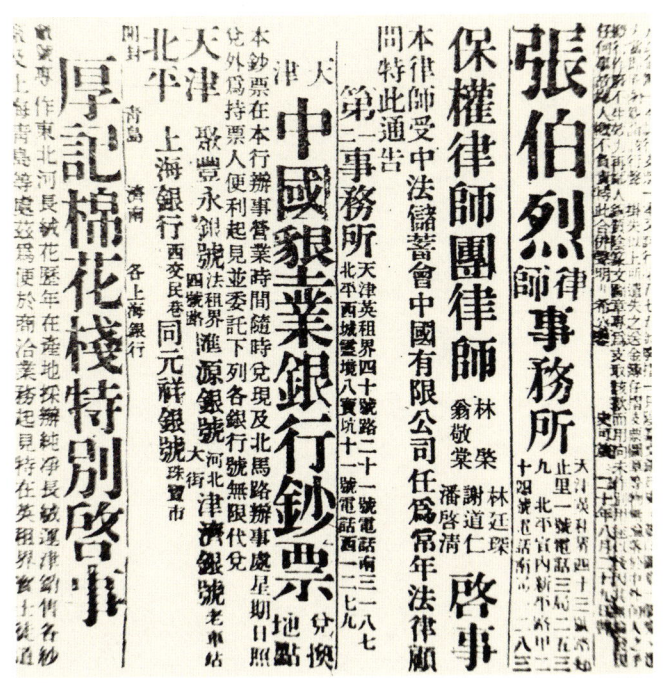

林棨、林廷琛、谢道仁律师团启事
Notice from the lawyers group of Lin Qi, Lin Tingchen and Xie Daoren

1930s, he served as the defense lawyer of the former Jiangxi Governor Chen Guangyuan to represent his family property disputes, and quite famous.

金殿选，满族，曾任合肥审判厅厅长、北京地方审判厅厅长等职。执业律师，除溥仪状告兴业银行案，还参与过著名的章遏云、倪道杰离婚案及张怀卿、张景韩离婚案。

Jin Dianxuan, the Manchus, once served as Director of Hefei Adjudicative Office, Director of Beijing Local Adjudicative Office. Practicing lawyers, in addition to Puyi's case against Xingye Bank, also participated in the famous divorce case of Zhang Eyun and Ni Daojie, and the divorce case of Zhang Huaiqing and Zhang Jinghan.

京剧名家章遏云，20世纪30年代与胡碧兰、孟丽君、雪艳琴并称为戏剧界四大坤旦、"女伶四大皇后"。1930年五六月间章遏云在大连、沈阳演出时，与原安徽督军倪嗣冲之子倪道杰相识，后经孙传芳、潘复介绍，两人在大连结婚。婚后，两人因琐事争吵不断，章遏云遂于1931年8月初在天津聘请律师李景光、林荣、林廷琛代理离婚诉讼，倪道杰则由金殿选代理。在金殿选的奔走、调解下，章倪双方最终确认因感情破裂、覆水难收而脱离关系，并表示愿以坦诚的态度私下了结脱离后的赡养费等相关事宜。重获自由的章遏云于1932年3月31日正式复出，直到20世纪80年代才告别舞台。

The famous Peking opera master Zhang Eyun, together with Hu Bilan, Meng Lijun, and Xue Yanqin, was called the "Four Queens" and "Four Queens of Actresses" in the theater industry in the 1930s. In May and June of 1930, Zhang Eyun met Ni Daojie, the son of the former Anhui Supervisor Ni Sichong, when performing in Dalian and Shenyang. After introduction by Sun Chuanfang and Pan Fu, the two married in Dalian. After their marriage, the two quarreled constantly over trivial matters. Zhang Eyun hired lawyers Li Jingguang, Lin Qi, and Lin Tingchen in Tianjin in early August 1931 to represent the divorce proceedings, while Ni Daojie was represented by Jin Dianxuan. Under the running and mediation of Jindianxuan, both Zhang and Ni finally confirmed that they had separated from the relationship due to the breakdown of their relationship and the overwhelming difficulties, and expressed their willingness to settle the alimony and other related matters after separation in a frank manner. Zhang Eyun, who had regained her freedom, officially returned on March 31, 1932, and did not bid farewell to the stage until the 1980s.

1932年9月，张作霖的四女儿张怀卿以夫妻感情不和为由，向河北天津地方法院提起诉讼，请求与张勋之子张景韩解除婚姻关系。12月6日，天津地方法院作出判决，准予两人解除婚约，并要求被告给付原告赡养费10万元。金殿选、张务滋、李怀亮为张景韩的代理律师，他们对解除婚约并无异议，但对赡养费的数额表示不服，由此上诉到河北高等法院天津分院。被上诉人张怀卿则聘请赵泉、陈璜为代理律师，双方你来我往，各执一词，缠讼多日，直到1933年3月。此案除张怀卿确已离婚外，并无最终判决。1992年，张怀卿在天津去世，享年81岁。

In September 1932, Zhang Zuolin's fourth daughter, Zhang Huaiqing, filed a lawsuit with the Hebei Tianjin District Court on the grounds that the husband and wife were not in harmony, requesting the termination of the marriage relationship with Zhang Xun's son Zhang Jinghan. On December 6, the Tianjin District Court issued a ruling, allowing the two to dissolve their marriage contract and demanding the defendant to pay the plaintiff's alimony of 100,000 yuan. Jin Dianxuan, Zhang Wuzi, and Li Huailiang were Zhang Jinghan's attorneys. They had no objection to the dissolution of the marriage contract, but expressed dissatisfaction with the amount of alimony, and therefore appealed to the Tianjin Branch of the Hebei High Court. The appellee Zhang Huaiqing hired Zhao Quan and Chen Huang as her attorneys. Both side entangled in litigation for many days until March 1933. There was no final judgment in this case, except that Zhang Huaiqing was indeed divorced. Zhang Huaiqing died in Tianjin in 1992 at the age of 81.

参与兴业银行案的孙观圻律师，字挹英，生于光绪元年（1875），江苏无锡人，清末曾获候补县知事资格。1913年出任江苏高等审判厅推事，1917年升任大理院推事，1921年8月出任天津地方审判厅厅长，一年后再次调任大理院推事。南京国民政府成立后，孙观圻曾短暂出任北平地方法院院长，随即在天津执业律师并长期担任开滦煤矿法律顾问。抗战胜利后，孙观圻出任天津地方法院院长。新中国成立以后，被天津市政协聘为特约委员。

Lawyer Sun Guanche, who participated in the Xingye Bank case, named Yiying, was born in 1875 in Wuxi, Jiangsu. He was qualified as an alternate county governor in the late Qing Dynasty. In 1913, he became a judge of the Jiangsu High Adjudicative Office. In 1917, he was promoted to the Judge of the Daliyuan. In August 1921, he became the director of the Tianjin Local Adjudicative Office. He was transferred to the Judge of the Daliyuan again a year later. After the establishment of Nanjing National Government, Sun Guanche briefly served as the president of the Beiping District Court, then practised as a lawyer in Tianjin and served as the legal counsel of the Kailuan Coal Mine for a long time. After the victory of Anti-Japanese War, Sun Guanche became the president of the Tianjin District Court. After the founding of the People's Republic of China, he was hired as a special committee member by the Tianjin CPPCC.

孙观圻执业天津期间，因对法律研究精深而颇有名气。鲜牡丹脱离领家案和曹书诚案是孙观圻执业初期承办的两起较为有名的案件。

During his practice in Tianjin, Sun Guanche was well-known for his in-depth legal research. The case of Xian Mudan leaving the leader and the case of Cao Shucheng were two of the more famous cases undertaken by Sun Guanche in his early practice.

鲜牡丹是20世纪20年代末天津有名的坤伶，深受观众青睐，然而大红大紫的背后是其领家李三姑（本名李鸿龄）及其姘夫刘凤桥对鲜牡丹的欺侮和压榨。于是从小被迫租给李三姑学戏的鲜牡丹伺机逃到了天津妇女协会，要求脱离领家，以重获人身自由。李三姑闻讯后，遂向河北地方法院提起诉讼，坚称鲜牡丹为其亲生，并派使女吴李氏代理出庭。1929年8月，法院开庭审理此案，双方律师展开了激烈的辩论。孙观圻律师不仅否定了吴李氏的证人资格，而且通过计算年龄戳穿了李三姑是鲜牡丹生母的谎言。法院最终宣判，驳回原告李三姑的请求，并判决她返还鲜牡丹翠圈一个、宝石戒指一个以及生活费银币1600元。

Xian Mudan was a famous actress in Tianjin in the late 1920s and was very popular with audiences. However, behind the popularity is the leader Li Sangu (real name Li Hongling) and her concubine Liu Fengqiao's bullying and squeeze of Xian Mudan. So Xian Mudan, who was forced to rent to Li Sangu to learn opera since childhood, fled to Tianjin Women's Association and asked to leave the leader in order to regain her personal freedom. After hearing the news, Li Sangu filed a lawsuit in the Hebei District Court, insisting that Xian Mudan is her own person, and sent the maid, Wu Lishi, to attend as an agent. In August 1929, the court opened a trial to hear the case, and the lawyers of the two sides had a heated debate. Lawyer Sun Guanche not only denied Wu Lishi's qualifications as a witness, but also debunked the lie that Li Sangu was Xian Mudan's biological mother by calculating her age. The court finally pronounced that the plaintiff Li Sangu's request was rejected, and she was ordered to return a fresh peony green ring, a gem ring, and 1,600 yuan for living expenses.

1928年7月，北洋大学采冶科四年级学生曹书诚在校被捕，次年11月由河北高等法院进行审判，这便是轰动一时的曹书诚案，而曹书诚的辩护律师就是孙观圻和张务滋。

In July 1928, Cao Shucheng, a fourth-year student of the Department of Mining and Metallurgy of Beiyang University, was arrested at the school. He was tried by the Hebei High Court in November the following year. This was the sensational case of Cao Shucheng. Cao Shucheng's defense lawyers were Sun Guanche and Zhang Wuzi.

曹书诚时为中国共产党在北洋大学内的秘密联络员，经常组织开会、传递情报。然而在1928年被校内国民党发觉，从河北省完县（今顺平县）、蠡县和龙华店寄来的三封密函也被截获了。经过药水检查，国民党确认曹书诚为"反革命"团体的省委发信人，并且将"图谋不轨"。比如蠡县来信中说："实行铁的纪律，以便将吾党的基础确确实实地建筑在工农群众中，成为真正清一色的共产阶级政党。""最近会议议决一个重要议案，即实际上积极预备武装，制买枪械，搜寻附近奉军逃兵的枪子炮弹，准备最近将来的武装暴动。"曹书诚随即被天津警备司令部逮捕，同时被指控意图倾覆中国国民党、预备暴动，且认定曹书诚为主要负责人，执行重要任务。

Cao Shucheng was the secret liaison of the Communist Party of China in Beiyang University, often organizing meetings and disseminating information. However, in 1928, he was discovered by the school's Kuomintang that three confidential letters sent from Wan County(now Shunpin County), Li County and Longhuadian in Hebei Province were also intercepted. After a potion inspection, the Kuomintang confirmed that Cao Shucheng was the sender of the provincial party committee of the "counter-revolutionary" group and that he would "conspiracy unruly". For example, Lixian's letter said, "Implement iron discipline, so that the foundation of our party can be truly built among the workers and peasants, and become a truly all-communist party." "Recently, an important resolution was decided at the meeting, it is actually actively preparing for arm, purchased firearms, searched for the guns and shells of deserters from the nearby army, and prepared for the armed riots in the near future." Cao Shucheng was arrested by the Tianjin Garrison Command and accused of intending to overthrow the Chinese Kuomintang and preparing for a riot, and Cao Shucheng was identified as the main person in charge to perform important tasks.

在孙观圻和张务滋律师的努力下，曹书诚最终仅以加入"反革命"团体、执行重要事务罪被判处两年有期徒刑，裁判确定前羁押日数以一日抵有期徒刑一日。

With the efforts of Sun Guanche and Zhang Wuzi, Cao Shucheng was finally sentenced to two years in prison only for joining a "counter-revolutionary" group and performing important affairs. The judge determined that the number of days in custody before was equal to one day in prison.

张务滋（1890—1965），字洽升，上海人。宣统三年（1911），北洋大学堂法科法律学门甲班毕业，进士出身，授翰林院庶吉士。民国元年6月开始在天津私立直隶法政学校任教。同年11月5日，与钱俊同一天被司法部授予律师证书，编号85。1915年6月离开直隶法政学校。1921年3月开始在北洋大学任教，直到七七事变爆发前夕。其间，张务滋还在今昆明路创办了一座私立燕达学校，也就是今天昆明路小学的前身。抗战胜利后，张务滋重返北洋大学，曾任副训导长一职。

Zhang Wuzi (1890-1965), named Qiasheng, was from Shanghai. In 1911, he graduated from the class A of the law department of Beiyang University. In June of the first year of the Republic of China, he began to teach in Tianjin Private Zhili School

张务滋律师
Lawyer Zhang Wuzi

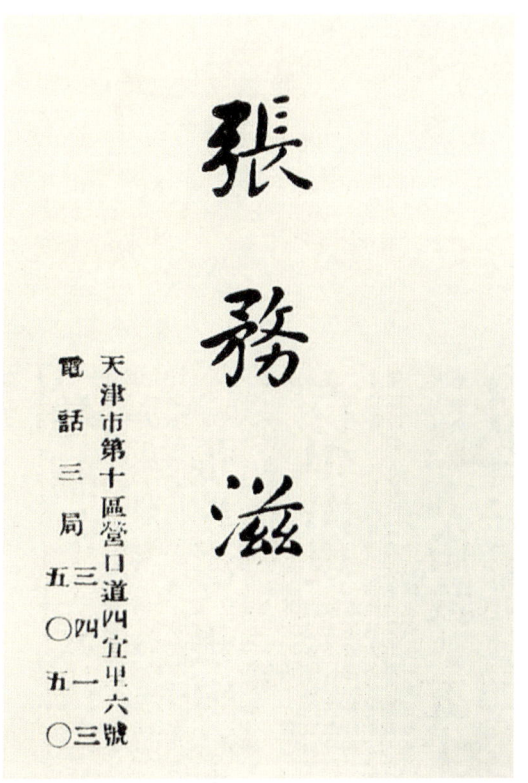

张务滋律师的名片
Business card of lawyer Zhang Wuzi

of Law and Politics. On November 5 of the same year, on the same day as Qian Jun, he was awarded a lawyer certificate by the Ministry of Justice, number 85. He left Zhili Law School in June 1915. He started teaching at Beiyang University in March 1921 until the July 7 Incident of 1937. In the meantime, Zhang Wuzi also founded a private Yanda School on Kunming Road, which is the predecessor of today's Kunming Road Primary School. After the victory of Anti-Japanese War, Zhang Wuzi returned to Beiyang University and served as the deputy dean.

除从事教育外，张务滋执业律师更是颇负盛名。他是著名的华洋商务律师，曾代理高介臣控诉美商兴泰洋行买卖合同欠款案，也曾担任袁世凯家族的法律顾问。张务滋"历办重案，拥有厚资"且"极富道德心，素日义侠性成，乐善不倦"，一年内办理各类义务案件不下一百种，为世人所称道。

In addition to his education, lawyer Zhang Wuzi is quite famous. He was a well-known Huayang business lawyer. He once represented Gao Jiechen in suing the American company Xingtai Foreign Company for arrears in the sale and purchase contract. He also served as the legal counsel of Yuan Shikai's family. Zhang Wuzi "has a history of dealing with serious cases and possesses a lot of money" and was "very ethical,

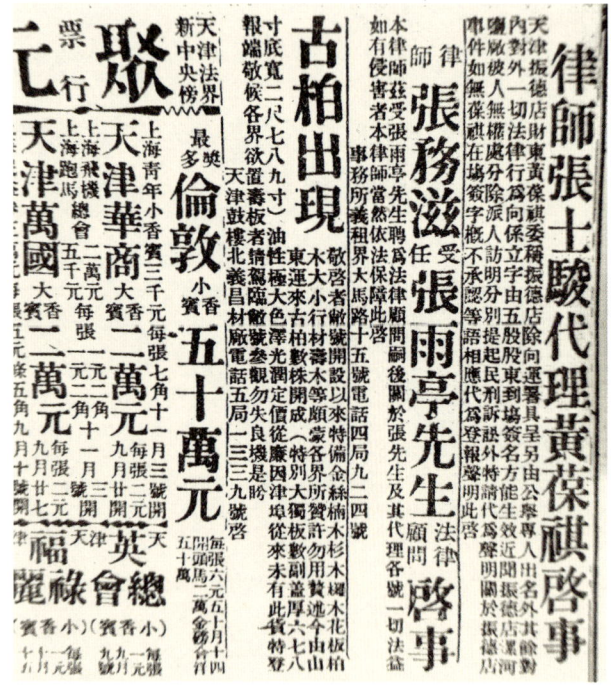

1931年9月9日张务滋律师受任法律顾问启事
Notice of lawyer Zhang Wuzi's appointment as legal counsel on September 9, 1931

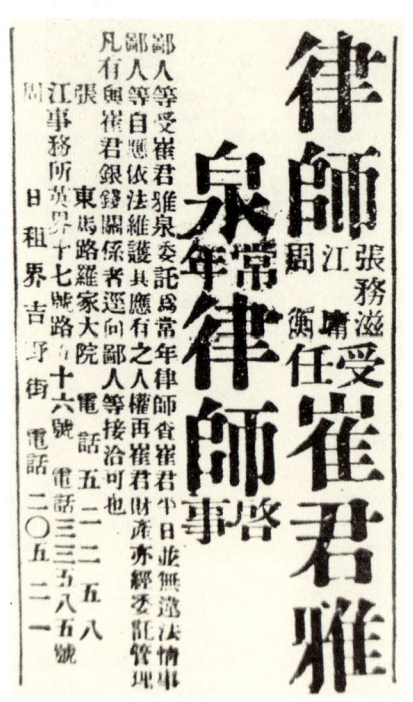

张务滋、江庸、周衡律师受托启事
Notice of entrustment of lawyers Zhang Wuzi, Jiang Yong and Zhou Heng

chivalrous, tireless". He handled more than one hundred kinds of voluntary cases in one year, which was praised by the world.

三、文绣、溥仪离婚案
3. Divorce Case of Wenxiu and Puyi

1931年秋，天津发生了中国历史上唯一一起皇妃起诉皇帝的离婚案，这便是轰动海内的文绣、溥仪离婚案。因文绣出宫时随身带了一把剪刀,故此事件又被称为"刀妃革命"。

In the autumn of 1931, Tianjin was the only divorce case in Chinese history where an imperial concubine sued the emperor. This was the Wenxiu and Puyi divorce case that caused a sensation in China. Because Wenxiu brought a pair of scissors when she left the palace, this incident was also known as the "sword concubine revolution".

文绣于宣统元年(1909)年末出生在北京方家胡同锡珍府邸。1922年11月,逊帝溥仪按照清室惯例,在不违反中华民国临时政府与清廷约定的情况下,娶婉容为后,纳文绣为妃。当时文绣早婉容一日进宫,以便在"皇帝"大婚时跪迎"皇后"。

Wenxiu was born at the Xizhen Mansion in Fangjia Hutong, Beijing at the end of 1909. In November 1922, Emperor Puyi, in accordance with the customs of the Qing Dynasty, did not violate the agreement between the Provisional Government of the Republic of China and the Qing court, after marrying Wanrong as his the Queen, Wenxiu became his concubine. At that time Wenxiu entered the palace as early as one day, so as to kneel and welcome the "Queen" when the "Emperor" got married.

进宫之初,因淑妃文绣忠厚善良、性格开朗且擅长诗文,所以溥仪对其十分宠爱,不仅经常与之谈话,还聘请专职的英语、汉语教师帮助她学习。不过,文绣的得宠,引起了婉容的忌妒。婉容是一个掩袖工谗、性情泼辣的女人,她与文绣常因生活琐事而争吵,并且总是霸道的婉容占上风,而溥仪也总是一边倒地偏袒婉容而指责文绣,甚至不允许文绣在公开场合露面。

At the beginning of entering the palace, because Wenxiu was loyal and kind, cheerful and good at poetry, Puyi loved her very much. Not only did she often talk with her, she also hired full-time English and Chinese teachers to help her learn. However, Wenxiu's favor, aroused Wanrong's jealousy. Wanrong was slanderous and aggressive woman. She and Wenxiu often quarrel over trivial matters in life, and Wanrong always prevailed. Puyi always favors Wanrong and accuses Wenxiu, even not allowing Wenxiu appeared in public.

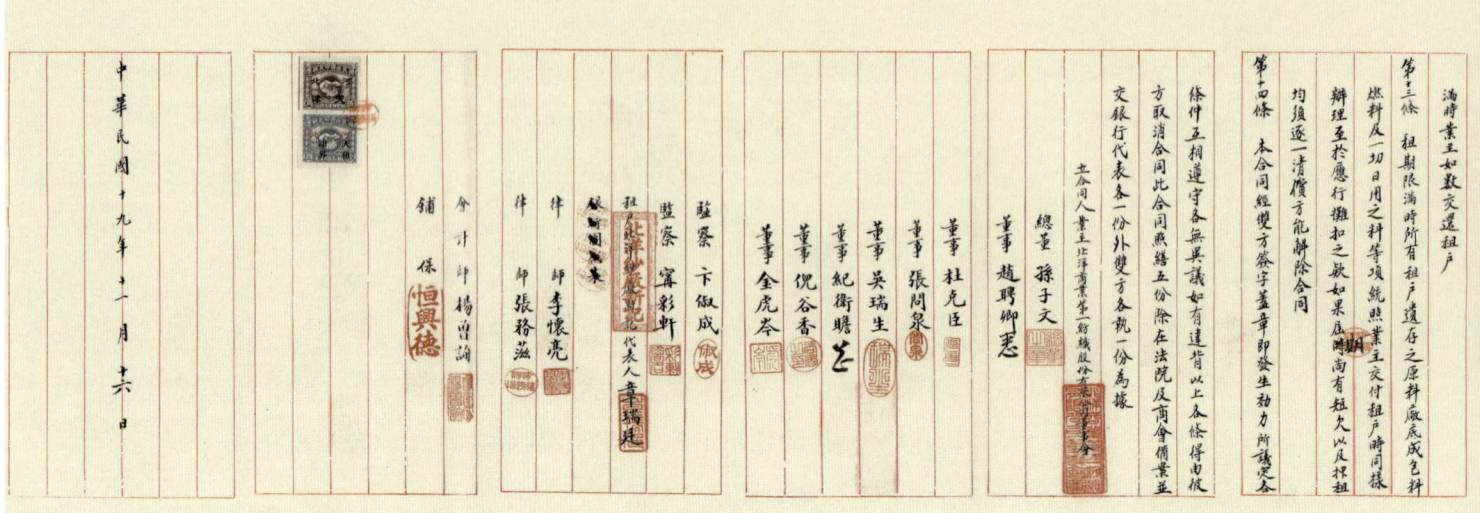

张务滋律师参与签订的北洋商业第一纺织股份有限公司与北洋纱厂新记合同

The new contract between Beiyang Commercial No.1 Textile Co., Ltd. and Beiyang Yarn Mill signed by lawyer Zhang Wuzi

1924年10月，冯玉祥发动北京政变，将溥仪赶出了紫禁城。次年2月，几经波折的溥仪住进了位于天津日租界的张园，同年3月5日，婉容、文绣也抵达了天津。或许当时没有人会想到，正是北京政变的发生，才使得溥仪从逊帝变成了中华民国的普通公民，也就为文绣提出离婚奠定了法律基础。

In October 1924, Feng Yuxiang launched a coup in Beijing and drove Puyi out of the Forbidden City. In February of the following year, Puyi, who had gone through many twists and turns, moved into Zhangyuan in the Japanese Concession of Tianjin. On March 5 of the same year, Wanrong and Wenxiu also arrived in Tianjin. Perhaps no one would have thought that it was the Beijing coup that made Puyi from Emperor to an ordinary citizen of the Republic of China, which laid the legal foundation for Wenxiu to file for divorce.

1929年7月，溥仪与婉容、文绣又迁到了静园居住，而他对文绣的精神虐待和摧残依然没有

1934	1935	1936	1937	1938	1939	1940	1941	1942	1943	1944	1945	1946
1960	1961	1962	1963	1964	1965	1966	1967	1968	1969	1970	1971	1972
1986	1987	1988	1989	1990	1991	1992	1993	1994	1995	1996	1997	1998
2012	2013	2014	2015	2016	2017	2018	2019	2020	2021	……		

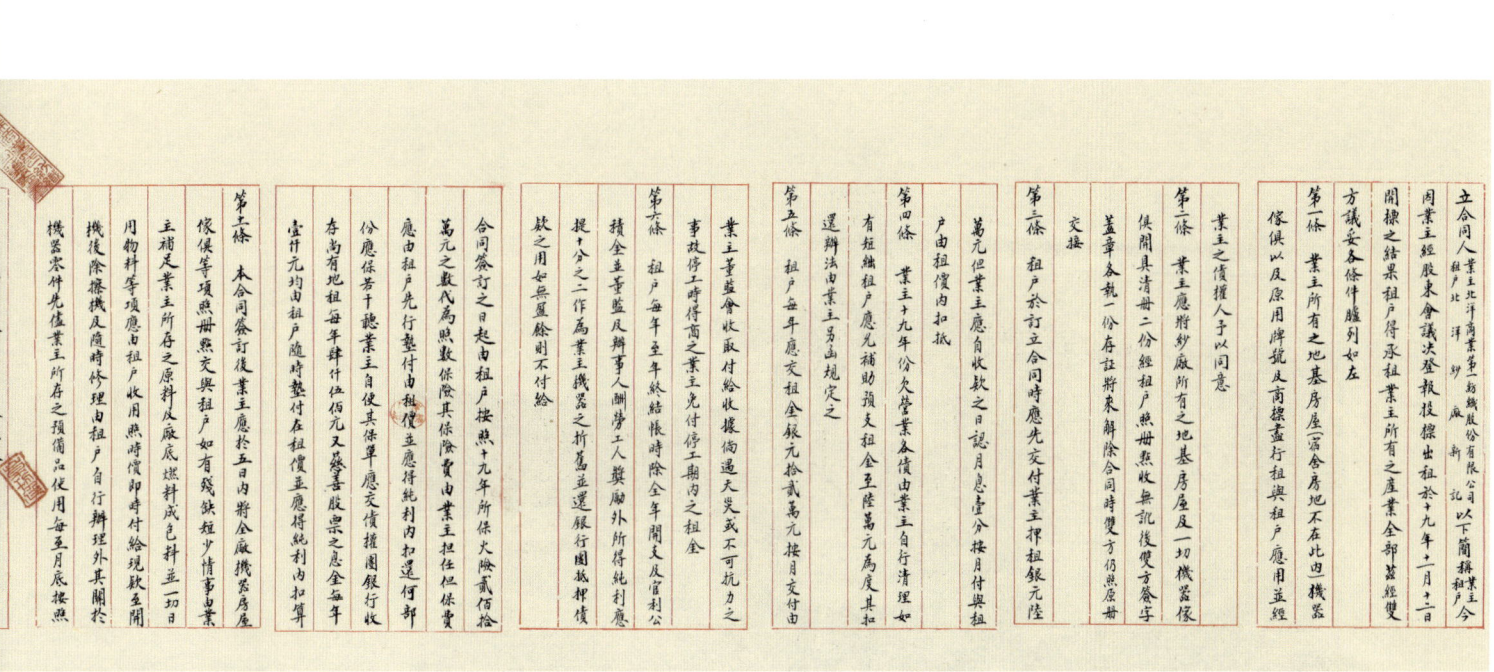

减弱，从而使文绣多次自杀未遂。溥仪发觉后，除责令太监严密监视外，还准许文绣的胞妹、老庆王的孙媳妇文珊进宫劝导。文珊的不断来访，给文绣带来了生机，一则不再自寻烦恼，二则找到了逃脱的机会。

In July 1929, Puyi, Wanrong, and Wenxiu moved to Jingyuan, and his mental abuse and devastation to Wenxiu remained undiminished. As a result, Wenxiu attempted suicide many times. After Puyi found out, in addition to ordering the eunuch to monitor closely, he also allowed Wenxiu's sister and Lao Qingwang's granddaughter Wenshan to enter the palace to persuade her. Wenshan's constant visits brought hope to Wenxiu. One did not worry about herself, and the other found a chance to escape.

1931年8月25日中午，文绣再次自杀未遂，溥仪便令太监找文珊前来劝解。当日下午3时，文珊向溥仪、婉容说，文绣哭泣不止，劝说无效，望允许她陪其外出散心，溥仪当即同意。文

1921	1922	1923	1924	1925	1926	1927	1928	1929	1930	1931	1932	1933
1947	1948	1949	1950	1951	1952	1953	1954	1955	1956	1957	1958	1959
1973	1974	1975	1976	1977	1978	1979	1980	1981	1982	1983	1984	1985
1999	2000	2001	2002	2003	2004	2005	2006	2007	2008	2009	2010	2011

1926年溥仪、婉容与威林顿夫妇、庄士敦在张园

In 1926, Puyi, Empress Wanrong, and Willinton, Reginald Johnston in Zhangyuan

绣、文珊只带了太监赵长庆，乘溥仪的专车由日租界协昌里静园驶出，直奔国民饭店。文绣、文珊等人下车后，走进37号房间，刚刚落座，文珊便对赵长庆说："你先回去吧！淑妃留在这儿了，她还要控告皇上哪！"文绣从袖中取出三函，扔给跪在地上的赵长庆，说："今儿之事与你无关，你可拿着这几封信回去转告皇上！"

At noon on August 25, 1931, Wenxiu failed in suicide again, and Puyi ordered the eunuch to find Wenshan to come to persuade her. At 3 o'clock that day, Wenshan said to Puyi and Wanrong that Wenxiu was crying and the persuasion was invalid. She hoped to allow her to accompany Wenxiu out to relax, and Puyi immediately agreed. Wenxiu and Wenshan only took Zhao Changqing, the eunuch, and took Puyi's special car from Xiechang Lane Jingyuan in the Japanese Concession to the National Hotel. After Wenxiu, Wenshan and others got out of the car, they walked into room 37. Just after sitting down, Wenshan said to Zhao Changqing,"You go back first! Shufei stayed here, and she will sue the emperor!" Wenxiu took out three letters from her sleeves and threw them to Zhao Changqing, who was kneeling on the ground, and said, "The matter today has nothing to do with you. You can take these letters back and tell the emperor!"

赵长庆赶回静园后,将三封信交给溥仪,一封为文珊函,一封为律师张士骏、张绍曾函,一封为律师李洪岳函,均称"事帝九年,未蒙一幸,孤衾独抱,悉泪暗流,备受虐待,不堪忍受。今兹要求别居,溥仪于每月定若干日前往一次,实行同居,否则唯有相见于法庭",文绣提出了准备离婚的要求。

After Zhao Changqing hurried back to Jingyuan, he handed three letters to Puyi, one wrote by Wenshan, one wrote by lawyers Zhang Shijun and Zhang Shaozeng, and one wrote by lawyer Li Hongyue. They all stated that "the emperor didn't care for me for nine year, it is abused and unbearable. I now request to live apart. Puyi will go there once a month and live together, otherwise he will only meet in court." Wenxiu asked for a divorce.

溥仪阅后大怒,立即命令将文绣抓回来。众仆人、太监闻讯后乘车直奔国民饭店,又到老庆王府邸搜查文珊的居室,均无所获。而文绣与文珊早有戒备,已从国民饭店后门离开,躲入一法国律师家中。

Puyi was furious after reading it, and immediately ordered to brought Wenxiu back. After hearing the news, the servants and eunuchs drove straight to the National Hotel and went to the Laoqingwang residence to search Wenshan's room, but found nothing. Wenxiu and Wenshan had been on guard for a long time, and they had walked out of the back door of the National Hotel and hid in the home of a French lawyer.

文绣的行动使溥仪大惊失色。当晚,溥仪召开"御前会议",以求善策。与会遗老们认为,这是"圣朝"不能容忍的,但也无可奈何。最后决定委派林棨、林廷琛两位律师出面,与文绣的律师李洪岳、张士骏和张绍曾对话,以求和解。翌日,报载:"皇妃不堪帝后的虐待、太监的威逼,自杀未遂,设计逃出,聘请律师离婚,这是数千年来皇帝老爷宫中破天荒的一次妃子革命。"

Wenxiu's actions made Puyi pale in shock. That night, Puyi held a "Prince Meeting" in order to seek good strategies. The elders attending the meeting believed that this was intolerable by the "holy dynasty", but they were helpless. Finally, it was decided to appoint two lawyers, Lin Qi and Lin Tingchen, to talk to Wenxiu's lawyers Li Hongyue, Zhang Shijun, and Zhang Shaozeng to seek reconciliation. The next day, the newspaper reported, "The imperial concubine could not bear the abuse of the emperor, the threat of the eunuch, attempted suicide, make a plan to escape, and hire a lawyer for divorce. This is an unprecedented revolution in the palace of the emperor for thousands of years."

在这期间，双方律师一直处于紧张调解的过程中。最初几轮谈判，文绣占主动，溥仪不断让步，由不准分居到同意择地别居。唯文绣提出索要50万元生活费的问题，溥仪只同意按需支付，始终未能达成协议。为了给溥仪施加压力，律师为文绣代写了诉状，起诉到河北天津地方法院，要求裁决。溥仪担心到民国法院应诉有失皇家体统，因此只得让律师调解解决。双方律师经过反复磋商，终于在1931年9月13日达成离婚协议。协议书的主要内容是：一、自立约之日起，双方完全脱离婚姻关系；二、溥仪给文绣生活费5.5万元；三、允许文绣带走常用衣物和用品；四、文绣返回母家生活，永远不能再结婚；五、双方互不损害名誉；六、文绣撤回诉状，并保证今后不再起诉。

During this period, the lawyers of both parties have been in an intense mediation process. In the first few rounds of negotiations, Wenxiu accounted for the initiative, and Puyi continued to make concessions, from not allowing separation to agreeing to choose a place to live. Wenxiu raised the issue of asking for 500,000 yuan for living expenses. Puyi only agreed to pay as needed, but never reached an agreement. In order to put pressure on Puyi, the lawyer wrote a complaint for Wenxiu, and sued the Hebei Tianjin District Court for a ruling. Puyi was worried that the court of the Republic of China would lose the imperial decency, so he had to let a lawyer mediate. After repeated negotiations, the lawyers of the two parties finally reached a divorce agreement on September 13, 1931. The main contents of the agreement are: 1. Since the date of signing the contract, both parties will be completely separated from the marriage; 2. Puyi will provide Wenxiu with a living allowance of 55,000 yuan; 3. Wenxiu will be allowed to take away common clothing and supplies; 4. Wenxiu will return to live with her mother, can never get married again; 5. The two parties do not harm each other's reputation; 6. Wenxiu withdraws the complaint and promises not to prosecute in the future.

文绣和溥仪离婚后,手中约有5.5万元生活赡养费,分给玉芬、文珊、张家(袁世凯姨太太家,离婚期间文绣一直住在此处)各5000元;三位律师每人2000元;中间人齐子度、赵香玉、李寿如各1000元;外加租用国民饭店及赏给底下人的钱,计3000余元;最终文绣手中只剩下2.6万元左右。离婚后,文绣即迁入北京辛奇胡同,初为小学教师,一年后辞职,后迁居刘海胡同。

After divorced, Wenxiu had about 55,000 yuan in support for living expenses, which were distributed to Yufen, Wenshan, and Zhang's family (the home of Yuan Shikai's wife, Wenxiu stayed here during the divorce), each of 5,000 yuan; each of the three lawyers each were 2,000 yuan; the intermediaries Qi Zidu, Zhao Xiangyu, and Li Shouru each were 1,000 yuan; plus the money for renting the National Hotel and rewarding the people below, it was more than 3,000 yuan; in the end, Wenxiu left only about 26,000 yuan. After the divorce, Wenxiu immediately moved to Beijing Xinqi Hutong. She started as a primary school teacher, resigned a year later and later moved to Liuhai Hutong.

抗战胜利后,文绣与一名叫刘振东的少校军官结婚,并迁居西城白来斜街。1953年9月17日,文绣因心肌梗塞于晚10时去世,终年44岁,埋葬在北京安定门外土城的义地。

After the victory of Anti-Japanese War, Wenxiu married a major officer named Liu Zhendong and moved to Bailai Xiejie in Xicheng. On September 17, 1953, Wenxiu died of myocardial infarction at 10 o'clock in the evening. She was 44 years old at and was buried in the righteous land of Tucheng outside Andingmen, Beijing.

双方都聘请天津律师代理的这起"皇妃"与"皇帝"的离婚案件成了重要新闻。此案一方面体现了妇女运用法律武器保护自身权益的进步意识,另一方面也体现了律师所能发挥的重要作用。

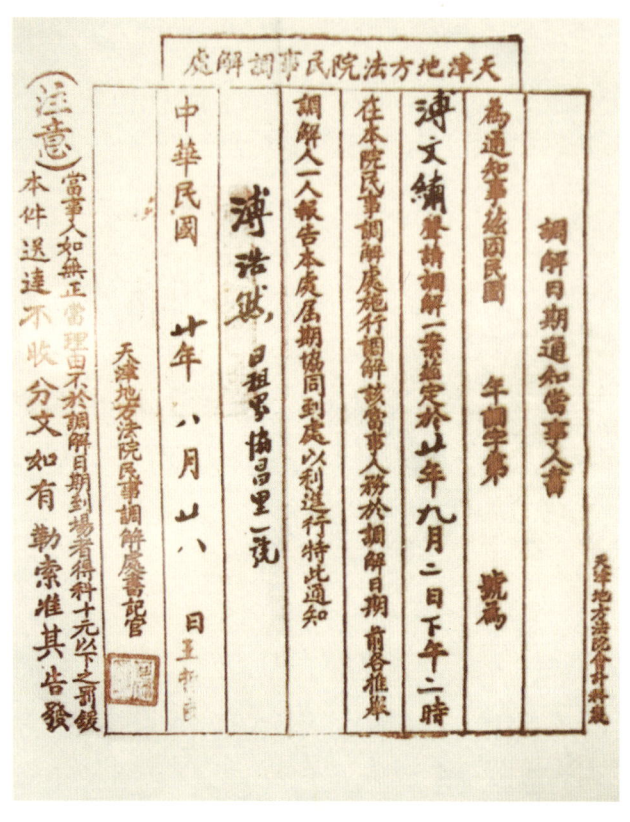

文绣、溥仪离婚调解通知书
Mediation notice of divorce of Wenxiu and Puyi

文绣离婚申请调解副状
Subsidiary of Wenxiu's divorce application mediation

The divorce case between the "imperial concubine" and the "emperor", which both sides hired lawyers from Tianjin, became important news. On the one hand, this case reflects women's progressive consciousness of using legal weapons to protect their rights and interests, on the other hand, it also reflects the important role that lawyers can play.

张绍曾（1890—1981），名省三，以字行，直隶蠡县（今河北省蠡县）人，保定优级师范毕业，在校时曾参加孙中山领导的同盟会，并亲眼见过孙中山先生。后考入天津直隶法政专门学校，五四运动时任天津学联评议部部长，作为各界联合会青年代表赴北京请愿，并赴上海参加全国学联活动。1920年毕业后，张绍曾留校任直隶法政专门学校附属初级中学教员，后在天津公立甲种商业学校担任党义和修身课教员，同时兼职做律师。

Zhang Shaozeng (1890-1981), named Xingsan tooking place of his name, born in Li County, Zhili(now Hebei Province). He graduated from Baoding Excellent Normal University. He participated in the Union League led by Sun Yat-sen and met Mr. Sun Yat-sen with his own eyes. Later, he was admitted to Tianjin Zhili School of Law and Politics. At the time of the May Fourth Movement, he served as the head of the evaluation department of the Tianjin Federation of Students. He went to Beijing to petition as the youth representative of various federations and went to Shanghai to participate in the activities of the National Federation of Students. After graduated in 1920, Zhang Shaozeng worked as a teacher in the junior high school affiliated to Zhili Law and Politics Special School. Later, he worked as a teacher of Party ethics and self-cultivation courses in Tianjin Public Class A Commercial School, as well as a part-time lawyer.

张绍曾与许多退隐天津的寓公有很深的交情，常年作他们的法律顾问；同时，张绍曾还有很多金融界、工商界的朋友，他们有法律方面的事，自然找张绍曾来处理。张绍曾还主张律师要遵循"三不"原则，即不先拿钱；不乘人之危，敲诈勒索；尽量作调解，争取不起诉。

Zhang Shaozeng had a deep friendship with many retired apartments in Tianjin and served as their legal counsel all the year round. At the same time, Zhang Shaozeng also had many friends in the financial and industrial and commercial circles. They had legal matters, so naturally they asked Zhang Shaozeng to handle them. Zhang Shaozeng also advocated a lawyer. It is necessary to follow the "three nos" principle, that is, do not take money firstly; do not take advantage of people's dangers, extortion and blackmail; try to mediate, and strive not to prosecute.

抗战胜利后，张绍曾当选天津律师公会会长。由于天津市市长张廷谔是他的盟兄弟，因此张绍曾又被委任为天津市政府观察处副处长。任职期间，他曾掩护过中共地下党员郭春源、张子光同志的工作。抗美援朝时期，张绍曾曾积极募捐救灾，并热心参加市政协组织的各项活动，曾任天津市第六届政协委员、民革中央委员、民革天津市第四届常委等职。

After the victory of Anti-Japanese War, Zhang Shaozeng was elected president of the Tianjin Bar Association. Since Tianjin Mayor Zhang Ting'e was his brother, Zhang Shaozeng was appointed as the Deputy Director of the Observation Department of Tianjin Municipal Government. During his tenure, he had covered the work of Guo Chunyuan and Zhang Ziguang who were underground members of the Communist Party of C. During Anti-Japanese War against the US and Aid Korea, Zhang Shaozeng had actively raised funds for disaster relief, and enthusiastically participated in various activities organized by the CPPCC. He used to be a member of the Sixth CPPCC in Tianjin, a member of the Central Committee of the Chinese Revolutionary Committee, and the Fourth Standing Committee of the Chinese Revolutionary Committee in Tianjin.

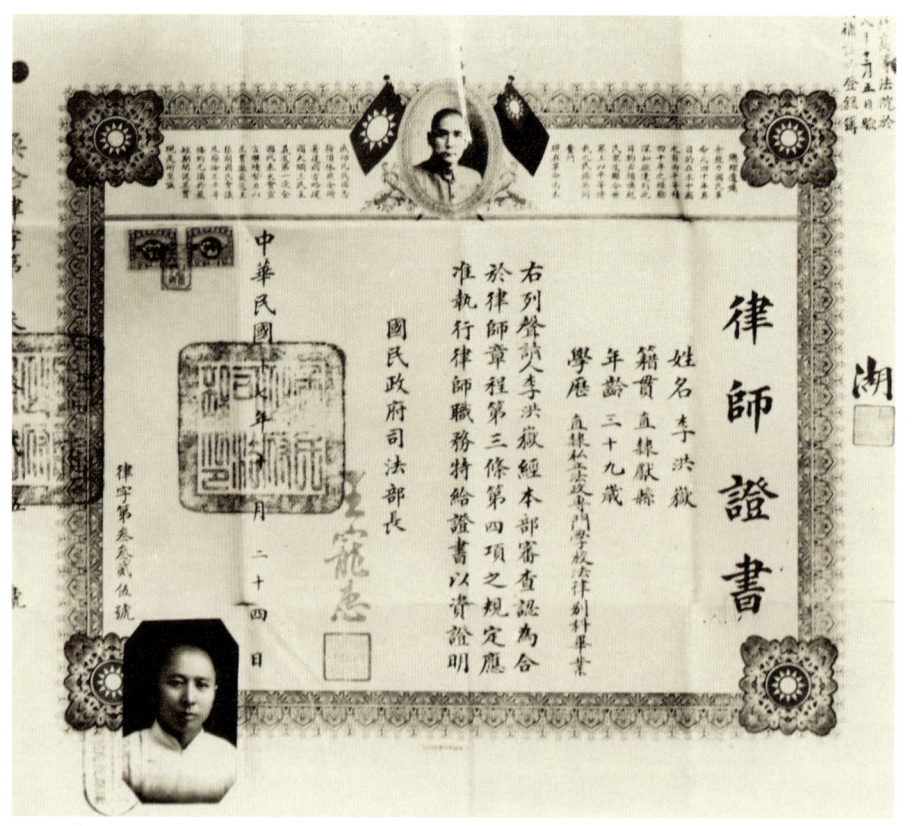

李洪岳 1928 年律师证书

Lawyer certificate of Li Hongyue in 1928

1934	1935	1936	1937	1938	1939	1940	1941	1942	1943	1944	1945	1946	
1960	1961	1962	1963	1964	1965	1966	1967	1968	1969	1970	1971	1972	
1986	1987	1988	1989	1990	1991	1992	1993	1994	1995	1996	1997	1998	
2012	2013	2014	2015	2016	2017	2018	2019	2020	2021	……		

四、施剑翘案
4. The Case of Shi Jianqiao

1935年11月13日下午,前直系军阀孙传芳在天津居士林突然被刺客枪杀,顿时震惊了全国。

On the afternoon of November 13, 1935, Sun Chuanfang, a former direct warlord, was suddenly shot and killed by an assassin in Jushilin, Tianjin, which shocked the whole country.

刺杀成功后,刺客随即向警察局自首,自称施剑翘,乃前直鲁军混成旅旅长施从滨的长女。因施从滨于1925年在蚌埠被孙传芳斩首,因此施剑翘伺机为父报仇。案发后,社会舆论对施剑翘多有同情,全国各地的声援电报不计其数,报纸、杂志争相报道,称赞她为"女中豪杰""巾帼英雄",并纷纷呼吁特赦施剑翘。与此同时,孙传芳的部下、原浙江督军卢香亭紧急召开记者会,要求严惩凶手,并停尸义园,由孙传芳的长子孙家振提起诉讼,孙观圻代理律师。施剑翘一方则由余棨昌和胡学骞担任辩护律师。1935年11月17日,天津地方法院开庭审理此案。

After the assassination was successful, the assassin immediately surrendered to the police station, claiming to be Shi Jianqiao, the eldest daughter of Shi Congbin, commander of the former Zhilu Army mixed brigade. Because Shi Congbin was beheaded by Sun Chuanfang in Bengbu in 1925, Shi Jianqiao waited for the opportunity to avenge her father. After the incident, public opinion sympathized with Shi Jianqiao. There were countless telegrams of support across the country. Newspapers and magazines rushed to report, praising her as a "female hero" and "heroine", and they called for an amnesty for Shi Jianqiao. At the same time, Lu Xiangting, Sun Chuanfang's subordinate and former Zhejiang Superintendent, urgently held a press conference to demand severe punishment of the murderer and placed the corpse in Yiyuan. Sun Chuanfang's eldest son, Sun Jiazhen, filed a lawsuit, and Sun Guanche represented the lawyer. On Shi Jianqiao's side, Yu Qichang and Hu Xueqian served as defense lawyers. On November 17, 1935, Tianjin District Court opened a court session to hear the case.

1921	1922	1923	1924	1925	1926	1927	1928	1929	1930	1931	1932	1933
1947	1948	1949	1950	1951	1952	1953	1954	1955	1956	1957	1958	1959
1973	1974	1975	1976	1977	1978	1979	1980	1981	1982	1983	1984	1985
1999	2000	2001	2002	2003	2004	2005	2006	2007	2008	2009	2010	2011

施剑翘女士
Ms. Shi Jianqiao

  根据当时的法律，杀人犯因案情有别可判十年以上有期徒刑及至死刑；若凶犯自首成立，可将刑期减为五年；若"情可悯恕"，则可减刑为两年半。由此，余荣昌、胡学骞两位律师为施剑翘据理力争，不过孙观坯律师也严正指出"情感不能置法律于不顾"，双方遂争执不下。1935年12月16日，天津地方法院作出一审裁决，施剑翘为报父仇，杀死孙传芳，理由成立，杀人后自首成立，但情不可悯，故判处有期徒刑十年。宣判后，孙家振与施剑翘同时提出上诉。

  According to the law at the time, the murderer could be sentenced to more than ten years imprisonment and to death depending on the circumstances of the case; if the perpetrator voluntarily surrenders, the sentence can be reduced to five years; if the "feeling is merciful", the sentence can be reduced to two and a half years. As a result, lawyers Yu Qichang and Hu Xueqian fought hard for Shi Jianqiao, but attorney Sun Guanche also sternly pointed out that "emotions cannot be ignored by

天津居士林旧貌
Old view of Tianjin Jushilin

the law." The two sides couldn't help but argue. On December 16, 1935, the Tianjin District Court made a first-instance ruling. Shi Jianqiao killed Sun Chuanfang in revenge for her father. The reason was established. After the murder, she surrendered, but she was unforgivable, so she was sentenced to ten years in prison. After the sentence was pronounced, Sun Jiazhen and Shi Jianqiao lodged an appeal at the same time.

  1936年1月28日，河北高等法院开庭复审。2月11日，迫于舆论压力，法官将刑期改为七年，不过施剑翘仍不服判决，向南京最高法院提出了上诉。经过数月的调查审核，最高法院终于在1936年8月25日作出终审判决，上诉驳回，维持河北高等法院之宣判。不过很快，南京国民政府主席林森签发的国府公告便送达了天津，文中称："据司法院呈称，施剑翘因其父施从滨曩年为孙传芳残害，痛切父仇，乘机行刺，并即时坦然自首，听候惩处。论其杀人行为，固属

1921	1922	1923	1924	1925	1926	1927	1928	1929	1930	1931	1932	1933
1947	1948	1949	1950	1951	1952	1953	1954	1955	1956	1957	1958	1959
1973	1974	1975	1976	1977	1978	1979	1980	1981	1982	1983	1984	1985
1999	2000	2001	2002	2003	2004	2005	2006	2007	2008	2009	2010	2011

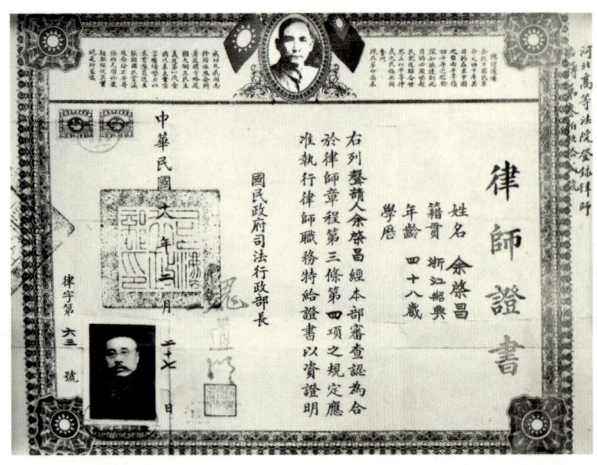

余棨昌 1929 年律师证书
Lawyer certificate of Yu Qichang in 1929

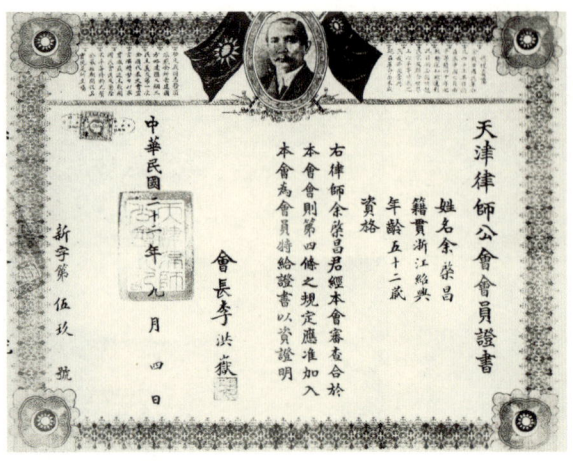

余棨昌 1933 年律师公会会员证书
Tianjin Bar Association membership certificate of Yu Qichang in 1933

触犯刑法，而以一女子发于孝思，奋力不顾，其志可哀，其情尤可原。现据各学校各民众团体纷请特赦，所有该施剑翘原判徒刑，拟请依法免其执行等语，兹依《中华民国训政时期约法》第六十八条之规定，宣告将原判处有期徒刑七年之施剑翘特予赦免，以示矜恤。"

On January 28, 1936, the Hebei High Court opened a court review. On February 11, under pressure from public opinion, the judge changed the sentence to seven years, but Shi Jianqiao still refused to accept the sentence and appealed to the Nanjing Supreme Court. After several months of investigation and review, the Supreme Court finally made a final judgment on August 25, 1936. The appeal was rejected and the sentence of the Hebei High Court was upheld. But soon, the government announcement issued by Lin Sen, chairman of the Nanjing National Government, was delivered to Tianjin. The article stated, "According to the Judicial Yuan, Shi Jianqiao took the opportunity to assassinate Sun Chuanfang because her father Shi Congbin was killed by Sun Chuanfang. And she immediately surrendered calmly and awaited punishment. On her murder, it is a violation of the criminal law, but her filial piety and desperately desperate are particularly understandable and forgivable. Now according to the requests of various schools and public organizations Amnesty, it is proposed to exempt her from execution according to law, in accordance with the provisions

1934	1935	1936	1937	1938	1939	1940	1941	1942	1943	1944	1945	1946
1960	1961	1962	1963	1964	1965	1966	1967	1968	1969	1970	1971	1972
1986	1987	1988	1989	1990	1991	1992	1993	1994	1995	1996	1997	1998
2012	2013	2014	2015	2016	2017	2018	2019	2020	2021	……		

of Article 68 of the *Law during the Political Training Period of the Republic of China*, it is declared that forgive Shi Jianqiao who was originally sentenced to seven years of imprisonment. Used to express pity and condolences."

特赦的结果是时任国民政府军事委员会副委员长的冯玉祥发挥的作用。1912年年初滦州起义爆发，施剑翘的四叔施从云任滦州革命军总司令，冯玉祥为总参谋长。后施从云为挽救起义部队而牺牲，冯玉祥一直感念在心。施剑翘案发生后，冯玉祥便联络于右任、李烈钧、张继、宋哲元等20多名国民党中央委员联名上书，吁请对施剑翘特赦。南京国民政府权衡利弊，遂于1936年10月14日签发了特赦令。

The result of the amnesty was influenced by Feng Yuxiang, the vice chairman of the National Military Commission. The uprising in Luanzhou broke out in early 1912. Shi Jianqiao's fourth uncle Shi Congyun served as the commander-in-chief of the Luanzhou Revolutionary Army, and Feng Yuxiang was the chief of the general staff. Shi Congyun sacrificed to save the uprising troops, Feng Yuxiang has always been grateful. After the case of Shi Jianqiao, Feng Yuxiang contacted more than 20 members of the Kuomintang Central Committee including Yu Youren, Li Liejun, Zhang Ji, Song Zheyuan to petition jointly, calling for an amnesty for Shi Jianqiao. Nanjing National Government weighed the pros and cons and issued an amnesty on October 14, 1936.

七七事变至新中国成立前的天津律师

TIANJIN LAWYERS IN THE PERIOD FROM THE JULY 7 INCIDENT OF 1937 TO THE FOUNDING OF THE PEOPLE'S REPUBLIC OF CHINA

百年律师在天津
ONE HUNDRED YEARS OF LAWYERS ACCUMULATED HISTORY FOCUSED ON TIANJIN

沦陷后的天津律师 / 224
TIANJIN LAWYERS AFTER THE OCCUPATION

一、英法租界的选择 / 226
1. Choice of Anglo-French Concession

二、律师的生存状态 / 228
2. The Living Condition of Lawyers

三、沦陷时期的天津律师公会 / 232
3. Tianjin Bar Association in the Occupied Period

《律师法》的实施与民国律师制度的最终完成 / 238
THE IMPLEMENTATION OF THE *LAWYERS LAW* AND THE FINAL COMPLETION OF LAWYER SYSTEM IN THE REPUBLIC OF CHINA

一、律师自由职业者身份的强化 / 239
1. Strengthening the Status of Lawyers as Freelancers

二、律师资格的获取 / 240
2. The Acquisition of Lawyer's Qualification

三、律师应履行的义务 / 242
3. Obligations of Lawyers

四、1945 年《律师法》对 1941 年《律师法》的修正 / 248
4. Amendments to the *Lawyers Law* of 1941 by the *Lawyers Law* of 1945

抗战胜利后的天津司法与律师 / 250
TIANJIN JUDICIAL AND LAWYERS AFTER THE VICTORY OF ANTI-JAPANESE WAR

一、抗战胜利后天津的司法活动 / 250
1. Judicial Activities in Tianjin after the Victory of AntiJapanese War

二、20 世纪 40 年代末的天津律师 / 259
2. Tianjin Lawyers in the Late 1940s

三、20 世纪 40 年代末的天津律师公会 / 264
3. Tianjin Bar Association in the Late 1940s

沦陷后的天津律师

TIANJIN LAWYERS AFTER THE OCCUPATION

七七事变以后,日军随即向平津发起进攻,7月29日开始攻击天津守军,30日午后天津陷落。8月1日,在日军的操纵下,管理天津的临时机构伪天津市治安维持会成立。9月,伪天津高等法院和伪天津地方法院成立,由伪维持会直接领导,方若任伪"两院"院长。因日军进攻天津时,天津地方法院(位于今河北区三马路南端)建筑被毁,案卷及相关律师资料也荡然无存,因此伪法院设在日租界旭街利津公司内,后迁到河北西窑洼天津看守分所旧址内办公,直到1942年2月迁至南马路188号。

After the July 7 Incident of 1937, the Japanese attacked Pingjin immediately. On July 29, they began to attack the Tianjin defenders. Tianjin fell in the afternoon on the 30th. On August 1, under the control of the Japanese army, the Tianjin Municipal Public Order Maintenance Committee, a temporary organization that manages Tianjin, was established. In September, the puppet Tianjin High Court and the puppet Tianjin District Court were established, under the direct leadership of the puppet Maintenance Council, and Fang Ruo served as the puppet president of the "two organizations". When the Japanese army attacked Tianjin, the building of the Tianjin District Court (located at the southern end of San Road, Hebei District) was destroyed, and the case file and relevant lawyer information were also gone. Therefore, the puppet court was set up in the Lijin Company in Asahi Street in the Japanese Concession and moved to West Hebei The office of Yaowa Tianjin Detention Branch was located on the old site until it moved to No.188 South Road in February 1942.

1934	1935	1936	1937	1938	1939	1940	1941	1942	1943	1944	1945	1946
1960	1961	1962	1963	1964	1965	1966	1967	1968	1969	1970	1971	1972
1986	1987	1988	1989	1990	1991	1992	1993	1994	1995	1996	1997	1998
2012	2013	2014	2015	2016	2017	2018	2019	2020	2021	……		

1937年12月14日，伪华北临时政府在北京成立，司法行政事务由伪法制部管理。次年1月，伪天津高等法院改为伪河北高等法院天津分院，伪天津地方法院名称不变；院长、推事、书记官等由伪法制部派遣。1940年3月30日，汪伪政府在南京成立，随即设立了伪华北政务委员会，管辖河北、山东、山西三省和北京、天津、青岛三个特别市。伪河北高等法院天津分院和伪天津地方法院同时隶属于伪华北政务委员会。同年5月，伪"两院"改由伪临时处理法务委员会领导，1943年11月又划归伪华北事务署。

On December 14, 1937, the puppet North China Provisional Government was established in Beijing, and judicial and administrative affairs were managed by the puppet Ministry of Legal Affairs. In January of the following year, the puppet Tianjin High Court was changed to the puppet Hebei High Court Tianjin Branch, and the name of the puppet Tianjin District Court remained unchanged; the president, judges, and clerks were dispatched by the puppet legal system. On March 30, 1940, the Wang Puppet Government was established in Nanjing, and then the puppet North China Government Affairs Committee was established to govern the three provinces of Hebei, Shandong, and Shanxi and the three special cities of Beijing, Tianjin, and Qingdao. The Tianjin Branch of the puppet Hebei High Court and the puppet Tianjin District Court are also affiliated to the puppet North China Political Affairs Committee. In May of the same year, the "two organizations" was replaced by the puppet temporary legal affairs committee, and in November 1943 it was placed under the puppet North China Affairs Office.

天津沦陷后，律师与其他行业一样进入了低潮期。他们或停止执业，另谋出路；或搬迁异地，辗转奔向后方；而留下来继续做律师的也不在少数，只是他们呈现出了不同于以往的特殊生存形态。

After the occupied of Tianjin, lawyers, like other industries, entered a low ebb. They may stop practicing and find another way out; or relocate to another place and rush to the rear; and there are not a few who stayed behind to continue to be lawyers, but they present a special living form different from the past.

1921	1922	1923	1924	1925	1926	1927	1928	1929	1930	1931	1932	1933
1947	1948	1949	1950	1951	1952	1953	1954	1955	1956	1957	1958	1959
1973	1974	1975	1976	1977	1978	1979	1980	1981	1982	1983	1984	1985
1999	2000	2001	2002	2003	2004	2005	2006	2007	2008	2009	2010	2011

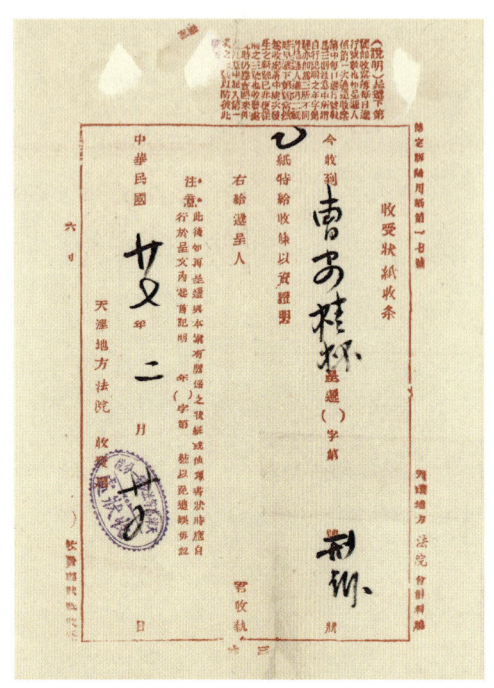 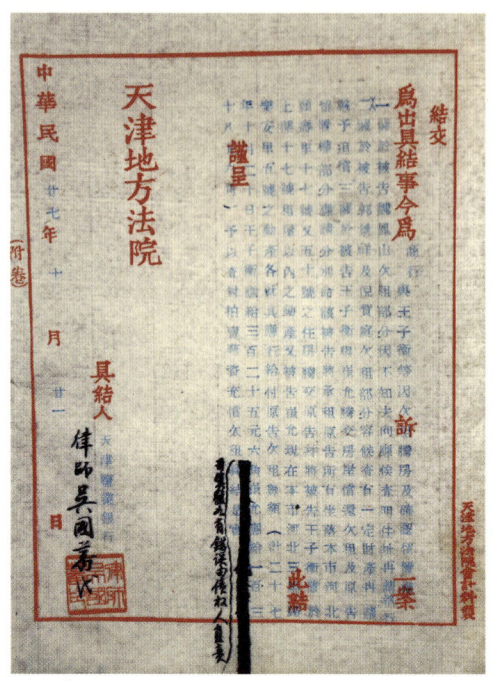

1938年2月伪天津地方法院受理案件证明
Proof of case accepted by puppet Tianjin District Court in February 1938

1938年伪天津地方法院具结书
Recognition of the puppet Tianjin District Court in 1938

一、英法租界的选择
1. Choice of Anglo-French Concession

天津沦陷之前，约有40%的律师活动在河北大经路（今中山路）的省（市）政府一带。陷落后，大部分律师进入了相对安全的英法租界。据《1941年天津律师公会会员录》统计，当时在英租界内设立事务所的律师有55人，是人数最多的区域，法租界则有31人。

Before occupied of Tianjin, about 40% of the lawyers' activities were in the province (city) area of Hebei Dajing Road (now Zhongshan Road). After the fall, most lawyers entered the relatively safe Anglo-French concession. According to statistics from the *Members of the Tianjin Bar Association in 1941*, there were 55 lawyers in the British Concession, which was the largest number of lawyers, while there were 31 in the French Concession.

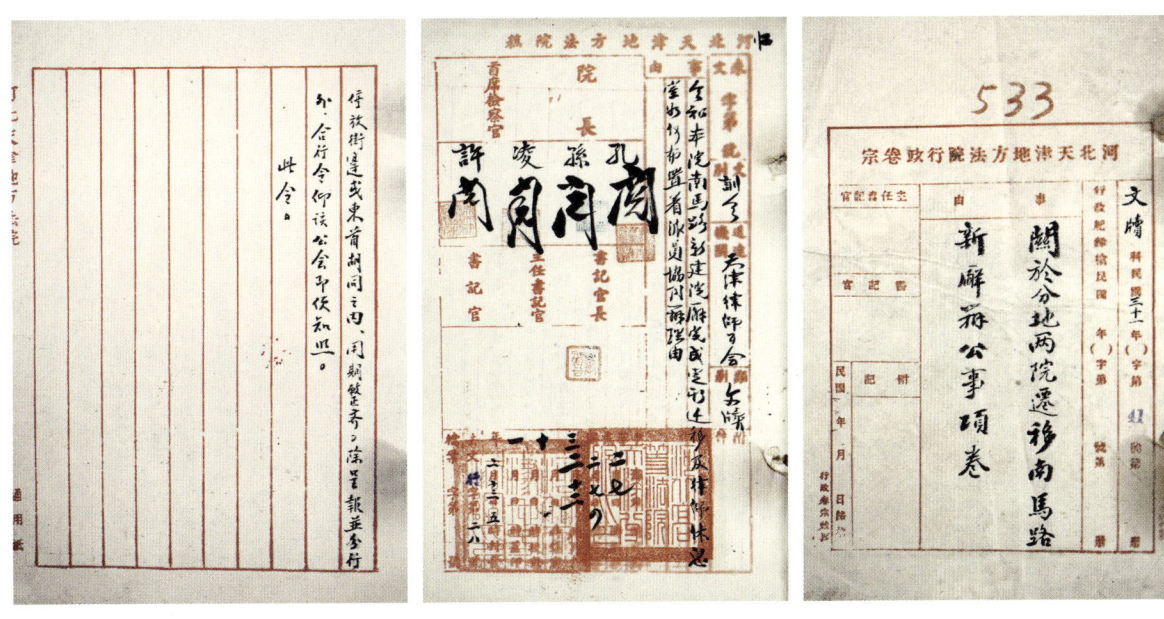

1942年伪天津地方法院移至南马路办公事
In 1942, the puppet Tianjin District Court moved to South Road for office

中国律师之所以选择英法租界，除了相对安全的生存环境外，还能找到更多的业务，有利于维持生计。这一时期，以房地产买卖为代表的非诉讼案件成了天津沦陷后租界内律师代理的一大主业。租界人口的激增和货币状况的不稳定使不少商人从事房地产投机，而代办律师就可从中获得大笔佣金。此外，成立大契，律师要收公证费；代买方登报声明置产，要收手续费；代理产权人向法院登记所有权，要按产值酌收代办费等。由此，许多律师都与会计师合作，在重要的地点开办联合事务所。比如李洪岳和王芝邺在今滨江道基泰大楼开办宗正联合事务所，徐维藩和宋翰云在今建设路寿德大楼开办中信法律联合事务所，张靖远与罗耀枢在中街（今解放北路）新华信托储蓄银行大楼开办信成法律会计联合事务所等。

　　The reason why Chinese lawyers choose the Anglo-French concession is that in addition to a relatively safe living environment, they can also find more business, which is conducive to their livelihood. In this period, non-litigation cases represented by real estate sales have become one of main business represented by lawyers in the concession after the fall of Tianjin. The rapid increase in the population of the concession and the instability of the currency situation have caused many businessmen to engage in real estate speculation, and the agent lawyers can obtain large commissions from them. In addition, for the establishment of a major contract, the lawyer must charge a notarization fee; the buyer will be required to charge a handling fee for the declaration of the purchase of the property on behalf of the buyer; when the property owner registers the ownership with the court, the agency fee must be charged according to the value of the output. As a result, many lawyers have worked with accountants to open joint firms in important locations. For example, Li Hongyue and Wang Zhicun opened Zongzheng Joint Office in Jitai Building on Binjiang Road, Xu Weifan and Song Hanyun opened CITIC Law Joint Office in Shoude Building on Jianshe Road, Zhang Jingyuan and Luo Yaoshu in Zhongjie (now Jiefang North Road) Xinhua Trust & Savings Bank The building opened Xincheng legal and accounting joint office, etc.

1941年12月7日太平洋战争爆发，第二天清晨，日本军队进入并接管了英租界，加之此前法国维希傀儡政府的成立，英法租界的优势也一去不复返了。

The Pacific War broke out on December 7, 1941. In the early morning of the next day, Japanese troops entered and took over the British concession. In addition to the establishment of the French Vichy puppet government, the advantages of the British and French concessions were gone.

二、律师的生存状态
2. The Living Condition of Lawyers

随着民族危机的加深，天津律师越发坚守民族底线，坚定民族气节，"凭借中央遗留之中国法律，保障并非自己沦陷之中国民权，以为明日之抗战"，虽不免"一经出头代理得胜，则代理律师或被殴打，或被敌宪兵逮捕，或被残杀"，却依然苦苦支撑，以尽匹夫之责。

With the deepening of the national crisis, Tianjin lawyers have increasingly adhered to the national bottom line and strengthened national integrity. Relying on the legacy of the Chinese law to protect the rights of the citizens who were not under their own occupation, they believed that Anti-Japanese War in the future would inevitably be victorious in the beginning, and the lawyers would be beaten, or arrested by the enemy's military police, or killed. Still struggling to support, in order to fulfill the responsibilities of ordinary people.

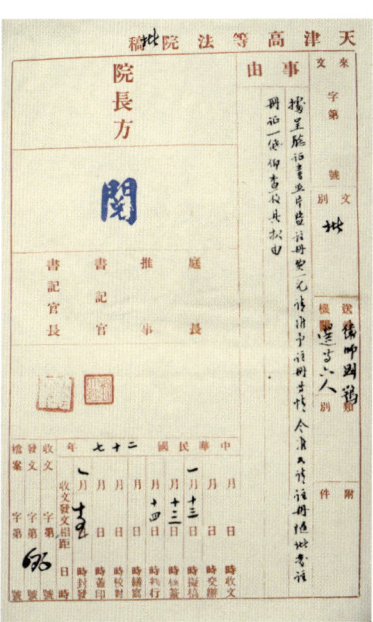
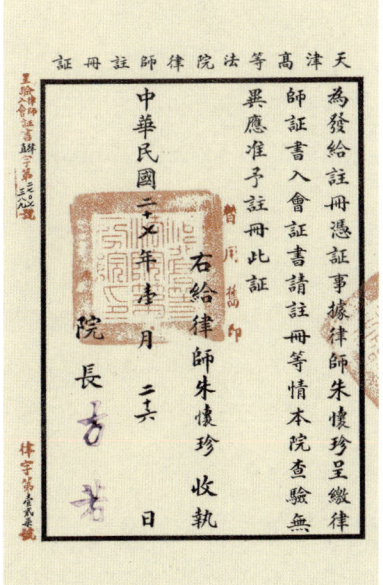
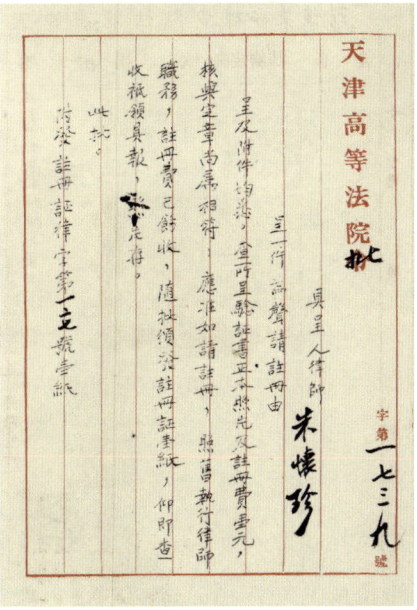

1938年伪天津高等法院准予朱怀珍律师注册

In 1938, the puppet Tianjin High Court granted the registration of lawyer Zhu Huaizhen

有的律师以身份为掩护，积极参加中国共产党领导的抗日斗争。比如胡毓枫律师经常与法商学校的进步青年共同参加中共地下党组织的各类活动，并以律师身份作掩护，到津北王庄、双口、渔坝口等地宣传抗日救亡，后不幸被害，年仅40岁。

Some lawyers actively participated in the anti-Japanese struggle led by the Communist Party of China under the cover of identity. For example, lawyer Hu Yufeng often participates in various activities organized by the CCP's underground party with progressive youths from the School of Law and Business, and as a lawyer, he travels to Wangzhuang, Shuangkou, Yubakou and other places in Jinbei to promote anti-Japanese and national salvation, and was later killed in only 40 years old.

另有一些律师同样利用自己的合法身份支持抗日活动。比如大律师张务滋将不愿在敌伪学校教书的教师聘用到燕达学校，并在教学过程中抵制奴化教育，宣传抗日书籍，并积极介绍青年学生到大后方继续深造。张务滋的爱国行为引起了日寇的怀疑，日伪文教部甚至将其传讯批捕。大律师张士骏同样借助其身份，出资护送学生、技术人才及其家属800余户转移至大后方，并掩护中华民族解放先锋队（简称"民先"）成员到其家中避难。

Other lawyers also used their legal status to support anti-Japanese activities. For example, Zhang Wuzi, founded Yanda School in order to solve the work problem of teachers who are unwilling to teach in schools of the enemy. During the teaching process, he resisted enslavement education, promoted anti-Japanese books, and actively introduced young students to the rear of the university to continue their studies. Zhang Wuzi's patriotic behavior aroused the suspicion of the Japanese invaders, and the puppet Ministry of Education and Culture even sent him for interrogation. Barrister Zhang Shijun also used his identity to escort more than 800 students, technical talents and their family members to the rear, and protected members of the Chinese National Liberation Vanguard ("Minxian") to take refuge in his home.

大部分律师还是采取了一种在其职业及能力范围之内，积极维护当事人权益的做法，并在很大程度上起到了为天津百姓伸张正义的作用。处理经济问题、解决经济纠纷是这一时期律师

1934	1935	1936	1937	1938	1939	1940	1941	1942	1943	1944	1945	1946
1960	1961	1962	1963	1964	1965	1966	1967	1968	1969	1970	1971	1972
1986	1987	1988	1989	1990	1991	1992	1993	1994	1995	1996	1997	1998
2012	2013	2014	2015	2016	2017	2018	2019	2020	2021	……		

的主要工作。比如金银首饰同业公会会员同义金店为避免因停业而造成债权等方面的纠纷，就聘请了张恩寿律师代理该号出兑以及承兑人续租等方面的法律事务。

Most lawyers still adopted a practice of actively safeguarding the rights and interests of the parties within the scope of their profession and ability, and to a large extent played a role in upholding justice for the people of Tianjin. Dealing with economic problems and resolving economic disputes are the main tasks of lawyers in this period. For example, Tongyi Gold Store, a member of the Gold and Silver Jewelry Trade Association, hired lawyer Zhang Enshou to represent the bank's cashier and the acceptor's lease renewal in order to avoid disputes over creditor's rights due to the suspension of business.

当然也有一些律师，"自堕其人格，看了人家的'眼前富贵'，就生羡慕之心，半途失节"。还有一些"黑律师"，拉案子不问事件大小，给钱就干，办起事来不问青红皂白，有缝就钻，通过制造假证、串通威胁等手段榨取委托人的钱财。

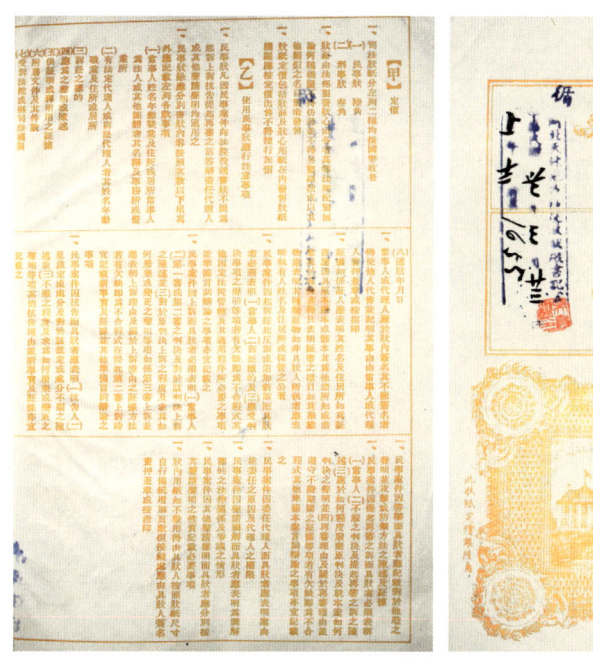
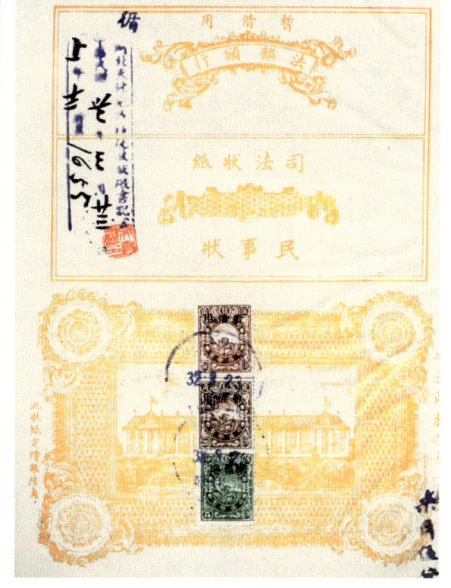

1943 年天津民事司法状纸
Tianjin civil judicial pleadings in 1943

Of course, there are some lawyers who "degenerate themselves into their own personalities, and when they see others' 'prosperity in front of them', they are envied and lost in the middle." There are also some "fake lawyers" who do not ask about the size of the incident, and do what they pay for. When they do things, they don't ask for anything, but drill if there are gaps. They squeeze the client's money through creating names, creating false certificates, and colluding.

三、沦陷时期的天津律师公会
3. Tianjin Bar Association in the Occupied Period

天津沦陷后，日寇占领了天津律师公会位于黄纬路诚安里27号的会址，公会只能暂时转移到诚安里4号办公，之后又被日本商会占用，公会活动也不得已陷入低潮。虽然此时大部分律师因日军封锁而无法正常参加公会活动，但公会的主要成员，如会长和各评议员，仍然可以借助租界的庇护，与日伪政府周旋，以维持会务。

After the fall of Tianjin, the Japanese invaders occupied the meeting site of the Tianjin Bar Association in Cheng'an Lane, Huangwei Road. The association could only temporarily move to No.4 Cheng'an Lane, and was later occupied by the Japanese Chamber of Commerce. The activities of the Association also had to fall into a low ebb. Although most of the lawyers were unable to participate in the activities of the guild due to the Japanese military blockade, the main members of the guild, such as the chairman and members of the council, could still use the shelter of the concessions to deal with the puppet governments to maintain the affairs of the meeting.

1940年10月1日，天津律师公会向伪河北天津地方法院呈报了1940年9月22日天津律师公会会员大会改选的职员名单，其中会长李洪岳，副会长田淇清、朱道孔，评议员朱德武、耿运枢、王庭兰、胡学骞、李维祺、白鋆、夏彦邦、冯景旺、李兆庚，干事邢忠烈、刘玉峰、薛万选等。

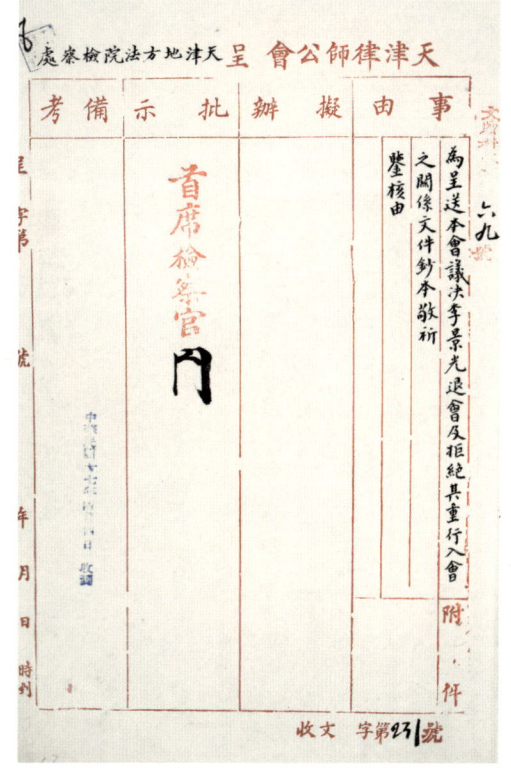
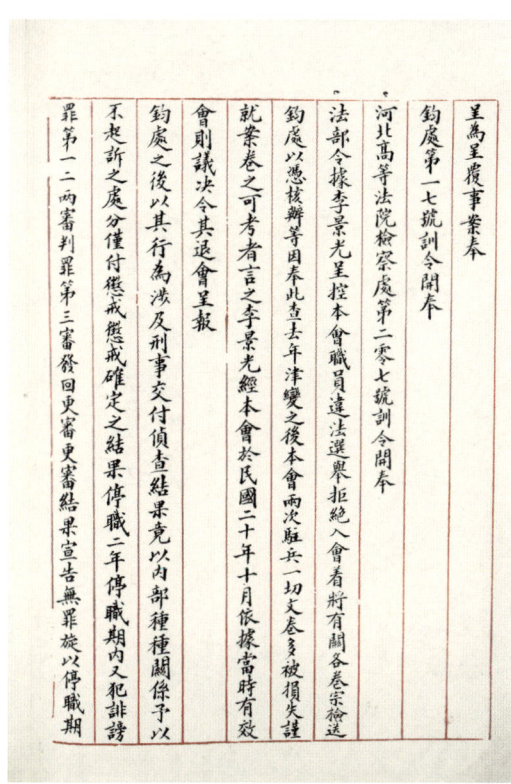
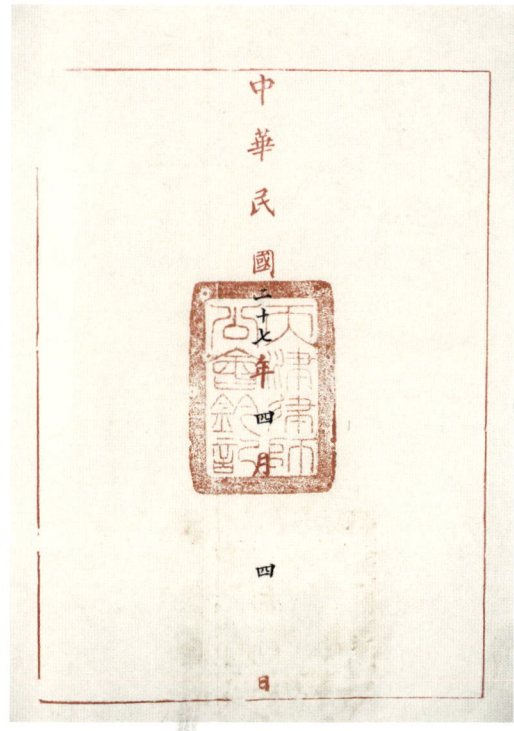
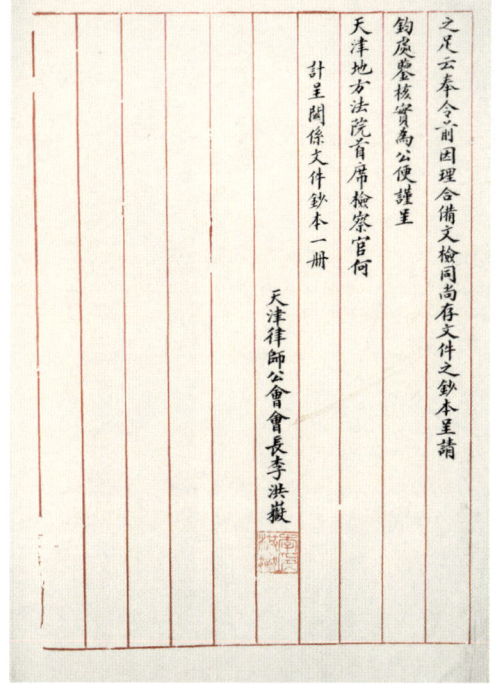

天津律师公会致伪天津地方法院检察处呈报

Report from the Tianjin Bar Association to the Procuratorate Department of the puppet Tianjin District Court

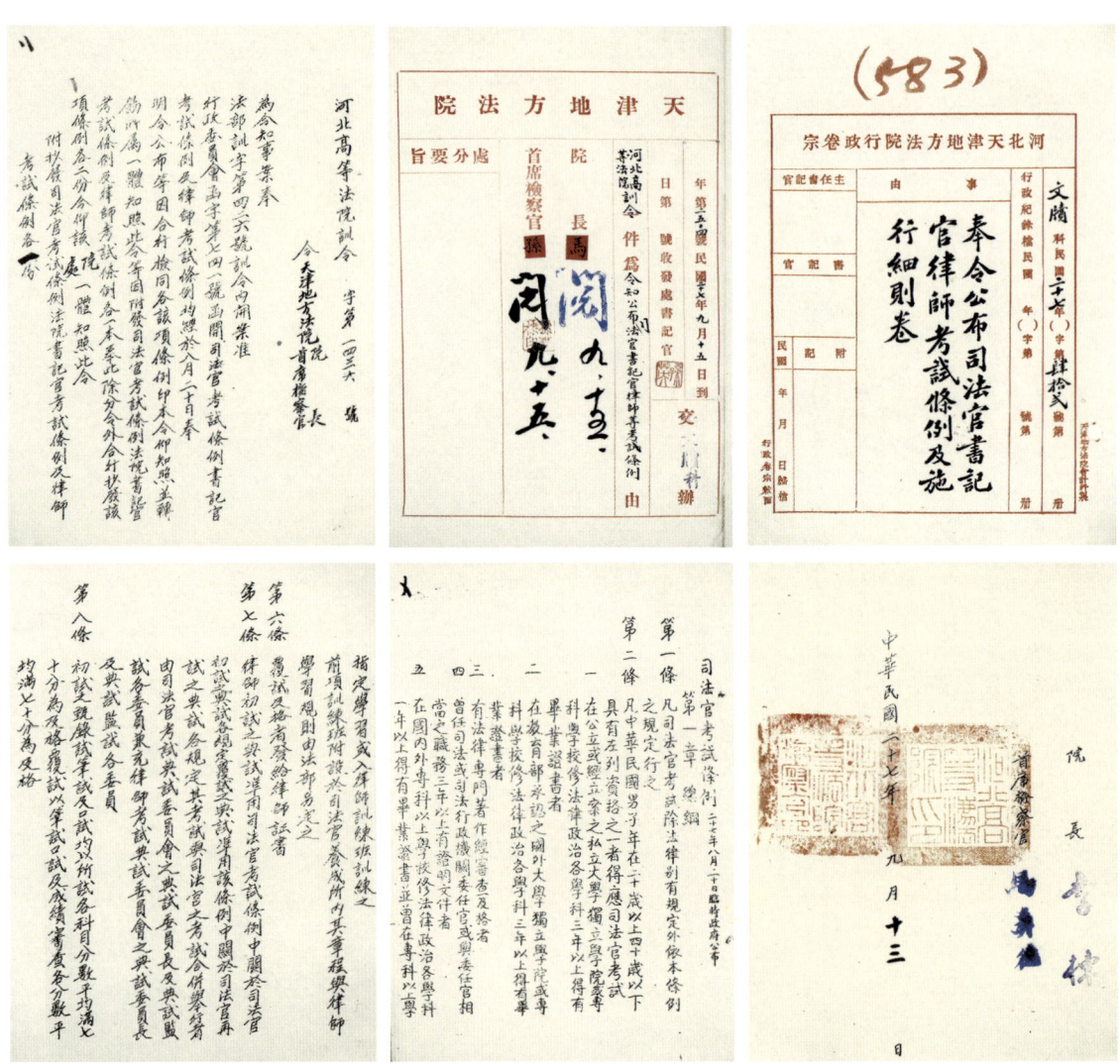

1938年伪河北天津地方法院公布司法考试条例事
In 1938, the puppet Hebei Tianjin District Court announced the judicial examination regulations

On October 1, 1940, the Tianjin Bar Association submitted to the puppet Hebei Tianjin District Court the list of staff re-elected at the Member's General Assembly of the Tianjin Bar Association on September 22, 1940. Among them, chairman Li Hongyue, vice chairmen Tian Qiqing and Zhu Dakong, comment Members Zhu Dewu, Geng Yunshu, Wang Tinglan, Hu Xueqian, Li Weiqi, Bai Yun, Xia Yanbang, Feng Jingwang, Li Zhaogeng, and officers Xing Zhonglie, Liu Yufeng, Xue Wanxuan, etc.

1934	1935	1936	1937	1938	1939	1940	1941	1942	1943	1944	1945	1946
1960	1961	1962	1963	1964	1965	1966	1967	1968	1969	1970	1971	1972
1986	1987	1988	1989	1990	1991	1992	1993	1994	1995	1996	1997	1998
2012	2013	2014	2015	2016	2017	2018	2019	2020	2021	……		

从1937年下半年开始，日寇加强了对华北的法西斯统治，并以"自首"和策动告密的方式瓦解华北的抗日力量，同时在天津实行"清乡"。于是，一些投机求荣之人，"向日本军事机关投函诬陷者尤夥，人人谈虎色变，咸具戒心"。面对这样的局面，天津律师公会于1938年2月18日从法律的角度拟订了三项办法，向伪天津地方法院请愿。三项办法包括：匿名告发函件概置之不理；具名告发者，先传讯告发人，倘无其人，即以匿名信视之，若有其人，令其具结负诬告责任，再传集原被双方，于短期内送交法院，依法核办；如告发现行犯，扭送宪兵或特务机关者，即将原被双方暂行扣留，于短期内送交法院核办。经过律师公会的多方奔走，该办法终于得到了伪地方法院和日本军部的批准。

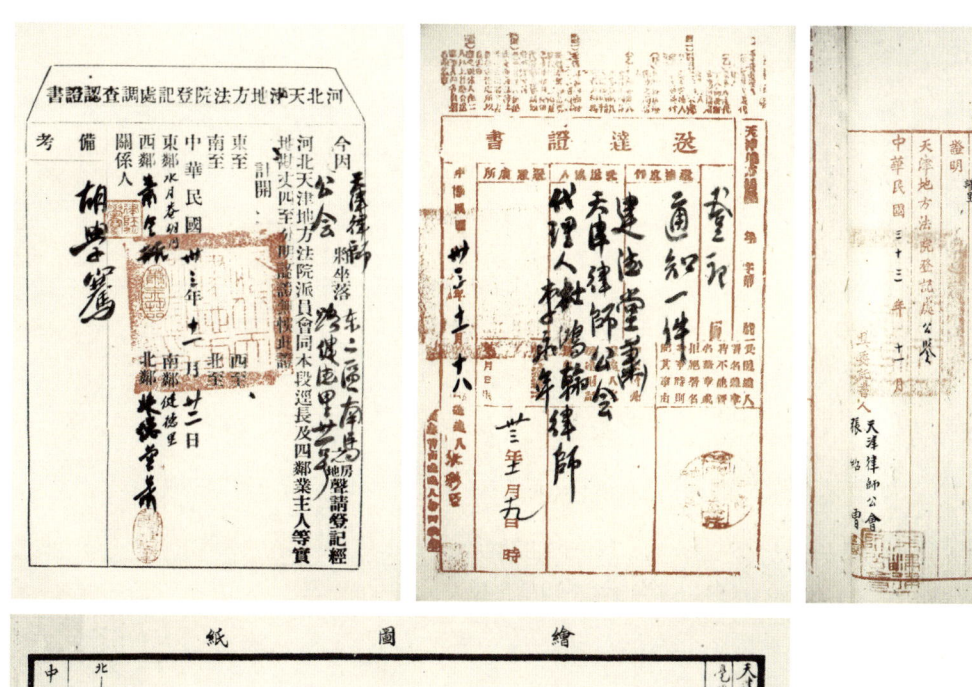

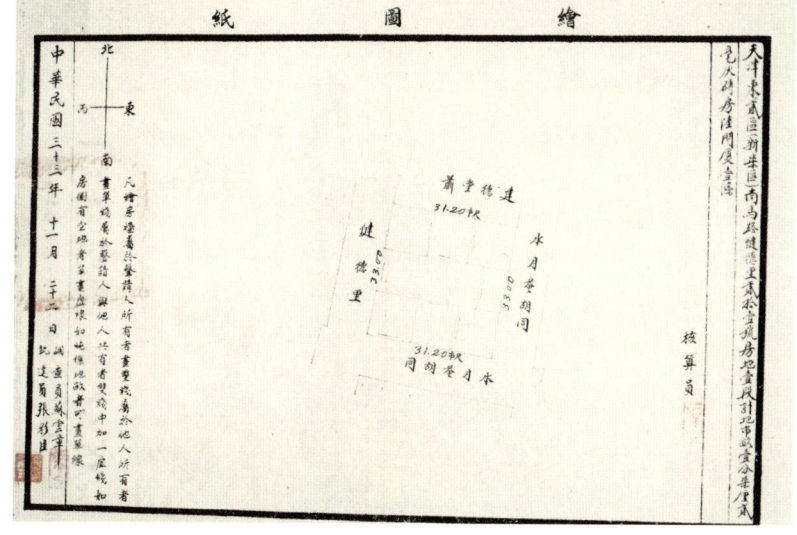

1944 年天津律师公会所有权转移事
The transfer of ownership of Tianjin Bar Association in 1944

1921	1922	1923	1924	1925	1926	1927	1928	1929	1930	1931	1932	1933
1947	1948	1949	1950	1951	1952	1953	1954	1955	1956	1957	1958	1959
1973	1974	1975	1976	1977	1978	1979	1980	1981	1982	1983	1984	1985
1999	2000	2001	2002	2003	2004	2005	2006	2007	2008	2009	2010	2011

Beginning in the second half of 1937, the Japanese invaders strengthened their fascist rule over North China, and used the methods of "surrendering" and instigating whistleblowers to dismantle the anti-Japanese forces in North China, and at the same time implemented "clearing the countryside" in Tianjin. As a result, some speculative people, "a lot of people write letters to Japanese military agencies to flatter, everyone talks about it, and they are very wary". Faced with such a situation, the Tianjin Bar Association drafted three measures from a legal perspective on February 18, 1938, and petitioned the puppet Tianjin District Court. The three methods include: Disregarding the anonymous notification letter. If the name is reported, the informant shall be summoned first. If there is no one, the informant shall be regarded as anonymous. It shall be sent to the court within a short period of time for verification in accordance with the law. If the accused is found to have committed a crime and sent to the gendarmerie or the secret service, it will be temporarily detained by both parties and shall be sent to the court for verification in a short period of time. After a lot of efforts by the Bar Association, the method was finally approved by the puppet District Court and the Japanese Military Ministry.

为协助日寇筹划"大东亚圣战"的资金，日伪政府在天津实行经济统制以实现日本以战养战的目的。他们责令市营自来水管理处修改水价，将普通用水由每千加仑1.2元增为2.9元，责令天津交通股份有限公司将车票价格由每一路线0.5元改为2元，由此民众的生活负担日益沉重。面对这样的变故，律师公会出于保障会员生活的目的提出"（律师）收取公费最高额之限制现已不适用，且官吏薪金以及其他有给职之报酬均随经济状态屡有增加，倘律师公费仍按多年以前之限制而不予变通，实不免相形见绌"。随后，律师公会出面与伪河北高等法院检察处协商，最终达成了"以公费之最高额暂行增加一倍，待经济状况恢复常态即行取消"的意见。

In order to assist the Japanese invaders in planning the funds for the "Greater East Asian Holy War", the puppet government exercised economic control in Tianjin to achieve the purpose of Japan's war with war. They ordered the municipal puppet-tap water management office to modify the water price, increasing ordinary water from 1.2 yuan per thousand gallons to 2.9 yuan, and ordered the puppet Tianjin

Communications Co., Ltd. to change the ticket price from 0.5 yuan per route to 2 yuan. The burden of life is getting heavier. In the face of such a change, the Bar Association has proposed that "the maximum amount of public expense (charged by the lawyers) is no longer applicable for the purpose of protecting the lives of its members, and the salaries of officials and other rewards for employment have increased with the economic status. Attorneys' public expenses are still inconsistent with the restrictions that existed many years ago, which inevitably pales in comparison". Subsequently, the Bar Association came forward to negotiate with the Prosecutor's Office of the puppet Hebei High Court, and finally reached an opinion that "the maximum amount of public expense will be temporarily doubled, and it will be cancelled when the economic situation returns to normal".

《律师法》的实施与
民国律师制度的最终完成

THE IMPLEMENTATION OF THE *LAWYERS LAW* AND THE FINAL COMPLETION OF LAWYER SYSTEM IN THE REPUBLIC OF CHINA

  1927年7月23日，南京国民政府司法部公布并施行了《律师章程》，以代替北洋政府时期的《律师暂行章程》，加之随后颁布的《甄别律师委员会章程》《高等考试司法官律师考试条例》《律师惩戒委员会规则》和《律师公会标准会则》，从而形成了更具规范化的民国律师制度。不过，随着社会的发展，《律师章程》已不能适应社会发展的需要，于是国民政府司法行政部于1935年完成了《律师法草案》，几经修改，终于在1940年12月24日由立法院审议通过。1941年1月11日，国民政府公布实施了全新的《律师法》，《律师章程》也就此废止。不久以后，《律师登录规则》《律师惩戒规则》《律师检核办法》《律师公会平民法律扶助实施办法大纲》《外国人在中国充任律师办法》等法律法规相继出台，共同构建起20世纪40年代的律师制度，也标志着民国律师制度的完备，并进入了一个相对稳定的成熟时期。

  On July 23, 1927, the Ministry of Justice of Nanjing National Government promulgated and implemented the *Regulation of Lawyers* to replace the *Provisional Regulation of Lawyers* of Beiyang Government. In addition, with the subsequent *Statutes of the Screening Lawyers Committee*, the *Examination Regulations of Higher Examination for Magistrates and Lawyers*, the *Rules of the Lawyers Disciplinary Committee* and the *Standards Rules of the Bar Association* formed a more standardized lawyer system of the Republic of China. However, with the development of society, the *Regulation of Lawyers* can no longer meet the needs of social development. Therefore, the Ministry of Justice and Administration of the National Government completed the *Lawyers Law* in 1935, which was revised several times and finally passed by the Legislature on December 24, 1940. On January 11, 1941, the National Government promulgated and implemented the brand-new *Lawyers Law*, and the *Regulation of Lawyers* was abolished. Soon after, laws and regulations such as *Rules for Lawyers Registration*, *Lawyers' Disciplinary Rules*, *Measures for Examining Lawyers*, *Outline for the Implementation of Bar Assistance for Civilians of Bar Association* and *Measures for Foreigners to Serve as Lawyers in China* were promulgated one after another, which jointly established the lawyer system in the 1940s, and also marked the perfection of the lawyer system in the Republic of China and entered a relatively stable mature period.

一、律师自由职业者身份的强化
1. Strengthening the Status of Lawyers as Freelancers

从民国初年《律师暂行章程》开始,律师的自由职业者身份就已被确立,直到《律师法》的出台,这一身份特征又得到了较大幅度的提升。《律师章程》第一章"职务"中规定:"律师受当事人之委托或法院之命令得在通常法院执行法定职务,并得依特别之规定,在特别审判机关行其职务;律师得受当事人之委托,为契约、遗嘱之证明或代订契约等法律文件。"反观《律师法》第二十条规定,律师受当事人之委托或法院之命令,得在法院执行法定职务,并办理其他法律文件。由此可见,《律师法》扩大了律师办理法律文件的范围,丰富了律师的执业内容,从而进一步强化了律师自由职业者的身份。

The lawyer's status as a freelancer has been established since the *Provisional Regulation of Lawyers* in the early years of the Republic of China. Until the promulgation of the *Lawyers Law*, this identity has been greatly improved. The first chapter of the *Regulation of Lawyers* stipulates, "Lawyers may perform statutory duties in ordinary courts when entrusted by the parties or ordered by the courts, and may perform their duties in special judicial organs according to special regulations. Lawyers may be entrusted by the parties to prove contracts, wills or contract and other legal documents." On the other hand, Article 20 of the *Lawyers*

Law stipulates that lawyers may perform their statutory duties and handle other legal documents in the court when entrusted by the parties or ordered by the court. It can be seen that the *Lawyers Law* expands the scope of lawyers' handling of legal documents, enriches lawyers' practice content, and further strengthens the status of lawyers as freelancers.

二、律师资格的获取
2. The Acquisition of Lawyer's Qualification

关于获取律师资格，《律师法》第一条规定了两种方式：一是通过律师资格考试，二是通过检核。不过，在《律师法》颁布后，真正通过考试获取律师资格的仅一人，而通过检核获取的有2284人，足见二者在实践中的差别。

With regard to obtaining the lawyer's qualification, Article 1 of the *Lawyers Law* stipulates two ways: one is to pass the lawyer's qualification examination, and the other is to pass the examination. However, after the promulgation of *Lawyers Law*, only one person actually obtained lawyer qualification through examination, while 2284 people obtained lawyer qualification through examination, which shows the difference between them in practice.

根据《律师法》的规定，曾任推事或检察官，或毕业于公立大学、经立案之私立大学、独立学院之法律专业，讲授主要法律科目满两年以上的教授（满两年）、副教授（满三年）、讲师（满五年），办理民刑案件满四年以上且成绩优良的司法行政官等都可通过检核，直接获得律师资格。随即出台的《律师检核办法》又具体指出，推事或检察官也包括候补推事和候补检察官，而主要法律科目则指民法、商事法规、刑法、民事诉讼法、刑事诉讼法、强制执行法、破产法和国际私法。

According to the provisions of the *Lawyers Law*, professors (full two years), associate professors (full three years), lecturers (full five years) who have served as judges or prosecutors, or graduated from legal profession of public universities, private universities and independent colleges, who have taught major legal subjects for more than two years, and judicial administrators who have handled civil and criminal cases for more than four years and have achieved excellent results can pass the examination and obtain the lawyer qualification directly. The *Measures for Examining Lawyers*, which was promulgated immediately, specifically pointed out that judges or prosecutors also include alternate judges and alternate prosecutors, while the main legal subjects refer to civil law, commercial regulations, criminal law, civil procedure law, criminal procedure law, enforcement law, bankruptcy law and private international law.

相较于《律师章程》,《律师法》不再允许只取得毕业证书的普通学生直接获得律师资格,更强调了律师要求学历与司法实践并重的职业特征。

Compared with the *Regulation of Lawyers*, the *Lawyers Law* no longer allowed ordinary students who have only obtained graduation certificates to obtain lawyer qualifications directly, and emphasized the professional characteristics that lawyers require equal emphasis on academic qualifications and judicial practice.

与此同时,《律师法》还明确规定了七种不能获得律师资格的情况,包括背叛国家且证据充足者,曾经被判处有期徒刑及以上者,受律师惩戒处分中除名处分者,担任公务员而受到开除惩戒者,亏空公款者,破产宣告还未复权者以及吸食鸦片或其代用品者。这些新规弥补了《律师章程》的不足,也有助于提升律师队伍的整体形象。

At the same time, *Lawyers Law* also clearly stipulated seven situations in which lawyers could not be qualified, including those who betray the country and have sufficient evidence, those who have been sentenced to fixed-term imprisonment or above, those who have been removed from the disciplinary punishment of lawyers, those who have been dismissed and punished as civil servants, those who have lost public funds, those who have not been reinstated after bankruptcy declaration, and those who smoke opium or its substitutes. These new regulations made up for the shortcomings of the *Regulation of Lawyers* and helped to enhance the overall image of the lawyers.

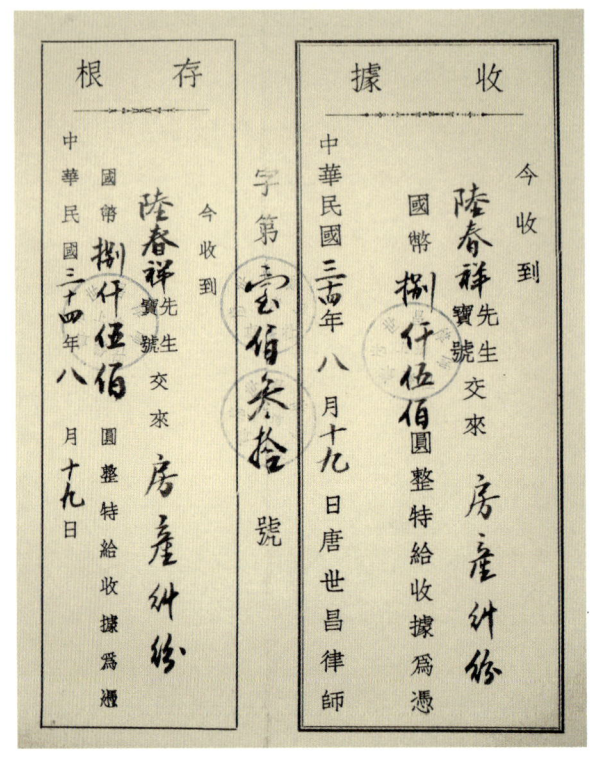

1945年8月的律师收费收据
Receipt of lawyer's fees in August 1945

三、律师应履行的义务
3. Obligations of Lawyers

律师的义务是指律师在执业过程中应遵守的禁止性规定和职业道德规范，《律师法》对此类义务进行了更加丰富的阐释。

The obligations of lawyers refer to the prohibitive regulations and professional ethics that lawyers should abide by in the course of practicing. The *Lawyers Law* provides a richer interpretation of such obligations.

（一）忠于职守的义务
(a) The Obligation to Be Loyal to One's Duties

律师与委托人之间事实上是一种契约关系，为使律师在履行契约的过程中承担更多的义务，《律师法》作出了律师应忠于职守、尽职尽责的规定。

In fact, the relationship between lawyers and clients is a contractual relationship. In order to enable lawyers to assume more obligations in the process of fulfilling the contract, the *Lawyers Law* stipulates that lawyers should be loyal to their duties and perform their duties.

《律师法》第二十二条规定，律师没有正当理由，不得推辞法院的指令。第二十三条规定，律师在接受委托后，应该忠实的搜求证据，深入了解案情。第二十四条规定，没有正当理由，不得随意终止与当事人的契约；如果律师有正当理由需与委托人解除契约的，必须于审期前十日通知委托人，并且必须在委托人同意的情况下，才能正式解除契约。这些条款要求律师对于法院的指令和当事人的委托必须做到尽职尽责，没有正当理由，不得推脱。

Article 22 of the *Lawyers Law* stipulates that a lawyer shall not resign the court's order without a valid reason. Article 23 stipulates that after accepting an entrustment, a lawyer should faithfully search for evidence and gain a thorough understanding of the case. Article 24 stipulates that the contract with the client shall not be terminated without justified reasons; if the lawyer has a justified reason to terminate the contract with the client, he must notify the client ten days before the trial period, and the client must agree to officially terminate the contract. These clauses require lawyers to be responsible for the court's orders and client's entrustment, and cannot shirk without justified reasons.

对于没有履行好忠于职守义务而造成委托人损失的律师，《律师法》要求其对委托人进行赔偿，即第二十五条所规定，律师如果因为懈怠或疏忽，导致委托人受损害的，需负赔偿责任。同时，该律师还可能遭到惩戒的处分。

For lawyers who fail to perform their duty of loyalty and cause losses to their clients, the *Lawyers Law* requires them to compensate their clients, that is, as stipulated in Article 25, if lawyers suffer damages to their clients due to their slack or negligence, they shall be liable. At the same time, the lawyer may also be punished.

（二）诚实信用的义务
(b) The Obligation of Good Faith

诚实、讲信用是律师执业的基本原则，也是《律师法》对律师应尽义务作出的重要规定。其中第二十八条规定，律师对于法院及委托人，不得有蒙蔽或欺诱行为；第二十九条规定，律师不得有足以损及自身名誉或信用之行为。这是《律师法》对律师道德的约束，要求律师具有良好的执业操守。不过，这两条规定有许多模糊的概念，很难执行，不似法律条款，只能说代表了立法者的一种美好企盼。

Honesty and trustworthiness are the basic principles of lawyers' practice, and they are also important provisions of the *Lawyers Law* on the obligations of lawyers. Among them, Article 28 stipulates that lawyers shall notdeceive the court and their clients. Article 29 stipulates that lawyers shall not conduct acts that would damage their reputation or credibility. This is the restriction on lawyers' ethics under the *Lawyers Law* and requires lawyers to have good professional ethics. However, these two provisions have many vague concepts and are difficult to implement. They are not like legal provisions. They can only be said to represent a good hope of legislators.

（三）禁止兼职的义务
(c) The Obligation to Prohibit Part-time Jobs

关于律师的兼职，《律师法》第三十条和第三十一条规定，律师不得兼任公务员，但可出任学校的教员或者中央与地方的民意代表或者中央与地方的特定的临时职务；也不得兼营商业，但可在所登录的高等法院或分院的许可下，兼营与职务无碍的商业项目。

Regarding the part-time job of lawyers, Article 30 and Article 31 of the *Lawyers Law* stipulate that lawyers shall not serve as civil servants, but they may serve as school teachers or representatives of the central and local public opinion or specific temporary positions at the central and local levels; they are not allowed to work concurrently Commercial, but with the permission of the registered high court or branch, it can concurrently operate commercial projects that are not hindered by the position.

在律师经手的业务中，有不少涉及公务机关对当事人权益的侵害。如果兼任公务员，难免会影响律师活动的公正性，因此《律师法》规定律师不能兼任公务员。至于兼营商业，律师所受委托常与商业活动有关，既涉及商业秘密，也涉及商业利益。如果律师以兼营商业的身份接受他人委托，就难免会与委托人发生利益上的冲突；同时，兼营商业还会分散律师执业的精力，因此《律师法》又规定律师不能随意兼营商业。

Many of the businesses handled by lawyers involve infringements on the rights and interests of clients by public agencies. If they serve as civil servants, it will inevitably affect the fairness of lawyers' activities. Therefore, the *Lawyers Law* stipulates that lawyers cannot serve as civil servants. As for concurrent business operations, the entrustment of lawyers is often related to commercial activities, involving both commercial secrets and commercial interests. If a lawyer accepts the entrustment of others as part-time business, it is inevitable that there will be conflicts of interest with the client; at the same time, part-time business will also distract lawyers from practicing. Therefore, the *Lawyers Law* also stipulates that lawyers cannot freely engage in business .

（四）回避的义务
(d) The Obligation to Avoid

为保证律师能够公正地执行任务，《律师法》规定律师必须履行回避义务。这种回避包括事务性回避与职务性回避两种。

In order to ensure that lawyers can perform their tasks fairly, the *Lawyers Law* stipulates that lawyers must perform the obligation of avoidance. This kind of avoidance includes two types: transactional avoidance and official avoidance.

《律师法》第二十六条规定，有以下三种情形的，不得提供法律服务，如果有委托人请求的，律师也应当拒绝：第一，曾接受委托人的相对人的委托的，或者接受过委托人的相对人的赞助的；第二，在担任推事或检察官时处理的案件；第三，在仲裁程序中，以仲裁人的资格处理的案件。第三十二条又规定，律师不得与执行职务区域内之司法人员往还应酬。由此可见，凡是案件中能够引起律师与其私下交易、暗箱操作的人都应被列入事务性回避的名单中，从而尽可能地保证司法公正。

Article 26 of the *Lawyers Law* stipulates that in the following three circumstances, legal services are not allowed. If the client requests, the lawyer should also refuse: First, he has accepted the entrusts of client's counterparts, or has accepted the supports of the client's counterparts; Second, cases handled while serving as judges or prosecutors; Third, cases handled as arbitrators in arbitration proceedings. Article 32 also stipulates that lawyers are not allowed to repay the judicial personnel in the area where they perform their duties. It can be seen from this that all persons who can cause private transactions and black-box operations with lawyers should be included in the list of transactional avoidances, so as to ensure judicial justice as much as possible.

职务性回避则多为律师自身的人际关系所致。《律师法》第三十七条规定，司法人员在离职后三年内，不得在曾经供职的法院管辖区域内从事律师职业；第三十八条规定，律师在注销登记后一年内，不得在曾经执行律师业务的区域内的法院充任司法官；第三十九条规定，与法院院长或首席检察官有配偶、五亲等内血亲或三亲等内姻亲关系的律师，不能在该法院登录。这三条是对律师有过特殊从业经历或与特殊人员有亲属关系，需进行回避的规定。

The duty-based avoidance is mostly caused by the lawyer's own interpersonal relationship. Article 37 of the *Lawyers Law* stipulates that within three years after resignation, judicial personnel shall not engage in the profession of lawyers within the jurisdiction of the courts where they once served. Article 38 stipulates that within one year after logging off, lawyers shall not be allowed to engage in judicial officer within the region where they once served as lawyer. Article 39 stipulates that lawyers who have a spouse, blood relatives within the five relatives, or in-laws within the three relatives with the president of the court or the chief prosecutor cannot be registered in the court. These three articles are requirements for recusal for lawyers who have special experience or have kinship with special personnel.

（五）消极诉讼的义务

(e) The Obligation for Negative Litigation

《律师法》第三十四条规定，律师不得挑唆诉讼，或以不正当的方法招揽诉讼；第三十五条规定，律师不得代理当事人为显无理由之起诉、上诉或抗告。这就意味着律师不能采取积极主动的态度去开展业务，只能被动地履行职责，履行消极诉讼的义务。

Article 34 of the *Lawyers Law* stipulates that lawyers shall not instigate litigation or solicit litigation by improper methods. Article 35 stipulates that lawyers shall not represent the client for unreasonable prosecution, appeal or protest. This means that lawyers cannot take a proactive attitude to conduct business, but can only passively perform their duties and perform passive litigation obligations.

事实上，律师的使命在于保护当事人的合法权益，防止其他团体或个人对当事人造成侵害；而在侵害发生的情况下，则帮助当事人通过合法程序，要求赔偿或补偿，并以其对于法律条款及法律程序的熟悉，保护当事人的诉讼权益，防止司法机构在审判中的偏颇。然而《律师法》要求律师必须履行消极诉讼义务的规定，无疑是在"开倒车"。

In fact, the mission of a lawyer is to protect the legal rights of the client and prevent other groups or individuals from infringing upon the client; and in the event of an infringement, to help the client to pass legal procedures to claim compensation or salvation, and with his familiarity with legal terms and legal procedures protects the litigant rights and interests of litigants and prevents judicial institutions from being biased in trials. However, the requirement that lawyers must perform passive litigation obligations in the *Lawyers Law* is undoubtedly "reversing".

四、1945年《律师法》对1941年《律师法》的修正
4. Amendments to the *Lawyers Law* of 1941 by the *Lawyers Law* of 1945

在《律师法》制定颁布后，鉴于抗战的特殊时期，其针对性囿于国统区之内。不过随着国际国内形势的变化，如美英等国与中国改定新约，宣布放弃领事裁判权；抗战迎来最后的大反攻阶段，全国即将光复，国民政府将还都南京等，国民政府遂于1945年对《律师法》进行了大幅度的改动，在调整立法体例、整理法条后，条文从四十八条增至五十一条。

After the *Lawyers Law* was enacted and promulgated, in view of the special period of Anti-Japanese War, its pertinence was limited to the Kuomintang Controlled Area. However, with the changes in the international and domestic situation, such as the United States, Britain and other countries amending the new treaty with China, announcing the abandonment of consular jurisdiction; Anti-Japanese War ushered in the final stage of the counter-offensive, the country is about to recover, the national government will return to Nanjing and so on. As a result, the National Government made substantial changes to the *Lawyers Law* in 1945. After adjusting the legislative style and sorting out the legal provisions, the provisions were increased from 48 to 51.

1945年修正案在第一条律师资格的规定中增加了第三款规定：具备《法院组织法》第三十三条第四款或第三十六条第五款资格的，也可通过检核直接获得律师资格。《法院组织法》第三十三条第四款为在专科以上学校修习法律三年以上毕业，曾担任荐任级别的司法行政官，办理民、刑事两年以上成绩优良的；第三十六条第五款为曾任立法委员三年以上的。据此，司法行政人员和立法委员也具备了参与检核而直接获得律师资格的条件。不过这样一来，政府官员就可以在毫无司法经验的背景下充任律师，实为《律师法》的一大倒退。

In the 1945 amendment, paragraph 3 was added to Article 1 of the Law on Lawyers' Qualification. Those who have the qualification of Article 33, paragraph 4, or Article 36, paragraph 5 of the *Organic Law of the Court* can also obtain the lawyer's qualification directly through examination. Referring to the *Organic Law of the Court*, the content of Article 33, paragraph 4, is that he graduated from a college or above to study law for more than 3 years, served as a judicial administrator at the recommendation level, and handled civil and criminal affairs for more than 2 years with excellent results. Paragraph 5 of Article 36 refers to those who have served as legislators for more than 3 years. According to these two paragraphs, judicial administrators and legislators also have the conditions to participate in the examination and directly obtain the qualification of lawyers. However, as a result, government officials can also act as lawyers without judicial experience, which is a great retrogression of the *Lawyers Law*.

抗战胜利后的天津司法与律师

TIANJIN JUDICIAL AND LAWYERS AFTER THE VICTORY OF ANTI-JAPANESE WAR

一、抗战胜利后天津的司法活动

1. Judicial Activities in Tianjin after the Victory of Anti—Japanese War

1945年8月抗战胜利后，南京国民政府派贾艮任天津地方法院院长。在当年12月1日接收了日伪时期的天津地方法院后，国民政府对前法院人员及法院组织机构作了重大调整。除地方法院外，原河北省高等法院设在天津的第一分院也得到恢复，到1948年3月改称河北高等法院天津分院。

After the victory of Anti-Japanese War in August 1945, Nanjing National Government appointed Jia Gen as the president of the Tianjin District Court. After accepting the Tianjin District Court during the puppet regime on December 1 of that year, the Nationalist Government made major adjustments to the former court personnel and court organization. In addition to the district court, the first branch of the Hebei High Court in Tianjin was restored, and in March 1948 it was renamed the Tianjin Branch of the Hebei High Court.

1945—1946年，国民政府先后颁布了《处理汉奸案件条例》及《惩治汉奸条例》。天津对汉奸的一审设在河北高等法院第一分院，其中最著名的就是1945年的审判方若汉奸案。

From 1945 to 1946, the Nationalist Government successively promulgated the *Regulations on Handling Traitors Cases* and the *Regulations on Punishing Traitors*.

1934	1935	1936	1937	1938	1939	1940	1941	1942	1943	1944	1945	1946
1960	1961	1962	1963	1964	1965	1966	1967	1968	1969	1970	1971	1972
1986	1987	1988	1989	1990	1991	1992	1993	1994	1995	1996	1997	1998
2012	2013	2014	2015	2016	2017	2018	2019	2020	2021	……		

1945年审判汉奸方若
Trial of traitor Fang Ruo in 1945

The first instance of the traitor in Tianjin was set up in the First Branch of the Hebei High Court. The most famous of these was the 1945 Fang Ruo traitor case.

方若，字药雨，浙江定海人。光绪二十年（1894）来津，后赴《国闻报》任编辑。光绪二十九年（1903），日本驻津领事馆在日租界旭街开办《天津日日新闻》，方若任经理。其妻汤小豹系日女所生，故与日人过从甚密。方若借此关系，揽下日租界垫土修路工程而发迹，成为津门巨富。

Fang Ruo, whose courtesy name was Yaoyu, was born in Dinghai, Zhejiang. He came to Tianjin in 1894 and later worked as an editor for *Guowen Newspaper*. In 1903, the Japanese Consulate in Tianjin opened the *Tianjin Daily News* in Asahi Street, Japanese Concession, and Fang Ruo served as the manager. His wife, Tang Xiaobao, was born to a Japanese woman, so she had a close relationship with the Japanese. With this relationship, Fang Ruo succeeded in taking over the construction of roads in the Japanese Concession and became a wealthy man in Tianjin.

1937年8月20日，方若执掌伪天津法院，31日伪高、地两级法院成立后，又充任伪"两院"

院长。三个月后，孔嘉璋接任伪院长，方若改任伪政府参事。1941年12月太平洋战争爆发，英美对日宣战，天津英租界为日伪政府接管，改称特别区。1942年3月，方若转任该区伪署长，7月升任伪华北政务委员会委员。1945年2月，改任该会顾问，直至日本投降。

On August 20, 1937, Fang Ruo took charge of the puppet Tianjin court. After the establishment of the puppet high and prefectural courts on the 31st, he served as the puppet president of the "two organizations". Three months later, Kong Jiazhang took over as the puppet president, Fang Ruo changed to the puppet government counselor. In December 1941, the Pacific War broke out. Britain and the United States declared war on Japan. The British concession in Tianjin was taken over by the Japanese and puppet government and was renamed a special area. In March 1942, Fang Ruo was transferred to the district director. In July, he was promoted to a member of the puppet North China Political Affairs Committee. In February 1945, he was appointed as the consultant of the association until Japan surrendered.

1945年12月6日，方若因汉奸罪被国民政府军统局捕送河北高等法院第一分院。方若对其担任伪职供认不讳，并写有《自述书》。在职八年，方若提倡"中日亲善"，并引以为豪。1944年5月3日他接受《天津华北新报》采访时宣称："我们的主旨，希望挽回人心，脱离联俄死路，而与同文同种日本敦睦邦交，共谋捍卫东亚大计。"足见其卖国之坚定。

On December 6, 1945, Fang Ruo was arrested by the Bureau of Investigation and Statistics of the Military Commission of the Nationalist Government and sent to the First Branch of the Hebei High Court for the crime of traitor. Fang Ruo confessed to his previous puppet posts, and wrote *The Book of Self Report*. During his eight years in office, he advocated "goodwill" between China and Japan, and was proud of it. On May 3, 1944, he declared in an interview with the *Tianjin North China News*, "Our main purpose is to save people's hearts and break away from the dead end of the alliance. We have established diplomatic relations with Japan of the same language and the same species, and conspired to defend the grand plan of East Asia." This shows his firm idea of tredson.

在审期间，法院也收到了徐世章、雍剑秋、丁懋英、张务滋等天津乡绅的具结证词，证明"日寇加诸人民之暴行，（方若）尚知设法维护"。如1937年8月日军拟强占江苏、浙江两义园，1941年9月日本浪人强占广仁堂房屋、田地，均经方若与敌军交涉而免予侵占。1941年1月，天津女医院院长丁懋英被日军宪兵队逮捕，同年12月燕达学校校长张务滋被日伪文教部传讯扣押，均经方若具保释放，理由是"念其衰年，法外准予保释"。

During the trial, the court also received confirmed testimony from Tianjin squires such as Xu Shizhang, Yong Jianqiu, Ding Maoying, Zhang Wuzi, etc., proving that "the atrocities committed by the Japanese invaded the people, (Fang Ruo) still knew how to defend", such as the Japanese army's proposed occupation in August 1937. In Jiangsu and Zhejiang Liangyi Gardens, in September 1941, the Japanese Ronin forcibly occupied the houses and fields of Guangrentang, but they were exempted from occupying them through negotiations with the enemy. In January 1941, Ding Maoying, the director of Tianjin Women's Hospital, was arrested for the Japanese military police. In December of the same year, Zhang Wuzi, the principal of Yanda School, was summoned and detained by the puppet Ministry of Culture and Education. Both were released by Fang Ruo on the grounds that "the release was granted due to old age."

1948年3月20日，河北高等法院天津分院判决："方若通谋敌国，反抗本国，处有期徒刑七年，褫夺公权五年。全部财产除酌留家属必需生活费外没收。"方若不服判决，上诉至南京最高法院，并以"年高气衰，感患失眠、咳嗽等症，精神疲惫"为由，申请具保，停止羁押。同年6月26日，最高法院作出终审判决："原判决撤销，方若通谋敌国，图谋反抗本国，处有期徒刑五年，褫夺公权五年。"其理由是"对此年已八十岁之被告，仍处以有期徒刑七年，量刑显有未当"。1949年7月，天津市人民法院作出"方若通敌叛国，迫害人民，处有期徒刑三年，缓刑五年"的判决。1954年，方若在天津病逝。

On March 20, 1948, the Tianjin Branch of the Hebei High Court sentenced as follow, "Fang Ruo conspired against the enemy country and rebelled against his own country. He was sentenced to seven years' imprisonment and deprived of public power for five years. All his property must be confiscated except for his family

天津地方法院欢迎居正、夏勤两院长莅临视察（与高、地两院职员合影）

The Tianjin District Court welcomed Presidents Ju Zheng and Xia Qin to visit and inspect (a photo with the staff of the high court and district court)

members. Appealed to the Supreme Court of Nanjing, and applied for insurance and ceased detention on the grounds of young age, dysphoria, insomnia, coughing, and mental exhaustion". On June 26 of the same year, the Supreme Court made a final judgment, "The original judgment was revoked. Fang Ruo conspired against the enemy country and attempted to rebel against his country. He was sentenced to five years imprisonment and five years of deprivation of public power." The reason was that "He was eighty years old this year. The defendant was still sentenced to seven years' imprisonment, and the sentence was clearly improper." In July 1949, the Tianjin Municipal People's Court ruled that "Fang Ruo treason with the enemy and persecuted the people was sentenced to three years imprisonment and five years probation." In 1954, Fang Ruo died of illness in Tianjin.

抗战胜利后，朝阳学院迁回北平，并于1946年秋在原址复校。1947年3月1日，曾任朝阳学院校董事长的司法院院长居正和曾任该校代院长的最高法院院长夏勤专程从南京赶赴北平参加庆祝活动。活动结束后，他二人在河北高等法院院长邓哲熙的陪同下，到天津视察河北高等法院第一分院和天津地方法院。

After the victory of Anti-Japanese War, Chaoyang College moved back to Beiping, and reopened at the original site in the autumn of 1946. On March 1, 1947, Ju Zheng, Dean of the Judicial Yuan, who was the chairman of Chaoyang College, and Xia Qin, Dean of the Supreme Court, who was the acting dean of the school, made a special trip from Nanjing to Beiping to participate in the celebration. After the event, the two of them, accompanied by Deng Zhexi, President of Hebei High Court, went to Tianjin to inspect the First Branch of Hebei High Court and Tianjin District Court.

1947年3月3日上午9时10分，居正一行乘加挂专列离开北平，当时预计11时1刻抵达天津。天津市副市长张子奇、秘书长梁子青，河北高等法院天津分院院长刘荣松，天津地方法院院长贾良，律师公会代表及高、地两院全体职员约200人齐集东火车站迎接。因列车在廊坊稍作停留，故延至12时抵津。宾主双方稍作寒暄，随即登车赴河东大陆银行，出席高、地两院举行的欢迎宴会。

居正一行步入欢迎会场
Ju Zheng and his party stepped
into the welcoming venue

At 9:10 a.m. on March 3, 1947, Ju Zheng and his party boarded a special train and left Beiping. They were expected to arrive in Tianjin at 11:15. About 200 people including Zhang Ziqi, Deputy Mayor of Tianjin, Liang Ziqing, Secretary-General, Liu Rongsong, President of Tianjin Branch of Hebei High Court, Jia Gen, President of Tianjin District Court, representatives of the Bar Association and all staff of the high court and district court, greeted at East Railway Station. Because the train stopped in Langfang for a while, it was postponed to arrive in Tianjin at about 12 o'clock. The host and the guest exchanged a little greeting, and then boarded the car and rushed to the Hedong Mainland Bank to attend the welcome banquet held by the high court and district court.

入席前，居正、夏勤在大陆银行会议室接受各报记者的采访。居正简要介绍了此次北行

1934　1935　1936　1937　1938　1939　1940　1941　1942　1943　1944　1945　1946
1960　1961　1962　1963　1964　1965　1966　1967　1968　1969　1970　1971　1972
1986　1987　1988　1989　1990　1991　1992　1993　1994　1995　1996　1997　1998
2012　2013　2014　2015　2016　2017　2018　2019　2020　2021　……

的目的，称完全为朝阳学院复校问题而来，顺便视察华北司法行政及探访旧日好友。记者问："目前各地司法人员均感缺乏，未悉在朝阳学院以外，如何增加司法人才？"居正答："目前各大学均设有法律系，将来司法人才不致缺乏。"问："中华民国宪法颁布，居正院长以为如何？"答："很好，我甚为满意。"问："我国可否亦实行选举法官制度？"答："法官选举一事，目前只有美苏两国实行，因我国人民文化程度尚嫌不够，尚需稍候时日。"当记者问及审理烟犯和汉奸之事时，夏勤答："关于烟毒案件，因为司法独立，自然应归法院审理，由军法审理是不对的。目前仅京、沪、江苏三地，声请最高法院复判的汉奸案即有500余件，若以全国计当有5000余件，最高法院计设10所，推检人员有50名，分别赶办，约于今年年底即可办理完毕。"采访结束后，宾主双方步入宴会厅。

Before joining, Ju Zheng and Xia Qin were interviewed by reporters from various newspapers in the conference room of the Mainland Bank. Ju Zheng briefly introduced the purpose of this trip to the north, which was entirely for the reinstatement of Chaoyang College. By the way, he inspected the judicial administration of North China and visited the old friendship. The reporter asked, "Currently, there is a lack of judicial personnel in various places. I have not known how to increase judicial personnel outside of Chaoyang College?" Ju Zheng replied, "At present, every university has a law department, and there will be no shortage of judicial

居正在宴会前致辞
Ju Zheng delivered a speech before the feast

personnel in the future." Asked, "The Republic of China What does President Ju Zheng think about the promulgation of the constitution?" Replied, "Very good, I am very satisfied." Asked, "Can China also implement a system of electing judges?" Replied, "The election of judges is currently only implemented in the United States and the Soviet Union. Because the education level of our people is not enough, we still have to wait a while." When the reporter asked about the trial of tobacco criminals and traitors, Xia Qin replied, "With regard to tobacco and drug cases, because of the independence of the judiciary, it should naturally be heard by the court. It is wrong to be tried by military law. At present, there are more than 500 cases of traitorous traitors in Beijing, Shanghai, and Jiangsu. If there are more than 5,000 cases in the country, the Supreme Court will set up 10 and recommend There are 50 inspectors, who will be rushed to handle them separately, and the procedures will be completed around the end of this year." After the interview, both the host and the guest entered the banquet hall.

下午4时，居正、夏勤由邓哲熙陪同，到南马路河北高等法院第一分院和天津地方法院视察。两位院长、首席检察官、书记官率领"两院"全体职员，在法院前大院内列队迎接。全体合影后，众人来到第一法庭，居正、夏勤讲话40分钟。地方法院院长贾艮致答谢词后，居正一行又分别视察了"两院"的各个办公室，并不时向职员们询问工作、生活上的一些具体问题。5时许，居正一行视察完毕。

At 4 in the afternoon, Ju Zheng and Xia Qin, accompanied by Deng Zhexi, went to the First Branch of the South Road the First Branch of Hebei High Court and the Tianjin District Court for inspection. The two presidents, the chief prosecutor, and the clerk led all the staff of the "two organizations" to greet them in a line in the former compound of the court. After taking a group photo, everyone came to the First Court and Ju Zheng and Xia Qin spoke for 40 minutes. After Jia Gen, the president of the district court, gave a speech of thanks, Ju Zheng and his entourage inspected the offices of the "two organizations" and asked the staff about specific work and life issues from time to time. At about 5 o'clock, the inspection by Ju Zheng and his party was completed.

1934	1935	1936	1937	1938	1939	1940	1941	1942	1943	1944	1945	1946
1960	1961	1962	1963	1964	1965	1966	1967	1968	1969	1970	1971	1972
1986	1987	1988	1989	1990	1991	1992	1993	1994	1995	1996	1997	1998
2012	2013	2014	2015	2016	2017	2018	2019	2020	2021	……		

二、20世纪40年代末的天津律师
2. Tianjin Lawyers in the Late 1940s

（一）执业人数逐步增加
(a) The Number of Practitioners is Gradually Increasing

按照《律师法》及《律师法实施细则》的规定，天津律师公会要定期编写会员录并呈报给天津市社会局和地方法院备查，从而也为后人留下了一笔宝贵的资料。根据1946年4月天津市社会局的记载，在天津执业的律师共有19人。当年11月编印的《天津律师公会会员录》记载在天津地方法院管辖内的执业律师共有270人。1947年9月为304人，1948年10月为339人。由此可见，抗战胜利后在天津地区执业的律师人数在稳步回升，律师业得到了迅速恢复。

In accordance with the *Lawyers Law* and the *Implementation Rules of the Lawyer Law*, the Tianjin Bar Association must regularly compile a membership record and submit it to the Tianjin Municipal Social Bureau and the district court for inspection, thus leaving a precious piece of information for future generations. According to the records of Tianjin Municipal Social Bureau in April 1946, there

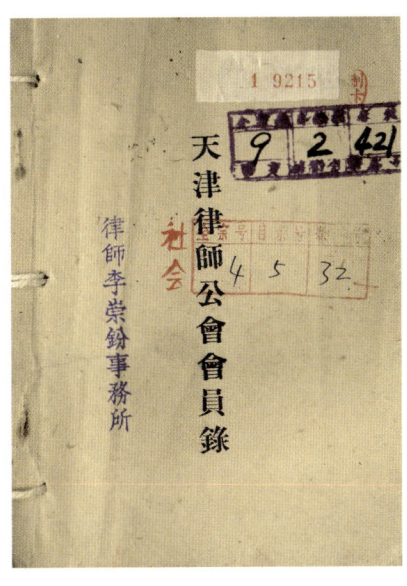
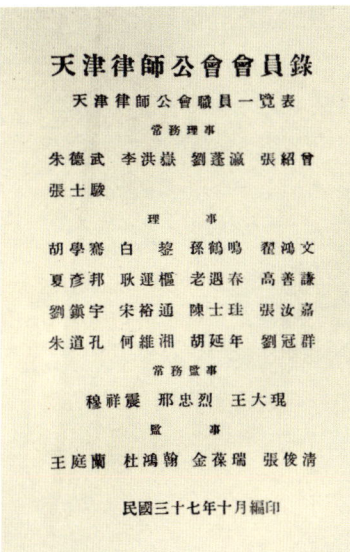
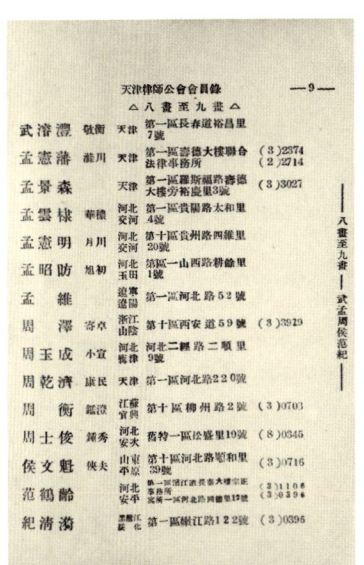

1948年《天津律师公会会员录》
1948 *Panel of Tianjin Bar Association*

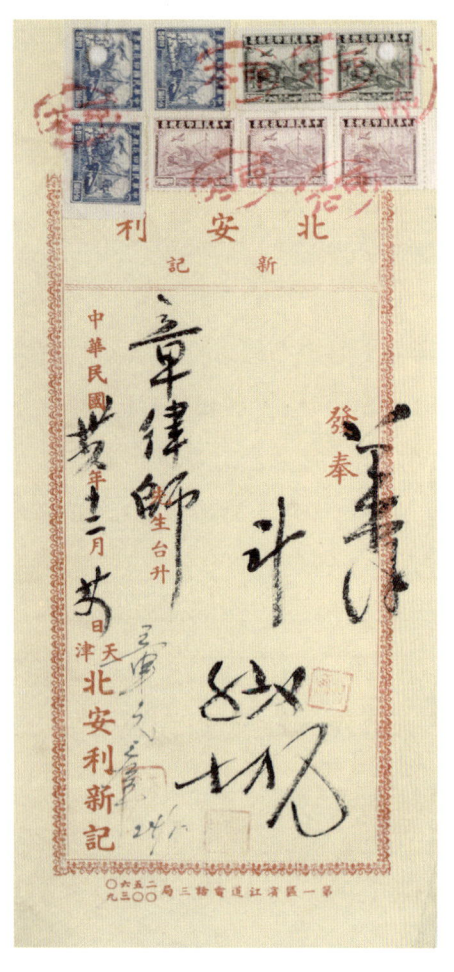

1947年北安利新记给章律师出具的发票
In 1947, the new invoice issued by Beianli Xinji to lawyer Zhang

were 19 lawyers practicing in Tianjin. The *Membership Record of the Tianjin Bar Association* compiled and printed in November of that year recorded a total of 270 practicing lawyers within the jurisdiction of the Tianjin District Court. The Tianjin Bar Association's membership record compiled in September 1947 recorded a total of 304 practicing lawyers within the jurisdiction of the Tianjin District Court. The Tianjin Bar Association's membership records compiled in October 1948 recorded a total of 339 practicing lawyers within the jurisdiction of the Tianjin District Court. This shows that after the victory of Anti-Japanese War, the number of lawyers practicing in Tianjin has steadily picked up, and the legal profession has recovered rapidly.

（二）科班出身较多，水平参差不齐

(b) There are many Academic Backgrounds, and the Level is Uneven

大多数律师都是法律专业科班出身，只有少部分律师是非法律专业毕业，如政治、经济类专业。其中有一部分毕业于当时的名校，如朝阳大学、东吴大学、北京大学、北洋大学，绝大多数毕业于地方院校或是学堂，水平参差不齐。

Almost all lawyers have graduated from law majors, but there are also a small number of lawyers who graduated from non-law majors, such as politics and economics. Some of them graduated from prestigious universities at the time, such as Chaoyang

1934	1935	1936	1937	1938	1939	1940	1941	1942	1943	1944	1945	1946
1960	1961	1962	1963	1964	1965	1966	1967	1968	1969	1970	1971	1972
1986	1987	1988	1989	1990	1991	1992	1993	1994	1995	1996	1997	1998
2012	2013	2014	2015	2016	2017	2018	2019	2020	2021	......		

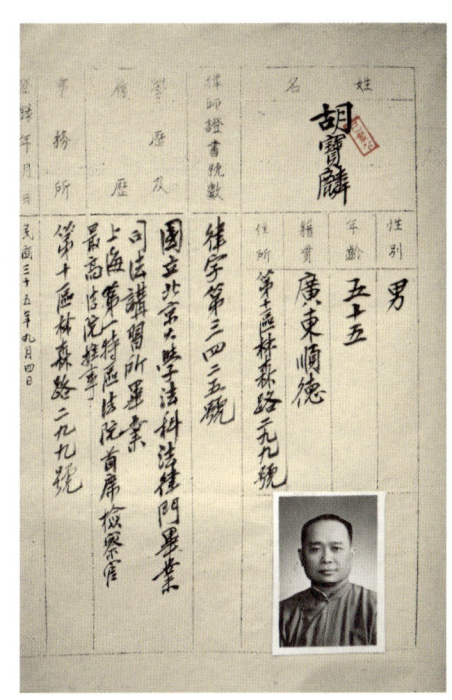

毕业于北京大学法科的胡宝麟律师
Lawyer Hu Baolin graduated from Peking University Law Department

University, Soochow University, Peking University, Beiyang University, etc. Most of them were graduated from local colleges or schools, and the level was uneven.

除了获得本科学历之外，还有一些律师获得了硕士、博士，甚至还有一部分具有国外留学的背景。其中绝大多数是留学日本，如张汝嘉毕业于日本法政大学，张宗芙毕业于日本明治大学法科，李震彝毕业于日本早稻田大学政治经济科，阮性言毕业于日本东京大学法政速成科，何维湘毕业于日本东京大学政治科，周衡毕业于日本明治大学法科，付同德为明治大学法学士，李宜琛为日本早稻田大学大学院民法研究四年，蔡枢衡为日本东京中央大学法学部本科毕业，法学部大学院（研究院）研究二年。此外，还有少量律师在其他国家留学，如王书纶，英国伦敦大学法硕士肄业，英国牛津大学农业经济研究院毕业；黄宗法，美国密西根大学法学士、哥伦比亚大学法学硕士、纽约大学法理学博士；阮笃成，法国都鲁斯大学法学硕士；郑怀德，法国巴黎大学法学硕士；丁作韶，法国巴黎大学法学博士；袭钺，法国巴黎大学法科毕业，哥伦奥布大学法学博士等。

In addition to obtaining a bachelor's degree, some lawyers have obtained master's and doctoral degrees, and some even have a background of studying abroad. Most of them are studying in Japan. For example, Zhang Rujia graduated from Hosei University, Zhang Zongfu graduated from Meiji University, Japan, Li Zhenyi graduated from Waseda University, Japan, graduated from the political and economics department, Ruan Xingyan graduated from the University of Tokyo, Japan law and politics fast-track course, He Weixiang graduated from Japan Department of Political Science, University of Tokyo, Zhou Heng graduated from Meiji University Law Department, Fu Tongde holds a Bachelor of Laws from Meiji University, Li Yichen graduated from Waseda University Graduate School of Civil Law for four years, Cai

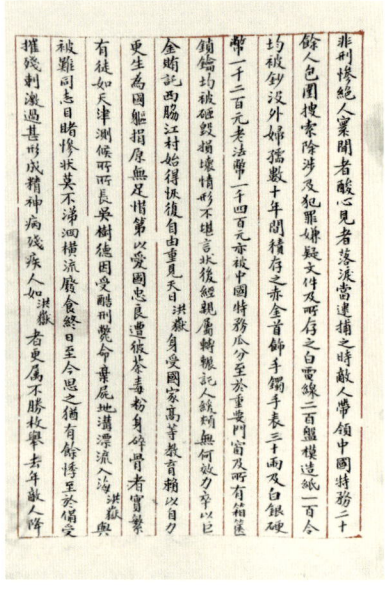
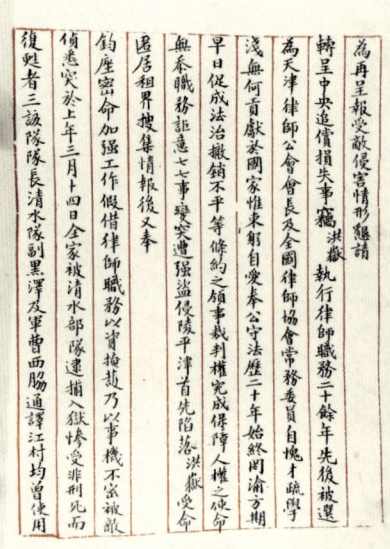
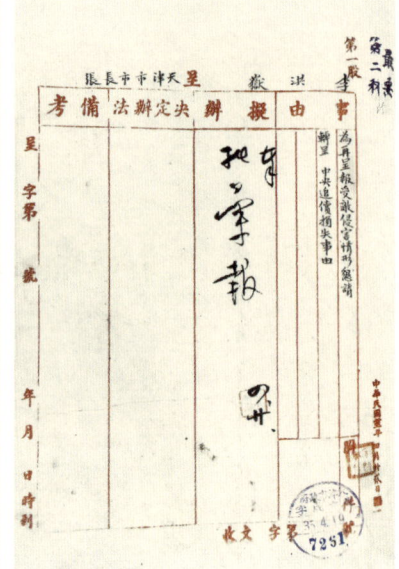
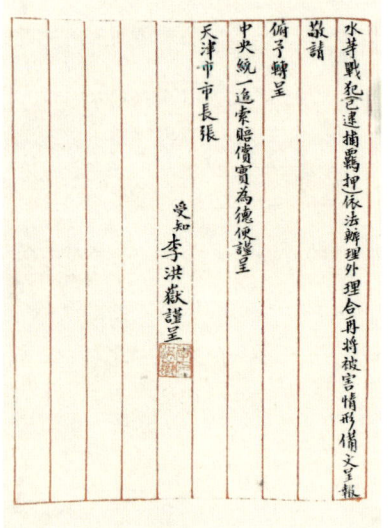
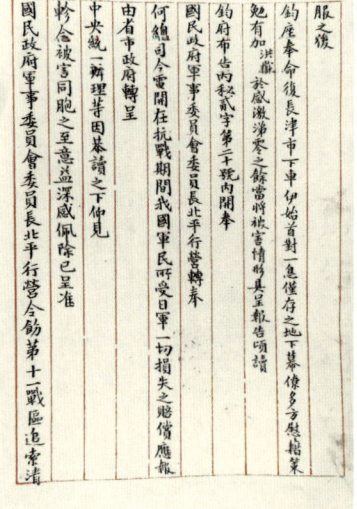

1946年4月天津律师公会会长李洪岳呈请天津市市长转呈中央为受敌侵害情形追偿损失事

In April 1946, Li Hongyue, chairman of the Tianjin Bar Association, petitioned the mayor of Tianjin to submit to the central government to recover losses for the victim's infringement during Anti-Japanese War

Shuheng graduated from Tokyo Chuo University, Japan Faculty of Law, Graduate School of Law (Graduate School) Study for two years. In addition, there are a small number of lawyers studying in other countries, such as Wang Shulun, a master's degree in law from the University of London, and a graduate of the Agricultural Economics Institute of Oxford University in the United Kingdom; Huang Zongfa, a Bachelor of Laws from the University of Michigan, a Master of Laws from Columbia University, and a Doctor of Jurisprudence from New York University Ruan Ducheng, Master of

Laws from the University of Durres, France; Zheng Huaide, Master of Laws from the University of Paris, France; Ding Zuoshao, Doctor of Laws from the University of Paris, France; Xiyue, Law graduate of the University of Paris, France, Doctor of Laws from the University of Columbus, etc.

（三）经历丰富，职业流动性明显

(c) Rich Experience and Obvious Career Mobility

从律师公会会员录的履历来看，很少有律师仅从事律师一项职业，大部分还从事其他职业，如各个地方法院、检察院的推事、检察官，军法处的军法官，还有一些是大学教员。此外还有许多人担任过地方政府官员，甚至高级政府官员，如参议会议员、国会议员等。

It can be seen from the member lists of the bar associations that very few lawyers are engaged in only one profession as lawyers, and most of them have engaged in other professions. The common are judges and prosecutors of various district courts and procuratorates, Military judges of the Military Law Division, and some are university faculty members. In addition, there are many people who have served as local government officials, including many senior government officials such as members of the Senate and Congress.

（四）收入水平相对较高

(d) Relatively High Income

20世纪40年代末，国民政府经济政策混乱，滥发纸币，物价飞涨，律师费用也随之水涨船高。天津律师无论是分收酬金还是总收酬金相比于其他律师公会都比较高。相较于公务员，律师的收入也十分丰厚，无疑是一个高收入行业。

Due to the chaotic economic and fiscal policies of the National Government in the late 1940s and excessive currency issuance, prices directly led to soaring prices. Therefore, lawyers' fees have also risen. Tianjin lawyers both charge higher fees than other bar associations in terms of split remuneration and total

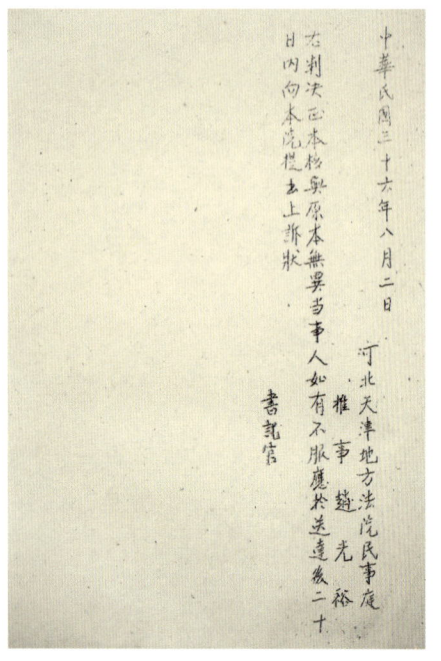 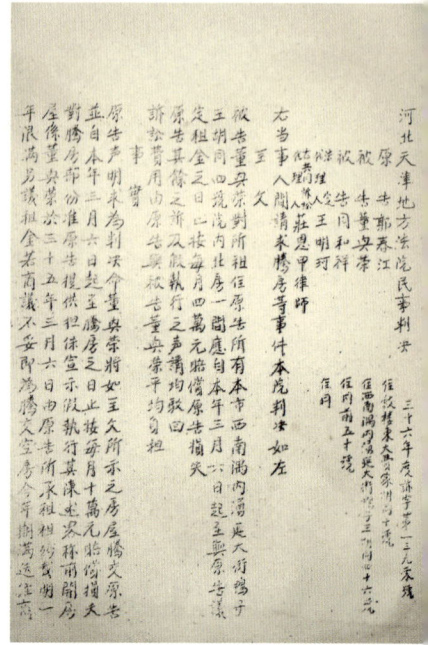

1947年8月天津地方法院民事判决书
Judgment of Tianjin District Court in August 1947

remuneration. Compared with civil servants, the income of lawyers is also very generous, and it is undoubtedly a high-income industry.

三、20世纪40年代末的天津律师公会
3. Tianjin Bar Association in the Late 1940s

（一）天津律师公会的重建
(a) Reconstruction of Tianjin Bar Association

日本投降以后，天津律师公会在迪化道（今鞍山道）71号重新设立会址。1946年3月27日，重建后的天津律师公会第一届会员大会在私立河东中学礼堂召开，会议通过了《天津律师公会章程》。根据1945年1月12日国民政府修订的《律师公会章程订立办法》第七章对酬金的新规定，《天津律师公会章程》第七章第二十九条规定："会员受当事人之委托，办理诉讼事件，

1934	1935	1936	1937	1938	1939	1940	1941	1942	1943	1944	1945	1946
1960	1961	1962	1963	1964	1965	1966	1967	1968	1969	1970	1971	1972
1986	1987	1988	1989	1990	1991	1992	1993	1994	1995	1996	1997	1998
2012	2013	2014	2015	2016	2017	2018	2019	2020	2021	……		

其收受酬金办法分左列两种，由当事人自择，以契约定之。"其中有讨论案情不得逾国币1200元/小时，民事出庭费不得逾国币12800元/次，刑事出庭费不得逾国币8000元/次的内容。

After Japan surrendered, the Tianjin Bar Association re-established a new venue at No. 71, Dihua Road (now Anshan Road). On March 27, 1946, the rebuilt Tianjin Bar Association's first Member's General Assembly was held in the private Hedong Middle School Auditorium. The meeting passed *The Constitution of Tianjin Bar Association*. Pursuant to the new regulations on remuneration in Chapter 7 of the *Measures for Formulation of the Constitution of the Bar Association* amended by the National Government on January 12, 1945, Article 29 of Chapter 7 of *The Constitution of Tianjin Bar Association* stipulates that "Members are entrusted by the parties to handle litigation events. There are two methods for receiving remuneration, which can be chosen by the parties and determined by contract." Among them, the case for

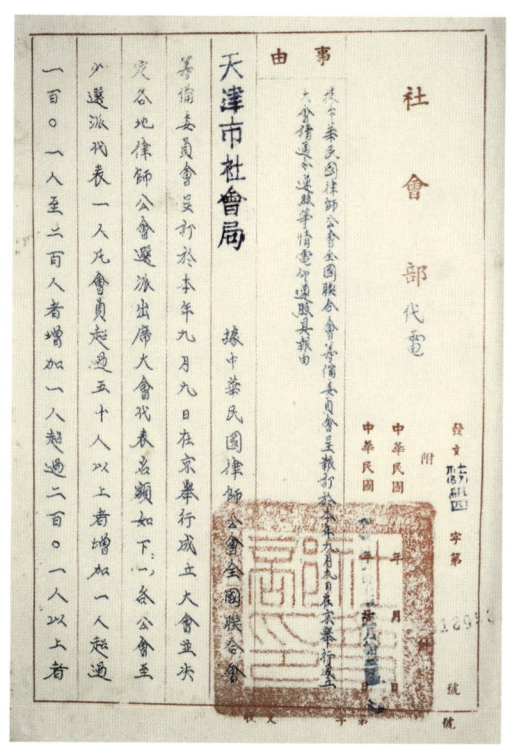
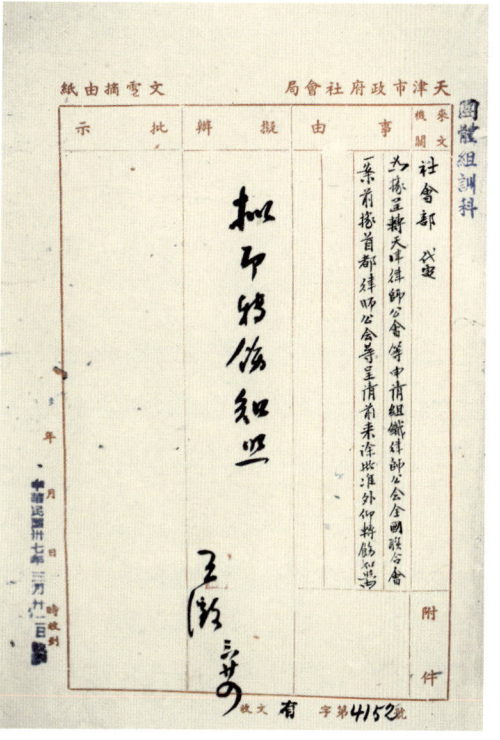

1948 年天津律师公会组织律师公会全国联合会事
In 1948, Tianjin Bar Association organized the National Federation of Bar Associations

全国律师联合会第一届代表大会在北平召开
The First Congress of the National Lawyers Association was held in Beiping

discussion shall not exceed 1200 yuan per hour, and the civil court fee shall not exceed the national currency. 12,800 yuan/time, the criminal court fee shall not exceed the national currency 8,000 yuan/time.

　　1946年7月23日，国民政府司法行政部为《公布出庭伪法院律师停止职务年限》发出公告，公告规定："查在抗战期间出庭伪组织法院执行职务之律师……兹定自1945年9月3日战事结束之日起，停止执行职务一年，期限届满，准予复业。"8月13日，国民政府公布了《处理伪组织所发律师证书办法》，其中规定："一、伪组织所发律师证书，一律无效；二、战前已领证书之律师，曾换领伪证书者，如未依照《惩治汉奸条例》判罪，得自1946年9月3日起，缴销伪证书，并检齐下列证件，呈由所在地法院查明，呈转司法行政部，请补领新证书：（一）战前取得律师资格之证明文件；（二）现任荐任官两人之证明书，证明并无《律师法》第二条第一款情事（背叛中华民国证据确实者）。……请补领新证书期间，至1946年12月31日截止。"上述法律、公告和办法，天津律师公会及会员律师都照例执行。

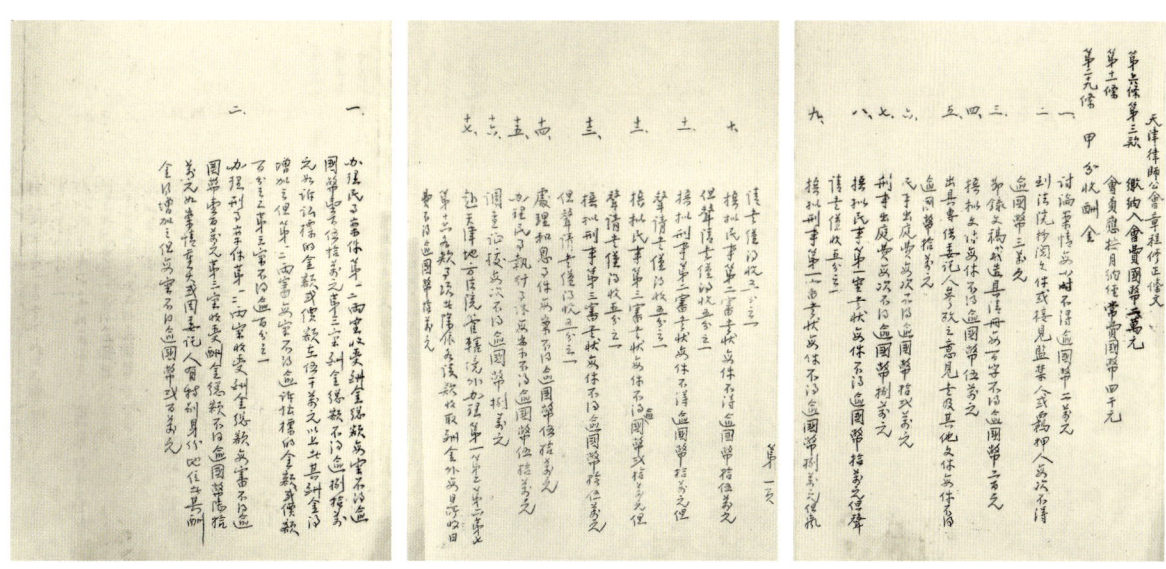

1946年8月《天津律师公会章程》修正条文
Amendments to *The Constitution of Tianjin Bar Association* in August 1946

On July 23, 1946, the Ministry of Justice and Administration of the National Government issued an announcement for the *Announcement of the Length of Time for Lawyers Appearing in Puppet Courts to Cessate their Duties*. The announcement stipulated, "Check for lawyers who appeared in puppet court during Anti-Japanese War and organized the puppet courts to perform their duties... It is hereby determined from September 3, 1945, the day of the end of the Japanese war, the performance of duties will be suspended for one year, and the period will expire." On August 13, the National Government announced the *Measures for Handling Lawyer Certificates Issued by Puppet Organizations*, which stipulated, "1. Lawyers issued by puppet organizations Certificates are all invalid; 2. Lawyers who have received certificates before the war and who have renewed fake certificates who have not been convicted in accordance with the *Punishment for Traitors Act* may hand in the fake certificates and check the following certificates from September 3, 1946. The submission shall be verified by the district court and forwarded to the Ministry of Justice and Administration, and a new certificate shall be obtained: (1) Certificate of qualification as a lawyer before the war; (2) Certificates of the two currently recommended officers, certifying that there is no article in the *Lawyers Law*

Article 2 Paragraph 1 (Those who betrayed the authenticity of the evidence from the Republic of China)... Please apply for a new certificate until December 31, 1946." The above-mentioned laws, announcements and methods are implemented by the Tianjin Bar Association and its member lawyers as usual.

（二）律师公会的任务

(b) Tasks of the Bar Association.

《天津律师公会章程》第四条规定了律师公会的任务：关于平民法律扶助之实施事项；关于法令修改或司法事务之建议事项；关于法律教育之提倡事项；关于法学研究及刊物出版事项；关于会员品德与风纪之整饬事项；关于会员共同利益之维护增进事项；关于行政及司法机关委托或咨询事项；关于《律师法》暨本《章程》所规定之其他事项。

Article 4 of *The Constitution of Tianjin Bar Association* stipulates the tasks of the Bar Association: Matters concerning the implementation of legal assistance for civilians; Matters concerning the revision of laws or recommendations on judicial matters; Matters concerning the promotion of legal education; Matters concerning legal research and publications; Matters concerning the rectification of members' morality and discipline; Matters concerning the maintenance and promotion of the common interests of members; Matters concerning entrustment or consultation by administrative and judicial agencies; Matters concerning other matters stipulated in the *Lawyers Law* and this *Constitution*.

（三）律师公会的职员及选举

(c) Staff and Election of the Bar Association

按照《天津律师公会章程》第十五至二十条的规定，公会设置职员：理事二十一人，执行公会一切会务，并互选常务理事五人，轮流处理日常事务，对外代表公会；候补理事七人，于理事缺额时依次递补；监事七人，监察公会一切事务，并互选常务监事三人，处理日常监察事务；候补监事三人，于监事缺额时依次递补；理、监事及候补理、监事均任期两年，连选得连任一次。公会设书记长一人，事务员无定额，视事务之繁简而定，由理事会雇用，受理事指挥，监督办理文书、记录、会计、庶务及其他事务，前项人员于办理监事会事务时应受监事的指挥、监督。

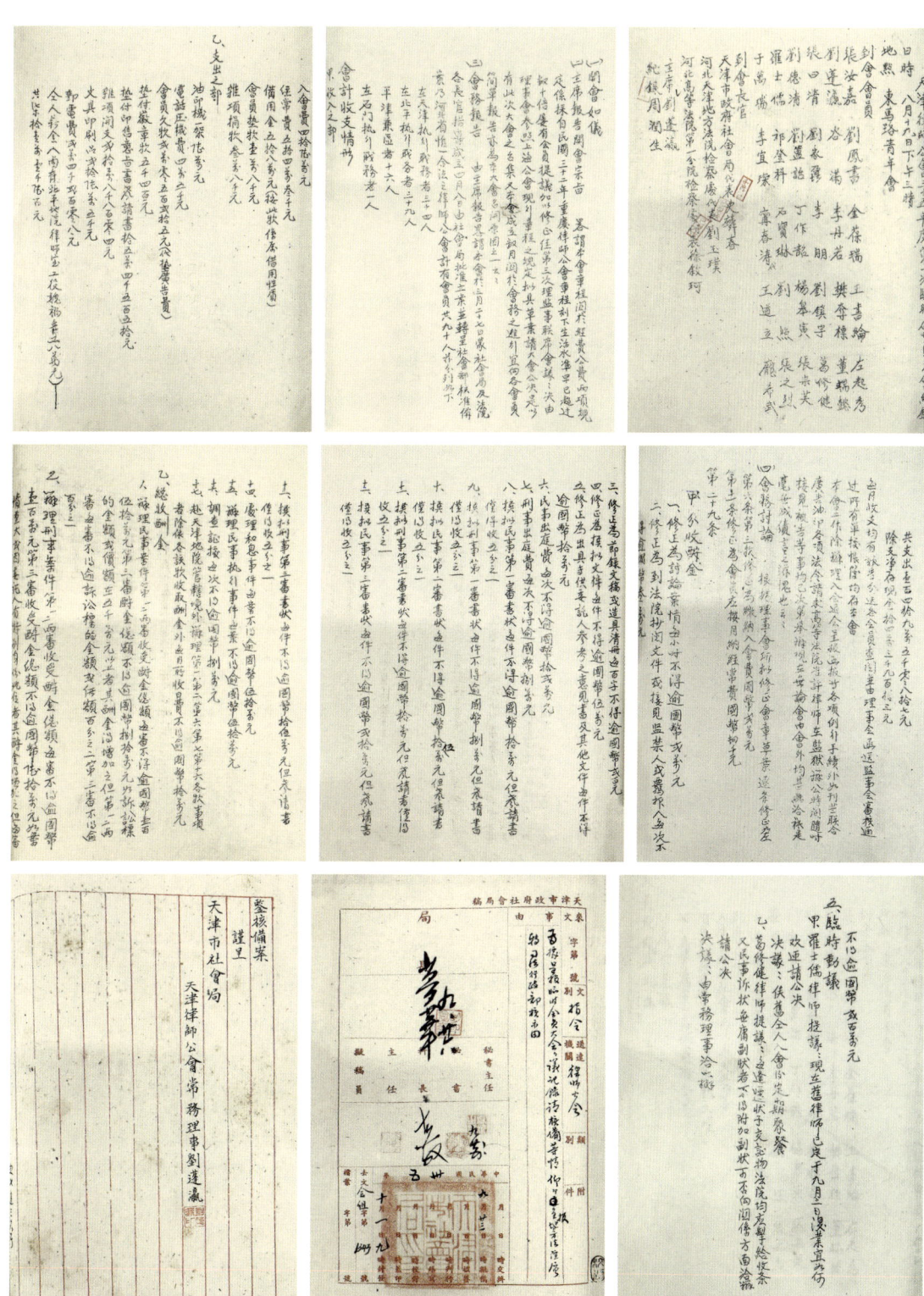

1946年天津律师公会三十五年度第一次临时会员大会纪录

Records of the year 35 first temporary Member's General Assembly of the Tianjin Bar Association in 1946

In accordance with Articles 15-20 of *The Constitution of Tianjin Bar Association*, the association has staff members, twenty-one directors perform all the affairs of the association, and the executive directors are selected from each other, and five people take turns to handle daily affairs and represent the association externally; alternate seven members of council will be replenished in turn when the director is vacant; seven supervisors will supervise all the affairs of the committee and elect three standing supervisors from each other to handle daily supervision affairs; three alternate supervisors will be filled in order when supervisors are vacant; The term of office of directors, supervisors and alternates is two years, and they may be re-elected once. The committee has a secretary-general and no fixed number of clerks. Depending on the complexity of the affairs, they are hired by the board of directors to accept and direct the affairs, supervise the handling of documents, records, accounting, general affairs and other affairs. The personnel mentioned in the preceding paragraph shall handle the affairs of the board of supervisors. Under the command and supervision of supervisors.

1946年9月22日，天津律师公会第一届第二次临时会员大会在大沽路天津市立第二中学礼堂召开。两次会议选举产生了天津律师公会第一届职员，分别是常务理事刘蓬瀛、于万瑞、李宜琛、朱德武、李洪岳、张绍曾、张士骏七人，理事王书伦、左起秀、宁岛涛、罗士儒、黄宗法、张汝嘉、孙鹤鸣、老遇春、张务滋、白鋆、胡学骞、耿运枢、崔鸿文、高善谦十四人，候补理事李丹若、吴燮昌、刘镇宇、陈士阜、李伯熏、胡延年、夏延邦七人，常务监事金葆瑞、张德良、穆祥震三人，理事张德清、尹福保、王庭兰、杜鸿翰四人，候补监事田淇清、王天伟、王大琨三人。

On September 22, 1946, the Second Temporary Member's General Assembly of the First Tianjin Bar Association was held in the auditorium of Tianjin Second Middle School on Dagu Road. The two meetings elected the first staff of the Tianjin Bar Association, including executive directors Liu Pengying, Yu Wanrui, Li Yichen, Zhu Dewu, Li Hongyue, Zhang Shaozeng, Zhang Shijun, and directors Wang Shulun, Zuo Qixiu, Ning Daotao, Luo Shiru, Huang Zongfa, Zhang Rujia, Sun Heming, Lao Yuchun,

1934	1935	1936	1937	1938	1939	1940	1941	1942	1943	1944	1945	1946
1960	1961	1962	1963	1964	1965	1966	1967	1968	1969	1970	1971	1972
1986	1987	1988	1989	1990	1991	1992	1993	1994	1995	1996	1997	1998
2012	2013	2014	2015	2016	2017	2018	2019	2020	2021	……		

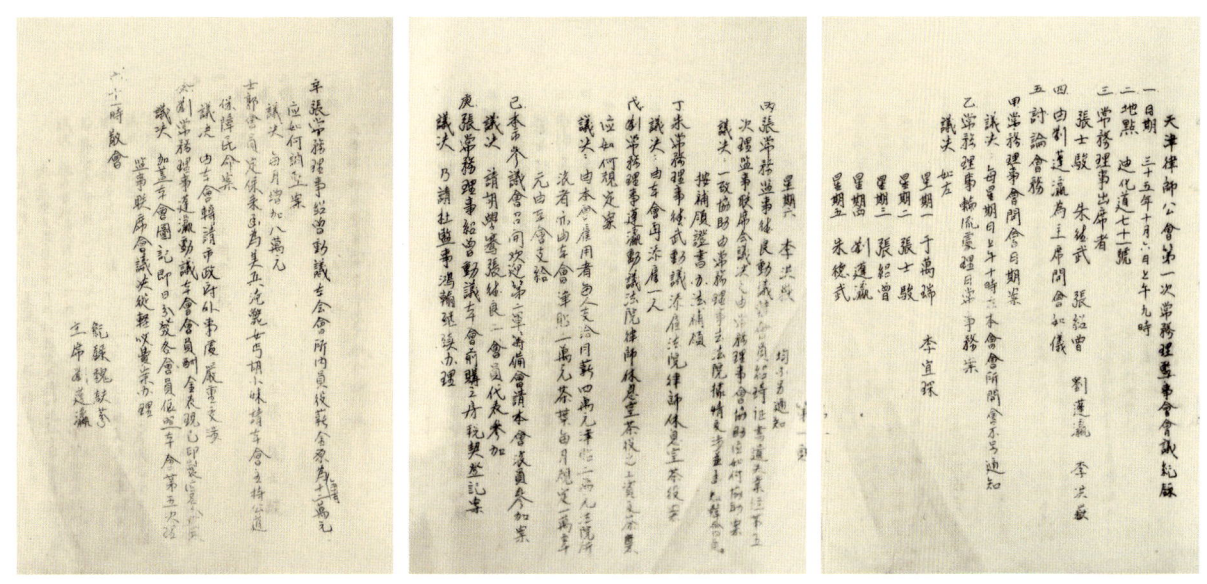

1946年10月6日天津律师公会第一次常务理监事会会议纪录
Minutes of the first meeting of the Tianjin Bar Association's Executive Board of Supervisors on October 6, 1946

Zhang Wuzi, Bai Yun, Hu Xueqian, Geng Yunshu, Cui Hongwen, Gao Shanqian 14 people, alternate director Li Danruo, Wu Xiechang, Liu Zhenyu, Chen Shifu, Li Boxun, Hu Yannian, Xia Yanbang 7 people, executive supervisor Jin Baorui, Zhang Deliang and Mu Xiangzhen, 4 directors Zhang Deqing, Yin Fubao, Wang Tinglan and Du Honghan, and 3 alternate supervisors Tian Qiqing, Wang Tianwei and Wang Dakun.

（四）律师公会会议

(d) Bar Association Meeting

根据《天津律师公会章程》第二十一至二十七条的规定，公会会议分为四种：

According to Articles 21-27 of *The Constitution of Tianjin Bar Association*, the Association's meetings are divided into four types:

1. 会员大会，每年春季举行一次，由理事会确定日期召开，在开会两个星期前登报通告并专函各会员。如理监事联席会认为必要，或经会员十分之二以上书面请求并记明提议事项及理由者，应召开临时会员大会，并在开会一星期前登报通知且专函各会员。

1921	1922	1923	1924	1925	1926	1927	1928	1929	1930	1931	1932	1933
1947	1948	1949	1950	1951	1952	1953	1954	1955	1956	1957	1958	1959
1973	1974	1975	1976	1977	1978	1979	1980	1981	1982	1983	1984	1985
1999	2000	2001	2002	2003	2004	2005	2006	2007	2008	2009	2010	2011

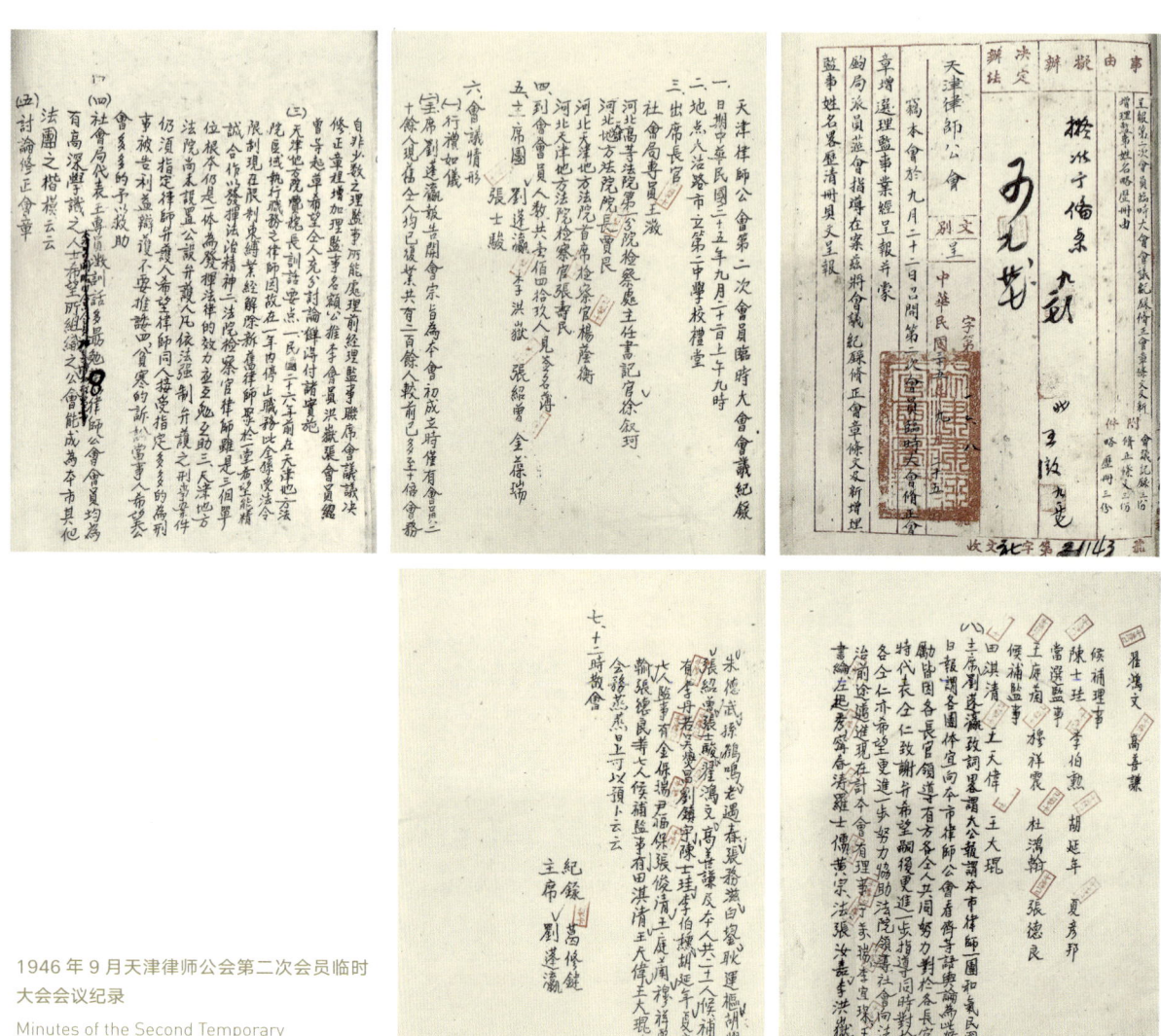

1946年9月天津律师公会第二次会员临时大会会议纪录

Minutes of the Second Temporary Member's General Assembly of Tianjin Bar Association in September 1946

1. The Member's General Assembly is held once a year in the spring and is held on a date set by the board of directors. Two weeks before the meeting, a notice and a special letter will be issued to all members. If the Board of Directors and Supervisors deems it necessary or the member has requested a written request of two-tenths or more of the members and stated the proposed items and reasons, a temporary Member's General Assembly shall be convened, a notice and a special letter to each member shall be posted one week before the meeting.

1934	1935	1936	1937	1938	1939	1940	1941	1942	1943	1944	1945	1946
1960	1961	1962	1963	1964	1965	1966	1967	1968	1969	1970	1971	1972
1986	1987	1988	1989	1990	1991	1992	1993	1994	1995	1996	1997	1998
2012	2013	2014	2015	2016	2017	2018	2019	2020	2021	……		

2. 理事会，每月举行一次，由常务理事召开，并通知监事列席。如经理事三分之一提议，则应召开临时会。

2. The board of directors is held once a month and is convened by the standing directors, and the supervisors are notified to attend as non-voting delegates. If one-third of the manager proposes, an ad hoc meeting should be held.

3. 监事会，每月举行一次，由常务监事召开。如经监事三分之一以上提议，则应召开临时会。

3. The board of supervisors is held once a month and is convened by the standing supervisors. If proposed by more than one-third of the supervisors, a temporary meeting shall be convened.

4. 理监事联席会，常务理监事认为必要时会同召开。会员大会有三分之一以上会员出席方得开会，如出席会员不足法定人数再行召集时，其缺席者应于会员总数内扣除计算。理事会、监事会及理监事联席会有二分之一以上理监事出席方得开会，候补理事、监事均得列席。遇有理事、监事缺席时，得分别临时补充议决，但不得超过缺席人数的二分之一。会员大会主席由出席会员互推，理事会主席由常务理事互推，监事会主席由常务监事互推，理监事联席会主席由常务理监事互推。会议事项与理事、监事或会员有关系者应停止其表决权，但得陈述事实或意见。公会各种会议均在会期一星期前呈报天津市社会局及天津地方法院首席检察官。

4. A joint meeting of directors and supervisors shall be convened when the executive directors and supervisors deem necessary. At the Member's General Assembly, more than one-third of the members can attend the meeting. If there is less than a quorum, the absentee shall be deducted from the total number of members. The board of directors, the board of supervisors and the joint board of directors and supervisors shall have more than one-half of the directors and supervisors attending the meeting, and alternate directors and supervisors shall be present as nonvoting delegates. When directors and supervisors are absent, they may make supplementary decisions separately, but they shall not exceed one-half of the number of absentees. The chairman of the

Member's General Assembly is recommended by the members present, the chairman of the board of directors is recommended by the standing directors, the chairman of the board of supervisors is recommended by the standing supervisors, and the chairman of the joint board of directors and supervisors is recommended by the standing directors and supervisors. Meeting matters related to directors, supervisors or members shall stop their voting rights, but may state facts or opinions. All meetings of the Association are reported to the Municipal Social Bureau and the Chief Prosecutor of Tianjin District Court one week before the meeting.

（五）公会会员

(e) Members of the Bar Association

1. 会员的入会与退会

1. Members' Enrollment and Withdrawal

根据《天津律师公会章程》第五至九条的规定，凡律师呈准天津地方法院登录者，得入会为公会会员；会员入会履行以下手续：填具入会申请书，并附二寸半身相片两张，交验律师证书及呈准天津地方法院登录证件，缴纳入会费国币五万元；会员入会后，由公会发给入会证书

1946年10月27日天津律师公会第四次常务理事会会议纪录

Minutes of the Fourth Executive Council Meeting of Tianjin Bar Association on October 27, 1946

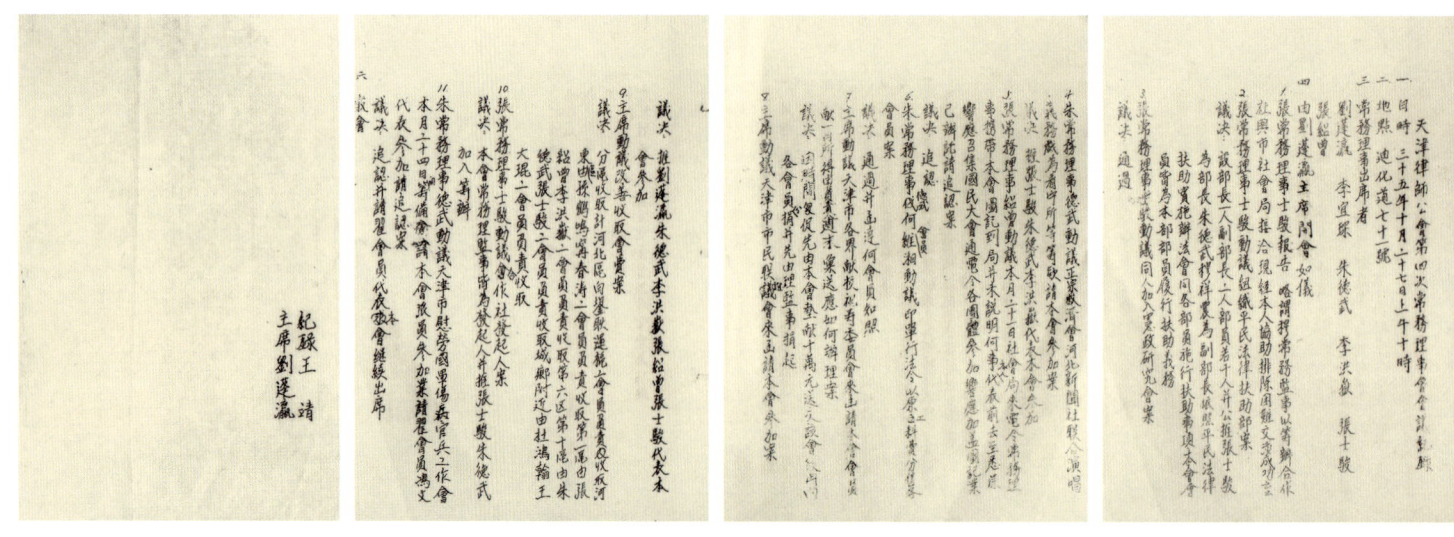

并登记于会员名簿；会员如经法院注销登录者，应令其退会；会员送请惩戒，其情节重大者，得经会员大会或理监事联席会议之决议令其暂时退会，但应经天津地方法院首席检察官之核准并呈报天津市社会局备案。

According to Articles 5-9 of *The Constitution of Tianjin Bar Association*, all lawyers who are approved to register in Tianjin District Court are allowed to join the association; members shall complete the following procedures: Fill in an application for membership and attach two two-inch half-length photos, submit the lawyer certificate and submit the registration certificate to Tianjin District Court, and pay the membership fee of 50,000 yuan; After the member joins the association, the association will issue the membership certificate and register it in the member directory; If the member is cancelled by the court, it shall be ordered to withdraw from the association; If the members request disciplinary action, if the circumstances are serious, they may be temporarily withdrawn by the resolution of the Member's General Assembly or the joint meeting of directors and supervisors, but they shall be approved by the chief prosecutor of Tianjin District Court and reported to the Tianjin Municipal Social Bureau for record.

2. 会员的权利与义务

2. The Rights and Obligations of Members

根据《天津律师公会章程》第十至十四条的规定，会员有发言权、表决权、选举权及被选举权。会员应按月缴纳经常费国币一万元。会员欠缴经常费逾三个月经催告不理者，由会员大会或理监事联席会议之决议令其退会，但应经天津地方法院首席检察官之核准并呈报天津市社会局备案。会员应轮流办理平民法律扶助事宜，会员事务所迁移应立即报告公会。

According to Articles 10-14 of *The Constitution of Tianjin Bar Association*, members have the right to speak, vote, vote and be elected. Members should pay 10,000 yuan for regular monthly fees. If a member owes regular fees for more than three months and is urged for disregard, the Member's General Assembly or the joint meeting of directors and supervisors shall order him to withdraw from the meeting, but it shall be approved by the chief prosecutor of Tianjin District Court and reported to the Tianjin Municipal Social Bureau for record. Members shall take turns to handle matters concerning legal assistance to civilians. The relocation of the member firm shall be reported to the association immediately.

（六）公会会员的酬金

(f) Members' Remuneration

根据《天津律师公会章程》第二十八条的规定，会员受当事人之委托，办理诉讼案件，其收受酬金办法分下列两种，由当事人自择，以契约定之。

According to Article 28 of *The Constitution of Tianjin Bar Association*, members are entrusted by the parties to handle litigation cases. There are two methods for receiving remuneration, which are chosen by the parties and determined by contract.

1. 分收酬金

1. Remuneration

一、讨论案情，每小时不得逾国币一万两千元。二、到法院抄阅文件或接见监禁人或羁押人，每次不得逾国币两万元。三、节录文稿或造具清册，每百字不得逾国币一千元。四、撰拟函件，每件不得逾国币四万元。五、出具专供委托人参考之意见书及其他文件，每件不得逾国币八万元。六、民事出庭费，每次不得逾国币十二万元。七、刑事出庭费，每次不得逾国币八万元。八、撰拟民事第一审书状，每件不得逾国币十万元，但申请书仅得收五分之一。九、撰拟刑事第一审书状，每件不得逾国币六万元，但申请书仅得收五分之一。十、撰拟民事第二审书状，每件不得逾国币十万元，但申请书仅得收五分之一。十一、撰拟刑事第二审书状，每件不得逾国币八万元，但申请书仅得收五分之一。十二、撰拟民事第三审书状，每件不得逾国币十万元，但申请书仅得收五分之一。十三、撰拟刑事第三审书状，每件不得逾国币十二万元，但申请书仅得收五分之一。十四、处理和息事件，每案不得逾国币五十万元。十五、处理民事执行案件，每案不得逾国币五十万元。

1. Discussing the case shall not exceed 12,000 yuan per hour. 2. Going to the

court to read and copy documents or interview with prisoners or detainees shall not exceed 20,000 yuan each time. 3. The list of excerpted manuscripts or creations shall not exceed 1,000 yuan per hundred characters. 4. Each piece of the proposed letter shall not exceed 40,000 yuan. 5. Issue opinions and other documents exclusively for the client's reference, each of which shall not exceed 80,000 yuan. 6. The fee of representation in civil case in the court shall not exceed 120,000 yuan each time. 7. The fee of representation in criminal case in the court shall not exceed 80,000 yuan each time. 8. Each petition of the first civil trial shall not exceed 100,000 yuan, but only one-fifth of the application form will be accepted. 9. Each pleading for drafting the first criminal trial shall not exceed 60,000 yuan, but only one-fifth of the application is accepted. 10. Each pleading of the second civil trial shall not exceed 100,000 yuan, but only one-fifth of the application form is accepted. 11. Each pleading written for the second criminal trial shall not exceed 80,000 yuan, but only one-fifth of the application will be accepted. 12. Each of the draft civil third-instance pleadings shall not exceed 100,000 yuan, but only one-fifth of the application form will be accepted. 13. Each petition for drafting the third criminal trial shall not exceed 120,000 yuan, but only one-fifth of the application form will be accepted. 14. When handling peace and interest incidents, each case shall not exceed 500,000 yuan. 15. In handling civil enforcement cases, each case shall not exceed 500,000 yuan.

2. 总收酬金

2. Total Remuneration

办理民事案件，第一二两审收受酬金总额，每审不得逾国币一百五十万元，第三审收受酬金总额不得逾国币八十万元。如诉讼标的金额或价额在五千万元以上者，其酬金得增加之。第一二两审，每审不得逾诉讼标的金额百分之二，第三审不得逾百分之一。办理刑事案件，第一二两审收受酬金总额，每审不得逾国币一百万元，第三审收受酬金总额不得逾国币六十万元。如案情重大或因委托人有特别身份地位者，其酬金得增加之，但每审不得逾国币一百二十万元。此外，会员办理非讼案件之酬金准用办理民事案件总酬金之规定，会员办理平民法律扶助事宜及各级法院指定办理之案件，均不得收受酬金。

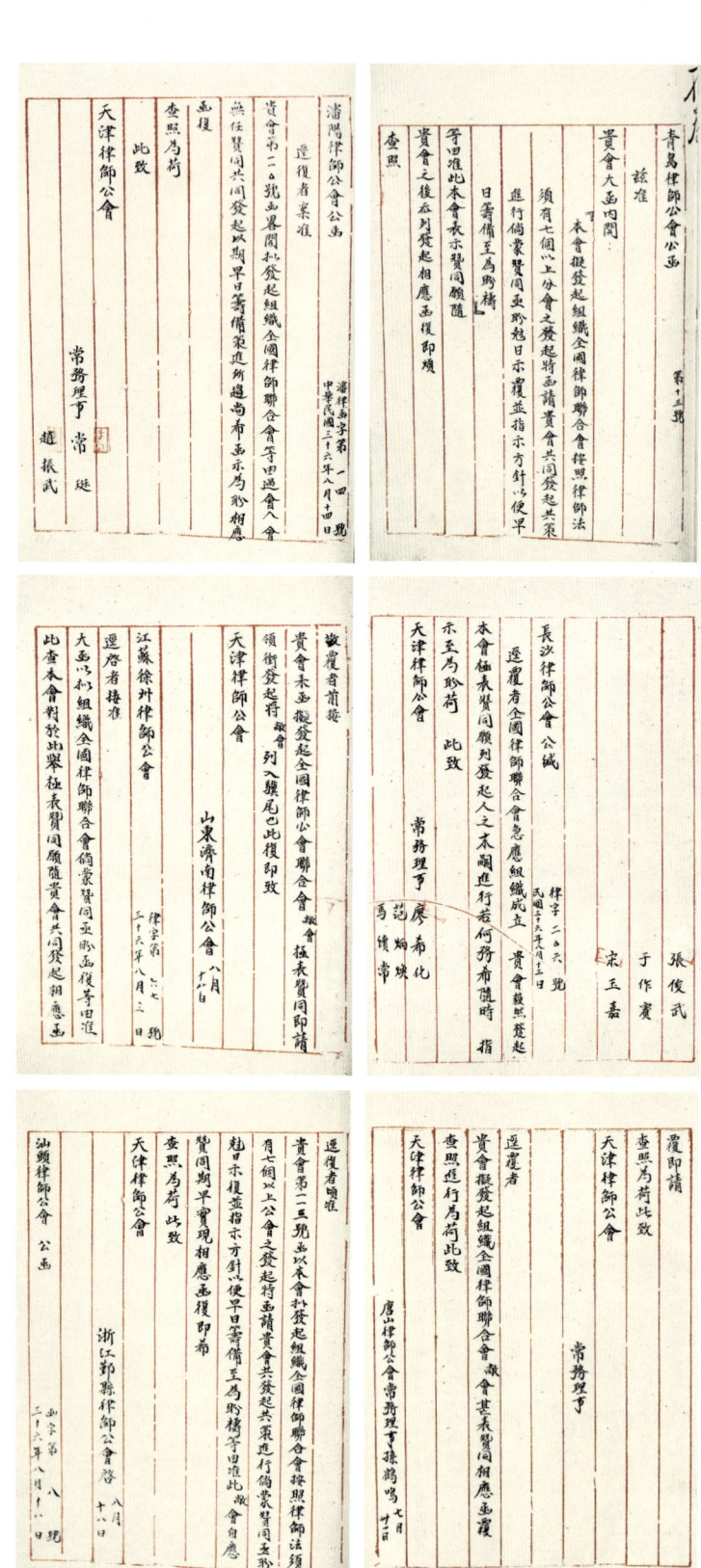

1947年8月全国各城市律师公会致天津律师公会函

Letters from the bar associations of cities across the country to the Tianjin Bar Association in August 1947

The total amount of remuneration received in the first and second trials of civil cases shall not exceed 1.5 million yuan per trial, and the total amount of remuneration received in the third trial shall not exceed 800,000. If the amount of the subject matter of the litigation is more than 50 million yuan, the lawyer's fee remuneration needs to be increased. The first and second trials shall not exceed 2% of the amount of the subject matter in the litigation, and the third trial shall not exceed 1%. The total amount of remuneration received in the first and second trials of criminal cases shall not exceed 1 million yuan per trial, and the total amount of remuneration received in the third trial shall not exceed 600,000 yuan. If the case is serious or the client has a special status, The remuneration may be increased, but it shall not exceed the national currency of 1.2 million yuan per trial. In addition, the remuneration of members for handling non-litigation cases shall be governed by the provisions of total remuneration for handling civil cases, and members shall not receive remuneration for handling civilian legal assistance matters and cases designated by courts at all levels.

（七）会员惩戒

(g) Members Punishment

根据《天津律师公会章程》第四十五条规定，会员违反本《章程》之规定，情节轻微者，得经会员大会或理监事联席会之决议命其注意，情节重大者，公会应负责检举。

According to Article 45 of *The Constitution of Tianjin Bar Association*, if a member violates the provisions of this *Constitution*, if the circumstances are minor, the Member's General Assembly or the joint board of directors and supervisors may order its attention. If the circumstances are serious, the association shall be responsible for reporting.

1947年8月全国各城市律师公会致天津律师公会函
Letters from the bar associations of cities across the country to the Tianjin Bar Association in August 1947

百年律师看天津

ONE HUNDRED YEARS OF LAWYERS
ACCUMULATED HISTORY FOCUSED ON TIANJIN

下册

天津市律师协会　编著

丁立莹　编译

天津出版传媒集团

天津古籍出版社

目 录
CONTENTS

百年律师看天津
ONE HUNDRED YEARS OF LAWYERS ACCUMULATED HISTORY FOCUSED ON TIANJIN

下 册
Volume 2

282 人民律师 整装起步
PEOPLE'S LAWYERS GET STARTED

318 春风化雨 重建新生（上）
THE SPRING WIND AND RAIN OF REBUILDING THE TIANJIN LAWYERS ASSOCIATION (I)

386 春风化雨 重建新生（下）
THE SPRING WIND AND RAIN OF REBUILDING THE TIANJIN LAWYERS ASSOCIATION (II)

428 新时代 新律师 新征程
NEW ERA, NEW LAWYER, NEW JOURNEY

546 后 记
POSTSCRIPT

人民律师
整装起步

**PEOPLE'S LAWYERS
GET STARTED**

百年律师看天津
ONE HUNDRED YEARS OF LAWYERS ACCUMULATED HISTORY FOCUSED ON TIANJIN

天津市司法局与天津市律师协会筹备委员会 / 284
TIANJIN MUNICIPAL BUREAU OF JUSTICE AND THE PREPARATORY
COMMITTEE OF THE TIANJIN LAWYERS ASSOCIATION

20 世纪 50 年代的律师代表 / 300
REPRESENTATIVES OF LAWYERS IN THE 1950S

20 世纪 50 年代的律师工作 / 309
LAWYERS' WORK IN THE 1950S

天津市司法局与
天津市律师协会筹备委员会

TIANJIN MUNICIPAL BUREAU OF JUSTICE AND THE PREPARATORY COMMITTEE OF THE TIANJIN LAWYERS ASSOCIATION

新民主主义革命时期的司法，服务于武装夺取政权，其制度尚不完善。新中国成立之后，司法作为一种有序、和平地解决纠纷的重要方式，越来越显示出它的重要性，不过需要逐步加以改革和完善。要彻底废除压迫人民的旧法律、法令和司法制度，建立和制定保护人民的法律、法令和司法制度，就要一切都白手起家，从头开始，任务十分艰巨。同时，社会上还存在着轻视司法工作和不敢轻易触及司法两种态度。

During the period of the New Democratic Revolution, the judicial system served the armed seizure of power, and its system was not yet formal. After the founding of the People's Republic of China, the judicial system, as an important way to resolve disputes in an orderly and peaceful manner, has increasingly demonstrated its importance and needs to be gradually reformed and improved. To completely abolish the old laws, decrees, and judicial systems that oppress the people, and establish and formulate laws, decrees, and judicial systems to protect the people. Everything must be built from scratch. It is a very difficult task. In society, there are two types of underestimating judicial work and not daring to touch it lightly.

1949年2月，中共中央发布了《关于废除国民党的六法全书与确定解放区的司法原则的指示》。4月1日，华北人民政府根据中共中央的指示也颁布了《废除国民党的六法全书及一切反动的法律训令》，彻底废除了旧的司法制度，为新中国成立后建立新的司法制度扫除了障碍。

1934	1935	1936	1937	1938	1939	1940	1941	1942	1943	1944	1945	1946
1960	1961	1962	1963	1964	1965	1966	1967	1968	1969	1970	1971	1972
1986	1987	1988	1989	1990	1991	1992	1993	1994	1995	1996	1997	1998
2012	2013	2014	2015	2016	2017	2018	2019	2020	2021			

In February 1949, the Central Committee of the Communist Party of China issued the *Instructions on the Abolition of the Kuomintang's Six Laws and the Determination of Judicial Principles in Liberated Areas*. On April 1, the North China People's Government also issued the *Abolition of the Kuomintang's Six Laws and All Reactionary Legal Orders* in accordance with the instructions of the Central Committee of the Communist Party of China, which completely abolished the old judicial system and wiped out the establishment of a new judicial system after the founding of the People's Republic of China.

1949年9月27日通过的《中国人民政治协商会议共同纲领》第十七条明确规定:"废除国民党反动政府一切压迫人民的法律、法令和司法制度,制定保护人民的法律、法令,建立人民司法制度。"为了维护人民法院的威信和保护人民群众的利益,打击旧律师和讼棍在社会上包揽词讼、欺骗群众的行为,1950年7月颁布的《人民法庭组织通则》第六条规定:"县(市)人民法庭及其分庭受理案件后,应保障被告有辩护和请人辩护的权利。但被告所请的辩护人,须经法庭认可后,方得出庭辩护。"1950年12月,中央人民政府发出《关于取缔黑律师及讼棍事件的通报》,明令取缔国民党的旧律师制度,解散旧的律师公会,禁止旧律师和讼棍活动。

Article 17 of the *Common Program of the Chinese People's Political Consultative Conference* adopted on September 27, 1949 clearly stipulates, "Abolish all laws, decrees and judicial systems that oppress the people by the reactionary Kuomintang government, formulate laws and decrees to protect the people, and establish people's justice System." In order to maintain the prestige of the people's courts and protect the interests of the people, and to combat the acts of old lawyers and shysters in soliciting litigation to deceive the people in society, Article 6 of the *General Rules for the Organization of the People's Courts* promulgated in July 1950 stipulates, "After the county (city) people's court and its chambers accept the case, they should guarantee the defendant's right to defend and call for defense. However, the defender requested by the defendant must be approved by the court before he can come to court for defense." In December, the Central People's Government issued the *Notice on the Banning of Black Lawyers and Shysters*, expressly banning the Kuomintang's old bar system, disbanding the old Bar associations, and prohibiting old lawyers and shysters activities.

1950年7月26日至8月11日，最高人民法院、最高人民检察院、法制委员会和司法部共同在北京召开了第一届全国司法会议，会议讨论了《人民法院暂行组织条例》《刑法大纲》《诉讼程序通则》《犯人改造暂时条例》《公司法》等草案。司法部将《京津沪三市辩护人制度试行办法（草案）》提交会议讨论，并要求各地酌情办理。1954年7月31日，司法部发出《关于试验法院组织制度中几个问题的通知》，决定在北京、上海、天津、重庆、武汉、沈阳等城市试办法律顾问处，试行开展律师工作。1955年年初，天津市高级人民法院抽调两名审判员兼任律师的辩护工作。

From July 26 to August 11, 1950, the Supreme People's Court, the Supreme People's Procuratorate, the Legislative Affairs Commission and the Ministry of Justice jointly convened the First National Judicial Conference in Beijing. The meeting discussed drafts such as the *Temporary Organizational Regulations of the People's Courts*, *Outline of Criminal Law*, *General Rules of Procedure*, *Temporary Regulations on the Reform of Prisoners*, and *Company Law*. The Ministry of Justice submitted the *Trial Measures for the Defender System in Beijing, Tianjin and Shanghai (Draft)* to the meeting for discussion, and requested all localities to handle it as appropriate. On July 31, 1954, the Ministry of Justice issued the *Notice on Several Issues in the Organizational System of Trial Courts*, deciding to pilot legal counsel offices in cities such as Beijing, Shanghai, Tianjin, Chongqing, Wuhan, and Shenyang to start lawyer work on a trial basis. At the beginning of 1955, the Tianjin Higher People's Court assigned two judges to serve as lawyers for the defense work.

在中国共产党的正确领导下，人民司法制度初步建立，中国律师真正成为了人民律师。天津成为最早开展人民律师工作的试点城市之一，天津律师业整装起步。

Under the correct leadership of the Communist Party of China, the people's judicial system has been initially established, and Chinese lawyers have truly become people's lawyers. Tianjin became one of the first pilot cities to carry out the work of people's lawyers, and Tianjin's lawyers started in their entirety.

新中国成立初期确立的审判机关与司法行政机关"合一制"一直延续到1955年。其间，

1934	1935	1936	1937	1938	1939	1940	1941	1942	1943	1944	1945	1946
1960	1961	1962	1963	1964	1965	1966	1967	1968	1969	1970	1971	1972
1986	1987	1988	1989	1990	1991	1992	1993	1994	1995	1996	1997	1998
2012	2013	2014	2015	2016	2017	2018	2019	2020	2021	......		

1954年9月20日第一届全国人民代表大会第一次会议通过了《中华人民共和国宪法》，其中第七十六条规定："人民法院审理案件，除法律规定的特别情况外，一律公开进行，被告人有权获得辩护。"

Article 76 of the *Constitution of the People's Republic of China* adopted at the first meeting of the First National People's Congress on September 20, 1954 stipulates, "People's courts shall hear all cases in public, except for special circumstances stipulated by law. The defendant has the right to be defended."

1954年国庆节游行队伍中的《宪法》模型

Constitution model on National Day in 1954

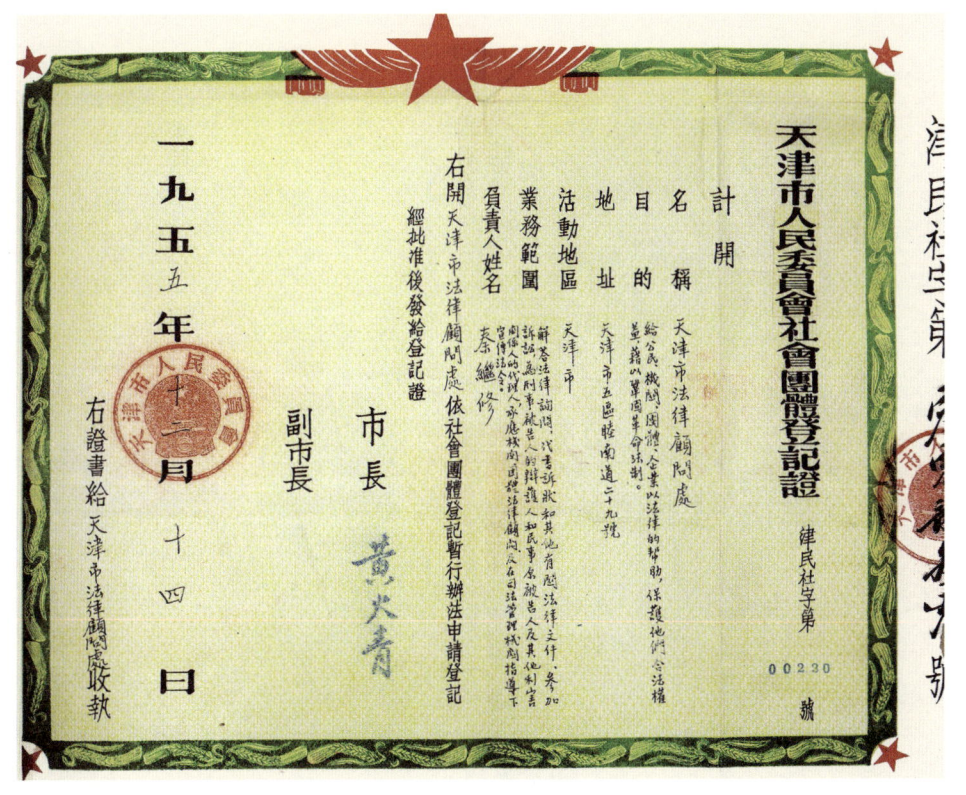

1955年12月天津市法律顾问处登记证

Registration certificate of Tianjin Legal Counsel Office in December 1955

287

1921	1922	1923	1924	1925	1926	1927	1928	1929	1930	1931	1932	1933
1947	1948	1949	1950	1951	1952	1953	1954	1955	1956	1957	1958	1959
1973	1974	1975	1976	1977	1978	1979	1980	1981	1982	1983	1984	1985
1999	2000	2001	2002	2003	2004	2005	2006	2007	2008	2009	2010	2011

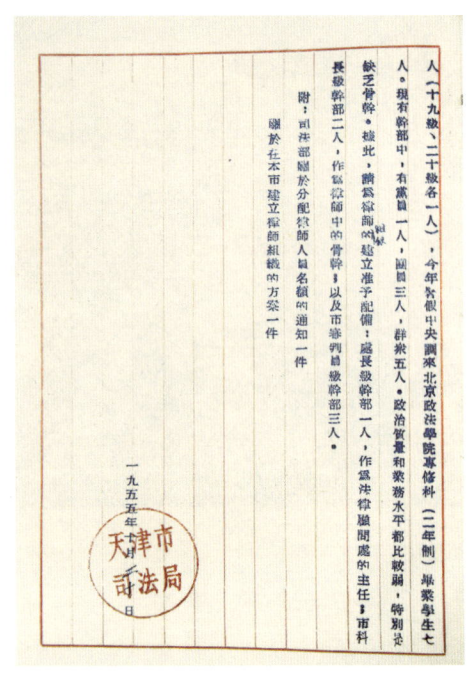
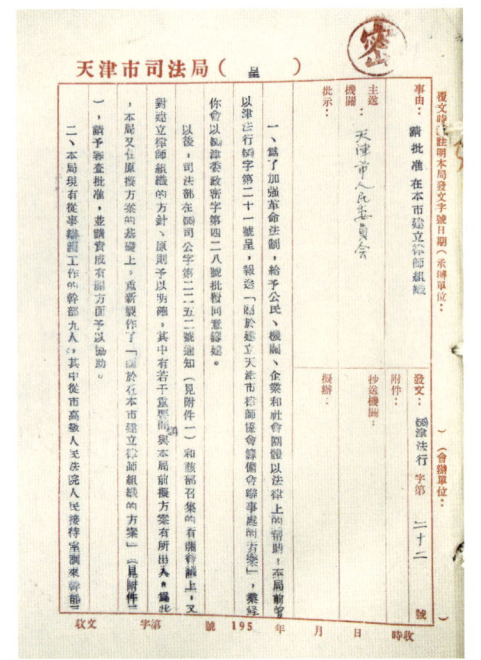

1955年10月天津市司法局呈送天津市人民委员会批准建立律师组织的请示

In October 1955, Tianjin Municipal Bureau of Justice submitted a request for approval to the Tianjin Municipal People's Committee for the establishment of a lawyer organization

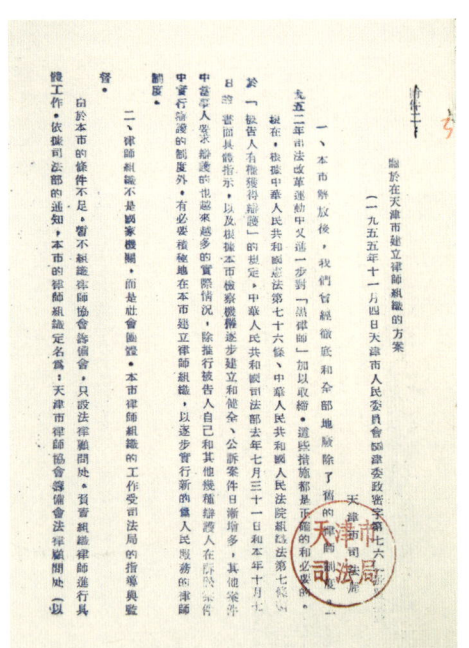
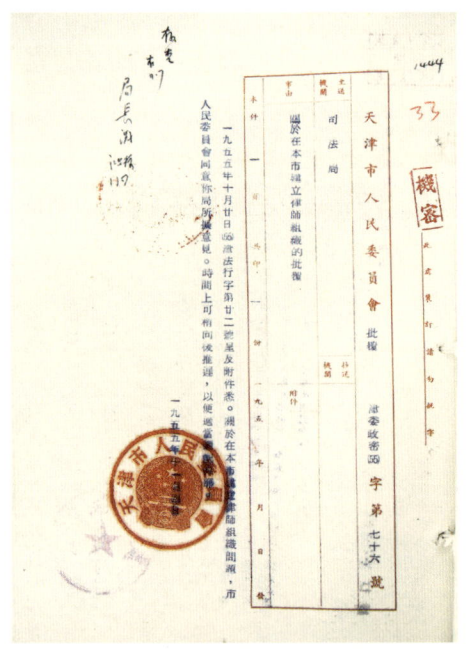

1955年10月天津市司法局呈送天津市人民委员会批准建立律师组织的请示所附的《关于在天津市建立律师组织的方案》（部分）（左）

Scheme for Establishing a Lawyer Organization in Tianjin (partial) attached to the request for approval for establishing a lawyer organization which Tianjin Municipal Bureau of Justice submitted to the Tianjin Municipal People's Committee in October 1955 (left)

1955年11月天津市人民委员会关于在天津市建立律师组织的批复（右）

Reply of Tianjin Municipal People's Committee on the establishment of a lawyers organization in Tianjin in November 1955 (right)

1934	1935	1936	1937	1938	1939	1940	1941	1942	1943	1944	1945	1946
1960	1961	1962	1963	1964	1965	1966	1967	1968	1969	1970	1971	1972
1986	1987	1988	1989	1990	1991	1992	1993	1994	1995	1996	1997	1998
2012	2013	2014	2015	2016	2017	2018	2019	2020	2021	……		

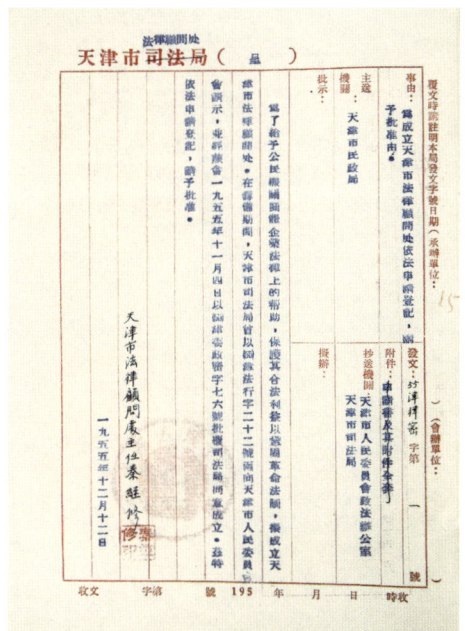
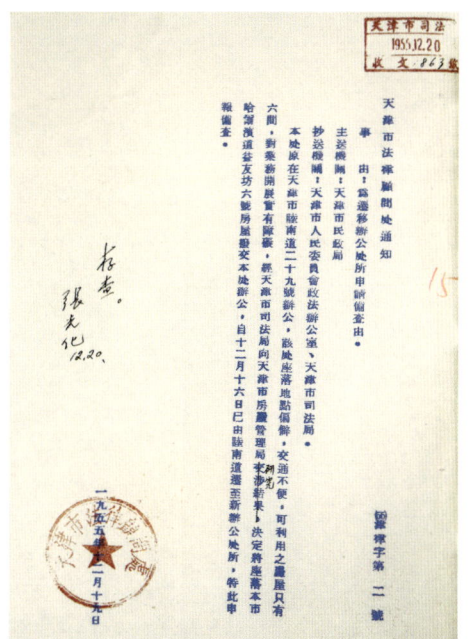

1955年12月天津市法律顾问处呈送天津市民政局批准成立天津市法律顾问处登记的请示（左）

In December 1955, Tianjin Legal Counsel Office submitted a request for the registration of Tianjin Municipal Civil Affairs Bureau to approve the establishment of Tianjin Legal Counsel Office (left)

1955年12月天津市法律顾问处迁移办公处的通知（右）

Notice on the relocation of Tianjin Legal Counsel Office in December 1955 (right)

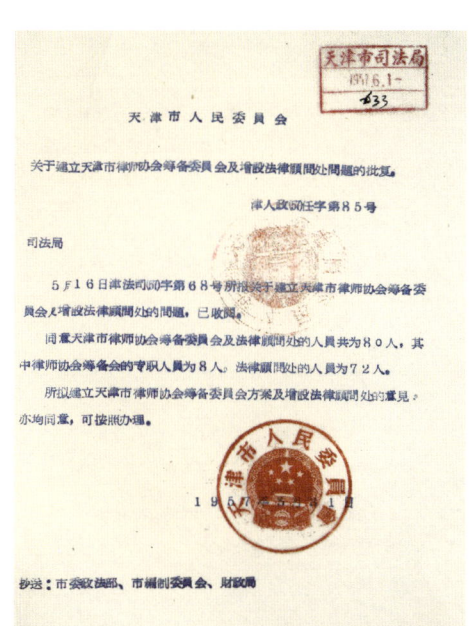

1957年5月关于建立天津市律师协会筹备委员会及增设法律顾问处问题的批复（左）

Reply of May 1957 on the establishment of the Preparatory Committee of the Tianjin Lawyers Association and the establishment of the legal counsel office (left)

1957年6月关于建立天津市律师协会筹备委员会，更改天津市法律顾问处、天津市法律顾问处分处名称的通知（右）

In June 1957, the notice regarding the establishment of the Preparatory Committee of the Tianjin Lawyers Association and the change of name of the Tianjin Legal Counsel Office and the Tianjin Legal Counsel Office Branch (right)

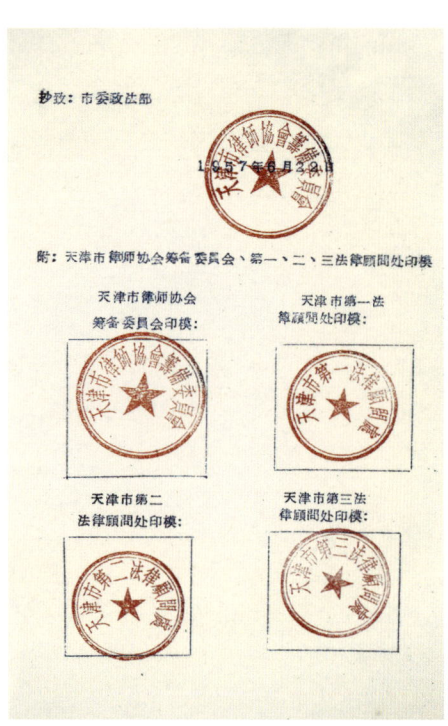
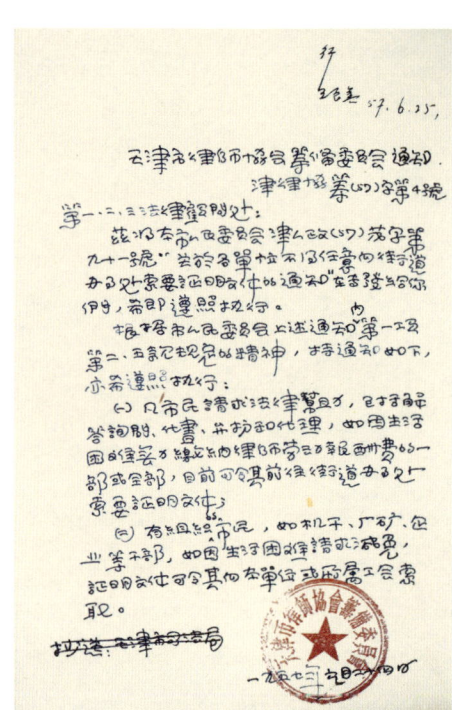

1957年6月关于建立天津市律师协会筹备委员会，更改天津市法律顾问处、天津市法律顾问处分处名称的通知（左）

In June 1957, the notice regarding the establishment of the Preparatory Committee of the Tianjin Lawyers Association and the change of name of the Tianjin Legal Counsel Office and the Tianjin Legal Counsel Office Branch (left)

1957年6月天津市律师协会筹备委员会转给第一、二、三法律顾问处的通知（右）

In June 1957, the notice of the Preparatory Committee of the Tianjin Lawyers Association transferred to the First, Second and Third Legal Counsel Office (right)

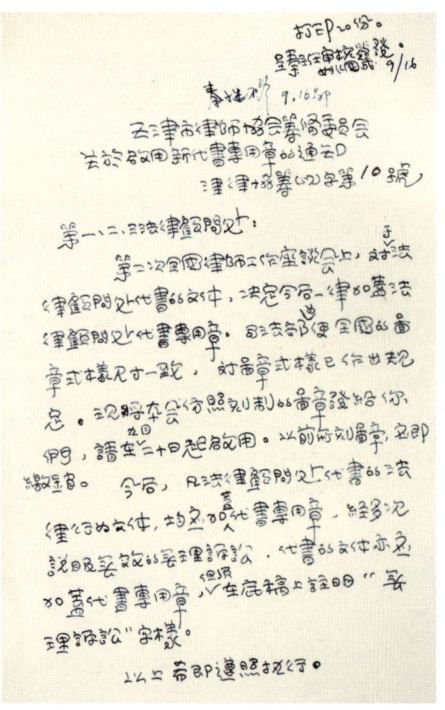
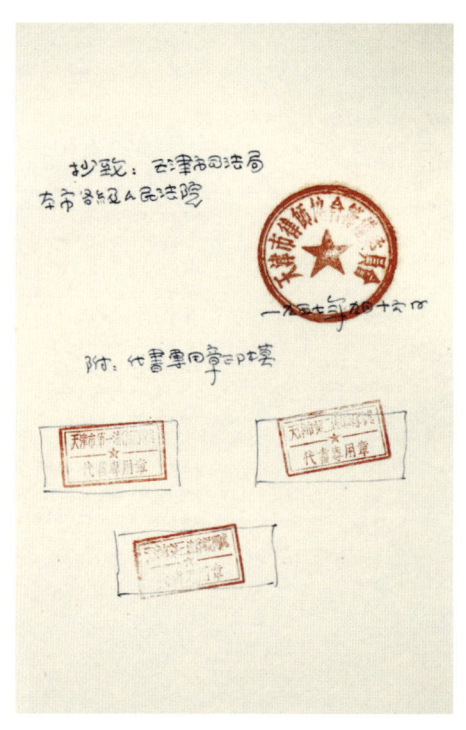

1957年9月天津市律师协会筹备委员会关于启用新代书专用章的通知

In September 1957, the notice on the use of the new special seal of the Preparatory Committee of the Tianjin Lawyers Association

1934	1935	1936	1937	1938	1939	1940	1941	1942	1943	1944	1945	1946
1960	1961	1962	1963	1964	1965	1966	1967	1968	1969	1970	1971	1972
1986	1987	1988	1989	1990	1991	1992	1993	1994	1995	1996	1997	1998
2012	2013	2014	2015	2016	2017	2018	2019	2020	2021	……		

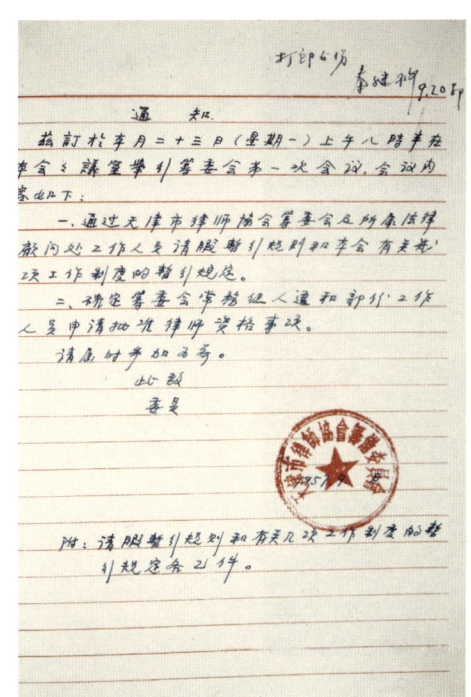

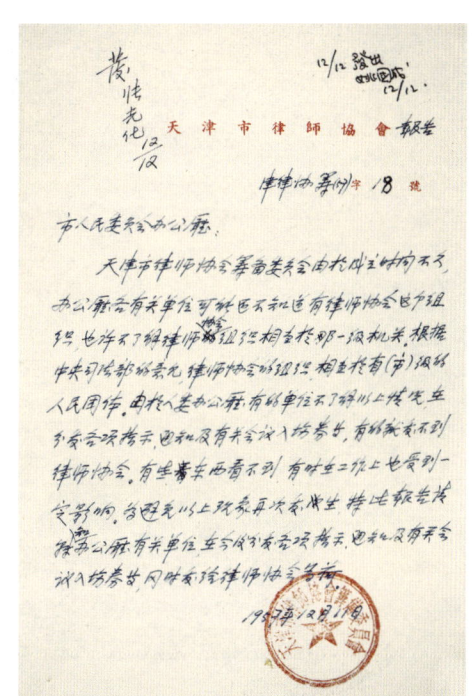

1957年9月关于召开天津市律师协会筹备委员会第一次会议的通知（左）

Notice on the First Meeting of the Preparatory Committee of the Tianjin Lawyers Association in September 1957 (left)

1957年12月天津市律师协会关于分发指示、通知及会议入场券事致天津市人民委员会办公厅的报告（右）

The Tianjin Lawyers Association's report to the General Office of the Tianjin Municipal People's Committee on the distribution of instructions, notices and meeting admission tickets in December 1957 (right)

天津市法律顾问处成立的报道

Report on the establishment of Tianjin Legal Counsel Office

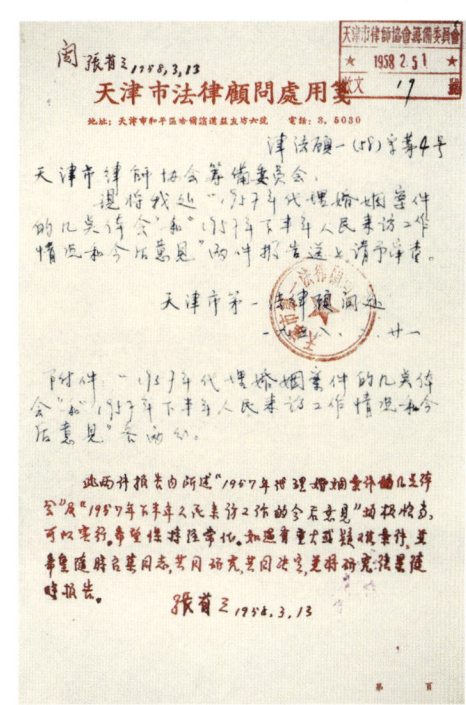

1958年2月天津市第一法律顾问处致天津市律师协会筹备委员会的报告

Report from Tianjin First Legal Counsel Office to the Preparatory Committee of the Tianjin Lawyers Association in February 1958

1921	1922	1923	1924	1925	1926	1927	1928	1929	1930	1931	1932	1933
1947	1948	1949	1950	1951	1952	1953	1954	1955	1956	1957	1958	1959
1973	1974	1975	1976	1977	1978	1979	1980	1981	1982	1983	1984	1985
1999	2000	2001	2002	2003	2004	2005	2006	2007	2008	2009	2010	2011

秦继修在天津市律师协会筹备委员会成立大会上讲话

Qin Jixiu delivered a speech at the inaugural meeting of the Preparatory Committee of the Tianjin Lawyers Association

王丹侠局长在天津市律师协会筹备委员会成立大会上讲话

Director Wang Danxia delivered a speech at the inaugural meeting of the Preparatory Committee of the Tianjin Lawyers Association

1934	1935	1936	1937	1938	1939	1940	1941	1942	1943	1944	1945	1946
1960	1961	1962	1963	1964	1965	1966	1967	1968	1969	1970	1971	1972
1986	1987	1988	1989	1990	1991	1992	1993	1994	1995	1996	1997	1998
2012	2013	2014	2015	2016	2017	2018	2019	2020	2021			

天津的司法行政工作始终由人民法院管理。1954年8月15日，中央司法部向各大区高分院，各省、市人民法院下达了《关于各省与中央直辖市审判机关与司法行政机关分立问题的意见》，指出："各高分院和各省、市法院首先应切实向同级党政建议，由于各省、市法院审判工作本已十分繁重，如继续兼管所属法院干部的管理、教育、训练、组织建设、财务以及陪审、民间调解、公证、律师等司法行政工作，根据几年来的经验证明，实难兼顾；同时参照苏联审判与司法行政工作分立的先进经验，今后应尽先将各省、市的审判机关与司法行政机关，根据具体情况的不同分别先后逐步分立。"要求河北等十八个省和京津沪三个直辖市，根据法院内原有的司法行政基础和各省、市的干部条件，立即着手建立省、市的司法厅（局）。同年9月15日，中央司法部又下达了《关于撤销各高分院司法行政机构的几项规定》，明确指出："今后各省、市司法行政工作，由司法部直接领导。"1955年4月26日，天津市司法局成立。1955年12月15日，根据天津市人民委员会批准的《关于在天津建立律师组织的方案》，市司法局设立了天津市法律顾问处，这是新中国成立后天津第一个律师组织，地址在睦南道29号，后迁址到哈尔滨道益友坊6号。

From the early days of the founding of the People's Republic of China, the "one system" of judicial organs and judicial administrative organs continued until 1955. The judicial administration in Tianjin was still managed by the People's Court. On August 15, 1954, the Central Ministry of Justice issued the *Opinions on the Separation of Judicial Authorities and Judicial Administrative Authorities between Provinces and Municipalities Directly under the Central Government* to the high branch courts of various regions, provinces and cities, stating that, "The municipal court should first make suggestions to the party and government at the same level. Because the trial work of the provincial and municipal courts is already very heavy. If you continue to supervise the management, education, training, organization construction, finance, jury, civil mediation, notarization, lawyers and other judicial administrative work of the affiliated court cadres, based on the experience of the past few years, it is really difficult to do both; at the same time, with reference to the advanced experience of the separation of judicial and judicial administrative work in the Soviet Union, in the future, the judicial organs and judicial administrative organs of various provinces and cities should be separated gradually according to the specific circumstances."

18 provinces including Hebei and 3 municipalities directly under the Central Government, including Beijing, Tianjin and Shanghai, should proceed to establish provincial and municipal judicial departments (bureaus) based on the original judicial administrative foundation in the courts and the cadre conditions of each province and city. On September 15 of the same year, the Central Ministry of Justice issued the *Several Provisions Regarding the Revocation of Judicial Administrative Institutions of the High Branches*, which clearly pointed out, "In the future, the judicial administrative work of all provinces and cities will be directly led by the Ministry of Justice." April 1955 on the 26th, the Tianjin Municipal Bureau of Justice was established; on December 15, 1955, in accordance with the *Plan on Establishing a Lawyers Organization in Tianjin* approved by the Tianjin Municipal People's Committee, the Municipal Bureau of Justice established the Tianjin Legal Counsel Office, which was after the founding of the People's Republic of China. The first lawyer organization in the city. The address was at No. 29 Munan Road, and later moved to No. 6 Yiyoufang, Harbin Road.

天津市法律顾问处成立后，1956年10月增设了一个法律顾问处分处，此后又出现了第三个法律顾问处。1957年6月，根据上级部署，天津市律师协会筹备委员会成立，在和平区睦南道43号（今24号）办公。截至1957年6月14日，天津市法律顾问处共有工作人员58人，包括主任4人，律师41人，会计、打字员等行政人员13人。其中取得正式律师资格的有23人，取得学习律师资格的有10人，其余8人的职务尚未正式确定。全国有19个省、市、自治区先后成立了律师协会，有专业律师和兼职律师近3000名。

After the establishment of the Tianjin Legal Counsel Office, a legal counsel disposition division was added in October 1956, and a third legal counsel division has since appeared. In June 1957, according to the deployment of superiors, the Preparatory Committee of the Tianjin Lawyers Association was established, and the office was located at No. 43 (currently No. 24) Munan Road, Heping District. As of June 14, 1957, the Tianjin Legal Counsel Office had a total of 58 people, including 4 directors, 13 accountants, typists and other administrative staff, and 41 lawyers. Among the lawyers, 23 have obtained the formal qualifications of lawyers, 10 have

1934	1935	1936	1937	1938	1939	1940	1941	1942	1943	1944	1945	1946
1960	1961	1962	1963	1964	1965	1966	1967	1968	1969	1970	1971	1972
1986	1987	1988	1989	1990	1991	1992	1993	1994	1995	1996	1997	1998
2012	2013	2014	2015	2016	2017	2018	2019	2020	2021	……		

位于和平区哈尔滨道益友坊 6 号的天津市法律顾问处

Tianjin Legal Counsel Office, No. 6, Harbin Road, Yiyoufang, Heping District

obtained the qualifications of learning lawyers, and the positions of the remaining 8 have not been officially determined. There are 19 provinces, municipalities, and autonomous regions across the country that have successively established lawyers associations, with nearly 3,000 professional and part-time lawyers.

1956年司法部《关于建立律师工作的请示报告》
1956 *Report on the Request for Instructions on Establishing Lawyers* by the Ministry of Justice

1956年史良部长在全国律师工作座谈会闭幕时的讲话

Minister Shi Liang's speech at the conclusion of the National Lawyers' Work Symposium in 1956

天津市法律顾问处分处
Tianjin Legal Counsel Office Branch

天津市法律顾问处分处工作场景
Work scene of Tianjin Legal Counsel Office Branch

1934　1935　1936　1937　1938　1939　1940　1941　1942　1943　1944　1945　1946
1960　1961　1962　1963　1964　1965　1966　1967　1968　1969　1970　1971　1972
1986　1987　1988　1989　1990　1991　1992　1993　1994　1995　1996　1997　1998
2012　2013　2014　2015　2016　2017　2018　2019　2020　2021　……

天津市法律顾问处分处工作场景
Work scene of Tianjin Legal Counsel Office Branch

20世纪50年代的律师代表

REPRESENTATIVES OF LAWYERS IN THE 1950S

根据天津市律师协会第一届会长郑振亚和20世纪50年代执业的老律师兰英、陈丽的回忆，天津市第一法律顾问处设在新华路，主任是秦继修、王良善；第二法律顾问处在北马路，主任是刘生；第三法律顾问处在解放南路原北京电影院附近，主任是傅金英。当时律师的来源有三条渠道，一是从各级法院抽调，如刘泗兴（后调任红桥区法律顾问处）、李金牛、兰英；二是从政法院校的教师或毕业生中分配或调入，如刘维贤、周奕文是从中国人民大学调来支援律师队伍的；三是司法局干部。三个法律顾问处约有律师、行政人员70人。兰英律师还捐献了一张珍贵的20世纪50年代律师与法官的合影，除上述律师外，还有侯新峰（后调任河北区法律顾问处）、路之岐、武宝锐、边文萍、魏国城、邱喜爱、黄惠莲、李煌、王士贤、刘怀亮、王力成、林中、左克、徐吾林、王鸣鸾、宋杰岑、蔡允正、郑萱、牟振邦、刘国佐、姚国成、傅国义、杨文渊、韩瀛、鞠炳阳、张同信、徐汤华、邵恺……当时的社会还不太重视律师，人们大多收入低，没有能力聘请律师；经济能力差的遇到法律问题，由居委会开出证明，不用花钱就可以聘请律师；一般咨询仅收5角钱，代书答辩状、上诉状收1元钱，复杂一些的代理可以收1.5元。

According to the memories of the old president Zheng Zhenya and the old lawyers Lan Ying and Chen Li who worked in the 1950s, the First Legal Counsel Office was located on Xinhua Road, and the directors were Qin Jixiu and Wang Liangshan; the Second Legal Counsel was located on North Road, and the director was Liu Sheng; the Third Legal Counsel was located near the original Beijing Cinema on Jiefang South Road, and the director was Fu Jinying. At that time, the sources of lawyers were three channels. One was from the courts at all levels, such as Liu Sixing (later transferred to the Hongqiao District Legal Counsel Office), Li Jinsheng, and Lan

1934	1935	1936	1937	1938	1939	1940	1941	1942	1943	1944	1945	1946
1960	1961	1962	1963	1964	1965	1966	1967	1968	1969	1970	1971	1972
1986	1987	1988	1989	1990	1991	1992	1993	1994	1995	1996	1997	1998
2012	2013	2014	2015	2016	2017	2018	2019	2020	2021	……		

Ying. The other was from the teachers or graduates of political and law colleges. For example, lawyers Liu Weixian and Zhou Yiwen were transferred from the faculty of Renmin University of China to support the lawyers. The third is the cadres of the Judicial Bureau. There are about 70 lawyers and administrative staff in the three legal counsel offices. Attorney Lan Ying also donated a precious photo of the lawyer and the judge in the 1950s. In addition to the above, there are Hou Xinfeng (later transferred to the Legal Counsel Office of Hebei District), Lu Zhiqi, Wu Baorui, Bian Wenping, Wei Guocheng, Qiu Xiai, Huang Huilian, Li Huang, Wang Shixian, Liu Huailiang, Wang Licheng, Lin Zhong, Zuo Ke, Xu Wulin, Wang Mingluan, Song Jiecen, Cai Yunzheng, Zheng Xuan, Mou Zhenbang, Liu Guozuo, Yao Guocheng, Fu Guoyi, Yang Wenyuan, Han Ying, Ju Bingyang, Zhang Tongxin, Xu Tanghua, Shao Kai… At that time, the society did not pay much attention to lawyers. Most people had low incomes and were unable to hire lawyers. Those with poor financial ability encountered legal problems. The residents committee could issue a certificate and they could hire lawyers without spending money. General consultations only charge 50 cents, and 1 yuan for replies and appeals; more complicated agents can charge 1.5 yuan.

1955年4月26日，经天津市人民委员会批准，天津市司法局在天津市高级人民法院司法行政处的基础上成立了，负责管理全市的司法行政工作。局内设一室四科，即办公室和一、二、三、四科，编制为55人。王赣愚任局长，李曼任副局长，办公地点在二区（今南开区）南马路182号。5月27日，市司法局迁至十区（今和平区）睦南道150号新址办公。

On April 26, 1955, with the approval of the Tianjin Municipal People's Committee, the Tianjin Municipal Bureau of Justice was established on the basis of the Judicial Administration Division of the Municipal Higher People's Court, which is responsible for the administration of the city's judicial administration. The bureau has one office and four departments, namely: Office, One, Two, Three, and Four subjects, with an establishment of 55 people. Wang Ganyu was the director and Li Man was the deputy director. The office was located at No. 182, South Road, Second District (now Nankai District). On May 27, the Municipal Judicial Bureau moved to a new office at No. 150 Munan Road, District X (now Heping District).

1921	1922	1923	1924	1925	1926	1927	1928	1929	1930	1931	1932	1933
1947	1948	1949	1950	1951	1952	1953	1954	1955	1956	1957	1958	1959
1973	1974	1975	1976	1977	1978	1979	1980	1981	1982	1983	1984	1985
1999	2000	2001	2002	2003	2004	2005	2006	2007	2008	2009	2010	2011

5月31日，天津市人民委员会批准了天津市司法局拟定的《关于建立天津市律师协会筹备委员会增设法律顾问处的请示报告》，指出："同意报告。人员共为80人，其中律师协会筹备委员会的专职人员为8人，法律顾问处的人员为72人。"6月6日，市司法局批准宋杰岑、牟振邦、尤秀民三人为律师。

On May 31, the Municipal People's Committee approved the *Request for Instructions on Establishing the Preparatory Committee of the Tianjin Lawyers Association and the Establishment of a Legal Counsel Office* drafted by the Municipal Bureau of Justice, stating, "Agree to the report, with a total of 80 personnel. Among them, there are 8 full-time staff in the preparatory committee of the Lawyers Association, and 72 staff in the legal counsel office." On June 6, the Municipal Judicial Bureau approved Song Jiecen, Mou Zhenbang, and You Xiumin as lawyers.

1956年1月5日，天津市人民委员会批复天津市司法局制定的《天津市律师收费暂行办法》。批复指出："准予试行。不在报纸上公布，可张贴在法律顾问处，供当事人阅览。"1月8日，市司法局批准天津市法律顾问处自1956年1月9日开始试收费。10月25日，天津市法律顾问处分处成立，编制17人，副主任刘生，位于城厢区（今红桥区）北马路220号。1957年3月30日，市司法局批准蔡允正、刘怀亮、武宝锐等20人为律师，批准郑萱、兰英、王鸣鸾等10人为学习律师。

On January 5, 1956, the Municipal People's Committee approved the *Interim Measures for Lawyers' Fees* formulated by the Municipal Bureau of Justice. The reply stated, "Trial is permitted. It will not be published in newspapers, but can be posted in the legal counsel office for the parties to read." On January 8, the Municipal Judicial Bureau approved the Municipal Legal Counsel Office to start trial fees on January 9, 1956. On October 25, Tianjin Legal Counsel Office Branch was established. The establishment of 17 people. Deputy Director was Liu Sheng. The address was located at No. 220, North Road, Chengxiang District (now Hongqiao District). On March 30, 1957, the Municipal Bureau of Justice approved 20 people including Cai Yunzheng, Liu Huailiang, and Wu Baorui as lawyers; and approved 10 people including Zheng Xuan, Lan Ying, and Wang Mingluan as study lawyers.

1934	1935	1936	1937	1938	1939	1940	1941	1942	1943	1944	1945	1946
1960	1961	1962	1963	1964	1965	1966	1967	1968	1969	1970	1971	1972
1986	1987	1988	1989	1990	1991	1992	1993	1994	1995	1996	1997	1998
2012	2013	2014	2015	2016	2017	2018	2019	2020	2021			

6月22日，天津市律师协会筹备委员会召开成立大会。秦继修任主任委员，张省三任副主任委员，潘长有、朱其华、王良善、刘生、傅金英、蔡允正、李金生、黄惠莲任委员；办公地址在和平区哈尔滨道益友坊6号，同年10月29日迁到了睦南道43号。大会同时决定，将天津市法律顾问处及其分处改称天津市第一、第二法律顾问处；一处主任王良善，二处主任刘生。6月24日，天津市第三法律顾问处成立，编制为13人，主任傅金英，办公地址在河西区解放南路289号。

On June 22, the Preparatory Committee of Tianjin Lawyers Association held an inaugural meeting. Qin Jixiu was the chairman and Zhang Xingsan was the vice chairman. Pan Changyou, Zhu Qihua, Wang Liangshan, Liu Sheng, Fu Jinying, Cai Yunzheng, Li Jinsheng and Huang Huilian served as committee members. Office address: No. 6, Yiyoufang, Harbin Road, Heping District; moved to No. 43, Munan Road on October 29 of the same year. At the same time, the conference decided to rename the Tianjin Legal Counsel Office and its branch offices to Tianjin First and Second Legal Counsel Offices. Wang Liangshan was the director of the first division; Liu Sheng was the director of the second division. On June 24, the Third Legal Counsel Office of Tianjin was established. The establishment was 13 people. Deputy Director: Fu Jinying. The office address was located at No. 289, Jiefang South Road, Hexi District.

9月17日，天津市委政法工作部批准天津市律师协会筹备委员会成立分党组，由秦继修、王良善、刘生三位同志组成，秦继修任书记。12月6日，天津市高级、中级人民法院，天津市司法局联合发出通知，根据"精简机构、紧缩编制"的精神，天津市高级、中级人民法院，天津市司法局决定于1957年12月5日合并办公。市司法局原有处室与高级人民法院督导研究室、中级人民法院人事科合并，改设宣传教育、审判监督、人事三个部门（名称尚未正式确定），高级、中级人民法院，市司法局统一设办公室。市司法局的干部除并入上述三个部门外，部分调至高级人民法院审判庭、律师协会筹委会和区法院。此后，天津市司法局系统整风"反右"运动转入反"右派"斗争阶段。斗争结束时，各法律顾问处被错划为"右派分子"的共15人，占70名律师工作人员的21%。其中有4人被判刑，投入劳改。

On September 17, the Political and Legal Work Department of the Municipal

Party Committee approved the establishment of a sub-party group by the Tianjin Lawyers Association Preparatory Committee. Composed of Qin Jixiu, Wang Liangshan, and Liu Sheng, Qin Jixiu was the secretary. On December 6, the Municipal High and Intermediate People's Court and the Municipal Bureau of Justice jointly issued a notice. The notice pointed out that, in accordance with the spirit of "simplifying the organization and tightening the staffing", the Municipal High and Intermediate People's Court and the Municipal Bureau of Jastice decided to merge on December 5, 1957. The original division of the Municipal Bureau of Justice, the Supervision and Research Office of the Municipal Higher People's Court, and the Personnel Section of the Intermediate People's Court were merged to form three departments: Publicity and Education, Trial Supervision, and Personnel (the names have not yet been officially determined). The high and intermediate people's courts and the Bureau of Justice have unified establishment offices. In addition to the cadres of the Judicial Bureau merged into the above three units, some are transferred to the Trial Chamber of the Higher People's Court, the Preparatory Committee of the Lawyers Association, and the District Court. Since then, the rectification and "anti-rightist" movement of the Municipal Bureau of Justice has turned into the "anti-rightist" struggle stage. At the end of this struggle, 15 people in the legal counsel offices were mistakenly classified as "rightists", accounting for 21% of the 70 lawyers. Four of them were sentenced to labor reform.

1958年11月，天津市律师协会筹备委员会和三个法律顾问处合并到天津市高级人民法院，撤销了机构，调离了人员，仅有三名审判人员以兼职律师的名义办理一些典型案件，基本停办了律师业务。

In January 1958, Tianjin Lawyers Association Preparatory Committee and the three legal counsel offices were merged into the Municipal Higher People's Court. The organization was abolished and the staff was transferred. Only three judges handled some typical cases in the name of part-time lawyers, the lawyer business was basically closed.

1934	1935	1936	1937	1938	1939	1940	1941	1942	1943	1944	1945	1946
1960	1961	1962	1963	1964	1965	1966	1967	1968	1969	1970	1971	1972
1986	1987	1988	1989	1990	1991	1992	1993	1994	1995	1996	1997	1998
2012	2013	2014	2015	2016	2017	2018	2019	2020	2021	……		

20世纪50年代的律师制度虽然建立两年就停止了，但老律师们留下的一些宝贵经验也的确在1979年恢复律师制度后发挥了"传、帮、带"的作用。1989年6月1日，武宝锐律师经过考核，再次获得了司法部颁发的中华人民共和国律师资格证书。这是1979年恢复律师制度后，经过考核颁发的第一批律师资格证书之一。据说自20世纪50年代就开始执业的武宝锐律师是民国时期天津著名律师张务滋的后人。

Although the lawyer system in the 1950s ceased after two years of establishment, some of the valuable experience they left behind played the role of "teaching, helping, and leading" after the restoration of the lawyer system in 1979. On June 1, 1989, attorney Wu Baorui passed the examination and again obtained the certificate of qualification for lawyers of the People's Republic of China issued by the Ministry of Justice. This is the first batch of lawyer qualification certificates issued after assessment after the restoration of the lawyer system in 1979. It is said that lawyer Wu Baorui, who started practicing in the 1950s, is a descendant of the famous Tianjin lawyer Zhang Wuzi during the Republic of China.

1921	1922	1923	1924	1925	1926	1927	1928	1929	1930	1931	1932	1933
1947	1948	1949	1950	1951	1952	1953	1954	1955	1956	1957	1958	1959
1973	1974	1975	1976	1977	1978	1979	1980	1981	1982	1983	1984	1985
1999	2000	2001	2002	2003	2004	2005	2006	2007	2008	2009	2010	2011

兰英律师

Lawyer Lan Ying

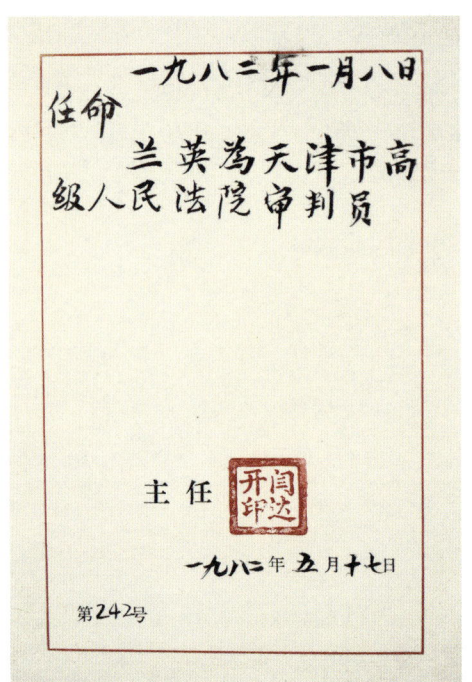

兰英同志的任命书

Letter of appointment from Comrade Lan Ying

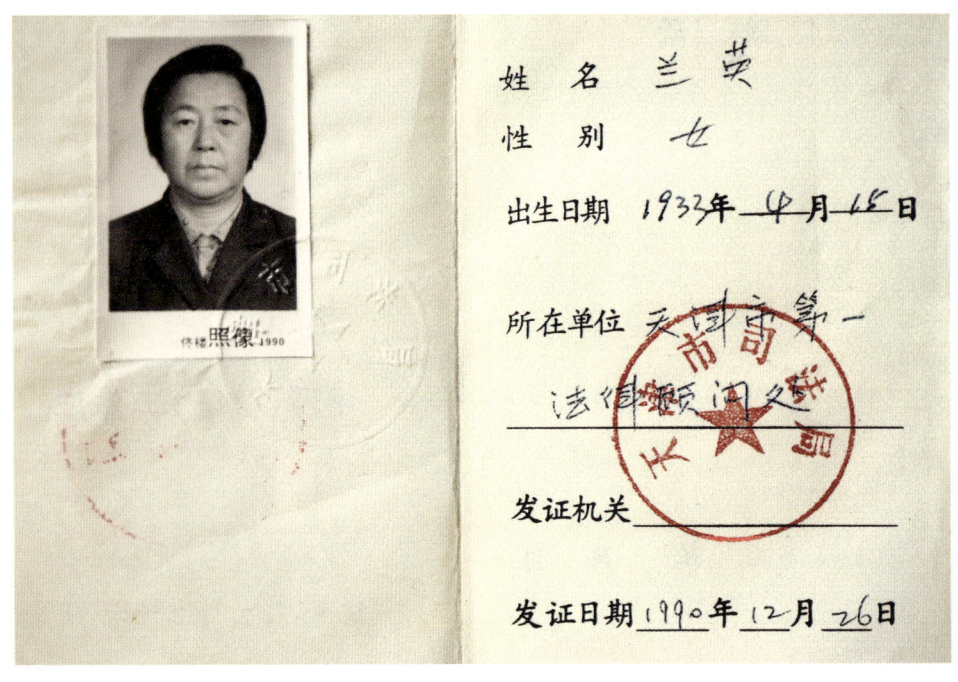

兰英律师的工作证（兰英律师提供）

Lawyer Lan Ying's work permit (provided by lawyer Lan Ying)

1934	1935	1936	1937	1938	1939	1940	1941	1942	1943	1944	1945	1946
1960	1961	1962	1963	1964	1965	1966	1967	1968	1969	1970	1971	1972
1986	1987	1988	1989	1990	1991	1992	1993	1994	1995	1996	1997	1998
2012	2013	2014	2015	2016	2017	2018	2019	2020	2021	……		

20世纪50年代部分法律工作者（含律师）合影

A group photo of some legal staffs (including lawyers) who worked in the 1950s

1988年，司法部召开20世纪50年代老律师会议。天津市有20位律师出席，这是在北京国谊宾馆（原国务院一招）楼前合影，其中包括侯新锋（左四）、邱喜爱（左五）、左克（左六）、郑萱（左八）、路之岐（左九）、刘维贤（左十）、徐汤华（左十一）、兰英（左十二）、徐吾林（左十四）、边文萍（左十五）、刘泗兴（左十八）

In 1988, the Ministry of Justice held a meeting of old lawyers in the 1950s. Twenty lawyers from Tianjin attended. This is a group photo in front of the Beijing Guoyi Hotel (formerly the First Guest House of the State Council). Hou Xinfeng (fourth from left), Qiu Xiai (fifth from left), Zuo Ke (sixth from left), Zheng Xuan (eighth from left), Lu Zhiqi (ninth from left), Liu Weixian (tenth from left), Xu Tanghua (eleventh from left), Lan Ying (twelveth from left), Xu Wulin (fourteenth from left), Bian Wenping (fifteenth from left), Liu Sixing (eighteenth from left)

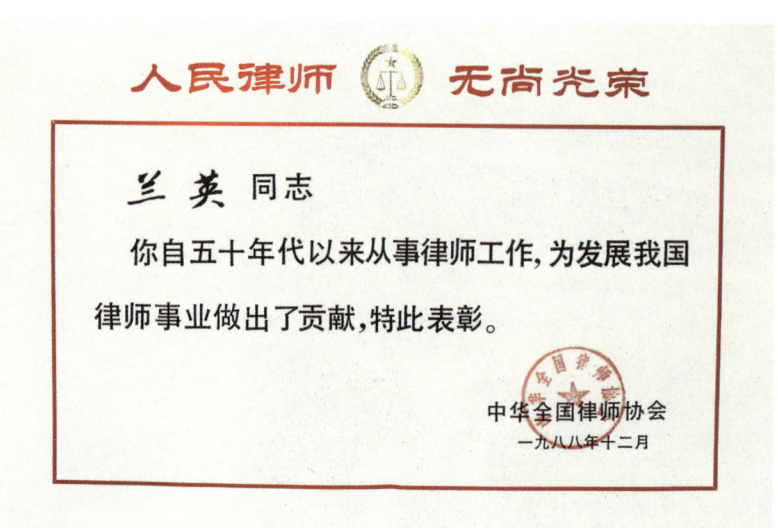

中华全国律师协会为20世纪50年代以来执业的兰英律师颁发的表彰证书

Certificate of commendation issued by All China Lawyers Association to practicing lawyer Lan Ying in the 1950s

老一辈律师代表兰英

Lan Ying is a representative of the older generation of lawyers

丁立莹律师在建设天津律师文史馆过程中记录老律师的口述历史

Lawyer Ding Liying recorded the oral history of old lawyers during the construction of Tianjin Lawyer's Culture and History Museum

20世纪50年代的律师工作

LAWYERS' WORK IN THE 1950S

1955年12月，天津开始建立法律顾问处，组建律师队伍。其主要任务是接受被告人委托或法院的指定，担任刑事案件的辩护人，出庭辩护；接受当事人的委托，担任民事案件的代理人参加诉讼；接待群众来访，解答法律咨询和提供法律帮助，代写各类法律事务文书等。

In December 1955, Tianjin began to establish a legal counsel office to form a team of lawyers. Its main tasks were: accepting the entrustment of the defendant or the designation of the court, acting as the defender of criminal cases, and appearing in court; accepting the entrustment of the parties, acting as the agent of civil cases to participate in the litigation; receiving people's visits, answering legal inquiries and providing legal assistance, writing all kinds of legal affairs documents.

据档案统计，在20世纪50年代短暂的执业中，律师开展的业务主要是接待群众来访，包括法律咨询、代写文书，诉讼代理也仅限于婚姻家庭、房屋、继承、债务、赡养收养、加工承揽、购销等。律师工作开展两年间，广大律师共接待群众来访23869人次，其中解答法律咨询14839人次，代写各种法律文书9030件。刑事案件出庭辩护742件，代理民事案件698件。民事案件以房屋案件最多，占45.12%；其次是债务、继承、析产案件，占20%；再次是赡养、抚养案件，占23.81%；离婚案件占11.03%。

According to archive statistics, in the short-lived practice in the 1950s, the main business carried out was to receive visits from the masses and legal consultation; to write documents; litigation agency was also limited to marriage and family, housing, inheritance, debt, support and adoption, processing contract, purchase and sale etc. According to the statistics of two years of working as lawyers, lawyers received 23,869 visitors, of which 14,839 legal inquiries were answered, and 9,030 legal documents were written on behalf of them. Represented the defendants in 742 criminal cases and represented the parties in 698 civil cases. In civil cases, housing cases accounted for 45.12%, followed by debt, inheritance, and property analysis cases, which accounted for a total of 20%; again, support and raise case accounted for 23.81%; divorce cases accounted for 11.03%.

1958年1月6日，天津市红桥区人民法院下发了有律师参与辩护的红法刑判（57）字第2157号刑事案件判决书。

On January 6, 1958, the Hongqiao District People's Court of Tianjin issued a case verdict in the form of Hongfa Criminal Judgment (57) Zi No. 2157 with lawyers participating in the defense.

公诉人天津市红桥区人民检察院检察长李杭指控被告人王树森破坏粮食政策及流氓罪，天津市第二法律顾问处律师韩瀛担任辩护人。

The prosecutor Li Hang, the chief prosecutor of the People's Procuratorate of Hongqiao District, Tianjin City, accused the defendant Wang Shusen of undermining the grain policy and crimes of hooliganism. Han Ying, a lawyer from the Second Legal Counsel Office of Tianjin, served as the defender.

法院查明，被告人王树森于1956年趁盲目流入津市之运输大车政府不供给饲料之机，以骗取、借、代卖等方式，取得李文起、高崇礼等10余人之饲料本，并以涂改数字、撕掉册页等手段，在第10门市部等处套购红粮1630斤、黑豆3340斤、玉米皮1660斤、麸子14225斤，后以每斤高于牌价1—7分的价格卖与刘静华、张连臣等人，从中非法牟取暴利843.90元。在同一时间内，被告还伙同王学敏、于云龙等人用上述手段套购麸子5686斤、玉米皮2700斤，以高于牌价两倍的价格卖给永兴农业合作社和宣家院农业合作社，从中非法牟利455.23元，三人均分。被告还利用自己家中粮本结存麸粉88斤、杂粮66.5斤之机，将买过粮食的粮折，先后撕掉8页，在第18门

1934	1935	1936	1937	1938	1939	1940	1941	1942	1943	1944	1945	1946
1960	1961	1962	1963	1964	1965	1966	1967	1968	1969	1970	1971	1972
1986	1987	1988	1989	1990	1991	1992	1993	1994	1995	1996	1997	1998
2012	2013	2014	2015	2016	2017	2018	2019	2020	2021	……		

市部套取粮票814.5斤、粮食264斤，卖给马振中等人，从中非法取利。被告共套取粮食、饲料等30648.5斤，取得非法利润1299.13元。被告将所得之款大部用于挥霍，每日大吃大喝，并诱骗10余名妇女通奸。特别严重的是将一名患有精神病的女教员诱至墙外猪圈内进行奸污。庭讯中以上事实被告均供认不讳。

The court found out the case that the defendant Wang Shusen took advantage of the opportunity that the government did not supply feed on the transportation cart that blindly flowed into Tianjin City in 1956, and obtained feed books from more than ten people including Li Wenqi, Gao Chongli, etc. by fraud, borrowing, or selling on behalf of others. By altering the numbers and tearing off the number of pages, 1630 kg of red grain, 3340 kg of black beans, 1,660 kg of corn husk, and 14,225 kg of bran were purchased at the tenth store and sold at Liu Jinghua, Zhang Lianchen and others by 1-7 points above the list price. And illegally made a huge profit of 843.90 yuan. At the same time, together with Wang Xuemin, Yu Yunlong and others used the above methods to buy 5,686 kilograms of bran and 2,700 kilograms of corn husks, sometimes twice the price of the brand, and sold them to the Yongxing Agricultural Cooperative. The Hexuanjiayuan Agricultural Cooperative, illegally profited 455.23 yuan from it, and the three people shared their salaries. The defendant also used his family's grain balance to save 88 kilograms of bran powder and 66.5 kilograms of miscellaneous grains to fold the grain that had been bought, tearing off 8 pages one after another. In the 18th store, they collected 814.5 kilograms of food stamps and 264 kilograms of grain, and sold them to Ma Zhenzhong and others to make illegal profits. The defendant bought a total of 30648.5 kilograms of grain and fodder, and obtained an illegal profit of 1,299.13 yuan. The defendant used most of the proceeds to squander, eat and drink every day, to lure more than a dozen women into adultery. The most serious thing was to lure a mentally ill female teacher to the pigpen outside the wall and raped her. In the court hearing, the defendant confessed to the above facts.

判决书认为，被告人王树森，一贯不务正业，生活腐化，虽经政府教育，但仍不知悔改，变本加厉地追求资产阶级生活方式，不顾国家法纪，公开破坏粮食政策，性质实属恶劣，已构成犯罪，应予惩处，特判决王树森破坏粮食政策，处有期徒刑十年。

The verdict held that the defendant Wang Shusen had always failed to do his job properly and had a corrupt life. Although he was educated by the government, he did not repent and pursued the bourgeois way of life more vigorously, despite the state's laws and regulations. Publicly undermining the grain policy is really bad in nature and has constituted a crime and should be punished. Wang Shusen was sentenced to ten years in prison for undermining the grain policy.

从这个案件可以看出，20世纪50年代律师参与辩护工作还是较为普遍的，不过那时候律师的辩护意见没有列明在判决书中。

It can be seen from this case that in the 1950s, lawyers' participation in defense work was still relatively common, but at that time, the lawyer's defense opinions were not listed in the judgment.

20世纪50年代的律师在民事诉讼庭审中

Lawyers in the 1950s in civil proceedings

1934	1935	1936	1937	1938	1939	1940	1941	1942	1943	1944	1945	1946
1960	1961	1962	1963	1964	1965	1966	1967	1968	1969	1970	1971	1972
1986	1987	1988	1989	1990	1991	1992	1993	1994	1995	1996	1997	1998
2012	2013	2014	2015	2016	2017	2018	2019	2020	2021	……		

20 世纪 50 年代的律师参与民事诉讼庭审

Lawyers in the 1950s in civil proceedings

1921	1922	1923	1924	1925	1926	1927	1928	1929	1930	1931	1932	1933
1947	1948	1949	1950	1951	1952	1953	1954	1955	1956	1957	1958	1959
1973	1974	1975	1976	1977	1978	1979	1980	1981	1982	1983	1984	1985
1999	2000	2001	2002	2003	2004	2005	2006	2007	2008	2009	2010	2011

20 世纪 50 年代的公审大会

Public trial conference in the 1950s

20 世纪 50 年代的公审大会现场

The scene of the public trial conference in the 1950s

20 世纪 50 年代的律师在刑事诉讼庭审辩护中

The lawyers in the 1950s were defending in the criminal court

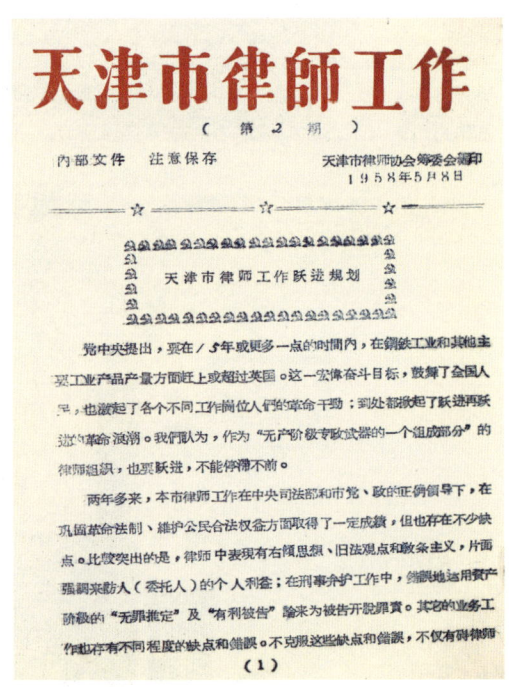

1958 年 5 月天津市律师工作跃进规划（部分）

Tianjin city lawyer's leap forward planning in May 1958 (partial)

1934	1935	1936	1937	1938	1939	1940	1941	1942	1943	1944	1945	1946
1960	1961	1962	1963	1964	1965	1966	1967	1968	1969	1970	1971	1972
1986	1987	1988	1989	1990	1991	1992	1993	1994	1995	1996	1997	1998
2012	2013	2014	2015	2016	2017	2018	2019	2020	2021	……		

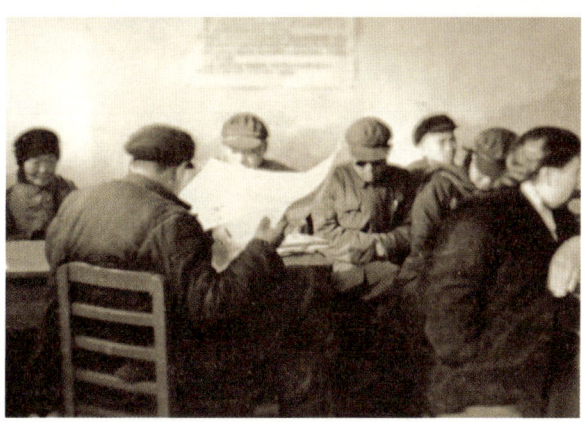

20世纪50年代的律师为群众宣讲法律
Lawyers in the 1950s preached legal to the masses

20世纪50年代的律师接待咨询
The lawyer reception and consultation in the 1950s

20世纪50年代法律顾问处的工作场景
Working scene of the legal counsel office in the 1950s

1956年7月10日，国务院批复了司法部《关于建立律师工作的请示报告》，文中称："国务院全体会议第二十九次会议原则上同意你部关于司法行政工作方面几个问题的请示报告，并且决议如下……同意司法部《关于建立律师工作的请示报告》，并且批准《律师收费暂行办法》，由司法部发布施行。"随后，司法部下发了《律师收费暂行办法》。同年7月20日，司法部部长史良签发了《关于发布施行律师收费暂行办法的通知》，这是新中国第一个关于律师收费的规定。此办法是为适应建立社会主义市场经济体制的要求，保障律师事务所和委托律师事务所办理法律事务的自然人、法人和其他组织的合法权益，规范律师服务收费行为，根据律师和价格的有关法律、法规而制定的办法。截至1957年2月底，天津已成立的两个法律顾问处共收费29201.83元。其中，解答法律咨询9993人次，减免收费5535人次，占55.4%，收费2237.93元；代写法律事务文书6212件，减免收费605件，占10%，收费1134.90元；刑事辩护案件684件，减免收费60件，经法院指定为被告进行辩护的案件203件，共占38.4%，收费5031.50元；代理民事案件531件，减免收费25件，占4.7%，收费10587.50元。天津市第三法律顾问处于同年6月24日成立后，即实行收费，截至当年年底，共收费3996.30元。

On July 10, 1956, the State Council approved the Ministry of Justice's *Request for Instructions on the Establishment of Lawyers*, and stated, "The 29th meeting of the plenary meeting of the State Council agreed in principle to your Ministry's decision on several issues concerning judicial administration. Request for instructions, and the resolution is as follows: …agree to the Ministry of Justice's *Request for Instructions on the Establishment of Lawyers*, and approve the *Interim Measures for Lawyers' Fees*, which will be issued and implemented by the Ministry of Justice." The Ministry of Justice issued the *Interim Measures for Lawyers' Fees*. On July 20 of the same year, Shi Liang, Minister of Justice of the People's Republic of China, issued the *Notice on the Interim Measures for Lawyers' Fees*, this is the first regulation of lawyers' fees in the People's Republic of China. This measure is to meet the requirements of establishing a socialist market economy system, protect the legal rights of law firms and natural persons, legal persons and other organizations that entrust law firms to handle legal affairs, regulate the behavior of lawyers' service fees, regulations made in accordance with relevant laws and regulations on lawyers and prices. As of the end of February 1957, the two legal counsel offices established in the city charged a total of 29,201.83 yuan.

Among them, 9993 legal inquiries were answered, 5535 fees were reduced or exempted, accounting for 2,237.93 yuan for 55.4%; 6212 legal affairs documents were written on behalf, 605 fees were reduced or exempted, accounting for 10%, 684 criminal defense cases, Charge 1134.90 yuan, and 60 fees were reduced or exempted. 203 cases were designated by the court to defend the defendant, accounting for 38.4%, and the fee was 5,031.50 yuan; 531 civil cases were represented, and 25 cases were reduced or exempted, accounting for 4.7%, and the fee was 10,587.50 yuan. Since its establishment on June 24 of the same year, the Municipal Third Legal Counsel Office has implemented fees, and as of the end of the year, the fees totaled 3,996.30 yuan.

1957年，在法律虚无主义和"反右"斗争扩大化的影响下，刚刚建立起来的律师制度遭到错误的批判，律师辩护被说成是"丧失阶级立场""为犯罪分子鸣冤叫屈，开脱罪责"，律师制度被说成是"资产阶级的制度"。法律顾问处逐步缩减，律师大都被调离政法部门。到1958年11月，天津市三个法律顾问处均合并到高级人民法院院内办公，只保留三名审判人员以兼职律师的名义办理少量典型的案件。司法部在1959年被撤销后，律师工作由人民法院代管，不过实际上已不再开展工作。

In 1957, under the influence of legal nihilism and the expansion of the "anti-rightist" struggle, the lawyer system that was just established was erroneously criticized. Lawyer defense were said to be the "lost class position" and "to cry out for the criminals and to excuse guilt", while the lawyer system was described as a "bourgeois system". The legal counsel office has gradually shrunk, and lawyers have been transferred from the political and legal departments. By November 1958, the three legal counsel offices in Tianjin were merged into the court of the Higher Court, leaving only three judges to handle some small and typical cases in the name of part-time lawyers. After the Ministry of Justice was abolished in 1959, the work of lawyers was managed by the people's court, but in fact the work of lawyers could no longer be carried out.

春风化雨 重建新生（上）

THE SPRING WIND AND RAIN OF REBUILDING THE TIANJIN LAWYERS ASSOCIATION (I)

法律顾问处的恢复与律师事务所的初步发展 /324
THE RESTORATION OF LEGAL
COUNSEL OFFICES AND THE INITIAL
DEVELOPMENT OF LAW FIRMS

改革开放后天津律师业的起步 /337
THE STARTING OF TIANJIN LAWYER INDUSTRY
AFTER THE REFORM AND OPENING-UP

天津市律师协会的成立及其在20世纪八九十年代的发展 /344
THE ESTABLISHMENT OF TIANJIN LAWYERS ASSOCIATION
AND ITS DEVELOPMENT IN THE 1980S AND 1990S

律师资格考试的确立与律师事务所体制的转变 /360
THE ESTABLISHMENT OF THE
LAWYER QUALIFICATION EXAMINATION
AND THE TRANSFORMATION OF THE LAW FIRM SYSTEM

律师业务的变迁 /369
CHANGES IN THE LAW PRACTICE

20世纪八九十年代的律师行业交流 /377
THE LAWYER INDUSTRY EXCHANGES IN
THE 1980S AND 1990S

1921	1922	1923	1924	1925	1926	1927	1928	1929	1930	1931	1932	1933
1947	1948	1949	1950	1951	1952	1953	1954	1955	1956	1957	1958	1959
1973	1974	1975	1976	1977	1978	1979	1980	1981	1982	1983	1984	1985
1999	2000	2001	2002	2003	2004	2005	2006	2007	2008	2009	2010	2011

在庆祝中国共产党成立一百周年的日子里，回顾尘封的档案，记忆里满是新中国律师40多年沧海桑田的变迁。42年前，新中国的律师制度恢复重建，春风化雨，滋润沃土；如今，新时代赋予律师新的使命，爱国敬业，铸就辉煌。

On the day of celebrating the founding of the Communist Party of China, looking through historical archives, the memory of the photo is 42 years of vicissitudes. 42 years ago, the lawyer system of the People's Republic of China was restored and rebuilt, and the spring breeze melted the rain and nourished the fertile soil. Now, the new era gave lawyers a new mission, patriotism, dedication, and glory.

伴随着改革开放的春风，天津律师从探索、起步到发展、前行，从无到有，从小到大，从少到多……走上了法制化的轨道，也取得了历史性的成就。

The start and development of Tianjin lawyers is also accompanied by the spring breeze of reform and opening up, and has since embarked on the track of the legal system. Grow out of nothing, from small to large, from less to more... historic achievements have been made.

党的十一届三中全会以后，随着"健全社会主义民主，加强社会主义法制"方针的确立，新中国的律师制度也获得了新生。1979年12月9日，司法部颁布了《有关律师工作的通知》，这一年也因此被视为新中国律师制度恢复重建的元年。

After the Third Plenary Session of the Eleventh Central Committee of the Communist Party of China, with the establishment of the principle of "improving socialist democracy and strengthening the socialist legal system", the lawyer system of the People's Republic of China has also been reborn. On December 9, 1979, the Ministry of Justice issued the *Notice on Lawyers' Work*. This year was the first year of the restoration and reconstruction of the lawyer system of the People's Republic of China.

1980年8月，五届全国人大常委会第十五次会议讨论通过了《中华人民共和国律师暂行条例》，并于26日正式颁布，标志着中国的律师制度进入了一个崭新的发展阶段。

1934	1935	1936	1937	1938	1939	1940	1941	1942	1943	1944	1945	1946
1960	1961	1962	1963	1964	1965	1966	1967	1968	1969	1970	1971	1972
1986	1987	1988	1989	1990	1991	1992	1993	1994	1995	1996	1997	1998
2012	2013	2014	2015	2016	2017	2018	2019	2020	2021	......		

In August 1980, the 15th meeting of the Standing Committee of the Fifth National People's Congress discussed and passed the *Interim Regulations on Lawyers of the People's Republic of China*, which was formally promulgated on the 26th, marking that China's lawyer system has entered a new stage of development.

1978年3月5日第五届全国人大通过的《中华人民共和国宪法》中第四十一条规定"被告人有权获得辩护"

Article 41 of the *Constitution of the People's Republic of China* adopted by the Fifth National People's Congress on March 5, 1978 stipulated that "the defendant has the right to be defended"

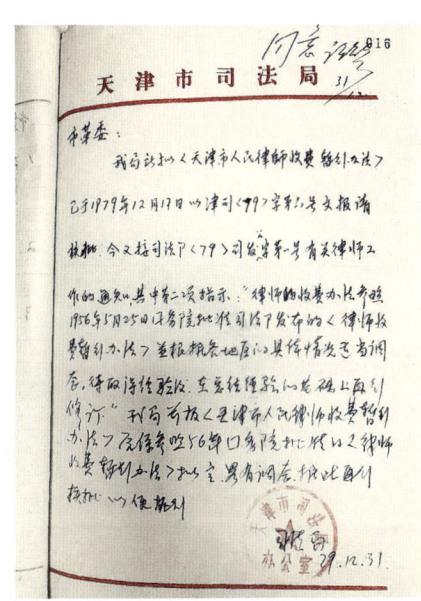

1979年天津市司法局转发司法部颁布的司法公字第1号《有关律师工作的通知》，这是恢复律师制度后关于律师工作的第一个文件规定

In 1979, the Municipal Bureau of Justice forwarded Judicial Gongzi No. 1 *Notice on Lawyers' Work* issued by the Ministry of Justice. This is the first document on lawyers' work after the restoration of lawyer system

1980年中央书记处接见全国司法行政工作座谈会全体成员合影

A group photo of the Central Committee meet all members of the National Symposium on Judicial Administration In 1980

1980年12月中央政法干校第十八期律师班结业留影
Photo of the end of the 18th Lawyer Class of the Central Political and Legal Cadre School in December 1980

班结业留念 一九八〇年十二月廿日

法律顾问处的恢复与
律师事务所的初步发展

THE RESTORATION OF LEGAL COUNSEL OFFICES AND THE INITIAL DEVELOPMENT OF LAW FIRMS

"文革"结束以后,天津市司法局积极恢复重建,王良善、武兆吉是恢复重建司法局的筹备组负责人。随着司法部的恢复,全国各地纷纷按照要求恢复重建了法律顾问处,而这也成为了当时唯一一种法律服务机构。

After the end of the "Cultural Revolution", the Tianjin Municipal Bureau of Justice actively restored and rebuilt. Wang Liangshan and Wu Zhaoji were the leaders of the preparatory group for the restoration and reconstruction of the Municipal Bureau of Justice. After the restoration and reconstruction of the Ministry of Justice, the legal counsel offices were restored and rebuilt in various places in accordance with the requirements. At that time, the legal service organization had only one form of legal advisory office.

1979年12月15日,天津市第一法律顾问处成立,标志着律师制度在天津的恢复重建。1981年5月10日,经天津市编制委员会批准,天津市第一法律顾问处更名为天津市法律顾问处,受天津市司法局组织领导和业务监督。同时,各区、县司法局分别设立法律顾问处,承担本地区的法律顾问工作,并受各区、县司法局的组织领导和业务监督。到1981年年底,全市共有法律顾问处17个,其中律师58名、实习律师8名、其他人员41名。

On December 15, 1979, Tianjin First Legal Counsel Office was established,

天津市编制委员会《关于调整法律顾问处机构设置和人员编制的通知》

Notice on Adjusting the Organizational Structure and Staffing of the Legal Counsel Office by Tianjin Municipal Organization Committee

1983年9月天津市中级人民法院召开严厉打击刑事犯罪分子宣判大会

In September 1983, Tianjin Intermediate People's Court held a strike hard public judgment meeting to crackdown criminals

marking the restoration and reconstruction of the lawyer system in Tianjin. On May 10, with the approval of the Municipal Organization Committee, the Tianjin First Legal Counsel Office was renamed Tianjin Legal Counsel Office, which was subject to the organizational leadership and business supervision of the Municipal Bureau of Justice. The District and County Judicial Bureaus established legal counsel offices respectively to be responsible for the legal advisory work in the region, and is subject to the organizational leadership and business supervision of the district and county judicial bureaus. By the end of 1981, there were 17 legal counsel offices in the city. Among them, there were 58 lawyers and 8 trainee lawyers, 41 other personnel.

第一法律顾问处成立后，曾为天津司法作出杰出贡献的赵光裕又开始了执业律师生涯。赵光裕1943年8月毕业于中国大学法科法律学系，新中国成立前曾任河北天津地方法院民庭推事，河北长芦盐务局、中国盐业公司法律顾问；新中国成立后任河北省人民法院审判员、天津市人民法院审判员、天津市公证处公证员。执业律师期间，赵光裕以"用法体现道德，手段反映品

1934	1935	1936	1937	1938	1939	1940	1941	1942	1943	1944	1945	1946
1960	1961	1962	1963	1964	1965	1966	1967	1968	1969	1970	1971	1972
1986	1987	1988	1989	1990	1991	1992	1993	1994	1995	1996	1997	1998
2012	2013	2014	2015	2016	2017	2018	2019	2020	2021	……		

质"为座右铭,同时培养了包括王天举在内的众多杰出律师,可谓桃李满天下。

After the establishment of the First Legal Counsel Office, Zhao Guangyu, who had made outstanding contributions to Tianjin justice, began to practice as a lawyer again. Zhao Guangyu graduated from the Faculty of Law of the University of China in August 1943. Before the founding of the People's Republic of China, he served as the civil judge of the Hebei Tianjin District Court, and the legal adviser of the Hebei Changlu Salt Bureau and the China Salt Company. After the founding of the People's Republic of China, he served as thejudge of People's Court of Hebei Province, judges of Tianjin People's Court, notaries of Tianjin Notary Office. During his practice as a lawyer, Zhao Guangyu took "usage to reflect morality and means to reflect quality" as his motto, and at the same time trained many outstanding lawyers including Wang Tianju. Can be described as peaches and plums all over the world.

赵光裕律师

Lawyer Zhao Guangyu

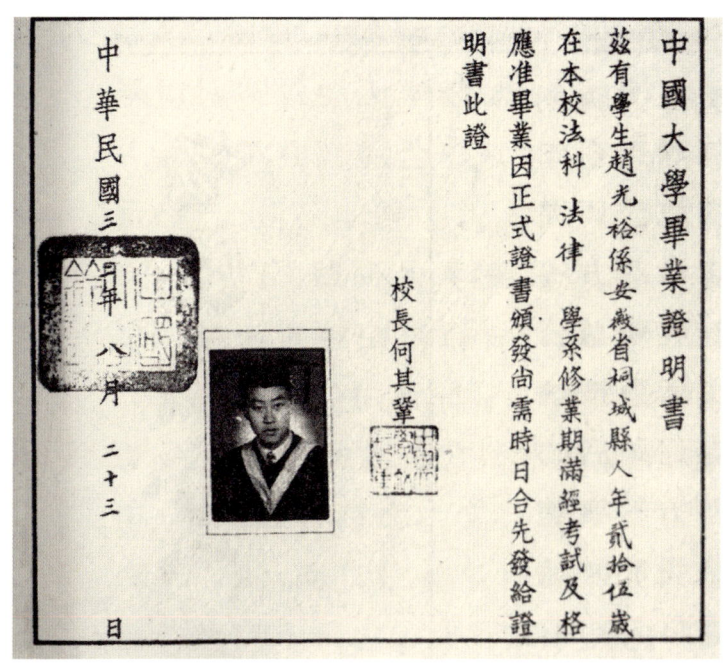

1943 年赵光裕中国大学法科法律学系毕业证书

Graduation certificate of Zhao Guangyu, Faculty of Law, University of China in 1943

新中国成立后的赵光裕
Zhao Guangyu after the founding of the People's Republic of China

天津市第一法律顾问处承办的渤海2号沉船案是在新中国律师制度刚刚恢复，政策、机构还不健全的情况下发生的一起震惊中外的重大案件。

The Bohai No. 2 shipwreck case undertaken by the Tianjin First Legal Counsel Office was a major case that shocked China and foreign countries when the lawyer system of the People's Republic of China had just been restored and the policies and institutions were not yet sound.

1979年11月25日凌晨3点35分，渤海湾发生了新中国成立后损失最为严重的海难，石油部海洋石油勘探局"渤海2号"钻井船在迁往新井位的拖航中于东经119度37分48秒、北纬38度41分30秒的渤海海面翻沉，导致72人死亡，直接经济损失3700万元。经调查，此次沉船是由冒险拖航造成的。1980年9月，天津市中级人民法院开庭审理了事故责任人渎职一案。

At 3:35 a.m. on November 25, 1979, the most devastating shipwreck occurred in the Bohai Bay since the founding of the People's Republic of China. The Offshore Petroleum Exploration Bureau of the Ministry of Petroleum "Bohai 2" drill ship moved eastward during the towing to the new well site. The Bohai Sea at 119 degrees, 37 minutes, 48 seconds and 38 degrees, 41 minutes and 30 seconds north latitude overturned, causing 72 deaths and direct economic losses of 37 million yuan. After investigation, the shipwreck was caused by risky towing. In September 1980, the

Tianjin Intermediate People's Court opened a trial to hear the case of the person responsible for the accident.

  天津市第一法律顾问处董师凯、常维仕、徐承斌、郝纯源四名律师作为辩护人出庭参加诉讼，这是律师制度恢复后律师第一次参与刑事案件的重要实践。不过，正如首席辩护律师董师

石油部海洋石油勘探局钻井平台
Drilling platform of Offshore Petroleum Exploration Bureau, Ministry of Petroleum

检察院讨论渤海 2 号沉船案
Procuratorate discusses the case of Bohai No. 2 shipwreck

凯后来所说，当时的人们对于给"坏人"辩护，还是心存忌惮的。由于案情重大，因此全国多家媒体都对该案进行了持续深入的报道，律师作为辩护人随着案情的广泛传播也为公众知晓。那时的律师有一个共识，即办理刑事、民事案件是律师的看家本领，参加庭审是最基本的锻炼，而参与重大案件的诉讼活动对律师能力和声誉的提升更是不言而喻的。

Four lawyers, Dong Shikai, Chang Weishi, Xu Chengbin, and Hao Chunyuan from the Tianjin First Legal Counsel Office, appeared in court as defenders to participate in litigation. This was the first important practice in which lawyers participated in criminal cases after the restoration of the lawyer system. However, as the chief defense lawyer Dong Shikai later said, people at that time were still afraid of

1934	1935	1936	1937	1938	1939	1940	1941	1942	1943	1944	1945	1946
1960	1961	1962	1963	1964	1965	1966	1967	1968	1969	1970	1971	1972
1986	1987	1988	1989	1990	1991	1992	1993	1994	1995	1996	1997	1998
2012	2013	2014	2015	2016	2017	2018	2019	2020	2021	……		

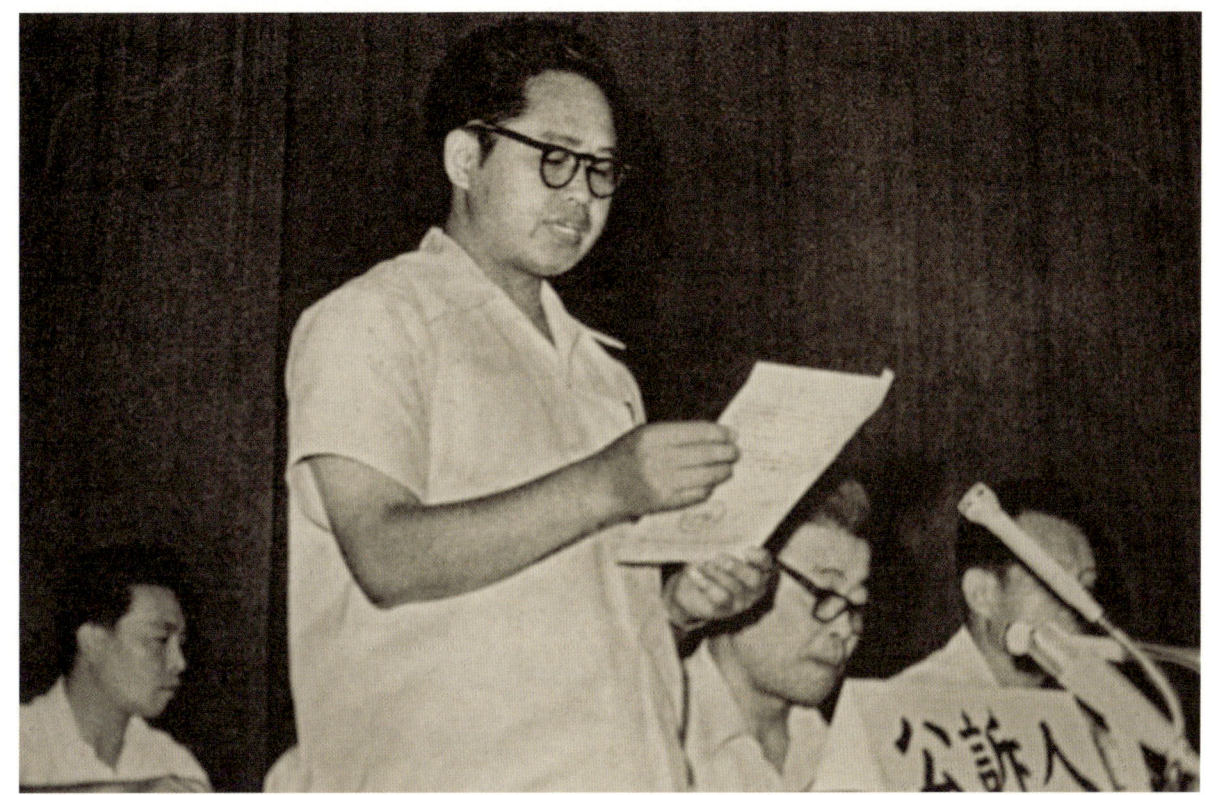

公诉人
Prosecutor

defending "bad guys". Due to the seriousness of the case, many media across the country have carried out continuous and in-depth reports on the case, and lawyers as defenders have become known to the public as the case has spread widely. At that time, lawyers had a consensus that handling criminal and civil cases was a lawyer's housekeeping skills, and participating in court trials was the most basic exercise. Participating in litigation activities in major cases was also self-evident.

1984年，经市委政法委批准，天津市司法局建立了天津市第二法律顾问处，编制20人。天津市法律顾问处又改回第一法律顾问处，编制71人。从1985年至1990年，天津市司法局批准成立了若干家律师事务所。其中包括以特邀律师为主的集体所有制的天津市塘沽区第二律师事务所，在第一法律顾问处内部成立的天津市专利律师事务所、天津市侨务律师事务所（不另设机

董师凯、常维仕、徐承斌、郝纯源四名辩护律师在法庭上辩护

Four defense lawyers Dong Shikai, Chang Weishi, Xu Chengbin, and Hao Chunyuan defended in court

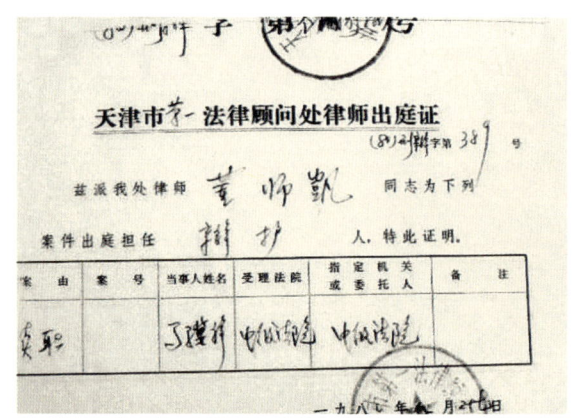

律师出庭辩护通知书

Notice of lawyer appearing in court to defend

律师出庭证

Lawyer appearance certificate

1934 1935 1936 1937 1938 1939 1940 1941 1942 1943 1944 1945 1946
1960 1961 1962 1963 1964 1965 1966 1967 1968 1969 1970 1971 1972
1986 1987 1988 1989 1990 1991 1992 1993 1994 1995 1996 1997 1998
2012 2013 2014 2015 2016 2017 2018 2019 2020 2021 ……

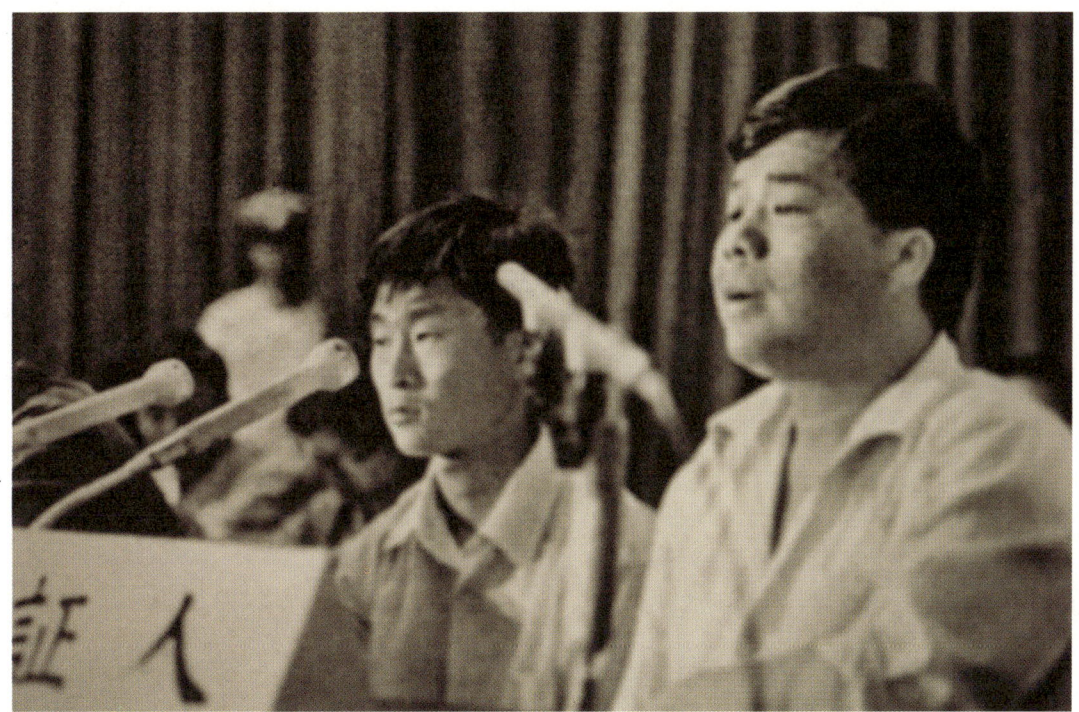

证人
Witness

审判
Trial

《工人日报》刊登的渤海2号沉船案消息
News of the Bohai No. 2 shipwreck case published in *Workers Daily*

丁立莹律师向董师凯律师收集案件资料
Lawyer Ding Liying collected case data from Lawyer Dong Shikai

构，仅指定几位律师从事与专利和侨务相关的业务工作，对外可以挂牌）以及在第二法律顾问处内成立的天津市对外经济律师事务所。

In 1984, with the approval of the Political and Legal Committee of the Municipal Party Committee, the Municipal Bureau of Justice established the Tianjin Second Legal Counsel Office. The establishment was 20 people. The original Municipal Legal Counsel Office was renamed the First Legal Counsel Office, with an establishment of 71 people. From 1985 to 1990, the Tianjin Municipal Bureau of Justice approved the establishment of several law firms. For example: The No. 2 Law Firm of Tanggu District, Tianjin, which was collective ownership and among them are mainly specially-invited lawyers, established Tianjin Patent Law Firm and Tianjin Overseas Chinese Affairs Law Firm within the First Legal Counsel Office (no separate organization, designated several lawyers are engaged in patent and overseas Chinese affairs business, which can be listed externally), and Tianjin Foreign Economic Law Firm established in the Second Legal Counsel Office.

1985年9月28日，经市政府批准，天津经济技术开发区律师事务所成立。此后，隶属天津市政法管理干部学院的第一法律顾问处第二接待室改建为天津市第四律师事务所，南开大学恢复

1934	1935	1936	1937	1938	1939	1940	1941	1942	1943	1944	1945	1946
1960	1961	1962	1963	1964	1965	1966	1967	1968	1969	1970	1971	1972
1986	1987	1988	1989	1990	1991	1992	1993	1994	1995	1996	1997	1998
2012	2013	2014	2015	2016	2017	2018	2019	2020	2021	……		

了天津市第六律师事务所，隶属于第二法律顾问处的天津联合业余大学接待站改建为天津市第七律师事务所，同时在天津市妇女联合会成立了天津市第八律师事务所，恢复了河西区第二律师事务所，设立了南开区第二律师事务所、东郊区第二律师事务所、塘沽区第二律师事务所，并在塘沽区成立了天津市海事海商律师事务所等。到1990年年底，全市律师工作机构已达45个，律师1032名，体制上国办所与合作所并存。天津初步形成了一支以专职为主、兼职和特邀律师为辅的律师队伍。

In addition, with the approval of the Municipal People's Government, on September 28, 1985, Tianjin Economic and Technological Development Zone Law Firm was established. After that, the second reception room of the First Legal Counsel Office under the Tianjin Municipal Law Management Cadre College was transformed into

天津市第一法律顾问处（王金安律师提供）
Photo of Tianjin First Legal Counsel Office
(provided by lawyer Wang Jin'an)

1921	1922	1923	1924	1925	1926	1927	1928	1929	1930	1931	1932	1933
1947	1948	1949	1950	1951	1952	1953	1954	1955	1956	1957	1958	1959
1973	1974	1975	1976	1977	1978	1979	1980	1981	1982	1983	1984	1985
1999	2000	2001	2002	2003	2004	2005	2006	2007	2008	2009	2010	2011

在天津市对外经济律师事务所门前合影

A group photo in front of Tianjin Foreign Economic Law Firm

the fourth law firm of Tianjin. Approved Nankai University to restore the Tianjin Sixth Law Firm, approved the Tianjin United Amateur University Reception Station under the Tianjin Second Legal Counsel Office to be transformed into Tianjin Seventh Law Firm. At the same time, the Tianjin Eighth Law Firm was established in Tianjin Women's Federation. And the Hexi District Second Law Firm was restored. Established Nankai District No. 2 Law Firm, Dong Suburban No. 2 Law Firm, Tanggu District No. 2 Law Firm. And established Tianjin Maritime affairs Law Firm in Tanggu District and many more. By the end of 1990, the city had 45 lawyers' working institutions and 1032 lawyers. The state-run offices and cooperative offices coexist in the system, initially forming a team of lawyers mainly full-time, supplemented by part-time and specially invited lawyers.

改革开放后
天津律师业的起步

THE STARTING OF TIANJIN LAWYER INDUSTRY AFTER THE REFORM AND OPENING-UP

从1981年1月开始,天津市司法局开展了为期四个半月的律师招聘工作。经过报名、考试、体检、政审等环节,市司法局最终录取了专职律师43人、兼职律师工作人员20人。同时,根据司法部(1981)司发公字269号文件的精神,天津市司法局还为专职律师、兼职律师、实习律师、律师业务工作人员统一颁发了律师工作证。到当年11月份,天津律师共办结刑事辩护案件875件,代理民事案件226件,接待群众来访、解答法律咨询5471人次,代写法律文书2061件。

From January 1981 to April 16, the recruitment of lawyers by the Municipal Bureau of Justice basically ended. After registration, examination, physical examination, political review, etc., 43 full-time lawyers and 20 part-time lawyers staff were admitted. In accordance with the spirit of the Ministry of Justice (1981) Sifagongzi No. 269, the Tianjin Municipal Bureau of Justice issued a unified lawyer's work permit. The scope of distribution includes: lawyers, part-time lawyers, trainee lawyers, and lawyer business staff. On November, Tianjin lawyers settled 875 criminal defense cases, represented 226 civil cases, received visits from the masses, answered legal inquiries, 5471 person-times, and wrote 2061 legal documents.

1982年1月13日,天津市司法局下发了《关于试行〈律师收费试行办法〉的通知》。《通知》要求各法律顾问处于当年3月10日前,将试行中的经验和问题呈报市司法局公证律师处。两天后,天津市高级人民法院、天津市司法局、天津市财政局又联合下发了《天津市各级人民法

天津市委组织部、天津市人事局关于天津市司法局公开招募律师有关问题的通知

Notice of the Organization Department of the Tianjin Municipal Committee of the Communist Party of China and the Municipal Personnel Bureau on issues concerning the open recruitment of lawyers by the Tianjin Municipal Bureau of Justice

1980年天津市司法局招聘律师简章

In 1980, Tianjin Municipal Bureau of Justice recruitment lawyer guide

1934	1935	1936	1937	1938	1939	1940	1941	1942	1943	1944	1945	1946
1960	1961	1962	1963	1964	1965	1966	1967	1968	1969	1970	1971	1972
1986	1987	1988	1989	1990	1991	1992	1993	1994	1995	1996	1997	1998
2012	2013	2014	2015	2016	2017	2018	2019	2020	2021	……		

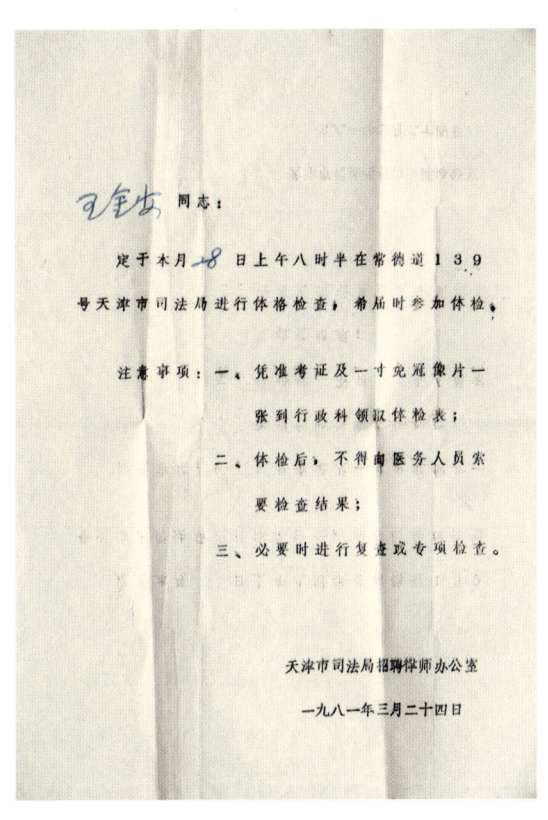

1981年天津市司法局招聘律师体检通知

Medical examination notice for recruitment of lawyers by Tianjin Municipal Bureau of Justice in 1981

院审理法人之间经济纠纷案件收取诉讼费用暂行规定的通知》。《暂行规定》共十四条，自1982年2月1日起施行。当年下半年，天津市司法局又连续下发了若干与律师工作相关的规定，如《关于严加制止冒充律师进行非法活动的通知》（7月15日）、《关于对专职律师工作人员进行考核及审批律师资格的意见》（8月13日）、《天津市律师守则（试行）》（10月6日）、《天津市兼职律师管理试行办法》。其中《守则》（共八条）和《办法》（共十条）对律师和兼职律师提出了严格的要求。12月4日，天津市司法局下发了《关于法院指定的辩护案件收费的通知》，指出："自1983年1月1日起，对法院指定辩护的一、二审案件，法律顾问处应向法院收取辩护费，每件壹拾伍元。"一系列的规定为天津律师业的平稳起步与良好发展作出了规范。

On January 13, the Municipal Bureau of Justice issued the *Notice on Trial Implementation of the Trial Measures for Lawyers' Fees*. The *Notice* requires all legal counsel offices to be present before March 10, and report the experience and problems in the trial implementation to the Notary Lawyer Office of the Municipal Bureau of Justice. On January 15, the Tianjin Higher People's Court, the Municipal Bureau of Justice, and the Municipal Finance Bureau jointly issued the *Notice of the Interim Provisions on the Collection of Litigation Fees in the Trial of Economic Dispute Cases between Legal Persons by the People's Courts of Tianjin at All Levels*. There are 14 articles in the *Regulations*, which came into effect on February 1, 1982. Since 1982, the Municipal Bureau of Justice has successively issued a number of regulations on the work of lawyers, including: *Notice on Strictly Stopping Illegal Activities Impersonating a Lawyer* (July 15), *Regarding the Assessment of Full-Time Lawyers Opinions on the Approval of Lawyers' Qualifications* (August 13),

Tianjin Lawyers Code (Trial) (8 articles in total, October 6), and *Tianjin City Part-Time Lawyers Management Trial Measures* (10 articles in total). The *Code* and *Measures* set strict requirements on lawyers and part-time lawyers. On December 4, the Municipal Bureau of Justice issued the *Notice on Charges for Defense Cases Designated by the Court*. The *Notice* pointed out, "Since January 1, 1983, the legal counsel office shall collect defense fees from the court for cases of first instance and second instance for which the court has designated defense, at a rate of one hundred and fifty yuan per case." A series of regulations set the standards for the steady start and sound development of Tianjin's lawyer industry.

1982年10月15日，经天津市编制委员会批准，天津市法律顾问处增加事业编制35名，各区、县法律顾问处增加事业编制134名，各区、县公证处增加行政编制61名，市政法干部学校增加行政编制20名。当年年底，在全市19所法律顾问处中，有三所法律顾问处应聘担任七家企事业单位的常年法律顾问。全市律师全年共办结刑事辩护案件1839件、各类民事和经济案件949件，解答法律咨询20349人次，代写法律文书6498件。全市律师的收费总额为120133元，公证收费32585元。

Approved by the Municipal Organization Committee on October 15 of the same year, the establishment of the judicial administration system was increased as follows: the Municipal Legal Counsel Office increased the establishment of 35, the district and county legal counsel offices increased a total of 134, the district and county notary offices increased the administrative establishment of 61; the municipal law cadre school increases the administrative establishment by 20. By the end of 1982, among the 19 legal counsel offices in the city, 3 legal counsel offices were employed as perennial legal advisors for 7 enterprises and public institutions; 1839 criminal defense cases and 949 various civil and economic cases were handled throughout the year, answered 20,349 legal inquiries, and wrote 6,498 legal documents. Tianjin lawyers' fees totaled 120,133 yuan; notarization fees were 32,585 yuan.

经过一年的发展，到1983年年底，天津律师总数增长到257人，其中被授予律师资格的有

115人、兼职律师54人、实习律师10人。律师应聘担任常年法律顾问的企事业单位有54家。全市律师全年共办结刑事辩护案件2710件、民事案件1218件、经济案件124件，承办非诉讼事务106件，解答法律咨询23114人次，代写法律文书8021件。

After a year of development, by the end of 1983, the total number of lawyers in the city had grown to 257. Among them: 115 were granted lawyer qualifications, 54 were part-time lawyers, and 10 were trainee lawyers. There are 54 enterprises and institutions for which lawyers are employed as perennial legal advisers. In the whole year, they handled 2,710 criminal defense cases, handled 1,218 civil agency cases, represented 124 economic cases, undertook 106 non-litigation incidents, and answered 23,114 legal inquiries, wrote 8021 legal documents.

发生在1984年的荷花女名誉权案是新中国成立后首例死者生前的名誉、人格权益是否仍受民法保护的案例，而这在当时还没有明确的立法。1984年4月18日至6月12日，天津《今晚报·副刊》连载小说《荷花女》。因小说中有关荷花女（吉文贞）之母陈秀琴同意其女作妾并遭流氓侮辱的情节失实，所以原告陈秀琴将小说作者和报社共同告上法庭。该案后经天津市中级人民法院和代理律师王宗华的积极调解而结案，最高人民法院还专门复函了天津市高级人民法院。该案的公正审理也成为了全国法院处理此类案件的典型。

The Lotus Girl's reputation right case that occurred in 1984 was the first case after the founding of the People's Republic of China on whether the reputation and personality rights of the deceased were still protected by the civil law. At that time, there was no clear legislation. From April 18 to June 12, 1984, the Supplement of Tianjin *Tonight News* serialized the novel *Lotus Girl*. Because the plot of Chen Xiuqin, the mother of the Lotus Girl (Ji Wenzhen) in the novel, who agreed to her concubine as a concubine and was insulted by hooligans, the plaintiff Chen Xiuqin took the novel author and the newspaper to court. The case was closed after the active mediation of Tianjin Intermediate Court and the attorney Wang Zonghua. The Supreme People's Court also specially replied to Tianjin Higher People's Court. The fair trial of this case has also become a typical case in the handling of such cases by courts across the country.

曲艺艺人荷花女

Quyi artist Lotus Girl

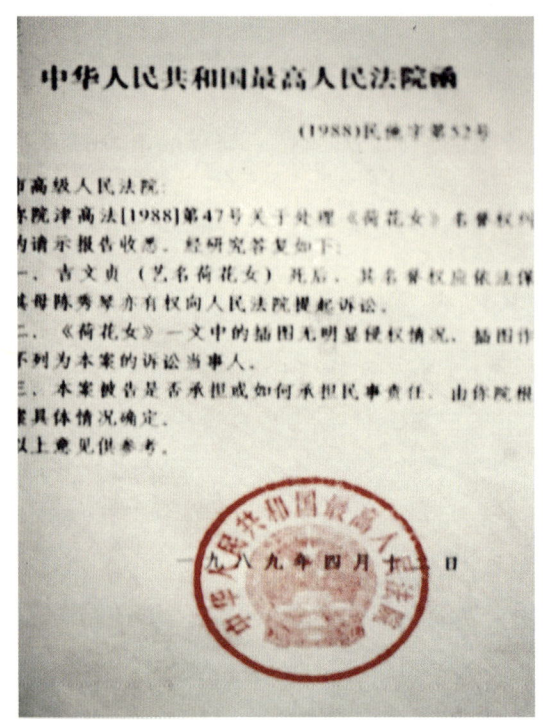

最高人民法院的专门复函

Special reply letter from the Supreme People's Court

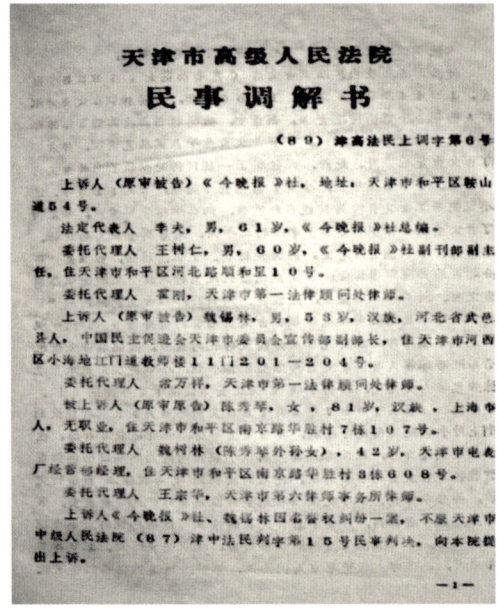

天津市高级人民法院关于荷花女案的民事调解书

Civil mediation letter of Tianjin Higher People's Court on the case of the Lotus Girl

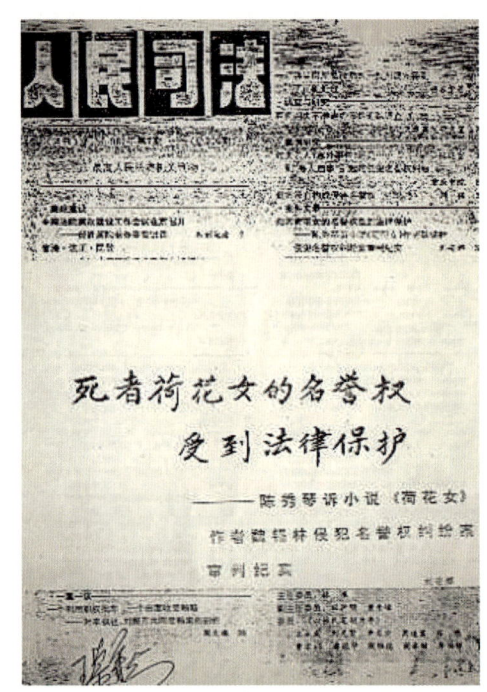

1989年第7期《人民司法》关于荷花女案的评论

Comment on the case of the Lotus Girl in the seventh issue of *People's Justice* in 1989

1934	1935	1936	1937	1938	1939	1940	1941	1942	1943	1944	1945	1946
1960	1961	1962	1963	1964	1965	1966	1967	1968	1969	1970	1971	1972
1986	1987	1988	1989	1990	1991	1992	1993	1994	1995	1996	1997	1998
2012	2013	2014	2015	2016	2017	2018	2019	2020	2021	……		

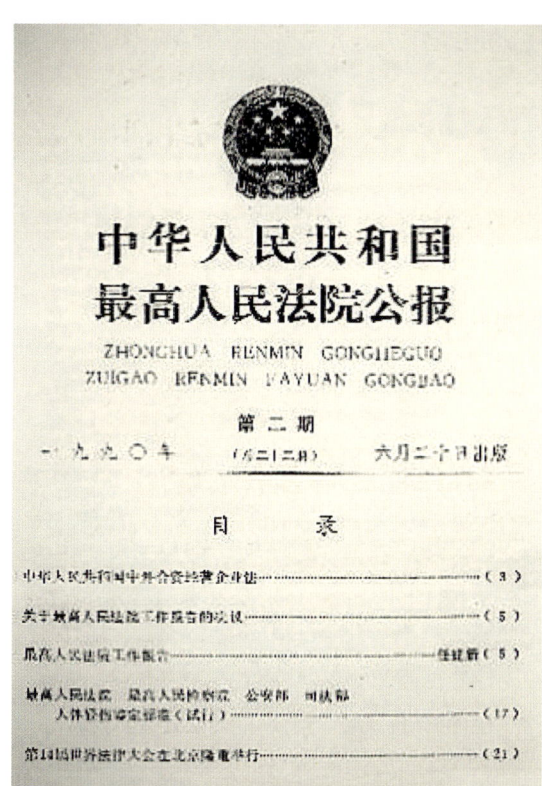

《最高人民法院公报》对荷花女名誉权案的报道
Report of the *Supreme People's Court Bulletin* on the Lotus Girl's reputation right case

天津市律师协会的成立及其在20世纪八九十年代的发展

THE ESTABLISHMENT OF TIANJIN LAWYERS ASSOCIATION AND ITS DEVELOPMENT IN THE 1980S AND 1990S

天津市律师协会成立于1984年10月21日；22日至24日，天津市第一届律师代表大会暨天津市律师协会成立大会在天津宾馆召开。出席会议的有正式代表133人、列席代表11人。大会通过了《天津市律师协会章程》，选举产生了由39人组成的天津市律师协会第一届理事会。会议推选陈以毅为天津市律师协会名誉会长，选举宋树涛、郑振亚、王丹侠、刘广炬、董师凯为常务理事，宋树涛任会长，郑振亚、王丹侠任副会长，刘广炬任秘书长。至此，天津市律师协会正式成立，天津律师有了自己的行业组织。此时，全市共有专职、兼职及特邀律师429人。

The Tianjin Lawyers Association was established on October 21, 1984. From October 22 to 24, 1984, Tianjin First Lawyers' Representative Conference as below the inaugural meeting of Tianjin Lawyers Association was held in Tianjin Hotel. There were 133 official representatives and 11 non-voting representatives. The conference passed the *Articles of Tianjin Lawyers Association* and elected the first council of the Tianjin Lawyers Association composed of 39 people. The meeting elected Chen Yiyi as the honorary chairman of the Tianjin Lawyers Association, Song Shutao, Zheng Zhenya, Wang Danxia, Liu Guangju, and Dong Shikai as executive directors, Song Shutao as the chairman, Zheng Zhenya and Wang Danxia as the vice chairman, and Liu Guangju as the secretary general. At this point, the Tianjin Lawyers Association was formally established, and Tianjin lawyers have their own industry organization. At this time, there are 429 full-time, part-time and specially invited lawyers in the city.

天津市律师协会的筹建工作早在1982年就开始了。当年3月30日，天津市政法干部学校在静海县党校举办了为期三个月的司法干部轮训班，对市局机关各处室、律协筹备组、各区县司法局、法律顾问处、公证处的80余人进行了轮训。轮训学习的主要内容是法理、刑法、民法、公证、律师专业法律知识等。与此同时，政法干部学校还举办了为期三个月的公证、律师、干部培训班，全市司法行政系统近100人参加了学习。学习内容以民法、刑法为重点，并涉及法理、婚姻法、刑事诉讼法、民事诉讼法、公证业务、律师业务等相关基础知识。5月13日，天津市司法局党组1982年第十三次会议讨论决定建立天津市司法学校筹备组。筹备组由王丹侠（兼）、冯哲贵、宋呈明、成丁、边文萍五人组成，王丹侠任组长，冯哲贵任副组长。会议还决定建立天津市律师协会筹备组。筹备组由郝双禄、武兆吉、张鳌、许培元、庞甦蔚、李守福、孙才斌七人组成，郝双禄任组长，武兆吉任副组长。

The preparations for the establishment of the Tianjin Lawyers Association began in 1982. On March 30, 1982, the Municipal Law Cadre School held a three-month rotation training course for judicial cadres at the Party School of Jinghai County. More than 80 people were trained in rotation. The content learned during the rotation training is: jurisprudence, criminal law, civil law, notarization, professional legal knowledge of lawyers, etc. At the same time, the Municipal Law Cadre School held a three-month training course for notarization, lawyers, and cadres. Nearly 100 people from the judicial administration system of the city participated in the study. The learning content focuses on civil law and criminal law, as well as basic knowledge of jurisprudence, marriage law, criminal procedure law, civil procedure law, notarization business, and lawyer business. On May 13, after discussion and decision at the 13th meeting of the Party Group of the Municipal Bureau of Justice in 1982, the Tianjin Judicial School Preparatory Group was established. The preparatory team consists of five people including Wang Danxia (concurrently), Feng Zhegui, Song Chengming, Cheng Ding, and Bian Wenping. Wang Danxia was the team leader and Feng Zhegui was the deputy team leader. The meeting also decided to establish a preparatory group for the Tianjin Lawyers Association, consisting of 7 people including Hao Shuanglu, Wu Zhaoji, Zhang Ao, Xu Peiyuan, Pang Suwei, Li Shoufu, and Sun Caibin. Hao Shuanglu was the team leader and Wu Zhaoji was the deputy team leader.

1984年10月21日天津市律师协会成立大会全体代表合影
A group photo of all the representatives of the founding assembly of Tianjin Lawyers Association on October 21,1984

天津市第一届律师代表大会
Tianjin First Lawyers Congress

1934	1935	1936	1937	1938	1939	1940	1941	1942	1943	1944	1945	1946
1960	1961	1962	1963	1964	1965	1966	1967	1968	1969	1970	1971	1972
1986	1987	1988	1989	1990	1991	1992	1993	1994	1995	1996	1997	1998
2012	2013	2014	2015	2016	2017	2018	2019	2020	2021	……		

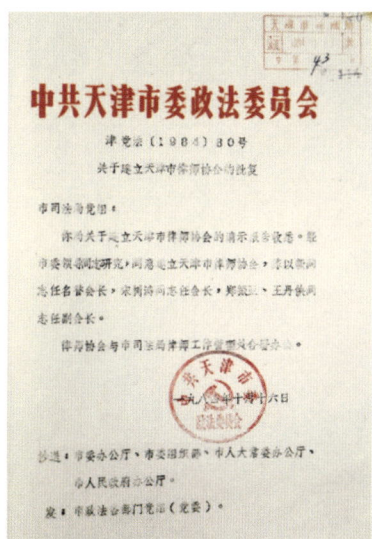

1984年10月16日中共天津市委政法委员会关于建立天津市律师协会的批复

Reply of the Political and Legal Committee of the Tianjin Municipal Committee of the Communist Party of China on the establishment of the Tianjin Lawyers Association on October 16, 1984

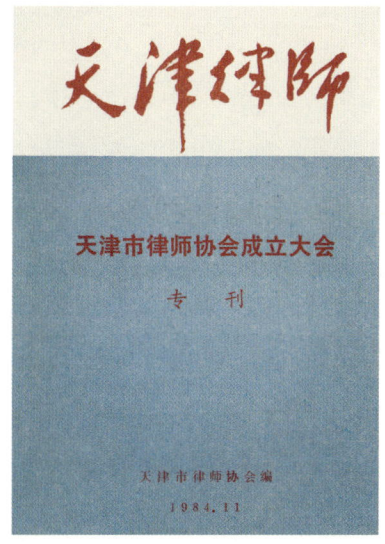

1984年11月《天津律师》天津市律师协会成立大会专刊

November 1984 Tianjin Lawyer special issue of the founding conference of Tianjin Lawyers Association

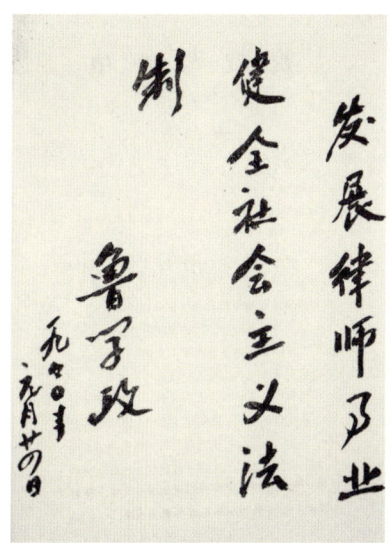

《天津律师》鲁学政题词

Lu Xuezheng wrote an inscription for Tianjin Lawyer

1921	1922	1923	1924	1925	1926	1927	1928	1929	1930	1931	1932	1933
1947	1948	1949	1950	1951	1952	1953	1954	1955	1956	1957	1958	1959
1973	1974	1975	1976	1977	1978	1979	1980	1981	1982	1983	1984	1985
1999	2000	2001	2002	2003	2004	2005	2006	2007	2008	2009	2010	2011

1986年7月中央领导接见全国律师代表合影

A group photo of the leaders of the central government meeting with lawyer representatives from across the country

　　1986年7月5日，第一次全国律师代表大会在北京召开，中华全国律师协会正式成立。乔石、陈丕显、彭冲、荣毅仁、郑天翔、杨易辰、康克清、钱昌照、王光英等中央领导同志出席了此次大会。天津市司法局派出郑振亚、何家惠、蒋龙祥、马锦华四名代表出席。大会选举出名誉会长刘复之、会长邹瑜、秘书长谭文玑。郑振亚被选为会议主席团成员，并当选中华全国律师协会第一届理事会理事。同年9月5日，天津市律师协会召开第六次常务理事会和第四次理事会。经过讨论，理事会决定同意宋树涛辞去会长职务，并选举郑振亚为会长，增选董师凯为副会长。

On July 5, 1986, the first National Lawyers Congress was held in Beijing, and the All China Lawyers Association was formally established. Qiao Shi, Chen Pixian, Peng Chong, Rong Yiren, Zheng Tianxiang, Yang Yichen, Kang Keqing, Qian Changzhao, Wang Guangying and other central leaders attended. The Tianjin Municipal Bureau of Justice sent four representatives, Zheng Zhenya, He Jiahui, Jiang Longxiang, and Ma Jinhua to attend the National Lawyers Congress. The meeting elected honorary chairman Liu Fuzhi, chairman Zou Yu, and secretary-general Tan Wenji. Comrade Zheng Zhenya was selected as a member of the presidium of the conference and was elected

1934	1935	1936	1937	1938	1939	1940	1941	1942	1943	1944	1945	1946
1960	1961	1962	1963	1964	1965	1966	1967	1968	1969	1970	1971	1972
1986	1987	1988	1989	1990	1991	1992	1993	1994	1995	1996	1997	1998
2012	2013	2014	2015	2016	2017	2018	2019	2020	2021			

as a member of the first council of the All China Lawyers Association. On September 5, 1986, Tianjin Lawyers Association held the sixth standing council and the fourth council. After discussion, it was decided that Song Shutao was agreed to resign as the chairman, Zheng Zhenya was elected as the chairman, and Dong Shikai was co-opted as the vice chairman.

1989年1月11日，天津市律师协会在八一礼堂召开了向20世纪50年代从事律师工作的老律师颁发荣誉证书大会。武宝锐、兰英等25名老律师荣获律师荣誉证书和纪念品。天津市人大常委会副主任李原参加了会议。同年，天津市律师协会成立了民事、刑事、非诉讼、法律顾问、国内经济、涉外业务六个专业委员会，天津律师从此走上了专业化道路。

On January 11, 1989, Tianjin Lawyers Association held a meeting in the Bayi Auditorium to award certificates of honor to the old lawyers who were engaged in the work of lawyers in the 1950s. Twenty-five old lawyers including Wu Baorui and Lan Ying received the lawyer's certificate of honor and souvenirs. Li Yuan, deputy director of the Standing Committee of the Municipal People's Congress, attended the

中华全国律师协会第一届理事会理事合影

A group photo of the first council members of the All China Lawyers Association

1986年7月5日第一次全国律师代表大会在北京人民大会堂召开，中华全国律师协会正式成立

On July 5, 1986, the First National Lawyers Congress was held in the Great Hall of the People in Beijing, and the All China Lawyers Association was formally established

郑振亚在工作交流中

Zheng Zhenya was in work communication

1934	1935	1936	1937	1938	1939	1940	1941	1942	1943	1944	1945	1946
1960	1961	1962	1963	1964	1965	1966	1967	1968	1969	1970	1971	1972
1986	1987	1988	1989	1990	1991	1992	1993	1994	1995	1996	1997	1998
2012	2013	2014	2015	2016	2017	2018	2019	2020	2021	……		

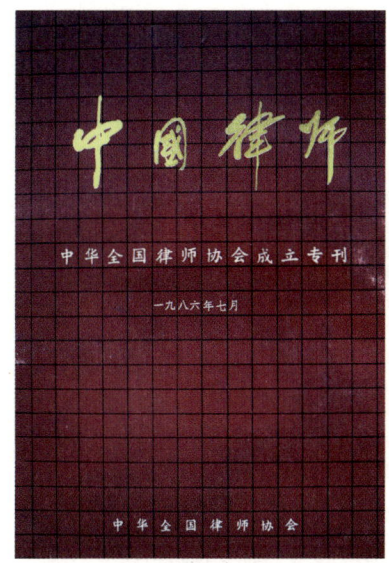

1986年7月《中国律师》中华全国律师协会成立专刊

July 1986 *Chinese Lawyer* All China Lawyers Association established a special issue

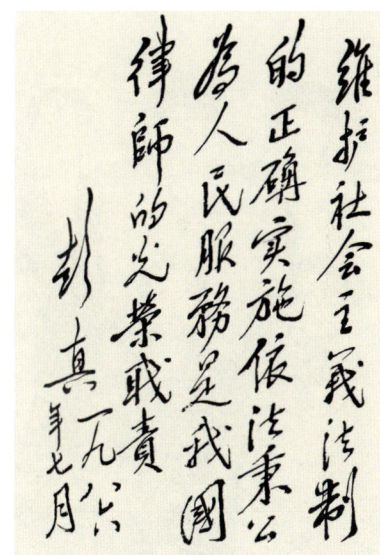

彭真题词

Inscription by Peng Zhen

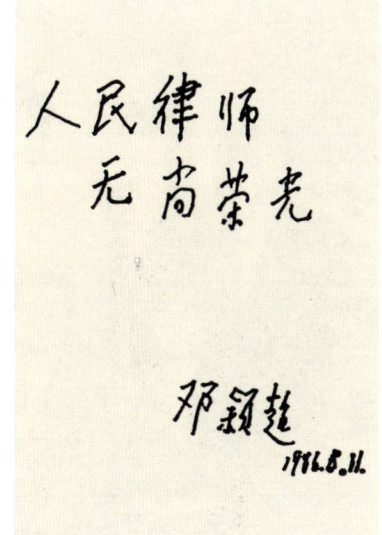

邓颖超题词

Inscription by Deng Yingchao

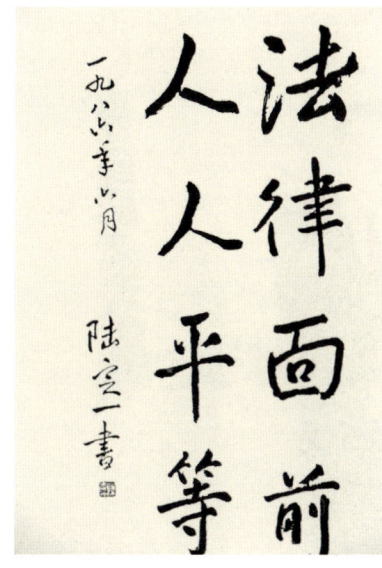

陆定一题词

Inscription by Lu Dingyi

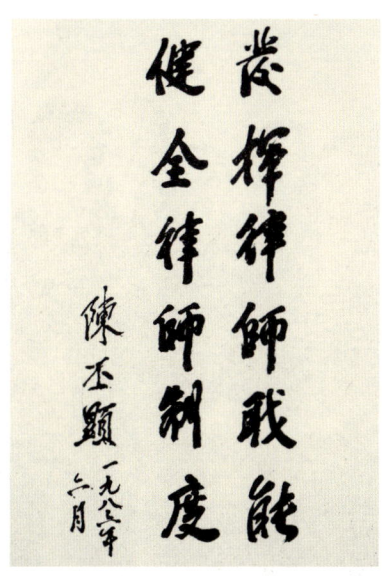

陈丕显题词

Inscription by Chen Pixian

《中国律师》书影

Chinese Lawyer copy

20 世纪 80 年代天津市司法局领导与部分律师合影

A group photo of the leaders of the Tianjin Municipal Bureau of Justice and some lawyers in the 1980s

20 世纪 80 年代天津市司法局领导与部分律师合影

A group photo of the leaders of the Tianjin Municipal Bureau of Justice and some lawyers in the 1980s

律师与司法局干警合影

Photo of lawyers and police officers from the Judicial Bureau

meeting. In this year, Tianjin Lawyers Association established six professional committees including civil, criminal, non-litigation, legal counsel, domestic economy, and foreign-related business, and Tianjin lawyers began to embark on a path of professionalization.

1989年12月4日，在《中华人民共和国宪法》颁布纪念日这一天，天津市第二届律师代表大会暨律师制度恢复十周年表彰大会在天津宾馆召开。134名正式代表和20余名列席代表参加了会议。大会表彰了11个先进集体、12名优秀律师和75名先进律师。同时大会选举产生了由59人组成的律师协会第二届理事会。

On December 4, 1989, on the anniversary of the promulgation of the *Constitution of the People's Republic of China*, the Second Tianjin Lawyers Congress and the Tenth Anniversary of the Lawyers System Restoration Commendation Conference was held in Tianjin Hotel. 134 official representatives and more than 20 non-voting representatives attended the meeting. The conference commended 11 advanced collectives, 12 outstanding lawyers and 75 advanced lawyers. At the same time, the conference elected the second council of the Lawyers Association composed of 59 people.

截至1989年年底，全市共有律师机构39家、律师941名，全市律师担任法律顾问2390家，办理刑事案件4373件、民事案件8195件、经济案件2656件、行政案件29件，办理非诉讼法律事务561件，全年业务总收入623.3万元。在随后的几年中，伴随着改革的深入，天津律师行业也得到了快速发展。

At the end of 1989, the city had 39 lawyer institutions, 941 lawyers. The city's lawyers acted as legal advisers to 2,390, handling 4,373 criminal cases, 8,195 civil cases, 2,656 economic cases, 29 administrative cases, and 561 non-litigation legal affairs. The total annual business income was 6,233 million yuan. In the following years, along with reforms, the lawyer industry also developed rapidly.

1990年4月22日，为期六天的第十四届世界法律大会在北京举行。天津市以法学会为主体，

1987年春节期间，律师与司法局干警在河西区司法局合影

During the Spring Festival in 1987, a group photo of lawyers and officers from the Judicial Bureau at the Judicial Bureau of Hexi District

在天津市律师协会、天津市高级人民法院的协助下，组成了由市领导、教授、律师、法官、检察官、法学研究人员等13个有关部门的36人参加的代表团出席了此次大会。代表团团长为王永臣，副团长为王诚熙、赵儒基。

On April 22, 1990, the Fourteenth World Law Conference was held in Beijing. It took 6 days. Tianjin was dominated by the Law Society. With the assistance of the Tianjin Lawyers Association and the Higher People's Court, a delegation of 36 people from 13 relevant departments including city leaders, professors, lawyers, judges, prosecutors, and law researchers was formed. Attended the conference. The head of the delegation is Wang Yongchen, and the deputy heads are Wang Chengxi and Zhao Ruji.

截至1990年年底，全市律师共为2471家政府机关、企事业单位担任常年法律顾问，办理刑

郑振亚在投票

Zheng Zhenya was voting

天津市第二届律师代表大会暨律师制度恢复十周年表彰大会

The Second Lawyers Congress in Tianjin and the Tenth Anniversary Commendation Conference for the Restoration of the Lawyer System

第二届律师代表大会领导，左起依次为秘书长何家惠，副秘书长李国樑，会长刘广炬，原会长郑振亚，副会长董师凯，常务理事谌炳炎、蒋龙祥，副会长高纪莉

Leaders of the Second Lawyers Congress, from left to right are Secretary-General He Jiahui, Deputy Secretary-General Li Guoliang, Chairman Liu Guangju, Former Chairman Zheng Zhenya, Vice Chairman Dong Shikai, Executive Manager Chen Bingyan, Jiang Longxiang, Vice Chairman Gao Jili

1989年天津市司法局工会首届代表大会合影

A group photo of the First Trade Union Congress of Tianjin Municipal Bureau of Justice in 1989

1990年7月全国司法行政法制工作会议（兰州）合影

A group photo at the National Judicial Administrative and Legal Work Conference (Lanzhou) in July 1990

1992年8月天津市司法行政工作会议全体代表合影

A group photo of all representatives at the Tianjin Judicial Administration Working Conference in August 1992

事辩护案件4054件，代理民事案件8343件，解答法律咨询28094人次，代写法律文书11588件。全市共有183个基层法律服务所为528个街乡村、企事业、个体户担任常年法律顾问，调解经济纠纷1174起，代理民事诉讼2553件，非诉讼代理1115件，解答法律咨询16657人次，代写法律文书6388件，开展法制宣传2030场次。

The city's lawyers acted as perennial legal consultants for 2,471 government agencies, enterprises and institutions, handled 4,054 criminal defense cases, represented 8,343 civil cases, answered 28,094 legal consultations, and wrote 11,588 legal documents. The city's 183 grassroots legal service offices have applied for permanent legal counsel for 528 villages, enterprises, and self-employed individuals. Adjusted 1,174 economic disputes, represented 2,553 civil litigation cases, represented 1,115 non-litigation cases, answered 16,657 legal consultations, wrote 6,388 legal documents, and carried out 2,030 legal publicity events.

1993年3月，天津市第三次律师代表大会召开。此时律师事务所已发展到65家，律师从业者1133名。在办理刑事、民事、经济案件的同时，广大律师大力开拓非诉讼业务领域，非诉讼法律事务大幅度增加，1993年年底达到了4718件。律师业务全年总收入也增长到了1989万元。20世纪90年代，在国家改革开放的大背景下，天津律师行业的改革工作也在不断加快。

In March 1993, the Third Lawyers Congress of Tianjin City was held. The number of law firms in our city has grown to 65, with 1,133 lawyers. While carrying out criminal, civil and economic cases, it vigorously explored the field of non-litigation business, and non-litigation legal affairs increased significantly, reaching 4,718 by the end of 1993. In 1993, the total income of the lawyer's business also increased to 19.89 million yuan. In the 1990s, under the background of the whole country's reform and opening up, the reform of the lawyer industry continued to accelerate.

1934	1935	1936	1937	1938	1939	1940	1941	1942	1943	1944	1945	1946
1960	1961	1962	1963	1964	1965	1966	1967	1968	1969	1970	1971	1972
1986	1987	1988	1989	1990	1991	1992	1993	1994	1995	1996	1997	1998
2012	2013	2014	2015	2016	2017	2018	2019	2020	2021	……		

陈丽律师（右一）在工作中
Lawyer Chen Li（first one of right） at work

天津市第三次律师代表大会
The Third Lawyers Congress in Tianjin

20 世纪 90 年代初的天津市律师协会
Tianjin Lawyers Association in the early 1990s

天津市律师协会成员在天津市司法局门前合影
Members of Tianjin Lawyers Association took a group photo in front of Tianjin Municipal Bureau of Justice

359

律师资格考试的确立与律师事务所体制的转变

THE ESTABLISHMENT OF THE LAWYER QUALIFICATION EXAMINATION AND THE TRANSFORMATION OF THE LAW FIRM SYSTEM

律师制度恢复之初，国家还没有统一的律师资格考试，要担任律师工作，只需进行七天的师资班培训。1981年1月21日，根据中央组织部、国家人事局、国家编制委员会、财政部、司法部《关于举办法律师资班的通知》的精神，经天津市编制委员会的批准，报给法律专业师资编制15名，暂列为行政编制，由天津市司法局统一管理，待政法干部学校正式建立后，转入干部学校编制。2月，司法部在中央政法干部学校举办了为期半年的法律师资培训班，主要是为当年秋季军队转业干部司法专业培训班准备师资力量。天津的李金生、路之岐、漆长全三人参加了此次师资培训班。

At the beginning of the restoration of the lawyer system, there was no unified lawyer qualification examination system. Those who worked as lawyers had to train for seven days in a teacher class. On January 21, 1981, in accordance with the spirit of the *Notice on Holding Legal Lawyers Class* by the Central Organization Department, the National Personnel Bureau, the National Editorial Board, the Ministry of Finance, and the Ministry of Justice, it was approved by the Tianjin Municipal Editorial Board and submitted to the legal professional faculty establishment. Fifteen were temporarily listed as administrative staff and managed by the Municipal Bureau of Justice. After the establishment of the municipal law management system, it will be transferred to the establishment of the municipal law management school. In February, the Ministry of Justice held a half-year training course for legal lawyers at the Central Political and Law Cadre School. Mainly prepared teachers for the judicial professional training class for demobilized military cadres in the fall of that year. In Tianjin, three people, including Li Jinsheng, Lu Zhiqi, and Qi Changquan, participated in the training courses for lawyers.

1986年4月12日，司法部发布了《关于全国律师资格统一考试的通知》，决定从1986年起实行全国范围的律师资格统一考试，考试合格者由司法部授予律师资格。当年9月27日和28日两天，律师资格全国统一考试在天津司法学校举行，天津市133名考生参加。此次考试规定只有律师事务所的专职律师和允许做兼职律师的人员才能报考，还属于"内部"性考试；1988年，这项考试开始面向全社会公开、公平选拔律师，为律师职业社会化创造了条件。此后，通过律师资格考试发展壮大律师队伍的方式渐渐超过了"归队""分配""招聘""特邀"，成为了主流。2002年，我国举行首届司法考试，将初任法官和初任检察官考试同律师资格考试合并，司法考试的历史进入了新纪元。

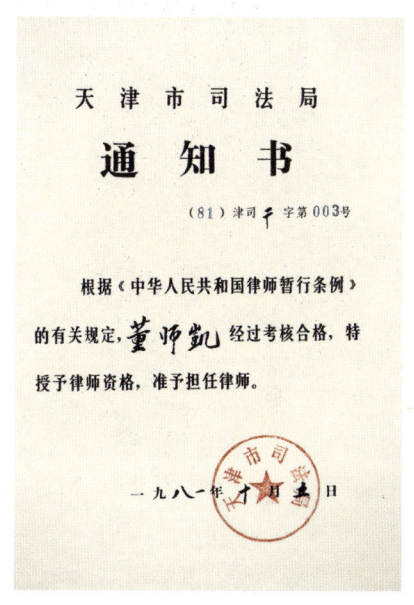

1981年10月天津市司法局授予董师凯的律师资格通知书

Notice of lawyer qualification granted to Dong Shikai by Tianjin Municipal Bureau of Justice in October 1981

1989年的律师资格证书

The lawyer's qualification certificate in 1989

法律职业资格证书
Legal professional qualification certificate

律师（特邀）工作证
Lawyer (invited) work permit

1997年全国律师资格考试考场
The 1997 National Lawyers Qualification Examination examination room

1997 年天津市部分考取律师资格人员合影

A group photo of some qualified lawyers in Tianjin in 1997

1999 年天津市司法局律师资格颁证宣誓仪式

In 1999, Tianjin Municipal Bureau of Justice Lawyer Qualification Certification Oath Ceremony

On April 12, 1986, the Ministry of Justice issued the *Notice on the Unified National Lawyers Qualification Examination*, which decided to implement a nationwide unified lawyer qualification examination from 1986. Those who pass the examination will be granted the qualifications of lawyers by the Ministry of Justice. On September 27th and 28th, a unified national examination was held at Tianjin Judicial School. 133 candidates from our city participated. This examination stipulated that only full-time lawyers in law firms and those who were allowed to work as part-time lawyers could apply for the examination. It was also an "internal" examination. By 1988, lawyers were selected openly and fairly for the whole society, opening up the possibility of professional socialization of lawyers. Since then, the way to develop and grow the lawyer team through the lawyer qualification examination has gradually surpassed the methods of "returning to the team," "allocation," "recruitment" and "special invitation" and has become the mainstream. By 2002, the first judicial examination of our country was held, and the examination for novice judges and prosecutors was merged with the qualification examination for lawyers, and the history of the judicial examination entered a new era.

1988年，遵照党的十三大报告关于"要改变国家包办律师事务的现状"的指示精神，全国各地逐步开展了律师体制改革工作。当年4月11日，天津市司法局下发了《关于建立"天津东方律师事务所"的通知》。《通知》指出，经局务会研究决定，并经司法部、天津市人民政府同意，决定成立天津东方律师事务所。4月19日，天津市政府又批转天津市司法局《关于我市律师体制改革的几点意见》，标志着天津以分配体制改革为重点的律师体制改革工作的开始，天津律师业从此进入了改革创新的阶段。

In 1988, in accordance with the instructions of the 13th National Congress of the Communist Party of China on "To change the status quo of state-run lawyers' affairs", various localities initiated the reform of the lawyer system. On April 11, 1988, the Municipal Bureau of Justice issued the *Notice on the Establishment of "Tianjin Dongfang Law Firm"*. The *Notice* pointed out that the Tianjin Dongfang Law Firm shall be established after the study and decision of the Bureau's Executive Council and the approval of the Ministry of Justice and the Municipal People's

Government. On April 19, 1988, with the approval of the Tianjin Municipal Bureau of Justice *Several Opinions on the Reform of the Lawyer System in Our City* by the Tianjin Municipal People's Government, our city took the lead in implementing the reform of the lawyer system focusing on the reform of the distribution system. The Tianjin law industry has entered a stage of reform and innovation.

5月23日，全国第一家合作制律师事务所——天津东方律师事务所举行开业典礼。天津市委常委、市委政法委书记鲁学政，司法部党组成员、全国律协常务副会长陈卓，司法部公律司司长丁增祺，天津市体改委、公检法、工商、税务、财政等有关部门的负责人，新华社、人民日报社等十余家媒体代表出席了这一典礼。鲁学政、陈卓亲自为天津东方律师事务所开业剪彩，市司法局局长赵儒基、副局长郑振亚分别介绍了该所的全体律师和成立情况，天津东方律师事务所主任李增产还举行了记者招待会。作为律师体制改革的试点，天津东方律师事务所首开不占国家编制，不由国家核拨经费，自收自支、自负盈亏、自我发展、自我约束的组织形式的先河。此后，国办所之外，合作所不断涌现，合作制律师事务所纷纷成立。

On May 23, Tianjin Dongfang Law Firm, the first cooperative law firm in the country, held an opening ceremony. Lu Xuezheng, Member of the Standing Committee of the Municipal Party Committee and Secretary of the Municipal Committee of Political and Legal Affairs, Chen Zhuo, Member of the Party Group of the Ministry of Justice and Executive Vice President of the National Lawyers Association, Ding Zengqi, Director of the Public Law Department of the Ministry of Justice, and persons in charge of relevant departments such as the Tianjin Municipal System Reform Commission, Public Security Bureau, Procuratorate, Court, Industry and Commerce Bureau, Taxation Bureau, Finance Bureau, etc. representatives from more than 10 news organizations including Xinhua News Agency and People's Daily attended the opening ceremony. Lu Xuezheng and Chen Zhuo cut the ribbon for the opening of the firm. Zhao Ruji, the director of the Municipal Bureau of Justice, and Zheng Zhenya, the deputy director of the Municipal Bureau of Justice, respectively introduced all the lawyers and the establishment of the firm to the guests. Li Zengchan, director of Dongfang Law Firm, held a press conference. As a pilot for the reform of the lawyer system, it is the first organization that does not account for the state's

天津市政府转呈天津市司法局《关于我市律师体制改革的几点意见》

Tianjin Municipal Government forwarded to the Tianjin Municipal Bureau of Justice *Several Opinions on the Reform of the Lawyer System in Our City* submitted to the Municipal Bureau of Justice

1988 年第一家合作制律师事务所——天津东方律师事务所成立

The first cooperative law firm, Tianjin Dongfang Law Firm, was established in 1988

天津市第一律师事务所曾是全国最大的律师事务所，是天津律师的"摇篮"

Tianjin No. 1 Law Firm was once the largest law firm in the country and the "cradle" of Tianjin lawyers

律师事务所分所执业许可证
Practicing license of law firm branch

establishment, does not allow the state to approve funds, and is self-receiving, self-financing, self-development, and self-discipline. After that, in addition to the state office, cooperative law firms began to emerge, and cooperative law firms were later established.

1988年7月26日,天津市司法局又下发了《关于贯彻执行〈天津市律师体制改革实施细则(试行)〉的通知》。《细则》包括总则、实行不同改革形式的有关原则规定等六章三十条内容,为天津的律师体制改革作出了规划。

On July 26, the Municipal Bureau of Justice issued the *Notice on the Implementation of the Detailed Rules for the Reform of the Lawyer System in Tianjin (Trial)*. The *Detailed Rules* include six chapters and 30 articles including general rules and relevant principles and regulations for implementing different reform forms, which laid out a plan for the reform of Tianjin's lawyer system.

1993年司法部发布了《关于深化律师工作改革的方案》,与国际接轨的合伙制律师事务所开始出现。在司法部方案的基础上,1994年,天津市司法局出台了《关于深化律师体制改革的实施办法》,规定了各律师事务所实行效益浮动工资,效益工资一般不能超过收入的40%,这便是直到现在还在广泛采用的"提成制"。这个《办法》同时提出了"解放思想,试办突破所有制的模式,发展不占国家编制和经费的多种模式的自律性律师事务所"。这一形式突破了原有律师机构的模式,符合当时加速建立适应社会主义市场经济需要的律师机构的改革精神。此后,不占国家编制、自愿组合、自收自支、自我约束、财产所有权归发起人所有的新型律师事务所开始成立。当时天津市批准成立了四方、天允、圆通、恒信、胜达、瀚洋、金旭七家律师事务所,到1995年,达到了40余家。

In 1993, the Ministry of Justice issued the *Plan on Deepening the Reform of*

Lawyers' Work. The partnership law firms that were in line with international standards began to appear. On the basis of the Ministry of Justice's plan, in 1994, the Tianjin Municipal Bureau of Justice issued the *Implementation Measures on Deepening the Reform of the Lawyers System*, and stipulated that law firms implement profitable variable wages, which generally cannot exceed 40% of their income. This is the "commission system" widely used until now. This *Measures* also proposes "emancipating the mind, piloting the establishment of a self-disciplined law firm that breaks through the ownership system and develops multiple models that do not account for the state's establishment and funding". The form broke through the model of the original law firm and was in line with the reform spirit of accelerating the establishment of a law firm adapted to the needs of the socialist market economy at that time. Since then, a new type of law firm that does not account for the state's establishment, voluntary combination, self-receipt, self-discipline, and property ownership belongs to the promoters began to be established. There are seven law firms including Sifang, Tianyun, Yuantong, Hengxin, Shengda, Hanyang, and Jinxu. By 1995, there were more than 40 self-regulatory law firms.

律师业务的变迁

CHANGES IN THE LAW PRACTICE

在律师制度恢复重建的初期，诉讼业务是多数律师事务所和律师的主要业务和看家本领。据统计资料显示，1980年，天津有律师事务所三家，律师50人，当年办理的业务主要有两类：一是刑事辩护，659件；二是民事代理，47件。1980—1989年的十年间，全市律师共办理刑事、民事、经济案件66345件。而作为后来在相当长的时间里律师业务主要开拓方向的非诉讼案件，1980年为0件，1981年为15件，至1989年九年间累计为2181件。

In the early days of the recovery and reconstruction of the lawyer system, litigation business was the main business and housekeeping skills of most law firms and most lawyers. Statistics show that in 1980, there were three law firms in Tianjin, with 50 lawyers. There were two main types of business handled that year: one was 659 criminal defense, and the other was 47 civil representation. During the ten years from 1980 to 1989, lawyers in the city handled 66,345 criminal, civil and economic cases. As a non-litigation case in which the lawyer's business was the main development direction for a long period of time, there were 0 case in 1980, 15 cases in 1981, and a total of 2,181 cases in the nine years to 1989.

律师制度恢复后，法律顾问业务得到了快速发展。1981年，天津市国际信托投资公司聘请第一法律顾问处的武宝锐律师任常年法律顾问，标志着天津律师制度恢复后，律师担任常年法律顾问的开端。到1981年年底，武宝锐律师共为公司审查与国内外缔结的合同42件，解答法律咨询8次，并对公司全体职工进行法制宣传，从而有效减少了公司的纠纷与诉讼，维护了公司的利益，同时也增强了职工的法制观念。法律顾问业务和非诉讼业务一样，在律师制度恢复后的相当长的时间里，是律师开拓业务的主要方向，也是律师和律师事务所生存的基本保障。特

律师执业证
Lawyer's license

天津市离退休法律工作者协会法律顾问证
Tianjin Retired Legal Workers Association Legal Counsel Certificate

在天津市第一招待所合影
A group photo at Tianjin No.1 Guest House

934	1935	1936	1937	1938	1939	1940	1941	1942	1943	1944	1945	1946
960	1961	1962	1963	1964	1965	1966	1967	1968	1969	1970	1971	1972
986	1987	1988	1989	1990	1991	1992	1993	1994	1995	1996	1997	1998
012	2013	2014	2015	2016	2017	2018	2019	2020	2021	……		

20 世纪 80 年代天津市司法局领导与部分律师合影

A group photo of the leaders of the Tianjin Municipal Bureau of Justice and some lawyers in the 1980s

别是在1988年律师体制改革以后，多数律师事务所实行自收自支的财务制度，法律顾问业务就显得越发重要了。据统计资料显示，1981年全市律师事务所仅有法律顾问1家，此后持续增长，1982年为8家，1988年为1982家，1989年为2390家。

In the development stage after the restoration of the lawyer system, the legal advisory business has developed rapidly. In 1981, Tianjin International Trust and Investment Company hired lawyer Wu Baorui from the First Legal Counsel Office as its permanent legal counsel. It is generally believed that this is the beginning of lawyers serving as perennial legal advisers after the restoration and reconstruction of the Tianjin lawyer system. By the end of the year, the lawyers had reviewed 42 contracts concluded between the company and domestic and foreign countries, answered 8 legal consultations, and conducted legal publicity to all employees of the company. This enabled the company to reduce disputes and litigation, maintained the company's economic benefits, and enhanced the legal concept of employees. The legal advisory business, like the non-litigation busines, has been the main direction for lawyers to expand their business during the initial recovery of the lawyer system for a long time, and is the basic guarantee for the survival of lawyers and law firms. Especially after the reform of the lawyer system in 1988, most law firms implemented a self-financing financial system, and the legal advisory business became more and more important. Previously, according to statistics, in 1981, the city's law firms had only one legal adviser. Since then, the number has continued to grow. There were 8 in 1982, 1,982 in 1988, and 2,390 in 1989.

相对于传统的诉讼业务，非诉讼业务为律师提供了更加广阔的发展空间。1993年，当时的对外经济贸易律师事务所的主要负责人之一吕常胜辞去公职，领衔创办了天津汇川律师事务所。这位有着在香港律师事务所研修、工作经历的带头人和他的律师事务所借鉴了香港律师操作房地产项目的业务模式，参与完成了天津市第一宗大型楼宇河川大厦的涉外销售，他们为天津律师业的发展推开了一扇新的窗户。1993年，天津环球磁卡股份有限公司作为天津市和中国制卡行业首家上市企业，其股票在上海证券交易所上市。天津金融律师事务所为上市提供了全程法律服务并出具了上市必备文件——法律意见书。这也是天津律师第一宗公司上市法律服务案例。

1988年10月第一法律顾问处成员合影(王金安律师提供)
A group photo of the First Legal Counsel Office in October 1988
(provided by lawyer Wang Jin'an)

Compared with traditional litigation business, non-litigation business provides lawyers with a broader space for development. In 1993, Lü Changsheng, one of the principal persons in charge of the Foreign Economic and Trade Law Firm at the time, resigned from public office and led the founding of Huichuan Law Firm. This leader with experience in studying and working in a Hong Kong law firm and his law firm drawing lessons from the business model of Hong Kong lawyers operating real estate projects, they participated in the completion of the foreign-related sales of Tianjin's first large-scale building, Hechuan Building. They opened a new window for the development of Tianjin's lawyers. In 1993, Tianjin Universal Magnetic Card Co., Ltd. was the first listed company in Tianjin and China's card manufacturing industry, and its stock was listed on the Shanghai Stock Exchange. Tianjin Finance Law Firm provided full legal services for listing and issued legal opinions as a necessary document for listing. This is also the first legal service case for a Tianjin lawyer to list a company.

1995年天津开展律师见证业务

In 1995, Tianjin started lawyer witness service

律师与天津市司法局工作人员合影

A group photo of lawyers and staff of the Tianjin Municipal Bureau of Justice

1921	1922	1923	1924	1925	1926	1927	1928	1929	1930	1931	1932	1933
1947	1948	1949	1950	1951	1952	1953	1954	1955	1956	1957	1958	1959
1973	1974	1975	1976	1977	1978	1979	1980	1981	1982	1983	1984	1985
1999	2000	2001	2002	2003	2004	2005	2006	2007	2008	2009	2010	2011

律师与司法局工作人员合影

A group photo of lawyers and staff of the Bureau of Justice

20世纪八九十年代的律师行业交流

THE LAWYER INDUSTRY EXCHANGES IN THE 1980S AND 1990S

20世纪80年代的律师十分重视对外交流工作。1983年2月27日，天津市法律顾问处副主任董师凯，律师赵光裕、丛英、韩建新、吕常胜应天津市科委之邀，参与研究了新加坡亿智企业集团与天津市合资建立天津科技咨询服务公司的相关事宜，并与该企业集团董事长杜亿春的法律顾问、美国联邦法院法官马丁进行了磋商，商谈后双方均表示满意。3月5日，天津市法律顾问处副主任郭一泓参加了以司法部副部长朱剑明为团长的一行十人的中国法律工作者代表团访问印度，为期11天。5月7日，天津市法律顾问处周荔律师参加了以中国法学会副会长王仲方为团长的一行四人的中国律师考察团访问美国加利福尼亚州和华盛顿州，为期21天。周荔也成为了新中国律师制度恢复后第一位代表天津出访的律师。

Lawyers in the 1980s attached great importance to foreign exchanges. On February 27, 1983, Dong Shikai, deputy director of the Municipal Legal Counsel Office, and lawyers Zhao Guangyu, Cong Ying, Han Jianxin, and Lü Changsheng were invited by the Municipal Science and Technology Commission to participate in the establishment of a joint venture between Singapore Yizhi Enterprise Group and Tianjin Municipal Science and Technology Consulting Service Company. Regarding matters, he discussed with the legal counsel of the chairman of the enterprise group Du Yichun and the judge of the US Federal Court, Mr. Martin, and both parties were satisfied after the discussion. On March 5th, Guo Yihong, deputy director of the Municipal Legal Counsel Office, participated in a 10-member delegation of Chinese legal workers headed by Zhu Jianming, Deputy Minister of Justice, to visit India, which lasted 11 days. On

最早代表天津律师出国访问的周荔律师
Lawyer Zhou Li, who was the first to represent Tianjin lawyers to visit abroad

周荔与部分律师在第一法律顾问处门前合影
Zhou Li and some lawyers took a group photo at the door of the First Legal Counsel Office

周荔律师访美纪念证明
Memorial certificate of lawyer Zhou Li's visit to the United States

20世纪80年代天津律师参与涉外交流活动
Tianjin lawyers participated in foreign exchange activities in the 1980s

May 7th, Lawyer Zhou Li from the Municipal Legal Counsel Office participated in a 4-member Chinese lawyers delegation headed by Wang Zhongfang, vice president of the Chinese Law Society, and visited California and Washington State in the United States for 21 days. Zhou Li has also become the first lawyer to travel on behalf of Tianjin after the restoration of the lawyer system of the People's Republic of China.

1985年5月1日至9日，以日本神户市市长宫崎辰雄为团长，包含七名律师协会成员的访华团到天津进行友好访问，市长李瑞环、副市长吴振亲切会见了访华团全体成员。司法部副部长朱剑明、中国法学会副会长王仲方也会见了访华团全体成员，天津市律师协会名誉会长陈以毅、天津市司法局局长宋树涛会见时在座。其间，七名访华团成员与天津律师就律师体制、制度，担任企业法律顾问的职责，律师资格的取得，办案的过程，经济纠纷的解决和依法治理城市等问题进行了广泛而深入的探讨。

From May 1 to 9, 1985, the delegation including seven members of the lawyers association headed by the Mayor of Kobe City, Miyazaki, Japan visited Tianjin for a friendly visit. Mayor Li Ruihuan and Deputy Mayor Wu Zhen cordially Meeting with all members of the visiting delegation; Vice Minister of Justice Zhu Jianming and Vice President of the Chinese Law Society Wang Zhongfang also met with all members of the visiting delegation. Chen Yiyi, Honorary Chairman of the Municipal Lawyers Association, and Song Shutao, Director of the Municipal Bureau of Justice were present at the meeting. During the period, the seven members of the delegation and Tianjin lawyers conducted extensive research and discussion on the lawyer system, institution, responsibilities as corporate legal advisers, acquisition of lawyer qualifications, process of handling cases, settlement of economic disputes, and governance of the city according to law.

1986年5月10日，应中国法学会会长王仲方的邀请，加拿大律师协会主席罗伯特·韦尔斯偕夫人来华访问，并专程到天津进行了为期三天的交流。其间，韦尔斯夫妇同天津市第二法律顾问处部分律师就律师在法律界的作用以及中加两国律师情况进行了座谈。天津市司法局局长赵儒基、副局长郑振亚，天津市律师协会会长宋树涛会见了来访客人。

On May 10, 1986, at the invitation of Wang Zhongfang, President of the Chinese Law Society, Robert Wells, President of the Canadian Lawyers Association, and his wife made a special visit to Tianjin during their visit to China. It lasted 3 days. During the visit, the Wells had a discussion with some lawyers of the Tianjin Second Legal Counsel Office on the role of lawyers in the legal profession and the situation of lawyers in the two countries. Zhao Ruji, Director of the Municipal

1986年郑振亚率韩惠英等律师访问日本

In 1986, Zheng Zhenya led lawyers such as Han Huiying to visit Japan

郑振亚一行在东京最高裁判所前

In 1986, Zheng Zhenya led Han Huiying and other lawyers to visit Japan in front of the Tokyo Supreme Court

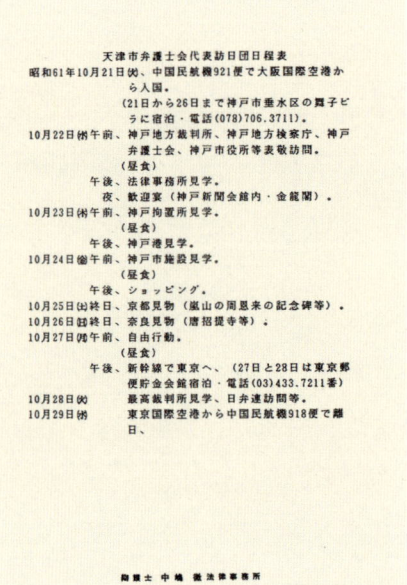

1986年郑振亚一行访问日本函件

Letter from Zheng Zhenya's visit to Japan in 1986

1934	1935	1936	1937	1938	1939	1940	1941	1942	1943	1944	1945	1946
1960	1961	1962	1963	1964	1965	1966	1967	1968	1969	1970	1971	1972
1986	1987	1988	1989	1990	1991	1992	1993	1994	1995	1996	1997	1998
2012	2013	2014	2015	2016	2017	2018	2019	2020	2021	……		

Bureau of Justice, Zheng Zhenya, Deputy Director of the Municipal Justice Bureau, and Song Shutao, Chairman of Tianjin Lawyers Association met with the visitors.

伴随着改革开放的深入和律师业务领域的拓展,律师行业间的交流不断深化。1991年4月27日至29日,由太平洋律师协会和中华全国律师协会联合主办的"中国及亚太地区投资和知识产权法律研讨会"在天津召开。来自苏联、南朝鲜、日本、马来西亚、菲律宾、泰国、澳大利亚、美国等14个国家和地区的200多名律师、学者参加了此次研讨会。大会向社会各界展示了天津,与会代表在会议期间参观了天津经济技术开发区,天津律师也与海内外的同行进行了充分的探讨与交流。

接待香港胡关李罗律师行代表团
Receiving the delegation of Hong Kong Woo, Kwan, Lee & Lo Law Firm

两岸交流
Cross-Strait exchange

与台湾律师交流
Cross-Strait exchange

接待日本名古屋律师
Reception of lawyers in Nagoya, Japan

接待泰国律师院代表团
Receiving a delegation of Thai lawyers

With the deepening of reform and opening up and the expansion of the lawyer's business field, the international exchanges between the lawyers industry were constantly deepening. From April 27 to 29, 1991, the "China and Asia Pacific Investment and Intellectual Property Law Seminar" co-sponsored by the Pacific Lawyers Association and the All China Lawyers Association was held in Tianjin. At that time, more than 200 lawyers, experts and scholars from 14 countries and regions including the Soviet Union, South Korea, Japan, Malaysia, the Philippines, Thailand, Australia, and the United States participated in the conference. The conference showcased Tianjin to all walks of life. During the conference, the participants visited the Tianjin Economic and Technological Development Zone. Tianjin lawyers and their counterparts from foreign and other regions also conducted thorough discussions.

为进一步拓宽律师对外交流的渠道，1993年，天津市律师协会与韩国仁川地方辩护士会结为友好姊妹协会，此后保持着每年一次的交流互访活动。1994年，天津市律师协会接待了美国、英国、加拿大、日本、韩国以及香港、台湾、澳门的律师代表团来访，经过友好协商签订的业务协作协议书就有六份，可以说是律师协会的对外交流年。这期间，也有很多律师走出了国门，以留学、出访、参加学术会议的形式与境外律师广泛接触，通过"引进来"和"走出去"，向全世界展示天津律师的风采。

In order to further broaden the channels for lawyers' foreign exchanges, in 1993, Tianjin Lawyers Association and the Incheon Local Advocate Association of Korea formed a sister association. Since then, the two cities' lawyers associations have maintained an annual exchange and visits. In 1994, Tianjin Lawyers Association received visits from lawyers from the United States, Britain, Canada, Japan, South Korea, Hong Kong, Taiwan, Macau and other countries and regions. There were six business cooperation agreements signed after friendly negotiations. It's the Foreign Exchange Year of the Lawyers Association. During this period, many lawyers also went out of the country to have extensive contacts with foreign lawyers in various forms such as studying abroad, visiting, and participating in academic conferences. Through "bringing in" and "Going Global", they showed Tianjin lawyers to all walks of life.

接待印度律师代表团

Receiving a delegation of Indian lawyers

1934	1935	1936	1937	1938	1939	1940	1941	1942	1943	1944	1945	1946
1960	1961	1962	1963	1964	1965	1966	1967	1968	1969	1970	1971	1972
1986	1987	1988	1989	1990	1991	1992	1993	1994	1995	1996	1997	1998
2012	2013	2014	2015	2016	2017	2018	2019	2020	2021	……		

接待巴基斯坦律师代表团
Receiving a delegation of Pakistani lawyers

春风化雨 重建新生（下）

THE SPRING WIND AND RAIN OF REBUILDING THE TIANJIN LAWYERS ASSOCIATION (II)

百年律师看天津
ONE HUNDRED YEARS OF LAWYERS ACCUMULATED HISTORY FOCUSED ON TIANJIN

《中华人民共和国律师法》的颁布
与律师制度改革的深化 / 388
THE PROMULGATION OF THE LAWYERS LAW OF THE
PEOPLE'S REPUBLIC OF CHINA AND THE DEEPENING OF
THE REFORM OF LAWYER SYSTEM

世纪之交的三次律师代表大会 / 392
THREE LAWYERS CONGRESSES AT THE
TURN OF THE CENTURY

律师业务的多元化发展与广泛的社会服务 / 400
DIVERSIFIED DEVELOPMENTS OF LAW
PRACTICE AND EXTENSIVE SOCIAL SERVICES

律师队伍的建设与发展 / 415
CONSTRUCTION AND DEVELOPMENT OF LAWYERS

一、党建工作 / 415
1. Communist Party of China Building Work

二、队伍建设 / 417
2. Team Building

三、人才培养 / 419
3. Personnel Training

世纪之交的律师行业交流 / 421
THE LAWYER INDUSTRY EXCHANGES
AT THE TURN OF THE CENTURY

《中华人民共和国律师法》的颁布与律师制度改革的深化

THE PROMULGATION OF THE *LAWYERS LAW OF THE PEOPLE'S REPUBLIC OF CHINA* AND THE DEEPENING OF THE REFORM OF LAWYER SYSTEM

1996年5月15日,经八届全国人大常委会第十九次会议审议通过,《中华人民共和国律师法》颁布,并于1997年1月1日起施行。《律师法》的颁布是我国律师事业发展中的一座新的里程碑。律师的身份也从"国家法律工作者"转变成了"社会法律工作者";律师不再是国家公职人员,而成了社会职业群体中的一员。与之配套的律师事务所,也随之出现了合伙制、合作制、国资所并存的格局,律师事业的发展跨入了崭新的时代。

On May 15, 1996, the *Lawyers Law of the People's Republic of China* was promulgated and went into effect on January 1, 1997 after being deliberated and adopted at the 19th meeting of the Standing Committee of the Eighth National People's Congress. The promulgation of the *Lawyers Law* is a new milestone in the development of my country's lawyers' career. The status of a lawyer has changed from a "national legal worker" to a "social legal worker". The lawyer is no longer a national public official, but a member of the social professional group. The corresponding law firm has also become a pattern of partnership, cooperation, and state-owned firms, and the development of the lawyer's career has entered a new era.

自1997年《律师法》实施以来,律师行业进入到一个规范发展的新时期,律师事务所的内部管理不断规范化,一些先进的管理理念和现代化的管理方法被运用到律师管理工作中,规模化的律师事务所开始出现并得到发展。律师的专业化分工不断提升，一批以房地产、金融、公司事务、知识产权、海事海商为主要业务内容的专业化律师事务所不断涌现。律师业务也深入到了重大经济社会活动以及立法、政府决策、参政议政、服务民生等各项工作中，天津律师业逐步走向了成熟。

Since the implementation of the *Lawyers Law* in 1997, the lawyer industry has entered a period of standardized development. The internal management of law firms has been continuously standardized. Some advanced management concepts and modern management methods have been used in the management of lawyers. Large-scale law firms began to appear and develop. The specialized division of labor in the law industry has continued to increase, and a number of specialized law firms with real estate, finance, corporate affairs, intellectual property rights, maritime affairs and maritime trade as their main business content have continued to emerge. The lawyer's business has also penetrated into major economic and social activities and legislation, government decision-making, participation in and discussion of politics, serving the people's livelihood, etc., and Tianjin's lawyer industry has gradually matured.

在改革与发展的进程中，天津律师迎来了新世纪。2000年8月，司法部在天津召开专题会议，对律师事务所的脱钩改制工作作出全面部署，下发了《律师事务所社会法律咨询服务机构脱钩改制实施方案》。随后，全国各地的律师事务所开始了脱钩改制工作。11月1日，天津市司法局在静海召开了天津市律师事务所脱钩改制工作会议，天津的律师体制再次进行重大变革，所有国办性质的律师事务所全部脱钩改制为合伙制或合作制，律师事务所成为了真正意义上的自主经营、自我发展、自负盈亏、自我约束的市场主体。当时，各项工作平稳进行，全市有66家律师事务所、331名律师在很短的时间内就办理了脱钩改制。到2001年，全市国资所的脱钩工作基本完成。

In reform and development, Tianjin lawyers ushered in a new century. In August 2000, the Ministry of Justice held a special meeting in Tianjin to make overall arrangements for the decoupling and restructuring of law firms, and issued the *Implementation Plan for the Decoupling and Restructuring of Law Firms' Social Legal*

2000年8月7日至8日全国司法行政系统中介机构
脱钩改制工作会议在天津召开

Working Conference on Decoupling and Restructuring of Intermediary Institutions of the National Judicial Administration System was held in Tianjin from August 7 to 8, 2000

Consultation Service Institutions. Subsequently, law firms across the country carried out decoupling restructuring. On November 1, the Tianjin Municipal Bureau of Justice held a meeting on the decoupling and restructuring of Tianjin law firms in Jinghai County. The Tianjin lawyer system has undergone major changes again. All state-run law firms have been decoupled and restructured into partnership or cooperative systems. Law firms have become market entities in the true sense of self-management, self-development, self-financing and self-restraint. At that time, various tasks were carried out smoothly. There were 66 law firms and 331 lawyers in the city underwent decoupling restructuring in a short period of time. By 2001, the decoupling of the city's state-owned assets offices was basically completed in that year.

2008年6月1日，新《律师法》开始实施。新《律师法》对律师进行了重新定义，由"为社会提供法律服务"变为"为当事人提供法律服务"，同时明确了律师的社会价值，即"律师三维护"：维护当事人的合法权益、维护法律正确实施、维护社会公平和正义，使律师职业的崇高性重新得到了认识。关于律师事务所的组织形式，新增了个人所，合作所退出了历史舞台，

全国司法行政系统中介机构脱钩改制工作会议
National Working Conference on Decoupling and Restructuring of Intermediary Institutions of the Judicial Administration

天津市律师事务所脱钩改制工作会议
Working Conference on Decoupling and Restructuring of Tianjin law firm

合伙所与个人所成为了律师事务所的主要形式，律师行业的发展又进入了一个新的时期。

On June 1, 2008, the new *Lawyers Law* came into effect. The new *Lawyers Law* redefines lawyers from "providing legal services to the society" to "providing legal services to clients", and clarifies the social value of lawyers, that is, the "three protections of lawyers": safeguarding the legal rights and interests of clients, maintain the correct implementation of the law, maintain social fairness and justice, and re-recognize the lofty nature of the lawyer's profession. Regarding the organizational form of law firms, individual firms have been added, cooperative firms have withdrawn from the stage of history, partnership firms and individual firms have become the main forms of law firms, and the development of the lawyer industry has entered a new era.

世纪之交的三次律师代表大会

THREE LAWYERS CONGRESSES AT THE TURN OF THE CENTURY

1997年6月8日至9日,天津市第四次律师代表大会召开。全市141名律师代表参加了大会。此时,天津律师事务所已发展到149家,其中国资所78家、合作所16家、合伙所55家,律师人数发展到2016名。

From June 8 to 9, 1997, the Fourth Lawyers Congress of Tianjin City was held. 141 lawyer representatives from the city attended the conference. At this time, Tianjin law firm has grown to 149, with 78 Chinese capital offices, 16 cooperative firms, 55 partnership firms, and the team of lawyers has grown to 2,016.

2002年6月14日至16日,天津市第五次律师代表大会召开。这次大会选举产生了全部由执业律师担任领导的新一届律师协会领导班子,实现了律师决策机构的职业化。同年12月28日,天津市律师协会会馆也正式启用,天津律师又有了自己的新家。

From June 14 to 16, 2002, the Fifth Tianjin Lawyers Congress was held. This conference elected a new lawyers association led by practicing lawyers, realizing the professionalization of lawyers' decision-making bodies. On December 28 of the same year, Tianjin Lawyers Association Hall was officially opened, and Tianjin lawyers had their new home.

2008年1月17日至19日,天津市第六次律师代表大会召开。大会选举出了41名理事、5名监事。与往届不同的是,这届律师协会增设了监事会,以加强协会对自身决策和执行的监督,确

天津市第四次律师代表大会
The Fourth Lawyers Congress in Tianjin

天津市第四次律师代表大会，天津律师界喜迎香港回归
The Fourth Lawyers Congress in Tianjin, Tianjin lawyers welcame the return of Hong Kong

天津市第五次律师代表大会合影
A group photo of the Fifth Lawyers Congress in Tianjin

1934	1935	1936	1937	1938	1939	1940	1941	1942	1943	1944	1945	1946
1960	1961	1962	1963	1964	1965	1966	1967	1968	1969	1970	1971	1972
1986	1987	1988	1989	1990	1991	1992	1993	1994	1995	1996	1997	1998
2012	2013	2014	2015	2016	2017	2018	2019	2020	2021	……		

天津市第五次律师代表大会投票
Voting at the Fifth Lawyers Congress in Tianjin

天津市第五次律师代表大会代表表决
Voting by representatives of the Fifth Lawyers Congress in Tianjin

天津市律师协会会馆启用仪式
Opening ceremony of Tianjin Lawyers Association Hall

天津市律师协会
Tianjin Lawyers Association

天津市律师协会办公室
Tianjin Lawyers Association Office

律师袍
Lawyer gown

保各项工作民主、规范、科学的运行。根据行业发展的特点,这届律师协会在原有11个专门委员会的基础上,又增设了行业创新与发展、青年律师工作、对外交流等专门委员会,进一步完善了律师协会的自律管理体系建设。在各个委员会的推动下,律师协会的上述各项工作也取得了显著成效。拓展业务是行业协会重要的职责之一,也是律师协会成立行业创新与发展委员会的主要目的。通过深入搭建法律服务需求市场对接平台,律师协会引导广大律师为重点领域开发、重大项目推进、各类企业发展提供法律服务。

From January 17th to 19th, 2008, the Sixth Lawyers Congress of Tianjin City was held. The conference elected 41 directors and 5 supervisors. Different from previous sessions, this session of the Lawyers Association has newly established a board of supervisors to strengthen the supervision of the association's own decision-making and implementation, and to ensure the democratic, standardized and scientific operation of various tasks. According to the characteristics of the development of the industry, on the basis of the original 11 special committees, this session of the Lawyers Association has added special committees for industry innovation and development, young lawyer work, and foreign exchange to further improve the construction of the Lawyers Association's self-discipline management system. Promoted by the work of the committee, the above-mentioned work has also achieved remarkable results. Business expansion is one of the important responsibilities of the industry association, which is also the main purpose of the Tianjin Lawyers Association to establish the Industry Innovation and Development Committee. Through in-depth establishment of a market docking platform for legal service demand, Tianjin Lawyers Association guides lawyers to provide legal services for the development of key areas, the promotion of major projects and the development of various enterprises.

天津市第六次律师代表大会
The Sixth Lawyers Congress in Tianjin

天津市第六次律师代表大会理事会第一次会议
The first meeting of the Tianjin Sixth Lawyers Congress Council

天津市第六次律师代表大会理事会第一次会议表决
Voting at the first meeting of the Tianjin Sixth Lawyers Congress Council

律师业务的多元化发展与广泛的社会服务

DIVERSIFIED DEVELOPMENTS OF LAW PRACTICE AND EXTENSIVE SOCIAL SERVICES

　　在深化改革的过程中，律师的服务领域持续拓宽，并朝着多元化方向发展。天津律师为第43届世界乒乓球锦标赛、"天交会"等重大活动提供法律支持，为企业改制、转轨提供法律服务，大力发展提存见证业务，积极开辟房地产交易、国有资产转让、金融、证券等新业务领域。同时，通过担任区、县政府法律顾问，广大律师为政府重大决策、对外开放、投资合作以及政务工作提供多样化的法律服务。律师不仅办理一般的刑事、民事案件，而且也办理投资贸易、不动产、股票、知识产权、海事海商、税务、高科技开发等业务，各类经济社会活动都有了律师的身影。

　　In the process of deepening reforms, lawyers' service areas have continued to expand. Lawyers have provided legal services for major events such as the 43rd World Table Tennis Championships and Tianjin Spring Commodities Fair, provided legal services for corporate restructuring and transformation, vigorously developed deposit witness business, and actively developed Real estate transactions, transfer of state-owned assets, finance, securities and other new business areas. At the same time, by serving as the legal adviser to the district and county governments, lawyers provide legal services for major government decisions, opening to the outside world, investment cooperation, and government affairs. Lawyers not only handle general criminal and civil cases, but also handle investment and trade, real estate, stocks, intellectual property, maritime affairs, taxation, high-tech

三八妇女节保障妇女权益宣传咨询公益活动
Women's Day Protection of Women's Rights
Publicity and Consultation Public Welfare Activities

development, and other businesses. Lawyers are present in various economic and social activities.

1997年5月28日，为加强法律援助工作，天津市成立了市级法律援助中心。此后，各区、县法律援助机构陆续成立，专业的律师法律援助队伍逐步建立，法律援助工作有了组织保障。

On May 28, 1997, in order to strengthen the legal aid work, Tianjin Legal Aid Center was established. Since then, legal aid agencies in various districts and counties have been established one after another, professional legal aid lawyers have been gradually established, and legal aid work has been organized and guaranteed.

在积极参与法律援助工作的同时，广大律师还热心公益事业，用爱心回报社会。1998年发生的特大洪灾牵动着天津律师的心，天津市律师协会于当年8月21日在天津市抗震纪念碑前举办了"天津律师界情系灾区、赈灾捐款"义务法律咨询活动，来自全市律师事务所的百余名律师参加了活动。在提供咨询的同时，广大律师还踊跃捐款，不到一小时，捐款数额就达到了20余万元，彰显了行业的社会责任心。

In actively participating in legal aid work, our city's lawyers are also enthusiastic about public welfare undertakings and repay society with love. The huge floods that occurred in 1998 touched the hearts of Tianjin lawyers. On August 21 of that year, Tianjin Lawyers Association organized the "Tianjin Lawyers Circle's Legal Consultation Activity for Disaster Relief Donations Obligation" compulsory legal consulting activities in front of the Tianjin Earthquake Monument. More than 100 lawyers from law firms participated in the event. While providing consultation, the lawyers also donated on the spot. In less than an hour at that time, the donation amount reached more than 200,000 yuan, demonstrating the social responsibility of the industry.

2000年前后，天津津华律师事务所、天津安信律师事务所的家庭法律顾问业务开展得如火如荼。针对公民家庭的需求特点和承受能力，律师事务所采用了收取较低签约费的方式，一般的家庭法律问题免费咨询，复杂的法律事务商议收费。2001年，仅津华律师事务所一家，就与340多户家庭签约，建立了法律顾问关系，一时成为业内与坊间热议的话题。2000年，全市律师事务所法律顾问达到6607家，这是全市法律顾问业务数量在这一阶段达到的最高峰。

Around 2000, the family legal advisory services of Jinhua and Anxin Law Firms were in full swing. According to the needs and affordability of citizens' families, law firms adopted lower signing fees, free consultation on general family legal issues, and negotiate fees for complex legal matters. In 2001, there was only one Jinhua Law Firm, which signed a contract with more than 340 families and established a legal counsel relationship, which became a hot topic in the industry and the public for a while. In 2000, the number of legal consultants of law firms in the city reached 6,607, which arrived the highest peak in the city at this stage.

2001年，中国加入了世界贸易组织（WTO），天津律师的很多工作便围绕此项工作展开。天津市律师协会在组建了行业规则、纪律维权和财务监督委员会后，又调整组建了民事经济、刑事辩护、电子商务、房地产、金融证券、海事海商和WTO法律咨询等业务委员会，并制定了相应的组织活动规则。为适应加入WTO的需要，有近千名律师接受了电子商务法律实务、美国法律制度和WTO系列讲座等方面的培训。在这一年，司法部律师公证司与全国律协、中央电视台联合举办的"首届全国律师电视辩论大赛"给全国观众留下了深刻印象，天津队最终获得了"最佳风格奖"。此次辩论赛给天津律师界带来的最大收获就是集中涌现出了一大批新人，他们后来很多都成为了律师事务所的主任或高级合伙人。

In 2001, China joined the World Trade Organization(WTO), and much of the work of Tianjin lawyers was carried out around this work. After the Tianjin Lawyers

2007年天津市司法局和天津市律师协会组织的"把法律交给群众，让律师走进万家"活动
In 2007, the "Give the Law to the Masses, Let Lawyers Enter in Every Family" organized by the Municipal Bureau of Justice and Tianjin Lawyers Association

Association established the industry rules, disciplinary rights protection and financial supervision committees, it adjusted and established the civil economy, criminal defense, e-commerce, real estate, financial securities, maritime affairs, and WTO legal consulting committees, and formulated corresponding committees rules for organizing activities. In order to meet the needs of WTO accession, nearly a thousand lawyers have received training in the e-commerce legal practice, the US legal system and WTO series of lectures. In this year, the "First National Lawyers TV Debate Competition" jointly organized by the Department of Lawyers and Notaries of the Ministry of Justice, the National Lawyers Association and China Central Television left a deep impression on the national audience. The Tianjin team finally won the "Best Style Award". The biggest gain that this debate brought to the Tianjin lawyers was that a large number of new people emerged in a concentrated manner, and many of them later became directors and senior partners of law firms.

2002年，天津市司法局制定了《关于在天津经济技术开发区实行公职律师试点工作的实施意见》，开展了公职律师与公司律师的试点工作；"天津律师网"的开通实现了律师行业管理与服务工作的网络化、信息化；天津市女律师联谊会、执业纠纷调解委员会、业务发展与继续教育委员会相继成立，律师行业的自律管理体系不断健全。

In 2002, the Tianjin Municipal Bureau of Justice formulated the *Implementation Opinions on the Pilot Work of Public Lawyers in Tianjin Economic and Technological Development Zone*, and carried out the pilot work of public lawyers and corporate lawyers; the "Tianjin Lawyer Website" was launched, and the lawyer industry management and service work has been networked and informatized; Tianjin Female Lawyers Association, the Practice Dispute Mediation Committee, and the Business Development and Continuing Education Committee have been established, and the industry's self-discipline management system has been continuously improved.

在"两结合"管理体制不断完善、行业自律管理职能不断健全的背景下，律师服务经济社会发展的能力也在不断提升。这一时期，天津律师为"海河工程"等重大项目提供法律服务，并将触角深入到经济建设的各个领域。广大律师有效地服务国企改制、金融证券业改革，为

34	1935	1936	1937	1938	1939	1940	1941	1942	1943	1944	1945	1946
60	1961	1962	1963	1964	1965	1966	1967	1968	1969	1970	1971	1972
86	1987	1988	1989	1990	1991	1992	1993	1994	1995	1996	1997	1998
12	2013	2014	2015	2016	2017	2018	2019	2020	2021	……		

21 世纪初天津部分女律师风采
Some female lawyers in Tianjin in the early 21 century

2004 年庆"三八"天津市女律师才艺展示大舞台
2004 "March 8th" Tianjin female lawyer talent show stage

"两会"建言献策,并在参与服务保障和改善民生的工作中充分发挥作用。律师的社会作用不断被社会各界所认识与肯定。

With the continuous improvement of the "two-combination" management system and the continuous improvement of industry self-discipline management functions, the ability of lawyers to serve economic and social development has also been continuously improved. During this period, Tianjin lawyers provided legal services for major projects such as the "Haihe Project" and extended their tentacles to various fields. Lawyers effectively serve the reform of state-owned enterprises and financial and securities reforms. Lawyers provide advice and suggestions for the "two sessions", and give full play to their role in participating in service guarantees and improving people's livelihood. The social role of lawyers is constantly recognized and affirmed by all walks of life.

2006年,天津市滨海新区开发开放纳入国家总体发展战略布局,天津市的法律服务行业也迎

天津律师积极参政议政

Tianjin lawyers participate in politics

来了发展的历史性机遇。为应对滨海新区开发开放，天津市律师协会组织开展了"海归律师滨海创业座谈会"，整合有海外教育背景的律师资源，为滨海新区的开发开放提供全方位的法律服务。同时又举办了"国有企业改制与律师服务""《破产法》与企业转制重组"座谈会，积极推荐律师为国企改制和民营经济发展提供法律服务。广大律师积极介入滨海新区金融改革和土地管理改革筹划工作，承接了建立渤海银行、天津港、空港物流加工区、滨海国际机场改扩建等基础设施建设工程的法律服务业务。据统计，2006年天津律师共担任法律顾问4625家，办理刑事诉讼案件3518件、民事案件12766件、经济案件5713件、行政案件409件，办理非诉讼法律事务11180件，全年业务总收入40137万元。律师的法律服务成为促进经济社会发展的重要力量。

In 2006, the development and opening up of Tianjin Binhai New Area was incorporated into the overall national development strategy layout, and Tianjin's legal service industry also ushered in a historic opportunity for development. In response to the development and opening up of the Binhai New Area, Tianjin Lawyers Association organized the "Symposium for Overseas Returned Lawyers to Start a Business in Binhai" to integrate the resources of lawyers with

与海外同行交流

Communication with overseas counterparts

overseas education backgrounds to provide a full range of legal services for the development and opening up of the Binhai New Area. Held the "State-Owned Enterprise Restructuring and Lawyers Service", "*Bankruptcy Law* and Enterprise Restructuring and Reorganization" symposiums, and actively recommended lawyers to provide legal services for the reform of state-owned enterprises and the development of private economy. The majority of lawyers actively participated in the financial reform and land management reform planning of Binhai New Area, and undertook legal services for the establishment of infrastructure construction projects such as Bohai Bank, Tianjin Port, Airport Logistics Processing Zone, and Binhai International Airport. In 2006, Tianjin lawyers served as legal advisors to 4,625 companies in total, handled 3,518 criminal cases, 12,766 civil cases, 5,713 economic cases, 409 administrative cases, handled 11,180 non-litigation legal affairs. The total annual business income is 401.37 million yuan. Lawyers' legal services have become an important force in promoting economic and social development.

在开展各类法律服务的过程中，广大律师集合各方面的优势，发挥团队作用，有效介入经济社会的各个领域。2005年，受天津市人大常委会法工委委托，天津市律师协会组织律师起草了《天津市制定地方性法规听证办法（草案）》，并由市人大常委会审议通过，在全国开创了律师协会接受委托起草地方性法规草案的先河。2006年，律师协会又接受市政府法制办和市国土房管局委托，完成了《天津市城镇房屋交易管理条例（草案）》的起草工作，并获得通过。广大律师在参与地方立法和法规修改工作中充分发挥了专业作用。在服务重大赛事和重大经贸活动中，律师也进行了有效参与。2007年组建了奥运律师顾问团，为2008年北京奥运会天津分赛区基础工程建设和各项组织工作提供法律服务。18家律师事务所参加了由天津市政府、全国工商联和美国企业成长协会共同主办的"中国企业国际融资洽谈会"。此后历届融洽会，律师均积极参与。

In the process of carrying out various legal services, lawyers in our city gather superior resources from various aspects, give full play to team advantages and effectively intervene in various fields of economy and society. In 2005, entrusted by the Legal Work Committee of the Standing Committee of Tianjin Municipal People's Congress, Tianjin Lawyers Association organized lawyers to draft the

高从善副局长（右）代表天津市司法局和奥运律师顾问团签署奥运律师顾问法律服务协议

Deputy Director Gao Congshan (right), on behalf of the Municipal Bureau of Justice and the Lawyers Advisory Group, signed the legal service agreement for Olympic lawyers and consultants

Hearing Measures for Formulating Local Laws and Regulations in Tianjin, which was reviewed and approved by the Standing Committee of the Municipal People's Congress. At that time, it was the first time in China that lawyers associations were entrusted to draft local laws and regulations. In 2006, Tianjin Lawyers Association was entrusted by the Legislative Affairs Office of the municipal government and the Municipal Bureau of Land and Housing Management to complete the drafting of the *Regulations on the Administration of Urban Housing Transactions in Tianjin (Draft)*, which was passed. Lawyers have fully played their professional role in participating in the revision of local legislation and regulations. At the same time, lawyers also participate effectively in serving major events and major economic and trade activities. In 2007, an advisory group of Olympic lawyers was set up to provide legal services for infrastructure construction and various organizational work in Tianjin Division of the 2008 Olympic Games. Eighteen law firms participated in the "International Financing Fair for Chinese Enterprises" co-sponsored by Tianjin Municipal Government, All-China Federation of Industry and Commerce and American Enterprise Growth Association. Since then, lawyers from all previous symposiums have actively participated.

"作家走近律师"启动仪式
The launching ceremony of "the Writer Approached the Lawyer"

律师的服务工作得到了社会各界的广泛关注。2007年年底,天津市司法局、天津市律师协会组织开展了"作家走近律师"活动。活动历时一年,以作家的视角看天津律师,从不同侧面记录律师的工作与行业发展,这种方式在当时引起了社会大众的强烈反响。

The lawyer's service has received extensive attention from all walks of life. At the end of 2007, Tianjin Municipal Bureau of Justice and Tianjin Lawyers Association organized the activity of "the Writer Approached the Lawyer", which lasted for one year. From the perspective of writers, Tianjin lawyers were seen and lawyers' work and industry development were recorded from different aspects, which caused different repercussions from the public at that time.

2008年以来,围绕服务天津市重点项目建设,天津市律师协会组建了律师顾问团,为第六届东亚运动会、天津夏季达沃斯论坛等活动提供全程法律服务，得到了市委、市政府的高度评价。围绕服务企业发展，律师协会组建了"中小企业法律服务团"，在全行业开展"百名律师进百家民营企业""律师进企业，牵手共发展"的专项活动，通过"一帮一、结对子"的形式，让律师主动深入企业，实实在在地为企业办实事。围绕服务新农村建设，律师协会组建了农村城镇化业务委员会，组织全市律师，特别是郊区县律师为天津推进农村示范工业园区、农业产业园区和农民居住社区联动建设，促进"三改一化"提供法律服务。

Since 2008, Tianjin Lawyers Association has organized a lawyers advisory team to serve the construction of key projects in our city to provide full legal services for the Sixth East Asian Games, Tianjin Summer Davos Forum, etc., and have been highly praised by the Municipal Party Committee and the Municipal Government; Enterprise development, the establishment of the "SME Legal Service Group", and special activities such as "a Hundred Lawyers Enter a Hundred Private Enterprises", "Lawyers Enter the Enterprise, and Develop Together with Hands" in the whole industry, through the form of "one group, one pair", let lawyers take the initiative to go deep into the company and actually do practical things for the company; centered on serving the construction of a new countryside, Tianjin Lawyers Association's Rural Urbanization Business Committee was established to organize lawyers from the whole city. In particular, lawyers in suburban counties promoted the joint construction of rural demonstration industrial parks, agricultural industrial parks and farmer residential communities for Tianjin and provides legal services in the trial of "three reforms and one transformation".

在各项工作有效开展的同时，天津律师继续深入参与各类公益事业，在助学、济困、赈灾等各个领域都有律师的身影。2008年"5·12"汶川大地震发生后，全市律师积极行动起来，主动要求为灾区捐款捐物，并通过各种渠道捐款92万余元。2009年迎来了新中国律师制度恢复重建30周年。12月27日，天津市律师协会在喜来登大酒店举办了天津律师制度恢复重建30周年纪念表彰大会暨天津律师协会2009年年会。来自全市各区、县的400余名律师参加了此次大会。会议对评选出的"十佳青年律师""十佳公益律师""十佳公益律师事务所"进行了表彰，并授予12位律师"律师事业特殊贡献奖"、46位律师"律师荣誉奖"。

While all the work is being carried out effectively, lawyers in our city continue to participate deeply in various public welfare undertakings, and have lawyers in various fields such as helping students, helping the poor and relieving the disaster. After the "512" Wenchuan Earthquake in 2008, lawyers in the whole city took active actions and volunteered to donate money and materials to the disaster areas, and donated more than 920,000 yuan through various channels. In 2009, it ushered in the 30th anniversary of the restoration and reconstruction of the lawyer system. On December 27, Tianjin Lawyers Association held the 30th anniversary commendation conference and 2009 annual meeting of Tianjin lawyers system restoration and reconstruction at Sheraton Hotel. More than 400 lawyers from all districts and counties in the city attended the conference. The meeting commended the selected "Top Ten Young Lawyers" "Top Ten Public Welfare Lawyers" and "Top

天津市纪念律师制度恢复重建30周年纪念表彰大会签名背板
Signature backboard for commemorating the 30th anniversary of the restoration of lawyer system

Ten Public Welfare Law Firms", and awarded 12 lawyers "Special Contribution Award for Lawyers" and 46 lawyers "Honor Award for Lawyers".

2011年7月27日,天津市法律服务中心正式落成并启用,为天津律师业的发展带来了新的动力。作为全国首家集法律援助接待、律师法律服务、法律服务人才交流于一体的专门服务群众的场所,服务中心的设立,增强了天津法律服务的能力与水平。位于法律服务中心内的律师协会新会馆设置有服务大厅、报告厅、多功能厅、健身厅、纪律法庭等新的场所,使新会馆集合了办公、会议、培训、文体、娱乐、健身等多功能于一身,进一步完善了律师协会的管理与服务功能。新会馆启用以来,为有效利用协会资源,开展了各类培训及文体活动,使每位会员真正享受到了协会"家"一样的温暖。2011年12月4日,天津市律师协会与天津电视台,天津电台滨海广播、经济广播,北方网在法律服务中心联合举办了"天津市法律服务中心开放日"系列宣传活动。此后,律师协会定期或不定期地在休息日、节假日和宣传日举办"法律服务中心开放日"活动,由多家知名律师事务所的律师为群众答疑解惑。为进一步扩大律师的服务范围,律师协会与北方网合作开办了《律师帮办》栏目,组织律师事务所实时在线,为网民提供法律咨询服务,打造"天津最大的网上法律服务平台",得到了社会各界的强烈反响。在各项工作的引导下,广大律师与律师事务所把强化法制宣传、服务为民作为职业价值的体现和追求目标,主动深入百姓之中,开展公益活动,并在众多律师事务所中将公益服务形成常态。

On July 27, 2011, Tianjin Legal Service Center was officially completed and opened, which brought new impetus to the development of the lawyer industry in Tianjin. As the first place in China that integrates legal aid reception, lawyers' legal service and legal service talent exchange to serve the masses, the establishment of the center has enhanced the ability and level of legal service in our city. The new guild hall of the Lawyers Association, located in the legal service center, has set up new places such as service hall, lecture hall, multi-function hall, fitness hall and disciplinary court, which makes the new guild hall integrate office, conference, training, style, entertainment and fitness, and further improves the management and service functions of the association. Since the opening of the new guild hall of the Lawyers Association, various trainings and cultural and sports activities have been carried out to make effective use of the resources of the association, so that every member can truly enjoy the warmth of the "home" of the lawyers association. On December 4, 2011, Tianjin Lawyers Association, Tianjin TV Station, Tianjin Radio Binhai Broadcast, Tianjin Radio Economic Broadcast and Tianjin Enorth jointly organized a series of publicity activities of "Tianjin Legal Service Center Open Day" in the Municipal Legal Service Center. Since then, Tianjin Lawyers Association has insisted on holding the "Open Day of Legal Service Center" regularly or irregularly on rest days, holidays and publicity days, where lawyers from many well-known law firms answered questions for the masses. In order to further expand the scope of lawyer services, Tianjin Lawyers Association cooperated with Enorth to launch the column of "Lawyers' Deputy Office", organized real-time online law firms, provided legal consulting services for netizens, and created "the largest online legal service platform in Tianjin", which received enthusiastic response from the society. Under the guidance of all the work, the lawyers and law firms in our city regard strengthening legal publicity and serving the people as the embodiment and pursuit of professional value, actively go deep into the people and carry out public welfare activities, and form a normal public welfare service mode in many law firms.

律师队伍的建设与发展

CONSTRUCTION AND DEVELOPMENT OF LAWYERS

一、党建工作

1. Communist Party of China Building Work

2003年11月，为加强律师行业的党建工作，经天津市委组织部批准，中共天津市司法局委员会律师协会工作委员会正式成立。律师协会党工委的成立，标志着天津律师行业管理在加强党的领导、紧密党的联系等方面进入了一个新的阶段。

In November 2003, with the approval of the Organization Department of the Municipal Party Committee, the Working Committee of the Lawyers Association of the Tianjin Municipal Bureau of Justice Committee of the Communist Party of China was established in order to strengthen the party building work in the lawyer industry. The establishment of the Party Working Committee of Lawyers Association marks that the management of the lawyer industry has entered a new stage in strengthening the leadership of the party and keeping close ties with the party.

自律师协会党工委成立以来，通过以党建引领和保障律师行业正确发展方向为指引，党的影响力和凝聚力不断增强，律师党员的先锋模范作用更加突出，2009年还实现了党的组织和党的工作在律师行业的全覆盖。几年来，通过开展"学习实践科学发展观""保持党的纯洁性教育""创先争优"等主题教育实践活动以及律师事务所党支部书记培训班、全市律师行业党建知识竞赛、"党员奉献五个一"等主题实践活动的举办，律师队伍的思想政治素质得到了切实加强，并且引导律师回馈社会、服务社会。

Since the establishment of the Party Working Committee of the Municipal Lawyers Association, the party's influence and cohesion have been continuously enhanced by leading and ensuring the correct development direction of the lawyer industry through party building, and the vanguard and exemplary role of lawyer party members has become more prominent. In 2009, the full coverage of the party organization and work in the lawyer industry was realized. In recent years, through carrying out educational practice activities such as "Studying and Practicing the Scientific Concept of Development", "Maintaining the Purity of the Party", "Striving for Excellence", holding training courses for party branch secretaries of law firms, knowledge contest on party building in the whole city's lawyer industry, and carrying out practical activities such as "Five Ones Contributed by Party Members",

党建工作

Communist Party of China building work

the ideological and political quality education of lawyers was strengthened, and lawyers were guided to give back and serve the society.

二、队伍建设
2. Team Building

1999年，适逢新中国律师制度恢复重建20周年，天津隆重举办了优秀律师报告会暨为从业20年律师颁发荣誉证书大会，为28名从1979年开始执业的律师颁发了荣誉证书。值得一提的是，这一年的5月28日至30日，天津市司法局和天津市第一中级人民法院共同举办了"99审改中法官、律师角色研讨会"。全市130余名法官、律师、法律界人士以及新闻媒体参加了会议。会议围绕审判改革的宏观思考，审判改革相关制度、证据制度，法官、律师角色等议题展开了广泛的交流与研讨。与会人员一致认为，司法公正有如天平，法官是秤盘，律师是秤盘上的砝码，实现天平的平衡，法官与律师都应在各自不同的岗位履行各自不同的职责。会议还向全市法官、律师发出了一份倡议书。

In 1999, coinciding with the 20th anniversary of the restoration and reconstruction of the lawyer system, Tianjin held a grand conference of excellent lawyers reporting conference and honorary certificates for lawyers who have worked for 20 years, and awarded honorary certificates to 28 lawyers who started practicing in 1979. It is worth mentioning that, from May 28 to May 30 of this year, Tianjin Municipal Bureau of Justice and Tianjin No.1 Intermediate People's Court jointly held the "Seminar on the Role of Judges and Lawyers in the Reform in 1999". More than 130 judges, lawyers, legal professionals and news media units attended the meeting. The meeting focused on macro-thinking of trial reform, related systems of trial reform, evidence system, roles of judges and lawyers, and conducted extensive exchanges and discussions. Participants agreed that judicial justice is like a balance, judges are scales, lawyers are weights on scales, and to achieve balance, lawyers and judges should perform their respective duties in different positions. The meeting also sent a proposal to judges and lawyers in the city.

为了提高律师队伍的素质，解决学历教育问题，从2003年开始，天津市律师协会委托天津市广播电视大学政法学院为天津律师举办了学制两年的本科学历教育班。在规范、整顿、净化与教育的过程中，律师队伍不断发展壮大。

In order to improve the quality of lawyers and solve the problem of academic education, since 2003, Tianjin Lawyers Association has entrusted the School of Political Science and Law of Tianjin Radio and TV University to hold a two-year undergraduate education class for Tianjin lawyers. In the process of standardization, rectification, purification and education, the team of lawyers continues to grow and develop.

2004年，全国律师行业开展了律师队伍集中教育整顿活动，从4月份开始一直持续到当年年底。天津律师在天津市司法局和天津市律师协会的组织下，开展了"三项教育"，加强了"三个规范"的教育整顿工作，取得了显著成效，律师队伍进一步得到净化。同年4月16日，为强化行业诚信和加强律师职业道德建设，天津律师执业责任保险、人身意外伤害保险签约仪式暨新闻发布会召开。通过为全市所有注册律师投保律师执业责任保险和人身意外伤害保险，律师行业的社会信用得到了进一步的提升，同时也保障了律师的执业权益。

In 2004, the national lawyer industry launched a centralized education and rectification campaign for lawyers. From April to the end of the year, under the organization of the Municipal Bureau of Justice and the Municipal Lawyers Association, Tianjin lawyers carried out the education and rectification work of "three educations" and strengthening "three norms". This work has achieved remarkable results, and the lawyer team has been further purified. On April 16th of this year, in order to strengthen the integrity of the industry and the construction of lawyers' professional ethics, the signing ceremony and press conference of Tianjin lawyers' practice liability insurance and personal accident insurance were held. By insuring all registered lawyers in the city with lawyer's practice liability insurance and personal accident insurance, we will further enhance the social credit of the lawyer industry and protect the lawyer's practice rights and interests.

三、人才培养

3. Personnel Training

律师服务领域的拓宽与对外交流的发展，需要更多的优秀人才加入到律师行业中来。1997年，天津律师界开展了天津首届律师人才信息交流会，为律师事务所与已经或即将取得律师资格的人员搭建交流平台。此后每年都会举办这样的信息交流会，很多行业内的优秀人才通过该渠道进入到了律师队伍中。

The expansion of lawyer service field and the development of foreign exchange require more talents to join the industry. In 1997, Tianjin lawyers launched the first Tianjin lawyers talent information exchange conference, which set up a communication platform for law firms and those who have obtained or will soon obtain lawyer qualifications. Since then, such information exchange meetings have been held every year, and many outstanding talents in the industry have entered the lawyers through this channel.

青年律师是律师业发展的未来。伴随着行业的发展，青年律师在整个队伍中的比重不断增加，如何更好地发挥他们的作用，对于行业持续健康发展具有重要的意义。为了给青年律师搭建更广阔的发展平台，2008年4月，共青团天津市律师协会工作委员会在全国率先成立，"青年律师法律服务团"也随之成立。服务团的成立，将分散在各个岗位上的青年律师团结到一起，形成了一支跨越各个执业领域和各个专业方向的律师团队。多年来，服务团律师深入社区、走上街头，普及法律知识，解答法律诉求，受到了广大人民群众的热烈欢迎，青年律师已将法律的触角伸向了社会的方方面面。为推动青年律师队伍实现整体协调发展，帮助广大青年律师解决后顾之忧，2009年5月，律师协会下发了《关于青年律师执业会费减免的通知》，决定对30岁以下、首次在津申请执业的专职律师实行第一个注册年度免缴律师会费、第二个注册年度减半缴纳律师会费的规定。该政策惠及每一位新入行的青年律师。

Young lawyers are the future of lawyers. With the development of the industry, the proportion of young lawyers in the whole team is increasing. How to play their role well is of great significance to the sustained and healthy development of the industry. In order to build a broader development platform for young lawyers, in

April 2008, the Working Committee of Tianjin Lawyers Association of the Communist Youth League was first established in China, and the "Young Lawyers Legal Service Group" was subsequently established. With the establishment of the service corps, the young lawyers scattered in their respective posts are condensed together, forming a team of lawyers spanning all fields of practice and all professional directions. Over the years, lawyers of the service corps have gone deep into the community and taken to the streets to popularize legal knowledge and answer legal demands, which have been warmly welcomed by the broad masses of the people, and young lawyers have extended their legal tentacles to all aspects of society. In order to promote the overall coordinated development of young lawyers and help the majority of young lawyers solve their worries, in May 2009, the Municipal Lawyers Association issued the *Notice on the Reduction and Exemption of Young Lawyers' Practice Fees*, and decided to implement the regulations of exempting lawyers' fees in the first registration year and paying lawyers' fees in half in the second registration year for full-time lawyers under 30 years old who applied for practice in Tianjin for the first time. This policy benefited every new young lawyer.

世纪之交的律师行业交流

THE LAWYER INDUSTRY EXCHANGES AT THE TURN OF THE CENTURY

1997年香港回归，天津市司法局、市律师协会与市公证协会共同举办了"97庆香港回归，天津—香港律师界法律与实务报告会"，两地律师就香港回归后相关法律事务的前瞻性课题进行了研究。此后，津港律师业务交流与合作的领域不断拓宽，往来日益频繁。1998年7月27日，香港律师在天津设立的首家办事处——香港简家骢律师事务所天津办事处开业。2004年5月13日至14日，在天津市司法局举办的"津港澳台法律服务合作与发展论坛"中，市司法局、律师协会与香港律师会、澳门律师公会分别签订了津港、津澳两地律师业交流与合作协议，天津嘉德恒时律师事务所与香港简家骢律师行签订了联营协议，使天津律师对外交流合作不断深化。

In 1997, after the return of Hong Kong, Tianjin Municipal Bureau of Justice, Tianjin Lawyers Association and Tianjin notarization association jointly held the "Celebrating the Return of Hong Kong in 1997, Tianjin-Hong Kong Law and Practice Conference". Lawyers from both sides had conducted a study on the forward-looking issues related to legal affairs after the return of Hong Kong. Since then, the areas of business exchanges and cooperation between Tianjin and Hong Kong lawyers have continued to expand, and exchange activities have become more frequent. On July 27, 1998, the first office of Hong Kong lawyers in Tianjin—— the Tianjin Office of Fred Kan & Co. opened. From May 13 to 14, 2004, in the "Tianjin-Hongkong-Macao-Taiwan Legal Services Cooperation and Development Forum" held at the Tianjin Municipal Bureau of Justice, the Municipal Bureau of Justice, Tianjin Lawyers Association, the Hong Kong Law Society and the Macau Bar Association have signed agreements on exchanges and cooperation between Tianjin, Hong Kong and Tianjin and Macao lawyers. Tianjin J.D.Hands Law Firm singed a joint venture agreement with

香港简家骢律师事务所天津办事处开业典礼
The opening ceremony of the Tianjin Office of Fred Kan & Co.

津港澳台法律服务合作与发展论坛
Tianjin-Hongkong-Macao-Taiwan Legal Service Cooperation and Development Forum

34	1935	1936	1937	1938	1939	1940	1941	1942	1943	1944	1945	1946
60	1961	1962	1963	1964	1965	1966	1967	1968	1969	1970	1971	1972
36	1987	1988	1989	1990	1991	1992	1993	1994	1995	1996	1997	1998
12	2013	2014	2015	2016	2017	2018	2019	2020	2021	......		

津港澳台法律服务合作与发展论坛

Tianjin-Hongkong-Macao-Taiwan Legal Service Cooperation and Development Forum

Fred Kan & Co., which made the foreign exchange of Tianjin lawyers continuously deepened.

2005年11月4日至5日,天津成功举办了"第五届中国律师论坛"。来自美国、西班牙、英国、澳大利亚、德国、韩国、日本、俄罗斯、新加坡、香港、澳门11个国家和地区的律师代表和国内500多家律师事务所的律师代表1200余人参加了此次论坛。论坛以"构建和谐社会与律师业发展"为主题,以"促进天津法律服务业跨越式发展,更好地服务滨海新区建设"为宗旨,向社会各界全面展示了天津经济社会发展的成果,进一步扩大了天津法律服务业的对外交流与合作。

From November 4 to 5, 2005, Tianjin successfully held the "Fifth China Lawyers Forum". More than 1,200 representatives from the legal profession from 11 countries and regions including the United States, Spain, the United Kingdom, Australia,

1921	1922	1923	1924	1925	1926	1927	1928	1929	1930	1931	1932	19
1947	1948	1949	1950	1951	1952	1953	1954	1955	1956	1957	1958	19
1973	1974	1975	1976	1977	1978	1979	1980	1981	1982	1983	1984	19
1999	2000	2001	2002	2003	2004	2005	2006	2007	2008	2009	2010	20

2005年第五届中国律师论坛

The Fifth China Lawyers Forum in 2005

天津律师在第五届中国律师论坛授奖仪式上

Awarding ceremony of Tianjin lawyers at the Fifth China Lawyers Forum

Germany, South Korea, Japan, Russia, Singapore, Hong Kong, and Macau and from more than 500 domestic law firms participated in the forum. With the theme of "Building a Harmonious Society and the Development of Lawyers" and the purpose of "promoting the leap-forward development of Tianjin's legal service industry and better serving the construction of Binhai New Area", this forum fully demonstrated the achievements of Tianjin's economic and social development to all walks of life. It further expanded the foreign exchanges and cooperation of Tianjin's legal service industry.

加强各种形式的对外交流,组织律师"走出去",并将国外资深律师或学者"引进来",是天津市律师协会对外交流工作委员会成立后的重点工作。行业对外交流工作呈现出了规模大、范围广、方式新的特点。面对新的挑战,除坚持固定的交流合作项目以外,律师协会还扩大了与美国、德国、英国等国家的交流范围,不断开辟新的合作项目。2008年,举办了首届"中国—德国律师国际论坛""中美法律研讨会",组织律师参加了"中英法律研讨会",并开展了美国俄克拉荷马城市大学律师培训项目;2009年,组织律师代表团拜访英国大律师公会,确定开展英国BPP律师培训项目;2010年,与中国政法大学中欧法学院、德国汉堡律师协会合作开展"法治国家中律师的作用与功能"律师职业培训项目。多种形式的国际交流开阔了天津律师的视野,加深了全世界对天津律师的了解,为天津律师更广泛地开展对外交流与合作创造了条件。

Strengthening various forms of foreign exchanges, organizing lawyers to "Going Global", and "bringing in" senior foreign lawyers or scholars are the key tasks after the establishment of the Municipal Lawyers Association's Foreign Exchange Working Committee. It can be said that the industry's foreign exchange work has shown the characteristics of large-scale, wide-ranging, and new methods. In the face of new challeges, besides the fixed exchange and cooperation projects, the Lawyers Association had also expanded the scope of exchanges with the United States, Germany, the United Kingdom and other countries, and constantly opened up new cooperation projects. In 2008, organized the "First Sino-German Lawyers International Forum", "Sino-US Law Seminar", organized lawyers to participate in the "Sino-British Law Seminar", and carried out the lawyer training program of Oklahoma City University in the United States; in 2009, organized lawyer delegation went to

Britain to visit the British Bar Association and decided to carry out the British BPP lawyer training project; in 2010, China Europe law school, China University of Political Science and Law and Hamburg Lawyers Association cooperated to carry out the lawyer professional training project named "the role and function of lawyers in a country ruled by law". Through various forms of international exchanges, Tianjin lawyers have broadened their horizons, deepened the understanding of Tianjin lawyers from all walks of life, and created conditions for Tianjin lawyers to conduct more extensive foreign exchanges and cooperation.

2008年首届中国—德国律师国际论坛

The First Sino-German Lawyers International Forum in 2008

1934	1935	1936	1937	1938	1939	1940	1941	1942	1943	1944	1945	1946
1960	1961	1962	1963	1964	1965	1966	1967	1968	1969	1970	1971	1972
1986	1987	1988	1989	1990	1991	1992	1993	1994	1995	1996	1997	1998
2012	2013	2014	2015	2016	2017	2018	2019	2020	2021	……		

2016 年天津市律师协会在西班牙交流工作

Tianjin Lawyers Association exchanges work in Spain in 2016

新时代 新律师 新征程
NEW ERA, NEW LAWYER, NEW JOURNEY

壮丽70年 辉煌40载

百年律师看天津
ONE HUNDRED YEARS OF LAWYERS ACCUMULATED HISTORY FOCUSED ON TIANJIN

新时代 新风貌 / 430
NEW ERA, NEW ASPECT

一、天津市第七次律师代表大会 / 430
1. The Seventh Lawyers Congress in Tianjin

二、天津市第八次律师代表大会 / 432
2. The Eighth Lawyers Congress in Tianjin

三、党的十八大、十九大以来律师行业再上新台阶 / 440
3. The Lawyer Industry has Reached a New Level since the 18th and 19th National Congress of the Communist Party of China

依法治国的担当 / 485
RESPONSIBILITY FOR THE RULE OF LAW

建党百年新征程 / 522
A NEW JOURNEY FOR THE CENTENARY OF THE COMMUNIST PARTY OF CHINA

一、百年征程，波澜壮阔；百年初心，历久弥坚 / 522
1. The Journey of a Century has been Magnificent; a Century Later, the Heart will Become Stronger with Time

二、促进依法行政 / 524
2. Promoting Administration According to Law

三、护航经济发展 / 525
3. Escorting Economic Development

四、服务对外开放，聚焦"一带一路"涉外法律服务 / 528
4. The Service is Open to the Outside World, Focusing on "The Belt and Road Initiative" Foreign-Related Legal Services

五、参与社会治理和"送法下乡"活动 / 532
5. Participating in Social Governance and Sending Law to the Countryside

新时代 新风貌

NEW ERA, NEW ASPECT

一、天津市第七次律师代表大会

1. The Seventh Lawyers Congress in Tianjin

党的十八大高举中国特色社会主义伟大旗帜，从战略全局上对我国经济发展作出了全面规划和部署，踏着新时代的步伐，天津律师事业的发展再上一个新台阶。第七届天津市律师协会带领全市广大律师，围绕全面建成小康社会的宏伟战略目标，全面落实经济建设、政治建设、文化建设、社会建设和生态文明建设的五位一体总布局，引领和推动新时代天津律师行业高质量发展。

The Eighteenth National Congress of the Communist Party of China held high the great banner of socialism with Chinese characteristics and made a comprehensive plan and deployment for my country's economic development from a strategic overall perspective. Following the pace of the new era, the development of Tianjin's lawyer career has reached a new level. The 7th Tianjin Lawyers Association led the city's lawyers to comprehensively implemented the five in one general layout of economic construction, political construction, cultural construction, social construction and ecological civilization construction around the grand strategic goal of building a moderately prosperous society in an all-round way. It led and promoted the high-quality development of Tianjin lawyer's industry in the new era.

天津律师行业的发展离不开各级领导的关心和重视，在各级领导的关怀、支持和全市广大律师的共同努力下，天津律师业呈现出良好的发展态势。从2012年到2015年，全市律师从5217

天津市第七次律师代表大会

The Seventh Lawyers Congress in Tianjin

人增长至7513人，增长了44%；律师事务所从563家发展至833家，增长了48%。全市律师共办理诉讼案件170519件，非诉讼法律事务38138件，担任政府、企事业单位法律顾问24347家，总收入60.06亿元，业务收入逐年增长，分别为29.8%、19.3%、43.8%和29.7%。三名律师担任中共天津市第十一次党代会代表，93名律师担任各级人大代表与政协委员，比第六届律师协会增长了35%。天津市律师协会也多次被评为天津市先进社会组织。

The development of Tianjin's lawyer industry is inseparable from the care and attention of leaders at all levels. With the care and support of leaders at all levels and the joint efforts of lawyers throughout the city, the Tianjin lawyer industry has shown a good development trend. From 2012 to 2015, the number of lawyers in the city increased from 5,217 to 7,513, an increase of 44%; law firms grew from 563 to 833, an increase of 48%. The city's lawyers handled 170,519 litigation cases, 38,138 non-litigation legal affairs, and acted as legal counsel for the government, enterprises and institutions in 24,347, with a total income of 6.006 billion yuan, and business income increased year by year, respectively 29.8%, 19.3%, 43.8% and 29.7 %. Three lawyers served as representatives of the 11th Party Congress of the Communist Party of China in Tianjin, and 93 lawyers served as representatives of the People's Congress at all levels and members of the CPPCC, an increase of 35% over the previous session. Tianjin Lawyers Association has also been rated as an advanced social organization in Tianjin for many times.

二、天津市第八次律师代表大会

2. The Eighth Lawyers Congress in Tianjin

2019年是新中国成立70周年及新中国律师制度恢复重建40周年，也是天津市律师行业挑战与机遇、发展与荣光并存的一年。第八届天津市律师协会坚持以习近平新时代中国特色社会主义思想为指导，深入学习贯彻党的十九大和十九届二中、三中、四中全会精神，深入贯彻落实习近平总书记对律师工作的重要指示，树牢"四个意识"，坚定"四个自信"，做到"两个维护"。在天津市司法局党委的坚强领导下，全市广大律师团结奋进，锐意进取，行业发展全面加速。

2019年6月16日天津市第八次律师代表大会召开
The Eighth Lawyers Congress in Tianjin was held on June 16, 2019

天津市第八次律师代表大会
The Eighth Lawyers Congress in Tianjin

2019 marks the 70th anniversary of the founding of the People's Republic of China and the 40th anniversary of the restoration of lawyer system. It is also a year where challenges and opportunities, development and glory coexist in Tianjin's lawyer industry. The 8th Tianjin Lawyers Association adhered to the guidance of Xi Jinping Thought on Socialism with Chinese Characteristics for a New Era, and thoroughly studied and implemented the spirit of the nineteen and nineteen sessions of the second, third and fourth plenary sessions of the party, and thoroughly implemented the important instructions of General Secretary Xi Jinping on the work of lawyers. It firmly adhered to the "Four Consciousnesses" and strengthened the "Four Matters of Confidence", and achieved "Two Upholds". Under the strong leadership of the Party Committee of the Municipal Bureau of Justice, the majority of lawyers in the city united and forged ahead with determination, and the development of the industry accelerated in an all-round way.

换届以来，各级领导高度重视律师工作，天津市司法局党委书记、局长王红卫，市司法局党委委员、副局长、市律师行业党委书记刘基智多次深入律师行业视察指导工作。在各级领导的关怀、支持和全市广大律师的共同努力下，天津律师业呈现出良好的发展态势。截至2020年6月，全市共有律师事务所899家（其中个人制所487家、普通合伙制所402家、特殊的普通合伙制所9家、国资制所1家），律师8274人（其中专职律师6653人、兼职律师212人、派驻律师419人、法律援助律师48人、公职律师681人、公司律师261人）。根据司法部数据显示，截至2019年年末，天津市律师人数占常住总人口比例为0.052%，居全国第三，仅次于北京和上海。全市律师担任党政机关、人民团体、企事业单位法律顾问9174家，办理诉讼案件87906件、非诉讼案件17398件，业务总收入23.78亿元，比上一年度增长9.1%。

Since the change of office, leaders at all levels have attached great importance to the work of lawyers. Wang Hongwei, secretary and director of the Municipal Bureau of Justice, and Liu Jizhi, member of the Party Committee and deputy director of the Municipal Bureau of Justice, and Secretary of the Party Committee of the Municipal Lawyers Industry have conducted inspections and guidance work in the lawyer industry for many times. With the support and joint efforts of the majority of lawyers in the city, Tianjin's lawyers have shown a good development trend. As of June 2020, there are a total of 899 law firms in the city (including 487 individual law firms, 402 general partnership firms, 9 special general partnership firms, and 1 state-owned firm), and 8,274 lawyers (including 6,653 full-time lawyers, 212 part-time lawyers, 419 assigned lawyers, 48 legal aid lawyers, 681 public lawyers, and 261 corporate lawyers). According to data from the Ministry of Justice, as of the end of 2019, the number of lawyers in Tianjin accounted for 0.052% of the total permanent population, ranking third in the country, second only to Beijing and Shanghai. The city's lawyers acted as legal advisers for party and government agencies, people's organizations, enterprises and institutions with a total number of 9,147. They handled 87,906 litigation cases and 17,398 non-litigation cases. The total business income was 2.378 billion yuan, and it was 9.1% higher than the previous year.

京津冀律师协会监事工作交流会
Work Exchange Meeting of Beijing, Tianjin and Hebei
Lawyers Association Supervisor

天津市律师协会惩戒委员会在工作中
The Disciplinary Committee of the Tianjin Lawyers Association is working

天津市律师协会宣传及文化建设委员会新媒体宣传工作座谈会
Culture and Propaganda Committee of Tianjin Lawyers Association and New Media Work Forum

1934	1935	1936	1937	1938	1939	1940	1941	1942	1943	1944	1945	1946
1960	1961	1962	1963	1964	1965	1966	1967	1968	1969	1970	1971	1972
1986	1987	1988	1989	1990	1991	1992	1993	1994	1995	1996	1997	1998
2012	2013	2014	2015	2016	2017	2018	2019	2020	2021	……		

天津市律师协会政府法律顾问专业委员会
Tianjin Lawyers Association Government Legal Advisory Committee

天津市律师协会法律援助与公益法律事务委员会工作部署会
Work deployment meeting of Tianjin Lawyers Association legal aid and public welfare legal affairs committee

第八届天津市律师代表大会第二次会议
The Second Congress of the Eighth Lawyers Congress in Tianjin

第八届天津市律师协会理事会第二次会议
The Second Meeting of the Eighth Council of Tianjin Lawyers Association

律师代表大会小组讨论
Group discussion at the Lawyers Congress

第八届天津市律师协会未成年人保护专业委员会第一次会议
The First Meeting of the Eighth Tianjin Lawyers Association Juvenile Protection Professional Committee

三、党的十八大、十九大以来律师行业再上新台阶

3. The Lawyer Industry has Reached a New Level since the 18th and 19th National Congress of the Communist Party of China

（一）律师行业党建工作取得新成效

(a) New Results of Party Building have been Achieved in the Lawyer Industry

"党建兴、行业兴；党建新、行业新。"天津市律师行业全面加强新时期党的建设，全市党员律师人数占比居全国领先地位，省（市）级以下律师行业党组织全覆盖、健全行业党建制度和抓实支部建设等工作均走在全国前列，得到了全国律师行业党委调研组的充分肯定。天津市律师协会成立了天津市律师行业党校，举办形式多样的学习座谈会、知识竞赛、文艺演出，切实发挥律师基层党组织的战斗堡垒作用和党员先锋模范作用，涌现出一批全国律师行业先进党组织和优秀党员。同时，以天津市党外律师统战示范基地为载体，律师协会加强理论武装，抓实行业统战工作，在南开区、河西区、西青区设立区级行业统战工作联络站，广泛开展专题培训等活动，团结、组织、引领党外律师，增进政治共识，保持正确方向。

"Party building prosperous and industry development; Party building new, industry new." Tianjin lawyer industry has comprehensively strengthened party building in the new era. The number of party members and lawyers in the city has a leading position in the country, and the party organizations of the lawyer industry below the provincial (municipal) level are fully covered. The work of improving the industry's party building system and realizing branch construction are in the forefront of the country, which has been fully affirmed by the research team of the national lawyer industry Party Committee. Tianjin Lawyers Association established the Tianjin Lawyers Industry Party School, held various forms of study seminars, knowledge contests, and theatrical performances to effectively play the role of a fighting fortress of the grassroots party organizations of lawyers and the vanguard and exemplary role of party members, and a number of advanced party organizations and outstanding party members in the national law industry have emerged. At the same time, using the Tianjin Non-Party Lawyers United Front Demonstration Base as a carrier, Tianjin Lawyers

2018年12月25日党建工作示范点授牌仪式暨律师行业党建工作推动会

December 25, 2018, Communist Party of China building work demonstration site award ceremony and lawyer industry Party building work promotion meeting

2019年7月24日西青区联络站成立揭牌仪式

Inauguration ceremony for the establishment of the Xiqing District Liaison Station on July 24, 2019

南开区联络站

Nankai District Liaison Station

Association strengthened theoretical arms and extensively carried out special training and other activities to unite, organize, and lead non-Party lawyers, enhance political consensus, and maintain the right direction.

2016年9月5日至6日，中共中央政治局常委、全国政协主席俞正声来到天津，深入律师事务所、企业、学校和宗教场所，考察、了解新的社会阶层人士和非公有制经济人士工作等方面的情况。

From September 5 to 6, 2016, Yu Zhengsheng, member of the Standing Committee of the Political Bureau of the CPC Central Committee and Chairman of the National Committee of the Chinese People's Political Consultative Conference, came to Tianjin to visit law firms, enterprises, schools and religious sites to investigate and understand the work of people from new social strata and non-public economy.

俞正声主席强调，新的社会阶层人士是统一战线工作的重要着力点，要着力培养一支与党同心同德的新的社会阶层代表人士队伍，建立完善新的社会阶层人士组织，健全发现、培养、选拔工作机制，为他们履职尽责积极创造条件；要建立经常性联系渠道，关注他们的利益诉求，引导他们不断增强对党和政府的向心力。

Chairman Yu Zhengsheng emphasized that people from the new social class are an important focus of united front work. We should focus on cultivating a new contingent of representatives of social strata who have the same mind as the party, establishing and improving organizations for people from new social strata, and improving the mechanisms for identifying, training the selecting people from new social strata, so as to create conditions for them to perform their duties actively. It is necessary to establish regular contact channels, pay attention to their interests, and guide them to continuously strengthen their centripetal force towards the party and the government.

9月5日下午，俞正声主席在天津市委领导及天津市司法局党委书记、局长张铁英，天津市律师协会会长杨玉芙等领导的陪同下，深入天津四方君汇律师事务所，详细了解律师从业、参与社会服务和党建工作的情况。俞正声主席还与四方君汇律师事务所合伙人会议主席马弘亲切交谈。

On the afternoon of September 5, accompanied by the leaders of Tianjin municipal Party committee, Zhang Tieying, Secretary of the Party committee and director of Tianjin Municipal Bureau of Justice, and Yang Yufu, President of Tianjin Lawyers Association, president Yu Zhengsheng went to Tianjin Join & High Law Office to learn more about lawyers' practice, participation in social services and Party building. Chairman Yu Zhengsheng also had a cordial conversation with Ma Hong, Chairman of the Partners Meeting of Tianjin Join & High Law Office.

2020年，全市律师行业党建工作实现全规范、全统领、全覆盖。

In 2020, the city's lawyer industry party building work achieved full standardization, full command, and full coverage.

截至2020年5月，全市党员律师有2538人，占律师总数的34.9%。市级律师行业党委一个，区级律师行业党委六个、党总支十个，律师事务所党委两个、党总支两个、独立支部327个、联合支部101个。市、区、基层党组织三级联动，全力推进行业党建工作全规范、全统领、全覆盖，不断提升行业党建工作整体水平。全行业深入开展"不忘初心、牢记使命"主题教育活动，组织召开主题教育动员部署会、工作推进会，开展巡回指导工作，在规定动作"六个一"的基础上，确定具有天津特色的"八个一"工作目标，切实发挥律师基层党组织的战斗堡垒作用和党员先锋模范作用，得到了全国律师行业党委巡回指导组的充分肯定。

As of May 2020, there are 2,538 party lawyers in our city, accounting for 34.9% of the total number of lawyers. There are 1 city-level lawyer industry party committee, 6 district-level lawyer industry party committees, 10 general party branches, 2 law firm party committees, 2 general party branches, 327 independent branches, and 101 joint branches. The city, district, and grassroots party organizations are linked at three levels to fully promote the overall leadership, full coverage and full standardization of party building work in the industry, and continuously improve the overall level of party building work in the industry. The whole industry has carried out in-depth education activities on the theme of "remain true to the Party's original aspiration and founding mission", organized thematic education mobilization deployment meetings, work promotion meetings, and carried out tour guidance work. On the basis of the stipulated action "Six Ones", it was determined that there are Tianjin characteristics. The "Eight Ones" work goal, to effectively play the role of a fighting fortress of the grassroots party organizations of lawyers and the vanguard and exemplary role of party members, has been fully affirmed by the itinerant steering group of the national lawyer industry party committee.

全国律协秘书处党小组到天津市律师协会开展调研

The Communist Party of China Group of the Secretariat of the National Lawyers Association went to Tianjin Lawyers Association to conduct research

党外律师开展专题培训活动
Special training for non-Party lawyers

中共北京盈科（天津）律师事务所党委选举大会
Beijing Yingke (Tianjin) Law Firm Communist Party of China Committee Election Conference

上海锦天城（天津）律师事务所党支部学习场景
Learning scene of Shanghai Allbright (Tianjin) Law Office Party branch

天津四方君汇律师事务所全体党员学习大会
The Party Committee of Tianjin Join & High Law Office organized a study conference for all party members

国浩（天津）律师事务所党组织学习场景
Party organization learning scene of Grandall Law Firm (Tianjin)

天津市律师协会坚持大抓基层、大抓支部，高度重视行业党的建设，常态化开展巡回检查，扎实推进全市律师事务所"党建进章程"和"四同步"工作。截至2020年年末，全市所有律师事务所均实现了"党建进章程"，新成立的律师事务所均按照"四同步"原则建立了党支部，实现了党对律师工作的全面领导。

Tianjin Lawyers Association insists on focusing on the grassroots and branches, attaches great importance to the party building of the industry, conducts regular inspections, and steadily promotes the "Party Building into the Constitution" and "Four Synchronizations" work of the city's law firms. As of the end of 2020, all law firms in the city have implemented the "Party Building into the Constitution", and the newly established law firms have established party branches in accordance with the "four synchronizations" principle, realizing the party's overall leadership of lawyers.

2020年4月9日天津市律师行业党委开展天津市律师行业党建工作示范点"回头看"巡回检查

On April 9, 2020, the Tianjin Lawyers Industry Party Committee carried out the demonstration point of the city's lawyers industry Party building work "Looking back" it inerant inspection

天津市律师协会坚持严规矩、强作风，以行业党校和统战工作实践创新示范基地为平台，开展律师事务所党组织书记全员轮训和"党外律师大讲堂"活动，组织部分律师事务所党支部书记赴外省市开展主题培训及党建工作交流，持续推送"空中党课""党建微课堂"，推进律师政治学习教育培训常态化、长效化。

Tianjin Lawyers Association adheres to strict rules and strong work style. It uses industry party schools and united front work practice innovation demonstration bases as a platform to carry out rotation training for all party secretaries of law firms and "Non-Party Lawyers Lecture Hall" activities, and organize party branch secretaries of some law firms to carry out thematic training and party building work exchanges in other provinces and cities, and continue to push the "air party class" and "party building micro-classes" to promote the normalization and long-term effect of lawyers' political learning education and training.

2020年，天津市律师协会聚焦规范管理，强化监督，深入开展规范律师执业行为专项教育整顿活动，组成了七个调研组赴全市部分律师事务所实地调研督导，修订完善了《天津市律师协会会员处分规则》，推进惩治律师低价恶意竞争工作，向全市律师事务所、广大律师发出了《关于抵制不正当低价竞争维护良好发展环境的倡议书》，号召广大律师坚决抵制律师执业环境中存在的不良现象，自觉维护律师行业公平竞争的发展秩序和良好的社会形象，推动天津律师业持续健康的发展。

In 2020, Tianjin Lawyers Association will focus on standardizing management, strengthening supervision, and in-depth development of special education and rectification activities to regulate the practice of lawyers. It has formed 7 research teams to conduct field surveys and supervision of some law firms in 16 districts of the city, and revised and improved the *Tianjin Lawyers Association Member Disciplinary Rules*, promoted the punishment of low-price and malicious competition by lawyers, and published the *Proposal on Resisting Unfair and Low-Priced Competition and Maintaining a Good Development Environment* to law firms and lawyers throughout the city, call on the majority of lawyers to resolutely resist the bad phenomenon in the practice environment of lawyers, consciously maintain the

规范律师执业行为专项教育整顿

Special education and rectification for standardizing lawyers' practice

1921	1922	1923	1924	1925	1926	1927	1928	1929	1930	1931	1932	
1947	1948	1949	1950	1951	1952	1953	1954	1955	1956	1957	1958	
1973	1974	1975	1976	1977	1978	1979	1980	1981	1982	1983	1984	
1999	2000	2001	2002	2003	2004	2005	2006	2007	2008	2009	2010	

2020年9月"学四史 知党情 强党性"天津律师事务所党组织书记在古田会议会址培训

September 2020, "Learning Four History, Knowing Party Affection and Strengthening Party Spirit" Tianjin Law Firm's Party Organization Secretary was trained at the Gutian Conference Site

2020年9月"学四史 知党情 强党性"天津律师事务所党组织书记在古田培训，全体学员在古田会议会址宣誓

September 2020, "Learning Four History, Knowing Party Affection and Strengthening Party Spirit" Tianjin Law Firm's Party Organization Secretary was trained in Gutian, and all the trainees took an oath at the Gutian Conference site

1934	1935	1936	1937	1938	1939	1940	1941	1942	1943	1944	1945	1946
1960	1961	1962	1963	1964	1965	1966	1967	1968	1969	1970	1971	1972
1986	1987	1988	1989	1990	1991	1992	1993	1994	1995	1996	1997	1998
2012	2013	2014	2015	2016	2017	2018	2019	2020	2021	……		

2020年9月"学四史 知党情 强党性"天津律师事务所党组织书记在古田培训,全体学员在松毛岭战役纪念碑前举行授旗仪式

September 2020, "Learning Four History, Knowing Party Affection and Strengthening Party Spirit" Tianjin Law Firm's Party Organization Secretary was trained in Gutian, and all the trainees held a flag-giving ceremony at the Songmaoling Battle Monument

2020年11月部分党外律师赴西柏坡参加"弘扬爱国奋斗精神、建功立业新时代"专题培训班
In November 2020, some non-Party lawyers went to Xibaipo to carry out a special training course on "Carrying forward the spirit of patriotic struggle and making meritorious achievements in the new era"

扶贫消费日,律师参与消费扶贫
The lawyers participated in poverty alleviation through consumption on Poverty Alleviation and Consumption Day

development order of fair competition in the lawyer industry and a good social image, and promote the sustainable and healthy development of Tianjin's lawyer industry.

（二）围绕中心服务大局，律师工作展现新作为

(b) Focusing on the Center and Serving the Overall Situation, the Work of Lawyers Shows New Deeds

天津市律师协会围绕党和国家中心工作，紧贴天津经济发展实际，深入搭建平台，为推进"一带一路"建设、京津冀协同发展、雄安新区等国家重点工作以及天津自贸实验区建设、深化国企改革等市级重点项目保驾护航；同时组织律师深入服务法治政府建设，做好党委、政府的法律参谋；积极化解社会各类矛盾纠纷，参与化解和代理涉法涉诉信访案件、刑事案件律师辩护全覆盖、扫黑除恶专项斗争等相关工作；不断拓宽行业服务社会民众渠道，着力推进律师参与覆盖城乡居民的公共法律服务体系建设和12348公共法律服务热线平台建设。

Tianjin Lawyers Association focuses on the work of the Party and the country, closely follows the actual development of Tianjin's economy, and builds a platform in depth to promote the construction of "the Belt and Road Initiative", the coordinated development of Beijing-Tianjin-Hebei, the Xiongan New Area and other national key tasks, as well as the construction of the Tianjin Free Trade Pilot Zone, deepen the reform of state-owned enterprises and other key municipal projects to escort, organize lawyers to serve private enterprises in depth; serve the construction of the rule of law government, do a good job in the legal counseling of the party committee and the government; actively resolve various social contradictions and disputes, participate in the resolution and representation of legal and litigation-related petition cases, achieve the full coverage of defense by lawyers in criminal cases, and launch the national special campaign of crackdown on gang crime and other related work; continue to broaden the channels for the industry to serve the public, and strive to promote the participation of lawyers in the construction of the public legal service system covering urban and rural residents and the 12348 public legal service hotline platform construction.

2019年1月22日天津市律师协会、公证协会、进出口商会战略合作研讨暨签约仪式

On January 22, 2019, Tianjin Lawyers Association, Notary Association, and Import and Export Chamber of Commerce Strategic Cooperation Seminar and Signing Ceremony

（三）加强行业自律管理，实现新突破
(c) Self-Discipline Management to Achieve New Breakthroughs

天津市律师协会不断提升履职能力，定期召开代表大会、理事会和会长会议，建立述职评议考核机制，推动各工作机构有效履职。同时加强机构建设，新增三个专门委员会和七个专业委员会；完善内部治理结构，成立了15个区律师工作委员会。各区律工委不断完善服务，积极开展形式多样、内容丰富的活动。律师协会还积极健全内部管理制度，组织制定、修订《天津律师诚信信息管理披露办法》等26项自律性规则、规范，协会自律管理纳入了规范化、制度化的轨道。

Tianjin Lawyers Association has continuously improved the ability to perform duties, held regular congresses, councils and chairperson meetings, established a work report, appraisal and assessment mechanism, and promoted the effective performance of duties by various working institutions. At the same time, we strengthened the construction of institutions, added three special committees and seven professional committees; improved the internal governance structure, and established 15 district lawyer working committees. The legal work committees of all districts continue to improve their services and actively carry out activities in various forms and rich in content. The Municipal Lawyers Association has also actively improved its internal management system, organized the formulation and revision of 26 self-discipline rules and regulations including the *Tianjin Lawyers' Credit Information Management and Disclosure Measures*, and the association's self-discipline management has been brought into a standardized and institutionalized track.

天津市律师协会着眼文化传承、书写未来，把新时代天津市律师行业文化建设摆在自律管理工作更加突出的位置，深入开展行业优秀文化传承培育活动。同时制定《天津市律师行业党建工作评选表彰办法》，修订《天津市律师协会会员表彰奖励办法》，使行业内评优表彰工作常态化、规范化；开展天津市律师行业统筹疫情防控和经济社会发展先进评选和"最美女律师"评选活动，充分展示天津律师的风采。

疫情期间表彰决定
Recommendation decision during the epidemic period

Tianjin Lawyers Association focuses on cultural heritage, writes the future, puts the cultural construction of the Tianjin lawyer industry in the new era in a more prominent position in the self-discipline management work, and in-depth development of the industry's outstanding cultural heritage and cultivation activities. At the same time, the *Tianjin Lawyers Industry Appraisal and Recognition Measures for Party Building Work* was formulated, and the *Tianjin Lawyers Association Recognition and Reward Measures for Members of the Tianjin Lawyers Association* were revised to normalize and standardize the evaluation and commendation work within the industry; to carry out the overall prevention and control of epidemic situation in Tianjin lawyer industry, carry out the selection of advanced collectives and individuals in economic and social development, carry out the selection activity of "the Most Beautiful Female Lawyer", and fully display the elegant demeanour of Tianjin lawyers.

（四）律师队伍建设和青年律师培养，提升新水平
(d) Improve the Team Building to a New Level

天津市律师协会坚守执业底线，健全和规范投诉处理程序，深入开展律师职业道德、执业纪律教育专项治理，不断净化律师队伍。加强对新执业律师及实习人员管理，系好律师执业的"第一粒纽扣"。同时加大行业培训培养力度，与全市12所高校开展"双师互进"合作，每年定期举办"天津律师大讲堂""区域律师培训班"，各专门、专业委员会开展各类培训研讨活动230次。

Tianjin Lawyers Association adheres to the bottom line of practice, improves and standardizes complaint handling procedures, in-depth development of professional ethics and practice discipline education for lawyers, and constantly purifies the lawyer team. Strengthen the management of new practicing lawyers and interns, and be the "first button" of lawyers' practice. At the same time, we increase the

2018年12月天津市律师协会与天津高校"双师互进"工作推动会
In December 2018, Tianjin Lawyers Association and Tianjin colleges and universities "Lawyers and Professors Mutual Advancement and Swap Positions" work promotion meeting

intensity of industry training and talent training, and cooperate with 12 colleges and universities in our city to carry out "Lawyers and Professors Mutual Advancement and Swap Positions" cooperation, and regularly hold "Tianjin Lawyers Lectures" and "Regional Lawyers Training Classes" every year, and various specialized and professional committees carry out various training seminars 230 times.

天津市律师协会持续加强人才培养,着力打造行业优质人才队伍,同时加大对青年律师的培养和帮扶,落实《天津市律师行业领军人才培养工程实施方案》《关于扶持培养青年律师发展的指导意见》,为各专业领域人才及青年律师成长成才搭建平台、提供保障。此外,律师协会还制定了《天津市律师协会关于发展我市律师事务所境外分支机构的指导意见(2020—2022)》,着力培养一批在业务领域、服务能力方面具有较强国际竞争力的涉外法律服务机构和人才,不断推动天津律师事务所提升综合竞争力。

Tianjin Lawyers Association continues to strengthen the training of talents, and strive to build a high-quality talent team in the industry. At the same time, increase the training and support for young lawyers, implement the *Tianjin Lawyer Industry Leading Talent Training Project Implementation Plan* and *Guiding Opinions on Supporting the Development of Young Lawyers* to build a platform and provide assurance for talents in various professional fields and young lawyers to grow and become talents. At the same time, the *Guiding Opinions of Tianjin Lawyers Association on the Development of Overseas Branches of Law Firms in Our City (2020-2022)* was formulated to focus on cultivating a group of foreign-related legal service institutions and talents with strong international competitiveness in business areas and service capabilities, and constantly promote Tianjin Law Firm to improve its comprehensive competitiveness.

为破解行业发展瓶颈,天津市律师协会联合相关高校举办了天津市律师行业"云招聘"等系列活动,帮助律师事务所吸收优秀人才,推动律师事务所在规模层次、管理制度、治理结构、发展模式等方面的改革创新。

In order to breaking the bottleneck of industry development, Tianjin Lawyers

Association and related universities organized a series of activities such as the "Cloud Recruitment" of the Tianjin lawyer industry to help law firms absorb outstanding talents, and promote law firms to reform and innovate in terms of scale, management system, governance structure, and development model.

第八届律师协会换届以来，为提升律师综合素质，天津市律师协会共组织开展涵盖律师职业技能、各领域专业知识在内的专题培训、讲座、研讨活动82次，律师职业素养与专业水平得到进一步的提升。

Since the eighth session of the Lawyers Association changed its term, it has strengthened industry training and focused on improving the overall quality of

天津市第二届"律政先锋"青年律师职业风采大赛
Tianjin Second "Legal and Politics Pioneer" Young Lawyers Professional Style Competition

1921	1922	1923	1924	1925	1926	1927	1928	1929	1930	1931	1932	193
1947	1948	1949	1950	1951	1952	1953	1954	1955	1956	1957	1958	195
1973	1974	1975	1976	1977	1978	1979	1980	1981	1982	1983	1984	198
1999	2000	2001	2002	2003	2004	2005	2006	2007	2008	2009	2010	201

天津市第二届"律政先锋"青年律师职业风采大赛
Tianjin Second "Legal and Politics Pioneer" Young Lawyers Professional Style Competition

评选"十佳青年律师"
Selected "Top Ten Young Lawyers"

天津市律师协会"一带一路"涉外法律服务暨涉外律师人才培养国际合作交流会
Tianjin Lawyers Association "the Belt and Road Initiative" foreign-related legal services and foreign-related lawyer talent training international cooperation exchange meeting

1934	1935	1936	1937	1938	1939	1940	1941	1942	1943	1944	1945	1946
1960	1961	1962	1963	1964	1965	1966	1967	1968	1969	1970	1971	1972
1986	1987	1988	1989	1990	1991	1992	1993	1994	1995	1996	1997	1998
2012	2013	2014	2015	2016	2017	2018	2019	2020	2021	……		

天津市律师协会"一带一路"涉外法律服务暨涉外律师人才培养国际合作交流会合影

A group photo of Tianjin Lawyers Association "the Belt and Road Initiative" foreign-related legal services and foreign-related lawyer talent training international cooperation exchange meeting

律师行业现场招聘会

Recruitment fair for lawyers

天津市公职律师与公司律师颁证宣誓仪式暨工作培训会
Tianjin city public lawyers and corporate lawyers certificates oath ceremony and training

天津市律师协会中小企业法律服务专业委员会公开遴选委员
Members of the Legal Service Professional Committee of Small and Medium-sized Enterprises of Tianjin Lawyers Association were publicly selected

律师参加各类培训活动
Lawyers participate in training activities

疫情期间实习人员线上面试
Online interview of interns during the epidemic

lawyers. Tianjin Lawyers Association organized a total of 82 special trainings, lectures, and seminars covering lawyers' professional skills and professional knowledge in various fields. The professional quality and professional level of lawyers have been further improved.

（五）律师执业保障和会员福利普惠取得新进展

(e) New Progress has been Made in the Protection of Lawyers' Practice and Membership Benefits

为着力解决律师执业与发展中遇到的突出问题、畅通律师维权渠道、加强法律职业共同体建设，天津市律师协会进一步完善了律师预约会见平台功能，并开通了远程会见系统。为规范行业竞争，律师协会出台了《天津市律师服务收费行业指引（市场调节价）》。为推进律师执业便利化，开通了"律师一卡通"，建立了律师电子身份识别；同时积极拓宽福利范围，组织开展律师年度体检，制定了《天津市律师协会会员互助金管理办法》，并开展春节大走访、大慰问，使会员切实感受到协会的温暖。

In order to focus on solving the outstanding problems encountered in the practice and development of lawyers, to unblock the channels for lawyers' rights protection, and to strengthen the construction of the legal professional community, Tianjin Lawyers Association further improved the function of the lawyers appointment meeting platform and opened a remote meeting system. In order to regulate industry competition, the Municipal Lawyers Association has issued the *Guidelines for the Fees of Lawyers Services in Tianjin (Market Adjusted Prices)*. At the same time, it promoted the facilitation of lawyers' practice, opened the "Lawyer Card", established lawyers' electronic identification; broadened the scope of benefits, organized annual physical examinations for lawyers, and formulated the *Administrative Measures for Mutual Aid Funds for Members of Tianjin Lawyers Association*; members really feel the warmth of the association.

天津市律师协会对标新形势、新要求，结合行业发展情况，修订《天津市律师协会章程》；健全完善相关制度，畅通联系服务律师渠道，直接听取广大会员呼声、心声，全面掌握律师事务所和广大律师生存发展状况，及时回应律师关切的问题。

The Association revised the *Articles of Tianjin Lawyers Association* in light of the new situation and new requirements of the standard and the development of the industry. Improve the relevant systems, unblock the channels of contacting service lawyers, directly listen to the voices and aspirations of the majority of members, fully grasp the survival and development of law firms and lawyers, and respond to the concerns of lawyers in a timely manner.

为着力加强和完善实习人员管理，天津市律师协会制定了《申请律师执业人员实习管理规则实施细则》《申请律师执业人员实习考核规程实施细则》，优化工作环节，丰富培训课程，加大对面试考官库和试题库的调整和优化,进一步推动考核评价的标准化、规范化、便利化。

Efforts to strengthen and improve the management of interns, formulate the *Implementation Rules for the Internship Management Rules for Applicants for Lawyers* and *Implementation Rules for the Internship Assessment Procedures for Applicants for Lawyers*, optimize work links, enrich training courses, and increase the number of interview examiners and test questions. Adjustment and optimization will further promote the standardization, normalization and facilitation of assessment and evaluation.

为努力优化律师执业环境,维护律师执业权利,天津市律师协会与天津市公安局监所管理总队多次召开工作联席会议,使"会见难"问题得到了基本解决。律师协会又与公安局、市司法局共同研发了全国首个刑事案件委托备案系统、全国首例具备"人脸识别、双重核验"功能的律师类电子证书和全国首个部署在公安机关以外的远程会见系统。

Strive to optimize the lawyer's practice environment and safeguard the lawyer's right to practice. Tianjin Lawyers Association and the Management Team of the Municipal Public Security Bureau's Supervision Office have held joint work meetings for many times, which has basically solved the problem of "difficult meetings" in our city. The Lawyers Association and the Municipal Public Security Bureau and the Municipal Bureau of Justice jointly developed the country's first criminal case filing system, the country's first lawyer's electronic certificate with the function of "face recognition and dual verification", and the country's first deployment outside the public security agency.

天津市司法局注重以信息化手段服务律师制度改革,不断推进"互联网+政务服务",设计研发了集智慧查询、智慧服务、智慧管理、智慧应用为一体的"天津市智慧律管系统",在基础性管理工作法治化、标准化、规范化的前提下,以实用、好用的功能设计,有效汇集多层数据,通过与公检法等相关单位的业务协同和数据交换,延伸诉讼便利化服务措施、提升身份鉴证智能化水平。该系统被评为"全国司法信息化建设与应用优秀案例"、司法部首届"数字法治、智慧司法"大比武信息化优秀示范案例一等奖、2019年度司法部亮点工作,2020年入选了

"天津市首批优秀大数据重点项目"。天津的数字法治和智慧司法在全国创造了四个第一：

The Tianjin Municipal Bureau of Justice pays attention to the reform of the lawyer system by means of informatization, and continuously promotes the "Internet+ government service", and has designed and developed the "Tianjin Smart Law Management System" that integrates smart inquiry, smart service, smart management, and smart application. On the premise of legalization, standardization and normalization of basic management work, with practical and easy-to-use functional design, effectively collect multi-layer data, and extend the facilitation of litigation through business collaboration and data exchange with relevant units such as the public, procuratorate, and law. Service measures, improve the level of intelligent identification verification, was named "National Judicial Information Construction and Application Excellent Case", the first prize of the Ministry of Justice's first "Digital Rule of Law Smart Judicial" competition, the 2019 Ministry of Justice highlights work, selected in 2020 "Tianjin's First Batch of Outstanding Big Data Key Projects". Tianjin's digital rule of law and smart justice has created four firsts in the country:

第一，大数据重点项目具有全国领先的网上审批、管理、公示等功能，率先实现真正意义上的网上审批，落实"放管服"改革和"一制三化"改革要求，为律师提供全流程网上服务，为百姓打造"淘宝式"律师查询平台，助力管理机关实现智慧管理、预警联动，目前访问量已近170万人次。疫情期间，全市全面实现许可事项"不见面办理"，在全国大部分省市推迟考核的情况下，天津如期开展线上考核，走在全国前列。

First of all, the key big data project has the nation's leading online approval, management, and publicity functions. Take the lead in realizing online examination and approval in the true sense, implement the reform requirements of "decentralization, management and service" and "one system, three modernizations", provide lawyers with full-process online services, create a "Taobao-style" lawyer inquiry platform for the common people, and help management agencies realizing smart management and early warning linkage, the current visit volume has reached nearly

1.7 million. During the epidemic, our city fully realized the "no-face handling" of licensing matters. In the case that most provinces and cities across the country postponed the assessment, the online assessment was carried out as scheduled, and it was at the forefront of the country.

第二，全国首例具备人脸识别功能的律师类电子证书是基于平台优质数据，借助支付宝实名认证和金融级生物识别技术，通过与公安可信身份认证平台（CTID）比对后生成的电子证书，具备"刷脸领取，双重核验"的特点，可以在全国全面覆盖所有律师证书类型，也是首次

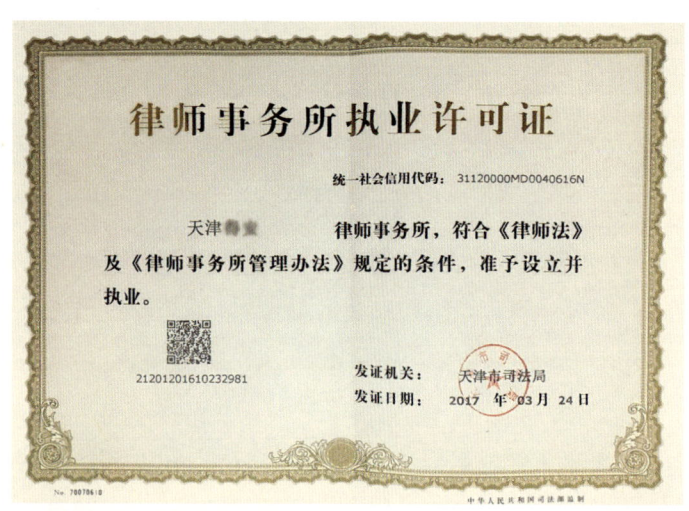

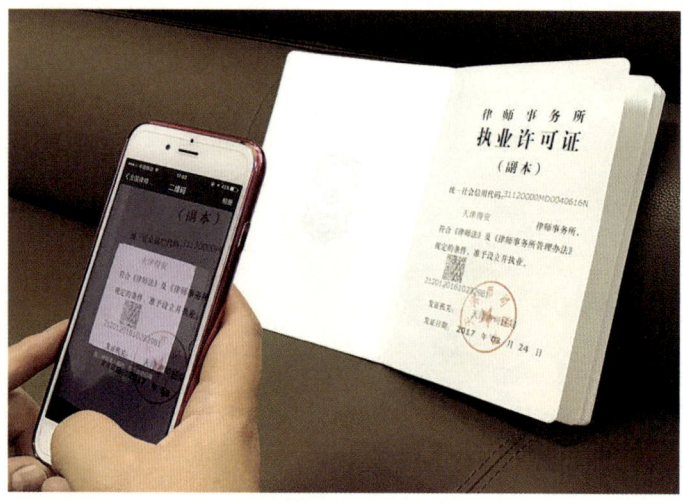

全国第一张新版（三证合一）律师事务所执业许可证
The country's first new version (three-in-one) law firm practice license

由公、检、法、司联合发文并召开新闻发布会确认效力的律师类电子证书。律师手持手机即可通行办案机关，令假律师无处遁形。目前，证书核验设备已部署到天津市各级法院、检察院、公安看守所和政务服务大厅等70多家单位，申领人数超过6000人，核验9万余人次，国务院新闻办、司法部、人民网、新华网和天津市媒体均进行了全方位报道。

Second, the country's first lawyer's electronic certificate with facial recognition function is based on the platform's high-quality data, using Alipay's real-name authentication and financial-grade biometric technology, and is generated after comparison with the Public Security Trusted Identity Authentication Platform (CTID). The certificate has the characteristics of "receiving by brushing the face and double verification", which can fully cover all types of lawyer certificates nationwide. It is also the first lawyer's electronic certificate that has been jointly issued by the public, procuratorate, law and department and held a press conference to confirm the validity. Lawyers can pass the case-handling agency with the mobile phone, and fake lawyers have nowhere to hide. At present, certificate verification equipment has been deployed to more than 70 units including courts at all levels, procuratorates, public security detention centers and government service halls in Tianjin. The number of applicants exceeds 6,000, and more than 90,000 person-times have been verified. Information Office of the State Council, Ministry of Justice, People's Daily Online, Xinhua Net and Tianjin media have all carried out comprehensive coverage.

第三是首个部署在公安机关以外的远程视频会见系统。基于2013年上线的律师预约会见平台，天津市率先将刑事诉讼文书格式申请了地方标准。2017年上线了全国首个刑事案件委托备案系统，将会见所需的律师证、委托书、介绍信全部电子化，率先实现"无纸化会见"，有效保障了律师的执业权利，同时也避免了随意会见、多人会见，既规范了律师执业行为，也提高了效率。目前已有效备案刑事案件6万余件，预约会见26万余人次。

The third nationwide case is the first remote video meeting system deployed outside the public security organs. Based on the lawyer appointment meeting platform launched in 2013, Tianjin took the lead in applying for local standards for the format of criminal litigation documents. In 2017, it launched the country's first criminal case filing system, and all the lawyers' certificates, power of attorney and letters of introduction required for the meeting were electronically realized, and the first to achieve "paperless meetings", which effectively protects lawyers' right to practice, and at the same time avoids random meetings and multi-person meetings. It not only regulates the practice of lawyers, but also improves efficiency. At present, more than 60,000 criminal cases have been effectively filed, and more than 260,000 appointments have been made.

2019年，天津市结合电子证书拓展应用，研发上线了全国首例部署在公安机关以外的"远程视频会见亭"。它采用加密视频传输技术，支持自动双向录像合成、间歇360度环视录像，具有首创、安全、灵活、易于推广的特点。目前，天津市司法局已与公安机关联合发文，将远程视频会见终端推广到全市看守所和各区司法局。首批调试联通的会见终端已经正式上线运行，效果良好，律师满意度高，并在当年8月底实现了全市看守所与律师任意两类终端之间"一对多"的视频会见，有效缓解了会见室不足的问题，也为疫情防控常态化情况下兼顾监所安全和律师执业权利保障提供了技术支撑。

In 2019, in conjunction with the expansion of the application of electronic certificates, our city developed and launched the country's first "remote video meeting booth" deployed outside the public security organs. It adopts encrypted video transmission technology and supports automatic two-way video synthesis and intermittent 360-degree surround view video recording. It is safe, flexible and easy to promote. At present, our bureau has jointly issued a document with the public security organs to promote the remote video meeting terminal to the city's detention centers and the district bureaus of justice. The first batch of meeting terminals for debugging and Unicom has been officially put into operation, with good results and high lawyer satisfaction. It is expected to be realized by the end of August. The city's "one-to-many" video meeting between any two types of terminals at the detention center and the lawyer's side effectively alleviates the problem of insufficient meeting rooms and provides technical support for the security of prisons and the protection of lawyers' rights to practice under the normalized

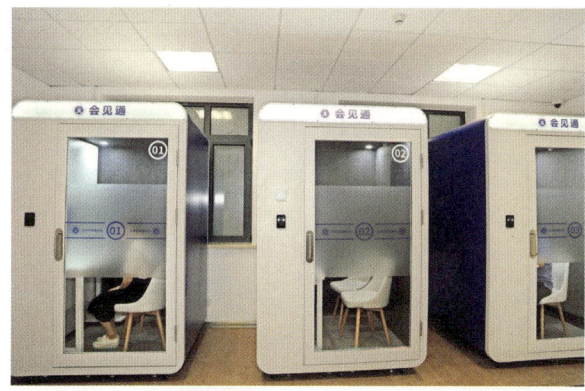
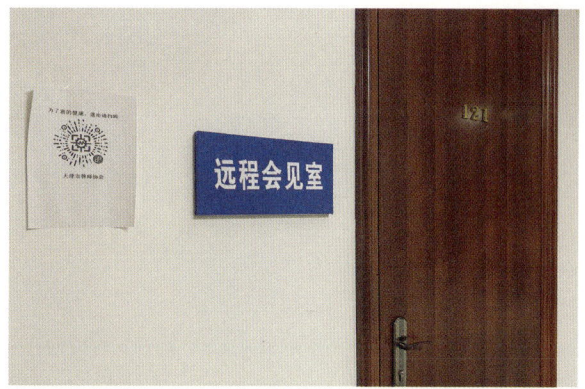
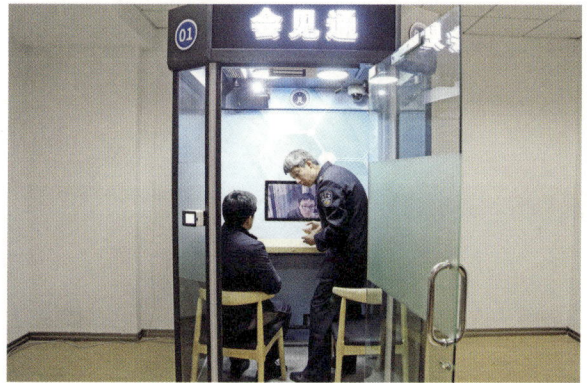
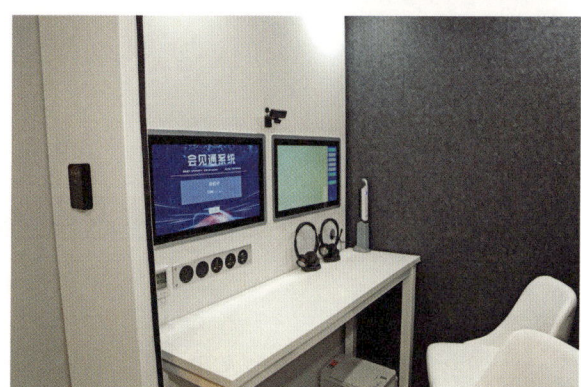
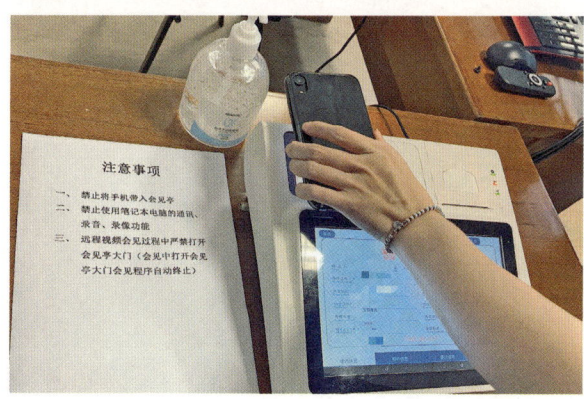

律师远程会见室
Lawyer's remote meeting room

situation of epidemic prevention and control.

第四是天津成为了全国首批律师业务数据采集汇聚试点城市。作为司法部确定的首批五个试点省市之一，天津充分调研，论证方案，积极投入研发力量，结合刑事案件委托备案系统取得的经验，研发上线了"天津市律师业务备案系统"，全面覆盖刑事诉讼、民事诉讼、行政诉讼、行政复议、仲裁、非诉讼法律事务、法律顾问、咨询和代书、公益法律服务九大类律师业务，以实现律师业务数据的全填报、全采集、全汇聚，并通过大数据分析，为科学决策提供参考。

Fourthly, Tianjin has become the first batch of pilot cities for collecting and gathering lawyer business data in China. As one of the first batch of five pilot

维护和保障律师执业权利联席会议
Joint Conference on Safeguarding and Protecting Lawyers' Practicing Rights

provinces and cities identified by the Ministry of Justice, our city has fully investigated and demonstrated plans, actively invested in research and development, combined with the experience gained in the criminal case filing system, developed and launched the "Tianjin Lawyer Business Filing System", a comprehensive covers nine major types of lawyer services, including criminal litigation, civil litigation, administrative litigation, administrative reconsideration, arbitration, non-litigation legal affairs, legal counsel, consultation and representation, and public welfare legal services. It will realize full reporting, full collection and full convergence of lawyer business data, through big data analysis, provide a reference for scientific decision-making.

天津市律师协会始终坚持需求导向、问题导向，并加强与公检法等办案部门的沟通协作和数据协同，进一步完善系统功能，延伸服务领域，探索更加丰富的诉讼便利化措施，让行政管理更高效、数据汇集更智慧、群众办事更便捷，为信息技术与律师工作深度融合提供原创的"天津方案"。

Tianjin Lawyers Association will continue to adhere to demand-oriented and problem-oriented, strengthen communication and collaboration with case handling departments such as public security, prosecution and law, and further improve system functions, extend service areas, explore and extend richer litigation facilitation measures, and let administrative management be more efficient, data collection be smarter, and people do things more conveniently, and the original "Tianjin Plan" is provided for the in-depth integration of information technology and lawyers' work.

（六）律师行业文化建设呈现新气象
(f) Cultural Construction of Lawyer Industry Presents a New Atmosphere

为传承律师文化，天津市律师协会建成了天津律师文史馆，集中展现天津律师业的起源和发展。同时，律师协会不断扩大对外宣传力度，在律师行业宣传领域广泛合作，开展形式多样的宣传活动，树立天津律师的良好执业形象。为丰富律师的文化生活，律师协会举办了"三八"女律师主题活动、天津律师"放飞梦想，律动津城"体育活动，组织律师开展足球、篮球、羽毛球、乒乓球以及艺术交流活动，为律师展示才干、放松身心提供机会和平台。

In order to pass on the lawyer culture, Tianjin Lawyers Association has built the Tianjin Lawyer's Culture and History Museum to show the origin and development of Tianjin's lawyer industry. The Municipal Lawyers Association has continuously expanded its external publicity efforts, extensively cooperated in the publicity field of the lawyer industry, and carried out various publicity activities to establish a good practice image of Tianjin lawyers. At the same time enrich the cultural life of lawyers, organize the "March 8" female lawyers theme activities, Tianjin lawyers "Flying Dreams and Moving Rhythm of Tianjin City" sports activities, organize lawyers to carry out football, basketball, badminton, ping-pong and art exchange activities, provide opportunities and platforms to show their talents and relax the body and mind.

天津律师文史馆正式开馆后，接待了全国律协，市委政法委、检、法、司，律师事务所以及天津大学、南开大学等众多单位超过1000人次的参观，成为宣传天津律师行业发展的重要窗口。

After the official opening of Tianjin Lawyer's Culture and History Museum, it received more than 1,000 visits from the National Lawyers Association, Tianjin Municipal Committee, Political and Legal Committee, Procuratorate, Court, Judicial Office, Law Firm, Tianjin University, Nankai University and many other units, and became an important window to publicize the development of Tianjin lawyer industry.

2019年年底，天津市律师协会组织了"壮丽70年，辉煌40载"庆祝展演主题纪念活动，用诗歌赞颂伟大时代，用舞蹈抒发爱国豪情，集中展示了天津律师行业40年来的发展历程和取得的辉煌成就。演出活动得到了天津市委领导，市司法局领导，市检察院、市公安局、全国律协等单位有关领导同志的关注，600余名律师代表参加了活动。

At the end of 2019, Tianjin Lawyers Association organized the theme commemorative activity of "70 Years of Magnificence, 40 Years of Glory", praising the great era with poetry, and expressing patriotism with dance, which concentratedly demonstrated the development and brilliant achievements of the lawyer industry in Tianjin over the past 40 years. The performance has attracted the attention of leaders of the Municipal Party Committee, the Municipal Bureau of Justice, the Municipal Procuratorate, the Municipal Public Security Bureau, the National Lawyers Association and other units. More than 600 lawyer representatives participated in the event.

天津市律师协会女律师工作委员会2021年三八妇女节在天津律师文史馆举行节日庆祝活动

The Female Lawyers Working Committee of Tianjin Lawyers Association held a holiday celebration event on March 8th in 2021 at the Tianjin Lawyer's Culture and History Museum

全国律协参观天津律师文史馆
The National Lawyers Association visited the
Tianjin Lawyer's Culture and History Museum

京津冀律师代表团参观天津律师文史馆
Beijing-Tianjin-Hebei lawyer delegation visited
Tianjin Lawyer's Culture and History Museum

1934	1935	1936	1937	1938	1939	1940	1941	1942	1943	1944	1945	1946
1960	1961	1962	1963	1964	1965	1966	1967	1968	1969	1970	1971	1972
1986	1987	1988	1989	1990	1991	1992	1993	1994	1995	1996	1997	1998
2012	2013	2014	2015	2016	2017	2018	2019	2020	2021	……		

天津市检察院参观天津律师文史馆

Visit to the Tianjin Lawyer's Culture and History Museum by the Municipal Procuratorate

天津市第二中级人民法院和天津海关参观天津律师文史馆

Visiting the Tianjin Lawyer's Culture and History Museum by the Municipal Second Intermediate People's Court and the Municipal Customs

律师制度恢复40周年庆典
40th anniversary celebration of the restoration of lawyer system

律师制度恢复40周年颁奖
Awarding for the 40th anniversary of the restoration of lawyer system

1934	1935	1936	1937	1938	1939	1940	1941	1942	1943	1944	1945	1946
1960	1961	1962	1963	1964	1965	1966	1967	1968	1969	1970	1971	1972
1986	1987	1988	1989	1990	1991	1992	1993	1994	1995	1996	1997	1998
2012	2013	2014	2015	2016	2017	2018	2019	2020	2021	……		

律师制度恢复 40 周年节目表演

Programs for the 40th anniversary of the restoration of lawyer system

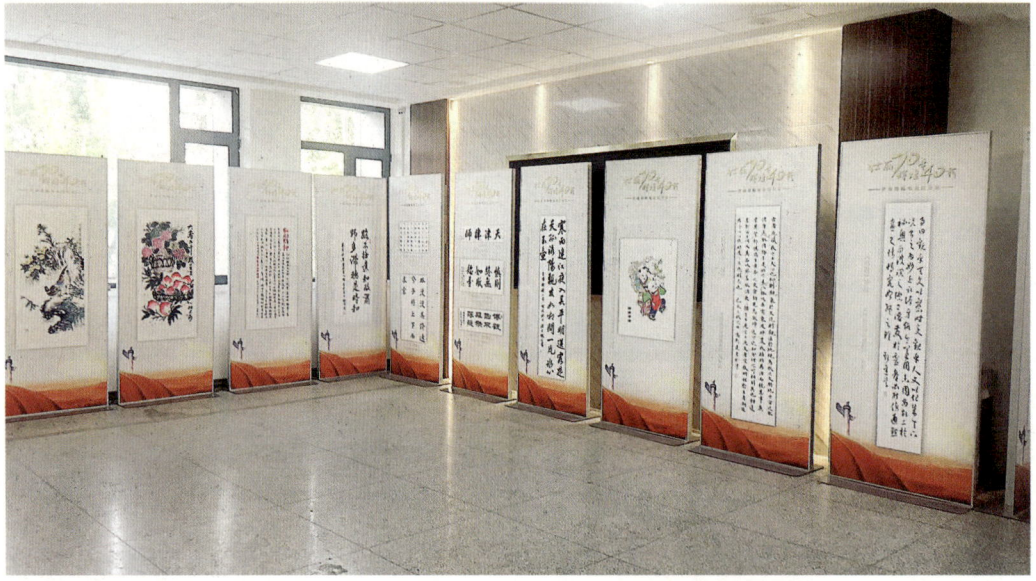

"壮丽70年，辉煌40载"天津律师书画摄影展
"70 Years of Magnificence, 40 Years of Glory" Tianjin lawyer calligraphy, painting and photography exhibition

"放飞梦想，律动津城"庆祝律师制度恢复重建40周年第二届天津律师羽毛球比赛

"Flying Dreams and Moving Rhythm of Tianjin City" to celebrate the 40th anniversary of the restoration and reconstruction of lawyer system, the 2nd Tianjin lawyer badminton competition

羽毛球比赛现场

Badminton match scene

2016年天津市律师协会足球队参加西班牙"律师世界杯"足球赛
2016 Tianjin Lawyers Association football team participated in the Spanish "Lawyers World Cup" football game

天津律师参加2017年京津冀律师书画摄影作品展
Tianjin lawyers participated in the 2017 Beijing-Tianjin-Hebei lawyers' painting, calligraphy and photography exhibition

天津律师羽毛球队参加第八届"京津沪渝粤琼"律师羽毛球赛

Tianjin lawyers badminton team participated in the 8th "Beijing-Tianjin-Shanghai-Chongqing-Guangdong-Hainan" lawyers badminton tournament

第十一届"京津沪渝粤琼"暨纪念律师制度恢复40周年律师羽毛球赛的赛旗由北京市律师协会传递给天津市律师协会

The flag of the 11th "Beijing-Tianjin-Shanghai-Chongqing-Guangdong-Hainan" and commemorating the 40th anniversary of lawyer system restoration lawyers badminton tournament was passed by the Beijing Lawyers Association to the Tianjin Lawyers Association

第十一届"京津沪渝粤琼"暨纪念律师制度恢复40周年
律师羽毛球赛全体参赛律师合影

The 11th "Beijing-Tianjin-Shanghai-Chongqing-Guangdong-Hainan" and commemorating the 40th anniversary of the restoration of lawyer system, a group photo of all participating lawyers in the lawyers badminton competition

依法治国的担当

RESPONSIBILITY FOR THE RULE OF LAW

随着各类活动的有效开展,天津市很多律师事务所与律师被司法部,天津市委、市委政法委及其他有关单位评选为先进集体或先进个人。才华当选全国人大代表,杨玉芙、何悦当选全国政协委员。在2012年召开的天津市第十次党代会上,有三名律师被选为党代表参加会议,实现了行业的历史性突破。截至2013年年底,全市有70余名律师担任了全国、市、区(县)三级人大代表、政协委员。广大律师通过有效发挥职业专长,认真履行职责,积极建言献策,为推动地方法治建设不断作出努力。

With the effective development of various activities, many advanced representatives have emerged from all walks of life in Tianjin. Many of the law firms and lawyers have been selected as advanced collectives and advanced individuals by the Ministry of Justice, the Tianjin Municipal Party Committee, and the Tianjin Municipal Political and Legal Committee and other related units. Cai Hua was elected as a deputy to the National People's Congress, and Yang Yufu and He Yue were elected as members of the National Committee of the Chinese People's Political Consultative Conference. At the Tenth Party Congress in Tianjin held in 2012, three lawyers from our city were selected as party representatives to participate in the meeting, achieving a historic breakthrough in the industry. As of the end of 2013, more than 70 lawyers in our city have served as national, city, district (county) people's congress representatives and members of the CPPCC. Lawyers make continuous efforts to promote the construction of local rule of law by effectively using their professional expertise, earnestly performing their duties, and actively offering advice and suggestions.

天津市律师行业创先争优活动总结表彰大会
Summary and commendation meeting of Tianjin lawyer industry pioneering and excellence activities

第十三届全国政协委员、第七届天津市律师协会会长、天津四方君汇律师事务所主任杨玉芙出席 2021 年 3 月的全国政协会议
Yang Yufu, member of the 13th National Committee of the Chinese People's Political Consultative Conference, Chairman of the 7th Tianjin Lawyers Association, and Director of Tianjin Join&High Law Office, attended the CPPCC meeting in March 2021

第十三届全国人大代表、第八届天津市律师协会会长、天津华盛理律师事务所主任才华在 2021 年 3 月的人大会议上发言
The representative of the 13th National People's Congress, the chairman of the 8th Tianjin Lawyers Association, and the director of Tianjin Huashengli Law Firm, Cai Hua, speaks at the National People's Congress in March 2021

天津市律师协会律师参政议政工作座谈会
Symposium on political participation and deliberation by lawyers of Tianjin Lawyers Association

推动律师服务创新，与其他现代服务业密切合作是新时期律师行业发展的主题。2014年以来，为加快律师行业改革创新步伐，充分发挥天津市滨海新区改革创新先试先行的政策优势，中华全国律师协会、天津市滨海新区人民政府、天津市司法局、天津市律师协会、天津市滨海新区中心商务区管委会共同签署了《关于建立天津市滨海新区律师服务创新示范基地协议》，在滨海新区建立了天津市滨海新区律师服务创新示范基地。2014年12月2日，在京津冀协同发展及投资与服务贸易便利化法治讲坛活动上，天津市滨海新区律师服务创新示范基地正式揭牌。示范基地将依托滨海新区雄厚的产业基础，推动律师行业为滨海新区经济发展、产业结构调整、企业转型升级提供创新型法律服务，更好地服务经济社会发展，探索可借鉴、可复制、可推广的经验，天津律师业也将迎来新的发展。

Promoting innovation in lawyer services and working closely with other modern service industries are the themes of the development of the lawyer industry in

京津冀协同发展及投资与服务贸易便利化法治讲坛暨天津市滨海新区律师服务创新示范基地成立

The Coordinated Development of Beijing-Tianjin-Hebei & Facilitation of Investment and Service Trade Legal Forum and establishment of Tianjin Binhai New Area Lawyers Service Innovation Demonstration Base

天津市滨海新区金融法律服务中心揭牌仪式

Inauguration ceremony of Financial Legal Service Center in Tianjin Binhai New Area

京津冀协同发展及投资与服务贸易便利化法治讲坛

The Coordinated Development of Beijing-Tianjin-Hebei & Facilitation of Investment and Service Trade Legal Forum

在天津市滨海新区律师服务创新示范基地合影

A group photo at the Tianjin Binhai New Area Lawyers Service Innovation Demonstration Base

the new era. Since 2014, in order to accelerate the pace of reform and innovation of the lawyer industry and give full play to the policy advantages of reform and innovation in Tianjin Binhai New Area, the All-China Lawyers Association, Tianjin Binhai New Area People's Government, Tianjin Municipal Bureau of Justice, Tianjin Lawyers Association, Tianjin Municipality The Administrative Committee of the Central Business District of Binhai New Area jointly signed the *Agreement on Establishing Tianjin Binhai New Area Lawyers Service Innovation Demonstration Base*, and established the Tianjin Binhai New Area Lawyers Service Innovation Demonstration Base in Tianjin Binhai New Area. On December 2, 2014, Tianjin Binhai New Area Lawyers Service Innovation Demonstration Base was officially unveiled at the Coordinated Development of Beijing-Tianjin-Hebei & Facilitation of Investment and Service Trade Legal Forum. The demonstration base will rely on the strong industrial foundation of Binhai New Area to promote the lawyer industry to provide innovative legal services for the economic development, industrial structure adjustment, and enterprise transformation and upgrading of the Binhai New Area, better serve the economic and social development, and explore experiences that can be used for reference, replicated and popularized, Tianjin's lawyer industry will also usher in new development.

2020年，天津市律师协会紧扣维护稳定的大局需要，积极发挥作用，按照一季度一会议的原则，组织开展各种学习培训活动，如三期"办理涉黑涉恶案件辩护与代理律师"专题业务培训、"学习全国扫黑办扫黑除恶法律政策文件视频培训会议材料"专题研讨会等，详细讲解相关法规政策，加强备案监督指导机制，帮助广大律师为维护社会公平正义、推进法治建设发挥更多积极的作用。

In 2020, Tianjin Lawyers Association will closely follow the overall needs of maintaining stability and play an active role. In accordance with the principle of one quarter, one meeting, various learning and training activities have been organized, such as the special business training for "Defending and Representing Lawyers Involved in Black and Evil Cases" and the symposium for "Learning the Video Training Conference Materials of the National Special Campaign of Crackdown on Gang

Crime Legal Policy Documents" to explain in detail relevant laws and policies, strengthen the filing supervision and guidance mechanism, and help lawyers play more active roles in safeguarding social fairness and justice and promoting the rule of law.

扫黑除恶专项斗争是党的十九大以来党中央作出的重大决策，事关社会大局稳定和国家长治久安。2019年7月6日至9日，全国扫黑办挂牌督办、天津扫黑除恶专项斗争1号案件——颜X等34人涉嫌犯组织、领导、参加黑社会性质组织等罪一案在天津市第二中级人民法院开庭。贾芳律师、枟桢律师作为辩护人之一参与庭审。君荐事务所的律师积极参与此次扫黑除恶斗争，严格以事实为依据、以法律为准绳开展辩护工作，在保障当事人诉讼权利的同时，也与公检法机关共同配合，顺利完成扫黑除恶第一案，展现了新时代律师应有的建设法治国家、服务大局的担当与使命。目前已有1015件律师代理的涉黑涉恶案件进行了备案，涉及代理律师616人。

National special campaign of crackdown on gang crime is a major decision made by the Communist Party of China Central Committee since the 19th National Congress of the Communist Party of China, which is related to the overall stability of society and the long-term stability of the country. From July 6 to July 9, 2019, listed for supervision by National Gang Crime Crackdown Office, the No.1 case of Tianjin Special Campaign of Crackdown on Gang Crime —— "34 people including Yan X suspected of organizing, leading, and participating in underworld organizations was heard at Tianjin No.2 Intermediate People's Court. Lawyer Jia Fang and lawyer Yunzhen participated in the trial as one of the defenders. The lawyers of Junjian Law Office actively participated in the crackdown on gang crime and carried out the defense work strictly based on facts and the criterion of law. While protecting the litigant rights of litigants, they also cooperated with the public, procuratorate and legal organs to successfully complete the fight against gangsters. The first case demonstrates the responsibility and mission that lawyers in the new era should have to build a country under the rule of law and serve the overall situation. At present, 1,015 cases involving the Major Campaign of Crime Crackdown case represented by lawyers have been filed, 616 lawyers were involved.

颜 X 等 34 人涉嫌犯组织、领导、参加黑社会性质组织等罪一案开庭审理

The case of 34 people including Yan X and others suspected of organizing, leading, and participating in a crime organization opened for trial

2020 年 7 月 25 日天津市办理涉黑涉恶案件辩护与代理律师专题业务培训

On July 25, 2020, Tianjin Municipality handles the special business training for defense and lawyers in Major Campaign of Crime Crackdown cases involving triads and crimes

天津市律师协会开展扫黑除恶相关法律政策文件专题研讨

Tianjin Lawyers Association launches a special seminar on laws and policies related to the Major Campaign of Crime Crackdown

  2020年,天津市律师协会持续做好律师参与和化解涉法涉诉信访案件律师服务工作。全年律师值班1500余次,律师服务团接待信访820余人次。同时,律师协会进一步做好矛盾纠纷化解工作,积极推进金融法律调解中心的建设,引导律师参与矛盾纠纷调解,为经济社会发展营造和谐稳定的社会环境。

  In 2020, the association will continue to carry out the work of lawyers in our city's lawyers participating in and resolving law-related petition cases. In 2020, lawyers were on duty more than 1,500 times, and the lawyer service team received more than 820 petitioners. Further did a good job in the resolution of conflicts and disputes, actively promoted the construction of the financial legal mediation center, and guide the participation of lawyers contradictions and disputes mediation work to create a harmonious and stable social environment for economic and social development.

  2019年7月,为响应司法部的号召,天津律师杨磊、王鹏、杜兆婷参加了由司法部律师工作局、中华全国律师协会和中国法律援助基金会共同组织实施的"援藏律师服务团"活动,来自

天津律师参与和化解涉法涉诉信访案件服务工作场景
The service work scenes of Tianjin lawyers participating in and resolving law-related complaints and petitions

全国22个省（自治区、直辖市）的68名援藏律师先后深入西藏7个市（地）、42个县（区）开展法律服务工作。杨磊、王鹏、杜兆婷作为首批援藏律师服务团天津地区的援助律师赴昌都市丁青县对口开展了为期一年的"1+1"法律援助服务。在服务期内，共办结法律援助案件4件，代书见证50人次，解答咨询244人次，培训600余人次，为当地政府提供法律服务23次，挽回经济损失约22万元。2020年7月23日，2020年度"援藏律师服务团"启动仪式在拉萨举行，天津2020年度"援藏律师服务团"律师贾存红与2019年度"援藏律师服务团"律师杜兆婷参加并完成交接。天津市司法局党委委员、副局长，市律师行业党委书记刘基智，天津市律师协会秘书处主要负责同志和援藏律师参加了启动仪式。

In July 2019, in response to the call of the Ministry of Justice, Tianjin lawyers Yang Lei, Wang Peng, and Du Zhaoting participated in the "Tibet-Aid Lawyers Service Group" jointly organized and implemented by the Lawyer Work Bureau of the Ministry of Justice, the All China Lawyers Association and the China Legal Aid Foundation. At the same time, 68 aid lawyers from 22 provinces (regions, cities) across the country went to 42 counties (districts) in 7 cities (prefectures) in Tibet to carry out legal services. Tianjin lawyer Yang Lei, Wang Peng, and Du

天津援藏律师服务团在西藏
Tianjin Tibet-Aid Lawyers Service Group in Tibet

Zhaoting, as the first aid lawyers from the Tianjin region of the Tibet-Aid Lawyers Service Group, went to Dingqing County, Changdu City to carry out a one-year "1+1" legal aid service. During the service period, a total of 4 legal aid cases were handled, 50 person-times were witnessed, 244 person-times were answered and consulted, more than 600 person-times were trained, 23 legal services were provided to the local government, and economic loss of 220,000 yuan was recovered. On July 23, 2020, the 2020 "Tibet-Aid Lawyers Service Group" kick-off ceremony was held in Lhasa. Tianjin 2020 "Tibet-Aid Lawyers Service Group" lawyer Jia Cunhong and 2019 "Tibet-Aid Lawyers Service Group" lawyer Du Zhaoting attended and completed the handover. Liu Jizhi, member of the Party Committee and Deputy Director of the Municipal Bureau of Justice, the main responsible comrades of the Secretariat of Tianjin Lawyers Association and Tibet-aid lawyers attended the launching ceremony.

2020年是非同寻常的一年，新冠病毒在全球肆虐，天津律师秉承依法正行、聚力同心的精神，与全国人民一道为抗击新冠肺炎疫情奋战在各条战线上。天津律师无论在党的基层建设方面，还是社会责任担当方面，都起到了积极示范引领作用。疫情发生伊始，律师协会迅速行动，第一时间成立了应对疫情工作领导小组，连续发布了《做好新型冠状病毒感染的肺炎疫情防控工作》等多个通知，设立了四个专项督察组，对全市16个区以电话询问、视频调度、随机抽查、现场了解等多种方式开展疫情防控的督察工作，推进全市律师行业做好防疫工作。律师

1934	1935	1936	1937	1938	1939	1940	1941	1942	1943	1944	1945	1946
1960	1961	1962	1963	1964	1965	1966	1967	1968	1969	1970	1971	1972
1986	1987	1988	1989	1990	1991	1992	1993	1994	1995	1996	1997	1998
2012	2013	2014	2015	2016	2017	2018	2019	2020	2021	……		

天津市司法局副局长刘基智为天津市律师协会部署疫情防控工作

Deputy Director Liu Jizhi of the Municipal Bureau of Justice deployed epidemic prevention and control work to the Tianjin Lawyers Association

协会紧扣抗击疫情，众志成城、超前谋划、果敢出击，云端会议部署抗疫工作，迅速发布《天津市律协为抗击新冠状病毒疫情捐赠倡议书》，研究制定了五项措施帮助会员渡过难关，减轻新冠肺炎疫情对律师行业造成的影响。其中"三减三免"会费减免政策的力度为全国律师行业之最，会员享受率为百分之百。

2020 is an extraordinary year. The novel coronavirus was raging around the world. The spirit of acting on the law and working together has led the lawyers of the city and the people of the whole country to fight on all fronts in the fight against the COVID-19 epidemic. Tianjin lawyers have played an active role as an example and leading role in the party's grassroots construction and social responsibility. At the beginning of the epidemic, Tianjin Lawyers Association acted quickly, established a leading group for the response to the epidemic as soon as possible, successively issued multiple notices such as *Doing a Good Job in the Prevention and Control of the Pneumonia Epidemic Caused by the Novel Coronavirus Infection*, and set up four special inspection teams to deal with The 16 districts carried out inspections of epidemic prevention and control through telephone inquiries, video scheduling, random inspections, and on-site understanding, and promoted the city's lawyers to do a good job in epidemic prevention. Tianjin Lawyers Association closely followed the fight against the epidemic, and made concerted efforts, advanced planning and bold attack in deploying anti-epidemic work through the cloud conference, quickly releasing the *Tianjin Lawyers Association Donation Proposal for Fighting the COVID-19 Epidemic*, and studying and formulating five measures to help members tide over the difficulties. Overcome difficulties and reduce the impact of the COVID-19 epidemic on the lawyer industry. Among them, the "three reductions and three exemptions" policy of membership fee reduction and exemption is the highest in the lawyer industry in the country, and the membership enjoyment rate is 100%.

疫情初期,天津市律师协会整合力量,发挥律师作用,积极抗击疫情。律师协会建立了全

天津市律师协会在疫情初期紧急召开应对疫情突发工作会议
Tianjin Lawyers Association urgently convenes a working meeting to respond to the outbreak in the early stage of the epidemic

三方携手，严防疫情输入，相关法律规定解读

Three parties join hands to strictly prevent the import of the epidemic, interpretation of relevant laws and regulations

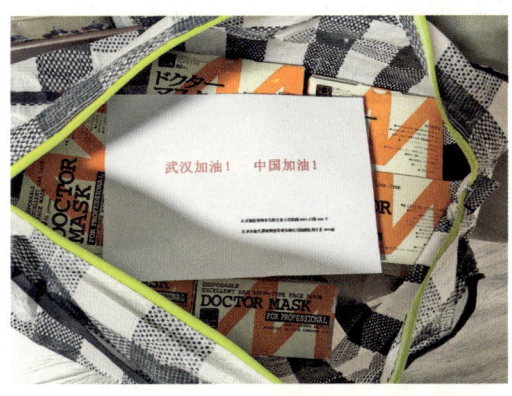

天津律师向抗疫一线捐款捐物

Lawyers in Tianjin donated money and materials to the front line against the epidemic

天津市律师协会编印的疫情防控法律汇编

Legal Compilation of Epidemic Prevention and Control published by Tianjin Lawyers Association

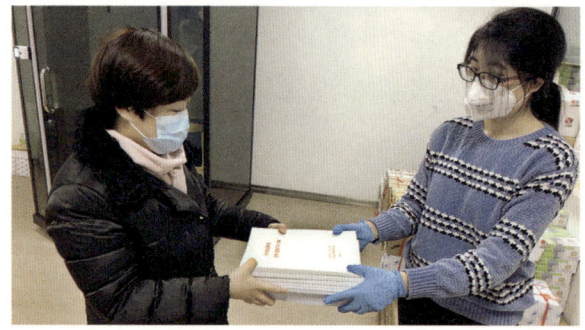 

天津市律师协会在疫情期间向律师配发口罩

Tianjin Lawyers Association distributed masks to lawyers during the epidemic

天津律师积极参与疫情防控工作
Tianjin lawyers took the initiative to participate in epidemic

天津律师在疫情期间开庭的场景
Tianjin lawyer's court scene during the epidemic

天津澍泽律师事务所疫情期间缴纳了一份特殊党费

Tianjin Shu Ze Law Office paid a special party fee during the outbreak

市应急法律服务三级响应机制，春节期间每天24小时电话值班；成立了天津市律师协会医疗卫生健康专业委员会；组建了市、区两级公益法律服务百人团93个，为党委、政府决策进行合法性审查、法律论证385件，编写法治宣传资料492篇；承办与疫情防控有关案件67件，为企业复工复产提供法律意见、建议2027件，解答群众法律咨询22033人次；制作了20期《助力企业复产复工公益法律服务讲堂》节目，助力疫情防控后期企业依法有序复工复产。疫情期间，天津市律师协会共捐款2291574.32元（含防疫物资123380元），以实际行动彰显了天津律师的大爱情怀和服务社会的使命担当。

At the beginning of the epidemic, it was the Tianjin lawyers associations that integrated their forces and played the role of lawyers to fight against the epidemic. The Municipal Lawyers Association has established a three-level response mechanism for emergency legal services in the city, and was on duty 24 hours a day during the Spring Festival; established a medical and health professional committee of the Municipal Lawyers Association; ninety-three 100-member public welfare legal service groups were formed at the municipal and district levels, 385 legal examinations and legal arguments were conducted for the decision-making of

1934	1935	1936	1937	1938	1939	1940	1941	1942	1943	1944	1945	1946
1960	1961	1962	1963	1964	1965	1966	1967	1968	1969	1970	1971	1972
1986	1987	1988	1989	1990	1991	1992	1993	1994	1995	1996	1997	1998
2012	2013	2014	2015	2016	2017	2018	2019	2020	2021	……		

天津市司法局和律师协会领导深入疫情防控一线慰问律师

Leaders of the Municipal Bureau of Justice and the Tianjin Lawyers Association visited the lawyers on the frontline of epidemic prevention and control

天津律师主动参与疫情防控工作
Tianjin lawyers took the initiative to participate in epidemic

1934	1935	1936	1937	1938	1939	1940	1941	1942	1943	1944	1945	1946
1960	1961	1962	1963	1964	1965	1966	1967	1968	1969	1970	1971	1972
1986	1987	1988	1989	1990	1991	1992	1993	1994	1995	1996	1997	1998
2012	2013	2014	2015	2016	2017	2018	2019	2020	2021	……		

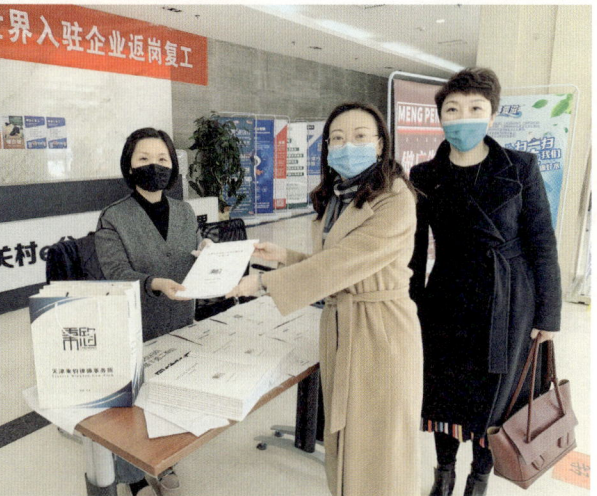

1921	1922	1923	1924	1925	1926	1927	1928	1929	1930	1931	1932	1933
1947	1948	1949	1950	1951	1952	1953	1954	1955	1956	1957	1958	1959
1973	1974	1975	1976	1977	1978	1979	1980	1981	1982	1983	1984	1985
1999	2000	2001	2002	2003	2004	2005	2006	2007	2008	2009	2010	2011

party committees and governments, and 492 publicity materials on the rule of law were prepared; 67 cases related to epidemic prevention and control were carried out, 2027 legal opinions and suggestions were provided for the resumption of work and production of enterprises, and 22,033 legal consultations were answered by the public; produced 20 issues of *Helping Enterprises to Resume Public Welfare Legal Services Lectures* to help enterprises in the later stage of epidemic prevention and control to resume work and production in an orderly manner. During the epidemic, Tianjin Lawyers Association donated a total of 2,291,574.32 yuan (including 123,380 yuan of epidemic prevention materials), which demonstrated the great love of Tianjin lawyers and their mission of serving the society through practical actions.

2020年，天津市律师协会坚持围绕中心、服务大局，积极搭建平台，着力推进律师参与服务重大战略项目，组织律师积极参与2020年天津融洽会暨民洽会。同时扎实做好"六稳"工作，允分发挥"公益法律服务团""中小外贸企业专项服务团"等职能作用和专业优势，不断总结经验，创新做法，聚焦企业应对疫情影响的难点问题，帮助企业和职工预防因疫情产生的风险，化解矛盾纠纷。

In 2020, Tianjin Lawyers Association adheres to the principle of centering on the work of the party committee and the government and takes active actions. The association actively built a platform to promote the participation of lawyers in major strategic projects, and organized lawyers to actively participate in the 2020 Tianjin R&D Fair and the People's Fair. Did a solid job of the "Six Stabilities", gave full play to the functions and professional advantages of the "Public Welfare Legal Service Group" and "Special Service Group for Small and Medium Foreign Trade Enterprises", constantly summed up experience, innovated methods, and focused on difficult issues for companies to deal with the impact of the epidemic, and helped companies and employees to prevent risks arising from the epidemic and resolved conflicts and disputes.

天津市律师协会积极响应市政府号召，持续推进律师行业服务保障法治化营商环境，开展中小企业法律专项服务活动，深入推进民营企业"法治体检"常态化、制度化，为企业投融资、劳务用工、兼并重组等重大生产经营事项提供法律建议和跟踪服务，帮助民营企业克服短期困难，有效防范和化解法律风险，保障经济社会安全平稳运行。

Tianjin Lawyers Association actively responded to the call of the municipal government, continued to promote the legal business environment in the lawyer industry, launched special legal service activities for small and medium-sized enterprises, and further promoted the normalization and institutionalization of the "Legal Physical Examination" of private enterprises, providing legal advice and follow-up services for major production and operation issues such as investment and financing, labor employment, mergers and acquisitions, etc., helping private enterprises overcome short-term difficulties, effectively prevent and resolve legal risks, and ensure the safe and stable operation of the economy and society.

党的十八大以来，党中央全面从严治党，加大反腐力度，诸多高官落马。在严惩腐败的同时，也要确保每一位落马高官得到公正的审判。2019年4月19日，天津市法律援助中心委派两名律师担任原公安部副部长孟XX涉嫌受贿罪的辩护人，经审理认定被告孟XX受贿金额高达人民币1446万余元，孟XX如实供述案件事实，认罪认罚。对其以受贿罪判处有期徒刑十三年六个月，并处罚金人民币200万元。孟XX当庭表示服从法院判决，不上诉。2020年1月6日，天津市法律援助中心再次委派两名律师担任原陕西省委书记赵XX涉嫌受贿罪的辩护人。被告赵XX非法收受财物7.17亿余元，其中2.91亿余元未实际取得，被告人当庭表示认罪悔罪。对其以受贿罪判处死刑，缓期两年执行，剥夺政治权利终身，并处没收个人全部财产，在其死刑缓期执行两年期满依法减为无期徒刑后，终身监禁，不得减刑、假释。赵XX当庭表示服从法院判决，不上诉。天津律师以坚定的政治立场和专业的法律素养，为被告人提供辩护，被告当庭表示服从法院判决，取得了良好的社会效果。

Since the 18th National Congress of the Communist Party of China, the CPC Central Committee has strictly managed the party in an all-round way, intensified anti-corruption efforts, and many senior officials have fallen. While severely punishing corruption, it is also necessary to ensure that every senior official who under investigation gets a fair trial. On April 19, 2019, two lawyers were appointed by Tianjin Legal Aid Center to act as defenders for the alleged bribery crime of former Deputy Minister of Public Security Meng XX. After the trial, it was determined that the defendant Meng XX had received bribes as high as 14.46 million yuan. Meng XX truthfully confessed the facts of the case, pleaded guilty and acknowledged punishment. He was sentenced to 13 years and 6 months imprisonment for accepting bribes and fined 2 million yuan. Meng XX expressed his obedience to the court's decision in court and did not appeal. On January 6, 2020, two lawyers were appointed by the Tianjin Legal Aid Center to act as defenders for the alleged bribery crime of former Shanxi Provincial Party Secretary Zhao XX. Defendant Zhao XX illegally received more than 717 million yuan of property, of which more than 291 million yuan was not actually obtained, and the defendant pleaded guilty and repented in court. He shall be sentenced to death for taking bribes with a two-year suspension of execution, deprived of his political rights for life and confiscated of all his personal property. He shall be sentenced to life imprisonment without commutation or parole after his death sentence is commuted to life imprisonment at the expiration of the two-year suspension of execution. Zhao XX said in court that he would obey the court's decision and would not appeal. Tianjin lawyers defended the defendant with a firm political stand and professional legal literacy. The defendant expressed his obedience to the court's judgment in court and achieved good social effects.

《民法典》出台以后，天津市律师协会以《民法典》的学习、宣传、实施作为推进"法治天津"建设的重要契机，组织成立了《民法典》宣讲团，深入机关、学校、社区、乡镇开展普法宣传和义务咨询，营造浓厚的法治氛围。

Since the promulgation of the *Civil Code*, Tianjin Lawyers Association has taken the study, publicity and implementation of the *Civil Code* as an important opportunity to promote the construction of "Tianjin under the rule of law". It has organized and set up a publicity group on the *Civil Code* to carry out legal publicity and voluntary consultation in government offices, schools, communities and towns to create a strong atmosphere of rule of law.

1934	1935	1936	1937	1938	1939	1940	1941	1942	1943	1944	1945	1946
1960	1961	1962	1963	1964	1965	1966	1967	1968	1969	1970	1971	1972
1986	1987	1988	1989	1990	1991	1992	1993	1994	1995	1996	1997	1998
2012	2013	2014	2015	2016	2017	2018	2019	2020	2021	……		

律师为交通银行天津分行宣讲《民法典》

Lawyers gave a lecture on *Civil Code* for Bank of Communications Tianjin Branch

律师为国家税务总局天津市税务局宣讲《民法典》

Lawyers gave a lecture on *Civil Code* for Tianjin Municipal Taxation Bureau of State Administration of Taxation

律师参加天津电视台组织的《民法典》普法宣传

Lawyers participated in the popularization of the *Civil Code* organized by the TV station

律师为西青区中北镇政府作"《民法典》主要内容梳理"专题讲座

Lawyer gave a special lecture on "combining the main contents of the *Civil Code*" for the Zhongbei Town Government of Xiqing District, Tianjin

1934	1935	1936	1937	1938	1939	1940	1941	1942	1943	1944	1945	1946
1960	1961	1962	1963	1964	1965	1966	1967	1968	1969	1970	1971	1972
1986	1987	1988	1989	1990	1991	1992	1993	1994	1995	1996	1997	1998
2012	2013	2014	2015	2016	2017	2018	2019	2020	2021	……		

律师为红桥区佳园南里社区义务讲解《民法典》

Lawyer explained the *Civil Code* for the obligation of Jiayuannanli Community, Hongqiao District, Tianjin

律师为河东区商务局宣讲《民法典》

Lawyers gave a lecture on the *Civil Code* for the Bureau of Commerce

律师为国家税务总局天津经济技术开发区税务局宣讲《民法典》

Lawyer gave a lecture on the *Civil Code* for the Tianjin Economic and Technological Development Zone Taxation Bureau of the State Administration of Taxation

律师为天津南站地区综合管理办公室各部门工作人员作《民法典》《行政法》专题讲座

Lawyers gave lectures on *Civil Code* and *Administrative Law* for staff of various departments of the Comprehensive Management Office of Tianjin South Railway Station

律师为天津市第十九中学宣讲《宪法》和《民法典》

Lawyer gave a lecture on the *Constitution* and the *Civil Code* for the 19th Middle School of Tianjin

律师为天津航空机电有限公司宣讲《宪法》

Lawyers preach the *Constitution* for Tianjin Aviation Electromechanical Co., Ltd.

2020年,天津市律师协会继续深化"法润天津"品牌,进一步招募、扩大12348公共法律服务热线律师团队,引导全市律师积极参与公共法律服务和12348热线咨询工作。律师协会还配合天津市司法局,组织律师对12348公共法律服务开展每周的质检工作,以确保律师对社会的法律咨询服务更加专业、规范、高效。同时组织律师做好老年人、农民工、残疾人等特殊群体的法律援助工作,组织律师定期赴天津市退休职工养老院法律服务基地、马三立敬老院开展法律咨询。为加强律师开展法律援助等公益活动的标准化和规范化建设,律师协会还印发了《律师公益法律服务手册》,进一步确保了律师参与公益活动服务的质量和水平。

In 2020, Tianjin Lawyers Association continued to deepen the "Farun Tianjin" brand, further recruited and expanded the 12348 legal service hotline lawyer team,

受援群众卧病在床,法律援助律师上门服务
The recipient was sick in bed, and the legal aid lawyers provides door-to-door services

1934	1935	1936	1937	1938	1939	1940	1941	1942	1943	1944	1945	1946
1960	1961	1962	1963	1964	1965	1966	1967	1968	1969	1970	1971	1972
1986	1987	1988	1989	1990	1991	1992	1993	1994	1995	1996	1997	1998
2012	2013	2014	2015	2016	2017	2018	2019	2020	2021	……		

在法律服务中心 12348 公共法律服务热线平台工作的律师

Lawyers working on the 12348 public legal service on-site platform of the Legal Service Center

2020 年 4 月 27 日天津市司法局召开 12348 公共法律服务律师经验分享和培训会，以加强对公共法律服务律师服务质量的检查和提升

On April 27, 2020, the Municipal Bureau of Justice held a 12348 public legal service lawyer experience sharing and training meeting to strengthen the inspection and improvement of the service quality of public legal service lawyers and guided the city's lawyers to actively participate in public legal services and 12348 hotline consultation. The Lawyers Association cooperated with the Bureau of Justice to organize lawyers to carry out weekly quality inspections on 12348 legal services to ensure that lawyers' legal consulting services to the society are more professional, standardized and efficient. Organize lawyers to provide legal assistance to special groups such as the elderly, migrant workers, and the disabled, and organize lawyers to regularly go to the legal service base of retirement homes for retired employees in Tianjin and Ma Sanli nursing home for legal consultation. Strengthen the standardization and standardization of public welfare activities such as legal aid carried out by lawyers, and publish the *Lawyers Public Welfare Legal Service Manual* to further regulate the quality of lawyers' participation in public welfare activities.

天津市律师协会认真落实党中央脱贫攻坚帮扶政策，加大教育扶贫援助力度，与对口帮扶地区建立长效工作机制，并按照天津市司法局的指示，积极探索脱贫攻坚与乡村振兴的有机衔接，进一步寻求业务职能和乡村振兴共同发展的契合点，实现脱贫工作、乡村振兴、职能发挥"齐步走"。为巩固好天津、承德两地帮扶工作取得的成效，进一步推动京津冀协同发展，2020年8月24日天津市司法局、天津市律师协会有关负责同志到河北省承德市下辖的承德县、兴隆县参加调研活动。截至2020年年末，天津市司法行政系统含律师协会已向承德市划拨帮扶资金90余万元，帮助兴隆县蓝旗营镇完成东风小学危房改造项目，并为东风小学师生捐助教学用品；同时又为承德县刘杖子村完成便民桥建设项目，切实解决了困扰村民多年的通行问题，受益群众149户、487人。

Tianjin Lawyers Association earnestly implemented the Party Central Committee's poverty alleviation and assistance policies, increased education and poverty alleviation assistance, established a long-term working mechanism with counterpart assistance areas, and actively explored the organic connection between poverty alleviation and rural revitalization in accordance with the instructions of the Municipal Bureau of Justice. Seek the joint point of the common development of business functions and rural revitalization, and realize poverty alleviation, rural revitalization, and functional performance "step by step." In order to consolidate

1934	1935	1936	1937	1938	1939	1940	1941	1942	1943	1944	1945	1946
1960	1961	1962	1963	1964	1965	1966	1967	1968	1969	1970	1971	1972
1986	1987	1988	1989	1990	1991	1992	1993	1994	1995	1996	1997	1998
2012	2013	2014	2015	2016	2017	2018	2019	2020	2021	……		

天津市律师协会为河北省承德县刘杖子村捐助 15 万元修建的"天津律师便民桥"

Tianjin Lawyers Association donated 150,000 yuan to build the "Tianjin Lawyers Convenience Bridge" for Liuzhangzi Village, Chengde County, Hebei Province

冯志东秘书长接受承德县刘杖子村党支部书记向天津市律师协会赠送的锦旗

Secretary General Feng Zhidong accepted the banner presented by the Party branch secretary of Liuzhangzi Village in Chengde County to Tianjin Lawyers Association

天津市律师协会现址

Current address of Tianjin Lawyers Association

the results of the assistance work in Tianjin and Chengde, and further promote the coordinated development of Beijing, Tianjin and Hebei, on August 24, 2020, the relevant responsible comrades of the Tianjin Municipal Bureau of Justice and the Tianjin Lawyers Association went to Chengde County and Xinglong County, Hebei Province to participate Up to now, the Tianjin Judicial Administration System including the Lawyers Association has allocated a total of more than 900,000 yuan in assistance funds to Chengde City. Convenient bridge construction project in Liuzhangzi Village of Chengde County, dilapidated house renovation project of Dongfeng Primary School in Lanqiying Town of Xinglong County, and teaching supplies donation project of Dongfeng Primary School teachers and students have effectively solved the traffic problems that have plagued villagers for many years and benefited the masses 149 households with 487 people.

2020年9月14日,天津市司法局、天津市律师协会赴甘肃省调研社会动员资金帮扶项目落实情况。天津市司法行政系统已向甘肃省划拨帮扶资金和物资共计134.21万元。为进一步落实市委部署的"多层全覆盖、有限无限相结合"的要求,市司法行政系统把有限援助资金用在刀刃上,发挥公证、律师等智力帮扶的无限力量,增进两地交往交融,确保将社会帮扶款、物用到脱贫攻坚的"关键处",用到受援地区老百姓的"心坎上"。调研组听取了帮扶资金和物资的拨付使用情况,实地考察了对口帮扶的甘肃省榆中县吕家岘村蓄水池等帮扶项目的建设情况。

On September 14, 2020, Tianjin Municipal Bureau of Justice and Tianjin Lawyers Association went to Gansu Province to investigate the implementation of social mobilization fund assistance projects. The judicial administrative system of Tianjin has allocated a total of 1.3421 million yuan in assistance funds and materials to Gansu Province. Further implement the requirements of "multi-layer full coverage, limited and unlimited combination" deployed by the Municipal Party Committee, use limited aid funds on the edge, give full play to the infinite power of intellectual assistance such as notaries and lawyers, enhance exchanges between the two places, and ensure social assistance. Funds and materials are used in the "key points" of poverty alleviation and the "hearts" of the people in the recipient areas. The research team listened to the appropriation and use of aid funds and materials,

调研组实地走访甘肃省榆中县吕家岘村蓄水池等帮扶项目建设情况
The research team visited the construction of the reservoir and other assistance projects in Lüjiaxian Village, Yuzhong County, Gansu Province

visited the construction situation of the reservoir in Lüjiaxian Village, Yuzhong County, Gansu Province, which was assisted by the counterpart.

第八届律师协会换届后，至2020年年底，天津市律师协会按照《天津市律师协会章程》组织召开了七次理事会、七次监事会、十七次会长会议以及各专门、专业委员会与区律工委工作会，谋划、部署、推进律师行业发展的各项工作。在巩固、深化行业管理成熟经验的基础上，结合行业发展情况，律师协会启动了《天津市律师协会章程》《天津市律师协会会费管理办法》的修订工作，着力健全和完善符合发展实际的行业自律管理规则体系。同时进一步规范申请律师执业人员的实习行为、制定实习人员面试考核规则、调整和优化实习人员集中培训课程，确保为律师队伍培养和输送合格人才。

After the eighth session of the Tianjin Lawyers Association, the Municipal Lawyers Association organized 7 councils, 7 supervisory committees, 17 chairman meetings and working meetings of various specialized and professional committees and district legal work committees in accordance with the *Articles of Tianjin Lawyers Association*. Plan, deploy, and promote the development of the industry; on the basis of consolidating and deepening the mature experience of industry management,

1934	1935	1936	1937	1938	1939	1940	1941	1942	1943	1944	1945	1946
1960	1961	1962	1963	1964	1965	1966	1967	1968	1969	1970	1971	1972
1986	1987	1988	1989	1990	1991	1992	1993	1994	1995	1996	1997	1998
2012	2013	2014	2015	2016	2017	2018	2019	2020	2021	......		

combined with the development of the industry, the revision work of the *Articles of Tianjin Lawyers Association* and *Tianjin Lawyers Association Membership Management Measures* was initiated, strive to improve the industry self-discipline management rule system that is in line with the development reality; further regulate the internship behavior of applicants for lawyers, formulate interns interview assessment rules, adjust and optimize the centralized training courses for interns, and ensure the training and delivery of qualified talents for the lawyer team.

天津经济社会发展中的每一个热词，如外商投资、企业改制、金融创新、城市基础设施建设与房地产开发以及开发区、新技术产业园区、滨海新区、自贸区等等都与律师业的发展紧密相关。尽管已经不再使用过去的对外经济律师事务所、专利律师事务所、侨务律师事务所、房地产律师事务所、金融律师事务所、海事海商律师事务所等名称，但已有越来越多的专业律师投入到了各个领域的法律服务中去。

Every hot word in Tianjin's economic and social development, such as foreign investment, enterprise restructuring, financial innovation, urban infrastructure construction and real estate development, development zone, new technology industrial park, Binhai New Area, free trade zone and so on, is closely related to the development of lawyer industry. Although the names of foreign economic law firm, patent law firm, overseas Chinese law firm, real estate law firm, financial law firm and maritime law firm in the past are no longer used, more and more professional lawyers have devoted themselves to legal services in various fields.

从非诉讼业务的统计数字来看，1990年以前，天津律师办理非诉讼法律事务的数量不超过1000件。此后增长迅速，1991年2850件，1994年5562件，1995年达到16228件。从1995年至今，多数年份在10000件以下，少数年份在10000件以上。从业务收入看，2013—2017年，非诉讼法律业务收入占全市律师业务收入的比例分别为14.37%、11.83%、14.45%、12.6%和15.12%。2013—2017年，全市律师办理民商事案件分别为20078件、25121件、25737件、32910件和40529件，总计144375件。办理民商事案件的业务收入占当年全市律师业务总收入的比例分别为47.3%、52.8%、55%、57.7%和57.9%。可以说，真正为律师业务撑起一片天的还是民商事业务。

1921	1922	1923	1924	1925	1926	1927	1928	1929	1930	1931	1932	1933
1947	1948	1949	1950	1951	1952	1953	1954	1955	1956	1957	1958	1959
1973	1974	1975	1976	1977	1978	1979	1980	1981	1982	1983	1984	1985
1999	2000	2001	2002	2003	2004	2005	2006	2007	2008	2009	2010	2011

Judging from the statistics of non-litigation business, before 1990, the number of non-litigation legal affairs handled by lawyers in the city did not exceed 1,000. Since then, there have been rapid growth, with 2,850 in 1991, 5,562 in 1994, and 16,228 in 1995. Since 1995, it has been below 10,000 in most years and more than 10,000 in a few years. From the perspective of business income, from 2013 to 2017, the proportion of non-litigation legal affairs business income to the city's lawyer business income was 14.37%, 11.83%, 14.45%, 12.6% and 15.12%. From 2013 to 2017, the number of civil and commercial cases handled by lawyers in the city was 20,078, 25,121, 25,737, 32,910, and 40,529, totaling 144,375. The proportion of business income from handling civil and commercial cases to the total income of lawyers in the city that year was 47.3%, 52.8%,

2010年天津夏季达沃斯筹备委员会办公室与天津四方君汇律师事务所签署法律服务方案暨合同
Tianjin Summer Davos Forum Preparatory Office and the director of Tianjin Join & High Law Office signed a legal service plan and contract

55%, 57.7% and 57.9%, respectively. It can be said that it is the civil and commercial business that really supports the lawyer business.

如今，律师的服务领域已扩展到政治、经济和社会生活的方方面面，律师服务水平不断提高，律师执业环境逐步改善，律师行业建设不断完善。律师制度恢复重建40多年来，天津律师队伍为经济社会发展、维护社会和谐稳定与推进"法治天津"建设作出了突出贡献，取得了显著成绩。

Nowadays, the service fields of lawyers have fully penetrated into various fields of politics, economy and social life. The service level of lawyers has been

2016年天津夏季达沃斯论坛筹备协调委员会律师法律
服务签约仪式在天津市政府举行
2016 Tianjin Summer Davos Forum Preparatory and Coordinating Committee Lawyers
Legal Services Signing Ceremony Held in Tianjin Municipal Government

continuously improved, the practice environment of lawyers has been gradually improved, and the construction of the lawyer industry has been continuously improved. Over the past 40 years since the restoration of the lawyer system, the Tianjin lawyer team has made outstanding contributions to economic and social development, maintaining social harmony and stability, and advancing the construction of "Tianjin under the rule of law", and has achieved remarkable results.

律师参与为企业"法治体检"活动

Lawyers participated in the "Legal Physical Examination" activities for enterprises

1934	1935	1936	1937	1938	1939	1940	1941	1942	1943	1944	1945	1946
1960	1961	1962	1963	1964	1965	1966	1967	1968	1969	1970	1971	1972
1986	1987	1988	1989	1990	1991	1992	1993	1994	1995	1996	1997	1998
2012	2013	2014	2015	2016	2017	2018	2019	2020	2021	……		

"检律"合力，助力民营经济发展

Prosecutors and lawyers join forces to help the development of the private economy

建党百年新征程

A NEW JOURNEY FOR THE CENTENARY OF THE COMMUNIST PARTY OF CHINA

一、百年征程，波澜壮阔；百年初心，历久弥坚

1. The Journey of a Century has been Magnificent; a Century Later, the Heart will Become Stronger with Time

2021年，中国共产党迎来百年华诞。中共中央《法治中国建设规划（2020—2025年）》中指出："当今世界正经历百年未有之大变局，我国正处于实现中华民族伟大复兴关键时期，改革发展稳定任务艰巨繁重，全面对外开放深入推进，人民群众在民主、法治、公平、正义、安全、环境等方面的要求日益增长，需要更好发挥法治固根本、稳预期、利长远的保障作用。"律师队伍作为法治建设的重要力量，经过百年沧桑变革，值此特殊的历史时刻，在中国共产党的伟大领导下，作好了承担新使命、踏上新征程的准备。国家"十四五"规划对完善律师制度、加快发展法律服务业、服务保障高质量发展也有明确要求。因此，新时代呼唤着新担当、新作为。在全面推进依法治国的进程中，律师将大有作为，也大有可为。

In 2021, the Communist Party of China will celebrate its 100th anniversary. The Central Committee of the Communist Party of China *Plan for the Construction of the Rule of Law in China (2020-2025)*, "The world today is undergoing major changes unseen in a century. Our country is in a critical period for achieving the great rejuvenation of the Chinese nation. The tasks of reform, development and stability are hard and arduous, and comprehensive opening up to the outside world is intensified. The people's requirements for democracy, the rule of law, fairness, justice, security, and the environment are increasing. The rule of law needs to be more effective in securing the foundation, stabilizing expectations, and benefiting the long-term." As an important force in the construction of the rule of law, a century of vicissitudes of change, at this special historical moment, under the great leadership of the Communist Party of China, we are ready to undertake a new mission and embark on a new journey. The national 14th Five-Year Plan also has clear requirements for improving the lawyer system, accelerating the development of the legal service industry, and guaranteeing high-quality development of services. Therefore, the new era calls for new responsibilities and new actions. In the process of comprehensively advancing the rule of law, lawyers have a lot to do and have a lot to do.

习近平总书记在其重要文章《坚定不移走中国特色社会主义法治道路 为全面建设社会主义现代化国家提供有力法治保障》中指出："要把拥护中国共产党领导、拥护我国社会主义法治作为法律服务人员从业的基本要求，加强教育、管理、引导，引导法律服务工作者坚持正确政治方向，依法依规诚信执业，认真履行社会责任，满腔热忱投入社会主义法治国家建设。要推进法学院校改革发展，提高人才培养质量。要加大涉外法学教育力度，重点做好涉外执法司法和法律服务人才培养、国际组织法律人才培养推送工作，更好服务对外工作大局。"天津律师始终紧紧围绕党和国家工作大局，积极服务法治实践，努力为"十四五"时期的发展开好局、起好步，以优异的成绩庆祝建党一百周年。

General Secretary Xi Jinping pointed out in his important article *Unswervingly Follow the Path of the Socialist Rule of Law with Chinese Characteristics, and Provide a Powerful Legal Guarantee for the Comprehensive Construction of a Modern Socialist Country*: "We must support the leadership of the Communist Party of China and support the socialist rule of law in our country as legal services. The basic requirements for personnel employment, strengthen education, management, and guidance, guide legal service workers to adhere to the correct political direction, practice honestly in accordance with laws and regulations, earnestly perform social responsibilities, and devote themselves to the construction of a socialist country under the rule of law. We must promote the reform and development of law schools. To improve the quality of talent training. We must increase the intensity of foreign-related legal education, focusing on the training of foreign-related law enforcement, judicial and legal services, and the training and promotion of legal talents in international organizations, so as to better serve the overall situation of foreign work." Tianjin lawyers have always been closely focusing on the party work in harmony with the overall situation of the country, actively serve the practice of the rule of law, and strive to provide legal protection for China's development during the 14th Five-Year Plan period, and celebrate the 100th anniversary of the founding of the party with outstanding achievements.

2020年，天津市律师协会坚持政治引领、党建先行，旗帜鲜明地把党的政治建设摆在首要位置，高标准地学习、宣传、贯彻党的十九届五中全会精神，坚定扎实推动全行业高质量的发展。

In 2020, Tianjin Lawyers Association insisted on political leadership and party building first, and clearly put the party's political building in the first place, studied, publicized, and implemented the spirit of the Fifth Plenary Session of the 19th Central Committee of the Party with high standards, and firmly promoted the high quality of the industry of lawyer.

二、促进依法行政
2. Promoting Administration According to Law

随着法治建设的不断深入，律师作为其中的一支重要力量，在服务政府方面发挥的作用越来越明显。例如，天津市南开区咸阳路污水处理厂搬迁项目是天津市民心工程之一。该项目在环境评估报告公示后，遭到了大量行政许可利害关系人的强烈异议。在这种情况下，西青区审批局决定进行听证。天津昊哲律师事务所在这一阶段介入到该项目中，从西青区审批局受理利害关系人异议，到拟定听证程序以及实际开展听证，全程提供法律服务，并协助组织、参与听证工作，使项目后续能够顺利进行，充分体现了律师在服务政府、服务社会中的积极作用。

With the continuous deepening of the construction of the rule of law, lawyers, as an important force in the construction of the rule of law in the country, play an increasingly prominent role in serving the government's administration. For example, the relocation project of the Xianyang Road Sewage Treatment Plant in Nankai District, Tianjin is one of Tianjin's civil engineering projects. After the environmental assessment report was publicized, the project received strong objections from a large number of administrative licensing stakeholders. In this case, Xiqing Approval Bureau decided to conduct a hearing. Tianjin Haozhe Law Firm was involved in the project at this stage, from the Xiqing Approval Bureau's acceptance of the interested parties' objections, to the drafting of the hearing procedures and the actual implementation of the hearing procedures, providing legal services throughout the entire process, and assisting in organizing and participating in the hearing work. The follow-up of the project can proceed smoothly, which fully reflects the active role of lawyers in serving the government and society.

三、护航经济发展

3. Escorting Economic Development

天津市律师协会紧紧围绕法律服务为人民的方针，引导广大律师持续推进民营企业"法治体检"、法律咨询进企业、法治宣传进企业、法律援助进企业等活动，为企业提供线上线下"清单式"公益普法宣讲，及时提供法律风险防控及法律问题解答服务，帮助企业有效防范风险。律师协会积极强化与工商联、企业协会、商会之间的信息联通、业务沟通，建立法律服务对接机制，及时解决企业法律服务需求。

Tianjin Lawyers Association closely focuses on the principle of providing legal services for the people, and guides lawyers to continue to promote the "Legal Physical Examination" of private enterprises, legal consultation into enterprises, rule of law publicity into enterprises, and legal aid into enterprises activities, and provide enterprises with online and offline "lists" public welfare law publicity

"一带一路"天津企业"走出去"服务联盟法律合作签约仪式
Signing ceremony for legal cooperation of "The Belt and Road Initiative" Tianjin enterprise "Going Global" service alliance

lectures provide timely legal risk prevention and control and answers to legal questions to help companies effectively prevent risks. The Lawyers association maintain close information and business communication with the Federation of Industry and Commerce, and business associations and chambers of commerce, establish a legal service docking mechanism, and promptly address corporate legal service needs.

2017年2月，石油管道工程公司应邀参加能源工程公司组织的浙江舟山液化天然气（LNG）海底管道施工工程招标投标。中标后因双方工程延迟、物价上涨等原因未能就合同条款达成一致，能源工程公司取消了石油管道工程公司的中标资格，并拒绝退还投标保证金及损失赔偿。石油管道工程公司委托天津开元律师事务所进行深入论证后，提起了诉讼，经宁波海事法院和浙江省高级人民法院的两审审理，最终判决能源公司应赔偿管道公司5928609元经济损失。律师们的努力维护了企业的合法权益，加快了管道公司的合规化管理建设，对改进大型国有企业的风险控制体系产生了积极的影响。

1934	1935	1936	1937	1938	1939	1940	1941	1942	1943	1944	1945	1946
1960	1961	1962	1963	1964	1965	1966	1967	1968	1969	1970	1971	1972
1986	1987	1988	1989	1990	1991	1992	1993	1994	1995	1996	1997	1998
2012	2013	2014	2015	2016	2017	2018	2019	2020	2021	……		

In February 2017, the Petroleum Pipeline Engineering Company was invited to participate in the bidding for the construction of the Zhejiang Zhoushan Liquefied Natural Gas (LNG) submarine pipeline organized by the Energy Engineering Company. After winning the bid, the two parties failed to agree on the terms of the contract due to project delays and price increases. The Energy Engineering Company cancelled the qualification of the Petroleum Pipeline Engineering Company and refused to return the bid bond and compensate for the losses. After the Petroleum Pipeline Engineering Company commissioned Tianjin Kaiyuan Law Firm to conduct in-depth demonstrations, it filed a lawsuit, which was heard by the Ningbo Maritime Court and the Zhejiang Higher People's Court. The final judgment was that the energy company should compensate the pipeline company for economic losses of 5,928,609 yuan. Safeguarding the legitimate rights and interests of enterprises, speeding up the construction of pipeline companies' compliance governance, and having a positive impact on improving the risk control system of large state-owned enterprises.

2020年突如其来的疫情导致各行各业的企业、公司停工停产，其中受疫情影响最大的莫过于文化演出行业。2020年1月，天津某文化传媒公司受疫情影响不得不取消了全部商业演出的承办，这也直接导致了公司经营困难，濒临破产。该公司向全体员工下发了《公司经营困难情况告知书》，向员工告知公司将采取减薪降薪的方式渡过困难期。公司员工张某因不满降薪的决定向仲裁院提出对公司的劳动仲裁申请，该公司委托天津相臣律师事务所的律师承办该案。律师依据疫情后政府和司法行政部门出台的一系列针对疫情期间产生问题的指导意见和规定，向法官提出疫情的出现属于不可抗力的客观事实，公司在尽量保证不影响员工生活的基础上提出减薪降薪是非常时期的非常方式，不应一概认定为违反《劳动合同法》的行为。最终，经过律师的陈述和答辩，劳动者和用人单位达成调解，公司避免了巨大损失，双方对案件结果均表示满意。

The sudden outbreak of the epidemic in 2020 has caused companies in all walks of life to suspend work and production. Among them, the industry most affected by the epidemic is the cultural performance industry. In January 2020, a cultural media company in Tianjin had to cancel the contracting of all commercial performances due to the epidemic. Work, which also directly led to the company's operating difficulties and on the verge of bankruptcy. The company issued the *Notice of Company Operating Difficulties* to all employees to inform employees that the company would take salary cuts to tide over the difficult period. Company employee Zhang filed an application for labor arbitration against the company to the Arbitration Court because of his dissatisfaction with the decision to lower his salary. The company entrusted lawyers from Xiangchen Law Firm to handle the case. Based on a series of guidelines and regulations issued by the government and judicial administrative departments to address the problems that occurred during the epidemic after the epidemic, the lawyer proposed to the judge the objective fact that the occurrence of the epidemic is force majeure, and the company proposed a salary cut on the basis of ensuring that it does not affect the lives of employees. Salary reduction is an extraordinary method in extraordinary times and should not be regarded as a violation of the *Labor Contract Law*. In the end, after the lawyer's statement and defense, the laborer and the employer reached a mediation, which reduced the company's huge losses, and both parties were satisfied with the outcome of the case.

四、服务对外开放，聚焦"一带一路"涉外法律服务

4. The Service is Open to the Outside World, Focusing on "The Belt and Road Initiative" Foreign-Related Legal Services

"十四五"期间，国内法治和涉外法治的统筹将成为一个重要的课题。为了适应更高水平的对外开放需要，更好地服务企业、维护公民个人的合法权益，坚定地维护国家主权安全和发展利益，律师将在涉外法治工作中发挥越来越大的作用。天津作为世界重要的港口城市，要面临的挑战尤为突出。

During the 14th Five-Year Plan period, the coordination of the domestic rule of law and foreign-related rule of law has become an important issue. In order to meet the needs of opening to the outside world at a higher level, better serve enterprises, safeguard the legitimate rights and interests of individual citizens, and firmly safeguard national sovereign security and development interests, lawyers will play an increasingly important role in foreign-related legal work. As an important port city in the world, Tianjin faces particularly outstanding challenges in this regard.

几年来，天津四方君汇律师事务所涉外法律服务团队积极探索涉外服务领域，努力提升服务品质，接受新加坡BIOCELIX公司、美国XPEL等非诉讼委托，在知识产权、投资股权争端等领域提供了高质量的法律服务；曾参与天津滨海国际机场与航空公司之间的债权债务处理，并与国际组织欧中发展协会和天津外经协会合作，不断探索中国企业"走出去"涉外法律服务的模式与方法。

In the past few years, the foreign-related legal service team of Tianjin Join & High Law Office has actively explored the field of foreign-related services and strived to improve the quality of services. It has accepted non-litigation commissions from Singapore BIOCELIX and US XPEL, providing high-quality legal services in intellectual property, investment and equity disputes and other fields. Participated in the settlement of claims and debts between Tianjin Binhai International Airport and related airlines, cooperated with international organizations Euro-China Development Association and Tianjin Association for Foreign Economic Relations, and constantly explore the foreign-related legal service models and methods of Chinese enterprises "Going Global".

北京观韬中茂（天津）律师事务所曾接受天津渤化公司的委托，指派精通涉外争议解决法律服务的律师团队承办了渤化公司与欧洲某公司的商事纠纷案件。渤化公司隶属于天津渤海化工集团，自营和代理各类商品及技术的进出口业务。在为一家汽车零部件公司提供进口代理服务时，渤化公司与欧洲某大型汽车部件供应商发生纠纷，双方对合同主体、质量及供货期限约定以及具体法律规定的理解存在差异，最终决定通过仲裁程序解决争议。外方在中国国际经济贸易仲裁委员会北京总会提出仲裁请求，要求渤化公司为第三方（真实供货方）延迟供货承担高额赔偿责任。律师们深知渤化公司既肩负着国有资产保值增值的重任，又承担着在国际市场打造"中国名片"的大计，因此对该案十分重视。经深入研究中外合同法律规定及对合同主体理解的异同，探讨涉外合同约定内容背后的法理，历时两年，经过数次沟通和开庭，中方不仅争取到了仲裁庭的支持，而且也获得了对方当事人的认同，最终仲裁庭驳回了欧洲公司的全部仲裁申请，渤化公司无须向对方进行任何给付，既避免了近百万欧元国有资产的损失，又在国际合作伙伴面前维护了中国企业的良好形象和应有的尊严。

Guantao Law Firm (Tianjin) accepted Bohua Company's entrustment to assign a team of lawyers proficient in foreign-related dispute resolution legal services to undertake a commercial dispute case involving Tianjin Bohua Company in a European company. Bohua Company is affiliated to Tianjin Bohai Chemical Group, which is engaged in the import and export business of various commodities and technologies by itself and as an agent. When providing import agency services for an auto parts company, Bohua Company had a dispute with a large European auto parts supplier. The two parties had differences in their understanding of the contract subject, quality and supply period agreement, and specific legal provisions, and finally it was decided to resolve the dispute through arbitration procedures, and the foreign party filed an arbitration request in Beijing CIETAC, demanding that Bohua Company be liable for high compensation for the third party (the real supplier) for delayed supply. Guantao's lawyers know that Bohua Company not only shoulders the important task of maintaining and increasing the value of state-owned assets, but is also related to the grand plan of creating a "Chinese business card" in the international market, and attaches great importance to this case. After in-depth study of the similarities and differences between Chinese and foreign contract laws and understanding of contract subjects, and discussing the legal principles behind the content of foreign-related contracts, it lasted for two years, after several communications and hearings, not only won the support of the arbitration tribunal, but also won the approval of the other parties. In the end, the arbitration tribunal rejected all arbitration applications of European companies. Bohua Company did not need to make any payment to the other party, which not only avoided the loss of nearly one million euros of state-owned assets, but also maintained the good image and application of Chinese companies in front of international partners.

2021年1月14日，天津市律师协会与天津市司法局、天津大学法学院合作设立了天津市涉外律师学院。这所学院依托天津大学法学院的优质师资和雄厚的科研力量，以国家发展需要和社会需求为导向,力图加快对新时代涉外律师领军人才的培养,推动涉外法律服务业的不断发展,创建更高水平的对外开放格局。

On January 14, 2021, Tianjin Municipal Bureau of Justice, Tianjin University Law School and Tianjin Lawyers Association jointly established Tianjin Foreign Lawyers College. Relying on the high-quality teachers and strong scientific research capabilities of Tianjin University Law School, this college is oriented to national development needs and social needs to accelerate the training of leading foreign-related lawyers in the new era, promote the continuous development of the foreign-related legal service industry, and promote higher horizontal opening up pattern.

天津市律师协会和天津大学法学院将进一步落实《天津市涉外律师人才培养合作协议》,开展交流合作,进一步提升天津市律师行业涉外法律服务的能力和水平。目前,天津市涉外律

2021年4月17日,由天津市律师协会委托天津大学法学院承办的"天津市涉外律师学院2021年第一期涉外律师培训班"开班合影
On April 17, 2021, a group photo of "the first training course for lawyers of foreign affairs in 2021" organized by law school of Tianjin University entrusted by Tianjin Lawyers Association

师呈现出年轻化、"海归"比例高的特点,发展潜力十分巨大。律师协会将始终把人才培养作为重点工作任务,努力打造一批政治素质高,通晓国际规则,具有国际眼光、国际视野的天津涉外律师领军人才。

Tianjin Lawyers Association and Tianjin University Law School will further implement the *Tianjin Foreign Lawyers Training Cooperation Agreement* to develop important content of exchanges and cooperation, and further enhance the level of foreign-related legal services in Tianjin's lawyers industry. At present, Tianjin foreign-related lawyers have shown the characteristics of being younger and having a high proportion of "returnees", and they have great potential for development. Tianjin Lawyers Association will always take the training of talents as a key task, and strive to create a group of leading foreign lawyers in Tianjin with high political quality, familiarity with international rules, and an international perspective.

五、参与社会治理和"送法下乡"活动
5. Participating in Social Governance and Sending Law to the Countryside

天津市律师协会倡议各律师事务所党组织开展党员先锋岗、志愿服务、"承诺践诺"等活动,引导广大律师,特别是党员律师、青年律师聚焦新时代党的依法治国方略,积极参与公益法律服务,特别是到基层、到乡村,"送法下乡",解决人民群众"急、难、愁、盼"的问题,为人民群众提供普惠均等、便捷高效、智能精准的现代公共法律服务,切实增强人民群众的获得感、幸福感、安全感。

Tianjin Lawyers Association proposes that the party organizations of all law firms carry out activities such as pioneering posts for party members, voluntary services, and promises, and guide lawyers, especially party member lawyers and young lawyers, to focus on the party's strategy of governing the country according to law in the new era, and actively participate in public welfare legal service activities. In particular, to send law to the countryside at the grass-roots

1934	1935	1936	1937	1938	1939	1940	1941	1942	1943	1944	1945	1946
1960	1961	1962	1963	1964	1965	1966	1967	1968	1969	1970	1971	1972
1986	1987	1988	1989	1990	1991	1992	1993	1994	1995	1996	1997	1998
2012	2013	2014	2015	2016	2017	2018	2019	2020	2021	……		

level to solve the problem of the people's "emergency and worry", provide the people with inclusive, convenient, efficient, intelligent and accurate modern public legal services, and effectively enhance the people's sense of gain, happiness, and security.

广大律师还紧紧围绕乡村振兴衔接办实事，积极开展"送法典进农村"活动，对乡村干部及广大农民进行《宪法》《民法典》的全面普及和教育，尤其突出与乡村振兴有关的农业现代化、农村现代化、农民现代化及土地承包经营权、宅基地使用权、婚姻家庭继承制度、环境

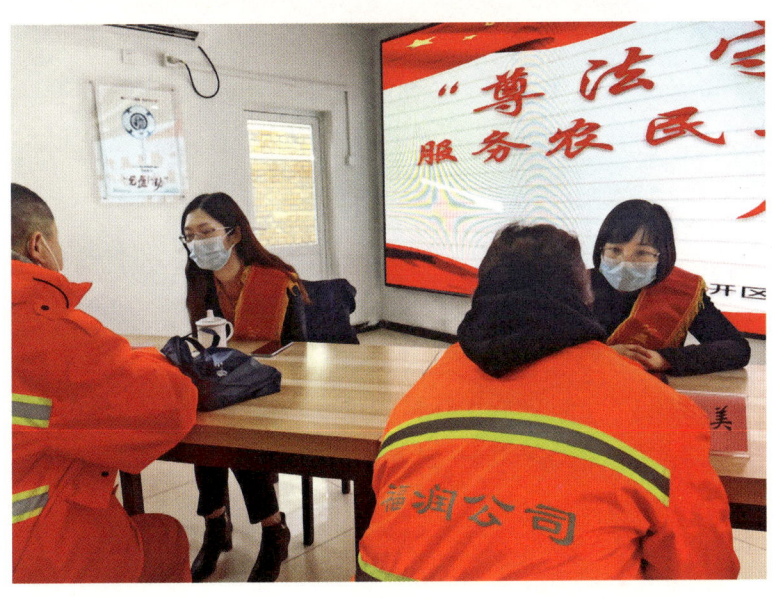

律师参加"遵法守法·携手筑梦"服务农民工公益法律服务

Lawyers participated in the public welfare legal service for migrant workers, which is "Obeying the Law and Building Dreams Together"

污染和生态破坏侵权责任等内容的宣讲。广大律师组织"乡村振兴依法治理大讲堂",开展面对面入户释法、解疑释惑、疏导情绪法律服务活动,服务保障民生。同时持续开展"遵法守法·携手筑梦"服务农民工公益法律服务行动,加强对农民工的关心关爱,符合法律援助条件的,做到应援尽援,维护其合法权益。

At the same time, work closely around the connection of rural revitalization. Lawyers actively carry out activities of "Sending Codes into the Countryside", and comprehensively popularize and educate rural cadres and farmers on the *Constitution* and *Civil Code*, with particular emphasis on agricultural modernization, rural modernization, farmers modernization and land contract management rights related to rural revitalization, propaganda of content such as the right to use homestead, marriage and family inheritance system, environmental pollution and ecological damage tort liability. The majority of lawyers carried out the "Lectures on Rural Rejuvenation and Governance by Law", carried out face-to-face legal service activities to explain the law, resolve doubts, and ease emotions, and serve to protect people's livelihood. Continue to carry out the public welfare legal service action of "Obeying the Law and Building Dreams Together" to serve migrant workers, strengthen the care for migrant workers, and ensure that they meet the requirements of legal assistance, and protect their legal rights and interests.

多年来,天津律师参与多项国家级和省市级重点项目的法律服务工作,更有多名律师不断探索新型法律服务领域的业务类型,国浩(天津)律师事务所为宁河区乡村公路工程PPP项目、赛达伟业发行CMBS工业地产项目资产证券化和城投公司融资债权发行等项目出具法律意见书。

Over the years, Tianjin lawyers have participated in legal services for a number of national, provincial and municipal key projects, and many lawyers have continued to explore new types of legal services. Grandall Law Firm (Tianjin) issued legal opinions for the PPP project of Ninghe District Rural Highway Project, the asset securitization issuance of Saidaweiye CMBS Industrial Real Estate Project and the financing bond issuance of City Investment Company.

1934	1935	1936	1937	1938	1939	1940	1941	1942	1943	1944	1945	1946
1960	1961	1962	1963	1964	1965	1966	1967	1968	1969	1970	1971	1972
1986	1987	1988	1989	1990	1991	1992	1993	1994	1995	1996	1997	1998
2012	2013	2014	2015	2016	2017	2018	2019	2020	2021	......		

天津市律师协会农村法律专业委员会赴津南区小站镇东西庄房村考察涉农法律服务实践基地

The Rural Legal Professional Committee of Tianjin Lawyers Association went to Dongxizhuangfang Village, Xiaozhan Town, Jinnan District to inspect the practice base of agricultural-related legal services

  与此同时，广大律师紧紧围绕服务基层一线办实事，他们在社区和便民警务站提供"法律超市"式法治宣传、法律咨询、律师调解等法律服务，帮助社区困难群众解决就业、就学、就医、社会保障等方面的法律问题，主动为低收入家庭、下岗失业人员、困难群体减免法律服务费。通过《宪法》《民法典》等法律知识的宣讲，积极引导人民群众依法理性表达诉求，化解矛盾纠纷，推动"守法光荣、违法可耻"良好氛围的形成，维护社会团结、和谐稳定，为经济社会发展大局提供优质高效的法律服务和法治保障。

  Closely work on the frontline of serving the grassroots. Lawyers provide legal services such as "law supermarket" publicity, legal consultation, and lawyer mediation in communities and convenient police stations to help people in difficulties solve legal problems encountered in employment, school, medical treatment, and social security. Low-income families, laid-off and unemployed

天津市律师协会与津南区小站镇东西庄房村村委会联合举办"法律精准帮扶、助力乡村振兴"共建共享活动，打造涉农法律服务优秀实践基地，助力乡村振兴发展

Tianjin Lawyers Association and the Dongxizhuangfang Village Committee, Xiaozhan Town, Jinnan District, jointly organized the "Accurate Legal Assistance, Helping Rural Revitalization" co-construction and sharing activity to create an excellent practice base for agricultural legal services and assist rural revitalization and development

天津律师深入乡村，"送法下乡"

Tianjin lawyers went to the countryside to "Sending Law to the Countryside"

persons, and disadvantaged groups take the initiative to reduce or exempt legal service fees. Through legal knowledge such as the *Constitution* and the *Civil Code*, actively guide the people to express their demands in a rational manner, resolve conflicts and disputes, promote the formation of a good atmosphere of honor and shame in law-abiding, maintain social unity, harmony and stability, and provide high-quality and efficient legal services and legal protection for the overall economic and social development.

除在以上方面发挥作用外，在自身完善和发展上，天津市律师协会聚焦"四化"发展，协同创新，针对全市律师事务所结构化问题，组织调研组分赴福建、湖南、浙江、上海、昆明等省市律师协会及当地律师事务所调研交流，充分吸收调研成果，并结合天津行业发展实际，有针对性地制订阶段重点工作计划以及解决行业发展短板的工作方案。同时组织律师事务所主任、合伙人举办律所规模化建设主题座谈会，帮助律师事务所吸收优秀人才、促进律师事务所强强联合，通过引导、推动等方式促进合并转型，激发"1+1＞2"的发展动力。

In addition to playing a role in the above aspects, in terms of self-improvement and development, Tianjin Lawyers Association focuses on the development of the "scale, standardization, specialization and internationalization", collaborative innovation, and organizes research teams to Fujian, Hunan, Zhejiang, Shanghai and Kunming and other provincial and municipal lawyers associations and local law firms conducted research and exchanges, fully absorbed the research results, combined with the actual development of the city's industry, and formulated targeted work plans for key phases and work plans to address shortcomings in industry development. At the same time, organize law firm directors and partners to hold a symposium on the large-scale construction of law firms to help law firms absorb outstanding talents, promote law firms' strong alliances, promote mergers and transformations through guidance and promotion, and stimulate "1+1>2" development motivation.

为深入开展党史学习教育，切实做到学史明理、学史增信、学史崇德、学史力行，推动习近平新时代中国特色社会主义思想入脑入心，天津市律师行业党委于2021年4月19日组织律师行业党委委员和天津市律师协会理事会、监事会中的党员律师赴西青区红色教育基地开展

天津市律师协会赴浙江省律师协会调研交流

Tianjin Lawyers Association went to Zhejiang Lawyers Association for research and exchange

天津市律师协会赴上海市律师协会调研交流

Tianjin Lawyers Association went to Shanghai Lawyers Association for research and exchange

天津市律师协会赴云南省昆明市律师协会调研交流
Tianjin Lawyers Association went to Kunming Lawyers Association in Yunnan Province for research and exchange

天津市律师事务所规模化发展主题沙龙
Thematic salon on the large-scale development of Tianjin law firms

天津市律师行业党委召开第八次党委会议，传达学习党的十九届五中全会精神

The Party Committee of the Tianjin Lawyers Association held the 8th Party Committee Meeting to convey and learn the spirit of the Fifth Plenary Session of the 19th Central Committee of the Party

天津市司法局党委书记、局长王红卫作"律师行业依法规范执业专项治理活动"动员部署

Wang Hongwei, Secretary of the Party Committee and Director of the Tianjin Municipal Bureau of Justice, mobilized and deployed the "Special Governance Activities for Lawyers to Standardize Practice in Accordance with Law"

"重走长征路"主题党日活动。活动弘扬和学习长征精神，旨在让全体党员以亲身实践，体会革命先辈坚定的政治信仰，铭记革命先辈的丰功伟绩，弘扬伟大的长征精神，进一步增强"四个意识"、坚定"四个自信"、做到"两个维护"。全体党员从长征精神中汲取经验、意志和力量，将学习成果转化为工作实效，切实将学党史、悟思想、办实事、开新局贯穿全过程，

1934	1935	1936	1937	1938	1939	1940	1941	1942	1943	1944	1945	1946
1960	1961	1962	1963	1964	1965	1966	1967	1968	1969	1970	1971	1972
1986	1987	1988	1989	1990	1991	1992	1993	1994	1995	1996	1997	1998
2012	2013	2014	2015	2016	2017	2018	2019	2020	2021	……		

从而大力推进天津律师行业的高质量发展。大家重温党史、感受党史、铭记党史，并且更加深刻地感悟共产党人的初心和使命，也更好地汲取攻坚克难、奋力前行的勇气和力量。大家纷纷表示，将牢记和弘扬伟大的长征精神，以饱满的热情，昂扬的斗志，时不我待、只争朝夕的精神，立足本职，扎实工作，践行共产党员的责任与担当，以优异的成绩迎接党的百年华诞。

In order to carry out in-depth study and education of party history, to earnestly learn history to be clear, to increase credit, to respect morality, and to practice history, and to promote Xi Jinping Thought on Socialism with Chinese Characteristics for a New Era into our mind, the Party Committee of the Municipal Lawyers Industry on April 19, 2021 Organize the party committee members of our city's lawyers industry and the party members and lawyers of the Tianjin Lawyers Association Council and board of supervisors to go to the red education base in Xiqing District to carry out the "Re-experience the Long March" theme party day activity. Carrying forward and learning the Long March Spirit aims to enable all party members to experience the strong political beliefs of the revolutionary ancestors, remember the great achievements of the revolutionary ancestors, carry forward the great Long March spirit, and further strengthen the "Four Consciousnesses" and strengthen the "Four Matters of Confidence", achieve "Two Upholds". By absorbing experience, will and strength from the Long March spirit, the results of learning will be transformed into actual work results, and the learning of party history, thinking, doing practical work, and opening up new situation will be carried out through the whole process, and vigorously promote the high-quality development of the lawyer industry in our city. Everyone revisited the history of the party, felt the history of the party, remembered the history of the party, and learned more deeply about the original aspirations and mission of Communist. From it, they can better absorb the courage and strength to overcome difficulties and move forward. Everyone said that they will keep in mind and carry forward the spirit of the Great Long March, with full enthusiasm, high morale, and the spirit of not waiting for the time and fighting for the day and night, based on their own duties and solid work, practice the responsibility of Communist, and welcome the party with outstanding achievements Centennial birthday.

1921	1922	1923	1924	1925	1926	1927	1928	1929	1930	1931	1932	1933
1947	1948	1949	1950	1951	1952	1953	1954	1955	1956	1957	1958	1959
1973	1974	1975	1976	1977	1978	1979	1980	1981	1982	1983	1984	1985
1999	2000	2001	2002	2003	2004	2005	2006	2007	2008	2009	2010	2011

"重走长征路"主题党日活动
"Re-experience the Long March" theme party day activity

1934	1935	1936	1937	1938	1939	1940	1941	1942	1943	1944	1945	1946
1960	1961	1962	1963	1964	1965	1966	1967	1968	1969	1970	1971	1972
1986	1987	1988	1989	1990	1991	1992	1993	1994	1995	1996	1997	1998
2012	2013	2014	2015	2016	2017	2018	2019	2020	2021	……		

在主题党日活动中宣誓

Take an oath in the theme party day activity

　　没有一个时代像法治中国这样如此成就律师行业，接下来，天津市律师协会将以党建为引领，不断提升政治站位，聚焦"一四五四三"工作目标，团结全市律师，以担当践行使命，以实干履行职责，共同努力，持续推进天津律师行业持续健康发展，为实现"两个一百年"奋斗目标和中华民族伟大复兴的中国梦、实现天津高质量发展作出新的更大的贡献！

　　There is no era like the great new era of the rule of law in China that has made the lawyer industry so successful. In the future, Tianjin Lawyers Association will take party building as the guide, continuously improve its political position, focus on the "One Four Five Four Three" work goals, and unite lawyers throughout the city. Continue to promote the sustainable and healthy development of the Tianjin lawyer industry by fulfilling the duties with hard work with joint effort, in order to make new, greater contributions in achieving the "Two Centenary" goals and the Chinese dream of the great rejuvenation of the Chinese nation, and in achieving Tianjin's high quality development.

天津市律师行业党委"重走长征路"主题党日活动合影
A group photo of party day activity with the theme of "Re-experience the Long March" by the Party committee of Tianjin Lawyers Association

1921	1922	1923	1924	1925	1926	1927	1928	1929	1930	1931	1932	1933
1947	1948	1949	1950	1951	1952	1953	1954	1955	1956	1957	1958	1959
1973	1974	1975	1976	1977	1978	1979	1980	1981	1982	1983	1984	1985
1999	2000	2001	2002	2003	2004	2005	2006	2007	2008	2009	2010	2011

后 记
POSTSCRIPT

  天津市第八届律师协会《百年律师看天津》编委会接过第七届律师协会的接力棒，在天津律师文史馆落成开放后，继续进行后期建设和档案文稿的整理工作。回首五年来，自 2016 年 3 月，第七届律师协会专门成立了文史馆建设领导小组，并委派律师协会文化及宣传委员会着手深入筹建天津律师文史馆，明晰天津律师业的发展沿革，传承律师文化。筹建的序曲就在挖掘、抢救律师业相关文物，收集、整理历史资料中迅速展开……

  The editorial board of the 8th Tianjin Lawyers Association *One Hundred Years of Lawyers Accumulated History focused on Tianjin* took over the baton of the 7th Lawyers Association. After the Tianjin Lawyer's Culture and History Museum was completed and opened, it continued to carry out post-construction and archive manuscript compilation. Looking back on the past five years, since March 2016, the 7th Lawyers Association has specially established a leading group for the construction of the Culture and History Museum, and appointed the Culture and Propaganda Committee of the Lawyers Association to start in-depth preparations for the establishment of the Tianjin Lawyer's Culture and History Museum, clarifying the development of Tianjin lawyer industry, inheriting lawyer culture. The prelude to be built is rapidly unfolding in the excavation and rescue of relevant cultural relics of the lawyer industry, and the collection and sorting of historical data...

  天津律师，迄今为止走过了百年。这一百年也是中国律师起源与发展的一百年，一个世纪的光阴淹没了多少尘封的往事？

1934	1935	1936	1937	1938	1939	1940	1941	1942	1943	1944	1945	1946
1960	1961	1962	1963	1964	1965	1966	1967	1968	1969	1970	1971	1972
1986	1987	1988	1989	1990	1991	1992	1993	1994	1995	1996	1997	1998
2012	2013	2014	2015	2016	2017	2018	2019	2020	2021	……		

天津律师文史馆

Tianjin Lawyer's Culture and History Museum

1921	1922	1923	1924	1925	1926	1927	1928	1929	1930	1931	1932	1933
1947	1948	1949	1950	1951	1952	1953	1954	1955	1956	1957	1958	1959
1973	1974	1975	1976	1977	1978	1979	1980	1981	1982	1983	1984	1985
1999	2000	2001	2002	2003	2004	2005	2006	2007	2008	2009	2010	2011

Tianjin lawyers have a history of 100 years. These centuries are also the centuries of the origin and development of Chinese lawyers. How many dusty past events have been submerged in the time of a century?

在2016年年初至天津律师文史馆落成的三年多的时间里，第七届律师协会筹备组工作人员均投入到建设中，第八届律师协会副会长丁立莹作为筹备的主要负责人员，具体参与了这项工作的开展。他们暂时放下业务上的工作，全身心投入到历史资料的收集整理、文史馆的设计规划之中。走访耄耋之年的律师，倾听他们如数家珍般讲述几十年前的法庭逸事；走进图书馆、博物馆、展览馆，从中找寻星星点点的线索；在档案馆翻阅浩瀚如海的各类卷宗，分辨着每一个繁体字、行草毛笔字；翻阅着全英文版的《京津泰晤士报》，用数千万像素的专业设备翻拍、扫描了数万张照片，分类存档……

牢记习近平总书记的指示

Keep in mind the instructions of General Secretary Xi Jinping

1934	1935	1936	1937	1938	1939	1940	1941	1942	1943	1944	1945	1946
1960	1961	1962	1963	1964	1965	1966	1967	1968	1969	1970	1971	1972
1986	1987	1988	1989	1990	1991	1992	1993	1994	1995	1996	1997	1998
2012	2013	2014	2015	2016	2017	2018	2019	2020	2021	……		

From the beginning of 2016 to the completion of the Tianjin Lawyer's Culture and History Museum for more than three years, all the staff of the 7th Lawyers Association's preparatory group have been involved in the construction. Ding Liying, the vice president of the 8th Lawyers Association, was the main person in charge of the preparation and specifically participated in the preparation. In order to carry out this work, they temporarily put aside their business work and devoted themselves to the collection and arrangement of historical data and the design and planning of the Culture and History Museum. Visit the lawyers in their old age and listen to them telling stories of the court decades ago familiarly and proudly; walk into libraries, museums, and exhibition halls to find clues; browse through the vast ocean of files in the archives to distinguish every traditional Chinese character and cursive brush writing; flipping through the English version of *Beijing-Tianjin Times*, using tens of millions of pixels of professional equipment to reproduce and scan tens of thousands of photos, classified and archived...

愈贴近，愈震撼；愈了解，愈自豪！

The closer you are, the more shocking you are; the more you understand, the more proud!

自清末民初华洋共处，到修律变法，政府更迭；从民族救亡，到新中国成立并恢复律师制度……百年沧桑，百年传承。故纸堆里映入眼帘的每一个新奇，都让我们无比惊喜：同治九年（1870）天津教案中洋律师的首次来华诉讼，中华讼师首次到伦敦越洋诉讼，"刀妃革命"的首次婚姻维权，天津律师首次为新民主主义革命先驱周恩来"莫须有入刑"案辩护，天津律师首次研究、翻译《罗马法》，天津在全国首次试办审判厅……每一个案件、事件都与天津和天津律师紧密相连，津沽大地，司法先行，开全国之先河。这座中西合璧、包容古今的大都会，自古至今都是海上、陆上丝绸之路的重要节点，也成就了中国律师制度的起源和发展。身为天津律师，我们为这片土地上曾经闪耀的如此璀璨的刀笔菁华而激动不已，挖掘的动力和使命感再次升腾。

From the coexistence of Chinese and foreigners in the late Qing Dynasty and the

百年律师看天津
One hundred years of lawyers accumulated history focused on Tianjin

天津由来

金朝（公元1115-1234年）在武清和杨柳青巡检驻兵，建立"直沽寨"，这是天津聚落的最早名称；元朝加强守备，改名"海津镇"。

"三官庙碑"记载：成祖文帝入靖内难，圣驾由此济渡沧州，因赐名天津……明永乐二年十一月二十一日（1404年12月23日），决定在小直沽设"天津卫"，1405年1月9日设"天津左卫"；1406年12月18日改"青州左护卫"为"天津右卫"。三卫关系平行，不相统属，都隶属于"五军都督府"。

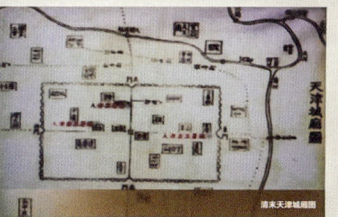

1793年8月11日美国使团抵达天津时马戛尔尼使团绘制的天津景象

1870年李鸿章任直隶总督时，将总督衙门迁至原三口通商大臣衙门旧址，现红桥区大胡同一带。八个告示牌分别写着：解审、验看、审录、考验、投文、放告、刷卷、敬文，可见征中国传统的诉讼审判程序。

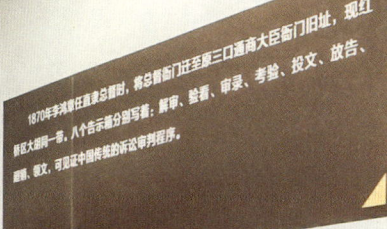

清末天津全部副海关直隶总督衙门辕门

清末天津街景

律师的起源

律师制度源起于西方。早在古罗马时期律师职业就已出现。传统中国并无替人代写诉状、沟通官员的个人师、刀笔先生等。邓析是春秋时期文明注重和谐，厌恶诉讼，因而至传入中国之前，讼师一直是国家严惩

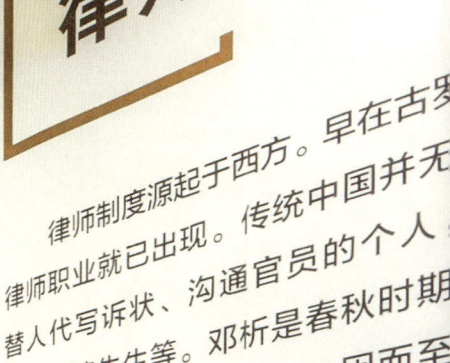

early Republic of China, to the revision of laws, and change of government; from national salvation to the establishment and restoration of the lawyer system in the People's Republic of China... a century of vicissitudes, a century of inheritance. Therefore, every novelty that came into view in the pile of papers surprised us: in 1870, Tianjin Religious Case, foreign lawyers first came to China for litigation, Chinese lawyers went to London for the first time overseas litigation, and the first marriage rights defense in the "Swordsman Revolution" case. Tianjin lawyer defended Zhou Enlai, a pioneer of the new democratic revolution, for the first time in the case of "no need to be imprisoned". Tianjin lawyers studied and translated the *Roman Law* for the first time; Tianjin trialed trial halls for the first time in the country... Every case and historical event are closely connected with Tianjin and Tianjin lawyers, Tianjin and Gu land, judicial first, set a precedent in the country. This metropolis that combines Chinese and Western cultures and embraces the past and the present has been an important node of the Silk Road on the sea and on the land since ancient times. It has also nurtured and sprouted the origin and development of the Chinese lawyer system. As lawyers in Tianjin, we are so excited about the brilliant Daobijinghua that once shined on this land, and the motivation and sense of mission to excavate rise again.

文史馆建设过程中，我们既要收集旧政权的档案材料，也要抢救、挖掘新中国成立后律师前辈的资料。

In the process of building the Museum of Literature and History, it is necessary to collect the archives of the old regime and rescue the data of the seniors who worked as lawyers after the founding of the People's Republic of China.

朔风伴着2016年的春季。这一天，经过第一任律师协会会长郑振亚的介绍，我们去采访兰英——一位85岁鲜为人知的老律师。兰英是20世纪50年代全国第一批执业律师，1958年调往天津市高级人民法院。20世纪80年代从市政法委退休后，适逢律师体制改革初期，她又短暂从事了律师工作，是新中国成立后经历过不同历史阶段的律师界老前辈，曾在1988年荣获中华全国律师协会颁发的"人民律师、无尚光荣"奖。

The new wind accompanies the spring of 2016. On this day, introduced by Zheng Zhenya, the first president of the Lawyers Association, we are going to interview Lan Ying, an 85-year-old little-known lawyer. Lan Ying was the first group of practicing lawyers in the country in the 1950s and was transferred to Tianjin Higher People's Court in 1958. After retiring from the Municipal Legal Committee in the 1980s, it coincided with the early stage of the reform of the lawyer system. She also engaged in short-term lawyer work. She is an old lawyer in the legal profession who has experienced different historical stages after the founding of the People's Republic of China. She was awarded the "People's Lawyer, Very Honor" Award issued by the All China Lawyers Association in 1988.

按照约定的时间，我们到了兰英律师的家，这是一栋建于20世纪80年代的楼房。

According to the agreed time, we arrived at Lawyer Lan Ying's house, which was a building in the 1980s.

一股温暖的气息扑面而来，一直暖到心里。那温暖来自老人简朴的家，来自一位85岁高龄的前辈律师的热情周到和责任担当。

A warm breath hits his face, and it keeps warming in his heart. The warmth comes from the simple home of the old lady, and the warmth and responsibility of an 85-year-old senior lawyer.

言谈中，老人仿佛又回到了60年前的那段时光，她的眼里闪着光芒，语气中充满了对逝去岁月的热爱和留恋。在回忆中，老人满怀荣耀并自豪地讲述了当年老法律顾问处办公室的样子，律师坐在凳子上出庭的情景，还绘声绘色地讲述了当时接待来访群众、宣传法律知识的情形。老人讲述最多的是其他律师做的事情，并且一再说："我在那个时候是律师助理，很多有能力的律师都在担任重要岗位……"

During the conversation, the old lady seemed to have returned to the time 60 years ago, her eyes were shining, and her tone was full of love and nostalgia for

1921	1922	1923	1924	1925	1926	1927	1928	1929	1930	1931	1932	1933
1947	1948	1949	1950	1951	1952	1953	1954	1955	1956	1957	1958	1959
1973	1974	1975	1976	1977	1978	1979	1980	1981	1982	1983	1984	1985
1999	2000	2001	2002	2003	2004	2005	2006	2007	2008	2009	2010	2011

the passing years. In the memory, the old lady gloriously and proudly described the appearance of the old legal counsel office, the scene of the lawyer sitting on a stool and appearing in court. She also vividly described the situation of receiving visitors and publicizing legal knowledge at that time. The old lady talked most about what other lawyers did, and she said repeatedly that, "I was a paralegal at that time, and many capable lawyers were in important positions..."

丁立莹副会长先后采访了十余位老律师，从他们的回忆中，我们能真切体味到老律师朴实的精神、崇尚法律的理念和那始终坚守信念的人格魅力。

Ding Liying, the vice president of the 8th Lawyers Association have interviewed more than ten old lawyers. From their memories, we can really appreciate the old lawyers' simple spirit, advocacy of the law, and the personality charm that has always adhered to their beliefs.

据一些史料记载，1919年，因有奸商勾结日本浪人殴打街头号召抵制日货的学生，激起社会公愤，天津的数千名学生因此奔赴直隶公署请愿。周恩来、马千里、于方舟等学生代表走进公署大门后即遭逮捕。当时北京的著名律师刘崇佑积极奔走，据理力争，在法庭上用精彩的辩护保护了学生。

According to some historical records, in 1919, because profiteers colluded with Japanese ronin and beaten students who called for boycotting Japanese goods on the street, this aroused public outrage. Thousands of students in Tianjin went to the Zhili Office to petition. Zhou Enlai, Ma Qianli, Yu Fangzhou and other student representatives were arrested when they walked through the door of the office. At that time, Liu Chongyou, a well-known lawyer in Beijing, rushed and fought hard and defended the students in court with a brilliant defense.

我们在查阅这个历史事件时，发现不同的出版物甚至史志有不同的记载。有的记载刘崇佑单独为周恩来辩护；有的记载与刘崇佑一起为周恩来辩护的还有天津律师张务滋；还有的说张务滋是主要辩护律师，对此，《大公报》还有过报道。不过，媒体的报道是否能够成为

1934	1935	1936	1937	1938	1939	1940	1941	1942	1943	1944	1945	1946
1960	1961	1962	1963	1964	1965	1966	1967	1968	1969	1970	1971	1972
1986	1987	1988	1989	1990	1991	1992	1993	1994	1995	1996	1997	1998
2012	2013	2014	2015	2016	2017	2018	2019	2020	2021	……		

2016年5月7日天津律师文史馆开工启动仪式

The commencement ceremony of Tianjin Lawyer's Culture and History Museum on May 7, 2016

2019年6月11日天津律师文史馆开馆仪式

On June 11, 2019, the opening ceremony of Tianjin Lawyer's Culture and History Museum

1921	1922	1923	1924	1925	1926	1927	1928	1929	1930	1931	1932	1933
1947	1948	1949	1950	1951	1952	1953	1954	1955	1956	1957	1958	1959
1973	1974	1975	1976	1977	1978	1979	1980	1981	1982	1983	1984	1985
1999	2000	2001	2002	2003	2004	2005	2006	2007	2008	2009	2010	2011

定论？因为他是天津民国时期执业律师"第一人"？各种说法不一，到底哪一个是事实？或更接近事实？

When we looked up this historical event, I found that different publications and even historical chronicles had different records. Some recorded that Liu Chongyou defended Zhou Enlai alone, and some recorded that Liu Chongyou defended Zhou Enlai together with Tianjin lawyer Zhang Wuzi. Others say that Zhang Wuzi is the main defense lawyer, *Ta-Kung-Pao* has reported on this. But can the media reports be conclusive? Because he was the "first lawyer" to practice in Tianjin during the Republic of China? There are different opinions. Which one is the fact? Or closer to the truth?

律师的职业敏感告诉我们，档案馆、博物馆中文献的原始记载甚至经过它们之间的交叉印证，或许才能接近正确答案。

The professional sensitivity of lawyers told us that the original records of archives, museums, and documents may be close to the correct answer even after cross-corroboration between them.

这一个细节的核实，我们用了整整六个月的时间。这段近百年前尘封的事件就在我们脑海里，各种记载的复印件摆在我们的案头，只要有机会，我们就会埋头在安静的档案馆里。岁月，静静地躺在一部部陈旧的卷宗里，宛若奔流不息的河；历史，时而波澜壮阔，时而平静如水，几代法律人筚路蓝缕，沐风栉雨，走过百年征程。天空没有翅膀的影子，但时光，已然飞过……

For six months for this verification of this detail, this dusty incident nearly a hundred years ago was in our mind. Copies of various records were placed on our desk. As long as we had the opportunity, we would bury my head in the quiet archives. Over the years, lying quietly in an old dossier, like a rushing river; history, sometimes magnificent, sometimes calm as water, generations of legal people walked through the journey of a century. There is no shadow of wings in the

1934	1935	1936	1937	1938	1939	1940	1941	1942	1943	1944	1945	1946
1960	1961	1962	1963	1964	1965	1966	1967	1968	1969	1970	1971	1972
1986	1987	1988	1989	1990	1991	1992	1993	1994	1995	1996	1997	1998
2012	2013	2014	2015	2016	2017	2018	2019	2020	2021	……		

sky, but time has already flown...

随着档案查阅的深入,一份1932年的《天津律师公会会员录》让我们眼前一亮。这里记载了七八百名会员的姓名、年龄、入会时间,第一页的前三个名字依次赫然写着梁锡纶53岁,1912年12月入会;钱俊,53岁,1912年12月入会。张务滋的名字靠后一些,他是1913年5月入会的,时年46岁。

With the deepening of the file access, a 1932 *Tianjin Bar Association Membership Record* made our eyes shine. The names, ages, and joining time of 700 or 800 members are recorded here. The first three names on the first page clearly read Liang Xilun, 53 years old, joined the club in December 1912; Qian Jun, 53 years old, joined the club in December 1912; Zhang Wuzi's name is a bit later. He joined the association in May 1913, at the age of 46.

这份档案至少证实了张务滋并非天津执业律师第一人,同时它也引起了我们对"他既是天津律师第一人,也是与刘崇佑共同为周总理辩护"的说法的进一步质疑。

This file at least confirmed the claim that Zhang Wuzi was not the first lawyer to practice in Tianjin, and at the same time raised our further doubts about the claim that "he was the first lawyer in Tianjin and also defended Premier Zhou together with Liu Chongyou."

而当丁立莹细细阅读中共党史编委会出版的《周恩来文集》,看到1912.10—1924.6卷第614页刊登的1920年7月17日的天津地方审判厅刑事判决书全文时,我们茅塞顿开。判决记载:"右列马千里、周恩来……被告人等,右委任辩护人刘崇佑律师、钱俊律师、兰兴周律师、梁锡纶律师(未到庭)……因私擅监禁、骚扰等案……"看到判决和辩护词,连是否到庭都有记载,结合档案馆关于天津律师梁锡纶、钱俊、兰兴周的记录,两者相互印证,最终得出结论:北京律师刘崇佑,天津律师钱俊、兰兴周、梁锡纶共四人参与了此案的辩护工作。

And when Ding Lingying read carefully the *Collected Works of Zhou Enlai* published by the Editorial Committee of the History of the Communist Party of China and saw the full text of the criminal verdict of the Tianjin Local Court of Justice on July 17, 1920, published on page 614 of Volume 1912.10-1924.6, we suddenly opened our mind. The judgment records, "The right sequence: Ma Qianli, Zhou Enlai... Defendants, etc., and the right appointed defenders: Attorney Liu Chongyou, Attorney Qian Jun, Attorney Lan Xingzhou, Attorney Liang Xilun (not in court)... Cases of imprisonment and harassment for private reasons..." Seeing the verdict and the defense, there are even records of whether they even appeared in court, combined with the archives' records of Tianjin lawyers Liang Xilun, Qian Jun, and Lan Xingzhou, the two confirmed each other, and finally came to the conclusion: Beijing lawyer Liu Chongyou, Tianjin lawyer Qian Jun, Lan Xingzhou, and Liang Xilun four people participated in the defense of this case.

收集的过程,也升华着我们自己。

The collection process also sublimated ourself.

当丁立莹和95岁的董师凯律师交流律师制度恢复之初就轰动全国的渤海2号案件时,老人说,1979年渤海2号沉船事件中,他为犯有渎职罪的被告人辩护。为"坏人"说"好"话,这在当时,是不被公众理解的,不过董师凯和同事一起,力排众议,以公正的辩护完成了工作。当我们询问老人是否留有照片时,老人激动又沮丧,说是记得当年的一本《人民画报》用整版刊登了案件发生和案件审理的图片报道,其中有他坐在辩护人席上的清晰照片。董师凯说:"如果能再找到这本画报该多好,这是我一生中最后的一个愿望了。"

When the 95-year-old lawyer Dong Shikai and Ding Liying discussed the Bohai No. 2 case that caused a national sensation when the lawyer system was restored, the old man said that in the 1979 Bohai No. 2 shipwreck incident, he defended the defendant who was guilty of dereliction of duty. Saying "good" words for "bad guys" was not understood by the public at the time, but Dong Shikai and his colleagues worked hard to overcome all opinions and completed the work with a fair defense. When we asked the old man if he had any photos, the old man was excited and frustrated, saying that he remembered that a copy of People's Pictorial that year published a full-

政法机关党支部天津律师文史馆主题党日活动

Communist Party branch of political and legal department of Tianjin held the theme party day activity at the Tianjin Lawyer's Culture and History Museum

page pictures report on the occurrence and trial of the case, and there was a clear picture of him sitting on the bench of the defender among these pictures. Dong Shikai said, "It would be great if I could find this pictorial again. This is the last wish in my life."

我们说:"我们帮您找!"

We said, "We'll help you find it!"

为了完成这个承诺,我们在网上搜、地摊找,逛书店、托朋友。最后,经乌鲁木齐市新华书店的一位朋友介绍,丁立莹律师从甘肃的一个旧书报收藏家手中买到了这本画报——1980年第11期的《人民画报》。它带着褶皱,穿越30年的时光,跨越数千公里来到天津。当我们将画报送给董老时,老人用颤抖的双手接过画报,两眼湿润。

1921	1922	1923	1924	1925	1926	1927	1928	1929	1930	1931	1932	1933
1947	1948	1949	1950	1951	1952	1953	1954	1955	1956	1957	1958	1959
1973	1974	1975	1976	1977	1978	1979	1980	1981	1982	1983	1984	1985
1999	2000	2001	2002	2003	2004	2005	2006	2007	2008	2009	2010	2011

In order to fulfill this promise, we searched the Internet, looked for street stalls, visited bookstores, and asked friends. Finally, through a friend of Xinhua Bookstore in Urumqi, Lawyer Ding Liying bought this pictorial from a collector of old books and newspapers in Gansu, the 11th issue of *People's Pictorial* in 1980. It came to Tianjin with its folds, traveling through 30 years of time, spanning thousands of kilometers. When we gave the pictorial to Mr.Dong, the old man took the pictorial with trembling hands, his eyes moist.

收集的过程，我们付出着，也得到着。

In the process of collecting, we paid and received.

看着那些民国初年的花名册，那些不同样式的律师印章、律师签名、诉讼状纸，那些竖版判决书的末尾，印着天津地方法院、河北天津地方法院、天津高等法院、直隶高等审判厅等等不同名称的印章，我们感慨万分。这些留在发黄的纸上用毛笔写就的名字、记载的事，承载着逝去的岁月，跨越悠悠百年，摆在我们面前。他们曾经生活在这里，曾经走过这里的路，曾经以法律的名义评判着生活中的是与非。

Looking at the roster from the early years of the Republic of China, the different styles of lawyer's seals, lawyer's signatures, litigation pleadings, and the end of those vertical verdicts are printed with Tianjin Local Court, Hebei Tianjin Local Court, Tianjin High Court, and Zhili High Court. Waiting for the stamps with different names, We were very moved. These names and records left on the yellowed paper and written with a brush carry the past years, spanning hundreds of years, and are placed in front of us. They have lived here, have walked the way here, and judged the right and wrong in life in the name of the law.

经过查阅文献的不断交叉确认，《周恩来文集》与《天津审判志》对周恩来"被捕""审判"过程的记载完全一致，该案的辩护律师终于有了明确的结论。百年前，中国共产党早期领导人领导的波澜壮阔的五四运动的一个重要篇章，就可以从这桩刑事判决说起，而为周恩来及中国共产党天津建党第一人于方舟烈士进行法庭辩护的，都是天津的著名律师……1920年7月17日，

1934	1935	1936	1937	1938	1939	1940	1941	1942	1943	1944	1945	1946
1960	1961	1962	1963	1964	1965	1966	1967	1968	1969	1970	1971	1972
1986	1987	1988	1989	1990	1991	1992	1993	1994	1995	1996	1997	1998
2012	2013	2014	2015	2016	2017	2018	2019	2020	2021	……		

天津地方审判厅最终判决"马千里、马骏等共犯妨害安全罪，处有期徒刑二月……周恩来、于方舟等共犯骚扰罪，处有期徒刑二月……"自1912年建立律师制度后，时隔7年，天津律师尚未达到成熟。律师业务类型也多是田间细物之争，参与这起刑事辩护，堪为律师辩护制度的开端。

After constant cross-confirmation by consulting the literature, the records of this process in the *Collected Works of Zhou Enlai* and *Tianjin Trial Records* are completely consistent, and the defense lawyers in the "arrest" and "trial" cases of Zhou Enlai finally came to a clear conclusion. It turned out that a hundred years ago, an important chapter of the magnificent May 4th Movement led by the early leaders of the Communist Party of China can start from this criminal sentence. The people who defended for Zhou Enlai and martyr Yu Fangzhou, the first person to establish the Communist Party of China in Tianjin, were all famous lawyers in Tianjin... On July 17, 1920, the criminal verdict of "Zhou Enlai and other representatives from all walks of life" was judged by the Tianjin local court. The case finally sentenced "Ma Qianli, Ma Jun and other accomplices to security crimes to be sentenced to fixed-term imprisonment... Zhou Enlai, Yu Fangzhou and other accomplices to harassment crimes to be sentenced to fixed-term imprisonment..." Since the establishment of the lawyer system in 1912, it has been 7 years. Tianjin lawyers have not yet reached maturity. The type of lawyer's business is mostly field disputes. Participating in this criminal defense can be the beginning of the lawyer's defense system.

时间的指针回拨至1919年。巴黎和会外交失败，自1919年5月4日起，以反帝爱国为主旋律的五四运动在全国范围迅速展开。第二年，天津各界联合会同天津学生联合会因反抗日本侵略而抵制日货，遭到北洋政府的镇压，警察殴伤多人亦逮捕了马千里、马骏、孟震候、夏琴西、周恩来、于方舟（于兰渚）、张砚庄（女）、郭隆真（女）等20余人。

The hands of time set back to 1919. The diplomacy of the Paris Peace Conference failed. Since May 4, 1919, the May Fourth Movement with anti-imperialist patriotism as its main melody spread rapidly across the country. In the turn of the May Fourth Movement, the Tianjin Federation of all walks of life and the Tianjin Student

Federation boycotted Japanese goods for resisting Japanese aggression. They were suppressed by the Beiyang government. The police beat many people and arrested more than 20 people, including Ma Qianli and Ma Jun, Meng Zhenhou, Xia Qinxi, Zhou Enlai, Yu Fangzhou (Yu Lanzhu), Zhang Yanzhuang (female), Guo Longzhen (female).

1920年4月29日，天津律师公会遂派出会长梁锡纶、副会长兰兴周、资深律师钱俊作为20余名代表的辩护律师。由于当时活跃于京津地区的刘崇佑律师名气很大，曾经为北京大学学生辩护，因此刘崇佑也被聘请到律师团队之中，由20余名代表共同委托的被捕人士之一天津商会职员夏琴西作为代表会主席承办与律师通信及签署委托状等事宜。关心国家命运的天津律师梁锡纶、兰兴周、钱俊和京津律师刘崇佑组成律师团，参与到了这场爱国辩护之中。

On April 29, 1920, the Tianjin Bar Association dispatched Chairman Liang Xilun, Vice Chairman Lan Xingzhou, and senior lawyer Qian Jun as defense lawyers with more than 20 representatives. Because lawyer Liu Chongyou, who was active in the Beijing-Tianjin area at that time, was famous and used to defend Peking University students, of course, lawyer Liu Chongyou was also hired into the team of lawyers. One of the arrested persons was commissioned by more than 20 representatives, Xia Qinxi, a staff member of the Tianjin Chamber of Commerce. As the chairman of the representative meeting, he undertook matters such as correspondence with lawyers and signing of power of attorney. Tianjin lawyers Liang Xilun, Lan Xingzhou, Qian Jun, and Beijing-Tianjin lawyer Liu Chongyou, who are concerned about the destiny of the country, formed a team of lawyers and participated in this patriotic defense.

法庭上，天津律师钱俊慷慨陈词："国势危亡，岂忍束手待毙？国民分子，天良而发，奋力呼号，热诚所激，不应受刑。"

In the court, Tianjin lawyer Qian Jun generously stated that, "The country is in danger, how can you bear to die? the nationals, for the sake of nature, screaming hard, motivated by enthusiasm, should not be tortured."

天津律师公会副会长兰兴周律师辩护称："检察官起诉之各项，殊与事实不符，委未允

1934	1935	1936	1937	1938	1939	1940	1941	1942	1943	1944	1945	1946
1960	1961	1962	1963	1964	1965	1966	1967	1968	1969	1970	1971	1972
1986	1987	1988	1989	1990	1991	1992	1993	1994	1995	1996	1997	1998
2012	2013	2014	2015	2016	2017	2018	2019	2020	2021	……		

当。""马千里等有无强暴胁迫,为本案构成之要件,马千里等虽系国民大会会员,究系与各同业公会共同之核议,自决抵制日货,对于一切行为,纯出自愿,焉得有强暴胁迫?"

Lawyer Lan Xingzhou, the vice chairman of the Tianjin Bar Association, defended that, "All the prosecutors' prosecutions are inconsistent with the facts, and the commission has not been approved." "Whether Ma Qianli and others have rape and coercion is an essential element of this case. Although Ma Qianli and others are members of the National Assembly, they had a joint agreement with various trade associations, decided to boycott of Japanese goods, and all acts are purely voluntary. How can there be violence and coercion?"

天津律师文史馆参观活动

Visit to Tianjin Lawyer's Culture and History Museum

经过多名律师的不懈努力，北洋政府在判决了各代表有期徒刑两个月后，不得不释放了爱国人士。出狱后的他们继续传播马克思主义、抵制日货，而周恩来从此也踏上了革命家的道路。

After the unremitting efforts of many lawyers, the Beiyang government had to release the patriots after sentenced the representatives to two months' imprisonment. After being released from prison, they continued to spread Marxism and boycott Japanese goods, while Zhou Enlai has since embarked on the road of revolutionaries.

天津是全国最早响应五四运动的城市。天津律师也是全国最早参与为在五四运动中被"逮捕、审判"的进步青年进行法庭辩护活动的。

Tianjin is the first city in the country to respond to the May Fourth Movement. Tianjin lawyers were also the first in the country to participate in court defense activities for progressive youths who were "arrested and tried" during the May Fourth Movement.

在北洋军阀黑暗统治、帝国主义百般欺凌的年代，天津律师公会派出的这个由会长、副会长和资深律师组成的爱国辩护团队，用法律武器捍卫了爱国和公正，用法律精神塑造了律师职业中不可或缺的灵魂和信仰，并在融通之中承上启下，构建了公民社会责无旁贷的法治梦想。

In the era of the dark rule of the Beiyang warlords and imperialist bullying, the patriotic defense team sent by the Tianjin Bar Association, composed of the chairman, vice-chairmen and senior lawyers, defended patriotism and justice with legal weapons, and shaped indispensable soul and faith in the lawyer's profession with the spirit of law, and linking up and down in the blending, construct the dream of the rule of law that is duty-bound in civil society.

1934	1935	1936	1937	1938	1939	1940	1941	1942	1943	1944	1945	1946
1960	1961	1962	1963	1964	1965	1966	1967	1968	1969	1970	1971	1972
1986	1987	1988	1989	1990	1991	1992	1993	1994	1995	1996	1997	1998
2012	2013	2014	2015	2016	2017	2018	2019	2020	2021	......		

2021年6月26日天津市律师行业召开庆祝中国共产党成立100周年主题报告会

On June 26, 2021, the lawyer industry in Tianjin held a theme report to celebrate the 100th anniversary of the founding of the Communist Party of China

1921	1922	1923	1924	1925	1926	1927	1928	1929	1930	1931	1932	1933
1947	1948	1949	1950	1951	1952	1953	1954	1955	1956	1957	1958	1959
1973	1974	1975	1976	1977	1978	1979	1980	1981	1982	1983	1984	1985
1999	2000	2001	2002	2003	2004	2005	2006	2007	2008	2009	2010	2011

浩然正气,律师之风骨。

Righteous, is the strength of a lawyer.

忆往昔大浪淘沙,看今朝壮怀激烈!新时代,律师必将践行五四精神,传承爱国传统,为"两个一百年"的奋斗目标和民族复兴的伟大中国梦奋力前进。

Recalling the big waves and scouring the sands of the past, and seeing the fierceness of the present! Lawyers in the new era will surely practice the spirit of the May Fourth Movement, inherit the patriotic tradition, striving for the "Two Centenary" goals and the great Chinese dream of national rejuvenation.

百年历史,薪火相传,离不开这一份份文件、一张张照片;我们要让这些零散的片段积聚到一起,让天津律师穿越百年的风云,在天津律师文史馆与今天的我们对视,迎接新时代美好的明天……

A hundred years of history, passed down from generation to generation, are inseparable from these documents and photos; we must let these scattered fragments accumulate, so that Tianjin lawyers can travel through the century of history and confront us today at the Tianjin Lawyer's Culture and History Museum. Welcome to the bright future of the new era...

编委会
Editorial board